Prior Consultation in International Law
A Study of State Practice

Volume 16, Procedural Aspects of International Law Series

The Procedural Aspects of International Law Series
RICHARD B. LILLICH, editor (1964–1977)
ROBERT KOGOD GOLDMAN, editor (1977–)

1. International Claims: Their Adjudication by National Commissions
RICHARD B. LILLICH (1962)

2. International Claims: Their Preparation and Presentation
RICHARD B. LILLICH and GORDON A. CHRISTENSON (1962)

3. The Role of Domestic Courts in the International Legal Order
RICHARD A. FALK (1964)

4. The Use of Experts by International Tribunals
GILLIAN M. WHITE (1965)

5. The Protection of Foreign Investment:
Six Procedural Studies
RICHARD B. LILLICH (1965)

6. International Claims: Postwar British Practice
RICHARD B. LILLICH (1967)

7. Law-Making in the International
Civil Aviation Organization
THOMAS BUERGENTHAL (1969)

8. UN Protection of Civil and Political Rights
JOHN CAREY (1970)

9. International Claims: Postwar French Practice
BURNS H. WESTON (1971)

10. International Law, National Tribunals, and the
Rights of Aliens
FRANK GRIFFITH DAWSON and IVAN L. HEAD (1971)

11. The Austrian-German Arbitral Tribunal
IGNAZ SEIDL-HOHENVELDERN (1972)

12. International Claims: Their Settlement by
Lump Sum Agreements
RICHARD B. LILLICH and BURNS H. WESTON (1975)

13. Evidence Before International Tribunals
Revised Edition
DURWARD V. SANDIFER (1975)

14. Improving Compliance with International Law
ROGER FISHER (1981)

15. International Claims: Contemporary European Practice
Edited by RICHARD B. LILLICH and BURNS H. WESTON (1982)

16. Prior Consultation in International Law
A Study of State Practice
FREDERIC L. KIRGIS, JR. (1983)

Prior Consultation in International Law

A Study of State Practice

Frederic L. Kirgis, Jr.

University Press of Virginia
Charlottesville

THE UNIVERSITY PRESS OF VIRGINIA

First published 1983

Library of Congress Cataloging in Publication Data

Kirgis, Frederic L.
Prior consultation in international law.

(The Procedural aspects of international law series;
v.16)
Includes index.
1. Prior consultation (International law) I. Title.
II. Series.
JX4471.K57 1983 341.3′3 82–17354
ISBN 0–8139–0971–6

Printed in the United States of America

To
my father, Frederic L. Kirgis
and the memory of
my mother, Kathryn B. Kirgis

Contents

Acknowledgments

I have had the benefit of research assistance, made possible by UCLA faculty research funds, in the preparation of chapters II, IV, and VI. Each research assistant's contribution is acknowledged at the beginning of the chapter reflecting his or her work. In each instance, I have reviewed the research and have done all the writing. Consequently, I am solely responsible for all errors and omissions.

In compiling the data for this book, I have had the help of more library personnel, government officials, and members of international organizations' secretariats than I can possibly mention. A few, however, have been so repeatedly helpful that I must single them out. These include Barbara Silvernail, the international documents librarian at UCLA; Sally Wiant, the law librarian at Washington and Lee University, and her staff—particularly Johanna Thompson and Judy Stinson, each of whom has been in charge of documents at crucial times in the preparation of the manuscript; Helen Philos, the librarian of the American Society of International Law; Ella Krucoff and Barbara Sloan, of the European Community Information Service in Washington, D.C.; Sir Joseph Gold, former General Counsel and Director of the Legal Department in the International Monetary Fund; Fernand Welter, in charge of education and cultural relations for NATO, and his staff; and Henri Smets, chief of the OECD Environment Directorate. By giving me access to materials I needed, each of these people has had a major hand in the preparation of this study.

The manuscript for this book has gone through several revisions and polishings, requiring a great deal of typing, retyping, and rearranging. This work has been done with impressive skill and unfailing good humor by Betty Durstine at UCLA and by Geraldine Saunders and Margaret Williams at Washington and Lee. I am greatly indebted to each of them.

Prior Consultation in International Law

A Study of State Practice

Chapter I

The Framework for the Study

A. The Utility of Prior Consultation

It is obvious that unilateral action by nations, or by entities subject to their control, can involve significant potential detriment to interests external to the acting state, even when the action does not violate prevailing substantive international norms. A United States president proclaims newly enunciated jurisdictional rights over continental shelf resources; the French government imposes new import restrictions in the wake of widespread internal disturbances and strikes; Brazil decides to construct a huge new dam on an international river; the Saudi Arabian government is in a position to invest heavily in the economies of other nations; a Chinese nuclear explosion may affect the environment of neighboring states; advanced technology permits outer space experiments that could interfere with other space uses. All of these instances have occurred. None involved action patently violative of substantive international law, but each involved potential detriment to external interests.

These and most of the other unilateral measures examined in this study involve actual or potential externalities, as economists use that term. Costs (detriments) are incurred that are external to the decisionmaker in the sense that they are borne primarily by others. The others in this case are foreign nationals, foreign states, or the international community in general; the costs are direct (for example, state *B*'s reduced export income when state *A* erects a new trade barrier to protect local producers), or indirect in the sense either of a secondary effect (state *C*'s producers have to compete against increased imports from state *B* as a result of *A*'s trade barrier), or of a burden shared by the entire international community, most of whom will be external to the acting state (as in the case of environmental harm to an international commons such as an ocean or outer space). To the extent that such potential detriments are not taken into account in making unilateral decisions whether or how to act, the total cost of the planned action will be underestimated. Some projects will be undertaken that could not be justified in cost-benefit terms if all costs had to be considered by the actor, and others will be undertaken in a manner unnecessarily inefficient from the world-community viewpoint.

A wide variety of substantive international norms may be characterized as attempts to preclude or limit unilateral conduct that would create significant externalities. This may be said, for example, of provisions of the General Agreement on Tariffs and Trade (GATT) limiting the parties' discretion as to the creation of new trade barriers,[1] and of customary and treaty rules restricting environmentally harmful conduct.[2] But such norms do not touch all externality-creating conduct, and even when they do, their scope and exact content may not be clear. Consequently, procedural norms assume considerable significance insofar as they oblige governments contemplating action to consider the potential effect on other states. To be effective, such norms must require some form of contact, in the form of adjudication of rights (including arbitration), conciliation, and / or consultation.

Unfortunately, dispute settlement through compulsory international adjudication seldom occurs, and almost never before the complained-of action is taken. Moreover, if the proposed unilateral measure does not violate substantive international law, the traditional forms of adjudication or arbitration provide no means for internalizing the measure's prospective external costs. Unless potentially affected states are to use self-help as a preventive remedy,[3] prior consultation (which could include some form of third-party conciliation) is left as the most prom-

[1] *See* GATT arts. II, III, VIII, XI, in IV CONTRACTING PARTIES TO GATT, BASIC INSTRUMENTS AND SELECTED DOCUMENTS 1(1969).

[2] *See, e.g.*, Bleicher, *An Overview of International Environmental Regulation*, 2 ECOLOGY L.Q. 1 (1972); Kirgis, *Technological Challenge to the Shared Environment: United States Practice*, 66 AM. J. INT'L L. 290 (1972).

[3] Some forms of self-help would not violate any existing international norms. An example would be the imposition of restrictions on new incoming foreign investment,

ising device to bring the cost of proposed unilateral action into the decision-making process. Decision makers in the acting state would be subjected to the arguments of governments (or, if feasible, of private parties)[4] representing interests most likely to bear any external costs, and would be called upon to respond directly to them, before the externally significant elements of the decision to act (or to permit nongovernmental persons to act) are irrevocably made. Given the weaknesses of the international legal system, this process of prior consultation with states or other parties that have their own interests to protect would seem a relatively efficient, peaceful means of achieving serious consideration of externalities, and thus of preserving the shared international community interest in seeing that the benefits of proposed action exceed all reasonably anticipated costs.

Perhaps one should ask at the outset whether those closely involved with affairs of state have asserted or acknowledged that there is indeed this measure of utility in prior consultations. If they have not, a study of consultation practice would have little practical significance. The point here is not to determine whether consultation has become the norm in the instances cited, but rather to examine whether those in a position to know from experience have treated prior consultation as a worthwhile procedural device. In fact, they have. A great many testimonials could be presented; a few should suffice.

It is now recognized at the highest levels of government that there is a measure of self-interest in taking the interests of other nations into account before acting unilaterally. In his message transmitting the 1977 international economic report to the Congress, the President of the United States said: "We have learned the importance of industrialized democracies taking into account the likely impact of their actions on other nations as they develop their economic policies. In an interdependent world,

in the absence of a specific treaty obligation to the contrary. *See generally* Note, *The Rising Tide of Reverse Flow: Would a Legislative Breakwater Violate U.S. Treaty Commitments?* 72 MICH. L. REV. 551 (1974). Other types of self-help, such as those involving armed force, would be unlawful under most circumstances.

[4] In some instances the interest of a private party uniquely affected by the prospective unilateral action may coincide substantially with those of his government. Consultation with such a private party would satisfy the goal of bringing the significant external costs into focus. *Cf.* The Mavrommatis Palestine Concessions, 1924 P.C.I.J., ser. A, No. 2, at 13–15.

a nation which disrupts the economies of its trading partners does so at its own eventual peril."[5] Of course,the likelihood of compliance with a norm designed to bring other nations' concerns into the decision-making process increases as the perception of one's self-interest in so doing increases.

A United States Secretary of State, recognizing the fragility of the international environment and the ineffectiveness of then-existing international mechanisms to protect it, declared in 1971: "[P]erhaps it is time for the international community to begin moving toward a consensus that nations have a right to be consulted before actions are taken which could affect their environment or the international environment at large. This implies, of course, that nations contemplating such actions would be expected to consult in advance other states which could be affected."[6] Similarly, a significant study prepared within the Organization for Economic Cooperation and Development (OECD) asserts that a prior notification and consultation process "is the most important procedure for dealing with transfrontier pollution."[7]

Another U.S. Secretary of State, referring to changes in national policy or new measures affecting transnational investments, has said that "there must be more effective bilateral consultation among governments to identify and resolve investment disputes before they become irritants in political relations."[8] More generally, a U.S. State Department official, referring to relations between the United States and Canada, has pointed out: "Independently and together our two Secretaries of State have stressed the need for open and frank consultation in advance of any action by one country that might affect the other. This joint commitment to seek together ways in which the objectives of one country can be met at the least

[5] International Economic Report of the President, Transmitted to the Congress January 1977, *reprinted in* 76 DEP'T ST. BULL. 129, 130 (1977).

[6] Address by William Rogers to the Panel on Science and Technology of the House Committee on Science and Astronautics, Jan. 26, 1971, U.S. Foreign Policy in a Technological Age, 64 DEP'T ST. BULL. 198, 200–201 (1971).

[7] Ad Hoc Group on Transfrontier Pollution, OECD Environment Committee, Study of Some Principles for Solving Problems of Transfrontier Pollution, Annex I, at 29 (OECD Doc. AEU / TFP / ENV / 74.1, 1974). The OECD has adopted prior consultation procedures in other fields as well. *See* LE THI MAI, ASPECTS JURIDIQUES DE LA NOTIFICATION ET DE LA CONSULTATION A L'OCDE 9–14 (1977).

[8] Statement delivered to U.N. General Assembly by Henry Kissinger, Sept. 1, 1975, Global Consensus and Economic Development, 73 DEP'T ST. BULL. 425, 433 (1975).

cost to the other is beginning to be implemented as we deal with specific issues."[9]

A revealing example of both the promise and the limitations of prior consultation appears in United Nations practice involving the Western industrialized countries and the postcolonial majority bloc. At the sixth special session of the General Assembly in the spring of 1974, there was minimal give and take before the developing countries obtained approval of the Declaration and Program of Action on the Establishment of a New International Economic Order.[10] The industrialized nations were offended and not at all inclined to accede to a new economic order that they felt others were attempting to impose on them. On the other hand, at the seventh special session, again devoted to the problems of economic development, genuine negotiations were held before adoption of a resolution on development and international economic cooperation. The United States, as the major capital-exporting state affected by the resolution, did not agree with all of its provisions.[11] Nevertheless, participation by the industrialized nations in the hammering out of its terms clearly led to a receptivity not to be found at the sixth special session. A high-ranking American representative, answering a question suggesting that the substantive outcome of the sixth and seventh special sessions was essentially the same in terms of U.S. interests, responded that the significant difference was in the "genuine process of negotiation in order to get an agreed result from which we all could go forward" at the seventh session, resulting in a softening of the tone of the proposals adopted.[12]

The prospect of increased economic cooperation had thus appeared. At the immediately following thirtieth regular session of the General Assembly, however, it became obvious that the genuine negotiations on specific proposals had not materially affected the underlying dichotomies of interest or the differing

[9] *United States-Canadian Relations: Hearing Before a Subcomm. of the House Comm. on Int'l Relations*, 94th Cong., 2d Sess. 5 (1976) (Statement of Richard D. Vine, Deputy Ass't Secretary for European Affairs).

[10] G.A. Res. 3201 and 3202, 6th Special Sess. U.N. GAOR Supp. 1 (A / 9559), at 3, 5, U.N. Doc. A / RES / 3201 (S-VI) (May 9, 1974); U.N. Doc. A / RES / 3202 (S-VI) (May 16, 1974), 13 INT'L LEGAL MATERIALS 715, 720 (1974).

[11] 73 DEP'T ST. BULL. 557–58 (1975).

[12] Thomas O. Enders, Assistant Secretary of State for Economic and Business Affairs, in 73 DEP'T ST. BULL, 569 (1975).

perceptions of political realities separating the Western developed world from most other member states.[13] The role of consultation had been simply to internalize (into the decision-making process of the majority) some of the external detriments to be anticipated if economic proposals reflecting only a narrow self-interest were to be adopted, and by so doing to alleviate a particular set of tensions that would have arisen. No further results could be claimed for the process.

Despite the growing number of participants and knowledgeable observers stressing the dispute-avoidance potentialities of prior consultation norms,[14] very few scholars have attempted serious analyses of existing normative expectations or the conditions in which presently piecemeal consultation practice is likely to develop into binding norms. The few extant efforts have been in limited subject areas.[15] This study attempts to fill

[13]The most dramatic, but not the only, manifestation of the continuing breach came with the adoption of General Assembly Resolution 3379(XXX), declaring Zionism to be a form of racism. *See* 73 DEP'T ST. BULL. 788–95 (1975).

[14]*See, e.g.,* OECD High Level Group on Trade and Related Problems, Report on Policy Perspectives for International Trade and Economic Relations 83 (1972); Decision of the Contracting Parties to GATT, BASIC INSTRUMENTS AND SELECTED DOCUMENTS, 9th Supp. 26, 27 (1961) (hereafter cited as BISD); Statement of the Managing Director of the International Monetary Fund (Mr. Witteveen) to ECOSOC, Nov. 26, 1974, in 3 IMF SURVEY 380–81 (1974); Statement of the Representative of the European Communities (Mr. Luyten) at the Tokyo Round of trade negotiations, Feb. 11, 1975, in 4 IMF SURVEY 71, 72 (1975); Panel on the Law of the Sea, *Principles for a Global Fisheries Management Regime* 14 (AM. SOC'Y OF INT'L L. STUD. IN TRANSNAT'L LEGAL POL'Y NO. 4, 1974); Gardner, *The Role of the UN in Environmental Problems,* 26 INT'L ORG. 237, 252 (1972); Committee of Experts on Air Pollution, Procedures for Consultation at National and International Level Prior to the Setting Up of Polluting Plant in Border Areas, Council of Europe Doc. EXP / Air (73)2, at 3 (1973); Utton, *International Environmental Law and Consultation Mechanisms,* 12 COLUM. J. TRANSNAT'L L. 56, 62–66 (1973); *Maritime Briefings: Hearings Before the House Comm. on Merchant Marine & Fisheries,* 93d Cong., 1st Sess. 158 (testimony of the Director of the Office of Maritime Affairs, U.S. Dep't of State, 1973); U.S. statement on direct satellite broadcasting, 73 DEP'T ST. BULL. 673, 675–76 (1975).

As indicated in the text, this is not to say that consultation always resolves differences, or that those close to state practice think prior consultation is advisable in all instances. On the problems of possible stalemate and of unequal negotiating strength, *see, e.g.,* remarks of the U.K. delegate in U.N. Conf. on the Law of Treaties, 1st Sess., U.N. Doc. A/CONF.39/11, at 420 (1969). The point is simply that a considerable body of knowledgeable opinion supports the presumption that, despite its deficiencies, in a variety of cases prior consultation is worth the time, effort, and expense.

[15]*See* Bourne, *Procedure in the Development of International Drainage Basins: The Duty to Consult and to Negotiate,* 1972 CAN. Y.B. INT'L L. 212; Sztucki, *International Consultations and Space Treaties,* in PROC. OF THE 17TH COLLOQUIUM ON THE LAW OF OUTER SPACE 147 (M. Schwartz ed. 1975). The latter work contains a brief historical introduction to the use of consultations in international practice.

the gap. It is a throwback to the genre of international legal scholarship practiced by the "publicists"; that is, it examines state practice and tries to synthesize and draw conclusions from it, rather than attempting to create new normative structures or to make value judgments about the governmental conduct being examined.

B. Methodology

1. Sources and Evidence of International Law Relating to Prior Consultation

The pages to follow will examine state practice in several forms—including, for example, the creation and observance of treaty obligations not only as indicative of normative expectations for parties, but as part of the international legal process that often creates expectations regarding even the rights and permissible behavior of nonparties; assertions of rights or duties outside the treaty context, and acquiescence or nonacquiescence; unilateral acts and declarations; resolutions and reports of national and international bodies; judicial decisions; national regulations; opinions of informed observers; and so on.[16]

Most of these are either generally accepted independent sources of international law or recognized ingredients of custom. If there remains any controversy about the normative significance of any of them, presumably it would concern technically nonbinding resolutions or the use of treaties as indicative of normative expectations for nonparties. As to the former, however, General Assembly resolutions—and even resolutions of other international bodies—are now widely acknowledged to be potential indicators of state practice if not actual embodiments of it, varying in significance according to such things as

[16]Specifics rather than generalities will be stressed. There are a great many multilateral and bilateral treaties and declarations containing general language calling for consultations on matters of mutual interest. These have not been considered significant for purposes of this study unless they have been applied by the parties as vehicles for prior consultations in identifiable situations or could reasonably be construed to require such consultations in specific contexts. For a stricter interpretation of such clauses, *see* J. Kusumowidagdo, Consultation Clauses as Means of Providing for Treaty Obedience 196–97, 301 (1981).

quantity and quality of consensus, normative character of the language, and consistency of deeds with the words.[17]

Concerning the use of treaties, the Vienna Convention recognizes certain well-defined instances in which rights or duties for nonparties may be created.[18] The present study goes further, however, treating the issue as one of determining whether a treaty commitment, or a series of such commitments involving as few as two states at a time, is such as to engender or affirm among nonparties a reasonable belief that the same or similar norms apply to them. That such could and does occur is not surprising, since mere declarations of intent, not embodied in treaties, can constitute legally relevant state practice, at least if the requisite opinio juris is present. The binding form of a treaty obligation supplies the opinio juris. If the obligation is expressly recognized by a significant number of states in one treaty or a series of similar ones, is generally observed by them in practice, and is not inherently applicable only to them, all the ingredients of custom are presumptively present.[19]

[17]The literature is bulky. *See, e.g.*, O. ASAMOAH, THE LEGAL SIGNIFICANCE OF THE DECLARATIONS OF THE GENERAL ASSEMBLY OF THE UNITED NATIONS (1966); J. CASTAÑEDA, LEGAL EFFECTS OF UNITED NATIONS RESOLUTIONS (1969); R. HIGGINS, THE DEVELOPMENT OF INTERNATIONAL LAW THROUGH THE POLITICAL ORGANS OF THE UNITED NATIONS (1963); Falk, *On the Quasi-Legislative Competence of the General Assembly,* 60 AM. J. INT'L L. 782 (1966); Schachter, *The Relation of Law, Politics, and Action in the United Nations,* 109 HAGUE ACADEMY, RECUEIL DES COURS 165 (1963). The General Assembly has asserted that "the development of international law may be reflected *inter alia*, by declarations and resolutions of the General Assembly." G.A. Res. 3232, 29 U.N. GAOR, Supp. (No. 31) at 141, U.N. Doc. A/9631 (1974); 69 AM. J. INT'L L. 249, 250 (1975) (adopted by consensus).

[18]Vienna Convention on the Law of Treaties, *opened for signature*, May 23, 1969, arts. 35, 36, 38, U.N. Doc. A/CONF.39/27; 63 AM. J. INT'L L. 875 (1969).

[19]For an enlightening evaluation of treaties as generators of custom, see A. D'AMATO, THE CONCEPT OF CUSTOM IN INTERNATIONAL LAW 103–66 (1971). *See also* 1 C. HYDE INTERNATIONAL LAW 12 (2d ed. 1945). *Cf.* Nottebohm Case, 1955 I.C.J. Rep. 3, 22–23 (reliance on superseded bilateral treaties and on draft multilateral convention); Advisory Opinion on Legal Consequences for States of the Continued Presence of South Africa in Namibia Notwithstanding Security Council Resolution 276, 1971 I.C.J. 16, 47, and Fisheries Jurisdiction Cases (Jurisdiction), 1973 I.C.J. 3, 18, *id.* at 49, 63 (provisions of unratified Vienna Convention on the Law of Treaties as reflecting custom); Fisheries Jurisdiction Cases (Merits), 1974 I.C.J. Rep. 3, 22, 29; *id.* at 175, 192–93, 198 (acceptance of provision of Convention on the High Seas as declaratory of established principles of international law, as stated in the Convention); U.S. Department of State, *Section-by-Section Analysis to the Foreign Sovereign Immunities Act of* 1975, 15 INT'L LEGAL MATERIALS 102, 113–14 (1976) (reliance on several treaties, some bilateral, to show that general international law no longer requires immunity of foreign state-owned property from execution); *but see* North Sea Continental Shelf Cases, 1969 I.C.J. 3, 42–44 (equidistance principle of Convention on the Continental Shelf not accepted as custom).

In the absence of a treaty obligation or normative declaration by an authoritative international body, state practice is often difficult to evaluate. The problem of proving the opinio juris crops up. Thus, a government may consult before acting, but may do so for reasons that have little or no legal significance. But there are a number of situations in which ad hoc consultations do have at least presumptive significance. The most obvious arises when State *B* asserts that State *A* must consult it before acting, and State *A* does so. This situation encompasses not only blunt demands by State *B*, but assertions in the form of requests couched in diplomatic language. Even when there is no express assertion, there is presumptive normative significance in prior consultation by State *A* if its short-term self-interest would have been served equally or better by acting without consultation. When it is unclear whether short-term self-interest would be served by nonconsultation, a consistent pattern of prior consultations by a significant number of states would be relevant.

2. Scope, Definitions, and Difficulties

The type of external detriment pertinent to this study is extranational: the reasonably foreseeable, nonminimal potential cost to interests not effectively represented by the acting or authorizing state, even though the precise magnitude of the cost (or the precise probability that there will be such a nonminimal cost) cannot be ascertained with certainty. Outside the

The less detailed, less technical the treaty obligation and the more states explicitly subject to it (because of its multilateral character or its repetition in a series of agreements), the more it lends itself to the assertion of rights and duties beyond the formal parties. *Cf.* S. S. Wimbledon Case, 1923 P.C.I.J., ser. A, No. 1, at 25 (reliance on treaties regulating Suez and Panama Canals to establish general principle regarding use of important international waterways in wartime). Prior consultation obligations generally are nontechnical, and thus often meet the former test. *See, e.g.*, the claim by nonparties to the 1974 OECD "Code of Good Conduct" (not a formal treaty) of the benefits of its prior consultation element, in GATT, BISD 21st Supp. 35, 40 (1975); Co-operation in the Field of the Environment Concerning Natural Resources Shared by Two or More States, Report of the Executive Director, U.N. Doc. UNEP / GC / 44, at 41 (1975) (prior consultation principles concerning use of shared resources could be derived from state practice as evidenced, inter alia, by bilateral and multilateral agreements); J. KUSUMOWIDAGDO, *supra* note 16, at 307 (1981) (consultation clauses in treaties of common interests as confirming the existence of custom); GRIFFIN, LEGAL ASPECTS OF THE USE OF SYSTEMS OF INTERNATIONAL WATERS, S. DOC. NO. 118, 85th Cong., 2d Sess. 63–72 (1958) (reliance on series of treaties to establish custom relating to prior consultation).

scope of the present work, however, is the obvious detriment to be anticipated by a state against which hostile or clearly retaliatory unilateral action is planned.[20] It has seemed fruitful instead to evaluate the decision-making process when imposition of a detriment is not the very purpose at hand.[21]

Also excluded is any examination of consultation practice relating to action clearly violating international law.[22] The concern is rather with conduct not patently unlawful—a more common phenomenon than clearly unlawful conduct, and therefore of much greater interest from the standpoint of international procedural law. If the lawfulness of the proposed conduct is genuinely arguable, it is within the scope of the study.

Consultations are irrelevant for present purposes when it is relatively clear that the initiating state could not effectively achieve its goal without the cooperation of the consulted states and the consultations are designed chiefly to work out a common position.[23] Such instances do not pose the problem of internalizing

[20]The reference here is to the subjective intent of the decision-making officials. It is not always clear, of course, whether the dominant motive for proposed action is hostility or retaliation, unless the action involves the use of armed force. As a rule of thumb for purposes of this study, measures are considered hostile or retaliatory when they are directed against a particular state or group of states in an atmosphere of confrontation, and seem to impose such costs on the state taking them that they probably would not be adopted if the dominant intent were not to bend or break the will of others.

Examples of such retaliatory action short of armed force include the enactment by the United States of the first Hickenlooper Amendment, 22 U.S.C. § 2370 (e) (1) (1970), and the imposition in 1974 by the United States of a quota on the import of meat from Canada after the latter had restricted imports from the U.S., 39 Fed. Reg. 40,741 (1974), 72 Dep't St. Bull. 44 (1975).

[21]It is nevertheless interesting to note that before the U.N. Charter imposed its restrictions on the legitimate use of armed force as an instrument of national policy, international law did attempt to require some form of consultation before a state went to war. *See, e.g.*, Treaty of Westphalia, October 24, 1648, arts. CXXIII, CXXIV, in Major Peace Treaties of Modern History 1648–1967, at 7, 46–47 (1967); League of Nations Covenant arts. 12, 13, 15; Arbitrage Entre le Portugal et l'Allemagne, July 31, 1928 (the Naulilaa Incident Arbitration), 2 UNRIAA 1013, 1019, 1027–28 (1949) (concerning armed reprisals). *Cf.* U.N. Charter arts. 33–38.

[22]An example was the resumption by the United States of the importation of Rhodesian chrome, in violation of binding Security Council decisions. *See* 50 U.S.C. § 98h-1 (1971 Supp.); Diggs v. Shultz, 470 F.2d 461 (D.C. Cir. 1972), *cert. denied*, 411 U.S. 931 (1973). The statute was later repealed.

[23]Examples would include consultations among commodity-consuming nations before a consumer-producer conference, U.S.-U.K. consultations with African nations before taking an initiative requiring the cooperation of contending parties in Southern Africa, U.S. consultations with its NATO allies regarding possible economic sanctions

the external cost of a decision when self-interest provides an incentive to proceed unilaterally. Moreover, consultations in such cases provide little or no evidence of an opinio juris, unless they are required by treaty—in which case it is the treaty that is important, and the consultations simply show that it is honored. Nevertheless, it is of interest to examine prior consultation practice involving political allies whose cooperation would normally be desired, when a state has the power and incentive to act without waiting for their input. That not only involves possible externalities, but tends to demonstrate a perceived duty if the government does consult.

Consultation means something more than notification, but less than consent. The term is used here as it has been in United Nations practice, where "the expressions 'in consultation with' or 'after consultation with' have a similar connotation as 'taking into account the views of' or 'bearing in mind the recommendations of' in the sense that these latter expressions do not require agreement with the views expressed or the recommendations made."[24] To consult in good faith is "to take into consideration the various interests involved, to seek to give them every satisfaction compatible with the pursuit of [the consulting state's] own interests, and to show that in this regard it is genuinely concerned to reconcile the interests of the other . . . State with its own."[25] That standard would not be met if the consulting state insists on its own position without contemplating any modification of it.[26] Nor would it be met if one party withholds essential information from the other or insists on acting before

to force Iran to release American hostages, and consultations among nations belonging to the European Communities before a meeting with nonmember states on international monetary reform.

[24]U.N. Doc. ST/LEG/8, at 269 (1962), relied upon by the Legal Counsel of the United Nations at a meeting of the Committee on Relations with the Host Country, Feb. 13, 1978. *See* 1978 U.N. JURIDICAL Y.B. 189, 190.

[25]Lake Lanoux Arbitration (France v. Spain), Nov. 16, 1957, 24 I.L.R. 101, 139.

[26]Some of the cases construing a duty to negotiate are illustrative, even though a duty to negotiate implies a more sustained effort to reach agreement than does a duty simply to consult. *See* the North Sea Continental Shelf Cases, 1969 I.C.J. 3, 47; Jugement du 26 Janvier 1972, Tribunal d'Arbitrage de l'Accord sur les Dettes extérieures allemandes, 24 REVUE HELLÉNIQUE DE DROIT INT'L 353, 383–88 (1971) (interpreting treaty obligation). The Lake Lanoux tribunal said conduct falling below the accepted international standard would include "an unjustified breaking off of the discussions, abnormal delays, disregard of the agreed procedures, systematic refusals to take into consideration adverse proposals or interests, and more generally, . . . violation of the rules of good faith." Lake Lanoux Arbitration, *supra* note 25, at 128.

there has been a reasonable opportunity to gather essential information. On the other hand, it is not necessary that there be lengthy discussions, or that the parties pursue negotiations with a view to reaching agreement.[27] Under some circumstances, the consultations could be carried out in writing, rather than face-to-face.[28] Whatever genuinely serves to bring into the decision-making process the extranational effects of the decision, as expressed by the representatives of those potentially affected, suffices as consultation even if there is no concentrated effort to reach mutual assent regarding the essential aspects of the proposed action.

The concern of this study is with a procedure that is likely to inject external cost assessment into the decision-making process; consequently, the only consultations of interest are those held before final decisions are made. But the actual moment of decision is not always clear: It may not be a matter of record; or the "final" decision may still be reopened under some (often undefined) circumstances; or the decision may have accrued by stages, no one of which settles all aspects of the matter.

Take the example of legislation proposed by the national executive and later enacted by the national legislature (which may or may not be independent of the executive) authorizing an administrative body to extend national jurisdiction for a

[27] *See* OECD Doc. ENV/TFP/78.17 at 7, 23 (1st rev. 1979). Consultation "may be a preliminary stage to a negotiation but differs from the latter when the country which initiates the consultation is merely seeking the opinion of the country(ies) concerned by the proposed activities or measures." OECD Doc. ENV(79)23, at 6 (1979). *See also* J. KUSUMOWIDAGDO, *supra* note 16, at 55–56.

Even "an obligation to negotiate does not imply an obligation to reach an agreement." Advisory Opinion on Railway Traffic Between Lithuania and Poland, 1931 P.C.I.J. ser. A/B, No. 42, at 116. *Cf.* Convention on a Code of Conduct for Liner Conferences, July 1, 1974, art. 11(6), in 13 INT'L LEGAL MATERIALS 912 (1974). The World Court has said: "Negotiations do not of necessity always presuppose a more or less lengthy series of notes and despatches; it may suffice that a discussion should have been commenced, and this discussion may have been very short; this will be the case if a dead lock is reached." The Mavrommatis Palestine Concessions, *supra* note 4, at 13. The issue was whether the applicant state had attempted to settle the dispute by negotiation before bringing it before the Court, as required by the relevant League of Nations mandate.

[28] *See* U.N. Doc. ST / LEG / 8, at 277–78 (1962). For municipal law decisions holding that a statutory duty to consult might be met by engaging in correspondence, see Attorney-General v. J.N. Perry Constructions, 6 Local Gvmt. Rep. of Austl. 385, 391 (1961); Port Louis Corp. v. Attorney-General of Mauritius, [1965] A.C. 1111, 1124, 1131–34 (Privy Council). *But see* Jugement du 26 Janvier 1972, *supra* note 26, at 390–91. The real shortcoming in the latter case was not that the exchange of views was in writing, but that neither side showed any willingness to compromise.

specialized purpose into adjacent ocean space and to define some of its attributes, to be effective at a later date. If consultations are held after any of these steps but before the effective date of the extension, are they prior to the relevant decision?[29] To take another example, if a national government decides in secret session to devalue the nation's pegged currency and then hurriedly consults with the Executive Directors of the International Monetary Fund (IMF) before actually carrying out the devaluation, has there been prior consultation? The answer would seem to turn in each case on whether, at the time of the consultation, there is still a meaningful opportunity to influence the manner in which the acting state seeks to achieve its objective. Thus if, for example, an administrative agency in the United States issues a proposed rule without having consulted foreign representatives, but then considers the views of affected foreign (as well as domestic) interests before issuing a final rule, there would be meaningful prior consultation.[30] To the extent, however, that the critical point of decision is not clear in any given situation, an educated guess has to be made if the available facts seem to warrant it; if they do not, this study draws no conclusion.

Sometimes a governmental decision on a matter having prospective external significance is passive, in the sense that it is a decision not to act, or not to regulate private activities within its control. There may even be no decision, as that term is usually understood, if a government simply has not faced the issue of controlling private conduct in externality-prone situations. Thus, a government might do nothing (deliberately or

[29] Philip Jessup has said that it is usually futile to enter into detailed consultations with potentially affected governments before new legislation is enacted and is to be applied in a specific instance. Jessup, *The Anti-Smuggling Act of 1935*, 31 AM. J. INT'L L. 101, 102 (1937). Consultations may indeed be premature when a legislature is likely to alter or reject legislation proposed by the executive, but there often comes a point before final enactment when meaningful consultations are possible. On the timing issue when a prior consultation standard is applied to the legislative process, see LE THI MAI, *supra* note 7, at 18–19.

[30] For example, in 1970 the United States Food and Drug Administration (FDA), after consulting only domestic interests, proposed that all eyeglasses sold in the United States be made of impact-resistant materials of a minimum thickness. *See* 35 Fed. Reg. 15,402 (1970). European manufacturers of fashion sunglasses, who supplied one-half of the U.S. market, complained to the FDA about the thickness requirement. As a result, that requirement was eliminated from the FDA's final position. *See* 36 Fed. Reg. 8939, 8940 (1971), and *see generally* Note, *The Restrictive Effects of Industrial Standards on International Commerce*, 4 LAW & POLICY IN INT'L BUSINESS 607, 611–12 (1972).

otherwise) to regulate private weather-modification activities near the boundaries of adjacent nations, even though the effects of the weather modification might spill over the border in ways considered undesirable by those on the other side. Such a situation is clearly relevant to this study, but it poses difficult fact-finding problems for the researcher. Because of the lack of data, only a few such cases are covered in this study.

Another troublesome problem is that of characterizing an assertion (in a treaty or otherwise) of an international duty to obtain the consent of affected states before acting in a given way. Is that simply another way of asserting that the contemplated act is in violation of a nonperemptory international norm, unless the norm is waived by the states for whose benefit it exists? Or should this be characterized as encompassing, a fortiori, an assertion of a duty to consult before acting? If the former, the assertion relates more to substance than to procedure, but if the latter, it is appropriate to consider it interchangeably (for purposes of this study) with an assertion limited to consultation. If the asserted duty to obtain consent is regarded by those involved simply as a more stringent alternative to consultations, or is an aberration in a string of assertions relating primarily to consultation, or is adopted by an international agency or conference essentially as a procedural mechanism without an express statement as to the lawfulness of the substantive conduct, it would seem to encompass an asserted duty to consult. In other cases, however, an assertion of a duty to obtain consent should be distinguished from an assertion of a duty to consult. The subject then would be lawfulness of the conduct qua conduct.

There is no comparable characterization problem when the asserted duty is simply to negotiate with potentially affected states. Negotiations encompass consultations, and a duty to negotiate does not imply that the contemplated conduct would be unlawful if the negotiations fail to produce agreement.

Finally, there is the problem of establishing the range of decisions to be covered. In a sense, almost every policymaking or policy-implementing decision a national government makes in the late twentieth century carries with it potential extranational effects. It is plausible to assume that in the great majority of cases involving essentially internal matters, the extranational effects will be sufficiently slight to render any but the most casual prior consultation inefficient: The transaction cost to both sides of holding the consultation would exceed any benefit from bringing the externality into the decision process. The focus will therefore be on decisions that have relatively visible, significant extranational implications, and even in such cases the study will neglect instances in which the impact is centered on one or a few individuals (for example, an isolated expropriation having relatively little political or economic effect in the investing state) or in which the detriment is essentially to national pride.[31]

Even within the scope of this study, it has been necessary to take representative instances of actual or potential unilateral conduct, rather than to examine all instances that could possibly be evaluated. The emphasis is on recent events, in order to facilitate perception of current norms and emerging trends. It is also on events that have achieved some notoriety, since those tend to be important and since useful data surrounding them are more likely to be available than in the case of less prominent events.

A few pertinent events that occurred or were reported too late to be included in the main body of the study appear in the Afterword. The most significant of these stem from the 1982 Conference of the International Law Association, including the Montreal Rules of International Law Applicable to Transfrontier Pollution.

[31] For one such example, see Handl, *Territorial Sovereignty and the Problem of Transnational Pollution,* 69 AM. J. INT'L L. 50 (1975).

Chapter II

International Watercourse Systems

A. Introduction

With about 214 international watercourse systems in the world serving a variety of purposes ranging from navigation to waste disposal, the opportunities for externality-creating unilateral action are legion. A dam or irrigation project upstream may not only affect navigation in a downstream state but change the ecology there. Industrial effluents pollute drinking water and restrict recreational uses downstream. Thermal pollution affects neighboring fisheries. Riverborne impurities pollute the oceans. Alteration of the banks of a boundary river may create a danger of flooding on the other side. The list could go on.

This chapter examines state practice relating specifically to freshwaters in international watercourse systems.[1] State practice arising from the use of relatively confined regional resources, but not relating exclusively to rivers, lakes, or other freshwaters, is covered in the next chapter. For example, practice broad enough to cover not only freshwater pollution, but air pollution and / or other disamenities, is discussed in the next chapter. Most of the practice stemming exclusively from the use of freshwaters, and thus most of the practice examined in this chapter, concerns rivers and lakes rather than groundwaters or aquifers.

There has been more scholarly inquiry into the existence of a prior consultation duty regarding international watercourses than into any other area covered by this study. The leading work is by Professor C. B. Bourne, who has concluded that

> international law imposes on a basin state the obligation to consult and to negotiate in good faith with co-basin states that object to a

I am grateful for the research assistance of Patricia Marrison, then a UCLA law student, in the preparation of this chapter.

[1] There is an ongoing debate over whether the proper subject of study and regulation is the international river, watercourse, drainage basin, or something else. The International Law Commission has opted for the international watercourse system concept, and that concept is accepted here even though much of the discussion necessarily concerns individual rivers and lakes. For the Commission's formulation, *see* [1980] 2 Y.B. Int'l L. Comm'n, Pt. 2, at 108–09, U.N. Doc. A/CN.4/SER.A /1980/Add.l (Part 2).

proposed work or utilization of waters on the ground that it might cause them serious injury. The law requires consultation and negotiation only for a reasonable time, so that a co-basin state cannot delay a project indefinitely by refusing to agree to it. It does not require a state to accept any reasonable terms offered to it by a co-basin state, nor does it require them to reach agreement.[2]

Other studies have come to similar conclusions.[3] A few have defined the duty more stringently. For example, Griffin concluded:

> (*a*) A riparian which proposes to make, or allow, a change in the existing regime of a system of international waters which could interfere with the realization by a coriparian of its right to share on a just and reasonable basis in the use and benefits of the system, is under a duty to give the coriparian an opportunity to object.
>
> (*b*) If the coriparian, in good faith, objects and demonstrates its willingness to reach a prompt and just solution by the pacific means envisaged in article 33(1) of the Charter of the United Nations, a riparian is under a duty to refrain from making, or allowing, such change, pending agreement or other solution.[4]

[2]Bourne, *Procedure in the Development of International Drainage Basins: The Duty to Consult and to Negotiate,* 1972 CAN. Y.B. INT'L L. 212, 233.

[3]*See* H. SMITH, THE ECONOMIC USES OF INTERNATIONAL RIVERS 152 (1931); G. GLOS, INTERNATIONAL RIVERS: A POLICY-ORIENTED PERSPECTIVE 144 (1961); Livingston, *Science, Technology, and International Law: Present Trends and Future Developments,* in 4 THE FUTURE OF THE INTERNATIONAL LEGAL ORDER: THE STRUCTURE OF THE INTERNATIONAL ENVIRONMENT 68, 86 (C. Black & R. Falk eds. 1972); Report of the Panel of Experts on the Legal and Administrative Aspects of International Water Resources Development, Management of International Water Resources: Institutional and Legal Aspects, U.N. Doc. ST/ESA/5, at 44 (Natural Resources / Water Series, No. 1, 1975); Report of the Comm. on Legal Aspects of the Conservation of the Environment, in REPORT OF THE 58TH CONF. OF THE INT'L LAW ASS'N, 1978, at 383, 407 (1980); *cf.* Report of Executive Director [of UNEP], Co-operation in the Field of the Environment Concerning Natural Resources Shared by Two or More States, U.N. Doc. UNEP/GC/44, at 8 (1975); J. KUSUMOWIDAGDO, CONSULTATION CLAUSES AS MEANS OF PROVIDING FOR TREATY OBEDIENCE 80 (1981).

O. SCHACHTER, SHARING THE WORLD'S RESOURCES 69–70 (1977), states that recent trends suggest the eventual emergence of a prior consultation rule and notes the additional details that would have to be filled in if such a rule is to be fully effective. The members of the Institute of International Law's Commission on pollution of rivers and lakes were divided on whether general custom requires notification and consultation when a pollution risk can be foreseen. *See* 58-I ANNUAIRE DE L'INSTITUT DE DROIT INT'L 239 (1979).

[4]GRIFFIN, LEGAL ASPECTS OF THE USE OF SYSTEMS OF INTERNATIONAL WATERS, S. DOC. NO. 118, 85th Cong., 2d Sess. 90–91 (1958). Griffin went on to say that a coriparian does not have a veto over changes in the river system; that is, it cannot frivolously object to a change and thereby render the change unlawful. *Id.* at 91.

Another eminent jurist defines the duty without reference to the likelihood of injury downstream. Jiménez de Aréchaga says, "[A]State which intends to proceed to the execution of works capable of affecting an international watercourse has a duty to give notice and consult the other riparian States."[5]

The trouble with these studies is that they do not systematically demonstrate that state practice has created the normative expectations embodied in their conclusions. Nor do they distinguish with sufficient particularity between situations that may raise different expectations regarding either the existence or the extent of a prior consultation duty. For example, Professor Bourne has demonstrated that when problems have arisen concerning the use of international watercourses, almost always there have been eventual negotiated settlements. The large number of river treaties attests to this.[6] But that does not demonstrate that these were *prior* negotiations in the sense that they occurred before final decisions were made regarding proposed unilateral acts, nor does it demonstrate that the parties asserted or acknowledged a duty to negotiate before making final decisions. The Griffin study set out primarily to demonstrate that the Harmon Doctrine no longer represents customary international law, if it ever did.[7] In the process, Griffin discussed several treaties, declarations, and resolutions tending to support a general norm of either prior consultation or prior consent, but he did not make some important distinctions; moreover, his study, published in 1958, does not reflect recent practice. Jiménez de Aréchaga, after setting forth the blanket consultation duty in *lex lata* terms, restated it as though it were *de lege ferenda*; moreover, he relied on only two indications of state practice.[8]

[5]Jiménez de Aréchaga, *International Law in the Past Third of a Century*, 159 HAGUE ACADEMY, RECUEIL DES COURS 1, 197 (1978).

[6]*See* Bourne, *supra* note 2, at 220.

[7]The Harmon Doctrine, formulated by the then–Attorney General of the United States, asserted that an upper riparian could do as it wished with waters within its territory, regardless of harm to lower riparian states. 21 Op. Att'y Gen. 274, 283 (1895). The Doctrine has now been thoroughly discredited. *See*, in addition to the Griffin study (note 4 *supra*), Utton, *International Water Quality Law*, in INTERNATIONAL ENVIRONMENTAL LAW 154, 155–69 (L. Teclaff & A. Utton eds. 1974). It has been replaced by the doctrine of equitable utilization, which, by stressing vague notions of reasonableness, lays bare the need for procedural constraints. For the doctrine of equitable utilization, see the Helsinki Rules, art. IV, in REPORT OF THE 52D CONF. OF THE INT'L LAW ASS'N, 1966, at 486 (1967).

[8]*See* Jiménez de Aréchaga, *supra* note 5, at 197–98. He relied on the Lake Lanoux

Thus, it seems essential to reexamine state practice, bringing existing studies up to date and examining critically the practice on which they were based. Since treaties in this field abound, and follow fairly consistent patterns of regulation, they are a particularly fruitful source and / or reflection of normative expectations regarding freshwater use, even for nonparties.[9] Some treaties no longer in force are mentioned, if they are part of a consistent pattern. Because a great many instances of state practice—whether in the form of treaties or otherwise—involve single watercourses within well-defined geographic regions, the discussion will proceed first by regions, and will then turn to nonregional normative assertions.[10]

B. Europe

As one would expect, there is a long history of bilateral, and occasionally multilateral, treaties regulating the uses of Europe's rivers. A substantial number set forth procedural requirements to be met before various unilateral measures may be taken. Relatively clear patterns emerge, with one norm rather consistently being applied to most uses of contiguous rivers—those forming or encompassing a boundary between states for all or substantial parts of their courses—and another norm for successive rivers.

The distinct normative pattern for contiguous European rivers calls for consent or formal agreement between the states opposite each other (or by any relevant river commission) before any measure is taken that is likely to alter significantly the water level, the rate of flow, or the course of the river.[11] If the

Case, discussed in the text at notes 61–67 *infra*, and on the Charter of Economic Rights and Duties, discussed in the text at note 194 *infra*.

[9]*See* Griffin, *supra* note 4, at 63; Vitányi, *The Regime of Navigation on International Waterways, Part I: The Beneficiaries of the Right of Navigation*, 5 Neth Y.B. Int'l L. 111, 160–66 (1974); *cf.* Bourne, *supra* note 2, at 223; F. Berber, Rivers in International Law 128–37 (1959) (expressing caution regarding the use of treaties as a source of custom, but using them nevertheless).

[10]Most of the treaties and other documents discussed in this chapter are summarized in two exhaustive reports by the U.N. Secretariat: Legal Problems Relating to the Utilization and Use of International Rivers, U.N. Doc. A/5409 (1963), and Legal Problems Relating to the Non-navigational Uses of International Watercourses, U.N. Doc. A/CN.4/274 (1974). The reports are reprinted in [1974] 2 Y.B. Int'l L. Comm'n, Pt. 2, at 33, 265, U.N. Doc. A/CN.4/SER.A/1974/Add.l (Part 2).

[11]As noted in chapter I, this is a more stringent norm than one requiring only prior consultation.

river is navigable, such measures would normally interfere with navigation, but the established normative pattern is not limited to navigable rivers or to measures that could affect only navigation. The list of European treaties establishing the prior consent norm for contiguous rivers covers such a span of time and cross section of states that the existence of at least a regional custom seems clear.[12] There are a few exceptions to the pattern,

[12]Some of the treaties below relate to successive as well as contiguous rivers. The list includes: (1) Prussia-Netherlands, June 26, 1816, art. 27(1), U.N. Doc. ST/LEG/SER.B/12,Treaty 203 (1963) (any alteration in course or in banks, or any diversion); (2) Belgium-Luxembourg, Aug. 7, 1843, art. 30, *id.* Treaty 152 (any new intake or change in river or in banks); (3) Austria-Germany, June 24, 1862, art. 58, *id.* Treaty 135 (any new conduit or watercourse diverting water from river); (4) Germany-Switzerland, March 10, 1879, art. 5(2), *id.* Treaty 217 (prior consultation regarding works likely to produce detrimental effect on flow or on banks, but parties have consistently reached agreement before acting; *see* U.N. Doc. A/5409, n. 616 (1963)); (5) U.K.-France, Sept. 4, 1913, Protocol art. 5, U.N. Doc. ST/LEG/SER.B/12, Treaty 24 (use for hydroelectric power; colonial treaty, applying to Sierra Leone and French Guinea); (6) France-Netherlands, Sept. 30, 1915, art. 3, *id.* Treaty 72 (any works capable of altering the "hydrographic regime"; colonial treaty, applying to French Guiana and Surinam); (7) Versailles Treaty, June 28, 1919, art. 359, in 2 MAJOR PEACE TREATIES OF MODERN HISTORY 1265, 1498 (F. Israel ed. 1967) (any works on the Rhine where it forms French-German border, subject to certain French rights to divert water or produce hydroelectric power if that would not interfere with navigation); (8)Poland, Russia, Ukraine, Mar. 18, 1921, Supp. Protocol to art. 2, 6 L.N.T.S. 169 (works by which waterways might be deteriorated); (9) Germany-Denmark, Apr. 10, 1922, art. 29, 10 L.N.T.S. 200 (new or major alteration of works if it would change water level); (10) Norway-Finland, Feb. 14, 1925, art. 1, 49 L.N.T.S. 379 (any detrimental change in specified waterways); (11) Germany-France, Aug. 14, 1925, art. 13, 75 L.N.T.S. 103 (any alteration in course or construction likely to modify flow of nonnavigable river); (12) Germany, France, Saar Territory, Nov. 13, 1926, Protocol art. 2, 77 L.N.T.S. 249 (any installation that might modify existing course across the frontier or change water level of River Saar); (13) U.S.S.R.-Turkey, Jan. 8, 1927, arts. 4(1), (2), (5), 10(1), U.N. Doc. ST/LEG/SER.B/12, Treaty 106 (choice of site and type of construction of dam); (14) Spain-Portugal, Aug. 11, 1927, art. 8, 82 L.N.T.S. 131 (any diversion not prohibited by the treaty); (15) Germany-Lithuania, Jan. 29, 1928, art. 2, 89 L.N.T.S. 337 (modifications in flood zone); (16) Norway-Sweden, May 11, 1929, art. 12(1), 120 L.N.T.S. 277 (any works likely to cause considerable inconvenience to navigation, timber floating, or fishing or considerable interference with water supply); (17) German Dem. Rep.–Poland, Feb. 6, 1952, art. 18 (1–3), 304 U.N.T.S. 160 (any new bridges or dams, and any changes in existing ones that would affect water level or navigability); (18) Bulgaria-Romania, Nov. 29, 1955, art. 6, U.N. Doc. A/CN.4/274, vol. 1, at 119 (navigation-improvement works altering conditions of Danube on the frontier; unclear whether the treaty entered into force); (19) France–Fed. Rep. Germany, Oct. 27, 1956, art. 7(1), U.N. Doc. ST/LEG/SER.B/12, Treaty 179 (any works in Saar frontier area subject to flooding); (20) France–Fed. Rep. Germany–Luxembourg, Oct. 27, 1956, art. 56, *id.* Treaty 123 (construction, operation, and maintenance of works and utilization of hydraulic resources on contiguous segment of Moselle); (21) U.S.S.R.-Afghanistan, Jan. 18, 1958, art. 19 (1–4), 321 U.N.T.S. 166 (any new bridges or dams likely to hinder navigation or influence water flow, and any change in existing ones that might alter water level); (22) Czechoslovakia-Poland, Mar. 21, 1958, art. 3(1), 538 U.N.T.S. 108 (any works that

but they are insignificant.[13]

The declarations on international watercourses of the Institute of International Law—primarily, though not exclusively, a European (nongovernmental) body—tend to support the proposition asserted above. In its Madrid Declaration of 1911, referring to uses other than navigation, the Institute said:

> I. When a stream forms the frontier of two States, neither of these States may, without the consent of the other, and without special and valid legal title, make or allow individuals, corporations, etc. to make alterations therein detrimental to the bank of the other State. On the other hand, neither State may, on its own territory, utilize or allow the utilization of the water in such a way as seriously

would affect the other's "water economy"); (23) Poland-U.S.S.R., Feb. 15, 1961, art. 20(1–3), 420 U.N.T.S. 161 (same as German Dem. Rep.–Poland, above); (24) Greece-Turkey, Jan. 19, 1963, arts. 19, 21, U.N. Doc. A/CN.4/274, vol. 1, at 136 (any work that might affect river's course, and any diversion for irrigation); (25) Hungary-Romania, June 13, 1963, art. 18(2), 576 U.N.T.S. 275 (construction or demolition of bridges or dams if water level would be changed); (26) Romania-Yugoslavia, Nov. 30, 1963, art.10(8), 512 U.N.T.S. 1 (any alteration in Iron Gates System on Danube that might affect other party's works); (27) Finland-U.S.S.R., Apr. 24, 1964, arts. 2, 9, 10, 537 U.N.T.S. 251 (measures that might adversely affect course, level, or flow, or that might create danger of flooding, cause significant loss of water, alter main channel, or interfere with navigation or timber floating; supersedes a similar treaty of Oct. 28, 1922, which had been revived on Feb. 10, 1947); (28) Poland-U.S.S.R., Feb. 16, 1965, art. 9, 552 U.N.T.S. 187 (any works that may affect use of water by other party); (29) Austria-Czechoslovakia, Dec. 7, 1967, art. 3(1), 728 U.N.T.S. 313 (any measures that would adversely affect water conditions in other state); (30) Finland-Sweden, Sept. 16, 1971, ch. 2, arts. 1–3 and ch. 3, art. 3, 825 U.N.T.S. 191 (new hydraulic works); (31) *cf.* France-Germany, July 16, 1975, art. 9, 80 REV. GEN. DE DROIT INT'L PUBLIC 1303 (1976) (parties will work together *[se concerteront]* before authorizing any appropriation of the water of the Rhine). See also the Barcelona Convention of Apr. 20, 1921, and its attached Statute, art. 10(6), 7 L.N.T.S. 37, requiring agreement among all riparian states or all members of an international river commission to close a "navigable waterway of international concern." There is one narrow exception, to be discussed later in this section. Eighteen of the twenty states that ratified or acceded to the Convention and Statute were European.

[13]For example, article 358 of the Versailles Treaty gave France certain rights to divert water from the Rhine or to produce hydroelectric power, provided that no interference with Rhine navigation resulted, and said that all proposed schemes "shall be laid before the Central Rhine Navigation Commission in order that it may assure itself that these conditions are complied with." *See* 2 MAJOR PEACE TREATIES OF MODERN HISTORY 1265, 1496–97 (F. Israel ed. 1967). The Rhine forms the border between France and Germany. There was no explicit requirement that the Commission give its consent to the proposed French measures. The precedential impact of this provision is diminished by the fact that this was a treaty dictated by France and its allies upon the defeated German state. Perhaps a more pertinent exception, though it applied to African rivers, was the Agreement between Belgium and the U.K., Nov. 22, 1934, art. 6, 190 L.N.T.S. 104 (prior notice and consultation regarding irrigation projects on contiguous rivers between Tanganyika and Ruanda-Urundi).

> to interfere with its utilization by the other State or by individuals, corporations, etc. thereof.
>
> The foregoing provisions are likewise applicable to a lake lying between the territories of more than two States.
>
> II. When a stream traverses successively the territories of two or more States:
>
> 1. The point where this stream crosses the frontiers of two States, whether naturally, or since time immemorial, may not be changed by the establishments of one of the States without the consent of the other.[14]

Paragraph II thus extends the prior-consent norm to a situation closely analogous to the contiguous-river situations we have considered: a physical alteration at the point where a successive river crosses the border. There is some European practice to support such a norm. In fact, it tends to support the norm as to long-term changes in the water level at the border, as well as to changes in the crossing point.[15]

In its 1961 Resolution on the Utilization of Non-Maritime International Waters, the Institute abandoned the distinction it had made in 1911 between contiguous and successive rivers.[16] The 1961 Resolution places primary emphasis on express or tacit agreement among interested states before any state undertakes works or utilization of waters "which seriously affect the possibility of utilization of the same waters by other States." Its pertinent articles provide:

> Article 5
>
> Works or utilizations referred to in the preceding article [quoted above] may not be undertaken except after previous notice to interested States.
>
> Article 6
>
> In case objection is made, the States will enter into negotiations with a view to reaching an agreement within a reasonable time.

[14]Set forth in English in U.N. Doc. E/ECE/EP/98/Rev.1, Annex 4, at 261 (1951), and in GRIFFIN, LEGAL ASPECTS OF THE USE OF SYSTEMS OF INTERNATIONAL WATERS, *supra* note 4, at 86.

[15]The treaties dissolving the Austro-Hungarian empire apply a prior-consent requirement to measures affecting "regions adjoining the frontier." *See* the treaties between Hungary-Romania, Apr. 14, 1924, arts. 1 & 2, 46 L.N.T.S. 41; Austria-Hungary, Mar. 11, 1927, arts. 1 & 2, 80 L.N.T.S. 67; Romania-Yugoslavia, Dec. 14, 1931, arts. 1 & 2, 135 L.N.T.S. 31. *Cf.* Lithuania-Poland, May 14, 1938, art. 18, 191 L.N.T.S. 373 ("common waters," broadly defined).

[16]Like the 1911 Declaration, *supra* note 14, this Resolution does not apply to navigation. It appears in English in 49-II ANNUAIRE DE L'INSTITUT DE DROIT INT'L 381 (1961), and in 56 AM. J. INT'L L. 737 (1962).

For this purpose, it is desirable that the States in disagreement should have recourse to technical experts and, should occasion arise, to commissions and appropriate agencies in order to arrive at solutions assuring the greatest advantage to all concerned.

Article 7

During the negotiations, every State must, in conformity with the principle of good faith, refrain from undertaking the works or utilizations which are the object of the dispute or from taking any other measures which might aggravate the dispute or render agreement more difficult.

Article 8

If the interested States fail to reach agreement within a reasonable time, it is recommended that they submit to judicial settlement or arbitration the question whether the project is contrary to the above rules.

If the State objecting to the works or utilizations projected refuses to submit to judicial settlement or arbitration, the other State free, subject to its responsibility, to go ahead while remaining bound by its obligations arising from the provisions of Articles 2 to 4.[17]

The Resolution contemplates that judicial settlement or arbitration could be a substitute for agreement, and that works or utilization could proceed if potentially affected, nonconsenting states refuse to submit to judicial settlement or arbitration. There is little or no state practice attaching such specific consequences to a refusal to submit to judicial settlement or arbitration, and the treaties mentioned above suggest that prior consent—not something closer to prior consultation—is still required for alterations in the level, course, or flow of contiguous rivers. The excerpt from the 1911 Declaration quoted above seems a more accurate reflection of European state practice regarding such alterations than does the 1961 Resolution.

On the other hand, it is not possible at present to extract a prior consent norm from European treaty practice regarding pollution of contiguous (or successive) rivers, nor does a prior consent norm presently apply to either pollution or changes in water level of contiguous lakes. There is evidence, however, that a prior consultation norm exists. We shall examine contiguous lakes first.

[17] 1961 Resolution, *supra* note 16, arts. 5–8.

The European contiguous lakes attracting the most regulatory attention have been Lake Constance and Lake Geneva.[18] In 1960 the Land (state) of Baden-Württemberg, the Free State of Bavaria, Austria, and Switzerland concluded a convention on pollution control in Lake Constance, containing the following provision:

> In particular, the riparian States shall inform each other, in sufficient time, of water utilization projects that could adversely affect the interests of another riparian State in maintaining the salubrious condition of the lake's water. Such projects shall not be put into effect until after there have been joint discussions among the riparian States, unless delay would endanger life or unless the other states have expressly consented to their immediate execution.[19]

In 1966 another agreement concerning Lake Constance was concluded among Austria, the Federal Republic of Germany, and Switzerland. It expressly preserves the pollution-control measures of the 1960 convention, and provides a procedural mechanism for regulating withdrawals of water from the lake. Under the 1966 Convention, "riparian States shall, before authorizing withdrawals of water, afford one another in good time an opportunity to express their views" when planned withdrawals exceed designated rates. When an objection is raised that the projected withdrawal would adversely affect important interests of the other riparian states and could not be offset by compensation, a joint consultative committee is to be established. If that fails to produce agreement, and further diplomatic efforts also fail, the matter ultimately may be submitted to an arbitration commission, whose decision is binding.[20]

These two treaties set up a comprehensive prior consultation system for Lake Constance, without requiring prior consent. They recognize the impropriety of purely unilateral action significantly affecting a common lake, while taking account also

[18] Lake Lanoux, the subject of a well-known arbitration pertinent to this study, lies wholly within France. The Lake Lanoux case is discussed later in this chapter.

[19] Convention on the Protection of Lake Constance Against Pollution, Oct. 27, 1960, art. 1(3), U.N. Doc. ST/LEG/SER.B/12, Treaty 127 (1963). The Convention entered into force on Dec. 10, 1961. The quotation in the text is the author's unofficial translation from the French.

[20] Agreement Regulating the Withdrawal of Water from Lake Constance, Apr. 30, 1966, Final Protocol, arts. 7–11, 620 U.N.T.S. 198.

of the distinctions between such a body of water and a contiguous river, with its narrower banks, running water, and—sometimes—greater diversity of potential uses.[21]

The French-Swiss convention on pollution control in Lake Geneva is less explicit on prior consultation than are the Lake Constance treaties. It requires the parties to cooperate closely to protect Lake Geneva from pollution, and establishes a joint commission with the power, inter alia, to recommend measures to prevent future pollution and to examine any matter related to pollution of the lake.[22] The duty to cooperate in the prevention of pollution, combined with the establishment of a commission designed to facilitate pollution-control cooperation, implies that neither party may lawfully act unilaterally, without offering to consult the other or the commission, in such a manner as to threaten a significant increase in the lake's pollution. The implied duty to consult in such a situation stems in part from the recognized good-faith obligation of a party to a treaty to refrain from acting in a way that seriously jeopardizes accomplishment of the treaty's purposes[23] and in part from the express duty in the treaty to cooperate in preventing pollution.[24]

The 1920 Peace Treaty between Russia and Estonia went further than the more recent Western European treaties, requiring consent of the other party before lowering by more than one foot, or raising by any amount, the water level of

[21] When a proposed project has threatened serious pollution of Lake Constance, action has apparently been withheld until the approval of the other parties has been obtained. *See* Kiss & Lambrechts, *La Lutte Contre la Pollution de l'Eau en Europe Occidentale,* 15 ANN. FRANÇAIS DE DROIT INT'L 718, 732–33 (1969). It is not clear, however, whether such practice has created an expectation among the parties that prior approval is required.

[22] Convention Concerning the Protection of the Waters of Lake Geneva (Lac Léman) Against Pollution, Nov. 16, 1962, arts. 1, 3, in OECD, ENVIRONMENTAL PROTECTION IN FRONTIER REGIONS 418 (1979) (hereafter ENVIRONMENTAL PROTECTION).

[23] *See, e.g.,* the International Law Commission's commentary to article 23 of its draft articles on the law of treaties, [1966] 2 Y.B. INT'L LAW COMM'N 211, U.N. Doc. A/CN.4/SER.A/1966/Add.l.

[24] *Cf.* Kiss & Lambrechts, *supra* note 21, at 733, suggesting that commissions are often used for prior consultation, despite the absence of an express duty to do so. The Technical Subcommission for Lake Geneva has been used for prior study of several significant projects. *See* Droz, *Protection of Lake Leman Waters Against Pollution,* in ENVIRONMENTAL PROTECTION, *supra* note 22, at 393, 406–07.

A consultation duty for projects affecting the Genevese aquifer may be implied from the Arrangement Concerning the Protection, Utilization and Recharging of the Franco-Swiss Genevese Aquifer, Jan. 1, 1978, art. 2, *id.* at 427 (functions of Joint Operations Board).

either of two named boundary lakes.[25] This treaty, no longer in force, is significant as a step in the European development of a norm against purely unilateral action significantly affecting contiguous lakes, but does not fit into any pattern calling for prior consent in such cases. Its only real support is found in the Institute of International Law's 1911 Madrid Declaration, which expressly applied the provisions of its paragraph I to contiguous lakes lying between more than two states. Paragraph I supplied essentially a prior-consent regime for those measures it did not purport to prohibit. Thus, if the Madrid Declaration represented custom, the prior-consultation treaty regime set up in 1960 and 1966 for Lake Constance would be a retreat from the more stringent customary rule. It is most unlikely that the parties regarded what they were doing as a step toward greater unilateralism. Aside from the 1920 treaty mentioned above, there was not and is not sufficient state practice in Europe to equate sizeable boundary lakes with boundary rivers for purposes of attaching a prior consent requirement.

Nevertheless, since all European treaties dealing specifically with frontier lakes, as well as the Madrid Declaration, apply a standard of prior consultation or something greater, it is reasonable to conclude that a customary prior-consultation norm does exist in Europe. That there are not many treaties to refer to is simply a function of the paucity of major contiguous lakes.

On the question of river pollution, European state practice does not set more stringent procedural standards for contiguous rivers than for successive ones, even though some of the treaties requiring prior consent for measures affecting the level, course, or flow of contiguous rivers are broad enough to encompass measures affecting water quality.[26] These treaties are not sufficiently pervasive to establish a general European norm regarding water quality in contiguous rivers; they do fit, however, into a broader pattern, discussed below, establishing the less stringent prior-consultation norm when measures are planned that could harmfully pollute either contiguous or successive rivers.

[25] Peace Treaty between Russia and Estonia, Feb. 2, 1920, annex 2 to art. 16, 11 L.N.T.S. 29.

[26] *See* the following treaties cited in note 12 *supra*: Norway-Finland, Feb. 14, 1925; Norway-Sweden, May 11, 1929; Czechoslovakia-Poland, Mar. 21, 1958; Finland-U.S.S.R., Apr. 24, 1964, arts 4, 9, 10; Poland-U.S.S.R., Feb. 16, 1965; Austria-Czechoslovakia, Dec. 7, 1967.

One significant treaty—between the Netherlands and the Federal Republic of Germany regarding their contiguous and successive rivers other than the Rhine, Ems, and Dollard—requires notification to the Dutch-German boundary waters commission before any measure is taken that might substantially affect the use and management of water resources in the territory of the other party; if that party objects to the measure, work on it must be postponed pending deliberations within the commission, unless the delay would endanger seriously the interests of the party proposing the measure.[27] Although the requirement is not limited to pollution-engendering measures, these are among its most important applications.[28]

The Nordic Convention on the Protection of the Environment[29] refers expressly to environmentally harmful discharges into watercourses and lakes, without distinguishing between contiguous and successive watercourses. It assumes, but does not require, that national officials will examine "the permissibility of environmentally harmful activities which entail or may entail considerable nuisance in another Contracting State." When such an examination is being conducted, "consultations shall take place between the States concerned if the government of the [potentially affected] State so requests."[30] Moreover, even if there is no official environmental assessment, persons in any contracting state may challenge a proposed activity in a court or administrative body of the proposing state.[31]

[27] Frontier Treaty between The Netherlands and the Federal Republic of Germany, Apr. 8, 1960, arts. 60–62, 508 U.N.T.S. 14.

[28] *See* Kiss & Lambrechts, *supra* note 21, at 726–27.

[29] Nordic Convention on the Protection of the Environment, Feb. 19, 1974, 13 INT'L LEGAL MATERIALS 591 (1974). The convention entered into force on Oct. 5, 1976, among Denmark, Finland, Norway, and Sweden. The reference to watercourses and lakes is in art. 1.

[30] *Id.* art. 11. As of April 1979, only Sweden among the contracting states had a mandatory environmental assessment procedure, although environmental assessments of major projects were regularly conducted in Finland and Norway. They were carried out on a somewhat less regular basis in Denmark. *See Hearing on S. Res. 49, Before a Subcomm. of the Senate Comm. on Foreign Relations*, 95th Cong., 1st Sess. 39 (1977); OECD Doc. ENV / Min(79)3, at 9 (1979); OECD, ENVIRONMENTAL IMPACT ASSESSMENT 33–36, 49–51, 53–57 (1979). The OECD member governments have declared that "prior assessment of the environmental consequences of significant public and private activities should be an essential element of policies applied at the national, regional and local levels." OECD Declaration on Environmental Policy, Nov. 14, 1974, in OECD AND THE ENVIRONMENT 21, 22 (1979). *See also* OECD Declaration of Anticipatory Environmental Policies, May 8, 1979, *id.* at 23.

[31] Nordic Convention, *supra* note 29, art. 3. For a preconvention case in which Norway consulted Sweden (under circumstances amounting to recognition of a duty) regarding

The treaties concluded in the early 1960s to alleviate pollution of the Moselle, Saar, and Rhine—each partly contiguous and partly successive—created river commissions to promote cooperation among the parties, but imposed no express duty of prior consent or of prior consultation.[32] The commissions have the power to propose measures to prevent further pollution, and can meet at any time at the request of one (or, in the case of the Rhine Commission, two) of the Parties. As in the case of the convention concerning Lake Geneva, discussed above, there is an implied duty to offer to consult the appropriate commission, or the parties it represents, before a party to one of these treaties adopts measures threatening increased pollution of the river.[33]

The 1976 Rhine convention on chemical pollution contains prior consultation requirements, to be carried out within the commission created by the 1963 Rhine treaty, for the establishment of emission standards for certain particularly harmful substances and of national programs to control less harmful pollutants.[34] It does not require consultation each time a pol-

proposed new discharges into a boundary fjord having the characteristics of a contiguous river, see OECD Secretariat, *Pollution in the Iddefjord,* in ENVIRONMENTAL PROTECTION, *supra* note 22, at 447, 454–55, 460.

[32] *See* Protocol on the Establishment, Composition and Functions of the International Commission for the Protection of the Moselle Against Pollution, Dec. 20, 1961, *summarized in* U.N. Doc. A/CN.4/274, vol. 1 at 114 (1974); Protocol Concerning the Establishment of an International Commission for the Protection of the Saar Against Pollution, Dec. 20, 1961, summarized *id.* at 131; Agreement Concerning the International Commission for the Protection of the Rhine Against Pollution, Apr. 29, 1963, *summarized id.* at 115.

[33] The argument is particularly strong regarding the Moselle, since the separate Convention Concerning the Canalization of the Moselle, Oct. 27, 1956, art. 55, U.N. Doc. ST/LEG./SER.B/12, Treaty 123 (1963), requires the three Moselle riparian states to cooperate with each other to prevent pollution. They are the three represented on the Moselle Commission. Consultations in the Moselle Commission have been held regarding thermal pollution from several proposed nuclear power plants. *See* ENVIRONMENTAL PROTECTION, *supra* note 22, at 269–70, 277.

Treaties comparable in many respects to those involving the Moselle, Saar, and Rhine are the Convention Between Italy and Switzerland Concerning the Protection of Italian-Swiss Waters Against Pollution, April 20, 1972, in 11 INTERNATIONAL PROTECTION OF THE ENVIRONMENT 5688 (B. Rüster & B. Simma eds. 1977), and the Agreement on Fishing in Waters of the Danube Among the Soviet Union, Bulgaria, Romania, and Yugoslavia, Jan. 29, 1958, arts. 7, 11–13, in A SOURCE BOOK ON SOCIALIST INTERNATIONAL ORGANIZATIONS 1104 (W. Butler ed. 1978). These are less clear than the others, however, regarding their respective commissions' authority to consider, and make recommendations on, specific measures that could result in new pollution.

[34] Convention on the Protection of the Rhine Against Chemical Pollution, Dec. 3, 1976, arts. 3, 5, 6, in 16 INT'L LEGAL MATERIALS 242 (1977).

lutant is to be discharged. A separate treaty on pollution of the Rhine by chlorides attempts to prevent any net increase in chloride ions discharged into the river, but includes an escape clause permitting some increases after an opinion from the commission has been requested.[35] In effect, the participants agreed that consultation with the commission will be sought before an increase in pollution of the Rhine by chlorides is permitted.

The 1911 Madrid Declaration of the Institute of International Law, in the paragraph dealing with contiguous rivers (quoted in the text above), was framed in terms of an outright prohibition against measures that would "seriously . . . interfere with . . . utilization by the other State or by individuals, corporations, etc. thereof." That prohibition would include pollution-engendering measures. On this point, the Institute's 1961 Resolution is closer to the mark. If it is shorn of its recommendatory language regarding judicial settlement or arbitration—language that clearly goes beyond existing practice—it sets forth a duty to negotiate, without distinguishing between pollution of contiguous and successive rivers.

In 1979 the Institute addressed itself specifically to river and lake pollution. After defining pollution in such a way as to limit it to injurious changes in water composition or quality, the Institute said that "States bordering the same hydrographic basin shall, as far as practicable, especially through agreements" resort to the following devices (inter alia):

> [N]otify the States concerned in due time of any activities envisaged in their own territories which may involve the basin in a significant threat of transboundary pollution; . . .
>
> . . . consult with each other on actual or potential problems of transboundary pollution of the basin so as to reach, by methods of their own choice, a solution consistent with the interests of the States concerned and with the protection of the environment.[36]

Since the norm would apply to potential problems as well as to actual ones, and since it is coupled with a prior notification norm, it would require prior consultation in appropriate cases.

[35]Convention on the Protection of the Rhine Against Pollution by Chlorides, Dec. 3, 1976, art. 3, *id.* 265. The signatories to both conventions are the Federal Republic of Germany, France, Luxembourg, the Netherlands, and Switzerland.

[36]Institute of International Law, *Resolution on Pollution of Rivers and Lakes*, 1979, art. VII, in 58–II ANNUAIRE DE L'INSTITUT DE DROIT INT'L 197, 201 (1979). *Cf.* Economic Commission for Europe, *Declaration of Policy on Prevention and Control of Water Pollution, Including Transboundary Pollution*, April 23, 1980, para. 13, U.N. Doc. E/ECE/1014 (1980).

European Community (EC) law goes a significant step further than the Institute's recommendations, by establishing prohibitions against the discharge into the "aquatic environment" of specified harmful substances beyond designated limits, and by restricting discharges of other, somewhat less harmful, substances. There are some exceptions to the prohibitions. A licensing system, administered by national authorities, is established to monitor the discharge rules. Transfrontier groundwaters are protected by a special regulatory scheme that requires the licensing authority of each member state to inform the other member states concerned before a license is issued. At the request of any member state concerned, consultations must be held before the license is issued, and the Commission may participate if it wishes.[37]

The European Communities also rely on prior notification and consultation procedures regarding some other potential freshwater pollutants. Article 37 of the Euratom Treaty calls for notification to the Commission, and an opinion by it, regarding any plan by a member state to dispose of radioactive waste; articles 41 and 43 of the same treaty require notification by enterprises, and a response by the Commission to the state concerned, regarding proposed nuclear power stations and installations concerned with the nuclear fuel cycle;[38] and in 1982 the Council was moving toward a prior consultation procedure when a power station is likely to affect the territory of another member state.[39] Apart from any such formal procedure, consultations have been held regarding several proposed nuclear power stations among the Moselle and the Rhine.[40]

[37] *See* Council Directive 76/464/EEC, May 4, 1976, in 19 O.J. EUR COMM. (No. L 129) 23 (1976); Council Directive 80 / 68/ EEC, Dec. 17, 1979, art. 17, in 23 *id.* (No. L 20) 43 (1980). The 1979 directive supersedes the earlier one as to groundwater, and requires member state compliance within two years. The "aquatic environment" includes (in addition to groundwater) surface water, territorial waters, and internal coastal waters. *See also* chapter III at note 40. Council of Europe, Draft European Convention for the Protection of International Watercourses Against Pollution, April 4, 1974, in 11 INTERNATIONAL PROTECTION OF THE ENVIRONMENT 5785 (B. Rüster & B. Simma eds. 1977), would set minimum quality standards for contiguous and successive rivers, subject to some exceptions.

[38] European Atomic Energy Community Treaty, March 25, 1957, 298 U.N.T.S. 167, article 37, expressly mentions water pollution. As to the other consultation requirements, *see* EC Doc. COM(76) 576 (Final) at 3, 12, and Annex I (1976).

[39] *See* 22 O.J. EUR. COMM. (No. C 149) 2 (1979).

[40] *See* 20 *id.* (No. C 277) 15 (1977) (proposed French station at Cattenom); *see also* note 33 *supra* (others on the Moselle); Lammers, *New International Legal Developments*

Thus far, the discussion of practice has suggested that there is a norm, at least in Europe, requiring consent of riparian states before potentially injurious measures, other than those strictly involving pollution, are taken affecting contiguous rivers (or successive rivers at the border crossing); and that a prior consultation norm applies to (*a*) potentially injurious uses (including those involving pollution) of contiguous lakes, and (*b*) potentially harmful pollution-engendering uses of contiguous or successive international rivers or groundwaters, at least in the absence of an internationally sanctioned regulatory scheme. It remains to be seen what procedural standard applies to nonpolluting uses of successive rivers.

At least one writer has concluded, primarily on the basis of European practice, that as to maintenance of navigability on a successive river, "[n]o alteration of the natural flow of river waters which is likely to prejudice the legitimate interests of a co-riparian State should be carried out without the consent of that State."[41] There are some significant European treaties, discussed below, to support that proposition.

The Statute attached to the Barcelona Convention of 1921, a multilateral treaty drafted and ratified primarily by European governments,[42] requires prior agreement among all riparian states, or all members of the international river commission if there is one, before a "navigable waterway of international concern" is closed to navigation. No distinction is drawn between contiguous and successive waterways, or between contiguous and successive segments of the same waterway. The Statute does contain a narrow exception. If there is no international commission on which nonriparian states are represented, the Statute provides that a riparian state may close a waterway to navigation if the navigation on it is of very small importance and if the state can show a greater economic value from the

Concerning the Pollution of the Rhine, 27 NETH. INT'L L. REV. 171, 186 (1980). The Rhine consultations have included Switzerland, a nonmember of Euratom. *See also* chapter III at notes 20–27.

[41] Vitányi, *The Regime of Navigation on International Waterways: Substantive Rights and Duties* (Part III), 7 NETH. Y.B.INT'L L. 3, 89 (1976). Although the language sounds precatory, its context demonstrates the author's belief that this is an existing customary obligation.

[42] The Barcelona Convention and Statute on the Regime of Navigable Waterways of International Concern, Apr. 20, 1921, 7 L.N.T.S. 35, was ratified or acceded to by twenty parties, of which all but two were European. One of the European parties was the United Kingdom, which participated on behalf of the British Empire.

alternative use than from navigation. To invoke the exception, the state must give prior notice to other riparian states and allow them an opportunity to appeal to a dispute-settlement procedure set forth in the Statute.[43] Thus, at least for parties to the Statute and Convention, prior consent would be required before a state could take the rather drastic step of closing a significant international navigable waterway, or even a relatively insignificant navigable waterway if nonriparian states are sufficiently interested to have become members of an applicable river commission.[44] But the Statute and Convention do not expressly require consent or consultation before action that might interfere with navigation without shutting it off completely.

The Final Act of the Congress of Vienna in 1815—the starting point for the development of European river law—went further than the Barcelona Statute and Convention by providing, "The Powers whose territories are separated or traversed by the same navigable river undertake to settle by common agreement all questions affecting navigation thereon."[45] That would call for prior consent not only of a contiguous or successive river is to be closed to navigation, but whenever a proposed measure would affect navigation.

The conventions regulating navigation on the Danube and the Elbe, adopted in the early 1920s, were consistent with the Final Act of the Congress of Vienna. The two conventions treated, in virtually identical terms, installations that could interfere with navigation. The Danube Convention provided:

> The riparian States shall supply the International Commission with a summary description of all works to be carried out on the portion of the waterway situated within their own frontiers which they consider necessary for their economic development, especially works designed to prevent inundation and those undertaken for purposes connected with irrigation and the utilisation of hydraulic power.

[43] Statute, *supra* note 42, art. 10(6).

[44] In Territorial Jurisdiction of the International Commission of the River Oder, 1929 P.C.I.J. ser. A, No. 23, at 22, the World Court held that the administrative powers of the Oder Commission stemming from the Barcelona Convention could not be asserted against Poland, a nonparty. Norms embodied in the Convention or Statute could still bind nonparties, if the norms did not require states to subject themselves to a given administrative body.

[45] Final Act of the Congress of Vienna, June 9, 1815, art. 108, *as quoted in Int'l Law Ass'n,* REPORT OF THE 56TH CONFERENCE 122 (1974). *See also* the Oder Commission Case, *supra* note 44, at 27.

> The Commission may not forbid the construction of such works except in so far as they may be detrimental to navigation.[46]

If the Commission made no observation within two months of the notice, the proposed works could be carried out. In effect, the Commission's tacit consent was required if the proposed works somehow would be detrimental to navigation.

Germany withdrew from the Elbe Commission in 1936. When the Federal Republic of Germany began building the Geesthacht Dam on the lower Elbe in the late 1950s, its government made the decision apparently without consulting either the German Democratic Republic or the then-recognized authority for East Germany, the Soviet Union. Clearly it did so without the consent of either of them. The Federal Republic did offer to discuss the matter at the technical level with the East German authorities after the basic decisions had been made but before the dam was completed.[47] Such an offer does not amount to an expression of willingness to admit the affected government into the basic decision-making process.

After World War II, a new Danube Convention was concluded among the Eastern European nations with interests in the river. Although the new convention did not include among its parties all the parties to the earlier one, its Supplementary Protocol asserted that the earlier Danube Convention was no longer in force.[48] The Western allies protested that the earlier convention was not terminated, but, as a practical matter, the administrative mechanisms—involving a new Danube Commission and greater power in the riparian states to set navigational rules for nonriparians—are those of the postwar convention.[49] The new convention dilutes the authority of the Danube Commission to deal with works that might hinder nav-

[46]Convention Instituting the Definitive Statute of the Danube, July 23, 1921, art. 14, 26 L.N.T.S. 173. The comparable provision relating to the Elbe was in Convention on the Navigation of the Elbe, Feb. 22, 1922, art. 41, 26 L.N.T.S. 219.

[47]*See* 3 M. Whiteman, Digest of International Law 902–03 (1964). The abnormal political situation involving the two Germanys at the time of the Geesthacht Dam incident impairs its precedential value.

[48]*See* Convention Regarding the Regime of Navigation on the Danube, Aug. 18, 1948, 33 U.N.T.S. 196, and Supplementary Protocol, *id.* 222.

[49]For discussion of events leading to the new convention and of the Western allies' position, see 3 M. Whiteman, Digest of International Law 887–901 (1964); R. Baxter, the Law of International Waterways 135–37 (1964). Austria ultimately ratified the 1948 convention and participated in the new Danube Commission.

igation by saying that the Danubian states undertake "not to obstruct or hinder navigation on the navigable channels of the Danube, [and that] [t]he Danubian states shall consult the Danube Commission on matters referred to in this article" (which also includes provisions for the maintenance of navigable channels).[50] For the last sentence to be effective, it must mean that the consultation is to be held before the navigational hindrance or maintenance scheme is accomplished. But such a prior consultation requirement, of course, is not tantamount to the tacit consent norm contained in the earlier Elbe and Danube Conventions.

There is no treaty relating to the Rhine that requires consent of a commission or of interested states before action is taken that could interfere with navigation. The applicable treaty does call for exchange of information among parties before hydrological works are carried out, in order that the works may be suitable to them.[51] Moreover, the practice has developed of consulting the Central Commission for the Navigation of the Rhine before executing works that might interfere with navigation.[52] The Commission sometimes asks for modifications and approves them,[53] but neither the Commission nor the states involved apparently consider the Commission's approval to be required.

Practice over a number of years between Belgium and the Netherlands involving their navigable waterways—rivers and canals—also supports only a prior consultation regime. First, there were the long-running disputes between the two countries involving diversions of the Meuse for navigable canals. Although Belgium at one point asserted that Dutch plans for the Juliana Canal could not be executed without its consent, the Dutch went ahead anyway and the Belgian government later

[50] Danube Convention, 1948, *supra* note 48, art. 3. The Eastern European states on the Danube have also agreed that "the Contracting Parties which build and operate such installations [as dams which might change the hydrological and hydrobiological regime of the river] shall work out in good time and jointly implement the plan of measures which would ensure the normal migration of fish." Agreement on Fishing in Waters of the Danube, *supra* note 33, art. 5.

[51] Navigation on the Rhine is still regulated by the Mannheim Convention of Oct. 17, 1868, as amended. It appears in an English translation in 32 Brit. Parl. Papers 33 (Cmd. 2421) (1963–64 sess.). The provision on exchange of information is article 29.

[52] *See* Walther, *Le Statut International de la Navigation du Rhin*, 2 Eur. Y.B. 3, 19–20 (1956).

[53] *See* International Navigable Waterways, U.N. Doc. UNITAR /74/ST/6, at 91 (1975).

proceeded with its own Albert Canal without waiting for Dutch consent. In each instance, however, there were consultations at the planning stage.[54]

In 1963, Belgium and the Netherlands agreed to construct a system of canals and locks connecting the Scheldt and the Rhine. They agreed, inter alia, to maintain the water level in the canal from Antwerp harbor to the eastern Scheldt at a given level "so far as possible," and to consult each other before adopting any measures that might affect that level. In addition, the Netherlands agreed to consult Belgium before closing a preexisting navigable waterway or making major changes in its quality.[55]

This patchwork of treaty obligations and other state practice produces the following regime for measures potentially affecting navigation on European successive waterways: At a minimum, prior consultation with other riparian states, or with a river commission if there is one, must be undertaken before any measure is adopted that could significantly interfere with navigation on an already-navigable waterway. Prior consent is required only if the proposed measure would completely close a significant waterway to navigation. Despite some evidence that a prior consent requirement might extend to any significant interference with navigation, the practice to that effect is not sufficiently consistent to establish such a customary European norm.

With respect to nonpolluting measures that could affect the level, course, or flow of nonnavigable successive rivers, there is very little to suggest that prior consent would be required in the absence of a specific treaty obligation. Any support for a prior consent duty stems almost entirely from European treaties relating to rivers that are contiguous in part and successive in part. The treaties in such instances normally apply a prior consent requirement to most or all segments of rivers lying between the two states or within either of them, unless the contiguous segments are insignificant in relation to the river systems covered by the treaties.[56]

[54] *See* The Diversion of Water from the Meuse, 1937 P.C.I.J. ser. A/B, No. 70, at 14–15. The Meuse is both a contiguous and a successive river.

[55] Treaty Concerning the Connection Between the Scheldt and the Rhine, May 13, 1963, arts. 15 and 33(2), 540 U.N.T.S. 3.

[56] *See* the following treaties, note 12 *supra:* Norway-Finland, Feb. 14, 1925; Germany–France–Saar Territory, Nov. 13, 1926; Norway-Sweden, May 11, 1929; Finland-U.S.S.R.,

On the other hand, European treaties dealing with successive nonnavigable rivers typically apply only a prior consultation requirement.[57] There also have been consultations without benefit of treaty obligations when unilateral measures affecting nonnavigational uses of successive rivers either were planned or could feasibly have been adopted.[58]

Relevant declarations concerning successive rivers also support the prior consultation duty, but not a prior consent re-

Apr. 24, 1964; Poland-U.S.S.R., Feb. 16, 1965; Austria-Czechoslovakia, Dec. 7, 1967; Finland-Sweden, Sept. 16, 1971. *Cf.* West Germany–East Germany, Sept. 20, 1973, in 11 INTERNATIONAL PROTECTION OF THE ENVIRONMENT 5693 (B. Rüster & B. Simma eds. 1977) (prior consultation re measures on frontier waters).

One treaty requiring consent before construction of hydroelectric works on a purely successive river was the Convention Between France and Italy on the River Roya, Dec. 17, 1914, arts. 1 & 3, *discussed in* F. BERBER, RIVERS IN INTERNATIONAL LAW 86 (1959). That treaty appears to have been superseded by the Treaty of Peace of Feb. 10, 1947, 49 U.N.T.S. 126, which modified the French-Italian frontier in such a way that most of the Roya is now in French territory. *See* U.N. Doc. A / 5409, n. 435 (1963).

[57] *See* (*1*) Spain-France, May 26, 1866, art. 11, U.N. Doc. ST/LEG/SER.B/12, Treaty 185 (works likely to change flow or volume downstream; this was the treaty involved in the Lake Lanoux arbitration, discussed later in this chapter); (*2*) U.K.-Belgium, Nov. 22, 1934, Gr. Brit. T.S. No. 42 (CMD. 5778) (irrigation diversions; colonial treaty, applying to Tanganyika and Ruanda-Urundi); (*3*) Austria-Yugoslavia, May 25, 1954, art. 4, 227 U.N.T.S. 128 (any new Austrian installations that might divert water from the Drava basin or affect it to the detriment of Yugoslavia; of primary significance to the nonnavigable portion of the Drava); (*4*) Netherlands–Federal Republic of Germany, Apr. 8, 1960, arts. 60–62 508 U.N.T.S. 14 (any measures that may substantially affect use and management of water resources in other's territory; applies to some waterways that are contiguous and successive, but primarily to purely successive ones); (*5*) Bulgaria-Turkey, Oct. 23, 1968, arts. 1 & 2, 807 U.N.T.S. 117 (implies prior consultation regarding structures and installations); (*6*) Bulgaria-Greece, July 12, 1971, arts. 1 & 2, U.N. Doc. A/CN.4/274, at 166 (1974) (implies prior consultation with river commission as to generation of electric power and utilization of waters of rivers crossing parties' territories). *Cf.* France-Switzerland, Aug. 27, 1926, art. 3, 71 L.N.T.S. 63, and Spain-Portugal, Aug. 30, 1927, art. 10, 82 L.N.T.S. 131 (consultation before one party carries out prearranged hydroelectric project in its own territory).

[58] For example: (*1*) When Bavarian authorities in 1923 planned to divert water from a Danube tributary, Austria protested and eventually reached a settlement with Bavaria. F. BERBER, RIVERS IN INTERNAIONAL LAW 79 (1959). (*2*) When Austria in 1926 blocked the course of the Walchen (a successive river) by constructing a power station, there had been negotiations since 1920 regarding the effect on Bavarian nonnavigational uses; the Bavarian authorities abandoned their original claim that a successive waterway could not be blocked without the consent of the downstream state. Sevette, Legal Aspects of Hydro-Electric Development of Rivers and Lakes of Common Interest, U.N. Doc. E/ECE/136, at 100–101 (1952). (*3*) The Agreement between Austria and Germany, Oct. 16, 1950, U.N. Doc. ST/LEG/SER.B/12, Treaty 136, regarding diversion of certain successive waterways, resulted from consultations in lieu of feasible unilateral Austrian action. *See* Sevette, *supra,* at 106–07. (*4*) A similar situation is reflected in the Agreement between Greece and Yugoslavia, June 12, 1970, U.N. Doc. A/CN.4/274, vol. 1, at 165 (1974).

quirement. In 1954, the Committee on Electric Power of the Economic Commission for Europe (ECE) recommended that a state proposing to construct a hydroelectric project in its own territory that was likely to have serious repercussions on the territory of other states should first communicate the relevant information to them and, if they raise objections, should endeavor through negotiations to reach agreement with them.[59] As already noted, insofar as the Institute of International Law purported in 1961 to set forth mandatory rules, it adopted essentially a prior notification and prior consultation regime to be pursued when any state proposes works or utilization of waters "which seriously affect the possibility of utilization of the same waters by other States."[60]

Particulary significant in this respect is the Lake Lanoux Arbitration in 1957 between France and Spain.[61] Lake Lanoux lies on the southern slope of the Pyrenees, in French territory. Its only outlet is the River Carol, which flows for about 25 kilometers within France and then crosses into Spain. Beginning in 1917, the French authorities considered various plans to divert Lake Lanoux waters from the River Carol basin to that of the River Ariège. Spain, on several occasions, asserted a right of prior notification and (somewhat inconsistently) a right either to be consulted or to require that its consent be obtained, pursuant to article 11 of the Additional Act to the 1866 Treaty of Bayonne.[62] Finally, in 1949, the parties agreed to establish a Mixed Commission of Engineers to study the matter. When another French diversion plan was formulated in 1950, the Spanish government requested that work be postponed until after a meeting of the Mixed Commission. The French government replied that although the Additional Act did not require works likely to affect the water system to be suspended at the request of a party, it could assure Spain that the project was not imminent and that it would agree to a meeting of the Mixed Commission. France also asserted that since it planned

[59]ECE Comm. on Elec. Power Recommendation No. 4, May 26, 1954, U.N. Doc. E/ECE/EP/147, *reprinted in* U.N. Doc. A/CN.4/274, vol. 2, at 205 (1974).

[60]*See* text at notes 16–17 *supra*.

[61]Lake Lanoux Arbitration (France v. Spain), Nov. 16, 1957, 24 I.L.R. 101 (1957), *digested in* 53 AM. J. INT'L L. 156 (1959), *and in* 3 M. WHITEMAN, DIGEST OF INTERNATIONAL LAW 1066–73 (1964).

[62]*See, e.g.* 24 I.L.R. at 105, reporting one instance in which Spain asserted a right to be consulted and one in which it said that its consent was required. Article 11 of the Additional Act is quoted in the text below.

to restore to the Carol the full amount of any water diverted, Spain had no legitimate interest in the matter under the Additional Act and work would not have to be delayed until the Mixed Commission had finished its studies. After further sparring, a new mixed commission met in December 1955. At that meeting, France proposed the scheme ultimately at issue in the arbitration: accumulation of waters in Lake Lanoux, diversion and use for hydroelectric power into the River Ariège, and an underground tunnel to return an equivalent amount of water from the Ariège to the Carol upstream from any Spanish use. Spain continued its opposition to any diversion, so the meeting and a subsequent one in March 1956 ended without agreement. At that point, France began work on the diversion project.

Clearly, then, there was consultation before the diversion project began, and it occurred under an assertion of right by Spain based on article 11 of the Additional Act to the Treaty of Bayonne, which provides in part:

> When in one of the two States it is proposed to construct works or to grant new concessions which might change the course or the volume of a watercourse of which the lower or opposite part is being used by the riparian owners of the other country, prior notice will be given to the highest administrative authority of the Department or of the Province to which such riparian owners are subject . . . , so that, if they might threaten the rights of the riparian owners of the adjoining Sovereignty, a claim may be lodged in due time with the competent authorities, and thus the interests that may be involved on both sides will be safeguarded.[63]

Such language clearly implies a duty to consider a "claim" in good faith—a form of consultation. In fact, France went further and negotiated despite its assertion that no harm would be done by the proposed measure.

The arbitral tribunal, composed of eminently qualified persons,[64] rejected Spain's argument that consent of the downstream state was required before the upstream state could utilize the resource in its own territory, since that could paralyze the exercise of territorial jurisdiction on the part of the latter state. Speaking in terms not restricted to practice under article 11, the tribunal said:

[63] Additional Act to the Treaty of Bayonne, May 26, 1866, art. 11, U.N. Doc. ST/LEG/SER.B/12, Treaty 185 (1963). The quotation in the text is from the English translation in 24 I.L.R. at 103 (1957).

[64] Messrs. Petrén, Bolla, De Luna, Reuter, and De Visscher.

> That is why international practice prefers to resort to less extreme solutions by confining itself to obliging the States to seek, by preliminary negotiations, terms for an agreement, without subordinating the exercise of their competence to the conclusion of such an agreement. . . .
>
> . . . States are today perfectly conscious of the importance of the conflicting interests brought into play by the industrial use of international rivers, and of the necessity to reconcile them by mutual concessions. The only way to arrive at such compromises of interests is to conclude agreements on an increasingly comprehensive basis. International practice reflects the conviction that States ought to strive to conclude such agreements: there would thus appear to be an obligation to accept in good faith all communications and contacts which could, by a broad comparison of interests and by reciprocal good will, provide States with the best conditions for concluding agreements.[65]

This, of course, is a finding that under existing state practice, apart from any treaty obligation (and not necessarily limited to Europe), there is an obligation to engage in meaningful preliminary negotiations, but no duty to obtain the agreement of other interested states if their consent proves unobtainable after a good-faith effort.

The tribunal then turned to the specific provisions of the Additional Act of 1866 and made several points relevant to this study. First, it reiterated its rejection of Spain's argument that prior agreement was required by the Act, and said: "one can but admit that there does exist a duty of consultation and of bringing into harmony the respective actions of the two States when general interests are involved in matters concerning waters."[66] Next, it supplied important corollaries to the duty to consult:

> [I]n order for negotiations to proceed in a favourable climate, the Parties must consent to suspend the full exercise of their rights during the negotiations. . . .
>
> . . . [T]he possibility of prejudicing the course or the volume of the water mentioned in Article 11 cannot in any case be left exclu-

[65] 24 I.L.R. at 128, 129–30 (1957).

[66] *Id.* at 133. When French authorities began work on a diversion project affecting the (successive) River Err in 1973 without consulting the Spanish authorities, the latter again complained. Consultations were then held under article 11 of the Additional Act, in time to protect Spanish interests. *See* Smets, *Joint Water Resource Management in the Llivia Enclave in the French / Spanish Pyrenees*, in ENVIRONMENTAL PROTECTION, *supra* note 22, at 314, 318–22.

sively to the discretion of the State which proposes to execute those works or to grant new concessions. . . . A State which is liable to suffer repercussions from work undertaken by a neighbouring State is the sole judge of its interests; and if the neighbouring State has not taken the initiative, the other State cannot be denied the right to insist on notification of works or concessions which are the object of a scheme.[67]

The two major corollaries—restraint from action during negotiations (which presumably could not be prolonged unreasonably by the other state) and denial of unbridled discretion to determine whether other states' interests would be affected—are significant whenever there is a duty of prior consultation, not just under the terms of the treaty at issue in the Lake Lanoux Case. On the other hand, the unqualified language about the right to insist on notification almost certainly was intended to apply only to the type of works or concessions covered by article 11—those that might change the course or volume of an international watercourse.

To summarize European practice, then, prior consent of the interested riparian states is required when a measure is contemplated that would pose a significant risk of an appreciable change in the navigability, level, course, or flow of a contiguous river or an analogous segment of a successive river (but not if the only threat is that of pollution), or that would close a navigable successive river to navigation, when navigation is an important use of the river.[68] The same duty probably applies when a measure would alter the course of a successive river at the point where it crosses the border. In all other situations involving a significant risk of appreciable harm to watercourse interests in other states, a prior consultation norm (as embellished by the Lake Lanoux decision) applies.[69] The Lake Lanoux

[67] 24 I.L.R. at 134, 138 (1957). The tribunal also set forth some standards for the good-faith conduct of negotiations in cases of this sort. *See* chapter I, note 26 *supra*.

[68] When a river is partly contiguous and partly successive, European practice tends to treat it as contiguous—and therefore subject to the prior consent requirement—if its contiguous segment represents a significant part of its total course. *See* text at note 56 *supra*.

[69] This would include situations in which the proposed measure is to be taken on a national tributary of a contiguous river, unless the latter represents a significant part of the combined courses of the two rivers. *See* note 68 *supra*. Measures on a wholly national tributary of a successive river should be subject to the same norm as the main river, bearing in mind that the risk of harm to other states may be lessened in such cases and that the duty to consult would normally arise only if there is a significant risk of appreciable harm. For discussion of European consultation practice involving

decision leaves undecided whether, in the absence of a treaty, a downstream state may demand that it be notified early in the planning stages of *any* proposed works affecting the watercourse. Probably the duty to notify arises only when there is reason to assume that the downstream state, acting in good faith, might contend that a significant risk of appreciable harm is presented. Any reasonable doubt must be resolved in favor of notification. In some cases, such as those involving noticeable changes in the course, volume, or water quality of an international watercourse, that assumption would arise from the very nature of the project.

C. Africa and Asia

If one excludes purely European state practice relating to African and Asian colonies and territories, relevant practice in Africa and Asia tends to be limited to a few major rivers and lakes.[70] It is difficult to distill unambiguous patterns from this rather episodic practice, but in general it supports the European norms discussed above.

A leading example relating to African contiguous rivers appears in the 1972 Convention promulgating the Statute of the Senegal River. For most of its course, the river runs along the Senegal-Mauritania border. Under the 1972 Convention, any project affecting the river requires prior consultation with, and approval by, the contracting states.[71] That is consistent with a 1926 treaty between South Africa and Portugal prohibiting construction of hydraulic works on the boundary sectors of the Kunene and Kavango rivers without the other government's prior consent.[72]

tributaries, *see* Sevette, Legal Aspects of Hydro-Electric Development of Rivers and Lakes of Common Interest, U.N. Doc. E/ECE/136, at 9–10 (1952).

[70] Treaties between European states on behalf of their colonial possessions reflected European norms rather than norms generated in the territories affected by the treaties. *See* notes 12 and 13 *supra*.

[71] Convention relative au statut de fleuve Senégal, Mar. 11, 1972, art. 4, Journal Officiel de la République Islamique de Mauritanie, July 26, 1972, at 212. The Convention entered into force in November 1972. In practice, the consultation and approval functions are carried out by the relevant river commission, the Organisation pour la mise en valeur du fleuve Senegal. *See* Parnall & Utton, *The Senegal Valley Authority: A Unique Experiment in International River Basin Planning*, 51 Indiana L.J. 235, 240 n.15 (1976). The 1972 Convention replaced an earlier Senegal River treaty set forth in 3 Basic Documents of African Regional Organizations 1019 (L. Sohn ed. 1972).

[72] South Africa–Portugal, July 1, 1926, art. 18, 70 L.N.T.S. 316.

The prior consent regime was applied rather consistently by the United Kingdom in its treaties with indigenous governments in Africa and the Indian subcontinent. In each instance the United Kingdom, with its overwhelming bargaining power, stood to gain from the prior consent requirement.

In the 1906 treaty between Great Britain and the Independent State of the Congo, the latter undertook not to construct or allow any work on the Semliki (Isango) River that would diminish the volume of water entering Lake Albert, a contiguous lake, without the consent of the Sudanese government.[73] The 1934 treaty between Afghanistan and the U.K. (on behalf of India) prohibited construction of any new irrigation channel from the Arnawai Khwar above its boundary segment, without the consent of the local British authorities.[74] In both of these instances, British interests were directly benefited.

The 1902 British treaty with Ethiopia is particularly noteworthy, not only for its terms but for the way in which they were applied. In it, Ethiopia agreed not to construct or allow any work across the Blue Nile, Lake Tsana, or the Sobat that would arrest the flow into the Nile, except in agreement with the British government and the government of the Sudan.[75] That provision was invoked by the British in 1927 when Ethiopia made preliminary contact with financing and engineering firms for the construction of a dam at Lake Tsana without informing the British government. Interestingly, the British Foreign Secretary protested, but asserted only the right to be consulted, not the right of veto apparently accorded by the language of the 1902 treaty.[76] The Ethiopian government conceded that it had a duty to consult (based on the treaty) before concluding any contract, but made no mention of any duty to obtain British consent.[77] Thus, the practical construction of the

[73]Great Britain–Independent State of the Congo, May 9, 1906, art. 3, U.N. Doc. ST/LEG/SER.B/12, Treaty 5 (1963). Batstone, *Utilisation of the Nile Waters*, 8 INT'L & COMP. L.Q. 523, 534 (1959), explains the prior consent requirement by observing that the Congo's interests in the river were insignificant.

[74]Afghanistan-U.K., Feb. 3, 1934, Note No. 1, para. 3, 154 L.N.T.S. 350.

[75]Great Britain–Ethiopia, May 15, 1902, art. 3, U.N. Doc. ST/LEG/SER.B/12, Treaty 13 (1963). Batstone, *supra* note 73, argues that this and the 1906 treaty with the Congo were inconsistent with prevailing state practice, which did not recognize a veto power in lower riparians.

[76]210 PARL. DEBATES, H.C., (5th ser.) col. 35 (1927); [1927] 2 FOREIGN REL. OF THE U.S. 605.

[77][1927] 2 FOREIGN REL. OF THE U.S. 607.

1902 treaty by the parties supports only a prior consultation norm.

The 1929 treaty between the U.K. and Egypt provides that in the absence of a prior agreement with Egypt, no irrigation or power works are to be constructed on the Nile or its branches, or on the lakes from which it flows—insofar as these are in the Sudan or in countries under British administration—that would prejudice Egypt by reducing the quality of water arriving there, modifying the date of its arrival, or lowering its level.[78] This treaty, which appears ultimately to have been acknowledged by the Sudan as binding on it after its independence,[79] may well be explained by the eagerness of the British government to maintain good relations with the strategically important Egyptian government, resulting in the subordination of its then-diminishing interest in the Sudan to its interest as a global naval and mercantile power dependent on maintaining a trouble-free Suez Canal.[80]

The construction of the Aswan High Dam, creating a reservoir with waters backing onto Sudanese territory, provides a significant—though not wholly unambiguous—example of state practice. In 1952, the relevant Egyptian agency adopted a basic plan for the dam without consulting the Sudanese government. The latter subsequently complained that it was not given the details of the proposal until September 1954, when negotiations for financing the project were well along.[81] Arguably, a 1949 declaration by the Egyptian government, welcoming "the participation of the Sudan in the projects for the control of the Nile which were then under consideration," obligated Egypt to consult the Sudan before irrevocable decisions regarding the new Aswan Dam were made.[82] In any event, the Sudanese gov-

[78] U.K.-Egypt, May 7, 1929, Note No. 1, para. 4(b), 93 L.N.T.S. 44.

[79] *See* the Nile Waters Agreement, Nov. 8, 1959, preamble, 453 U.N.T.S. 51; Hosni, *The Nile Regime*, 17 REVUE EGYPTIENNE DE DROIT INT'L 70, 92 (1961). Shortly after Sudanese independence, however, the Sudanese Prime Minister apparently said that the Sudan did not consider itself bound by the 1929 treaty. *See* 3 M. WHITEMAN, DIGEST OF INTERNATIONAL LAW 1006 (1964); Okidi, *Review of Treaties on Consumptive Utilization of Waters of Lake Victoria and the Nile Drainage System*, 22 NAT. RESOURCES J. 161, 175–76 (1982).

[80] *Cf.* Batstone, *supra* note 73, at 531–32.

[81] *See* Garretson, *The Nile Basin*, in THE LAW OF INTERNATIONAL DRAINAGE BASINS 256, 274–75 (A. Garretson, R. Hayton, & C. Olmstead eds. 1967); S. Hosni, Legal Problems of the Development of the River Nile 69 (1957) (Ph. D. dissertation, N.Y.U.).

[82] The quote is from S. Hosni, *supra* note 81, at 159. Hosni's conclusion that the

ernment asserted a right to be consulted in a timely fashion, and Egypt responded with negotiations leading to the Nile Waters Agreement of 1959.[83] Construction of the dam was not begun until 1960. Consequently, consultation took place before irrevocable steps had been taken, though not before detailed plans had been made. Moreover, the consultation was in response to a claim of right based on an arguable Egyptian recognition of a duty to consult. The incident is therefore normatively significant and tends to support a rule of consultation, at least before final action is taken.

Other treaty and nontreaty Asian-African practice is consistent, for the most part, with the prior consultation norm regarding successive rivers. For example, the Indus Waters Treaty of 1960, concerning rivers primarily successive, contains this provision:

> If either Party plans to construct any engineering work which would cause interference with the waters of any of the Rivers [in the Indus Basin] and which, in its opinion, would affect the other Party materially, it shall notify the other Party of its plans and shall supply such data relating to the work as may be available and as would enable the other Party to inform itself of the nature, magnitude and effect of the work. If a work would cause interference with the waters of any of the Rivers but would not, in the opinion of the Party planning it, affect the other Party materially, nevertheless the Party planning the work shall, on request, supply the other Party with such data regarding the nature, magnitude and effect, if any, of the work as may be available.[84]

At first glance, this provision would appear insignificant. It does not expressly require consultation, and it requires self-generated notification of plans and available data only if, in the opinion of the acting party, the proposed project would affect the other party materially. Nevertheless, the clear implication is that

quoted language obligated Egypt not to undertake Nile River control works without the consent of the Sudan seems to go beyond reasonable inference. On the significance of unilateral declarations, *see* the Nuclear Test Cases, 1974 I.C.J. 253 and 457; Rubin, *The International Legal Effects of Unilateral Declarations*, 71 Am. J. Int'l L. 1 (1977).

[83] The Nile Waters Agreement (Egypt-Sudan), Nov. 8, 1959, 453 U.N.T.S. 51. For another instance of prior consultation on a proposed dam affecting Nile waters, *see* Okidi, *supra* note 79, at 176.

[84] Indus Waters Treaty (India-Pakistan), Sept. 19, 1960, art. 7(2), 419 U.N.T.S. 125, 55 Am. J. Int'l L. 797 (1961).

whenever the duty to notify applies (under either sentence of the provision above), there is a duty to consult. The purposes in supplying the required data might be to enable the other party to present its position intelligently to the proposing state, or to apprise it of the magnitude of its prospective loss so it could try to adapt to the new situation in ample time, or to give it a basis for retaliation. The latter purpose may be summarily dismissed. It is equally unlikely that the second purpose underlies the notification duty, since the entire thrust of the Treaty is cooperation, not adaptation to faits accomplis. That leaves only the consultation purpose.[85]

Nor does the provision appear to be illusory simply because its first sentence permits the acting party to make the judgment whether the engineering work would affect the other party materially. First, the exercise of judgment would have to be made in good faith. This would be so even if the differences in the applicable treaty provisions render inapplicable the Lake Lanoux tribunal's dictum that the nonacting state "cannot be denied the right to insist on notification of works or concessions."[86] Even more importantly, notification of available details must be made on request under the second sentence of the Indus Waters Treaty provision quoted above. Nothing seems to preclude a blanket request calling for notification whenever a proposed scheme would interfere with the waters.

Moreover, the annexes to the Indus Waters Treaty clearly require prior consultation in certain situations. These are: construction by India of new run-of-the-river hydroelectric plants on the western rivers or material changes in design of existing western river plants, and material changes in design of existing storage works by India.[87] On the other hand, the Treaty neither expressly nor by implication requires consultation before new potential pollutants are introduced into the waters.[88]

[85]Not all treaty provisions requiring prior notification imply prior consultation. To determine whether such an implication is justified, one must ascertain the purpose of the notification requirement.

[86]*See* text at note 67 *supra*.

[87]Indus Waters Treaty, *supra* note 84, Annexure D, paras. 6, 7, 9, 10, 12, 19, 20, 22; Annexure E, paras. 5, 6. There were prior consultations concerning the Salal hydroelectric plant on the Chenab. *See* 21 FOREIGN AFF. REC. (India) 162 (1975); 22 *id.* 281, 282 (1976).

[88]Article 4(10) contains a declaration of intent to prevent, "as far as practicable, undue pollution of the waters" and requires the parties to take all reasonable measures

Finally, it is significant to note that the Indus Waters Treaty is itself the result of long negotiations between India, Pakistan, and the World Bank, undertaken at a time when India had already taken some unilateral action to divert Indus Basin waters and had threatened (under a claim of right) to increase its diversions. Pakistan consistently asserted that a solution had to be found through negotiations or, failing agreement, through adjudication. After making its initial diversions without consultation, India later acquiesced in the demands for negotiations and threatened unilateral action only when the negotiations stalled.[89]

India has constructed on the Ganges, a successive river running from India through Bangladesh, a dam (barrage) at Farakka to divert water into the Hooghly River in order to flush out silt deposits interfering with navigability at the port of Calcutta. Bangladesh asserted that this diversion so depleted the Ganges flow during the November-May dry season that 400,000 acres of irrigated agricultural land were seriously affected and other uses of the lower Ganges (such as navigation and domestic uses) were disrupted. The diversion, however, was preceded by extensive negotiations with the Pakistani government (then in control of East Pakistan), beginning in 1951. India began construction of the dam in 1961 and completed it in 1975. The negotiations failed to produce a lasting agreement before the dam was put in operation, but it appears that they were conducted in good faith. They did produce an interim agreement permitting India a limited diversion in April-May 1975, but Bangladesh later alleged that after May 1975 India began to take the diversion canal's full capacity without further consultation. India replied, however, that its full-capacity diversion was only during the abundant water season and offered to consult concerning diversions during the next dry season.[90] A

to treat sewage and industrial wastes introduced into the waters. It says nothing about prior notification or consultation. Nor could a duty to consult regarding pollution be inferred from the existence of the Permanent Indus Commission, since it was not set up to deal with pollution problems.

[89] For descriptions of the circumstances leading to the Indus Waters Treaty of 1960, *see, e.g.*, A. Michel, The Indus Rivers 195–265 (1967); Baxter, *The Indus Basin*, in The Law of International Drainage Basins 443, 451–66 (A. Garretson, R. Hayton, & C. Olmstead eds. 1967).

[90] *See* the letter from the Permanent Representative of Bangladesh to the U.N., Aug. 26, 1976, U.N. Doc. A/31/195/Add.l, Annex, at 2 (1976); 22 Foreign Aff. Rec. (India) 55–57 (1976). The interim agreement appears in 21 *id.* 111 (1975).

settlement was finally reached in November 1977. A joint committee was established to implement the settlement and to examine any difficulty arising out of the operation of the Farakka barrage.[91]

Taken as a whole, then, the Ganges diversion situation supports the prior consultation norm for successive rivers. India did consult extensively before building a dam and diversion canal of a specified capacity; it proceeded to use the canal up to its capacity only when any damage to Bangladesh would be minimal; and it agreed to set up the joint committee to which Bangladesh could resort for consultation in the event of later difficulties.

A similar dispute arose, spanning almost the same period of time, between Iraq, on one hand, and Turkey and Syria on the other, concerning the waters of the Euphrates, another successive river. In 1975 Turkey began to fill the Keban Dam on its sector of the Euphrates, and was building or planning three more dams. Downstream, Syria was filling its dam at Tabqa. The combined effect was to reduce significantly the amount of irrigated farm land in Iraq. Negotiations on the sharing of Euphrates water had been carried on among the three states since 1962.[92] In the case of Turkey and Iraq, the negotiations appear to have been conducted pursuant to their 1946 treaty requiring Turkey to inform Iraq of its plans for the construction of conservation works, "in order that these works may as far as possible, be adapted, by common agreement, to the interests of both Iraq and Turkey."[93]

The treaty regime governing the Niger River Basin—primarily a successive river system—expressly requires states parties to consult the Niger River Commission before executing any works likely to pollute the waters or any modification likely to affect the biological characteristics of the fauna and flora. Moreover, as indicated below, if the treaty language is interpreted in light of its preparatory work, it would require consultations before any project is executed that is likely to have

[91] *See* the Agreement on the Sharing of the Ganges Waters, Nov. 5, 1977, 23 FOREIGN AFF. REC. (India) 215 (1977), 17 INT'L LEGAL MATERIALS 103 (1978).

[92] *See* 21 KEESING'S CONTEMP. ARCHIVES 27284 (Aug. 18–24, 1975); Los Angeles Times, July 13, 1973, pt. 8, at 1, col. 1.

[93] Treaty of Friendship and Neighbourly Relations Between Iraq and Turkey, Mar. 29, 1946, Protocol No. 1, art. 5, 37 U.N.T.S. 226. The dispute between Iraq and Syria apparently was settled in the summer of 1975. *See* Financial Times, Aug. 13, 1975, at 6, col. 2.

an appreciable effect on navigation or on the agricultural or industrial exploitation of the river system.

The Niger River regime consists of two treaties: the Act of Niamey, signed in October 1963, and the Agreement Concerning the Niger River Commission, signed in November 1964. Article 4 of the Act of Niamey, in force among the states of the Niger Basin, provides:

> The riparian states undertake to establish close co-operation with regard to the study and the execution of any project likely to have an appreciable effect on certain features of the regime of the River, its tributaries and sub-tributaries, their conditions of navigability, agricultural and industrial exploitation, the sanitary conditions of their waters, and the biological characteristics of their fauna and flora.[94]

Article 12 of the 1964 Agreement implements the above provision as follows:

> In order to achieve maximum co-operation in connection with the matters mentioned in Article 4 of the Act of Niamey, the riparian States undertake to inform the [Niger River] Commission . . . , at the earliest stage, of all studies and works upon which they propose to embark. They undertake further to abstain from carrying out on the portion of the River, its tributaries and subtributaries subject to their jurisdiction any works likely to pollute the waters, or any modification likely to affect biological characteristics of its fauna and flora, without adequate notice to, and prior consultation with, the Commission.[95]

The Act of Niamey reflects a compromise reached among the riparian states at the second of two conferences held in 1963. At the first conference, two governments—Mali and Cameroon—were not represented. The represented governments agreed provisionally to a prior consultation regime for virtually any project that could appreciably affect other uses of the waters.[96] The government of Mali, which had not participated in drafting that arrangement, considered it too weak and thus proposed

[94] Act Regarding Navigation and Economic Co-operation Between the States of the Niger Basin (the Act of Niamey), Oct. 26, 1963, art. 4, 587 U.N.T.S. 9.

[95] Agreement Concerning the River Niger Commission, Nov. 25, 1964, art. 12, 587 U.N.T.S. 19.

[96] For the text, see Schreiber, *Vers un Nouveau Regime International du Fleuve Niger*, 9 Ann. Français de Droit Int'l 866, 875, 885 (1963).

at the second conference that the Commission be given comprehensive powers to plan and approve development projects. A heated debate ensued, resulting in the last-minute compromise language of article 4, quoted above.[97] That language left open the possibility that a prior consent regime, or even a comprehensive, semiautonomous development-planning role for the Commission, would evolve under the rubric of "close co-operation." Prior consultation had been treated throughout the debate as the least common denominator to which all could agree; the only question was whether to go further. The language finally drafted did not expressly call for prior consultation only because it was hurriedly drafted in order to get agreement at the end of the conference, and express mention of a duty to consult could well have diminished the prospect that greater restrictions on unilateralism, favored by some delegations, would evolve.

Article 12 of the 1964 Agreement, also quoted above, appears to have been designed to keep open the option of enhancing the Commission's development role, while insuring that environmentally risky projects inappropriate for joint development would be subject to the prior consultation safeguard. Thus, the mention of a prior consultation duty only in the second sentence of article 12 should not be taken to negate a similar duty regarding measures potentially affecting navigation or agricultural and industrial exploitation, stemming from the Act of Niamey.

A broad prior-consultation obligation appears in the Statute Relating to the Development of the Chad Basin:

> Art. 5. The Member States undertake to abstain from taking, without prior consultation with the Commission, any measure likely to have an appreciable effect either on the extent of the loss of water or on the nature of the yearly hydrogramme and limnigramme and certain other features of the Basin, the conditions subject to which other riparian States may utilise the water in the Basin, the sanitary conditions of the waters or the biological characteristics of its fauna and flora.
>
> In particular, the Member States undertake to abstain from carrying out on the portion of the Basin subject to their respective jurisdiction any hydraulic works or soil scheme likely to have an

[97] *See id.* at 879–81.

appreciable effect on the flow of surface and subterranean water in the Basin without adequate notice to and prior consultation with the Commission. . . .

Art. 6. In order to achieve maximum co-operation in connection with the provisions of Article 5, the Member States undertake to inform the Commission, at the earliest stage, of all studies and projects upon which they propose to embark.[98]

The Chad Basin includes Lake Chad and watercourses leading to it. Lake Chad is a large, shallow lake with fingers extending into Chad. It also touches or enters Niger, Nigeria, and Cameroon. Because of the configuration of the lake and of the other watercourses, the physical situation more closely approximates a successive basin than a contiguous one. The prior consultation norm therefore fits the pattern established by European practice and by most of the African-Asian practice documented above.

In 1971, the Legal Office of the Food and Agriculture Organization (FAO) prepared a new draft Agreement on Water Utilization and Conservation in the Lake Chad Basin, which was revised into a "Final Draft Agreement" by the Chad Basin riparian states at a meeting in April 1972. As of early 1982, this agreement had not been adopted by them and apparently was not being actively considered. Nevertheless, it is of some interest, since it would have continued in force the prior consultation regime under article 5 of the Chad Basin Statute for any water diversion in excess of designated minimum rates, and would have required prior Commission approval for any diversion in excess of designated "safe maximum rates" or in excess of the minimum rates if the water would be diverted outside the Basin.[99] Thus, the proposed prior consultation norm would have fit into an intermediate position between lack of procedural regulation for measures likely to cause only minimal harm (or thought to be wholly within the sovereign prerogatives of the acting state) and a prior consent requirement for measures thought to have particularly significant implications for other states. However,

[98]Statute Relating to the Development of the Chad Basin, May 22, 1964, arts. 5–6, in 3 BASIC DOCUMENTS OF AFRICAN REGIONAL ORGANIZATIONS 1048 (L. Sohn ed. 1972), and in 11 INTERNATIONAL PROTECTION OF THE ENVIRONMENT 5637 (B. Rüster & B. Simma eds. 1977).

[99]*See* Sand, *Development of International Water Law in the Lake Chad Basin*, 34 ZEITSCHRIFT FÜR AUSLÄNDISCHES OFFENTLISCHES RECHT UND VÖLKERRECHT 74 n.110 and 75 n.115 (1974).

since the Chad Basin states apparently were not prepared to turn over a veto power to the Commission, the prior consultation norm remains in force for all potentially harmful diversions.

Another river system, primarily successive, for which there is relevant state practice is the Mekong. In 1957 the states of the Lower Mekong Basin established the Committee for Co-ordination of Investigations of the Lower Mekong Basin. It was designed to promote, coordinate, supervise, and control the planning and investigation of water resources development projects in the Lower Mekong Basin and to recommend criteria for the use of the waters.[100] The Committee's rules of procedure provide for regular meetings three times a year; special meetings could be convened at any time on the request of any one or more members or of the executive secretary of the relevant U.N. regional commission.[101] Although the Committee lapsed into desuetude with the fall of the Western-backed governments in Cambodia and South Viet Nam, it had functioned reasonably effectively until then. Despite the absence of any explicit prior consultation requirement in the Statute, a practice had been established of consulting through the Commission before commencing any significant development project on the main stream or any tributary.[102]

The Lower Mekong experience tends to support the principle, discussed above in the European context, that states parties to an agreement setting up a river commission have an implied duty to consult it (or at least to offer to consult) before taking unilateral action in its field of competence. That principle would apply to action by Senegal or Gambia for the development of the River Gambia, a successive river rising in Guinea and then running through Senegal and Gambia. The latter two states have established a joint authority to plan the development of the river for hydroelectric power and irrigation.[103] Any unilateral development project, undertaken without consulting the

[100] Statute of the Committee for Co-ordination of Investigations of the Lower Mekong Basin, Oct. 31, 1957, art. 4, U.N. Doc. ST/LEG/SER.B/12, Treaty 81 (1963).

[101] Rule 1, in U.N. Doc. ST/LEG/SER.B/12, at 269 (1963).

[102] *See* Menon, *Water Resources Development of International Rivers with Special Reference to the Developing World*, 9 INT'L LAWYER 441, 454 (1975). In 1978, Laos, Thailand, and Viet Nam decided to establish an Interim Committee for Coordination of Investigations of the Lower Mekong Basin, pending resumed participation by Kampuchea (Cambodia). *See* 15 U.N. CHRON., Apr. 1978, at 61.

[103] *See* 16 AFRICA INST. BULL. 197, 277 (1978).

joint authority or the other government, would obviously run counter to the expectations of the parties if it would interfere with the integrated development of the river.[104]

Practice in Palestine is colored by the animosities there. On September 2, 1953, Israel began diversion works on the west bank of the upper Jordan River in the demilitarized zone between Israel and Syria. The water was destined for a hydroelectric plant, and was to be returned to the Jordan River system at Lake Tiberias. Syria was neither notified nor consulted. The Israeli plan was communicated orally to the Chief of Staff of the U.N. Truce Supervision Organization (UNTSO) on July 31, 1953, and formally on September 2.[105] Thus, there was nothing more than informal prior notification to the UNTSO Chief of Staff, with whom prior consultations could have been undertaken even if direct Israeli-Syrian consultations would not have been politically feasible. Nevertheless, because of the abnormal political situation, the incident must be regarded as marginally significant at best.[106] Some years later, Israel acknowledged the principle of consultation (but not consent) before a river is diverted.[107]

Some river treaties in the African-Asian region recognize the possibility of harm to a lower riparian state's interests at the hands of an upper riparian, but provide no procedural safeguards. An example is the treaty between Iran and Afghanistan regarding the Helmand River. It requires Afghanistan, the upper riparian, to refrain from certain action that would render the water unusable for agricultural or domestic purposes in Iran, but does not require prior notification or consultation when proposed action might have that effect.[108]

If we move away from state practice involving individual

[104]The same may be said regarding the Kagera River Basin, following the agreement among Burundi, Rwanda, and Tanzania to create an organization for its development. *See* 14 AFRICA RESEARCH BULL. 4155 (1977).

[105]8 U.N. SCOR (633d mtg.) at 18, U.N. Doc. S/PV.633 (1953); *see also* U.N. Doc. S/3122, Annexes I & II (1953).

[106]*Accord*, F. BERBER, RIVERS IN INTERNATIONAL LAW 99 (1959). For further details, *see* S. SALIBA, THE JORDAN RIVER DISPUTE 84–108 (1968).

[107]*See* Louis, *Les Eaux du Jourdain*, 11 ANN. FRANÇAIS DE DROIT INT'L 823, 855 (1965). It is unlikely that Israel consulted Jordan before deciding in 1980 to build a canal from the Mediterranean to the Dead Sea. Jordan asserted that its consent was required. *See* Financial Times, Aug. 27, 1980, at 4, col. 6.

[108]Helmand River Water Treaty, Mar. 13, 1973, art. 6 (unpublished; copy on file with Frederic L. Kirgis, Jr.).

rivers, there is support for a prior consultation norm in article 5(2) of the African Convention on the Conservation of Nature and Natural Resources. It provides: "Where surface or underground water resources are shared by two or more of the Contracting States, the latter shall act in consultation, and if the need arises, set up inter-State Commissions to study and resolve problems arising from the joint use of these resources, and for the joint development and conservation thereof." Similarly, article 14(3) provides: "Where any development plan is likely to affect the natural resources of another State, the latter shall be consulted."[109] There are some exceptions to these and other duties in the Convention, excusing performance in cases involving "the paramount interest of the State," force majeure, and the defense of human life, and permitting derogations required in time of famine, for the protection of public health, and in defense of property.[110]

The Convention does not say whether "shared" water resources are those used concurrently (such as contiguous rivers), those used successively, or both. In the absence of any further indication of the parties' intent, the presumption should be that both types of water resource are covered. That would be consistent with the understanding of most governments as to the meaning of "shared natural resources" in the post-Stockholm U.N. debate over exploitation of resources in which two or more states have an interest.[111] The prior consultation norm in the Convention would run counter to the (primarily European) prior consent practice regarding nonpolluting uses of contiguous rivers, but would support prevailing African-Asian-European practice regarding successive rivers and pollution-engendering activities on contiguous rivers. The exceptions all fall into the category of emergency action. As later chapters of this book will show, nonconsultation in a true emergency is normally excused whether or not the interested states have expressly provided for it.

In 1973 the Asian-African Legal Consultative Committee

[109] African Convention on the Conservation of Nature and Natural Resources, Sept. 15, 1968, arts. 5(2), 14(3), in 5 INTERNATIONAL PROTECTION OF THE ENVIRONMENT 2037 (B. Rüster & B. Simma eds. 1976). The Convention entered into force on October 9, 1969.

[110] *Id.* art. 17.

[111] *See* text at notes 197–98 *infra.*

considered the law of international drainage basins. The rapporteur's draft contained the following provision:

> A state which proposes a change of the previously existing uses of the waters of an international drainage basin that might seriously affect utilization of the waters by another co-basin state must first consult with the other interested co-basin states. In case agreement is not reached through such consultation, the states concerned should seek the advice of a technical expert or commission. If this does not lead to agreement, resort should be had to the other peaceful methods provided by Article 33 of the United Nations Charter and, in particular, to international arbitration and adjudication.[112]

This is consistent with the African Convention on the Conservation of Nature and Natural Resources, in that it does not distinguish between contiguous and successive watercourses. It is also consistent with the declaration adopted by the Fourth Conference of Heads of State or Government of Non-Aligned Countries, to the effect that the participating countries "believe that co-operation between countries interested in the exploitation of [natural resources common to two or more states] should be developed on the basis of a system of information and prior consultations within the frame work of the normal relations existing between them."[113]

To summarize African-Asian practice, there is much less support than in Europe for a prior consent regime regarding prospective changes in the navigability, course, water level, or flow of contiguous rivers. The European norm finds support in the 1972 Senegal River Convention, but other treaties and declarations—notably the African Convention on the Conservation of Nature and Natural Resources—do not support a prior consent regime for contiguous watercourses. There is, however, a rather consistently applied African-Asian norm requiring consultation with interested states before embarking on any new or intensified use of contiguous or successive watercourses that could have an appreciable, adverse effect on the interests of another state.

[112] ASIAN-AFRICAN LEGAL CONSULTATIVE COMMITTEE, REPORT OF THE 14TH SESS. 107 (1973).

[113] Documents of the Fourth Conf. of Heads of State or Government of Non-Aligned Countries, Algiers, Sept. 5–9, 1973, in U.N. Doc. A/9330, at 72 (1973). This declaration paved the way for the U.N. General Assembly's adoption of G.A. Res. 3129 (XXVIII). *See* text at note 192 *infra*.

D. The Americas

Relations between the United States and Canada provide a particularly rich source of relevant practice. The 3,000-mile border encompasses stretches of contiguous rivers and lakes, as well as an abundance of successive rivers flowing both north and south, so that each nation is sometimes the upper riparian, sometimes the lower.

Around the turn of the century there were a number of proposed and actual unilateral measures affecting contiguous and successive U.S.-Canadian waters.[114] Particularly significant for purposes of this study was the Chicago diversion. Before 1900 Chicago had been polluting its Lake Michigan drinking water with its own sewage. In that year, it completed a canal diverting Lake Michigan water to carry its sewage into the Mississippi River basin. This lowered the water level of the Great Lakes, including a lowering of six inches at the port of Montreal—a serious effect, since it limited the size of ships able to use that port.[115] There appears to have been no prior consultation with Canadian officials.[116] However, when Chicago again applied to the U.S. government for a permit in 1912 to increase its diversion, the United States informed the Canadian government of the hearing on the application, and the Canadian government appeared. The application was denied.[117] Chicago applied again in 1925; the Canadian government was again invited to participate in the hearing, but declined to do so. Instead it sent a note protesting the proposed diversion on the ground that under customary international law the United States could not permanently divert the waters without the consent of the co-basin state.[118] That contention has not been accepted

[114]One turn-of-the-century instance may be quickly dismissed. In 1900, Canada proposed to build the Gut Dam on the contiguous portion of the Saint Lawrence River. U.S. consent was obtained in 1903. The instance is of marginal normative significance to this study, since the project could not feasibly have been carried out without using an island on the U.S. side of the river. Thus, U.S. concurrence was necessary if the project was to be undertaken at all. *See generally Report of the Agent of the United States Before the Lake Ontario Claims Tribunal*, Sept. 27, 1968, *in* 8 Int'l Legal Materials 118, 119 (1969).

[115]*See* H. Smith, The Economic Uses of International Rivers 44–47 (1931).

[116]*Id.* at 50; Bourne, *supra* note 2, at 221.

[117]H. Smith, *supra* note 115, at 51.

[118]*Id; Bourne, Canada and the Law of International Drainage Basins,* in Canadian Perspectives on International Law and Organization 468, 476 (R. MacDonald, G. Morris, & D. Johnston eds. 1974).

by the United States, and has been abandoned by Canada in its more recent protests against new proposals to increase the Chicago diversion.[119]

Whenever a new proposal has been made in recent years, the U.S. government has acknowledged its willingness to consult, but has not recognized any duty to obtain Canadian consent.[120] Before enactment of the Water Resources Development Act of 1976, which authorized a five-year increase in the Chicago diversion, the State Department informed the appropriate congressional committee that adoption of the bill "without consultation with Canada, could, in the view of the Department, lead to a serious bilateral problem."[121] Such a statement is very close to an acknowledgment of an international duty to consult. The State Department did notify the Canadian government of the proposed legislation shortly after it was introduced, and passed along to the Congress Canada's response opposing the bill. No hearings were held, and the legislation was enacted without what the State Department felt was ample opportunity for its views or those of the Canadian government to be made known.[122] Nevertheless, before deciding on any increased rate of diversion, the United States conducted investigations into the projected effects, both on its own and in the U.S.-Canadian International Joint Commission (IJC) and acknowledged that Canadian views would be considered.[123]

Lake Michigan is not a boundary lake, though of course it is part of the Great Lakes system, which includes boundary lakes. Thus, the U.S.-Canadian practice stemming from the Chicago diversion might be compared with normative practice in other

[119] *See* Bourne, *supra* note 118, at 476. The more recent protests have been based on direct U.S. treaty obligations to Canada, including those stemming from the Boundary Waters Treaty, Jan. 11, 1909, United States–Canada, 36 Stat. 2448, 12 BEVANS 319. Arguably, article 2 bestows a right to object to Lake Michigan diversions "which would be productive of material injury to the navigation interests on [the Canadian] side of the boundary." *See* State Department Solicitor's note, June 5, 1926, *quoted in* D. PIPER, THE INTERNATIONAL LAW OF THE GREAT LAKES 99 (1967). But article 2 simply speaks of the intention of each party not to surrender any right "which it may have" to make an objection, and does not spell out the effect of such an objection.

[120] *See, e.g.,* the exchange of notes reprinted in 11 EXTERNAL AFFAIRS (Canada) 324–26 (1959).

[121] 1976 DIGEST OF UNITED STATES PRACTICE IN INT'L LAW 387.

[122] Letter to the author, Dec. 27, 1977, from the Environmental Officer, Office of Canadian Affairs, U.S. Department of State.

[123] *See* 1977 DIGEST OF UNITED STATES PRACTICE IN INT'L LAW 613, 616–17.

parts of the world relating to successive rivers.[124] In that framework it is consistent for the most part (after the original diversion in 1900) with practice elsewhere involving acquiescence in a duty to consult, but not in a duty to obtain prior consent, before diverting water from a noncontiguous watercourse to the detriment of a co-basin state.[125]

A situation analogous to that of the Chicago diversion arose in 1905 when Canada protested a proposed diversion from the Birch Lake Basin in Minnesota. Birch Lake is near the boundary and is connected with the Lake of the Woods and the Rainy River, both of which are on the boundary. It was feared that the proposed diversion would affect navigation on both of them. The matter was referred to the then-existent International Waterways Commission for investigation and was ultimately settled by agreement as part of the 1909 Boundary Waters Treaty.[126] The outcome was thus consistent with a prior consultation norm, and would tend to support a prior consent norm if the parties treated agreement as a condition precedent to the right to proceed. Whether they did is not clear.

The Chicago diversion, the proposed Birch Lake diversion, and proposed diversions from successive rivers on both sides of the border led to the negotiations culminating in the 1909 Boundary Waters Treaty.[127] Article 3 provides, subject to some exceptions, that no "uses or obstructions or diversions, whether temporary or permanent, of boundary waters on either side of the line, affecting the natural level or flow of boundary waters on the other side of the line, shall be made except . . . with the

[124]The closest analogy would be to the fingers of Lake Chad. *See* text at note 98 *supra*.

[125]SMITH, *supra* note 115, at 50, and Bourne, *supra* note 2, at 221, say that the proposed diversions were not accompanied by adequate attempts to consult Canada. *But see* D. PIPER, *supra* note 119, at 102. A full opportunity afforded a foreign government to participate in a hearing on an application for a permit allows it to present its views to a relevant decision maker. Until the 1976 Act, Canada was consistently presented either with that opportunity or with an opportunity for diplomatic consultations. Though the opportunity given it in 1976 was inadequate, the U.S. State Department acknowledged that legitimate Canadian expectations had been frustrated by the Congress' hasty action and did its best to rectify the situation.

[126]*See* Johnson, *The Canada–United States Controversy over the Columbia River*, 41 WASH. L. REV. 676, 699 (1966), *reprinted in* THE LAW OF INTERNATIONAL DRAINAGE BASINS 167, 186 (A. Garretson, R. Hayton, & C. Olmstead eds. 1967).

[127]Boundary Waters Treaty, Jan. 11, 1909, United States–Canada, 36 Stat. 2448, 12 BEVANS 319.

approval [of] the International Joint Commission." Each member of the Commission is appointed by his or her own government. *Boundary waters* are defined as contiguous waters, and do not include tributaries. Article 4 applies to successive waterways, and provides that neither state will permit the construction of any works that would raise the natural level of the waters on the other side of the boundary without the special agreement of the other or the approval of the International Joint Commission. Article 3 is thus consistent with the prior consent norm regarding contiguous waterways, and article 4 is consistent with the extended version of that norm—though it does not cover all physical alterations at the boundary, since it mentions only increases in water levels.

The exceptions to the article 3 consent rule relate primarily to governmental aids to navigation, "provided that such works are wholly on its own side of the line and do not materially affect the level or flow of the boundary waters on the other." Both governments have followed the practice of consulting each other on request, whenever a project might raise any question of "material effect."[128] Thus, consultation has supplanted unilateral determinations of the impact proposed navigational aids might have on the other state.

Article 9 supplies means for prior consultation in cases not falling within article 3 or 4:

> The High Contracting Parties further agree that any other questions or matters of difference arising between them involving the rights, obligations, or interests of either in relation to the other or to the inhabitants of the other, along the common frontier between the United States and the Dominion of Canada, shall be referred from time to time to the International Joint Commission for examination and report, whenever either the Government of the United States or the Government of the Dominion of Canada shall request that such questions or matters of difference be so referred.[129]

[128] 1976 DIGEST OF UNITED STATES PRACTICE IN INT'L LAW 384, 386. One such instance involved conultations before the U.S. government constructed an ice boom on the U.S. side of the Saint Mary's River. *Id.*

[129] The Commission's conclusions under article 9 are not binding; thus, any reference under that article is purely consultative. In practice, however, the Commission's recommendations under article 9 are normally followed. *See* Cohen, *The Regime of Boundary Waters—The Canadian–United States Experience,* 146 HAGUE ACADEMY, RECUEIL DES COURS 219, 272–73 (1975).

On its face, this indicates that the Commission should take up a proposed unilateral measure affecting any U.S.-Canadian successive river whenever either nation requests it. In practice, matters are referred to the Commission under article 9 only with the consent of both governments. It would clearly be a breach of article 9, however, if either government were to reject a request by the other to refer a matter, including a matter involving proposed unilateral action by the rejecting state.[130]

Since the entry into force of the 1909 Treaty, there has been ample (but not perfectly consistent) practice—some of it required by the Treaty, some not—supporting the prior consent norm for changes in the navigability, level, course, or flow of contiguous waterways and the European extension of that norm when a measure would alter the level or course of a successive river at the boundary. For example, the Lake of the Woods Convention prohibits diversion of waters from that contiguous watershed to any other watershed without the approval of the International Joint Commission.[131] Development of the contiguous portion of the Saint Lawrence River for navigation and hydroelectric power was pursuant to prior agreement between the two nations. There was also prior approval by the International Joint Commission for the joint power project in the international rapids section.[132] There have been a number of occasions when a governmental unit proposed a dam on a successive river that might have raised the water level on the other side of the boundary; approval of the Commission has been sought in such cases under article 4 of the 1909 Treaty.[133] On

[130] *See* Bourne, *supra* note 118, at 492.

[131] Convention on Regulation of Level of Lake of the Woods, Feb. 24, 1925, United States–Canada, art. 11, 44 Stat. 2108, 6 BEVANS 14, 43 L.N.T.S. 251. Before this Convention had been formulated, a Canadian diversion plan for domestic uses in Winnipeg from Shoal Lake, a contiguous lake near the Lake of the Woods, had been submitted to the Commission for its prior approval, which was given. *See* Jordan, *The International Joint Commission and Canada–United States Boundary Relations*, in CANADIAN PERSPECTIVES ON INTERNATIONAL LAW AND ORGANIZATION, *supra* note 118, at 522, 532.

For the European extension of the prior consent norm regarding border alterations of a successive river, *see* text at note 15 *supra*.

[132] *See* Jordan, *supra* note 131, at 529–30; 3 M. Whiteman, DIGEST OF INTERNATIONAL LAW 909–18 (1964); Agreement Relating to the Saint Lawrence Seaway Project for the Construction of Certain Navigation Facilities, Aug. 17, 1954, United States–Canada, 5 U.S.T. 1784, 234 U.N.T.S. 210. The Agreement requires consultation before either party embarks on certain designated activities. *See* arts. 4(b), 5, 6(b).

[133] *See* Jordan, *supra* note 131, at 529. As to the proposed Ross Dam on the Skagit River, a source of controversy in the 1940s and again in the 1970s and 1980s, *see* 1977 DIGEST OF UNITED STATES PRACTICE IN INT'L LAW 621–25; 5 INT'L ENVT'L REP., CURRENT

the other hand, the Saint Lawrence Seaway agreement requires only prior consultation in the case of proposed measures that might affect shipping.[134]

The 1978 Agreement on Great Lakes Water Quality gives the International Joint Commission extensive coordinating, advisory, and recommendatory powers to improve water quality. It does not expressly require the parties to obtain the approval of, or even to consult, the Commission before allowing any activity that might introduce new or increased pollution into the Great Lakes. However, the Commission's advisory and recommendatory authority extends, inter alia, to any matter relating to the quality of Great Lakes boundary waters and to all matters covered by the annexes to the agreement. There are twelve annexes encompassing a wide range of potentially polluting activities, including such things as dredging and discharge of various polluting substances and wastes. The Commission is to report at least biennially to the parties, and they are then to consult on the Commission's recommendations. In addition, "consultations may be held at the request of either Party on any matter arising out of the implementation of this Agreement."[135] This provision, couched in permissive terms, does not broadly require consultations on request. But, as in the case of the Lake Geneva convention,[136] there is an implied duty to consult within the Commission before either party undertakes an activity that could frustrate the agreement's water quality goals. Moreover, in the case of U.S.-Canadian pollution problems along the frontier—including the Great Lakes frontier waters—article 9 of the 1909 Boundary Waters Treaty would require each party to join in the other's request for referral to the International Joint Commission.

Practice involving purely successive U.S.-Canadian river basins has usually involved consultation, often through the Commission, when the proposed measure on one side of the boundary might lower the water level or affect water quality on the other side. These instances have arisen out of proposed works on such waterways as the Columbia-Kootenay, the Richelieu, the

REP 177 (1982) (IJC gave Seattle and British Columbia a year to negotiate concerning Ross Dam).

[134] Art. 6(b), note 132 *supra*.

[135] Agreement on Great Lakes Water Quality, Nov. 22, 1978, United States–Canada, arts. 7, 10(1), annexes, 30 U.S.T. 1383.

[136] *See* text at note 22 *supra*.

Souris, the Similkameen, and the Poplar River systems,[137] though in two instances—involving the Garrison diversion project on the Souris and the Poplar River Generating Station—the consultations had not reached a meaningful stage before construction began. Paradoxically, those two cases strengthen the norm rather than weaken it, since the Commission attached legal consequences to what it regarded as the failure by Canada and the United States to engage in adequate prior consultations. In the Poplar River case the Commission said:

> There has developed between the Governments of Canada and the United States a broad framework of cooperative interaction aimed at resolving problems along the International Boundary, hopefully before they become serious irritants between the two countries. The principle of prior notice and consultation is one element of this broad framework. Both Governments have also strongly supported the principle in several international fora. These are described in recent correspondence between the Commission and the Governments on the important role of prior notice and consultation in Canada–United States relations. . . . The reference of January 12, 1948, under which this apportionment study is being made, is an integral part of the notice and consultation process between the two countries. Under international law, if adequate prior notice and consultation have occurred, and construction has subsequently commenced, the project is generally accorded the status of an existing use and will generally occupy a preferred position over projected uses in determining equitable utilization.

International law has dealt only minimally with the effect of

[137] *See* Johnson, *supra* note 126 (Columbia-Kootenay); Cohen, *supra* note 129, at 277 (Richelieu); L. Bloomfield & G. Fitzgerald, Boundary Waters Problems of Canada and the United States 154, 166 (1958) (proposed Canadian diversion from the Souris; Similkameen); *United States–Canadian Relations: Hearing Before a Subcomm. of the House Comm. on Int'l Relations*, 94th Cong., 2d Sess. at 6, 9, 12 (1976), and H.R. Rep. No. 94–1335, 94th Cong., 2d Sess. 31–32, 34 (1976) (proposed Garrison diversion project on the Souris in North Dakota); *S. Res. 49: Hearing Before a Subcomm. of the Senate Comm. on Foreign Relations*, 95th Cong., 1st Sess. 22 (1977) (proposed Canadian power development on the Poplar); 1978 Digest of United States Practice in Int'l Law 1120–21 (proposed Canadian logging on Kishinena Creek).

The U.S. Department of the Interior announced that no work would be done on parts of the Garrison project potentially affecting rivers flowing into Canada, unless there is assurance that the United States can meet its commitments under the 1909 Treaty. *See* Council on Environmental Quality, 10th Ann. Rep. on Environmental Quality 629 (1979).

The Poplar River referral, Aug. 2, 1977, alluded to article 4 of the 1909 Treaty (approval of the IJC before raising the water level) as well as to water quality implications. It came after conditional Canadian licenses had been issued to build the dam in question but before final specifications had been prepared.

failure to give adequate prior notice and consultation of proposed activities. Only the [International Law Association's] 1966 Helsinki Rules on the Uses of the Waters of International Rivers . . . deal with this issue. . . . Article XXIX reads as follows:

> "1. With a view to preventing disputes from arising between basin States as to their legal rights or other interests, it is recommended that each basin State furnish relevant and reasonably available information to the other basin States concerning the waters of a drainage basin within its use of, and activities with respect to such waters.
>
> 2. A State, regardless of its location in a drainage basin, should in particular furnish to any other basin State, the interests of which may be substantially affected, notice of any proposed construction or installation which would alter the regime of the basin in a way which might give rise to a dispute as defined in Article XXVI. The notice should include such essential facts as will permit the recipient to make an assessment of the probable effect of the proposed alteration.
>
> 3. A State providing the notice referred to in paragraph 2 of this Article should afford to the recipient a reasonable period of time to make an assessment of the probable effect of the proposed construction or installation and to submit its views thereon to the State furnishing the notice.
>
> 4. If a State has failed to give the notice referred to in paragraph 2 of this Article, the alteration by the State in the regime of the drainage basin shall not be given the weight normally accorded to temporal priority in use in the event of a determination of what is a reasonable and equitable share of the waters of the basin."

Article XXVI of the Rules states that "this Chapter relates to procedures for the prevention and settlement of international disputes as to the legal rights or other interests of basin States and of other States in the waters of an international drainage basin." The Commission is in full agreement with and supports this principle of the effect of failure to give adequate prior notice and consultation set forth in the Helsinki Rules.

In the case of the Poplar River Generating Station, the United States Government acknowledged receipt of information concerning the project in September 1974. Construction of the SPC plant and dam began in the late summer of 1975. While some communication did take place prior to the actual construction, the process of prior notice and consultation was not fulfilled. This is due, in large part, to the unavailability of adequate information regarding the impacts of the project which would serve as a basis for consultations. Indeed, much of this information is only now being developed. And, until such time as an adequate information base exists, meaningful consultations cannot begin.

Thus, in the case of the Poplar River Generating Station, as with the Garrison Diversion Unit in North Dakota which the Commission investigated under another reference, the Governments have not effectively utilized the process of prior notice and consultation. Rather there has been ongoing construction coupled with an undertaking by the appropriate Government for modifications to the project in the light of existing international obligations, IJC recommendations and any resulting bilateral agreements. These conditions were attached to the license to [the Saskatchewan Power Corporation] by the Government of Canada for the Poplar River Generating Station.

In view of the above, the Commission does not consider the Poplar River Generating Station an existing use for the purposes of this apportionment study because the obligation of prior consultation was not fulfilled until a reasonable effort to develop an adequate information base was completed.[138]

As part of the settlement of the Columbia River dispute, the two nations agreed to a moratorium on diversions of Columbia Basin waters for other than consumptive uses without the consent of the other, if the diversion would alter the flow across the boundary.[139] This is consistent with the European consent norm for physical alterations of a successive waterway at the border. As we have seen, though, U.S.-Canadian practice does not consistently require consent in such cases.

The United States and Mexico do not share nearly as many watercourses as the United States and Canada, but those they do share are precious because of the arid conditions surrounding them. Claims and counterclaims have centered on the Rio Grande and the Colorado River, though there have been a few relevant incidents not involving either of those major watercourses.[140] The Rio Grande is a contiguous river for a long

[138] INT'L JOINT COMM'N REPORT ON WATER APPORTIONMENT IN THE POPLAR RIVER BASIN 69–71 (1978). The Helsinki Rules are further discussed in the text at notes 184–90 *infra*.

[139] Treaty Relating to Cooperative Development of the Water Resources of the Columbia River Basin, Jan. 17, 1961, United States–Canada, art. 13(1), 15 U.S.T. 1555, 542 U.N.T.S. 244.

[140] For example, the Rose Street canal was constructed in 1919 by the city of Douglas, Arizona, extending into an arroyo on the Mexican side of the boundary, for purposes of flood runoff. It was preceded by discussions with local Mexican officials. 6 M.

stretch of its course, forming the boundary between Texas and Mexico, but it also flows for a great distance within the United States before it reaches the border. The Colorado is a successive river.

Proposals in the late nineteenth century to construct dams on the portion of the Rio Grande wholly within U.S. territory led to the now-discredited Harmon Doctrine, by which the Attorney General of the United States attempted to justify existing and future U.S. diversions.[141] Despite its ostensible adherence to the Harmon Doctrine, the U.S. Department of State entered into consultations in 1895 with the Mexican government regarding a dam proposed to be built by a private company on the Rio Grande at Elephant Butte, New Mexico. The matter was referred to the U.S.-Mexican International Boundary Commission, which recommended that a dam be built instead at El Paso, Texas. The United States government ultimately obtained an injunction against construction of the Elephant Butte dam, and it was never built.[142]

In 1905 the U.S. Congress rejected a proposal for a dam at El Paso and instead enacted a statute providing for construction of a dam on the Rio Grande near Engle, New Mexico. The Mexican Embassy protested. In its reply, the U.S. Department of State did not admit any duty toward Mexico under international law, but said the United States government was nevertheless disposed to act in accordance with principles of equity and friendliness between neighbors. The result was the conclusion of the 1906 U.S.-Mexican treaty, which was essentially favorable to the U.S. position, but which required the delivery of 60,000 acre feet per year of Rio Grande water above Juarez, Mexico.[143] Thus, the United States did enter into prior consultations with Mexico.

By 1940 substantial irrigation diversions were being con-

Whiteman, DIGEST OF INTERNATIONAL LAW 262–65 (1968).

In 1957 the Mexican state of Baja California began construction of a highway involving earth fills in two canyons draining into the United States. Discussions—primarily technical, but eventually at the diplomatic level—were held before completion of the project, regarding possible failure of the earth fill and consequent flooding of U.S. territory. Some modifications were made as a result of the discussions. *Id.* at 260–62.

[141] *See* note 7 *supra*.

[142] *See* Simsarian, *The Diversion of Waters Affecting the United States and Mexico*, 17 TEXAS L. REV. 27, 36–41 (1939); Griffin, *supra* note 4, at 63–65.

[143] *See* Simsarian, *supra* note 142, at 42–46; U.S.-Mexico, May 21, 1906, 34 Stat. 2953, 9 BEVANS 924.

structed on both sides of the contiguous portion of the Rio Grande. It is not clear whether they were preceded by intergovernmental consultations; such evidence as is available suggests that they were not.[144] In any event, they were not preceded by agreement between the two governments. At the same time, however, the United States was investigating a possible flood storage project on the Rio Grande at Zapata, Texas. The Mexican government proposed that such unilateral projects be abandoned, and that joint storage projects be investigated. The U.S. government replied that it would welcome any concrete suggestions from the Mexican government, and that the American Boundary Commissioner was prepared at any time to discuss the lower Rio Grande water problem with his Mexican counterpart.[145] This led to exchanges of memoranda on proposed solutions, and ultimately to the 1944 U.S.-Mexican Water Treaty.[146]

Because the Colorado River is purely successive, the United States has consistently been able to take unilateral action that could harm Mexican interests, without any significant capability on Mexico's part to take similar action. Most of the problems have involved diversions for agriculture or for potation that would reduce the quantity of the water reaching Mexico, or increase its salinity, or both. At least until 1973, consultation practice appears to have been inconsistent.

In August 1922, when the Colorado River compact was being negotiated among interested states of the United States, Secretary of State Charles Evans Hughes quoted with approval from a 1919 report of an interdepartmental committee consisting of representatives of the State, War, Treasury, and Interior departments, stating that "The construction of a high-line canal capable of diverting all the waters of the Colorado River and using them in the United States without leaving any for Mexican lands might be considered a menace to the Mexican interests and should only be undertaken after exhausting all means for an amicable settlement satisfactory to the Republic of Mexico and the interests therein."[147] That sounds very much

[144] *See* [1940] 5 FOREIGN REL. OF THE U.S. 1032, 1035–36 (U.S. project in Willacy County, Texas, and Mexican project known as the Retamal Heading).

[145] *Id.* at 1032–36.

[146] [1942] 6 FOREIGN REL. OF THE U.S. 551–57; 3 M. Whiteman, DIGEST OF INTERNATIONAL LAW 966–73 (1964); U.S.-Mexico, Nov. 14, 1944, 59 Stat. 1219, 9 BEVANS 1166, 3 U.N.T.S. 313.

[147] Letter of Charles Evans Hughes to Herbert Hoover, Secretary of Commerce,

like an acknowledgment of a duty to consult when the proposed diversion would have the capacity to divert the entire flow of the river.

On the other hand, the United States constructed the Wellton-Mohawk Irrigation and Drainage District project in southwestern Arizona in 1961 apparently without consulting the Mexican government.[148] Mexico complained that the water returned to the Colorado River from the project was too saline to be acceptable under the 1944 Water Treaty (which, however, was silent on water quality) and was contaminated, contrary to general international law.[149] The Colorado River salinity problem continued to be an irritant in U.S.-Mexican relations until agreement was reached in 1973 guaranteeing delivery to Mexico of water sufficiently nonsaline to eliminate the adverse effect of the Wellton-Mohawk project. The 1973 agreement also contains the following provision: "With the objective of avoiding future problems, the United States and Mexico shall consult with each other prior to undertaking any new development of either the surface or the groundwater resources, or undertaking substantial modifications of present developments, in its own territory in the border area that might adversely affect the other country."[150] The "border area" is not defined, but it is clear from the context that it is not limited to the immediate U.S.-Mexican boundary. Consultations apparently could be conducted through the International Boundary and Water Commission or through normal diplomatic channels.[151]

Arguably, the 1973 agreement represents United States acquiesence in repeated Mexican assertions that the Wellton-Mohawk project violated its rights. One result of that assertion-acquiesence process was the U.S. promise to engage in consultations before embarking on any similar project in the future. Thus, it is a particularly significant indicator of current normative expectations regarding changes in the water quality of a successive river.

Aug. 17, 1922, in H.R. Doc. No. 359, 71st Cong., 2d Sess. 261, 265 (1930).

[148] Interview with State Department official, April 1974.

[149] *See* the summary of the Mexican position in the THIRD ANN. REP. OF THE U.S. COUNCIL ON ENVIRONMENTAL QUALITY 84 (1972).

[150] Agreement Approving Minute 242 of the International Boundary and Water Commission, Aug. 30, 1973, para. 6, 24 U.S.T. 1968, *reprinted in* 12 INT'L LEGAL MATERIALS 1105 (1973).

[151] *See* Lobato, *Legal Considerations, Interpretations and Projections of Minute 242*, 15 NAT. RES. J. 35, 38–39 (1975).

Inter-American practice not involving the United States includes a number of treaties and declarations calling for consent of the interested states before the waters of contiguous rivers are utilized.[152] On the other hand, some Latin American treaties and resolutions apply a single standard to contiguous and to successive rivers—that of prior consultation, rather than prior consent.[153] When these treaties and resolutions address themselves separately to successive rivers, they have generally—but not always—adopted a prior consultation standard.[154]

[152]*See* (*1*) Costa Rica–Nicaragua, Apr. 15, 1858, art. 8, 5 J. MOORE, INTERNATIONAL ARBITRATIONS 4706 (1898), U.N. Doc. A/5409, at 482 (1963) (contracts of canalization or transit injuring the "natural rights" of Costa Rica; *see* text at note 155 *infra*); (*2*) Brazil-U.K., Oct. 27 and Nov. 1, 1932, para. 1(vi), 177 L.N.T.S. 128 (works risking alteration of river's course and any canalization, irrigation, or hydroelectric project re border between Brazil and British Guiana); (*3*) Brazil-Uruguay, Dec. 20, 1933, art. 20, 181 L.N.T.S. 69 (any plant on contiguous or successive river that could cause an appreciable and permanent change in rate of flow); (*4*) Declaration of Montevideo, 1933, by the states represented at the Seventh Int'l Conf. of American States (except the U.S., and subject to reservations by Mexico and Venezuela), art.2, 3 M. Whiteman, DIGEST OF INTERNATIONAL LAW 936 (1964), U.N. Doc. A/5409, vol. 3, Annex I, at 2 (1963) ("no state may, without the consent of the other riparian state, introduce into [contiguous] water courses of an international character, for the industrial or agricultural exploitation of their waters, any alteration which may prove injurious to the margin of the other interested state"); (*5*) Act of Asunción, June 3, 1971, Argentina, Bolivia, Brazil, Paraguay, and Uruguay, para. 1, U.N. Doc. A/CN.4/274, at 178 (1974) ("In contiguous international rivers, which are under dual sovereignty, there must be a prior bilateral agreement between the riparian States before any use is made of the waters"); (*6*) Act of Santiago, June 26, 1971, Argentina–Chile, para. 3; *id.* at 180 (similar to Act of Asunción); (*7*) Act of Buenos Aires, July 12, 1971, Argentina–Bolivia, *id.* at 183 (also similar). The Declaration and the Acts are not in the form of treaties.

[153]*See* (*1*) Guatemala–El Salvador, Dec. 14, 1951, art. 19, 131 U.N.T.S. 132 (parties are to "co-ordinate" their activities to protect water resources in frontier regions); (*2*) Guatemala-Honduras, Aug. 22, 1956, art. 19, 263 U.N.T.S. 66 (same); (*3*) Declaration of Buenos Aires, July 9, 1971, Argentina–Uruguay, paras. 3–5, U.N. Doc. A/CN.4/274, at 181 (1974) (general declaration regarding utilization of international rivers); (*4*) La Plata Treaty, Argentina–Uruguay, Nov. 19, 1973, arts. 14, 17–22, in 13 INT'L LEGAL MATERIALS 251 (1974) (contiguous river so wide it approximates a bay); (*5*) Statute of the Uruguay River, 1975, Argentina–Uruguay, art. 36, U.N. Doc. A/CN.4/348, at 164 (1981) (environmental protection); (*6*) Resolution I of the fifth meeting of the Inter-American Council of Jurists, Feb. 1965, para. 8(e), in INTER–AMERICAN JURIDICAL COMM., INDUSTRIAL AND AGRICULTURAL USE OF INTERNATIONAL RIVERS AND LAKES, OAS Doc. OEA/Ser.I/VI.2, at 1 (1965).

[154]*See* (*1*) Guatemala–El Salvador, and (*2*) Guatemala–Honduras, *supra* note 153 (both impliedly imposing a duty to consult); (*3*) Joint Declaration of Buenos Aires, Sept. 23, 1960, Argentina, Brazil, and Uruguay, U.N. Doc. A/5409, at 162 n.228 (1963) (promise by Brazil to consult others before carrying out any hydraulic works that might alter the regime of the Uruguay River, which runs through Brazil before it becomes a boundary river); (*4*) Resolution I of the fifth meeting of the Inter-American Council of Jurists, *supra* note 153, para. 8(e); (*5*) Act of Santiago, June 26, 1971, *supra* note 152, paras. 5–7; (*6*) Declaration of Buenos Aires, July 9, 1971, *supra* note 153, paras.

The Costa Rica–Nicaragua treaty of 1858 has engendered some interesting practice demonstrating differing expectations regarding contiguous and noncontiguous waterways. It gave Nicaragua exclusive jurisdiction over the waters of the contiguous San Juan River, subject to a right of free navigation in favor of Costa Rica, and it said in article 8 that Nicaragua would not enter into any new arrangement for canalization or transit "without first hearing the opinion of the Government of Costa Rica as to the disadvantages which the transaction might occasion the two countries; provided that . . . if the transaction does not injure the natural rights of Costa Rica, the vote asked for shall be only advisory."[155]

The treaty was interpreted by President Grover Cleveland, sole arbitrator in the Costa Rican–Nicaraguan Boundary Arbitration of 1888:

> The Republic of Nicaragua remains bound not to make any grants for canal purposes across her territory without first asking the opinion of the Republic of Costa Rica, as provided in Article [8, above]. The natural rights of the Republic of Costa Rica alluded to in the said stipulation are the rights which, in view of the boundaries fixed by the said Treaty of Limits, she possesses in the soil thereby recognized as belonging exclusively to her; the rights which she possesses in the harbors of San Juan del Norte and Salinas Bay; and the rights which she possesses in so much of the River San Juan as lies more than three miles below Castillo Viejo. . . . These rights are to be deemed injured in any case where the territory belonging to the Republic of Costa Rica is occupied or flooded; where there is an encroachment upon either of the said harbors injurious to Costa Rica; or where there is such an obstruction or deviation of the River San Juan as to destroy or seriously impair the navigation of the said River or any of its branches at any point where Costa Rica is entitled to navigate the same.
>
> The Treaty . . . does not give to the Republic of Costa Rica the right to be a party to grants which Nicaragua may make for interoceanic canals; though in cases where the construction of the canal will involve an injury to the natural rights of Costa Rica, her opinion or advice, as mentioned in Article 8 of the Treaty, should be more than "advisory" or "consultative." It would seem in such cases that her consent is necessary.[156]

3–5; (7) Act of Buenos Aires, July 12, 1971, *supra* note 152. The exceptions are discussed in the text at notes 160–66 *infra*.

[155] Costa Rica–Nicaragua, *supra* note 152.

[156] 2 J. Moore, International Arbitrations 1945, 1966–67 (1898).

On August 5, 1914, the United States and Nicaragua signed a treaty granting the United States the right to construct and operate an interoceanic canal by way of the San Juan River or by any route over Nicaraguan territory, and granting certain other rights. Costa Rica protested that it had been neither notified nor consulted, and asserted that its consent was required by reason of article 8 of the 1858 treaty, as construed by President Cleveland. The dispute was submitted to the Central American Court of Justice, which held that Costa Rica's rights had been violated. It said that Costa Rica should have been consulted, and that its consent would have to be obtained if the canal was to be constructed by way of the San Juan River. This was because "the realization of that work over that route necessarily implies the occupation of the Costa Rican shore or the consequent inundation of her territory as well as the use of the Costa Rican affluents, etc., and in case, for canal purposes, the waters of the San Juan River should be diverted, Costa Rica's right to navigate that river and its affluents . . . would be rendered nugatory."[157] If the United States had exercised its option to construct the canal elsewhere over Nicaraguan territory, it would have been required to consult Costa Rica, but the latter's opinion would not have been binding.[158]

There is one significant instance of nontreaty practice in Central America regarding a contiguous lake. The government of El Salvador in early 1952 formulated plans to construct a hydroelectric dam within its own territory on an outlet of Lake Guija. The lake straddles the boundary with Guatemala, and the proposed dam would inundate some Guatemalan land. El Salvador notified the Guatemalan government of its plans and entered into negotiations with it. After receiving what appeared to be Guatemalan agreement in principle, but without any formal consent to the specific proposal, El Salvador began construction of the dam in 1953.[159] Since no formal agreement was reached, and since the informal agreement was later questioned by a successor Guatemalan government, it would be question-

[157] Costa Rica v. Nicaragua, Central American Court of Justice, 1916, in 11 AM. J. INT'L L. 181, 223 (1917).

[158] The Court noted that in the past Nicaragua had repeatedly complied with its obligation under the 1858 treaty to consult Costa Rica.

[159] Despatch No. 714, U.S. Embassy in San Salvador to U.S. Dept. of State, MS. Dept. of State file 816.2614/6–1858 (1958), and annexed pamphlet, EL SALVADOR COMISION EJECUTIVA HIDROELECTRICA DEL RIO LEMPA, EL LAGO DE GUIJA: HISTORIA Y CONSIDERACIONES TECNICAS DEL APROVECHAMIENTO INTERNACIONAL DE SUS AGUAS 10–13 (1958).

able to consider this an example of prior consent practice. On the other hand, it clearly reflects and bolsters expectations of prior consultation.

Two noteworthy but inconclusive Latin American instruments arguably espouse a prior consent norm for potentially harmful uses of successive rivers. One, the 1933 Montevideo Declaration, asserts in article 2, inter alia, that no state may, without the consent of the other riparian state, "introduce into [contiguous watercourses], for the industrial or agricultural exploitation of their waters, any alteration which may prove injurious to the margin of the other interested state." Article 3 begins by saying, "In the cases of damage referred to in the foregoing article an agreement of the parties shall always be necessary." It then provides that when compensable damages are involved, the works may proceed only after compensation is set in accordance with the procedure indicated later in the Declaration. Article 4 says that the same principles as those established in articles 2 and 3 for contiguous rivers shall be applied to successive rivers. Articles 7–10 enunciate a system of prior notification, a procedure for establishing a Mixed Technical Commission "to pass judgment" if demanded within three months by the notified state, and a further dispute settlement procedure if agreement is not reached on the basis of the Commission's report.[160]

Article 2 might be interpreted to require consent only when there may be a change in water quality injurious to the territory of the other state, but perhaps it extends also to changes in course, flow, or water level. Article 3 seems to require more than tacit consent in "cases of damage referred to" in article 2. It does not say what is meant by "damage," nor who has the burden of proving it. Perhaps "damage" means any encroachment on the other state's equitable apportionment of the waters, since a portion of article 2 not quoted above seems to adopt the equitable apportionment principle—but, of course, equitable apportionment is itself an imprecise notion. How the provisions for prior notification and dispute settlement fit in with the article 3 agreement requirement is also murky; perhaps it was contemplated that the parties would usually be able to agree on everything except specific compensation amounts, and that

[160]Montevideo Declaration, *supra* note 152, arts. 2, 3, 4, 7–10. The United States did not subscribe to the Declaration.

those amounts would be reached through the dispute-settlement procedure before work began.

The Lauca River dispute concerned the Montevideo Declaration's application to successive rivers, but its outcome did not resolve many of the questions. The Lauca rises in Chile and flows into Bolivia. In 1939 Chile announced that it would study a proposal to divert water from the Lauca to irrigate Chilean land outside the watershed. Bolivia then initiated an exchange of diplomatic correspondence, ultimately proposing in 1957 that a Mixed Technical Commission be established as envisioned in the Montevideo Declaration and asserting that the project could not proceed absent an agreement with Bolivia. Chile agreed to set up the Commission and acknowledged the applicability of the Montevideo Declaration. But when the Commission found that Chile would divert only 47 percent of the river water, Chile concluded that there was no damage to Bolivia within the meaning of the Declaration and that it was therefore free to proceed. (Apparently Chile would have conceded that there was "damage" if the loss to the watershed had exceeded 50 percent.) Moreover, Chile asserted that Bolivia had not made timely proposals of its own, thus eliminating any need for further recourse to the Declaration's dispute settlement procedure.[161] Chile went ahead. After further diplomatic exchanges in which Bolivia asserted and Chile denied that the project should be suspended pending agreement between the parties, Chile completed it in 1961. Bolivia thereupon broke off diplomatic relations, but restored them in 1975.

Thus, Chile resisted repeated assertions that an agreement with Bolivia was required by the Montevideo Declaration before the diversion project could be executed, but did acquiesce in the demand that it engage in essentially a consultative process through submission of the matter to the Mixed Technical Commission (even though water quantity, not quality, was at issue). The result suggests that the Montevideo Declaration requires at least prior consultation, if demanded, for a contemplated diversion of a successive river. But it does not necessarily establish that a diversion may lawfully proceed without the lower riparian's consent, since Bolivia preserved its position by ob-

[161] For the facts and the Chilean argument, see Lecaros, *International Rivers—The Lauca Case*, 3 INDIAN J. INT'L L. 133, 144–50 (1963). A briefer account appears in 3 M. Whiteman, DIGEST OF INTERNATIONAL LAW 1038–39 (1964).

jecting and breaking off relations. Chile's attitude does seem to acknowledge that consent would be required if two conditions are met: The diversion exceeds an equitable share (which Chile apparently calculated at one-half when only two states were interested), and the objecting state is making a good faith effort to reach agreement. But, as suggested above, the uncertainties in determining an "equitable share" give any such norm a distinctly ephemeral nature.

The second possible source of a prior consent standard for Latin American successive rivers appears in the Inter-American Juridical Committee's 1965 Draft Convention on Industrial and Agricultural Use of International Rivers and Lakes.[162] Its relevant provisions are based on article 2 of the Montevideo Declaration and on its procedures for prior notification and dispute settlement. As in the case of the Declaration, it is not clear from the face of the instrument (or from the report of the Juridical Committee) how the prior consent language meshes with the provisions for prior notification and consultation through a Joint Commission. Interestingly, however, the Inter-American Council of Jurists, then the parent body of the Juridical Committee, had requested the Committee only to draw up a procedure for notification or consultation, not for prior consent.[163] Moreover, the Juridical Committee's Draft Convention has never been adopted by the Organization of American States (OAS) or by any American states. Thus, it is only marginally significant as an indicator of normative expectations.[164]

One significant treaty, the 1978 Amazon Pact, deals with utilization of the successive rivers in the Amazon region without expressly requiring either consent or consultation before unilateral measures are adopted that might adversely affect other states on the river system. The Pact proclaims "that the exclusive use and utilization of natural resources within [the parties'] respective territories is a right inherent in the sovereignty of each state and that the exercise of this right shall not be subject to any restrictions other than those arising from International

[162] OAS Doc. OEA/Ser. I/VI.2, *supra* note 153, at 17.

[163] *See* the Juridical Committee's report, *supra* note 153 at 4.

[164] *But see also* the Resolution adopted by the Tenth Conference of the Inter-American Bar Association, Nov. 19, 1957, *reproduced in* GRIFFIN, *supra* note 4, at 89. It says that states are under a duty to refrain from making changes in their parts of international waterways that might adversely affect uses by other riparian states, in the absence of agreement with the affected states or an international judicial or arbitral decision.

Law."[165] This proclamation should be read not only in light of state practice (which may in fact cause a prior consultation duty to "arise from International Law"), but in light of other provisions of the Pact that call for joint efforts to promote harmonious development of the region, exchange of information on conservation measures, and cooperation in fields covered by the Pact, as well as those providing for regular and special meetings of foreign ministers and diplomatic representatives.[166] Thus, the Pact does not preclude prior consultation—including prior consultation based on a claim of right—and contains the principles and means to support it. Its failure to go further is presumably attributable to Brazil's apprehension that its economic development would be delayed if it recognized a prior consultation norm for successive rivers.

That apprehension underlies Brazil's claim that it not only has no duty to obtain the consent of its lower riparian, Argentina, before constructing a dam on a successive river, but that it also has no duty to consult. In the early 1970s, Brazil was planning the Itaipu Dam on the Paraná River, just 100 kilometers upstream from the Argentine border. Brazil contemplated that the dam would create a lake 100 kilometers long, none of it in Argentine territory. Brazil already had constructed twenty-two small dams on the Paraná and had consulted Argentina about some of them. Argentine officials were particularly concerned about the Itaipu Dam, however, because of its size and proximity to Argentina. It was feared that it could cause climate modification, disappearance of some fish species, impairment of navigability downstream, modification of the river's course, and pollution of the drinking water for six major cities.[167]

Despite Argentine insistence that it had a right to be consulted, Brazil steadfastly maintained that any prior consultation duty applied only to contiguous rivers and other resources shared simultaneously, not successively.[168] The dispute blocked inclu-

[165] Treaty for Amazonian Cooperation, (the Amazon Pact), July 3, 1978, art. 4, 17 Int'l Legal Materials 1045 (1978).

[166] *Id.* arts.1, 7, 15, 20, 21.

[167] *See* 6 Latin America 197 (1972).

[168] *See* Report of the [U.N. Environment Programme] Governing Council on the Work of Its 2d Sess., 29 GAOR Supp. (No. 25) at 35–37, U.N. Doc. A/9625 (1974); U.N. Docs. A/PV.2315/Corr.l, at 1–6 (1974), and UNEP/GC/44, at 4 (1975). The Brazilian government said it considered the Act of Asunción, *supra* note 152, "a perfect clarification of the norms to be applied in the utilization of each type of watercourse."

sion of a prior notification and consultation provision in the U.N. Declaration on the Human Environment in 1972,[169] and later impeded efforts in the U.N. General Assembly and in the U.N. Environment Programme to formulate specific norms on the subject.[170] Although Argentina and Brazil, at one point, patched up the dispute with a bilateral agreement calling for the "furnishing [of] mutual official and public knowledge of the technical data regarding the works to be undertaken by the States within their national jurisdictions with the purpose of preventing sensible harm which may be caused in the human environment of the neighbouring area," Argentina soon repudiated the agreement on the ground that Brazil had violated it.[171]

Brazil, under prior governments, had espoused the principle of prior consultation by joining in the Montevideo Declaration. It also adopted the Joint Declaration of Buenos Aires in 1960 with Argentina and Uruguay, saying that it would "in accordance with international doctrine and practice, consult with the other riparian States before carrying out any hydraulic works which may alter the present regime of the Uruguay River."[172] There was, however, some reason for the Brazilian concern in the 1970s about the delays inherent in a prior consultation obligation. Prior consultations often, but not inevitably, interfere with otherwise-attainable timetables. Moreover, as indicated above, the Montevideo Declaration could be read to mean that work on the Itaipu Dam could not begin until an agreement with Argentina and / or dispute settlement regarding compen-

U.N. Doc. A/CN.4/294, at 16 (1976). The Act of Asunción calls for prior agreement concerning use of contiguous rivers, but is silent as to any procedural prerequisite to the use of successive rivers. Brazil did consult Paraguay, the contiguous riparian on the Paraná at Itaipu, and reached agreement with it. Consultations with Argentina were undertaken after steps had been taken to proceed with the dam, but before it was too late to affect the magnitude of the project. *See* Financial Times, Jan. 5, 1978, at 4, col. 1; 13 LATIN AMERICAN POLITICAL REP. 290 (1979).

[169] *Compare* paragraphs 7 and 8 of the fundamental principles prepared by the Intergovernmental Working Group on the Declaration on the Human Environment, U.N. Doc. A/CONF.48/PC.12, Annex I, at 3 (1971) (duty to consult before activity that may damage the environment outside the acting state), with paragraph 20 of the revised draft principles, U.N. Doc. A/CONF.48/PC.16, Annex III, at 4 (1972) (watered-down duty to supply information), and with the Declaration, U.N. Doc. A/CONF.48/14, chapter 1 (1972) (no mention even of duty to supply information).

[170] For discussion of these efforts, see text at notes 191–198 *infra*.

[171] *See* Cano, *Argentina, Brazil, and the De La Plata River Basin: A Summary Review of Their Legal Relationship*, 16 NAT. RES. J. 863, 873–74 (1976).

[172] U.N. Doc. A/5409 at 162 n.228 (1963).

sation had been concluded. The Inter-American Juridical Committee's 1965 Draft Convention could be read the same way, and the 1961 Resolution of the Institute of International Law implied that a state proposing to act may go ahead in the absence of agreement with affected states only if it has proposed judicial settlement or arbitration and the other states have declined.[173] Some writers lend support to the Brazilian concern.[174]

On the other hand, a prior consultation obligation does not inherently imply a duty to desist until a solution is finally reached. It simply implies that nothing more than preparatory work will be undertaken until the consulted state has had an ample opportunity to present its views and until those views have been considered in good faith. Argentina has recognized that any right to be consulted carries with it an "obligation not to delay or impede without justification the programs and projects of exploration, use, exploitation and development of the natural resources of the State or States which intend to undertake the activity."[175] Argentina, Canada, and others have acknowledged that a right to be consulted before shared resources are exploited is not tantamount to a right of veto.[176] The Lake Lanoux Tribunal said that although "the Parties must consent to suspend the full exercise of their rights during the negotiations," an obligation to consult does not imply an obligation to reach agreement.[177] The OECD Principles Concerning Transfrontier Pollution, discussed more fully below, call for prior consultations, with the caveat that they "should not enable a country to unreasonably delay or to impede the activities or projects on which consultations are taking place."[178] The most thorough

[173] *See* note 16 and accompanying text *supra*.

[174] *See* Sevette, Legal Aspects of Hydro-Electric Development of Rivers and Lakes of Common Interest, U.N. Doc. E/ECE/136, at 210–11 (1952) (prior agreement required if risk of serious and lasting injury); GRIFFIN, *supra* note 4, at 91 (duty to refrain pending agreement or other peaceful solution); S. SALIBA, THE JORDAN RIVER DISPUTE 70 (1968) (prior consent norm). *Cf.* F. BERBER, RIVERS IN INTERNATIONAL LAW 155 (1959) (prior consent norm in Europe only).

[175] Draft Principles of Conduct submitted by Argentina, U.N. Doc. UNEP/IG.2/4, Annex II, at 3–4 (1976) (issued as an attachment to U.N. Doc. UNEP/GC/74 (1976)).

[176] *See* U.N. Docs. A/C.2/SR.1647, at 3 (1974) (Argentina); A/C.2/SR.1569, at 17 (1973) (Canada); A/C.2/SR.1570, at 7 (1973) (Libya).

[177] 24 I.L.R., 101, 128, 134 (1957). *See* text at notes 65–67 *supra*.

[178] Principle 8, *in* OECD Doc. C(74)224 (1974), 14 INT'L LEGAL MATERIALS 242 (1975). *See also* Smets, *The OECD Approach to the Solution of Transfrontier Pollution Problems*, in ENVIRONMENTAL LAW: INTERNATIONAL AND COMPARATIVE ASPECTS 3, 8 (J. Nowak ed. 1976): "Such consultation should aim at an agreement although the activity could be initiated without this agreement provided that adequate time for diligent consultation

doctrinal study to date on consultations involving international drainage basins is in accord.[179] So long as no veto power is implied, a prior consultation norm does not necessarily involve significant delays—as, for example, when a proposed project would require a substantial lead time anyway.

The clear trend of expectations is reflected in the OECD Principles and the other sources outlined in the paragraph just above. Since these expectations tend to undermine the apparent reason for Brazil's rejection of a duty to consult regarding the Itaipu Dam, they tend also to undermine the normative significance of Brazil's assertions. Moreover, insofar as Brazil's position rests on the proposition that there is a community of interest in contiguous rivers that is lacking in successive rivers, it is further undermined by the World Court's statement to the contrary in the River Oder case.[180]

Interestingly, after construction of the Itaipu Dam was well under way, Brazil, Argentina, and Paraguay agreed that:

> [S]uch eventual major harmful effects as may be caused to the Paraná River . . . must be foreseen, insofar as possible, and . . . their gravity and classification shall not be determined unilaterally by [the states involved]. Within the spirit of cooperation and good neighborliness which inspires the relations among the three countries, concrete cases shall be examined within the shortest possible time, compatible with the nature of the eventual major harmful effects and their analysis.[181]

This amounts to an agreement to consult regarding "major harmful effects" before they can occur, if possible. Although the agreement was not reached until it was too late to affect

in good faith was provided." To the same effect is a Note by the OECD Secretary-General on transfrontier pollution problems, in OECD Doc. C(77)28, at 13, n. 2 (1977). *See also* SUMMARY OF DISCUSSIONS OF THE CONFERENCE ON THE AVOIDANCE AND ADJUSTMENT OF ENVIRONMENTAL DISPUTES 6 (Am. Soc'y of Int'l Law 1974) ("Consultation does not imply a right of veto or unreasonable delay").

The OECD Principles are in the form of recommendations to member states, which do not include Argentina and Brazil. Nevertheless, they are expressions of the expectations of governments whose views regarding appropriate conduct are not without influence on the shaping of international norms recognized by other states as well.

[179] Bourne, *supra* note 2, at 233.

[180] In the Case Relating to the Territorial Jurisdiction of the International Commission of the River Oder, 1929 PCIJ ser. A, No. 23, at 27, the Court stressed state navigation practice recognizing "a community of interest of riparian States" when "a single waterway traverses or separates the territory of more than one State."

[181] Agreement on Paraná River Projects, Oct. 19, 1979, Argentina, Brazil, Paraguay, para. 5(g), in 19 INT'L LEGAL MATERIALS 615 (1980). Annex II to the Agreement records understandings reached after the sort of consultations contemplated by paragraph 5(g).

the dam's design, the language is broad enough to create expectations in similar cases that an effort will be made to foresee and mutually examine major harmful effects further in advance than that.

In general, then, practice in the Americas—like practice in Africa and Asia—predominantly supports the European practice outlined in section B above, except that inter-American practice supporting a prior consent norm for measures affecting contiguous rivers is somewhat less consistent than European practice, and there is little inter-American practice dealing specifically with the closing of a successive river to navigation. There is perhaps a somewhat stronger argument in Latin America than in Europe for a prior consent norm regarding significant pollution-engendering uses of contiguous and successive rivers, stemming primarily from the Montevideo Declaration. It is far from certain, however, that such a norm does exist, partly because of ambiguities in the Montevideo Declaration and partly because of a dearth of prior consent practice involving specific watercourses.

E. Nonregional Practice

If the resolutions of the Institute of International Law and the Barcelona Convention of 1921 are treated as essentially European measures, the significant nonregional instruments dealing with the procedural aspects of international waterway development are the 1923 Geneva Convention on hydraulic power, the 1966 Helsinki Rules of the International Law Association, the resolutions and documents generated within the United Nations on the exploitation of shared resources, and the documents of the OECD on transfrontier pollution. They will be examined seriatim.

The 1923 Convention provided: "If a Contracting State desires to carry out operations for the development of hydraulic power which might cause serious prejudice to any other Contracting State, the States concerned shall enter into negotiations with a view to the conclusion of agreements which will allow such operations to be executed."[182] This provision did not dis-

[182]Geneva Convention Relating to the Development of Hydraulic Power Affecting More than One State, Dec. 9, 1923, art. 4, 36 L.N.T.S. 75. The parties were the British Empire (including its African territories and some others), New Zealand, Siam (Thailand), Austria, Denmark, Greece, Hungary, the Free City of Danzig, Panama, Iraq, and Egypt. U.N. Doc. A/5409, at 70 (1963).

tinguish between contiguous and successive rivers. It represented the lowest common procedural denominator to which the parties could agree for all types of international rivers. An initial draft had called for obligatory prior agreement by the interested states, but that was unacceptable to many of those represented at the conference.[183] The result was a provision requiring prior negotiations to try to reach agreement, but not requiring actual consent. It applied, of course, only to hydroelectric development, and then only if the project might cause serious prejudice to another contracting state. Since very few of the contracting states were riparian to the same watercourse, the Convention had little practical effect as a matter of treaty law. Nevertheless, it is significant as an expression of prevailing expectations among the parties, reflecting carefully negotiated norms to which they subscribed.

Article 29 of the 1966 Helsinki Rules of the International Law Association (I.L.A.) has been quoted above in connection with the U.S.-Canadian International Joint Commission's report in the Poplar River Case.[184] It says that a state "should" notify interested basin states of any proposed construction or installation that would alter the basin's regime in such a way that a dispute might arise and should allow a reasonable time for them to submit their views. These provisions, couched in precatory terms, reflect a withering of the procedural norm first proposed by the Association's relevant committee. It had originally proposed a prior consent obligation regarding any new work or change in previously existing use of an international river.[185] Two years later the committee reduced this not only to prior consultation but to a recommendation rather than a statement of obligation.[186] With some language changes, it remained a recommendation in the final version.

The provisions as finally adopted represent a compromise between those members of the committee who wished to follow the formula adopted by the Institute of International Law in 1961—with its implication that work could proceed in the absence of agreement only if the affected states have declined an offer of judicial settlement or arbitration—and those who op-

[183] *See* Sevette, *supra* note 174, at 155–60.

[184] Article 29 appears in REPORT OF THE 52D CONF. OF THE INT'L LAW ASS'N, 1966, at 484, 518–19 (1967) and is quoted in the text preceding note 138 *supra*.

[185] *See* REPORT OF THE 47TH CONF. OF THE INT'L LAW ASS'N, 1956, at 244, 247 (1957).

[186] *See* REPORT OF THE 48TH CONF. OF THE INT'L LAW ASS'N, 1958, at 99, 100 (1959).

posed either the notion of prior notification or the attaching of consequences to a refusal to submit to third-party dispute settlement.[187] The thrust of the compromise was to enunciate preferred prior notification and consultation norms, but to minimize the opprobrium for failure to comply with them. Interestingly though, the same article sets forth a sanction for failure to give the contemplated notification—loss of equitable apportionment priority for the project—and this sanction was applied by the U.S.-Canadian International Joint Commission in the Poplar River case.[188]

It is instructive to compare the 1966 Helsinki provisions with article 18 *bis* of the same Rules, added by the Association in 1974. It provides:

> 1. A riparian State intending to undertake works to improve the navigability of that portion of a river or lake within its jurisdiction is under a duty to give notice to the co-riparian States;
>
> 2. If these works are likely to affect adversely the navigational uses of one or more co-riparian States, any such co-riparian State may, within a reasonable time, request consultation. The concerned co-riparian States are then under a duty to negotiate;
>
> 3. If a riparian State proposes that such works be undertaken in whole or in part in the territory of one or more other co-riparian States, it must obtain the consent of the other co-riparian State or States concerned. The co-riparian State or States from whom this consent is required are under a duty to negotiate.[189]

These provisions—stated in the form of duties and drawing a distinction, as a practical matter, between successive and contiguous rivers—appear to reflect in part the traditional European emphasis on navigational uses, but may also reflect the growing acceptability of prior consultation (shorn of any implication of a duty to submit to third-party dispute settlement) as a procedural norm for international waterway development.[190] The same duties would seem to apply, a fortiori, if a

[187]*See* REPORT OF THE 52D CONF., *supra* note 184, at 520–22.

[188]*See* Helsinki Rules, art. 29(4), *supra* note 184; Int'l Joint Comm'n Report, *supra* note 138.

[189]REPORT OF THE 56TH CONF. OF THE INT'L LAW ASS'N, 1974, at xiii (1976).

[190]On the European navigational emphasis, see the committee report in *id.* 114, 127–28. By 1976, some members of the I.L.A.'s Water Resources Law committee had concluded that "international law does impose an obligation on a State to negotiate with co-basin States about any development that might have substantial harmful effects in their territory." REPORT OF THE 57TH CONF. OF THE INT'L LAW ASS'N, 1976, at 250 (1978). *See also Articles on Regulation of the Flow of Water of International Watercourses*, arts. 7, 8, *in* REPORT OF THE 59TH CONF. OF THE INT'L LAW ASS'N, 1980, at 362, 368–69 (1982).

riparian state proposes works for purposes other than improving navigability and those works are likely to affect adversely the navigational uses of any co-riparian state.

The I.L.A.'s tortuous path toward prior consultation as an agreed norm has been mirrored in the United Nations. As we have seen, the U.N. Conference on the Human Environment omitted a provision on prior consultation from its 1972 Declaration on the Human Environment, even though such a provision had been prepared by the Conference's Intergovernmental Working Group.[191] The General Assembly took up the matter and in 1973 adopted its Resolution 3129, which recited the need to pursue the elaboration of international environmental norms, and then "considered" that "co-operation between countries sharing [natural resources common to two or more states] and interested in their exploitation must be developed on the basis of a system of information and prior consultation within the framework of the normal relations existing between them."[192] The debate in the Second Committee clearly indicated a general understanding that a normative principle, not just a desired goal, was being proposed.[193] It was clear, of course, that among the principal "common" or "shared" resources would be international watercourse systems. Most representatives seemed to assume, though it was never made explicit, that this would include successive as well as contiguous watercourses.

A year later, the General Assembly adopted the Charter of Economic Rights and Duties of States. It provides in article 3: "In the exploitation of natural resources shared by two or more countries, each State must co-operate on the basis of a system of information and prior consultations in order to achieve optimum use of such resources without causing damage to the legitimate interest of others."[194] The sponsors of the Charter

[191] *See* note 169 *supra*, and accompanying text.

[192] G.A. Res. 3129, para. 2, 28 U.N. GAOR, Supp. (No. 30) at 48, U.N. Doc. A/9030 (1973). The vote was 77–5–43.

[193] *See e.g.*, U.N. Docs. A/C.2/SR.1564, at 23 (1973) (Yugoslavia, which introduced the draft resolution on behalf of the 53 sponsors); A/C.2/SR.1565, at 19–20 (Argentina); A/C.2/SR.1566, at 5 (the Netherlands); *id.* at 18 (Mexico); A/C.2/SR.1567, at 27–28 (Paraguay, in opposition); A/C.2/SR.1568, at 10–11 (Algeria); A/C.2/SR.1569, at 16 (Uruguay, in opposition); *id.* at 17 (Canada); *id.* at 20 (Brazil, in opposition); A/C.2/SR.1570, at 3 (Ethiopia, in opposition); *id.* at 5 (Chile).

[194] G.A. Res. 3281, art. 3, 29 U.N. GAOR, Supp. (No. 31) at 50, U.N. Doc. A/9631 (1974). The vote was 120–6–10. Although the United States voted against the Charter as a whole, it voted in favor of this article, which was adopted by separate votes of 97–7–25 in the Second Committee and 99–8–29 in the General Assembly.

amended it in the Second Committee to delete preambular language declaring that a fundamental purpose of the Charter was to codify and develop rules, but the language of article 3 remained mandatory. It seems clearly to reflect the normative expectations of the great majority of U.N. member states.

In early 1974, the U.N. Environment Programme began a struggle to refine further these prior notification and consultation norms. The Governing Council entrusted a working group with the task, but it took the group until 1978 to produce an agreed text. Although the working group's explanatory note sounds as though the principles were drafted without intent to codify or develop international law, the Governing Council approved the text, "Desiring to promote and develop international law regarding the conservation and harmonious exploitation of natural resources shared by two or more States."[195] The principles obviously take account of trends in state practice, including practice embodied in resolutions and recommendations of international organizations.

Principle 6 of the agreed text provides in part:

> 1. It is necessary for every State sharing a natural resource with one or more other States:
>
> (*a*) to notify in advance the other State or States of the pertinent details of plans to initiate, or make a change in, the conservation or utilization of the resource which can reasonably be expected to affect significantly the environment in the territory of the other State or States; and
> (*b*) upon request of the other State or States, to enter into consultations concerning the above-mentioned plans; and
> (*c*) to provide, upon request to that effect by the other State or States, specific additional pertinent information concerning such plans; and
> (*d*) if there has been no advance notification as envisaged in sub-paragraph (*a*) above, to enter into consultations about such plans upon request of the other State or States.[196]

[195] 33 U.N. GAOR, Supp. (No. 25) at 154, U.N. Doc. A/33/25 (1978). The text was approved by consensus, with four delegations declining to join in it.

[196] Draft Principles of Conduct in the Field of the Environment for the Guidance of States in the Conservation and Harmonious Utilization of Natural Resources Shared by Two or More States, U.N. Doc. UNEP/IG.12/2, at 9, 12 (1978), in 17 INT'L LEGAL MATERIALS 1097, 1098 (1978). Principle 7 says that exchange of information, notification, and consultations are carried out in "good faith and in the spirit of good neighbourliness and in such a way as to avoid any unreasonable delays."

Although the agreed text contains no definition of shared natural resources, one definition seems to have had substantial support: "The term 'shared natural resource' means an element of the natural environment used by man which constitutes a biogeophysical unity and is located in the territory of two or more States."[197] This seems broad enough to include successive as well as contiguous waterways—a position that comports with the International Law Commission's view that, at least for non-navigational purposes, waters of an international watercourse are shared natural resources to the extent that their use in the territory of one state affects their use in the territory of another state within the same watercourse system.[198]

In deference to continuing resistance from Brazil and a few others, and out of a sense of caution, the U.N. General Assembly in its thirty-fourth session simply took note of the principles in the agreed text, rather than approving them. It did so, however, "without prejudice to the binding nature of those rules already recognized as such in international law."[199]

The U.N. Legal Counsel, referring to the resolutions on shared resources adopted by the various U.N. organs, has suggested that:

> [T]hose resolutions and the discussions regarding them will, in case of a dispute, be used largely as expressing the legal principles according to which prior consultations and exchange of technical information are necessary prerequisites for any potentially damaging use of international rivers. Past practice has already affirmed these principles, and the adopted resolutions have certainly given them more weight, and may even have consecrated them as legal principles.[200]

[197] Report of the Intergovernmental Working Group of Experts on Natural Resources Shared by Two or More States, 5th sess., U.N. Doc. UNEP/IG.12/2, at 7 (1978), in 17 INT'L LEGAL MATERIALS 1094, 1097 (1978). For another definition that clearly would include successive waterways, see INTERNATIONAL UNION FOR CONSERVATION OF NATURE AND NATURAL RESOURCES (IUCN), WORLD CONSERVATION STRATEGY § 19 (1980).

[198] Draft article 5(1) on the law of the non-navigational uses of international watercourses, [1980] 2 Y.B. INT'L L. COMM'N, pt. 2, at 120, U.N. Doc. A/CN.4/SER.A/1980/Add.l(Part 2).

[199] G.A. Res. 34/186, 34 U.N. GAOR Supp. (No. 46) at 128, U.N. Doc. A/34/46 (1979). *See also* [1980] 2 Y.B.INT'L L. COMM'N, pt. 2 at 125, U.N. Doc. A/CN.4/SER.A/1980/Add.l (Part 2).

[200] Suy, *Innovations in International Law-Making Process*, in THE INTERNATIONAL LAW AND POLICY OF HUMAN WELFARE 187, 193 (R. MacDonald, D. Johnston, & G. Morris eds. 1978).

Another potentially significant U.N. effort is the work of the International Law Commission on the nonnavigational uses of international waterways. At this writing the Commission had concluded, at least provisionally, that a general principle of international law requires negotiations seeking agreement among riparian states regarding their use of international freshwater resources.[201] Such a duty would go further than a mere consultation duty, but would encompass it. The duty would apply to uses that might deplete or alter the flow of a watercourse at or beyond an international boundary. The Commission's Special Rapporteur has also proposed articles that would apply a pure consultation duty to potentially polluting uses.[202]

In 1977 the United Nations Water Conference was held in Mar del Plata, Argentina. It produced the Mar del Plata Action Plan, which contained recommendations for regional cooperation in the development of shared water resources. Among the recommendations were those calling for joint committees to facilitate such things as resource management and pollution prevention, exchange of information to avoid foreseeable damage, and general cooperation in recognition of the growing economic, environmental, and physical interdependencies across international frontiers.[203]

The OECD has addressed the prior notification–prior consultation question in the context of transfrontier pollution, which, as defined by the OECD Council, would include pollution of contiguous or successive watercourses if the origin of the pollution is in one country and the effects are at least partly felt in an area under the national jurisdiction of another country. The principle of information and consultation formulated by the OECD in 1974 provides:

> Prior to the initiation in a country of works or undertakings which might create a significant risk of transfrontier pollution, this

[201][1980] 2 Y.B. INT'L L. COMM'N, pt. 2, at 115–17, U.N. Doc. A/CN.4/SER.A/1980/Add.l(Part 2). The Commission extracted the principle partly from the Lake Lanoux Arbitration, note 61 *supra*, but also by analogy from the North Sea Continental Shelf and Fisheries Jurisdiction Cases. As to these latter cases, see chapter III at notes 62–64, and chapter IV at notes 38–39.

[202]*See* Schwebel, Third Report on the Law of the Non-Navigational Uses of International Watercourses, draft art. 10(10), U.N. Doc. A/CN.4/348, at 221 (1981), and the comment, *id.* at 235. *See also* draft art. 9(4), *id.* at 152 (collection and dissemination of data when, inter alia, a question of water quality is raised). Judge Schwebel has since resigned as the Commission's Special Rapporteur.

[203]Report of the United Nations Water Conference, U.N. Doc. E/CONF.70/29, at 52–53 (1977).

country should provide early information to other countries which are or may be affected . . . , and should invite their comments.

Countries should enter into consultation on an existing or foreseeable transfrontier pollution problem at the request of a country which is or may be directly affected and should diligently pursue such consultations on this particular problem over a reasonable period of time.

Countries should refrain from carrying out projects or activities which might create a significant risk of transfrontier pollution without first informing the countries which are or may be affected and, except in cases of extreme urgency, providing a reasonable amount of time in the light of circumstances for diligent consultation. Such consultations held in the best spirit of co-operation and good neighbourliness should not enable a country to unreasonably delay or to impede the activities or projects on which consultations are taking place.[204]

In 1977 the OECD Council reiterated, in slightly different form, the principle of prior information and consultation in such cases.[205] The OECD Secretary-General added that transnational information and consultation procedures of the sort contemplated "may have become—or are in the process of becoming—a custom reflected in the practice of States and in international agreements."[206] Although the OECD couched its

[204] Recommendation of the Council on Principles Concerning Transfrontier Pollution, paras. 6–8, OECD Doc. C(74)224 (1974), in 14 INT'L LEGAL MATERIALS 242 (1975). Spain reserved its position on these paragraphs. A "significant risk of pollution" means that the product of probability times potential damage is significant. Thus, the greater the pollution probability, the less the damage would have to be, and vice versa. Letter to the author from Henri Smets, Director of the Environment Directorate, OECD, Feb. 13, 1978. No matter how great the probability, a risk of minimal damage could presumably be ignored. The OECD has sometimes expressed this by referring to a substantial risk of "appreciable" harm. *See* chapter III, note 155 *infra*.

For the OECD's definition of transfrontier pollution, see OECD Doc. C(77)28 (Final), Annex, introductory para. (c) in 16 INT'L LEGAL MATERIALS 977, 979 (1977).

[205] *See* OECD Doc. C(77)28(Final), Annex para. 8(a), *supra* note 204. *See also* Annex para. 9(a), calling on countries of origin to supply information to persons elsewhere who are exposed to a significant risk of transfrontier pollution. Another paragraph calls for them to have the same procedural rights as persons within the country. In some countries that would include the right to participate in a hearing before a pollution-risk activity is undertaken.

More specific recommendations for cooperation appear in the Recommendation of the Council for Strengthening International Cooperation on Environmental Protection in Frontier Regions, OECD Doc. C(78)77(Final), in 17 INT'L LEGAL MATERIALS 1530 (1978). It calls for environmental impact studies of proposed frontier-region activities to assess the effects on both sides of the frontier, and calls upon authorities on both sides to collaborate in the assessment.

[206] Note by the OECD Secretary-General, *supra* note 178, at 13.

principle in terms of a recommendation to member states, the Secretary-General's note left no doubt that it was felt to reflect the clear trend in the practice even of nonmember states.[207]

Some shortcomings in the 1974 OECD formulation have been pointed out. For example, it does not apply to an increase in pollution from an existing source.[208] This deficiency appears to have been corrected in the 1977 formulation, which refers to "matters of transfrontier pollution or significant risk of such pollution," without limiting it to new sources. Both formulations allow the acting state to determine in the first instance whether the risk is significant enough to provide information about it, but if the receiving state has information indicating such a risk (whether the information comes from the acting state or not), the 1977 formulation calls upon the acting state to consult on request. Moreover, the Lake Lanoux tribunal made it clear that the acting state does not have the exclusive discretion to determine whether the interests of other states are likely to be affected;[209] at the very least, it would have to exercise good faith in determining that the risk is insignificant and that it therefore need not supply information. Thus, the OECD principle is not illusory. It strengthens existing state practice supporting a prior consultation norm for activities posing objectively significant pollution risks to contiguous or successive watercourses.

F. Synthesis: Watercourses

The law of international waterways has been most fully developed in Europe, where a rather distinct pattern of procedural norms can be identified. European practice applies a prior consent norm to activities posing significant risks of adverse change to contiguous rivers, and a (lesser) prior consultation norm to such activities affecting successive rivers. There are three exceptions in Europe: (*a*) activities likely to change the course or level of a successive river at the border must have the consent of the adjoining state; (*b*) if navigation is a significant use of a

[207] OECD recommendations do not have formal legislative effect. However, the great detail in which the consultation principle was negotiated indicates that it was regarded as a standard by which to judge the legitimacy of conduct (of member governments, at least), rather than a mere statement of goals. *See* Smets, *supra* note 178, at 8.

[208] *See* McCaffrey, *The OECD Principles Concerning Transfrontier Pollution: A Commentary*, 1 Envtl. Pol'y & L. 2, 4–5 (1975).

[209] *See* text at note 67 *supra*.

successive waterway, the consent of at least the riparian states is required before the waterway may be closed to navigation; and (*c*) in the absence of a specific treaty obligation requiring consent, activities posing a substantial risk of appreciable environmental harm, but no risk of other harm, are still subject merely to the prior consultation norm even on contiguous rivers. Contiguous European lakes are generally subject only to a prior consultation norm. Proposed schemes affecting international lakes or watercourses must be notified to other interested states whenever there is reason to assume that those states might, in good faith, assert a substantial risk of appreciable harm.[210]

The distinction between contiguous and successive rivers is less clear in non-European practice. More support for it can be found in the Americas than in Africa and Asia. Despite some inconsistencies in the Americas—such as the prior consent requirement in the Columbia River treaty and the Brazilian refusal to concede even a prior consultation duty regarding successive rivers—inter-American practice seems consistent with the European norms outlined above.[211] In Africa and Asia, however, the customary norm appears to be that of prior consultation, even as to contiguous rivers.

At the level of general, rather than special (regional), custom, there is a clear common denominator—consultation with interested states is required before activities are undertaken that could reasonably be expected to cause a change in the watercourse appreciably damaging their interests. There is probably a corollary, as in Europe, requiring prior notification when a good faith claim of significant risk of harm is foreseeable.

The distinction between contiguous and successive rivers does not represent general custom. As a rule, however, general custom is less important than regional custom in the law of drainage basins, since all states interested in any given basin will

[210]*See* note 204 *supra* for an explanation of the terminology used here.

[211]There are two possible caveats: (*a*) the European prior consent norm for activities likely to change the course or level of a successive river at the border is not supported by consistent practice elsewhere, except along the U.S.-Canadian boundary. (*b*) The principal support for the prior consent norm regarding the closing of navigable waterways is the Statute attached to the Barcelona Convention of 1921. *See* note 42 *supra*, and accompanying text. The great majority (though not all) of parties to the Convention and Statute were European. The Convention and Statute purport to set forth general, not regional norms. Nevertheless, since practice outside Europe is so meager, the Convention and Statute might well be regarded as representing only European norms.

usually be within the same region.[212] General custom becomes important primarily when state practice is inconclusive in a particular region and there is no reason to regard practice elsewhere as unsuited to basins in that region.

[212]The primary exception would be the state whose nationals use a waterway of another region for navigation.

Chapter III

Air Basins, Partially Enclosed Seas, and Similar Resources

A. Introduction

The preceding chapter has considered the use of resources—rivers and lakes—having greater significance for states bordering them (or their tributaries) than for nonriparian states, at least as to many of their uses. The present chapter examines the use of other resources—air sheds, sea areas limited by natural features, and some freshwaters[1]—that are analogous in the sense that some or all of their uses are of special interest to a few states in a given region.[2] The focus is on uses relatively unique to the partially enclosed areas, in the sense that they peculiarly affect surrounding states. Uses of such areas that would affect states without particular regard to their territorial proximity are discussed in chapter IV. Thus, for example, new territorial-sea and fishery claims in semienclosed seas are not discussed in this chapter unless they might encroach upon similar claims of other littoral states or specially affect those states because of their community of interest in the well-defined sea area.

For the most part, unilateral acts peculiarly affecting partially enclosed areas have fallen into these categories: acts posing transboundary environmental risks; those extending exclusive or preferential jurisdictional claims to the possible detriment

[1] As indicated in chapter II, practice affecting freshwaters is examined here if the practice relates to regional resources generally, and not solely to freshwater resources.

[2] An air shed or a partially enclosed sea may cover a relatively vast region. Sweden, the recipient of "acid rain" from across the North Sea, has pointed out that sulfur pollutants remain airborne long enough to affect an area with a radius up to two thousand kilometers. Swedish Royal Ministry for Foreign Affairs and Royal Ministry of Agriculture, Air Pollution Across National Boundaries: The Impact on the Environment of Sulfur in Air and Precipitation 87 (1971). Nevertheless, it is analytically useful to distinguish uses of resources of particular interest to a region from uses primarily affecting the global commons.

of other littoral states; and exploitation of "common pool" resources. These will be considered region by region, although the practice in some regions is rather sparse. As in chapter II, nonregional practice will be examined after each region has been considered.

B. Europe

In a 1973 report to the Council of Europe, a group of legal experts examining European practice relating to air pollution observed that "there is no rule in ordinary international law that requires a state to consult another one before authorising potentially polluting plant to be set up close to a common border."[3] Nevertheless, there are clear indications—beginning before 1973 but becoming stronger since then—that a prior consultation norm has developed in such situations, and it may even extend to long-range air pollution.

Particularly significant is the Convention on Long-Range Transboundary Air Pollution, adopted in 1979 by the High-Level Meeting Convened by the Economic Commission for Europe (ECE), and applied provisionally by the thirty-one signatories even before ratification.[4] It requires intergovernmental consultations, on request, when there is a significant risk of long-range transboundary air pollution from activities carried on or contemplated within a party's territory. It also requires

[3]Report of Committee of Experts on Air Pollution, Procedures for Consultation at National and International Level Prior to the Setting Up of Polluting Plant in Border Areas, Council of Europe Doc. EXP/Air (73) 2, at 4 (1973). The Report, however, noted some prior consultation practice among local authorities in European states. *See id.* at 4, 29, 33, 50–51. Professor Kiss, chairman of the Committee, had not changed his view by 1976, though he found a "moral obligation" for U.N. members to cooperate through prior consultations. A.–C. Kiss, Survey of Current Developments in International Environmental Law 31 (IUCN Environmental Policy and Law Paper No. 10, 1976). *See also Conseil Europeen de Droit de l'Environnement Res. No. 3, Consultation Procedures Prior to the Installation of Polluting Establishments in Frontier Regions*, Dec. 13, 1975, para. 1 (Kiss and Prieur, rapporteurs), in OECD, Environmental Protection in Frontier Regions 227 (1979) (hereinafter cited as Environmental Protection); *Report of the Comm. on Legal Aspects of the Conservation of the Environment*, in Report of the 58th Conf. of the Int'l Law Ass'n, 1978, at 383, 408 (1980) (insufficient state practice based on legal conviction to extend prior consultation rule to cases of air pollution in one state injuring persons or property in another).

[4]Convention on Long-Range Transboundary Air Pollution, Nov. 13, 1979, arts. 5 and 8(b), in 18 Int'l Legal Materials 1442 (1979); editorial note, *id.*; Resolution on Long-Range Transboundary Air Pollution, para. 1, *id.* at 1450. The two non-European ECE members, Canada and the United States, are among the signatories.

such consultations as a matter of course when a party considers major alterations in national policies or industrial development that would be likely to cause significant changes in long-range air pollution.

The trend leading to the 1979 convention was set in motion in 1971, when the Council of Europe adopted a Resolution on Air Pollution in Frontier Areas.[5] It said that competent authorities should inform each other in good time about installations likely to pollute the atmosphere beyond the frontier, and that the authorities on the other side of the frontier should be able to comment on the projects. Those comments were to be given the same consideration as if they had been made by local inhabitants.

In 1973 the Final Resolution of the Council of Europe's Conference of Ministers Responsible for Regional Planning urged states to ensure that their planning authorities consult their counterparts in neighboring states when preparing plans concerning frontier territories;[6] in 1975 the Parliamentary Assembly of the Council of Europe recommended prior consultation through frontier commissions for projects that might affect the environment in neighboring frontier regions; in 1976 the European Ministers of Local Government approved a draft European outline convention that became the European Outline Convention on Transfrontier Cooperation Between Territorial Communities or Authorities,[7] signed by Council of Europe members in 1980; and in 1978 the OECD Council recommended:

> Countries concerned should ensure that the administrative authorities participating in [organized concertation among regional and local authorities in adjacent frontier regions] inform and consult one another regularly and in good time on any environmental protection issue arising in the frontier regions concerned and which might create difficulties between such regions.[8]

[5]Council of Europe Res. (71)5, 19 EUR. Y.B. 263 (1971).

[6]*See* OECD Ad Hoc Group on Transfrontier Pollution, Study of Some Principles for Solving Problems of Transfrontier Pollution, OECD Doc. AEU/TFP/ENV/74.1, Annex II, at 33–34 (1974).

[7]May 21, 1980, Europ. T.S. No. 106; *see also* Parliamentary Assembly of the Council of Europe, Recommendations 784 (1976) and 802 (1977), *reprinted in* 18 INTERNATIONAL PROTECTION OF THE ENVIRONMENT 9238 and 9255 (B. Rüster, B. Simma, & M. Bock eds. 1979).

[8]OECD Council Recommendation for Strengthening International Cooperation on Environmental Protection in Frontier Regions, pt. II, para. 11, OECD Doc. C(78)77(Final), in 17 INT'L LEGAL MATERIALS 1530 (1978).

Moreover, the ECE Seminar on Environmental Impact Assessment recommended in 1979 that member governments assess the transboundary effects of their proposed major activities, and that they "discuss with potentially affected countries or, in the case of the global commons, with an appropriate international organization, for the purpose of preventing or at least minimizing environmental harm."[9] These consultations, as well as those contemplated in the preceding paragraph, would cover virtually any significant prospective disamenity, including air pollution.

These measures reflect a very substantial body of European practice involving actual consultations and coordinated transfrontier planning, sometimes conducted by national authorities but often by local ones on both sides of a boundary. Frequently, formal or informal agreements to consult or coordinate are involved. The transfrontier consultation and planning practice has been applied most consistently by France, West Germany, and Switzerland among themselves, and by the Benelux countries among themselves.[10] It has also been followed in instances involving the Netherlands and West Germany; Belgium and West Germany; and West Germany, Austria, and Czechoslovakia.[11] Members of the European Community are required to coordinate their regional development programs through their Regional Policy Committee, though their "coordination" amounts

[9]*See* the Report of the Seminar, para. 48, in 6 Envt'l Pol'y & L. 40, 42 (1980).

[10]Instances are discussed in Bothe, *International Legal Problems of Industrial Siting in Border Areas and National Environmental Policies*, in OECD, Transfrontier Pollution and the Role of States 79, 92 (1981); Kiss, *Problemes Juridiques de la Pollution de l'Air*, in Hague Academy Colloquium: The Protection of the Environment and International Law 145, 195–96 (A.–C. Kiss ed. 1975); Report of the Committee of Experts, *supra* note 3, at 4, 29, 33, 50–51. *See also* Report of the Third Benelux Intergovernmental Conference, Oct. 20–21, 1975, in 23 Eur. Y.B. 295 (1975); *Agreement Setting up a Tripartite Intergovernmental Commission for the Upper Rhine Region*, Mar. 5, 1975, in Environmental Protection, *supra* note 3, at 259; Prieur, *Regional Planning in Frontier Areas*, *id.* at 110, 128, 129, 147; OECD Environment Directorate, Transfrontier Pollution 1975–1978: Measures Related to OECD Recommendation C(74)224 on Principles Concerning Transfrontier Pollution 19 (1979). For an instance in which the Belgian Foreign Minister acknowledged that his government would not decide on the siting of an oil refinery in the Liege area without consulting the Dutch authorities, *see* 12 Rev. Belge de Droit Int'l 326 (1976). *See also* 5 Int'l Envt'l Rep., Current Rep. 480 (1982).

[11]Bothe, *Local Co-operation on Transfrontier Environmental Problems*, in Environmental Protection, *supra* note 3, at 91, 96–97; Engelhardt, *Co-operation on Environmental Matters Between Bavaria and Austria and Between Bavaria and Czechoslovakia*, *id.* at 462, 463–69, 473–74; Lietzmann, *Co-operation in the Field of Transfrontier Pollution within the Euregio Rhine-Maas*, *id.* at 475, 483–88, 490; Prieur, *supra* note 10, at 128–29.

to consultation in the final planning stages.[12] Some instances can be found—even within the Community—in which consultation requests from one side of a boundary have been ignored or rejected by authorities on the other side.[13]

The 1974 Nordic Convention on the Protection of the Environment[14] refers not only to pollution of fresh waters, as mentioned in chapter II, but also to adverse effects on other water resources (which would include adjacent sea areas), air pollution, noise, changes in temperature, and so forth. It provides, inter alia: "Where the permissibility of environmentally harmful activities which entail or may entail considerable nuisance in another Contracting State is being examined by the Government or by the appropriate Minister or Ministry of the State in which the activities are being carried out, consultations shall take place between the States concerned if the Government of the former State so requests."[15] Although the Convention does not require states parties to make environmental impact assessments, it proceeds on the assumption that such assessments will ordinarily be made. In fact, they are regularly made for significant projects in all four Nordic states, with the possible exception of Denmark.[16] Moreover, the Nordic Convention must be read in conjunction with the 1974 OECD Declaration on Environmental Policy, which says that "prior assessment of the environmental consequences of significant public and private activities should be an essential element of policies applied at the national, regional and local levels."[17] Thus, the expectation

[12] *See* Council Reg. 724/75/EEC, Mar. 18, 1975, art. 6, in 18 O.J. EUR. COMM. (No. L 73) 1 (1975), *as amended*, Council Reg. 214/79/EEC, Feb. 6, 1979, art. 6, in 22 *id.* (No. L 35) 1 (1979). *See also* Council Dec. 75/185/EEC, Mar. 18, 1975, in 18 *id.* (No. L 73) 47 (1975); Council Res. of Feb. 6, 1979, para. 3, in 22 *id.* (No. C. 36) 10 (1979); Prieur, *supra* note 10, at 129–30. The French transfrontier cooperation policy on regional planning is outlined, *id.* at 125.

[13] For an example involving local authorities in France and West Germany, see Hulshoff, *Protection of the Environment in the Saar-Lorraine Region*, in ENVIRONMENTAL PROTECTION, *supra* note 3, at 266, 271–72.

[14] Nordic Convention on the Protection of the Environment, Feb. 19, 1974, 13 INT'L LEGAL MATERIALS 591 (1974). *See* chapter II, notes 29–31.

[15] Nordic Convention, *supra* note 14, art. 11. *See also* article 3, which permits persons in one contracting state to challenge proposed activities in another.

[16] *See* OECD Doc. ENV/Min(79)3, at 9 (1979). In Denmark there is piecemeal legislation requiring environmental assessment, or permitting the Environment Minister to intervene, in a variety of cases. *See* OECD, ENVIRONMENTAL IMPACT ASSESSMENT 33–36 (1979).

[17] OECD Declaration on Environmental Policy, Nov. 14, 1974, para. 9, in OECD AND THE ENVIRONMENT 21 (1979). *See also* OECD Council Recommendation on Assessment of Projects with Significant Impact on the Environment, May 23, 1979, OECD

among the Nordic countries is that environmental assessments will normally be made for major public and private activities, and that they will encompass prior intergovernmental consultations on request.

In the same vein, in 1976 the Nordic countries established guidelines concerning safety conditions for nuclear installations in border areas. The guidelines require notification of a nuclear installation's proposed location, and of any proposed license (or amendment of a license) to construct and / or operate a nuclear installation, unless the country proposing it deems the installation of minor significance to safety conditions in the neighboring country. Notification must be given in time to enable any comments by the neighboring government to be considered by the approving authority, and intergovernmental discussions on safety aspects must be held at the request of either government.[18] The obvious loophole may not be as wide as might appear, since the acting country clearly would have to exercise good faith in deciding that an installation would be of only minor significance to safety in the neighboring country.[19]

Apart from the Nordic guidelines, there is a substantial body of European practice involving consultations before final plans are made to construct nuclear power stations near frontiers. For example, the Federal Republic of Germany has entered into agreements with Denmark and the Netherlands to consult regarding safety and other conditions before making final decisions as to location, construction, or operation of nuclear installations within 30 kilometers of their common borders; similar agreements have been signed by France and Switzerland in 1979 and by Portugal and Spain in 1980.[20] These agreements

Doc. C(79)116; Convention on the Law of the Sea, Dec. 10, 1982, art. 206, U.N. Doc. A/CONF.62/122 (1982) (assessment if reason to expect substantial harm to marine environment).

[18]Guidelines for Nordic Co-operation Concerning Nuclear Installations in the Border Areas Between Denmark, Finland, Norway, and Sweden in Respect of Nuclear Safety Conditions, Nov. 15, 1976, §§ 1, 2, 4, in 19 NUCLEAR L. BULL. 38 (1977).

[19]The Lake Lanoux Tribunal, construing article 11 of the Treaty of Bayonne between France and Spain, refused to allow France to be the sole judge of whether its proposed river diversion would prejudice Spain, and thus of whether it was required to consult Spain. *See* chapter II at note 67. Unlike the language of that article, the language of the Nordic guidelines seems to entrust the discretion to the proposing state. At the very least, however, the Lake Lanoux principle would require that the discretion be exercised in good faith. On the principle of good faith in international law, see G. SCHWARZENBERGER AND E. BROWN, A MANUAL OF INTERNATIONAL LAW 118–19 (6th ed. 1976).

[20]*See* Agreement Between Denmark and the Federal Republic of Germany Regu-

omit the loophole found in the Nordic guidelines.

Some other European environmental treaties do not specifically mention siting nuclear plants, but are broad enough to cover it. Thus, the 1960 Lake Constance Convention calls for joint discussions among riparian states before projects are executed that could adversely affect the salubrious condition of the lake's water.[21] Pursuant to this provision, consultations were held between the Austrian and Swiss governments concerning a proposed Swiss nuclear power plant in the vicinity of Rüthi, near the Austrian border. The plant's cooling waters could have affected Lake Constance. After the consultations, the project was postponed indefinitely.[22] Treaty-based consultations have also been held concerning several proposed nuclear power stations along the Moselle and the Rhine, as well as in the Ardennes area on the French-Belgian border.[23]

Switzerland has also consulted the German government regarding proposed nuclear plants near the Swiss-German border, and the two governments have agreed to exchange information on plans for any new nuclear plants in the border area. It is not clear whether the exchange could affect the siting decision, but it unquestionably could affect safety and pollution-control decisions.[24] There are also Dutch-German, Dutch-Belgian, and French-German agreements calling for consultations before final safety-related decisions are made regarding nuclear installations in those border areas. Only under the Dutch-Bel-

lating the Exchange of Information on the Construction of Nuclear Installations Along the Border, July 4, 1977, arts. 1–6, in 17 INT'L LEGAL MATERIALS 274 (1978). The similar agreement between the Netherlands and the Federal Republic of Germany appears in 6 ENVT'L POL'Y & L. 192 (1980). The other agreements are mentioned, *id.* at 164.

Stein, *The OECD Guiding Principles on Transfrontier Pollution*, 6 GA. J. INT'L AND COMP. L. 245, 251 (1976), says that pre-1974 Swedish construction of a nuclear power plant near Copenhagen prompted elaboration of the prior notification and consultation provisions of the OECD Principles. *See* chapter II, text at note 204, and *see* this chapter, text at note 143 *infra*.

[21]Convention on the Protection of Lake Constance Against Pollution, Oct. 27, 1960, art. 1(3), U.N. Doc. ST/LEG/SER.B/12, Treaty 127 (1963). Another example is the French–West German–Swiss border area Tripartite Commission. *See* 22 NUCLEAR L. BULL. 34 (1978).

[22]*See* Handl, *An International Legal Perspective on the Conduct of Abnormally Dangerous Activities in Frontier Areas: The Case of Nuclear Power Plant Siting*, 7 ECOLOGY L.Q. 1, 28–30 (1978). Handl points out that the Swiss decision to postpone the project may not have been based solely on Austrian objections.

[23]*See* chapter II at note 40; 22 NUCLEAR L. BULL. 34 (1978).

[24]EUR. PARL. DOC. 392/75/Annex, at 80–81 (1975).

gian agreement, however, is it clear that the health-safety consultations could affect the actual siting of the plant.[25]

Consultations have also been held in the absence of a preexisting agreement. This occurred in the first Swiss-German consultations, mentioned above. It also occurred between Czechoslovakia and Austria, between Spain and Portugal, and in other (unpublicized) cases.[26] Like treaty-based consultations, however, the discussions have not always been held in time to influence such things as the size and the general location of nuclear plants.[27] Moreover, nontreaty consultations do not consistently occur when the plant would be near a boundary abutting an ocean space rather than the land territory of another state.[28]

As noted in chapter II, European Community law also requires consultation before certain nuclear installations are constructed. Articles 41 and 43 of the Euratom Treaty require prior consultation with the European Commission when member states plan nuclear power stations or industries engaged in the nuclear fuel cycle.[29] Moreover, as this was written, the Council of the European Communities was considering a prior consultation procedure proposed by the Commission for the siting of power stations (other than those covered by the Euratom Treaty provisions above) that are likely to affect the territory of another member state.[30]

[25] Brief descriptions of the agreements appear in *id.* 68–69 (Dutch-German and Dutch-Belgian agreements) and in 20 O. J. EUR. COMM. (No. C 277) 15 (1977) (Parliamentary question and the Council's answer, regarding the French-German agreement).

[26] *See* Handl, *supra* note 22, at 28 n.136; OECD ENVIRONMENT DIRECTORATE, *supra* note 10, at 20 n.4; OECD Doc. ENV(79)23(Final) at 13 n.5 (1980); *Report of the Comm. on Legal Aspects of the Conservation of the Environment, supra* note 3, at 401–02. The Czech-Austrian consultations stemmed from an Austrian demand for a joint safety evaluation. *See* Handl, *The Principle of "Equitable Use" as Applied to Internationally Shared Natural Resources: Its Role in Resolving Potential International Disputes over Transfrontier Pollution,* 1978–79 REV. BELGE DE DROIT INT'L 40, 62 n. 98. Spain and Portugal have an understanding that there will be consultations. *See* 20 NUCLEAR L. BULL. 32 (1977). *See also* chapter II note 40 *supra.*

[27] For such a case involving the proposed French nuclear plant at Chooz, near the Belgian border, see 3 INT'L ENVT'L REP., CURRENT REP. 276 (1980).

[28] For example, when the U.K. considered the implications of building a reprocessing plant at Windscale, on the Irish Sea, it apparently perceived no duty to consult the Irish government. For a discussion of the Windscale inquiry, see Greenhalgh, *After Parker: A Review of the Windscale Inquiry and Subsequent Developments,* 20 IAEA BULL., No. 6, at 2 (1978).

[29] European Atomic Energy Community Treaty, March 25, 1957, 298 U.N.T.S. 167.

[30] The proposed regulation is in 22 O.J. EUR. COMM. (No. C 149) 2 (1979). *See also*

The European Communities have not limited their attention to power stations and nuclear fuel. After a long delay, the Council has adopted a directive that requires consultations about certain industrial activities involving dangerous substances that may pose risks to the population or environment in the area of the activities, including risks in another member state.[31]

There has been extensive Western European waste disposal practice, involving both radioactive and nonradioactive wastes. Before the early 1970s there were a number of instances in which European states discharged low-level radioactive waste into relatively enclosed seas without any apparent consultation. For example, in 1952 the United Kingdom began to dispose of such waste from its Windscale reprocessing plant by means of a pipeline extending three kilometers offshore in the Irish Sea. Published descriptions of the precautions taken do not mention prior consultation with the Irish government or with any official outside the United Kingdom.[32] Although the point of discharge would suggest that the principal risk was to interests in the U.K., the project did introduce low-level radioactivity into a relatively enclosed international area at a time when the effect was not fully understood. The same thing appears to have been done, without consultation, by France, Italy, the Netherlands, and Sweden.[33] Another example, not involving radioactive materials, was the dumping and land-based discharge of toxic wastes into the Baltic Sea before 1973.[34]

the Council Resolution concerning the mutual exchange of information at Community level on the siting of power stations, Nov. 20, 1978, in 21 *id.* (No. C 286) 1 (1978).

[31] *See* 15 BULL. EUR. COMM., No. 6, at 41 (1982).

[32] *See* EUR. CONSULT. ASS., 10th Sess., vol. 3, Doc. 833, at 1, 6 (1958); Dunster, *The Disposal of Radioactive Liquid Wastes into Coastal Waters, in Industrial Radioactive Waste Disposal: Hearings Before a Subcomm. of the Joint Comm. on Atomic Energy*, 86th Cong., 1st Sess., vol. 2, at 1396, 1397–99 (1959); L. HYDEMAN & W. BERMAN, INTERNATIONAL CONTROL OF NUCLEAR MARITIME ACTIVITIES 67–69 (1960); Howells, *Discharges of Low-Activity, Radioactive Effluent from the Windscale Works into the Irish Sea*, in SYMPOSIUM ON THE DISPOSAL OF RADIOACTIVE WASTES INTO SEAS, OCEANS AND SURFACE WATERS 769, 771 (IAEA, 1966) [hereinafter cited as SYMPOSIUM].

[33] *See the discussions (which do not mention international consultations) in Study Panel, Assessing Potential Ocean Pollutants* 42–43 (N.A.S. 1975); EUROPEAN NUCLEAR ENERGY AGENCY, RADIOACTIVE WASTE MANAGEMENT PRACTICES IN WESTERN EUROPE 71–74 (OECD 1971). The French disposal was in the English Channel. It is discussed in Avargues & Jammet, *Etude du site marin de la Hague en relation avec le rejet d'effluents radioactifs*, in SYMPOSIUM, *supra* note 32, at 787.

[34] The pre-1973 practice is discussed, without mentioning consultations, in Reintanz, *The Baltic—Speical Pollution Problems*, in 3 NEW DIRECTIONS IN THE LAW OF THE SEA 219 (R. Churchill, K. Simmonds, & J. Welch eds. 1973); *see also* Deese, *Law of the Sea and High Level Radioactive Waste Disposal: A Potential Geologic Option Under the Deep Seabed?*

Beginning in the early 1970s, however, European practice began to change, particularly as the result of a series of treaties. One relevant instrument, the Euratom Treaty,[35] antedated the 1970s. It requires consultation about plans to dispose of radioactive waste, so the European Commission may determine whether the project is likely to contaminate the water, soil, or airspace of another member state.[36] In the treaties of the 1970s, disposal of certain noxious substances directly into sea areas is prohibited—unless, in some cases, they are nontoxic or rapidly rendered harmless—while a group of less deleterious substances may be dumped under regulated conditions, usually involving national licensing. There is no transnational consultation requirement as to the latter substances. As to the former, the treaties recognize that dumping may have to be carried out occasionally when there is no better alternative; in such cases prior consultation is required with potentially affected states, unless the emergency is such that there is no time to do so.[37] Prior consultation procedures have also been devised to impose a check on a national government's proposed disposal of an otherwise-prohibited substance on the ground that it is nontoxic or rapidly rendered harmless.[38]

in *Radiological Contamination of the Oceans: Hearings Before a Subcomm. of the House Comm. on Interior and Insular Affairs*, 94th Cong., 2d Sess. 823, 940 n.27 (1976).

[35] European Atomic Energy Community Treaty, Mar. 25, 1957, 298 U.N.T.S. 167.

[36] *Id.* art. 37.

[37] [Oslo] Convention for the Prevention of Marine Pollution by Dumping from Ships and Aircraft, Feb. 15, 1972, art. 9, in 11 INT'L LEGAL MATERIALS 262 (1972) (Northeast Atlantic); Protocol for the Prevention of Pollution of the Mediterranean Sea by Dumping from Ships and Aircraft, Feb. 16, 1976, art. 9, in 15 *id.* at 300 (1976).

The [Helsinki] Convention on the Protection of the Marine Environment of the Baltic Sea Area, Mar. 22, 1974, art. 9, in 13 *id.* at 546 (1974), contains a blanket dumping prohibition, subject to two exceptions. One is a force majeure clause permitting dumping under certain dire circumstances, without expressly requiring prior consultation; the other allows dumping of dredged spoils. The force majeure clause is similar to [London] Convention on the Prevention of Marine Pollution by Dumping of Wastes and Other Matter, Dec. 29, 1972, art. 5(1), 26 U.S.T. 2403, *reprinted in* 11 INT'L LEGAL MATERIALS 1294 (1972). Such clauses recognize that prior consultation is not practicable in a true emergency. The Helsinki Convention apparently does not permit the kind of dumping permitted (after consultation) under the Oslo Convention and the Mediterranean Protocol. The second exception to the Helsinki Convention's dumping prohibition, relating to dredged spoils, allows them to be dumped within the dumping state's territorial waters, or outside them if there is prior consultation. Helsinki Convention, *supra*, art. 9(2) and Annex 5, Reg. 1, para. 2(b).

For the low-level radioactive-waste ocean-disposal procedure adopted by the OECD's Nuclear Energy Agency, see chapter IV at notes 140–41.

[38] Such a procedure is in force as an interim measure under the Oslo Convention. *See* IMCO Doc. LDC IV/8. Annex 1 (1979). A comparable procedure has been proposed

European practice also evinces a trend toward prior consultation, on request, for the disposal of nonprohibited polluting substances from land-based sources into relatively enclosed sea areas when other treaty states are likely to be affected.[39] A comparable procedure appears in the European Council Directive on the protection of groundwater against pollution from certain dangerous substances. It establishes two lists, one containing substances that ordinarily are not to be discharged, and the other containing less harmful substances that may be discharged under permits issued by national authorities. Potentially affected member states are to be notified before permits are issued. If any member state requests consultations, they must be held, and the Commission is entitled to participate.[40]

Another European Council Directive, involving disposal of waste from the titanium dioxide industry, requires prior authorization not only from the competent authority in the member state where the waste is produced and initially discharged, but also from the authority in the member state upon whose territory it is ultimately to be discharged.[41] If authorization has been given but certain detrimental effects of the disposal appear, the disposing state is to take remedial action. Before it

for the Mediterranean Dumping Protocol, IMCO Doc. LDC IV/8, at 2 (1979).

[39] [Paris] Convention for the Prevention of Marine Pollution from Land-Based Sources, Feb. 21, 1974, art. 9, in 13 INT'L LEGAL MATERIALS 352 (1974) (Northeast Atlantic); Protocol for the Protection of the Mediterranean Sea Against Pollution from Land-Based Sources, May 16, 1980, art. 12(1), in 19 INT'L LEGAL MATERIALS 869 (1980). In these instruments the consultation provisions supplement internationally agreed upon national licensing systems.

The Convention for the Protection of the Mediterranean Sea Against Pollution, Feb. 16, 1976, art. 14, in 15 INT'L LEGAL MATERIALS 290 (1976), contains a general provision requiring consultations at the request of any party if the request is supported by two other parties.

[40] Council Directive 80/68/EEC, Dec. 17, 1979, art. 17, in 23 O.J. EUR. COMM. (No. L 20) 43 (1980). The Directive has superseded, in part, Council Directive 76/464/EEC, May 4, 1976, in 19 O.J. EUR. COMM. (No. L 129) 23 (1976). That Directive set up a prior-authorization scheme, to be administered by national officials, regarding the discharge of certain dangerous substances into the aquatic environment of the Community. The aquatic environment includes surface water, territorial waters, internal coastal waters, and groundwater. *See* chapter II at note 37. *See also* Council Directive 75/439/EEC, June 16, 1975, in 18 O.J. EUR. COMM. (No. L 194) 23 (1975), which deals with disposal of waste oils in the manner of the 1976 Directive.

There is a catchall Council Directive on Toxic and Dangerous Waste, Mar. 20, 1978, in 21 O.J. EUR. COMM. (No. L 84) 43 (1978), which applies to harmful wastes not covered by specific Community rules. It neither establishes standards nor requires prior consultation.

[41] Council Directive 78/176/EEC, Feb. 20, 1978, art. 4, in 21 O.J. EUR. COMM. (No. L 54) 19 (1978).

does so, it must consult other interested member states.[42] This procedural safeguard, like that attached to last-resort ocean dumping of otherwise-prohibited substances, serves to bring inclusive interests into the decision-making process when extraordinary action, potentially harmful in itself, must be taken.

There is a substantial amount of European practice relating to jurisdictional extensions (territorial waters, fishery zones, continental shelf rights, etc.) into relatively enclosed sea areas. Three recurring situations are of particular interest: (*a*) extensions in such areas as the North Sea, the English Channel, or the Baltic Sea that affect the interests of other littoral European states but that do not potentially overlap their jurisdictional claims;[43] (*b*) such extensions that do potentially encroach on a similar claim that could reasonably be made by another littoral state; and (*c*) exploitation of resource deposits straddling the actual or putative demarcation line between continental shelf rights of two or more European states.

The European Fisheries Conference was held in London from December 3, 1963, to March 2, 1964. The sixteen participating Western European states negotiated the European Fisheries Convention.[44] Fourteen of them ultimately signed it; one other (Norway) had already entered into a comparable bilateral fishery agreement with the U.K., the state principally interested in its coastal fishery.[45] The European Fisheries Convention (which applied to such relatively enclosed areas as the North Sea, the Irish Sea, and the English Channel as well as to the Atlantic Ocean) adopted a six-plus-six formula, with traditional distant-water fishing rights preserved in the outer six-mile area except when the coastal state's population was overwhelmingly dependent on the coastal fishery. In the latter case, approval of

[42] Council Directive 78/176/EEC, *supra* note 41, art. 8.

[43] As indicated at the beginning of this chapter, the present discussion omits any reference to consultations with nonlittoral states, even if they are affected by the extension in a relatively enclosed sea area. It also omits any reference to consultations with "littoral" states when the sea area is relatively open. Thus, for example, the Anglo-Icelandic difficulties surrounding Iceland's fishery zone extensions are examined in chapter IV rather than in this chapter. To the extent that European practice relates equally to relatively enclosed and relatively open sea areas—as in the case of the European Fisheries Convention—it is discussed in both chapters.

[44] European Fisheries Convention, Mar. 9, 1964, 581 U.N.T.S. 57. One Eastern European state—Poland—later acceded to the Convention.

[45] *See* 4 M. WHITEMAN, DIGEST OF INT'L LAW 1039–40, 1180–81. The other nonsigner was Iceland. *See* chapter IV notes 23–28 and 35–37 *infra*, for discussion of Iceland's fishery zone extensions.

the other contracting parties was required if the outer six-mile area was to become an exclusive zone. A state not overwhelmingly dependent on its coastal fishery could issue conservation regulations for the outer six-mile area, but only if it first informed the other contracting parties and consulted them at their request.[46] A transitional period was provided for phasing out traditional rights within the inner six-mile zone.

For purposes of assessing Western European practice concerning nonoverlapping claims, two features of the European fisheries arrangement are noteworthy. First, the European Fisheries Conference was itself a multilateral consultation among states interested in fishing off their own and each other's coasts. Instead of proceeding unilaterally—a step each of them must have considered—they strived for (and fourteen of them reached) agreement on extended fishery zones. Second, the consultation provision in the Convention regarding conservation regulations in the outer six-mile area demonstrates the expectation—later found to be a customary duty in the Fisheries Jurisdiction Cases[47]—that there must be consultation with interested states before the coastal state takes potentially adverse action in a nonexclusive (preferential) maritime zone. Interestingly, when the parties to the European Convention began to implement the Convention in the mid-1960s, they expressed their willingness to consult without waiting for requests from other states and without limiting consultations to states parties to the Convention.[48]

When the Norwegian government decided in August 1974 that its fishing interests required a 50-mile exclusive fishery zone and four trawler-free pockets off its coast, it announced that it would seek negotiations with the other interested states before taking any action. It then consulted the United Kingdom, West Germany, France, East Germany, Poland, and the Soviet Union. At one point the Commission of the European Communities apparently threatened retaliation if Norway were to act without giving adequate time for negotiations.[49] The negotiations continued, with Norway ultimately reducing considerably the ex-

[46] European Fisheries Convention, *supra* note 44, art. 5(2).

[47] *See* Chapter IV notes 38–39 *infra*.

[48] *See e.g.*, 696 PARL. DEB., H.C. (5th ser.) 947 (1964); Windley, *International Practice Regarding Traditional Fishing Privileges of Foreign Fishermen in Zones of Extended Maritime Jurisdiction*, 63 AM. J. INT'L L. 490, 501 (1969).

[49] EUROPEAN REP., Jan. 18, 1975, External Relations, at 3.

tent of the proposed trawler-free areas and the periods when they would be closed to fishing.[50] The Norwegian law came into force on January 31, 1975, after all the negotiations had been successfully concluded.[51]

Within the 200-mile fishery zones presently claimed by the European Community states, intra-Community conservation measures are to be adopted collectively pursuant to the common fisheries policy. Nevertheless, the United Kingdom and Ireland delayed the policy's entry into force on the ground that it did not reserve sufficient fishery rights to the individual states. As an interim procedural safeguard, the E.C. Council adopted in 1976 a resolution contemplating some temporary unilateral conservation measures if the member state sought the approval of the Commission beforehand and continued to consult it thereafter.[52]

While the definitive Community policy was pending, the U.K. and Ireland took several conservation steps affecting the fishing interests of other member states. These were interim measures, taken in most cases after seeking the approval of the Commission and after the projected unilateral steps had been discussed in the context of a broader Council discussion on proposed Community conservation rules.[53]

The United Kingdom's record, however, was not spotless. When it adopted its Fishing Nets (North-East Atlantic) Order in 1977, it failed to seek prior Commission approval.[54] Moreover, when the U.K. enlarged its "Norway Pout Box" in the North Sea in 1978, it again failed to seek the Commission's prior approval, and when it established new minimum net-mesh sizes in 1979, the Commission alleged that the U.K. had allowed it inadequate time to consider the measure.[55] France contested

[50] *See* BULL. LEGAL DEV. (Oct. 4, 1974) at 2; *id.* (Oct. 18, 1974) at 2; Financial Times, Dec., 2, 1974, at 26, col. 8; *id.* Dec. 7, 1974, at 11, col. 3; *id.* Jan. 22, 1975, at 7, col. 4; 18 O.J. EUR. COMM. (No. C. 86) 8 (1975).

[51] *See* BULL. LEGAL DEV. (Mar. 19, 1975) at 43.

[52] Council Res. of Nov. 3, 1976, Annex VI, unpublished, but *quoted in* 1977 E.C.J. REP. at 945.

[53] On the Irish fifty-mile conservation measures in 1977, *see* 10 BULL. E.C., No. 2, at 24 (1977); *id.*, No. 3, at 41; *id.*, No. 5, at 53. On the 1977 U.K. measures affecting herring and Norway pout, *see* The Times (London), June 28, 1977, at 1, col. 6; *id.*, July 1, 1977, at 1, col. 1; EUROPE, June 29, 1977, at 4; Financial Times, Oct. 26, 1977, at 28, col. 3; 10 BULL. E.C., No. 7/8, at 47 (1977). On the 1979 U.K. measures affecting net-mesh sizes, *see* Financial Times, Mar. 23, 1979, at 31, col. 1; 12 BULL. E.C., No. 6, at 65 (1979).

[54] *See* 12 BULL. E.C., No. 10, at 106 (1979); 22 O.J. EUR. COMM. (No. C. 280) 5 (1979).

[55] *See* 12 BULL. E.C., No. 7/8, at 45 (1979).

the 1977 Order, and the Commission challenged all three British measures in the European Court of Justice. The Court held all three measures unlawful, treating the Council's 1976 resolution as a binding application of the general duty of cooperation in article 5 of the European Economic Community (EEC) Treaty.[56]

Throughout, the U.K. remained willing to consult its European Community partners about their historic fishing rights in a contemplated twelve-mile exclusive zone it wished to establish on a long-term basis, and asserted that it would act unilaterally only if it failed to get acceptable Community action.[57] If this is considered with the other Western European practice outlined above, one finds a prior consultation duty in Western Europe, at least for definitive, nonoverlapping conservation measures and probably for interim ones.

When Western European states have extended their territorial waters to twelve miles, they have done so after (or in conjunction with) discussions within the United Nations framework.[58] Nevertheless, they have not followed a consistent practice of holding specific consultations with the littoral Western European states. This may be explained by the fact that their territorial sea claims have not in themselves restricted preexisting patterns of fishing or navigation by the littoral states.[59]

There seems to be no prior consultation norm among littoral Eastern European states when a nonoverlapping jurisdictional extension occurs, whether the extension is limited to conservation or is more comprehensive. The most that can be said is that the extensions in recent years have followed negotiations

[56] *See* France v. United Kingdom, 27 Comm. Mkt. L. R. 6, 23–24 (1980); Commission v. United Kingdom, 30 *id.* at 219 (1981); Commission v. United Kingdom, 33 *id.* at 543 (1982).

[57] *See* Financial Times, Nov. 23, 1978, at 37, col. 2; *id.*, June 28, 1979, at 25, col. 4.

[58] An example is the Italian twelve-mile claim in 1974, after the first substantive session of the Third U.N. Conference on the Law of the Sea. Even the French claim in 1971 came after considerable discussion of twelve-mile territorial seas in the U.N. Seabeds Committee. *See* 2 S. ODA, THE LAW OF THE SEA IN OUR TIME: THE UNITED NATIONS SEABED COMMITTEE 1968–1973, at 175 (1977); 26 U.N. GAOR, Supp. (No. 21) at 35–36, U.N. Doc. A/8421 (1971).

[59] *See, e.g.*, the 1971 French law, 11 INT'L LEGAL MATERIALS 153 (1972). *See also* Quéneudec, *France*, in 3 NEW DIRECTIONS IN THE LAW OF THE SEA, *supra* note 34, at 257, 258–59. It is not clear whether France consulted its European neighbors before asserting its 1971 claim. R.-J. DUPUY, THE LAW OF THE SEA 165 n.17 (1974), reports that at the international level, "[C]onciliation between the interests in protection of the riparian State and the interest of the international community in the matter of maritime and aerial navigation has been invoked."

in the Third U.N. Conference on the Law of the Sea.[60]

The discussion above has focused on conservation measures and extensions that are applied uniformly around the coasts of the claiming state. Another kind of jurisdictional extension—the drawing of closing lines across bays—usually has not evoked prior consultation in either Eastern or Western Europe.[61]

On the other hand, there is sufficient practice in Eastern and Western Europe to establish a consultation requirement before there is any attempt to exercise rights under an ocean-space jurisdictional claim in such a way as to encroach on a potentially overlapping claim of another state. This stems in part from the judgment in the North Sea Continental Shelf Cases.[62] The Court held that Denmark and the Netherlands could not simply maintain continental shelf rights out to the equidistance line with West Germany, a nonparty to the 1958 Continental Shelf Convention, but were instead obligated to enter into meaningful negotiations with the German government. The duty to negotiate stemmed from the 1945 Truman Proclamation on the continental shelf, which recognized the need to agree on delimitation with adjacent states, and from the negotiation principle recognized in U.N. Charter Article 33.[63] The Court noted, with

[60]This is true of the extended fishery claims in the Baltic in 1977–78. It is clear that at least one, the Soviet claim, was made without specific notice to, or consultation with, other Baltic states. *See* Los Angeles Times, Apr. 17, 1978, pt. I, at 12, col. 1; 13 BULL. LEGAL DEV. 122 (1978). (A much earlier version of the same Soviet claim was enforced without prior notice against Swedish vessels in the Baltic. *See* Swedish Note to the Soviet Union, July 18, 1951, in B. MacChesney, *Situation, Documents and Commentary on Recent Developments in the International Law of the Sea*, 51 U.S. NAVAL WAR COLLEGE INT'L L. STUDIES 441, 496–97 (1957).) On the other hand, once the exclusive fishery claims in the Baltic were made, the littoral states have recognized the need to cooperate with each other in establishing conservation measures within each zone. *See* L. GELBERG, MARITIME COOPERATION OF THE BALTIC STATES: LEGAL PROBLEMS 102–04 (1981). The Agreement between Poland and Sweden on Baltic Fisheries, Feb. 1, 1978, arts. 3 and 4, *id.* at 173, requires bilateral consultations before fishing allotments are made within each party's zone. For recommendations by the International Baltic Sea Commission regarding conservation, see 21 INTERNATIONAL PROTECTION OF THE ENVIRONMENT 168–91 (B. Rüster, B. Simma, & M. Bock eds. 1981).

The 1976 Albanian fifteen-mile territorial sea claim was preceded by warnings in the Third Law of the Sea Conference, and perhaps by off-the-record consultations there, but available materials do not show specific consultations with neighboring states. For Albania's public pronouncements, see THIRD U.N. CONF. ON THE LAW OF THE SEA, OR, vol. 1, at 100, and *id.*, vol. 2, at 113 (1975).

[61]*See* Chapter IV note 96 *infra*. *But see* the Fisheries Convention Between Spain and Portugal, Feb. 21, 1969, art. 4(2), in 21 INTERNATIONAL PROTECTION OF THE ENVIRONMENT, *supra* note 60, at 65.

[62]1969 I.C.J. 3.

[63]*Id.* at 47–48.

apparent approval, that the International Law Commission's Committee of Experts in 1953 had endorsed the same principle for lateral delimitation of territorial sea boundaries when the equidistance principle would not lead to an equitable solution.[64]

Denmark, the Netherlands, and West Germany did negotiate, and ultimately agreed.[65] With one possible exception, other European states with continental shelf claims in confined areas have entered into intergovernmental negotiations rather than—or at least before—making potentially overlapping unilateral claims. In most cases this has resulted in agreed delimitations.[66]

[64] *Id.* at 34. Report of the Committee of Experts, U.N. Doc. A/CN.4/61/Add.l, *reprinted in* [1953] 2 Y.B. INT'L L. COMM'N 77, 79, U.N. Doc. A/CN.4/SER.A/1953; 4 M. WHITEMAN, DIGEST OF INT'L L. 325–26 (1965).

[65] Treaty Between the Federal Republic of Germany and Denmark, Jan. 28, 1971, 10 INT'L LEGAL MATERIALS 603 (1971); Treaty Between the Netherlands and the Federal Republic of Germany, Jan. 28, 1971, *id.* at 607.

[66] Delimitation agreements: (*1*) U.K.–Norway, Mar. 10, 1965, 551 U.N.T.S. 213; (*2*) Finland–U.S.S.R., May 20, 1965, 566 U.N.T.S. 31; (*3*) U.K.–Netherlands, Oct. , 1965, 595 U.N.T.S. 106, *as amended*, Nov. 25, 1971, 11 INT'L LEGAL MATERIALS 744 (1972); (*4*) U.K.–Denmark, Oct. 6, 1965, 595 U.N.T.S. 113, as amended, Nov. 25, 1971, 11 INT'L LEGAL MATERIALS 723 (1972); (*5*) Denmark–Norway, Dec. 8, 1965, 634 U.N.T.S. 71, *as amended*, Apr. 24, 1968, 643 U.N.T.S. 414; (*6*) Denmark–Netherlands, Mar. 31, 1966, 604 U.N.T.S. 209; (*7*) Finland–U.S.S.R., May 5, 1967, 640 U.N.T.S. 111; (*8*) Italy-Yugoslavia, Jan. 8, 1968, 7 INT'L LEGAL MATERIALS 547 (1968); (*9*) Norway–Sweden, July 24, 1968, U.N. Doc. ST/LEG/SER.B/16 at 413 (1974); (*10*) Declaration by German Democratic Republic–Poland–U.S.S.R., Oct. 23, 1968, 7 INT'L LEGAL MATERIALS 1393 (1968); (*11*) Poland–German Democratic Republic, Oct. 29, 1968, Straburzynski, *Sovereign Rights to the Sea-Bed Resources and the Declaration on the Continental Shelf of the Baltic Sea*, 5 POL. Y.B. INT'L L. 61, 69 (1972–73); (*12*) Poland–U.S.S.R., Aug. 28, 1969, 769 U.N.T.S. 75 (these last two agreements carry out the policy established in the tripartite Declaration, no. 10 *supra*); (*13*) Italy–Tunisia, Aug. 20, 1971, 5 NEW DIRECTIONS IN THE LAW OF THE SEA 247 (R. Churchill, M. Nordquist, and S. Lay eds. 1977); (*14*) U.K.–Federal Republic of Germany, Nov. 25, 1971, *id.* at 731; (*15*) Finland–Sweden, Sept. 29, 1972, U.N. Doc. ST/LEG/SER.B/18, at 439 (1976) (*16*) France–Spain, Jan. 29, 1974, 5 NEW DIRECTIONS, *supra*, at 251; (*17*) Italy-Spain, Feb. 19, 1974, *id.* at 261; (*18*) Greece-Italy, May 24, 1977, 12 BULL. LEGAL DEV. 119 (1977).

Conflicting claims submitted to arbitration: U.K.-France (negotiations began in 1964; agreed to arbitrate in 1974; awards in 1977 and 1978). *See* Symmonds, *British Off-Shore Continental Shelf and Fishery Limit Boundaries: An Analysis of Overlapping Zones*, 28 INTL & COMP. L. Q. 703, 707 (1979); 18 INT'L LEGAL MATERIALS 397 (1979).

Protracted negotiations: Norway-U.S.S.R. concerning the Barents Sea, beginning in 1974, STAFF OF HOUSE COMM. ON FOREIGN AFFAIRS, 96TH CONG., 2D SESS., REPORT ON NATO AND WESTERN SECURITY IN THE 1980S: THE EUROPEAN PERCEPTION 14 (Comm. Print 1980). Negotiations punctuated by unilateral claims, resulting in an agreement to arbitrate: U.K.-Ireland (concerning area around Rockall Island), The Times (London), Sept. 13, 1974, at 2, col. 1; *id.* Feb. 19, 1977, at 19, col. 8; 1980 BRIT. Y.B. INT'L L. 456–57.

European domestic legislation on continental shelf claims either is silent regarding delimitation or expressly refers to agreements to be made with opposite or adjacent states. For examples of the latter type, see the Italian Act of July 21, 1967, art. 1, in

The one exception involved the conflicting unilateral Greek and Turkish claims to the Aegean continental shelf, originally asserted without prior consultation. But Greece and Turkey eventually agreed (before exploitation by either of them) to negotiate in good faith and to refrain from any further unilateral acts that might prejudice the negotiations.[67] They did negotiate. Thus, although Greek-Turkish practice would not support a European norm requiring consultation before a controversial continental shelf *claim* is made, it would support a norm requiring abstention from controversial exploitation until consultations can be held.[68]

There is a greater measure of consensus in Europe regarding the use of the equidistance line to delimit opposite or adjacent fishery zone claims than to delimit continental shelf claims.[69] The leading indicator of Western European practice is the European Fisheries Convention,[70] adopted in 1964. Article 7 established the median (or equidistance) line as the fishery boundary, in the absence of agreement with the opposite or adjacent state party. Similarly, after the Council of the European Communities decided that member states would extend their fishing zones to 200 miles after January 1, 1977, they did so subject to limits defined by the equidistance lines with other states' zones, or subject to agreement with opposite and adjacent states.[71] On those few occasions when a seemingly firm over-

U.N. Doc. ST/LEG/SER.B/15, at 370 (1970), and the Soviet Decree of Feb. 6, 1968, art. 2, *id.* at 441.

[67]For the agreement, Nov. 11, 1976, see 16 INT'L LEGAL MATERIALS 13 (1977). For earlier allegations by each side regarding the other's unilateral claims (not preceded by specific consultations), see U.N. Docs. S/PV.1949, at 7; S/PV.1950, at 7–10 (1976). There were heated discussions on delimitation between Greece and Turkey in the U.N. Seabeds Committee at least as early as 1973, but these do not seem to have been consultations on specific national proposals. *See* 2 S. ODA, *supra* note 58, at 242–43.

[68]It has been argued that a prior consent norm should be implied from a duty to seek agreement regarding continental shelf delimitation. *See* [1951] 1 Y.B. INT'L L. COMM'N 291, U.N. Doc. A/CN.4/Ser.A/1951 (Messsrs. Scelle, El Khoury, and Cordova). But it is difficult to find in European practice a conviction that consent would be required if, for example, extended negotiations proved fruitless.

[69]The same is true regarding use of the thalweg to delimit boundaries in contiguous rivers. The conclusions in the text concerning claims extending beyond the equidistance line apply as well to territorial claims beyond the thalweg.

[70]European Fisheries Convention, Mar. 9, 1964, 581 U.N.T.S. 57.

[71]*See e.g.*, Law No. 597 of Dec. 17, 1976, on the Fishing Territory of Denmark, art. 1(2), in 5 NEW DIRECTIONS, *supra* note 66, at 109; Danish Regulation No. 639, Dec. 22, 1977, *summarized in* 13 BULL. LEGAL DEV. 22 (1978); Irish Maritime Jurisdiction (Exclusive Fishery Limits) Order, Dec. 22, 1976, para. 4, 5 NEW DIRECTIONS, *supra* note

lapping claim has been announced, any attempt to enforce it has been stayed pending consultations.[72]

In Eastern Europe, Baltic fishery zones have not extended beyond the equidistance line. They have been negotiated where overlapping claims exist.[73] No unilateral claims have been asserted in the Caspian Sea, which has been divided into two maritime zones by the two littoral states—the Soviet Union and Iran.[74] Fisheries in the Black Sea are relatively insignificant, and apparently no potentially conflicting unilateral claims have been made.[75]

There is further European practice, some of which bestrides Western and Eastern Europe. When this is considered with the

66, at 120; British Fishery Limits Act 1976, § 1(3), *id.* at 123; Proclamation of the Fed. Repub. of Germany on the Establishment of a Fishing Zone in the North Sea, Dec. 21, 1976, para. 1, *id.* at 118; French Decree No. 77–130, on the Establishment of an Economic Zone, Feb. 11, 1977, art. 1, *id.* at 303; Netherlands State Practice for the Parliamentary Year 1976–1977, in 1978 NETH. Y.B. INTL L. 191, 228.

The potentially overlapping fishery zone claims of Ireland and the U.K. remained essentially undelineated while ongoing discussions were held. *See* Symmonds, *supra* note 66, at 733. Fishery conservation zones in the Bay of Biscay were established in 1970 only after agreement between France and Spain. *See* Quéneudec, *France*, in 3 NEW DIRECTIONS, *supra* note 34, at 257, 262.

[72]For example, when Denmark declared a 200-mile economic zone off Eastern Greenland in June 1980, thus creating a potential conflict with Iceland and Norway, it postponed indefinitely any attempt to enforce it in the disputed area until talks could be held. *See* The Times (London), June 2, 1980, at 6, col. 1.

[73]Financial Times, Dec. 23, 1977, at 17, col. 1. *See also* Carroz, *The Management of Living Resources in the Baltic Sea and the Belts*, 4 OCEAN DEV. & INT'L L. 213 (1977), discussing the Convention on Fishing and Conservation of the Living Resources in the Baltic Sea and the Belts. Swedish law authorizes a fishery zone claim to the equidistance line in the Baltic, U.N. Doc. ST/LEG/SER.B/118, at 349, 350 (1976), but when Sweden extended its actual fishing jurisdiction, it did so without fixing definite outer limits that could encroach on Soviet claims, and conducted negotiations with the Soviet government. 12 BULL. LEGAL DEV. 79, 133, 245 (1977). Poland similarly negotiated before adopting fishery zone legislation in December 1977, and made no unilateral claim to overlapping areas. 13 *id.* at 2 (1978). East Germany's Baltic fisheries zone extends only to the equidistance line, *id.* at 12, as does Denmark's, pending agreements with other Baltic states, *id.* at 44.

In April 1978, when the Soviet Union introduced interim conservation measures off its Baltic coast without prior consultation, the outer boundaries were left undefined pending negotiations with other Baltic states. *Id.* at 122.

For a collection of agreements on the Baltic Sea regime, see 2 V. SEBEK, THE EASTERN EUROPEAN STATES AND THE DEVELOPMENT OF THE LAW OF THE SEA, ch. 2 at 27 (1979).

[74]*See* W. BUTLER, THE SOVIET UNION AND THE LAW OF THE SEA 101–03 (1971); 1 V. SEBEK, *supra* note 73, at 450.

[75]1 V. SEBEK, *supra* note 73, at 458–59. *See also* the fishing agreement between the U.S.S.R., Bulgaria, and Romania, July 7, 1959, 2 *id.*, ch. 1, at 102; territorial waters boundary agreement between the U.S.S.R. and Turkey, Apr. 17, 1973, in 2 *id.*, ch. 2, at 27.

practice documented above, a European norm emerges requiring prior consultation—and perhaps even prior agreement—if a fishery zone claim is to be implemented that might overlap with another state's plausible claim (defined, in the absence of special circumstances, by reference to the equidistance line).[76] The same principle applies to potentially overlapping territorial sea claims, though the use of the equidistance line to judge the reasonableness of another state's claim is not as well established.[77]

[76]For example, before Norway and the Soviet Union enacted two-hundred-mile fishery zones in the Barents Sea, they negotiated a fishery agreement. *See* Traavik & Ostreng, Security and Ocean Law: Norway and the Soviet Union in the Barents Sea, 4 OCEAN DEV. & INT'L L. 343, 359–60 (1977). Although the agreement was negotiated after Norway had set in motion its parliamentary procedure to establish the zone, and was signed after the zone was proclaimed, there had been exploratory talks by Norway with interested states before its initial decision was made, and Norway had clearly expressed its willingness to consult further. *See* Financial Times, July 10, 1975, at 6, col. 5; *id.* Feb. 9, 1976, at 7, col. 8; *id.* Feb. 10, 1976, at 6, col. 5; *id.* Mar. 10, 1976, at 31, col. 1. (The agreement did not set the boundary, but alleviated the boundary problem by establishing a reciprocal access arrangement. Talks on setting the boundary began before the fishery zones came into force. *Id.* Dec. 13, 1976, at 4, col. 1.)

When Iceland established its two-hundred-mile fishery zone in October 1975, it recognized the equidistance line with Norway's Jan Mayen Islands as the temporary limit pending negotiation. There were negotiations and a tentative agreement before each announced potentially conflicting fishery claims in the summer of 1979. *See* 15 INT'L LEGAL MATERIALS 875 (1976); Financial Times, July 10, 1979, at 2, col. 6. They ultimately reached a definitive agreement, with Norway accepting a zone short of the equidistance line. *Id.*, May 13, 1980, at 3, col. 5.

Norway and Denmark have consulted as to their potentially overlapping economic zone claims between Greenland and Jan Mayen Island, where the issue is whether the island is entitled to any zone at all. Financial Times, June 11, 1980, at 2, col. 1.

[77]There have been several agreements delimiting European territorial seas. *See, e.g.*, (*1*) Denmark-Sweden, Jan. 30, 1932, 127 L.N.T.S. 62; (*2*) Norway–U.S.S.R., Feb. 15, 1957, 312 U.N.T.S. 322; (*3*) Poland–U.S.S.R., Mar. 18, 1958, 340 U.N.T.S. 94; (*4*) Finland-U.S.S.R., May 20, 1965, 566 U.N.T.S. 31; (*5*) U.S.S.R.–Turkey, Apr. 17, 1973, 2 V. SEBEK, *supra* note 73, at 27; (*6*) France–Spain, Jan. 29, 1974, 5 NEW DIRECTIONS, *supra* note 66, at 1; (*7*) Fed. Repub. Germany–German Dem. Repub., June 29, 1974, *id.* at 5. *See also* U.N. Doc. A/CN.4/71 and Add. 1–2, reprinted in [1953] 2 Y.B. INT'L L. COMMN 80–89, U.N. Doc. A/CN.4/SER.A/1953/Add.l, summarizing several pre-1953 European territorial-sea lateral-delimitation agreements. When agreements have not been reached, European governments have normally refrained from asserting unilateral territorial sea claims likely to encroach on reasonable claims of others. Thus, when France extended its territorial sea claim to twelve miles in 1971, it did so subject to the median-line principle. French Law No. 71–1060, Dec. 24, 1971, art. 2, in 11 INT'L LEGAL MATERIALS 153 (1972). *See also* Portuguese Law No. 2130, Aug. 22, 1966, art. 4, in U.N. Doc. ST/LEG/SER.B/15, at 112 (1970). Earlier in 1971, the British government rejected a demand by some members of Parliament to extend British territorial waters to twelve miles in the Straits of Dover, stressing that any such action would have to be preceded by an international agreement. Churchill, *United Kingdom*, in 3 NEW DIRECTIONS, *supra* note 34, at 281, 282.

On the question of mineral deposits straddling a continental shelf delimitation line, there are at least twelve Western European bilateral treaties requiring consultation, or consultation plus agreement or arbitration, before either government authorizes exploitation from its side of the line.[78] Some European continental shelf delimitation agreements are silent on the point, but there is no indication that practice under those agreements is inconsistent with the consultation norm. On the other hand, there is insufficient evidence of European consultation practice before a state exploits a common fishery, as distinguished from a common mineral resource deposit, to support an obligatory norm.[79]

C. AFRICA AND ASIA

The African Convention on the Conservation of Nature and Natural Resources provides, "Where any development plan is likely to affect the natural resources [soil, water, flora, and fauna] of another state, the latter shall be consulted."[80] The Convention

[78] (*1*) U.K.–Norway, Mar. 19, 1965, art. 4, 551 U.N.T.S. 213; (*2*) U.K.–Netherlands, Oct. 6, 1965, arts. 1 and 2, 595 U.N.T.S. 106, *as amended on another point*, Nov. 25, 1971, 11 INT'L LEGAL MATERIALS 744 (1972); (*3*) Denmark–Norway, Dec. 8, 1965, art. 4, 634 U.N.T.S. 71; (*4*) Italy–Yugoslavia, Jan. 8, 1968, art. 2, 7 INT'L LEGAL MATERIALS 547 (1968); (*5*) Norway–Sweden, July 24, 1968, art. 4, U.N. Doc. ST/LEG/SER.B/16, at 413 (1974); (*6*) Federal Republic of Germany–Denmark, Jan. 28, 1971, art. 2, 10 INT'L LEGAL MATERIALS 603 (1971); (*7*) Federal Republic of Germany–Netherlands, Jan. 28, 1971, art. 2, *id.* at 607; (*8*) Italy-Tunisia, August 20, 1971, art. 4, 5 NEW DIRECTIONS, *supra* note 66, at 247; (*9*) U.K.-Denmark, Nov. 25, 1971, art. 4, 11 INT'L LEGAL MATERIALS 723 (1972); (*10*) U.K.–Federal Republic of Germany, Nov. 25, 1971, arts. 3 and 4, *id.* 731; (*11*) France-Spain, Jan. 29, 1974, art. 4, 5 NEW DIRECTIONS, *supra* note 66, at 251; (*12*) Italy-Spain, Feb. 19, 1974, art. 2, *id.* at 261. The Declaration on the Continental Shelf of the Baltic Sea (German Dem. Repub.–Poland–U.S.S.R.), Oct. 23, 1968, 7 INT'L LEGAL MATERIALS 1393 (1968), says in paragraph 10 that the parties "will consult among themselves concerning questions of mutual interest in connection with the use of the continental shelf of the Baltic Sea."

Onorato, *Apportionment of an International Common Petroleum Deposit*, 26 INT'L & COMP. L.Q. 324 (1977), concludes on the basis of Western European practice that there is a duty not only to negotiate with a view to reaching agreement but to abstain from unilateral exploitation over the reasonable objection of the other interested state.

[79] In a related situation, there are consultation rules in the European Economic Community. Council Directives call upon member states to designate zones for special water-quality measures designed to conserve fisheries. When they propose to designate waters in the vicinity of, or crossing, a frontier with another member state, they are to consult that state. The Commission is entitled to participate in the consultations. Council Directives 78/659/EEC, Aug. 14, 1978, art. 10, in 21 O.J. EUR. COMM. (No. L 222) 1 (1978), and 79/923/EEC, Oct. 30, 1979, art. 10, in 22 *id.* 47 (1979).

[80] African Convention on the Conservation of Nature and Natural Resources, Sept.

for Co-operation in the Protection and Development of the Marine and Coastal Environment of the West and Central African Region does not contain such a clear consultation duty, but does have several provisions that call for cooperation, harmonization of policies, adoption of (unspecified) preventive measures, and dissemination of information.[81] Some or all of these provisions could form the basis for an asserted duty to consult, but it is too early to say whether they will be applied that way in practice.

In Asia, the Convention on Conservation of Nature in the South Pacific does not contain an explicit duty to consult before acting, but does require the parties to consult one another in order to give effect to the Convention and sets up an administering body, the South Pacific Commission. It also provides, among other things, that "Each Contracting Party shall carefully consider the consequences of the deliberate introduction into ecosystems of species which have not previously occurred therein."[82] The clear implication is that there must be consultation before a party does introduce new species.

Asian consultation practice regarding nonoverlapping extended jurisdictional claims peculiarly affecting other littoral states reflects differing expectations, depending on whether a claim is simply being asserted or is actually to be enforced. In one well-publicized instance, the Soviet Union did not consult the Japanese government before announcing in February 1977 that its new 200-mile fishing zone would include areas around the disputed Kurile Islands in the Sea of Okhotsk. Before the zone went into effect, however, there were negotiations between the two governments.[83] These negotiations preceded the then-

15, 1968, art. 14(3), in 5 INTERNATIONAL PROTECTION OF THE ENVIRONMENT 2037 (B. Rüster & B. Simma eds. 1976). Natural resources are defined in art. 3(1), *id.*

[81]Convention for Co-operation in the Protection and Development of the Marine and Coastal Environment of the West and Central African Region, Mar. 23, 1981, preamble and arts. 4–13, 16–17, in 20 INT'L LEGAL MATERIALS 746 (1981).

[82]Convention on Conservation of Nature in the South Pacific, June 12, 1976, art. 5(4), in 20 INTERNATIONAL PROTECTION OF THE ENVIRONMENT 10359 (B. Rüster, B. Simma, & M. Bock eds. 1979). The other relevant provisions are in art. 8. *See also* treaty between Australia and Papua New Guinea, Dec. 18, 1978, arts. 13, 21–23, 26–27, 30, in 18 INT'L LEGAL MATERIALS 291 (1979), dealing with environmental protection and conservation in the semienclosed sea area between the two.

[83]23 KEESING'S CONTEMP. ARCHIVES 28292 (1977); Financial Times, Mar. 1, 1977, at 6, col. 2; *id.*, Oct. 25, 1977, at 30, col. 6. Apparently the Soviet Union refused to negotiate with South Korea, a nonlittoral state, despite the latter's traditional fishing interest in the Sea of Okhotsk. *See* the remarks of Choung-il Chee in REGIONALIZATION OF THE LAW OF THE SEA 150 (D. Johnston ed. 1978).

proposed Japanese territorial sea extension to twelve miles and fishery zone extension to two hundred miles, and dealt with the Japanese plans as well as with implementation of the Soviet claim.[84] It is unlikely that the Japanese negotiated under any recognition of a duty to consult the Soviet government before enacting the 12- and 200-mile legislation, since the Soviet Union had not consulted it in the reciprocal situation and since the Japanese negotiators seem to have been primarily interested in using the impending Japanese claim as a bargaining tool to obtain an acceptable accommodation with the Soviets in the latter's 200-mile zone.[85] But the talks extended beyond July 1, 1977, the effective date of the Japanese legislation, causing the Japanese government to delay enforcement pending completion of the negotiations.[86] This suggests that the Japanese did feel obliged to negotiate before implementing their claims through specific measures that would harm identifiable Soviet fishing interests, and one must assume that the Soviet Union felt a similar obligation when it agreed to negotiate before implementing its February 1977 claim. An interim fishing agreement was, in fact, reached.

In addition to the Soviet Union, the Republic of Korea and the People's Republic of China were interested in Japan's fishery zone extension in the partially enclosed seas separating them from Japan. Because Japan did not want to disturb the fishing status quo with them, it excluded from its fishery zone the waters in which they were primarily interested—the East China Sea, an adjacent area of the Pacific Ocean, the Yellow Sea, and the western part of the Japan Sea.[87] Consequently, the consultation issue did not arise with those countries.

When the Soviet Union in 1957 designated the Bay of Peter the Great as internal waters (drawing a 108-mile closing line), it did not consult Japan. The Soviet Union said it had claimed historic bay status since 1901, but the Japanese government had not been aware of such a claim.[88]

There have been a number of other instances in which extended Asian jurisdictional claims have been made without prior

[84] *See* Yanai & Asomura, *Japan and the Emerging Order of the Sea—Two Maritime Laws of Japan*, 1977 Japanese Ann. Int'l L. 48, 66, 76.

[85] *Id.*

[86] *See* 23 Keesing's Contemp. Archives 28564 (1977).

[87] Yanai & Asomura, *supra* note 84, at 74.

[88] *See* the Japanese protests, 1958 Japanese Ann. Int'l L. 213–18; W. Butler, The Soviet Union and the Law of the Sea 108–10 (1971).

consultation. For example, when the Republic of Korea in 1952 drew the "Rhee Line," claiming sovereignty over areas ranging from 20 to 200 miles into the Sea of Japan, there was no prior consultation with Japan.[89] When the Republic of Korea in 1970 claimed seven continental-shelf mining zones in the East China Sea, including one in an area quite close to Kyushu Island, Japan, the Japanese government was not consulted. But Korea did not implement its claims, and ultimately agreed with Japan in 1974 on joint development of the bed of the East China Sea.[90] There apparently was no prior consultation when North Korea announced on August 1, 1977, that it was establishing a "military border" extending 50 miles into the Sea of Japan and 200 miles into the Yellow Sea.[91]

A strong case can be made that all the claims mentioned in the two preceding paragraphs, except perhaps the joint Korean-Japanese claim, violated substantive international law.[92] None of the claims was enforced without some form of consultation or an attempt to do so by the claiming state. Moreover, at least as to the China Seas, states in the region have said they intend to negotiate regarding potentially overlapping maritime zone claims.[93]

[89] *See* Park, *Fishing Under Troubled Waters: The Northeast Asia Fisheries Controversy*, 2 OCEAN DEVELOPMENT AND INT'L L.J. 93, 102 (1974); Oda, *A Consideration of the Problems of Conservation and Distribution of Marine Resources*, 18 ZEITSCHRIFT FÜR AUSLÄNDISCHES ÖFFENTLICHES RECHT UND VÖLKERRECHT 61, 74–75 (1957).

[90] *See* 1 S. ODA, THE LAW OF THE SEA IN OUR TIME: NEW DEVELOPMENTS 1966–1975, at 252 (1977); Kemp, *Threats from the Sea: Sources for Asian Maritime Conflict*, 19 ORBIS 1037, 1043–44 (1975); Los Angeles Times, May 12, 1978, pt. I, at 12, col. 1. Although Japan considered at least three protests from the People's Republic of China before the joint development plan was implemented, China claimed that there had not been real consultation and that use of the median-line principle is inappropriate in the absence of agreement. *See* Nakauchi, *Commentary*, *in* REGIONALIZATION OF THE LAW OF THE SEA, *supra* note 83, at 302, 304.

[91] *See* The Times (London), Aug. 2, 1977, at 4, col. 5; Park, *The 50-Mile Military Boundary Zone of North Korea*, 72 AM. J. INT'L L. 866, 867–68 (1978).

[92] The Bay of Peter the Great probably did not qualify as a historic bay. There has never been general acquiescence in two hundred-mile full-sovereignty claims such as that embodied in the Rhee Line. The Korean continental shelf claims in 1970 do not seem consistent with the natural prolongation theory of the North Sea Continental Shelf Cases, 1969 I.C.J. 3. The Korea-Japan-China situation in 1974 was complicated by the absence of diplomatic relations between Korea and China. Apparently Japan did try to consult China, but was rebuffed. *See* Landgon, *Japan-Soviet 200 Mile Zone Confrontation*, 9 PACIFIC COMMUNITY 46, 52 (1977). The North Korean "military border" extension interfered with high seas freedoms. It apparently also encompassed fishing rights, and was preceded by an unsuccessful attempt to discuss fishing with Japan. *Id.* at 57.

[93] *See* Park, *Maritime Claims in the China Seas: Current State Practices*, 18 SAN DIEGO L.

There is a substantial amount of Persian Gulf practice regarding potentially overlapping continental shelf claims. With isolated exceptions, assertions of unilateral oil deposit claims that could overlap those of opposite or adjacent states have amounted to nothing more than negotiating tactics. Negotiations have been held, and agreements reached.[94] The few exceptions involved unusual circumstances, and thus do not detract significantly from the norm in the Gulf.[95]

Elsewhere in the Asian-African region, the considerable number of maritime boundary delineation agreements and extended negotiations would also seem to attest to a norm calling for consultations in lieu of nonnegotiable, potentially overlapping claims.[96] Australia has articulated what many states have

REV. 443 (1981).

[94]*See* the agreements between (*1*) Bahrain–Saudi Arabia, Feb. 22, 1958, U.N. Doc. ST/LEG/SER.B/16, at 409 (1974); (*2*) Kuwait–Saudi Arabia, July 7, 1965, U.N. Doc. ST/LEG/SER.B/15, at 760 (1970); (*3*) Iran–Saudi Arabia, Oct. 24, 1968, 696 U.N.T.S. 189; (x) Abu Dhabi–Qatar, Mar. 30, 1969, U.N. Doc. ST/LEG/SER.B/16, at 403 (1974); (*5*) Iran–Qatar, Sept. 20, 1969, 787 U.N.T.S. 165; (*6*) Iran–Bahrain, June 17, 1971, 826 U.N.T.S. 227; (*7*) Iran-Oman, July 25, 1974, 14 INT'L LEGAL MATERIALS 1478 (1975); (*8*) Iran–United Arab Emirates, Aug. 13, 1974, 5 NEW DIRECTIONS, *supra* note 66 at 230. Earlier Persian Gulf claims were expressly made subject to negotiations with other Gulf states. *See* Oda, *The Continental Shelf*, 1 JAPANESE ANN. INT'L L. 15, 19–20 (1957). *See also* the territorial sea decrees of Saudi Arabia, Feb. 16, 1958, art. 7, U.N. Doc. ST/LEG/SER.B/15, at 114 (1970), and Kuwait, Dec. 17, 1967, art. 4, *id.* at 96; *cf.* Iran, Apr. 12, 1959, art. 4, U.N. Doc. ST/LEG/SER.B/16, at 10 (1974) (equidistance line).

[95]The first may not be an exception at all. There does not appear to have been consultation with Iraq before Iran and Kuwait issued a joint communique in January 1968, stating that they had delimited their continental shelves between themselves. The Iraqi government expressly reaffirmed its rights, but it is not clear that Iran and Kuwait ever intended to assert any claim against Iraq. *See* U.N. Doc. ST/LEG/SER.B/18, at 25 (1976). In 1970 Sharjah claimed that by a 1969 unpublished decree, it fixed its territorial sea around Abu Musa at twelve miles, thus claiming oil deposits previously within an offshore area claimed by Umm-al-Qaiwain. Apparently there was no prior consultation. *See* 5 NEW DIRECTIONS, *supra* note 66, at 235; Occidental Petroleum Corp. v. Buttes Gas and Oil Co., 331 F. Supp. 92, 99–100 n.11 (D. Cal. 1971). In 1971 Iran landed military forces on the Tumb Islands and Abu Musa, apparently with the intention of claiming mineral resources rights around them. 3 NEW DIRECTIONS, *supra* note 34, at 234. The use of force distinguishes the case from other maritime resource claims.

[96]*See* the delimitation agreements between (*1*) Indonesia-Malaysia, Oct. 27, 1969, 9 INT'L LEGAL MATERIALS 1173 (1970); (*2*) Australia-Indonesia, May 18, 1971, 10 *id.* 830 (1971); (*3*) Thailand-Indonesia, Dec. 17, 1971, U.N. Doc. ST/LEG/SER.B/18, at 437 (1976); (*4*) Indonesia-Malaysia-Thailand, Dec. 21, 1971, *id.* 429; (*5*) Australia-Indonesia, Oct. 9, 1972, 11 INT'L LEGAL MATERIALS 1272 (1972); (*6*) Australia-Indonesia, Jan. 26, 1973, U.N. Doc. ST/LEG/SER.B/18, at 444 (1976); (*7*) India–Sri Lanka, June 28, 1974, 5 NEW DIRECTIONS, *supra* note 66, at 326; (*8*) India-Indonesia, Aug. 8, 1974, *id.* 265; (*9*) India-Indonesia, Jan. 14, 1977, 23 FOREIGN AFF. REC. (India) 2 (1977); (*10*) India-Indonesia-Thailand, June 22, 1978, 13 BULL. LEGAL DEV. 151 (1978). *Cf.* Saudi Arabia–Sudan, May 16, 1974, U.N. Doc. ST/LEG/SER.B/18, at 452 (1976). The independent

practiced. Its official position is that adjacent and opposite states should use their best efforts to agree on delimitation, but if no agreement can be reached, they may establish an equidistance line between adjacent coasts and a median line between opposite ones.[97] China has also called for agreed solutions in such cases, but it has not set forth any fallback position (such as equidistance or median line) in case of a failure to agree.[98]

and self-governing island governments in the South Pacific pledged in advance to cooperate in establishing 200-mile zones. U.N. Doc. A/32/PV.11, at 25 (1977).

When Papua New Guinea in March 1978 declared an "interim" twelve-mile territorial sea in the Torres Strait overlapping a similar potential Australian claim, it had held negotiations with Australia but had not yet reached final agreement. Radio Australia Bull., Mar. 31, 1978. On the other hand, it is unlikely that Indonesia and Malaysia consulted each other before making overlapping twelve-mile territorial-sea claims in the Straits of Malacca in the 1960s, when there was extreme tension between the two governments. A settlement was reached in March 1970. *See* 17 KEESING'S CONTEMP. ARCHIVES 23962 (1970).

Bangladesh and India have held consultations to try to delimit their maritime boundaries. *See* 24 FOREIGN AFF. REC. (India) 122 (1978). Tunisia and Libya held a series of negotiations between 1968 and 1977 to try to delimit the continental shelf between them, before submitting the matter to the International Court of Justice. *See* their Special Agreement, Nov. 25, 1978, in 18 INT'L LEGAL MATERIALS 49, 50 (1979).

[97] *See Australian Practice in 1974–75*, in 6 AUSTL. Y.B. INT'L L. 187, 284 (1978). Australia had in mind the Timor Deep. *See* 2 S. Oda, *supra* note 58, at 278–79. Before Australia negotiated its partial delimitation agreements with Indonesia, it made unilateral claims extending only to equidistance or median lines. *See* Lumb, *Sovereignty and Jurisdiction Over Australian Coastal Waters*, 43 AUSTL. L.J. 421, 426, 434 (1969). Negotiations continued as to Timor Sea areas not covered by the agreements of the early 1970s. *See* Lumb, *Australia and the Law of the Sea: Recent Developments*, 26 INT'L & COMP. L.Q. 151, 158–59 (1980). For an account of the negotiations between Australia and Papua New Guinea, see Burmester, *The Torres Strait Treaty: Ocean Boundary Delimitation by Agreement*, 76 AM. J. INT'L L. 321, 326–29 (1982).

Japan's and New Zealand's 200-mile zones, both promulgated in 1977, attempt to avoid overlap with any prospective foreign claims by stopping at the equidistance or median lines. *See* Yanai & Asomura, *supra* note 84, at 78–79; Elkind, *Territorial Sea and Exclusive Economic Zone Bill 1977*, in 3 N.Z. RECENT LAW (n.s.) 241, 242 (1977). The equidistance line was also used by Madagascar to delimit its 1973 continental shelf claim, in the absence of any apparent overlapping claims. Its decree is in U.N. Doc. ST/LEG/SER.B/18, at 27 (1976). *See also* Iran's Fishing Zone Proclamation, Oct. 30, 1973, paras. 1 & 2, *id.* 334.

Some African and Midddle Eastern territorial sea claims have been made in the absence of agreement, but have tried to avoid possible encroachment on other states' claims. *See, e.g.*, South Africa's Territorial Waters Act, 1963, art. 6, in U.N. Doc. ST/LEG/SER.B/15, at 117 (1970); Kenya's Proclamation of June 6, 1969, *id.* at 95; South Yemen's Law of Feb. 9, 1970, art. 12, in U.N. Doc. ST/LEG/SER.B/16, at 25 (1974); Oman's Decree of July 17, 1972, art. 7, *id.* at 23; Morocco's Law of Mar. 2, 1973, art. 2, in U.N. Doc. ST/LEG/SER.B/18, at 29 (1976); Tanzania's Proclamation of Aug. 24, 1973, 2d para., *id.* at 31. *See also* the Conclusions of the African States Regional Seminar on the Law of the Sea, June 30, 1972, para. I(a)(6), in U.N. Doc. ST/LEG/SER.B/16, at 601–02 (1974).

[98] *See* 2 S. ODA, *supra* note 58, at 279.

Asian-African treaty practice regarding mineral deposits overlapping continental shelf delimitation lines is consistent with European practice. Except when joint exploitation regimes have been contemplated, the treaty practice requires consultation and / or agreement before exploiting such common pools.[99] As in Europe, there is insufficient prior consultation practice regarding exploitation of common fisheries to establish a customary norm.

D. The Americas

The U.S.-Canadian weather modification agreement requires prior notification, and consultation on request, regarding intentional weather modification activities planned by, or known to, either government that are to be conducted within 200 miles of the boundary or that, in the judgment of the notifying government, may significantly affect the atmosphere over the territory of the other party.[100] The Agreement recites that it rests

[99]Treaties requiring consultation and / or agreement: (*1*) Iran-Qatar, Sept. 20, 1969, art. 2(b), 787 U.N.T.S. 165; (*2*) Indonesia-Malaysia, Oct. 27, 1969, art. 4, 9 Int'l Legal Materials 1173 (1970); (*3*) Australia-Indonesia, May 18, 1971, art. 7, 10 *id.* 830 (1971); (*4*) Indonesia-Malaysia-Thailand, Dec. 21, 1971, art. 3, U.N. Doc. ST/LEG/SER.B/18, at 429 (1976); (*5*) Australia-Indonesia, Oct. 9, 1972, art. 7, 11 Int'l Legal Materials 1272 (1972); (*6*) Australia-Indonesia, Jan. 26, 1973, art. 6, U.N. Doc. ST/LEG/SER.B/18, at 444 (1976); (*7*) Japan–Repub. of Korea, Jan. 30, 1974, art. 2, 1 S. Oda, *supra* note 90, at 254, 256; (*8*) India–Sri Lanka, June 28, 1974, art. 7, 5 New Directions, *supra* note 66, at 326; (*9*) Iran-Oman, July 25, 1974, art. 2, 14 Int'l Legal Materials 1478 (1975); (*10*) India-Indonesia, Aug. 8, 1974, art. 3, 5 New Directions, *supra* note 66, at 265; (*11*) India–Sri Lanka, Mar. 23, 1976, art. 6, *id.* 333; (*12*) Australia–Papua New Guinea, Dec. 18, 1978, art. 6, 18 Int'l Legal Materials 291 (1979).

The agreement between Abu Dhabi and Qatar, Mar. 30, 1969, U.N. Doc. ST/LEG/SER.B/16, at 403 (1974), provides for the sharing of a common pool and for periodic consultations regarding its exploitation. A similar agreement is that between Saudi Arabia and the Sudan, May 16, 1974, art. 14, 5 New Directions, *supra* note 66, at 393. Some Persian Gulf agreements simply prohibit drilling within a stated distance on either side of the delimitation line: Iran–Saudi Arabia, Oct. 24, 1968, art. 4, 696 U.N.T.S. 189; Iran-Bahrain, June 17, 1971, art. 2, 826 U.N.T.S. 227; Iran–United Arab Emirates, Aug. 13, 1974, art. 2, *id.* 242.

[100]Agreement Relating to the Exchange of Information on Weather Modification Activites, Mar. 26, 1975, United States–Canada, arts. 1(b), 2(1), 4, 5, 26 U.S.T. 540, T.I.A.S. No. 8056. There is an exception in article 6 for weather modification in response to extreme emergencies. The basic duty applies not only to weather modification directly undertaken by the governments but to private plans notified to them. Persons intending to engage in weather modification in the United States are required to report their plans in advance to the National Oceanic and Atmospheric Administration. *See* 15 U.S.C. § 330a; 15 C.F.R. § 908.4 (1982). For the corresponding Canadian requirement, *see* Can. Stat., 19–20 Eliz. II ch. 59, § 3 (1971).

particularly on the special traditions of prior notification and consultation characterizing U.S.-Canadian relations, and says it does not imply the existence of any generally applicable rule of international law.[101] On the other hand, it asserts "the desirability of the development of international law relating to weather modification activities having transboundary effects."[102] Obviously, it contributes to that development.

The U.S.-Canadian weather modification agreement has not been emulated explicitly in the Americas or elsewhere—not even by the United States with its other immediate neighbor, Mexico. Nevertheless, there has been prior consultation by the United States with Cuba, Japan, the Philippines, and the United Kingdom regarding hurricane modification.[103] In broad terms, U.S. policy has been stated: "When we engage in this country in a weather modification project that could have an impact on foreign soil, we go through quite extensive discussions, using, of course, the State Department, with the nations that might be involved and offer to let their scientists work with ours so they understand the project."[104]

Going beyond weather modification, the United States and Canada have acknowledged that each should consult the other before taking or authorizing any action at or near the boundary that might adversely affect their shared resources. Article 9 of the 1909 Boundary Waters Treaty[105] contemplates joint referral to the U.S.-Canadian International Joint Commission of any

The notifying government would have to act in good faith in determining whether activities more than two hundred miles from the boundary may significantly affect the other's atmosphere. *See* note 19 *supra.*

[101] U.S.-Canadian Weather Modification Agreement, *supra* note 100, preamble and art. 7. There was some preagreement prior consultation practice with Canada involving cloud seeding over the Great Lakes. *See* Samuels, *International Control of Weather Modification Activities*, in CANADIAN PERSPECTIVES ON INTERNATIONAL LAW AND ORGANIZATION 360, 361 (R. MacDonald, G. Morris, and D. Johnston eds. 1974); *Weather Modification: Hearings Before a Subcomm. of the Senate Comm. on Foreign Relations*, 93d Cong., 2d Sess. 77 (1974) (statement of Professor H. Taubenfeld).

[102] U.S.-Canadian Weather Modification Agreement, *supra* note 100, preamble.

[103] *See* Weather Modification Hearings, *supra* note 101, at 77. Prior consultations on hurricane modification may have to be on a blanket basis, rather than hurricane-by-hurricane, because of the need to make quick decisions once a hurricane is formed. *See* Davis, *The United States and Mexico: Weather Technology, Water Resources and International Law*, 12 NATURAL RES. J. 530, 542 n.56 (1972).

[104] *Weather Modification: Hearings Before a Subcomm. of the House Comm. on Science and Technology*, 94th Cong., 2d Sess. 180 (1976) (statement of John W. Townsend, Jr., Assoc. Administrator, NOAA).

[105] Boundary Waters Treaty, Jan. 11, 1909, United States–Canada, 36 Stat. 2448, 12 BEVANS 319. *See also* chapter II, at notes 129–30 & accompanying text *supra.*

questions arising along the frontier—not just the questions involving waterways discussed in chapter II of this book. Some air pollution questions have been referred to it under that article, including questions regarding pollution risks from proposed projects.[106] Other bilateral consultations involving prospective transboundary problems have been held outside the Commission.[107] Moreover, the two countries have agreed to "continue and expand their longstanding practice of advance notification and consultation on proposed actions involving a significant risk or potential risk of causing or increasing transboundary air pollution," including proposed major industrial development and proposed changes of policy, regulations, or practices that may significantly affect transboundary pollution.[108] This is a step in their effort to work out a formal consultation procedure.

A number of instances have arisen in which the passage of U.S. vessels through Canadian straits posed serious environmental risks. Prior consultations have been held when the risk is novel and could involve spillage of pollutants carried as cargo.[109] For example, when the United States proposed in 1970 to trans-

[106] *See* 1976 DIGEST OF UNITED STATES PRACTICE IN INT'L LAW 590–92. *See also id.* at 382–86.

[107] Before President Carter in March 1980 announced a proposal to convert a number of power plants from oil to coal, the Canadian government requested and obtained consultations with the U.S. Department of State. Although Canada regarded these consultations as too late and too general to have a significant impact on the basic proposal, Canada did get a pledge from the U.S. government to consult further as details of the program were developed. Undated statement (March 1980) by the Assistant Deputy Minister, Canadian Environmental Protection Service; Canadian Embassy Press Release, Washington, D.C., Feb. 29, 1980. President Carter's proposal is in 16 WEEKLY COMP. OF PRES. DOC. 448 (Mar. 10, 1980).

[108] U.S.-Canadian Memorandum of Intent, Aug. 5, 1980, para. 3, T.I.A.S. No. 9856, *reprinted in* 20 INT'L LEGAL MATERIALS 690 (1981).

[109] When the risk was inherent in the use of Trident submarines, there apparently were no specific prior consultations. See the remarks of Mr. Epstein in 1 CANADA–UNITED STATES L.J. 99–100 (1978).

The distinction between risks from spillage and risks from the nature of the vessel may also be important under the Panama Canal Treaty, Sept. 7, 1977, art. 6(3), T.I.A.S. No. 10030, 16 INT'L LEGAL MATERIALS 1022 (1977). Under that provision, prior consultation through the U.S.-Panamanian Joint Commission on the Environment is to take place, with complete information supplied, "on any action taken in accordance with this Treaty which, in the judgment of *both*, might have a significant effect on the environment" (emphasis added). Since the United States concedes, and Panama would assert, that consultations are appropriate before pollutants are carried in bulk through narrow international passages under novel circumstances, the requirement that both parties concur would presumably be met in such cases. It presumably would not be met in cases like that involving the Trident.

fer nerve gas from Okinawa to the U.S. mainland via the Strait of Juan de Fuca, using only U.S. territorial waters in the strait, the Canadian government made representations to which the U.S. government responded. The Canadian Secretary of State for External Affairs said in Parliament that although the United States was not required by international law to submit to a Canadian veto over the passage, "I think the United States has a responsibility, which it is discharging, to consult with us about precautions."[110] This, of course, amounted to an assertion of a duty to consult, in which the United States acquiesced.

Similarly, there were consultations over a period of years regarding proposed U.S. tanker traffic bringing Alaskan oil through the Strait of Juan de Fuca.[111] On the opposite North American coast, when Maine environmental authorities were deciding whether to authorize construction of an oil refinery in Eastport, the Canadian government was in contact with the U.S. government regarding the pollution hazards posed if Head Harbor Passage, Canada, were to be used by oil tankers servicing the refinery.[112] However, the normative significance of the Head Harbor Passage consultations is diminished by Canada's assertion of a right to prohibit tanker passage as noninnocent. Whether or not that was a legally correct assertion, it gave the United States considerable incentive—exogenous to any perceived duty to consult—to seek agreement with the Canadian authorities.

When the Canadian government has been the acting or authorizing party in recent years, there have been consultations with the United States. For example, in 1976 a Canadian oil company was granted a permit to begin exploratory drilling in Arctic waters 120 miles northeast of the Alaskan-Canadian border. The area is covered with ice about ten months of the year,

[110] 7 CAN. PARL. DEB., H.C., 28th Parl., 2d Sess. 6640 (1970); *see also* 6 *id.* 6045.

[111] Beesley, *The Canadian Approach—Environmental Law on the International Plane*, 1973 SOUTHWESTERN LEGAL FOUNDATION SYMPOSIUM ON PRIVATE INVESTORS ABROAD 239, 270; Austin, *Remarks* in 1974 PROC. OF THE AM. SOC'Y OF INT'L L. 90; U.S.-Canadian Statement, Jan. 17, 1975, 72 DEP'T ST. BULL. 272 (1975).

When the privately operated tanker *Manhattan* made an experimental voyage through the Northwest Passage in 1969, there had been extensive prior arrangements between the American company and the Canadian government. Apparently there were also informal talks between the Canadian government and the U.S. State Department, though the latter did not reply to a Canadian request that permission be sought for the use of a U.S. Coast Guard icebreaker escort. See Dosman, *The Northern Sovereignty Crisis 1968–70*, in THE ARCTIC IN QUESTION 34, 38–40 (E. Dosman ed. 1976).

[112] 1976 CAN. Y.B. INT'L L. 362–63.

so that a blowout might not be capped for several months, until the summer thaw. The oil from such a blowout would be likely to come ashore in Alaska. Before granting the permit, the Canadian government consulted U.S. officials, and submitted the Canadian environmental assessment to the U.S. State Department for review.[113] Discussions with the United States continued before drilling under the permit began.[114]

Less clear cases involved new Canadian coal-burning power plants in Atikokan, Ontario, and on the East Poplar River in Saskatchewan, near the Minnesota and Montana borders, respectively. In 1977 the Ontario authorities approved construction of the Atikokan plant, apparently without prior consultation with the U.S. authorities and despite the fact that its air pollution would combine with existing pollution from an Atikokan iron ore processing plant to affect wilderness areas in Minnesota. At that point the U.S. Department of State sought consultations with the Canadian government. The talks were held when a change in the site or the installation of effective pollution control equipment was still possible, though it was unlikely that the Canadian government would accede to either request. Nevertheless, after the talks, the magnitude of the project was reduced somewhat.[115]

In the case of the Poplar River plant, prior notice was given to the U.S. government and some intergovernmental communication occurred, but construction went forward before the full impact could be assessed (and thus before detailed consultations could be held). Although representations by the U.S. government resulted in scaling down the initial phase from four 300-megawatt units to one, and influenced the installation of electrostatic precipitators, the International Joint Commission found the consultations inadequate and therefore declined to treat the plant as an existing use for water apportionment purposes.[116]

A particularly significant incident in U.S. practice involved Mexico. In December 1958 the U.S. Atomic Energy Commis-

[113] Washington Post, July 21, 1976, at A2, col. 1.

[114] 1978 CAN. Y.B. INT'L L. 392–94.

[115] *See* Washington Post, Sept. 10, 1977, at A2, col. 4; 4 INT'L ENVT'L REP., CURRENT REP., at 792 (Apr. 8, 1981).

[116] *See* INT'L JOINT COMM'N, WATER APPORTIONMENT IN THE POPLAR RIVER BASIN 70–71 (1978); 1 INT'L ENVT'L REP., CURRENT REP., at 96–97 (Apr. 10, 1978); *Contemporary Practice of the United States*, 72 AM. J. INT'L L. 620, 653–55 (1978). For more details *see* chapter II at notes 137–38.

sion (AEC) proposed to issue a license to a private firm to dispose of low-level radioactive waste approximately in the middle of the Gulf of Mexico. The Mexican government was invited to participate in the hearing on the proposed license, and did so. When the hearing examiner granted the license subject to AEC review, the Mexican government protested in a note to the Department of State. The State Department intervened in the AEC proceedings on behalf of the Mexican government and said, "Surely . . . those Mexican citizens have reason to expect . . . that their Government will have as effective a voice in the final decision as the Government of the American citizens who are also directly concerned. The mere fact that Mexican officials were invited to attend, and did attend, hearings on the license application does not give the Government of Mexico the effective voice in the final decision that the United States would expect if the situation were reversed."[117] Thus, there was a claim of right to be consulted in a more direct manner than simply through participation in a hearing (itself a form of consultation), and acquiescence by the United States in that claim.

When the United States in 1976 designated a site in the Gulf of Mexico for possible incineration of chemical wastes aboard a ship specially equipped for that purpose, it apparently did not consult the Mexican government, although it did hold a public hearing on the proposed site.[118] The site was roughly four hundred kilometers from the nearest Mexican shoreline, and the prevailing winds would render it quite unlikely that any resulting air pollution would reach Mexico. There is no indication that the Mexican government showed any interest in participating in the hearing, or that any request for consultation was made by that government. The minimal likelihood of adverse effect on Mexico, the uncertainty that the site would ever be used, and the Mexican lack of interest in the publicly announced hearings would distinguish this case from the earlier radioactive-waste precedent.

When the U.S. Congress enacted the Deepwater Port Act of

[117] 4 M. Whiteman, Digest of Int'l Law 612–13 (1965). The license application was ultimately denied, apparently because of the Mexican protest. *Id.* at 618. Moreover, the United States thereupon sharply curtailed all ocean disposal of radioactive waste.

[118] The EPA's Final Environmental Impact Statement on Designation of a Site in the Gulf of Mexico for Incineration of Chemical Wastes (1976) contains no indication of consultation with the Mexican government. Nor did the site designation procedures call for consultation with Mexico. *See id.* at 18–24. The hearing was held on Oct. 4, 1974, in Houston, Texas. *Id.* at 14.

1974, authorizing the issuance of licenses for supertanker ports beyond territorial waters, it requested the President to enter into negotiations with the governments of Canada and Mexico to protect the environmental and other interests of the people in those countries and in the United States.[119] The Senate report on the bill specifically recognized the environmental concerns of those neighboring nations.[120] The report and the Act reflect Congress's understanding that consultations are appropriate when legitimate transnational environmental concerns are involved, but they do not expressly acknowledge a duty to consult.

Section 115 of the U.S. Clean Air Act contemplates that a state-conducted public hearing will be held whenever the Environmental Protection Agency, upon receipt of a report from an international agency or a request from the Secretary of State, has reason to believe that any air pollutants emitted in the United States "cause or contribute to air pollution which may reasonably be anticipated to endanger public health or welfare in a foreign country" if the country extends reciprocal rights to the United States.[121] Canada has enacted reciprocal legislation.[122] The legislation in both countries provides reciprocating countries a right to be heard. Neither act expressly contemplates preventive action before the air pollution occurs, though each act does contemplate remedial action before actual harm is caused.[123] Unless they are applied quite liberally, the acts would not require consultations before decisions are made on endeavors potentially harmful to foreign residents.

The Clean Air Act was reexamined in Washington in 1981, with a view to relaxing some of its substantive standards. Canadian officials asserted a right to be consulted, and U.S. authorities discussed the matter with them in connection with a series of discussions on transboundary air pollution.[124]

When a significant environmental risk stems from a proposed U.S. government project, the National Environmental Policy Act requires the preparation of an environmental impact state-

[119] 33 U.S.C. § 1521 (1976).

[120] S. REP. NO. 1217, 93rd Cong., 2d Sess., *reprinted in* 1974 U.S. CODE CONG. & AD. NEWS 8589, 8595.

[121] 42 U.S.C. § 7415(a), *as amended in* 1977.

[122] *See* Can. Stat., 29 Eliz. II ch. 45, § 21.1 (1980).

[123] The legislative history of the U.S. act suggests that remedial, rather than preventive, action is required. *See* 111 CONG. REC. 24,941 (1965); H.R. REP. NO. 899, 89th Cong., 1st Sess. 5–6 (1965); S. REP. NO. 127, 95th Cong., 1st Sess. 57 (1977).

[124] *See* 4 INT'L ENVT'L REP., CURRENT REP. 921 (1981); *id.* at 1122.

ment, with an opportunity for comments by the public before a decision on the project is reached.[125] In 1976 the Council on Environmental Quality interpreted the Act to require an environmental impact statement regarding effects outside the United States.[126] In January 1979 the President issued an Executive Order requiring an impact statement or comparable assessment for many major federal actions significantly affecting the environment of the global commons or of other nations.[127] The President did not require that consultations be held with foreign governments. Nevertheless, the United States has joined in the OECD Council's recommendations to the effect that affected persons in neighboring countries should be heard in such cases.[128]

Unilateral maritime boundary delimitations among opposite or adjacent states in North America have been provisional, subject to negotiation and final agreement or third-party dispute settlement with the other states involved.[129] The United States acknowledges a duty to negotiate in such cases.[130] This is true

[125] 42 U.S.C. § 4332(2)(C) (1976).

[126] CEQ *Memorandum on the Application of the EIS Requirement to Environmental Impacts Abroad of Major Federal Actions*, Sept. 24, 1976, in 15 INT'L LEGAL MATERIALS 1428 (1976), and in 1976 DIGEST OF UNITED STATES PRACTICE IN INT'L LAW 586. The Act was applied to the proposed Darien Gap Highway through Panama and Colombia, in Sierra Club v. Coleman, 405 F. Supp. 53 (D.D.C. 1975), and 421 F. Supp. 63 (D.D.C. 1976).

[127] Exec. Order No. 12,114, 44 Fed. Reg. 1957 (1979), *reprinted in* 18 INT'L LEGAL MATERIALS 154 (1979).

[128] *See* the OECD Council recommendations in note 145 *infra*.

[129] *See* Minute No. 229 of the U.S.-Mexican International Boundary and Water Commission, Delineation of Provisional Maritime Boundaries Between the Exclusive Fishery Zones of the United States and Mexico in the Gulf of Mexico and the Pacific Ocean, Jan. 4, 1968, 7 INT'L LEGAL MATERIALS 320 (1968); Agreement on the Delimitation of the Continental Shelf Between Greenland and Canada, Dec. 17, 1973, 13 INT'L LEGAL MATERIALS 506 (1974); Notice of Proposed Canadian 200-mile Fishing Zones, Nov. 1, 1976, 110 Can. Gaz., Extra No. 101 (1976), *reprinted in* 15 INT'L LEGAL MATERIALS 1372 (1976); U.S. Announcement of Maritime Boundaries Between the United States and Canada, Nov. 1, 1976, 41 Fed. Reg. 48,619 (1976), *reprinted in* 15 INT'L LEGAL MATERIALS 1435 (1976), preceded by negotiations summarized in 1976 DIGEST OF UNITED STATES PRACTICE IN INT'L LAW 346; U.S.-Mexican Exchange of Notes on Provisional Maritime Boundaries, Nov. 24, 1976, in 1976 DIGEST OF UNITED STATES PRACTICE IN INT'L LAW 348–49, and U.S.-Mexican Treaty on Maritime Boundaries, May 4, 1978, 17 INT'L LEGAL MATERIALS 1073 (1978); U.S. Announcement of Provisional Fishery Conservation Zone, 42 Fed. Reg. 12937, 76 DEP'T ST. BULL. 273–74 (1977); U.S.-Cuba Maritime Boundary Agreement, Dec. 16, 1977, 17 INT'L LEGAL MATERIALS 110 (1978); summary of U.S. fishery negotiations, agreements, and claims in 1977 DIGEST OF UNITED STATES PRACTICE IN INT'L LAW 543–69.

[130] *See* Feldman & Colson, *The Maritime Boundaries of the United States*, 75 AM. J. INT'L L. 729, 731–32, 737–38 (1981).

even of the hotly disputed U.S.-Canadian maritime boundaries in the Beaufort Sea, Dixon Entrance, Strait of Juan de Fuca, and Gulf of Maine.[131] Delimitation practice in Central and South America is somewhat sparse, but does tend to support the proposition that there must be a reasonable effort to reach agreement through negotiation before a unilateral delimitation is made that might encroach on another state's claim.[132]

[131]*See Morin, Canada*, in 3 NEW DIRECTIONS, *supra* note 34, at 243, 246, discussing Canadian continental shelf delineation negotiations with the United States, Denmark (Greenland), and France (Saint Pierre and Miquelon Islands); Remarks of the Canadian Secretary of State for External Affairs, 1977 CAN. Y.B. INT'L L. 350–51, and 1978 *id.* at 386–89, discussing fishery zone negotiations with the United States and France; Swan, *That Gulf of Maine Dispute: Canada and the United States Delimit the Atlantic Coast Continental Shelf*, 10 NAT. RESOURCES LAW. 405, 406–16 (1977), and Feldman & Colson, *supra* note 130, at 754–63, discussing negotiations relating to delimitation of the Georges Bank continental shelf.

Gulf of Maine negotiations were first held in 1970 and were resumed in December 1975, thus antedating not only Canada's September 1978 claim to jurisdiction in the gulf beyond the equidistance line, but also each country's November 1976 initial claim. *See Outer Continental Shelf Lands Act Amendments of 1977: Hearings on H.R. 1614 Before the House Ad Hoc Select Comm. on Outer Continental Shelf*, 95th Cong., 1st Sess., pt 1, at 620–21, 624–45 (1977). The United States, however, asserted that Canada had not adequately attempted to reach an agreement before making its 1978 claim. *See* the U.S. note to the Canadian Embassy, 73 AM. J. INT'L L. 132 (1979). Canada resumed negotiations with the United States and ultimately agreed to submit the Gulf of Maine dispute to a chamber of the International Court of Justice. *See* Pickering, *Maritime Boundary and Resource Agreements*, 79 DEP'T ST. BULL., June 1979, at 7; Delimitation of the Maritime Boundary in the Gulf of Maine Area (Can. v. U.S.), 21 INT'L LEGAL MATERIALS 69 (1972) (order constituting chamber of Court, Jan. 20, 1982).

[132]The Gulf of Paria Treaty Between the U.K. (Trinidad) and Venezuela, Feb. 25, 1942, 205 U.N.T.S. 121, was the first continental shelf delimitation agreement anywhere. Other maritime boundary agreements have been concluded between Colombia-Ecuador, Ecuador-Peru, Peru-Chile, Argentina-Uruguay, and Colombia-Venezuela. *See* Hodgson and Smith, *Boundaries of the Economic Zone*, in LAW OF THE SEA: CONFERENCE OUTCOMES AND PROBLEMS OF IMPLEMENTATION 183, 190 (10th Ann. Conf. of the Law of the Sea Institute, 1976); 16 BULL. LEGAL DEV. 43 (1981). The Colombia-Ecuador Agreement, Aug. 23, 1975, is reprinted in 5 NEW DIRECTIONS, *supra* note 66, at 12. *See also* Treaty of La Plata River and Its Maritime Limits (Argentina-Uruguay), Nov. 19, 1973, art. 70, 13 INT'L LEGAL MATERIALS 251 (1974) (delimiting the maritime boundary in a "river" having the characteristics of a bay). The dispute between Colombia and Venezuela concerning delimitation in the Gulf of Venezuela was the subject of lengthy negotiations between the parties. *See* Wood, *Colombia's View of Maritime Legal Problems*, in THE SURGE OF SEA LAW 191, 193 (University of North Carolina Sea Grant Pub. UNC-SG-73-01, 1973). Venezuela's twelve-mile territorial sea legislation of July 27, 1956, provides that any overlap with another state's claim is to be resolved by agreement or other method recognized by international law. *See* U.N. Doc. A/CONF.19/5, at 34 (1960). Nicaragua has taken a comparable position regarding delimitation of its continental shelf, and Uruguay decreed in 1969 that the lateral delimitation of its continental shelf would be determined by the equidistance principle, "following appropriate international negotiation." 1 A. SZEKELY, LATIN AMERICA AND THE DEVELOPMENT OF THE LAW OF THE SEA 86 (1976).

Practice in the Americas is inconclusive regarding consultation before exploiting animate or inanimate resources in a pool straddling a maritime boundary.[133]

E. Nonregional Practice

The General Assembly resolutions and the agreed text of the U.N. Environment Programme (UNEP) on exploitation of shared resources, as well as the OECD resolutions on transfrontier pollution,[134] apply not only to international watercourse systems but to uses affecting common air sheds and partially enclosed seas.[135] These prescriptions, calling for transnational environmental cooperation based on a system of prior consultation, reflect expectations engendered by much of the regional environmental practice examined above.

As noted in the preceding chapter, the primary (perhaps the only) obstacle to more forceful assertions by the international community regarding a shared-resources prior-consultation duty has been the dispute over whether resources used only successively are "shared." That issue does not arise in the case of pollutants introduced into an air shed extending across an international boundary or directly into a partially enclosed sea bordered by more than one littoral state. Under any reasonable definition—including the one favored by several members of the UNEP Working Group of Experts on National Resources Shared by Two or More States[136]—such cases would involve the use of a shared resource.

The 1972 Stockholm Action Plan for the Human Environ-

[133]The Agreement Between Canada and Denmark Relating to the Delimitation of the Continental Shelf Between Greenland and Canada, Dec. 17, 1973, art. 5, 13 Int'l Legal Materials 506 (1974), contains a prior consultation requirement for exploitation of common mineral resources. The United States and Canada have negotiated at length regarding fish stocks off their east coasts and regarding common hydrocarbon pools. *See* 77 Dep't St. Bull. 896 (1977); Joint Report of the U.S. and Canadian Negotiators on Maritime Boundaries and Related Issues (unpublished, 1977). In 1981, President Reagan withdrew from Senate consideration the proposed Agreement on East Coast Fishery Resources, Mar. 29, 1979, Senate Comm. on Foreign Relations, Exec. V, 96th Cong., 1st Sess. 13 (1979). *See* 81 Dep't State Bull., June 1981, at 32–33.

[134]*See chapter II at notes* 192–205 *supra.*

[135]*See, e.g.*, U.N. Doc. UNEP/GC/44, at 40–41 (1975). The OECD Principles Concerning Transfrontier Pollution apply to partially enclosed seas only if the pollution would have an effect within the territory of another littoral country. Presumably that would include its territorial sea.

[136]*See chapter II at note* 197 *supra.*

ment contains one particularly pertinent recommendation, calling upon governments to "consult fully other interested States when activities carrying a risk of [climatic] effects are being contemplated or implemented."[137] This has been described as international recognition of an essential and basic principle of international environmental law.[138]

Despite these pronouncements, the 1975 World Meteorological Organization–U.N. Environment Programme (WMO/UNEP) Informal Meeting on Legal Aspects of Weather Modification thought it undesirable to impose a *duty* on states to consult others before engaging in weather modification activities. The meeting did conclude that consultation at the request of interested states would be "desirable" before major weather modification activities are undertaken. Moreover, it adopted a prior notification principle and tied it to prior consultation. The adopted principle provided, "States shall in good faith give adequate and timely notification of prospective major weather modification activities, within their jurisdiction or control, to WMO which should transmit such notification to all interested States." The report of the meeting explained that "timely" in this formulation meant that "the notified State is given the time to analyse the information and consult with the acting State before the activity is conducted."[139] In 1979 the WMO / UNEP Meeting of Experts on the Legal Aspects of Weather Modification adopted draft principles that include the notification principle in slightly stronger language than in 1975, and that go on to say:

> A State under whose jurisdiction or control major weather modification activities are planned or are taking place which can reasonably be expected significantly to affect the environment in areas

[137]Action Plan for the Human Environment, Recommendation 70, U.N. Doc. A/CONF.48/14 (1972), *reprinted in* 11 INT'L LEGAL MATERIALS 1421, 1449 (1972). Climatic risks, as distinguished from weather risks, involve possible long-term effects. Most climate changes are local or regional. REPORT OF THE STUDY OF MAN'S IMPACT ON CLIMATE, INADVERTENT CLIMATE MOFIFICATION 179 (1971).

[138]Beesley, *The Canadian Approach—Environmental Law on the International Plane*, 1973 SOUTHWESTERN LEGAL FOUNDATION SYMPOSIUM ON PRIVATE INVESTORS ABROAD 239, 273. Three Soviet jurists have asserted, "Surely no one government has the right to conduct [climate modification] experiments without consulting other interested nations." G. ZHUKOV, E. VASILEVSKAYA, & P. LUKIN, LEGAL ASPECTS OF THE UTILIZATION OF ARTIFICIAL SATELLITES FOR METEOROLOGICAL AND RADIO COMMUNICATION PURPOSES 67 (1970) (NASA translation, 1972).

[139]Report of the WMO / UNEP Informal Meeting on Legal Aspects of Weather Modification, Nov. 17–21, 1975, U.N. Doc. UNEP/GC/61, Annex 1, at 6–8 (1976).

> outside its national jurisdiction shall, upon the request of an interested State, enter into meaningful and timely consultation concerning such activities.[140]

This would seem to erode considerably the 1975 meeting's ostensible rejection of a prior consultation duty.

Nuclear explosions, particularly those in the atmosphere, pose obvious transnational pollution problems that are not completely solved by such instruments as the partial test ban treaty. Nuclear weapons tests normally are conducted in isolated areas, and thus are more appropriately discussed in the next chapter. But to the extent that nuclear explosions for peaceful purposes have been conducted or contemplated, they may well occur in reasonably finite air sheds or partially enclosed areas. One significant normative statement concerning such peaceful nuclear applications as oil and gas stimulation, energy storage, and various types of excavation appears in a 1977 report of an International Atomic Energy Agency (IAEA) Ad Hoc Advisory Group. It says that international arrangements for peaceful nuclear explosions should be made and "should take full account in accordance with international law of the interests of nonparticipating Third States whose territories may be affected environmentally or in respect of health and safety. Such States should be appropriately consulted at the earliest possible opportunity."[141] On the other hand, the Treaty for the Prohibition of Nuclear Weapons in Latin America permits peaceful nuclear explosions without expressly requiring prior consultation.[142] The IAEA's consultation standard probably should be read into the Treaty, since it reflects widely held expectations regarding respect for others whose proximity to the possible release of ra-

[140]Draft Principles of Conduct for the Guidance of States Concerning Weather Modification, U.N. Doc. WMO/UNEP/WG.26/4, para. VII (1979). The strengthened prior notification principle says that WMO "shall" transmit the notifications promptly to interested states. (*Id.* para. IV). Consequently, those states would be in a position to request the "meaningful and timely consultation" contemplated by para. VII.

The U.N. Environment Programme's Provisions for Cooperation Between States in Weather Modification, paras. 1(d) & (g), 35 U.N. GAOR, Supp. (No. 25) 117–18, U.N. Doc. A/35/25 (1980), contain recommendatory language ("should"), and hedge the notification provision so it applies only "to the extent possible."

[141]Report of the [IAEA] Ad Hoc Advisory Group on Nuclear Explosions for Peaceful Purposes 108 (1977). The Report was approved by the IAEA Board of Governors in September 1977.

[142]Treaty for the Prohibition of Nuclear Weapons in Latin America, Feb. 14, 1967, art. 18, 634 U.N.T.S. 281, 6 INT'L LEGAL MATERIALS 521 (1967). The Treaty does require prior notification to the IAEA and the relevant Latin American agency.

dioactivity gives them a clear interest in the matter. These expectations have been developed largely in the contexts of nuclear plant siting and radioactive waste dumping, but they would apply equally to nuclear explosions unburdened by national security considerations.

The OECD Council has recommended that member states, when they develop policies for the siting of major energy facilities (whether nuclear or not), assess the environmental impact of the facilities through the use of environmental impact statements or other comprehensive methods.[143] Less specifically, OECD governments and some others have undertaken to extend environmental assessments to other pollution-engendering activities.[144] To the extent that these assessments involve hearings or other means of consulting interests within the country of origin (as they would in the United States and in several other OECD countries with similar environmental practices), the right to be heard should extend to persons in neighboring countries who are likely to be affected.[145] Essentially the same

[143]OECD Council Recommendation Concerning the Reduction of Environmental Impacts from Energy Production and Use, Oct. 12, 1976, para. 2(v), OECD Doc. C(76)162 (Final), in OECD AND THE ENVIRONMENT 33 (1979).

[144]*See* OECD Declaration on Environmental Policy, Nov. 14, 1974, para. 9, in *id.* at 21; OECD Declaration of Anticipatory Environmental Policies, May 8, 1979, para. 1, *id.* at 23; OECD Council Recommendation on the Assessment of Projects with Significant Impact on the Environment, May 8, 1979, paras. 1, 2, OECD Doc. C(79)116 (1979). The 1974 Declaration was intended to be part of the developing international environmental law. *Id.* para. 7; *see also Report by the OECD Secretary-General*, ACTIVITIES OF OECD IN 1974, at 88, 89 (1975). OECD member states are increasingly adopting environmental impact assessment practices, in accordance with the Declaration. *See* OECD Doc. ENV/Min(79)3, at 9–10 (1979); OECD, ENVIRONMENTAL IMPACT ASSESSMENT 27–67 (1979).

The Convention for Co-operation in the Protection and Development of the Marine and Coastal Envronment of the West and Central African Region, *supra* note 81, contains an environmental impact assessment provision in art. 13, though it only requires the parties to endeavor to make such assessments.

The Persian Gulf states have said they will endeavor to provide environmental assessments of proposed projects posing significant risks of pollution in the Gulf. Kuwait Regional Convention for Cooperation on the Protection of the Marine Environment from Pollution, Apr. 4, 1978, art. 11(a), in 17 INT'L LEGAL MATERIALS 511 (1978).

[145]OECD Council Recommendation for the Implementation of a Regime of Equal Right of Access and Nondiscrimination in Relation to Transfrontier Pollution, May 23, 1977, para. 4, OECD Doc. C(77)28 (Final), in 16 INT'L LEGAL MATERIALS 977 (1977). *See also* OECD Council Recommendation for Strengthening International Cooperation on Environmental Protection in Frontier Reeions, pt. II, paras. 2–3, OECD Doc. C(78)77 (Final), 17 *id.* at 1530 (1978). Recent OECD pronouncements have stressed the need for public participation in environmental assessment. *See* the 1979 OECD Declaration, para. 7, and Recommendation, para. 5, *supra* note 144.

scheme, stated somewhat more cautiously, appears in the UNEP Draft Principles of Conduct relating to shared natural resources.[146] These procedures, of course, treat consultation with affected private persons and entities as equivalent to—or better than—consultation with their government.

The OECD Council has also said that "Co-operation between interested Member countries should be developed regarding coastal development in border areas and mutual exchange of information should take place; where mutual interests are concerned, consultations should take place at the request of one of the Member countries concerned."[147] The recommendation goes on to call for cooperative environmental assessment of significant public and private projects having environmental consequences in coastal areas within other countries.[148] The environmental assessment, of course, would provide a data base for the intergovernmental consultations, as well as opening the possibility of direct consultations with affected private parties.

The Convention on the Law of the Sea,[149] emanating from the Third U.N. Conference on the Law of the Sea, contains principles for partially enclosed seas. Article 123 enunciates a duty to cooperate regarding enclosed or semienclosed seas, through coordination of activities affecting fishing, the marine environment, and scientific research. On the question of delimiting territorial seas between opposite or adjacent states, article 15 prohibits either state from claiming beyond the median line without the agreement of the other, in the absence of a claim of historic title or other special circumstances.[150] It does not define "special circumstances," nor does it say what rules apply in such cases. Articles 74 and 83 on delimitation of exclusive economic zones and continental shelves, respectively, call for agreement "on the basis of international law . . . in order to achieve an equitable solution." If no agreement is reached within

[146] UNEP Draft Principles of Conduct in the Field of the Environment for the Guidance of States in the Conservation and Harmonious Utilization of Natural Resources Shared by Two or More States, principles, 4, 13, 14, U.N. Doc. UNEP/IG.12/2, at 9 (1978), in 17 INT'L LEGAL MATERIALS 1097 (1978).

[147] OECD Council Recommendation on Principles Concerning Coastal Management, Oct. 22, 1976, para. 22, OECD Doc. C(76)(161)(Final), in 16 INT'L LEGAL MATERIALS 983 (1977).

[148] *Id.* para. 23.

[149] Convention on the Law of the Sea, *supra* note 17.

[150] Article 15 reproduces the substance of article 12(1) of the Geneva Convention on the Territorial Sea and Contiguous Zone, Apr. 29, 1958, 15 U.S.T. 1606, 516 U.N.T.S. 205. *See also id.* art. 24(3).

a reasonable time, there is to be dispute settlement. Pending agreement or settlement, the states concerned are to make provisional arrangements.[151]

The delimitation problem was specifically addressed in the North Sea Continental Shelf Cases.[152] The International Court called for negotiations in lieu of firm, unilateral continental shelf claims based on the equidistance line.[153] Although those cases involved European parties, the Court's judgment did not turn on anything peculiar to European practice. Nor did the basic principle enunciated—negotiations in place of unilateral, potentially encroaching claims in an area where use of the equidistance line seems inequitable—turn on anything that would distinguish continental shelf claims from other maritime zone claims.

On the question of exploitation of common maritime resources, the Convention on the Law of the Sea would require interested states to seek agreement when a common fish stock overlaps two exclusive economic zones or one such zone and the area beyond.[154] It does not deal with overlapping mineral resources.

F. Synthesis: Regional Resources

Despite the observations to the contrary in 1973 by the Council of Europe's group of legal experts, a prior consultation norm has arisen in Western Europe regarding new activities near an international boundary if there is a substantial risk of appreciable transfrontier air pollution or other significant disamenity.[155] What may have been inconclusive in 1973 has become

[151]The Conference considered various moratorium proposals, to be applied while opposite or adjacent states seek agreement. No consensus was reached on a moratorium rule, but the Conference did recognize that such states should negotiate and should refrain from prejudicial activities during the negotiations. *See* Adede, *Toward the Formulation of the Rule of Delimitation of Sea Boundaries Between States with Adjacent or Opposite Coastlines*, 19 Va. J. Int'l L. 207, 237 (1979).

[152]1969 I.C.J. 3.

[153]*See* notes 62–64 *supra*, and accompanying text.

[154]Convention on the Law of the Sea, *supra* note 17, art. 63.

[155]The OECD Environment Committee has defined "appreciable" environmental effect as "a technically measurable effect resulting in some not inconsiderable and statistically significant adverse change in the state of the environment, with due regard for the environmental qualities which should enable the area concerned to fulfil its usual functions." OECD Doc. ENV/TFP/78.17, at 20–21 (1st rev. 1979). Under the

considerably more authoritative since then, as exemplified by the 1974 Nordic Convention on the Protection of the Environment and the extensive practice (including the 1976 Nordic guidelines) relating to nuclear installations in border areas.[156] It is also exemplified by consultations on regional plans in frontier areas. The 1979 Convention on Long-Range Transboundary Air Pollution[157] strengthens the norm, even as to activities outside frontier areas. Moreover, most Western European states have supported the efforts in the U.N. Environment Programme and the General Assembly to adopt principles on prior consultation regarding shared resources. Most of them have endorsed the OECD transfrontier pollution recommendations, adopted after 1973.

Outside Western Europe, the evidence of a similar regional custom is a bit less compelling. Nevertheless, some evidence does exist. Most Eastern European states, plus Canada and the United States, are signatories to the 1979 Convention on Long-Range Transboundary Air Pollution, and resolved to apply its provisions even before it enters into force. The African Convention on the Conservation of Nature and Natural Resources could be regarded as the basis for a customary consultation standard in that region when transnational injury to soil, water, flora, or fauna would be likely. There is no such broad norm in Asia, but in North America there is a bilateral U.S.-Canadian custom requiring consultation before activities posing significant air pollution hazards are undertaken near the frontier. This is a somewhat broader norm than the treaty obligation found in the U.S.-Canadian weather modification agreement.

There is some nonregional practice that tends to reinforce regional consultation standards regarding air pollution and similar disamenities. This includes the pronouncements of the U.N. General Assembly, UNEP, and the OECD, discussed in the preceding section and in chapter II.

Current Western European practice establishes a regional custom requiring intergovernmental consultations before par-

Lake Lanoux case (France v. Spain), Nov. 16, 1957, 24 I.L.R. 101, the determination whether there is a significant risk of such an effect does not lie within the exclusive discretion of the acting state. *Accord*, OECD Doc. ENV/TFP/78.17, *supra*, at 21.

[156]The norm is particularly evident regarding the siting of nuclear installations near a border, but it is not limited to that. *See* Bothe, *supra* note 10, at 86–89. The duty may not extend to such basic decisions as those establishing the size and general location of installations. *See* text at note 27 *supra*.

[157]*See* note 4 *supra*.

ticularly harmful substances are dumped into partially enclosed seas. Oddly, Western European treaties do not expressly require consultations before moderately harmful substances are dumped in a way that might affect littoral states, yet they do require them for land-based disposals under similar circumstances. One might argue that prior consultation norms relating to pollution of international watercourse systems apply by analogy to dumping of harmful but nonprohibited substances into relatively enclosed sea areas, when there is some discernable risk to the littoral states.[158]

The evidence is rather sparse outside Western Europe to support purely regional consultation norms when partially enclosed seas are threatened with pollution. U.S.-Canadian practice involving the use of straits, and the U.S. acquiescence in the Mexican claim of a right to be consulted regarding radioactive waste disposal in the Gulf of Mexico, probably establish a North American norm requiring consultation among the littoral states before an activity is undertaken that is particularly hazardous because of the substance involved or because of the fragile ecology of the area (as in the case of some straits). Any other non-European prior consultation norm would depend on general custom or specific treaty obligation.

There is considerable evidence that a general prior consultation custom has matured when there is a substantial risk of appreciable pollution in common air sheds or partially enclosed seas.[159] The General Assembly, UNEP, and OECD pronouncements are particularly authoritative in these areas, since the question of what is a "shared resource" does not arise as it does in the case of successive rivers. With respect to the dumping of pollutants into partially enclosed seas, the nonregional London Ocean Dumping Convention (which applies also to open seas), buttressed by the similar regional conventions requiring consultation before hazardous substances are dumped in exceptional circumstances, probably has ripened into general (nonregional) custom that applies when the dumping is not

[158]This argument stresses the physical similarities between relatively enclosed sea areas and international watercourse systems. *See* chapter II *supra*: *cf.* Moore, *Legal Aspects of Marine Pollution Control, in* MARINE POLLUTION 589, 598 (R. Johnston ed. 1976).

[159]Handl, *supra* note 26, at 61–63, concludes that there already is such a customary duty, at least if the affected state (which must be notified of the project) requests consultations. *Cf.* Montreal Rules of International Law Applicable to Transfrontier Pollution, and Comments, discussed in the Afterword to this book.

regulated by international standards or by internationally sanctioned national licensing procedures.[160]

A prior consultation norm clearly exists in two environmentally significant categories. One involves the use of radioactive materials (such as siting nuclear power plants, conducting peaceful nuclear explosions, and disposing of radioactive wastes) in a way that poses a significant risk of appreciable harm to another country, unless the use is directly related to national security.[161] The other is intentional climate modification near an international boundary. The argument for an existing norm is almost as convincing in the case of significant boundary-area weather modification activities that do not threaten long-term climate changes.[162]

Offshore jurisdictional claims are subject to a minimum procedural duty to consult before they are implemented in a way that might encroach on a reasonable jurisdictional claim of another state.[163] Probably, the procedural expectation goes further and calls for agreement before a claim is implemented in a manner that might encroach on a reasonable opposing claim, even though the North Sea Continental Shelf Cases held open the possibility of delimitation if attempts to reach agreement failed. Most shelf delimitations have been by agreement. The prior agreement norm appears in the provisions on delimitation of economic zones and continental shelves of the Convention on the Law of the Sea. It appears in modified form in the Convention's provision on delimitation of territorial seas.[164]

[160]These conventions appear to be specific applications of the broader principle that there will be consultations with states having specific treaty rights (or, perhaps, historic rights) before the acting state invokes a recognized escape clause, unless the need for quick action precludes effective consultation.

[161]*See* text at notes 18–28, 36, 117, and 141 *supra*. Even beyond the European regional context, the evidence is particularly strong regarding the siting of nuclear power stations near frontiers. *See* OECD Doc. ENV/TFP/78.17, at 14–15 (1st rev. 1979).

For an instance of nonconsultation when national security was involved, see the remarks of Mr. Epstein, note 109 *supra*.

[162]*See* text at notes 137–40 *supra*. Transnational climate modification, because of its long-term nature and the commonality of the atmospheric resource, would be a particularly clear case for application of the exploitation-of-shared-resources principle.

[163]This is not entirely a recent development. The principle of prior consultation in the event of potentially overlapping offshore pollution-control zones was recognized in the Final Act and Draft Convention of the Preliminary Conference on Oil Pollution of Navigable Waters, June 8–16, 1926, *reprinted in* 19 INTERNATIONAL PROTECTION OF THE ENVIRONMENT 9585 (B. Rüster, B. Simma, & M. Bock eds. 1979). Fourteen nations were represented at the conference. The draft convention never entered into force.

[164]*See* text at notes 150–51 *supra*.

There is also convincing evidence of a general custom requiring consultation before there is a depleting exploitation of a mineral deposit straddling a delimitation line.[165] The evidence is less compelling as to common fisheries, although one could argue forcefully that in the absence of decisive practice either way, the prior consultation norm relating to inanimate resources would extend to animate ones. The Convention on the Law of the Sea calls for prior consultation in the common fishery situation, buttressing that argument.

The evidence does not support an across-the-board norm requiring consultations with littoral states before any activity is undertaken in a partially enclosed area that might adversely affect them.[166]

[165] Lagoni, *Oil and Gas Deposits Across National Frontiers*, 73 AM. J. INT'L L. 215, 235, 237–38, 243 (1979), concludes, after a study of state practice, that there is such a customary duty. *Cf.* Onorato, *supra* note 78.

[166] For example: (*a*) When the Federal Republic of Germany established a requirement that its permission be obtained before pipelines are constructed across its continental shelf from another state's shelf, it did not consult other North Sea littoral states. Letter to the author from the Counselor of the German Embassy in Washington, May 12, 1975. There appear to have been no protests from the other governments. (*b*) There is no customary duty to consult a coastal state before a nuclear-powered ship enters its territorial sea in innocent passage, despite the risk if an accident should occur so close to the shore. *See* L. HYDEMAN & W. BERMAN, *supra* note 32, at 178–82; Convention on the Law of the Sea, *supra* note 17, art. 23.

Chapter IV

Nonregional Resources

A. Introduction

The preceding chapter dealt with uses of natural resources that peculiarly affect states in close proximity to each other. The present one will examine unilateral uses of essentially unenclosed areas often regarded as res communis—oceans and outer space. Although most of the ocean uses discussed in this chapter relate to the open seas, uses of partially enclosed ocean areas also are included insofar as their effect on other states does not stem inherently from the geographic proximity of those states. For example, if a jurisdictional extension into a partially enclosed sea affects the interests of nonlittoral as well as littoral states, the question of consultation with the affected states is addressed here, even though the resource might be considered primarily regional.[1]

B. Oceans

1. Jurisdictional Extensions

National decisions regarding jurisdictional claims in the oceans are often made in stages. Thus, there may be a governmental decision to introduce a bill in the legislature that would authorize an official to promulgate an extended fishery zone; later the bill is enacted, and still later the zone is promulgated. Perhaps yet another period elapses before a decision is made to enforce the zone by arresting noncomplying vessels. For purposes of determining whether meaningful prior consultations have occurred, if they do not precede the initial decision, the relevant questions are whether anything of real interest to the affected state remains to be decided when consultations are held, and whether there is any real prospect of influencing the

I am grateful for the research assistance of David Eandi and Scott Jordan, then UCLA law students, in the preparation of parts of this chapter.

[1] Because the significance of the measures examined in this chapter is not as localized as it is when the measures are unique to watercourses or partially enclosed areas, the discussion does not proceed by regions.

remaining decision significantly. In a number of cases, consultations have been held when the manner and timing of a decision's implementation apparently remained indeterminate. These consultations usually do involve matters of interest to the affected states, and one must assume that they could influence the final decision unless the circumstances strongly suggest otherwise.

Any discussion of the modern practice of ocean jurisdictional extensions must start with the Truman Proclamations of 1945 on the continental shelf and on fisheries.[2] The two proclamations were drafted and issued together, with Secretary of the Interior Harold Ickes as the driving force behind them. The process of making and implementing the decision to assert these claims was complicated by conflict between the Interior and State departments (with the latter generally urging caution and making some effort to consider the interests of other states) and by the death of President Roosevelt after he had made the basic decision to assert the claims, but before the proclamations were issued.[3]

The fisheries proclamation had its genesis in the 1930s, when concern developed in the United States over Japanese salmon fishing around Bristol Bay, Alaska. There was sentiment in Congress at that time to enact unilateral fishery legislation, but negotiations with the Japanese were held instead, and no unilateral action was taken until the 1945 proclamation.[4] Apparently, the only other discussions with foreign governments before the Roosevelt policy decision to go ahead were with Canada, Newfoundland, and Mexico regarding the fisheries proclamation.[5] President Roosevelt approved the draft statements of policy and the draft proclamations on March 31, 1945, subject to discussions being held with interested foreign governments. The results of the discussions were to be communicated to him before the proclamations would be issued.

The State Department then explained the proposed fisheries

[2]The proclamations appear in 4 M. WHITEMAN, DIGEST OF INT'L LAW 756 & 954 (1965).

[3]For narratives of the decision-making process leading to the issuance of the proclamations, see L. JUDA, OCEAN SPACE RIGHTS: DEVELOPING U.S. POLICY 12–17 (1975); Hollick, *U.S. Oceans Policy: The Truman Proclamations*, 17 VA. J. INT'L L. 23 (1976).

[4]*See* L. JUDA, *supra* note 3, at 12; *see also* Selak, *Recent Developments in High Seas Fisheries Jurisdiction Under the Presidential Proclamation of 1945*, 44 AM. J. INT'L L. 670, 671–72 (1950).

[5]*See* 1945 [2] FOREIGN RELATIONS OF THE UNITED STATES 1489–91.

policy to the governments of Canada, Newfoundland, Mexico, the United Kingdom, the Soviet Union, France, Norway, the Netherlands, Cuba, Iceland, Denmark, and Portugal; however, it communicated the draft statement of policy on the continental shelf only to Canada, Mexico, the United Kingdom, and the Soviet Union.[6] Most of the responses dealt with the proposed fisheries policy, but the U.K. did propose certain international arrangements regarding the continental shelf.[7] It has been alleged, with some support from the available documents,[8] that the United States' course of action had been set by Roosevelt's decision and Ickes's resolve to proceed at all costs. But it appears that the State Department did seriously consider the U.K. continental shelf proposal, and the fisheries proclamation, as finally issued, changed the draft in two respects urged by the British.[9] Thus, one must conclude that the consultations were meaningful in the sense that they could and did have some influence on the shape of the final decision, even though they probably could not have completely deterred the United States from going ahead. In fact, the United States never implemented the fisheries proclamation with any unilateral measures and, for thirty years thereafter, pursued fishery conservation goals primarily through international fishery organizations rather than by unilateral action.[10] One could infer that the interests expressed by foreign states in 1945 had some influence on this course of action.

As is well known, the Truman Proclamations precipitated a rash of jurisdictional extensions, many of which asserted considerably greater rights than those the United States had claimed. The first was the Mexican Declaration on the Continental Shelf, issued one month after the Truman Proclamation on the shelf.[11]

[6] 4 M. WHITEMAN, *supra* note 2, at 953; 1945 [2] FOREIGN RELATIONS OF THE UNITED STATES 1510, 1526.

[7] 1945 [2] FOREIGN RELATIONS OF THE UNITED STATES 1523–24.

[8] *See* Hollick, *supra* note 3, *passim* and at 44, 52; 1945 [2] FOREIGN RELATIONS OF THE UNITED STATES 1510–11, 1516–18, 1522.

[9] 1945 [2] FOREIGN RELATIONS OF THE UNITED STATES 1526–27; and compare the draft proclamation on fisheries, *id.* 1491–92, with the British comments, *id.* 1516–17, and with the final proclamation, 4 M. WHITEMAN, *supra* note 2, at 954–55.

[10] *See* Swygard, *Politics of the North Pacific Fisheries—with Special Reference to the Twelve-Mile Bill*, 43 WASH. L. REV. 269, 271–72 (1967). The United States did take a relatively minor unilateral step when it adopted a 12-mile fishery zone in 1966, but its primary conservation efforts remained within international organizations until Congress enacted the Fishery Conservation and Management Act of 1976, 16 U.S.C. §§ 1801 *et seq.* (1976).

[11] For the text of the Mexican Declaration, see U.N. Doc. ST/LEG/SER.B/1 at 13

The Declaration was never implemented.[12] The United States' note to Mexico after the Declaration suggests that no prior consultations occurred dealing specifically with its proposed terms,[13] although the discussions between the two countries before the Truman Proclamations must have touched on general Mexican intentions as well as those of the United States.

Chile and Peru first made their 200-mile maritime zone claims in 1947. Ecuador issued a similar decree in 1951, which was followed by the Declaration of Santiago, issued by all three governments in 1952.[14] A diligent search has uncovered no hint of prior consultation with the United States or any other potentially affected state regarding any of the three separate decrees, but it appears that neither the United States nor any other distant-water fishing state had existing fishing interests in the area, at least at the time of the 1947 claims.[15] There was a form of consultation just before the Declaration of Santiago, at a meeting of the Inter-American Juridical Committee that produced a draft article (to which the United States, Brazil, and Colombia objected) on a 200-mile economic zone.[16] The meeting gave the interested states an opportunity to express their positions, but they apparently did not discuss anything as spe-

(1951). For a summary of this and other claims in the ten years following World War II, see B. MacChesney, *Situation, Documents and Commentary on Recent Developments in the International Law of the Sea*, 51 U.S. Naval War College Int'l Law Studies 441 (1957).

[12]*See* 1 A. Szekely, Latin America and the Development of the Law of the Sea 66 (1976), noting that the Declaration claimed jurisdiction not only over the shelf but over the superjacent waters. To become law, the Declaration required a constitutional amendment that was not promulgated at that time. When the constitution finally was amended in 1960, the earlier claim to an epicontinental sea was dropped.

[13]*See* 1946 [11] Foreign Relations of the United States 1054.

[14]For texts, see B. MacChesney, *supra* note 11, at 265; U.N. Doc. ST/LEG/SER.B/1, at 6, 16, 301 (1951). It is not important for purposes of this study whether these were true territorial sea claims or claims more closely resembling the modern exclusive economic zone.

[15]*See* 1 A. Szekely, *supra* note 12, at 152; Loring, *The United States–Peruvian "Fisheries" Dispute*, 23 Stan. L. Rev. 391, 400 (1971). The United States clearly did have a prospective interest in the tuna fishing grounds off Chile and Peru. *Id.* The protest notes from the United States and others did not suggest that any prior consultations had taken place, nor did they assert a specific duty to consult—presumably because their authors wished to concentrate on the stronger assertion that the claims exceeded allowable international law limits, and perhaps also because they recognized that their economic interests were prospective only. For the protest notes, see B. MacChesney, *supra* note 11, at 448–50; 1951 I.C.J. Pleadings (2 Anglo-Norwegian Fisheries) 747, 750; (4 *id.*) 56, 589, 599, 602, 603, 605.

[16]*See* 4 M. Whiteman, *supra* note 2, at 68–69.

cific as a proposed Declaration. Diplomatic negotiations with the United States regarding the specific 200-mile claims of Chile, Ecuador, and Peru were not held until September 1955, after Ecuador and Peru had begun to enforce their claims against United States tuna boats which, by then, had begun to fish off their coasts.[17]

Some other Latin American countries were making extended jurisdictional claims at about the same time. In most cases, there is no indication of consultation before the claims were made.[18] But the claims were not immediately enforced; instead, they were in the nature of statements of position to be implemented in the future. Consultations then were held with the United States in various forums. For example, after the Costa Rican 200-mile decree of 1948, there were negotiations with the United States that led to a milder 1949 decree and to the creation of the Inter-American Tropical Tuna Commission.[19] In 1956 there were two Inter-American conferences at which ocean jurisdictional extensions were thoroughly discussed, though no general agreement was reached.[20]

Before the wholesale 12-mile territorial sea and 200-mile fishery (or economic) zone claims of the middle and late 1970s, other particularly significant jurisdictional extensions included

[17] *See generally* B. AUGUSTE, THE CONTINENTAL SHELF: THE PRACTICE AND POLICY OF THE LATIN AMERICAN STATES WITH SPECIAL REFERENCE TO CHILE, ECUADOR, AND PERU 105–47 (1960), especially at 144 n.137. Early seizures of U.S. fishing vessels are outlined in *Fishing Rights and United States–Latin American Relations: Hearing Before a Subcomm. of the House Comm. on Foreign Affairs*, 92d Cong., 2d Sess. 3, 40, 59–60 (1972). Before enforcement of the 200-mile claims, the United States had met with Ecuador about the latter's seizure of U.S. vessels within its 12-mile territorial sea. *See* 1 A. SZEKELY, *supra* note 12, at 192.

[18] There were consultations between the United States and El Salvador before the later adopted its constitution of Sept. 14, 1950, which claimed a 200-mile exclusive maritime zone (*see* 1950 [2] FOREIGN RELATIONS OF THE UNITED STATES 9P864), but that appears to have been an exception. For a collection of diplomatic notes suggesting lack of consultation before most decrees of this period were promulgated, see 1951 I.C.J. Pleadings (4 Anglo-Norwegian Fisheries) 570–605.

[19] *See* 1948 [9] FOREIGN RELATIONS OF THE UNITED STATES 263–68.

[20] *See* the Final Act of the Third Meeting of the Inter-American Council of Jurists, OAS Doc. CIJ-29 (1956); *U.S. Report on the Inter-American Specialized Conference on Conservation of Natural Resources*: *Continental Shelf and Marine Waters, Ciudad Trujillo*, 34 DEP'T ST. BULL. 894 (1956); F. GARCIA-AMADOR, THE EXPLOITATION AND CONSERVATION OF THE RESOURCES OF THE SEA 172–73 (2d ed. 1963). Venezuela adopted a 12-mile territorial sea only after the Ciudad Trujillo Conference, at which Venezuela had argued for the 12-mile rule. *See* Nweihed, *Venezuela's Contribution to the Contemporary Law of the Sea*, 11 SAN DIEGO L. REV. 603, 624 (1974).

the various Icelandic fishery zone extensions beginning in 1950, the widespread 12-mile fishery zone claims in the 1960s, the Canadian Arctic Waters Pollution Prevention Act in 1970, various U.S. conservation and pollution-control measures in the 1970s, the Brazilian 200-mile territorial sea claim in 1970–71, and the Norwegian establishment of trawler-free zones in 1975. These are discussed below.

In addition, virtually every coastal state has claimed the right to explore the continental shelf and exploit its resources, but these are not jurisdictional extensions in the strict sense, as they go no further than the "natural prolongation" of the land territory and do not claim more than the inherent right to explore and exploit the shelf.[21] No declaration of these rights is required by international law, and there is no evidence (after the Truman Proclamation) of state practice calling for consultation with interested states before an inherent continental shelf right is claimed.[22]

In October 1949, Iceland gave the United Kingdom notice of termination of the 1901 convention that had set three-mile fishery limits for Iceland. In April 1950, Iceland claimed a four-mile conservation zone off its north coast.[23] It is likely that negotiations were held in the interim.[24] When Iceland issued new regulations in March 1952 extending the four-mile limit to the entire coastline from straight baselines, it apparently did so without consulting the United Kingdom (although the British government knew that Iceland might take such a step following the International Court's decision in the *Anglo-Norwegian Fisheries* Case and had warned the Icelandic government not to do so).[25]

On June 1, 1958, about a month after the end of the 1958 Geneva Conference on the Law of the Sea, Iceland announced that on June 30 it would issue a decree claiming a 12-mile

[21] North Sea Continental Shelf Cases, 1969 I.C.J. 3, 22. There is no inherent right to full sovereignty over the shelf, and coastal states have not claimed such a right.

[22] This is to be distinguished from practice regarding new designations of species as sedentary for continental shelf exploitation purposes and new methods of enforcing continental shelf rights. These matters are discussed in the next section of this chapter.

[23] 4 M. WHITEMAN, *supra* note 2, at 1154–55.

[24] *See* 468 PARL. DEB., H.C. (5th ser.) 65 (1949) (written answer) (British government anticipated negotiations during the two years following the Icelandic notice of termination of the 1901 convention).

[25] *See* Green, *The Territorial Sea and the Anglo-Icelandic Dispute*, 9 J. PUB. L. 53, 63 (1960); 501 PARL. DEB., H.C. (5th ser.) 14, 913 (1952).

exclusive fishery zone. Iceland's position favoring extended fishery zones was discussed at the Conference, where unsuccessful attempts were made to reach general agreement on 12-mile zones. The United Kingdom issued an aide-mémoire on May 29, arguing that Iceland could not restrict high seas fishing rights. In addition, the British government and others informed the Icelandic government that they were prepared to enter into direct negotiations regarding fisheries around Iceland. It appears, however, that there were no direct discussions between Iceland and other interested states regarding Iceland's specific intentions between the end of the Conference and the June 1 announcement.[26] Between June 1 and June 30, the United Kingdom, France, and Sweden made further attempts to enter into substantive negotiations with Iceland.[27] These negotiations apparently did not begin until after the decree had been issued, but they did occur between the date of issuance and the September 1 effective date. During that time, Iceland's basic 12-mile claim was nonnegotiable, but the incidents of the claim, including the effective date, were discussed.[28]

The 1958 Geneva Conference dealt with a great many issues in addition to those relating to 12-mile zones. Among them was the issue of unilateral fishery conservation zones extending well beyond 12 miles. This issue was controversial, with some states fearing that the gates would be opened to extensive unilateral claims impinging on the traditional high seas freedom of fishing, and others (particularly the Latin American 200-mile maritime zone states) asserting that a mere right to establish "conservation zones" was inadequate. Once it became apparent that the conservation zone concept had considerable support, there was controversy over whether to attach a duty to consult other interested states as a condition precedent.[29] A compromise

[26]Green, *supra* note 25, at 68; *see also* 4 M. WHITEMAN, *supra* note 2, at 1157–59; 592 PARL. DEB., H.C. (5th ser.) 62–63 (1958) (written answer).

[27]*See* Gros, *La Convention sur la Pêche et la Conservation des Resources Biologiques de la Haute Mer*, 97 HAGUE ACADEMY, RECUEIL DES COURS 1, 77 (1959); 4 W WHITEMAN, *supra* note 2, at 1158–59.

[28]This is indicated in the U.K. memorandum *The Problem of the Fisheries Around Iceland*, 4 M. WHITEMAN, *supra* note 2, at 1169, 1170–71. The effective date (Sept. 1) appears, *id.* at 1163.

[29]*Compare* the proposal by Chile, Costa Rica, Ecuador, Peru, and seven others to eliminate the negotiation duty, [First] U.N. Conf. on the Law of the Sea, OR, vol. 5, U.N. Doc. A/CONF.13/41, at 56–57, 147, 153 (1958), *with* the responses of New Zealand, the Soviet Union, Pakistan, the U.K., Australia, and others stressing the importance of prior negotiations, *id.* at 63–67.

was reached, incorporating into article 7 of the Convention on Fishing and Conservation of the Living Resources of the High Seas a provision permitting a coastal state unilaterally to establish conservation measures adjacent to its territorial sea, provided that negotiations with the other states concerned have not led to an agreement within a "time certain" (six months).[30] The "time certain" replaced the vague "reasonable time" standard adopted in the International Law Commission's draft[31] and seemed to satisfy those states fearing that action could be delayed substantially by the prior negotiation requirement. The result was a provision that was regarded by most observers as new law, in the sense that it permitted a new form of jurisdictional extension into the high seas, but that attached prior consultations as a condition precedent to the exercise of the new right.[32]

The Convention came into force, but was not as widely ratified as the other three 1958 Conventions on the Law of the Sea. As a result, doubt was expressed whether its provisions had legal significance for nonparties.[33] By 1976, though, the U.S. State Department had taken the position that article 7 probably had become customary international law.[34] If that position is correct, the expectation thus created would not necessarily be limited to fishery conservation zones, but could extend to such claims as extended exclusive fishery zones and pollution control zones. It remains to be discussed, however, whether

[30]Convention of Fishing and Conservation of the Living Resources of the High Seas, Apr. 29, 1958, art. 7(1), 17 U.S.T. 138, T.I.A.S. No. 5969, 559 U.N.T.S. 285.

[31]*See* 1955 [2] Y.B. INT'L L. COMM'N 19, 30.

[32]To the effect that this was new law: 1955 [1]Y.B. INT'L L. COMM'N 102 (remarks of Sir Gerald Fitzmaurice); Sorensen, *Law of the Sea*, INT'L CONCILIATION NO. 520, p. 195 at 223–25 (1958); STAFF OF SENATE COMM. ON COMMERCE, 91st Cong., 2d Sess., TREATIES AND OTHER INTERNATIONAL AGREEMENTS ON OCEANOGRAPHIC RESOURCES, FISHERIES AND WILDLIFE 271, 287 (Comm. Print 1960) (views of Acting Secretary of State and Senate Comm. on Foreign Relations).

That the duty to negotiate was considered a condition precedent: 1955 [1] Y.B. INT'L L. COMM'N 113 (views of Sir Gerald Fitzmaurice and Mr. Liang, Secretary to the Commission); 1956 [1]Y.B. INT'L L. COMM'N 270 (commentary by the Commission); [First] U.N. Conf. on the Law of the Sea, OR, vol. 5, U.N. Doc. A/CONF.13/41, at 69 (1958) (concession by Ecuador that "many delegations had expressed the view that prior negotiation was indispensable").

[33]*See* Herrington, *The Future of the Geneva Convention on Fishing and the Conservation of the Living Resources of the Sea*, in THE LAW OF THE SEA: THE FUTURE OF THE SEA'S RESOURCES 62–63 (2d Ann. Conf. of the Law of the Sea Inst. 1967).

[34]1976 DIGEST OF UNITED STATES PRACTICE IN INT'L L. 355; Moore, *Foreign Policy and Fidelity to Law: The Anatomy of a Treaty Violation*, 70 AM. J. INT'L l. 802, 804 (1976).

state practice since 1958 supports the customary international law status of the negotiation requirement (and, a fortiori, the consultation requirement) in article 7.

To return to the Anglo-Icelandic fisheries dispute, it erupted in 1958 into a "cod war" in which British naval vessels attempted to protect British trawlers within the Icelandic 12-mile zone. In 1961 the U.K. finally recognized the zone in an exchange of notes that produced a stable situation until July 14, 1971. On that date, a new Icelandic government announced its plan to terminate the 1961 agreement and to extend its fishery zone not later than September 1, 1972. The U.K. responded with an aide-mémoire of July 17, 1971, asserting that there had been neither prior consultation nor advance warning to the British government.[35] Iceland indicated its willingness to discuss the matter, and talks were then held between Iceland and both the United Kingdom and the Federal Republic of Germany. When no agreement was reached, the Icelandic Althing (parliament) adopted a resolution on February 15, 1972, establishing the new 50-mile exclusive fishery zone effective September 1, 1972. The resolution urged that further discussions be held with the U.K. and Germany. Such discussions took place on several occasions before September 1, but no agreement was reached, and the resolution went into force as scheduled.[36]

From the start there was little chance that the consultations would persuade Iceland to preserve the status quo, but they did have some chance of producing agreements potentially less damaging to British and German interests than unilateral action imposing a 50-mile exclusive zone. It probably became impossible to preclude unilateral action after February 15, 1972, although the details of the fishery regime to be applied within the zone clearly remained negotiable. Negotiations followed, even though the basic nature, breadth, and effective date were already fixed. Thus, the situation was comparable to that existing between issuance of the Icelandic 12-mile decree of June 30, 1958, and its September 1, 1958, effective date. Both situations were similar to the pause for negotiations between President Roosevelt's 1945 decision to proceed with continental shelf

[35] *See* CMD. No. 5341, at 9 (1973).

[36] For summaries of the negotiations before and after the Althing resolution, see *id.* at 2–3; Bilder, *The Anglo-Icelandic Fisheries Dispute*, 1973 WISC. L. REV. 37, 55–57; 18 KEESING'S CONTEMP. ARCHIVES 25234–36 (1972); 19 *id.* 25869–71 (1973). The Althing resolution appears in 11 INT'L LEGAL MATERIALS 643 (1972).

and fishery conservation claims and President Truman's issuance of the proclamations.[37]

In the *Fisheries Jurisdiction* Cases, the International Court of Justice held that Iceland could not unilaterally extend its exclusive fishery zone beyond 12 miles, particularly against states such as the U.K. and Germany with historic fishing interests in the area and some economic dependence on the fishery.[38] The Court said that Iceland had only a preferential right and that "[i]t is implicit in the concept of preferential rights that negotiations are required in order to define or delimit the extent of those rights. . . . The obligation to negotiate thus flows from the very nature of the respective rights of the Parties."[39]

If these cases had been decided a mere three years later—after the Third U.N. Conference on the Law of the Sea had achieved general consensus on 200-mile exclusive economic zones and after the worldwide rush to adopt them—they surely would have upheld the Icelandic claim to an exclusive fishery zone, though probably the Court still would have required Iceland to negotiate to the extent that Iceland's harvesting capacity in the zone fell short of the maximum sustainable yield.[40]

Iceland's 1958 move to a 12-mile fishery zone antedated by five to eight years a series of comparable measures by other nations.[41] The question of 12-mile exclusive fishery zones was thoroughly discussed at the 1960 Geneva Conference on the Law of the Sea, where the U.S.-Canadian proposal for a 6-mile

[37]The Icelandic 200-mile fisheries claim in 1975 is discussed with similar claims of about the same period, at notes 87–89 *infra*.

[38]1974 I.C.J. 3, 27–28; *id.* at 175, 196–97.

[39]*Id.* at 32; *id.* at 201.

[40]*See* text at note 102 *infra*.

[41]There were a few 6- or 12-mile claims before 1958, not always preceded by consultations. *See e.g.*, U.N. Doc. A/CONF.19/5, at 34 (1960) (Venezuelan 12-mile territorial sea claim in 1956); Misra, *Territorial Sea and India*, 6 INDIAN J. INT'L L. 465, 468–72 (1966) (discussing India's 6-mile territorial sea claim in 1956). Apparently, there were no prior consultations in either case.

Compare the 1956 Soviet curtailment of salmon fishing in the Bering Sea and the Pacific. There had been negotiations with Japan, the only interested state. 4 M. WHITEMAN, *supra* note 2, at 1146, 1149. (Soviet-Japanese fishery negotiations continued after 1956, resulting in a steady curtailment of Japanese fishing in the Northwest Pacific and the Sea of Okhotsk. *See* Pond, Japan and Russia: The View from Tokyo, 52 FOREIGN AFFAIRS 141, 150 (1973).)

Another noteworthy incident about the time of the Soviet salmon fishing restriction involved the 1955 establishment of a fishery conservation zone by the People's Republic of China. Nongovernmental consultations were held with a Japanese fishing team after the decision but before enforcement. *See* Ohira & Kuwakara, *Fishery Problems Between Japan and the People's Republic of China*, 1959 JAPANESE ANN. INT'L. 109, 118–23.

territorial sea plus a 6-mile exclusive fishery zone failed by one vote to obtain the necessary two-thirds approval. After the Conference, Canada circulated a pamphlet to other governments urging acceptance of the six-plus-six formula and began a series of discussions with other nations on the same subject. When agreement could not be reached with the major powers, Canada announced in June 1963 that it intended to act unilaterally.[42] The Canadian government then pursued discussions with other interested states, including the United States, Norway, Denmark, the U.K., Portugal, Spain, Italy, and Japan, before and after a bill was formally introduced into the Canadian Parliament that provided for straight baselines with a 3-mile territorial sea and an additional 9-mile exclusive fishery zone.[43] The bill was enacted. It came into force on July 23, 1964, but states with traditional fishing interests were exempted, pending completion of negotiations.[44] The Canadian Secretary of State for External Affairs said in Parliament, "We are . . . convinced that we must carry forward our negotiations with these countries before we proclaim the base lines for our entire coast line."[45] Although the negotiations with countries not enjoying treaty rights (i.e., all except France and the United States) were aimed at eventually phasing out their fishing within the 12-mile zone,[46] it appears that their interests were given consideration within that overall constraint. Moreover, it appears that opposition expressed particularly by the United Kingdom and United States dissuaded Canada from drawing its straight baselines to enclose the Northwest Passage.[47] The other straight baselines were not put into force until 1967 and later.

[42] *See* Gottlieb, *The Canadian Contribution to the Concept of a Fishing Zone in International Law,* 1964 CAN. Y.B. INT'L L. 55, 64–71, 73–75; Legault, *Maritime Claims,* in CANADIAN PERSPECTIVES ON INTERNATIONAL LAW AND ORGANIZATION 377, 382–83 (R. MacDonald, G. Morris, & D. Johnston eds. 1974); Yogis, *Canadian Fisheries and International Law, id.* at 398, 403–05.

[43] *See* Gottlieb, *supra* note 42, at 74; Hollick, *United States and Canadian Policy Processes in Law of the Sea,* 12 SAN DIEGO L. REV. 518, 529 (1975); 1 CAN. PARL. DEB., H.C., 25th Parl., 1st Sess. 14–15, 768 (1962); 1 *id.*, 26th Parl., 1st Sess. 621 (1963); 3 *id.* at 3210; 1 *id.*, 26th Parl., 2d Sess. 7 (1964); 2 *id.*, at 1464; 4 *id.* at 3411.

[44] *See Canadian Practice in International Law, 1964,* in 1966 CAN. Y.B. INT'L L. 240–41.

[45] 4 CAN. PARL. DEB., H.C. 26th Parl., 2d Sess. 3409–10 (1964).

[46] Legault, *supra* note 42, at 383, 386. *See also* 6 CAN. PARL. DEB., H.C. 28th Parl., 2d Sess. 6183–85 (1970); 2 *id.*, 28th Parl., 3d Sess. 2189–90 (1970).

[47] McConchie & Reid, *Canadian Foreign Policy and International Straits,* in CANADIAN FOREIGN POLICY AND THE LAW OF THE SEA 158, 166 (B. Johnson & M. Zacher eds. 1977).

As noted in chapter III,[48] the European Fisheries Conference, held in London in 1963–64, adopted a six-plus-six formula when it adopted the European Fisheries Convention. A coastal state was empowered to displace even traditional distant-water fishing rights in the outer 6-mile zone if that state was overwhelmingly dependent on the coastal fishery and obtained the approval of the other contracting parties. A further provision, drawing on the 1958 Convention on Fishing and Conservation of the Living Resources of the High Seas, permitted a state not overwhelmingly dependent on its coastal fishery to apply conservation measures to the outer 6-mile zone after notifying the other contracting parties and consulting them if requested to do so.[49]

Spurred on by the trend toward 12-mile fishery zones and by the appearance in substantial numbers of Soviet trawlers off the coasts of Washington and Oregon, the United States enacted a 12-mile exclusive fishery zone in October 1966. This was preceded by discussions, at least with the Soviet Union, regarding fishing within 12 miles of the U.S. coast.[50] It is not clear whether consultations also took place with other interested states before October 1966. Perhaps not, since the State Department waited until December 29 to announce that it had notified interested governments of its willingness to consider their views on the continuation of their fisheries in the zone and indicated at the same time that "preliminary discussions" had just begun with Japan.[51] In any event, interested states were given the opportunity to consult before the legislation was enforced, and the statute provided for the continuation of traditional fishing rights.

Mexico followed the United States' lead in January 1967 by enacting a 12-mile fishery zone law. Discussions were held between the United States and Mexico after enactment of both countries' 12-mile legislation, but before either attempted to enforce its new zone against the other. An agreement was reached establishing reciprocal fishing rights for five years in the area

[48] *See* chapter III at notes 44–48.

[49] European Fisheries Convention, Mar. 9, 1964, art. 5(2), 581 U.N.T.S. 57.

[50] *See* 55 DEP'T. ST. BULL. 273–74 (1966). It is likely that the U.S.-Canadian discussions on Canada's 1964 fisheries legislation also covered fishing off the U.S. coasts. *See Fishing in U.S. Territorial Waters: Hearings Before the House Comm. on Merchant Marine & Fisheries*, 88th Cong., 2d Sess. 79 (1964).

[51] *See* 56 DEP'T. ST. BULL. 178 (1967).

between 9 and 12 miles off each coast.[52] In essence, the agreement turned the 9-to-12-mile zone into a preferential zone for five years. It required each government to consult the other before restricting fishing by the other's nationals in that zone to any greater extent than was originally set forth in the agreement.[53] That requirement was consistent with the regime established for the outer 6-mile area in the European Fisheries Convention and with the later decision in the *Fisheries Jurisdiction* Cases.

Some other contemporaneous 12-mile fishery zone claims were preceded by bilateral consultations, or by an expression of willingness to consult, with states having substantial interests. For example, when Denmark established a 12-mile exclusive fishery zone around the Faroe Islands in 1959, it had negotiated with the U.K. for several months and had arrived at an agreed compromise.[54] The South African government announced in December 1962 that it proposed to extend territorial waters to six miles and exclusive fishery jurisdiction to an additional six miles, but that it would consider sympathetically the representations of any state that might consider its interests affected.[55] On the other hand, when Australia extended its fishery zone to 12 miles effective January 31, 1968, it began discussions on continuation of Japanese fishing only in February of that year.[56] It appears, however, that there was no interruption of Japanese fishing at that point. Japan appears to have had a more substantial fishing interest in the area within 12 miles of the New Zealand coast at the time of the latter's 12-mile fishery extension

[52] U.S.-Mexico exchange of notes, Oct. 27, 1967, 18 U.S.T. 2724, T.I.A.S. No. 6359, 693 U.N.T.S. 175 (no longer in force). An agreement also was reached between Mexico and Japan before Mexico made any attempt to enforce its zone. *See* Sepúlveda, *Mexico and the Law of the Sea*, in THE CHANGING LAW OF THE SEA: WESTERN HEMISPHERE PERSPECTIVES 81, 82, 85 (R. Zacklin ed. 1974). *See also* Windley, *International Practice Regarding Traditional Fishing Privileges of Foreign Fishermen in Zones of Extended Maritime Jurisdiction*, 63 AM J. INT'L L. 490, 501 (1969).

[53] U.S.-Mexico exchange of notes, *supra* note 52, para. 8.

[54] *See* Gros, *supra* note 27, at 78–79: U.K.-Denmark exchange of correspondence, 8 INT'L & COMP. L.Q. 171–75 (1959).

[55] *See* 14 KEESING'S CONTEMP. ARCHIVES 19207 (1963). The six-plus-six zone was proclaimed in 1963.

[56] Japan's fishing interests off Australia were substantial enough to concern the Australians, but apparently were not as significant to Japan as its interests off some other coasts. *See* Leyser, *Fisheries Zones in the South-West Pacific*, 14 ARCHIV DES VÖLKERRECHTS 145, 153 (1969); Windley, *supra* note 52, at 503.

(January 1966). Discussions were not held until a few days before that zone came into force. They apparently did not involve real give and take regarding preservation of Japanese interests. The zone was enforced against Japanese fishing vessels before meaningful negotiations began.[57]

Despite the New Zealand–Japan exception, state practice in the 1960s reflected a widely shared expectation that there would be consultations with significantly interested states regarding continuation of their fishing activities (though perhaps only in diminished volume or for a temporary period) before a new fishery zone was enforced against them. It is doubtful, however, that practice in the 1960s would support a norm requiring consultations (*a*) any earlier than that, or (*b*) at any time regarding such basic matters as the nature, breadth, and effective date of the zone.

To the extent that an argument can be made to support an early, comprehensive consultation norm, it must rely, not on any consistent practice of direct, bilateral consultations, but on discussions at the 1958 and 1960 Conferences on the Law of the Sea regarding the desirability and legitimacy of 12-mile territorial seas and fishery zones. The Conferences did not merely discuss 12-mile territorial seas and fishery zones in the abstract; rather, they were held in a setting of announced intention on the part of several governments unilaterally to extend—or to consider extending—their territorial sea or fishery zone claims if no agreement could be reached.[58] At least one government expressly declined to exercise its statutory authority to extend its fishery jurisdiction, pending the outcome of the 1960 Conference.[59] Twelve-mile territorial sea claims were made shortly after the 1958 Conference by Panama, Iran, Libya, and the Sudan, apparently without consultations outside the Conference.[60] The People's Republic of China, which had not been invited to the Conference, joined the 12-mile territorial sea claimants shortly after the Conference ended. A Chinese spokesman asserted, however, that it was not necessary to hold prior consultations.[61]

[57] *See* Leyser, *supra* note 56, at 148–49; Foster, *New Zealand's Coastal Jurisdiction*, 1 Cal. Western Int'l L. J. 13 (1970).

[58] *See E.g.*, 4 Répertoire de la Pratique Française en Matière de Droit International Public 102 (A.-C. Kiss ed. 1962).

[59] *See* O'Higgins, *The Irish Maritime Jurisdiction Act, 1959*, in 9 Int'l & Comp. L.Q. 325, 331 (1960).

[60] *See* 4 M. Whiteman, *supra* note 2, at 118–20.

[61] Fu Chu, Concerning the Question of Our Country's Territorial Sea (Peking,

As a result of the failure to agree at the 1960 Conference, the Soviet Union for the first time enacted into law (on August 5, 1960) the 12-mile territorial sea it had claimed doctrinally theretofore.[62] Other 12-mile territorial sea claims were made over a span of about twelve years following the 1960 Conference. These included the 1967 Indian and Nigerian claims, neither of which expressly recognized any need to conduct direct, contemporaneous consultations with specially affected states.[63]

Even if the 1967 claims can be traced back to the 1958 and 1960 Conferences, the 12-mile territorial sea claims of Malaysia and Indonesia in the Strait of Malacca (November 16, 1971) could not be. The time lag between the Conferences and the claims was too great, even if the discussions at the Conferences otherwise could be considered prior consultations on the question of claims encroaching on high seas freedoms in international straits. Moreover, consultations in the 1960s regarding 12-mile claims into open seas would not relate to the claims in the Strait of Malacca.

To establish custom stemming from the 1958 and 1960 negotiations, it would be necessary to show not only that the negotiations related to the specific subsequent claims, but also that there was a widely shared perception that the negotiations were a prerequisite to valid 12-mile claims. Insofar as states did postpone their gestating claims until the Conferences had ended, however, they seem to have done so, not because they thought they had to, but because they thought it inexpedient to anticipate unilaterally what might soon be agreed upon in a multilateral forum. Thus, the Conferences did not reflect or establish a prior consultation norm for extended jurisdictional claims.

The 1970s saw maritime jurisdictional claims expand far beyond 12 miles. One of the most significant claims was that authorized by the Canadian Arctic Waters Pollution Prevention Act, introduced in the House of Commons on April 8, 1970. The Act asserted a right to issue subsequent regulations con-

1959), *translated in* 1 J. COHEN & H. CHIU, PEOPLES CHINA AND INTERNATIONAL LAW: A DOCUMENTARY STUDY 470, 477 (1974).

[62] *See* W. BUTLER, THE SOVIET UNION AND THE LAW OF THE SEA 44 (1971).

[63] *See* INDIAN J. INT'L L. 584 (1967) (Indian claim), and U.N. Doc. ST/LEG/SER.B/ 15, at 103 (1970) (Nigerian claim). Nigeria extended its claim to 30 miles in 1971, apparently without prior consultations, and to 50 miles in 1974. The latter claim was preceded by consultations at the Third U.N. Conference on the Law of the Sea. *See* note 91 *infra*.

trolling shipping; prescribing standards of vessel construction, navigation, and operation; and prohibiting or restricting passage in shipping safety-control zones extending as much as one hundred miles into the Arctic waters.[64]

On March 11, 1970, the Canadian government communicated to the U.S. embassy its decision to introduce the bill, and some discussion between representatives of the two governments apparently took place then. On March 20, President Nixon telephoned Prime Minister Trudeau, reportedly in anger because Canada was planning to act against U.S. interests without adequate consultation.[65] It is unclear whether these contacts on March 11 and 20 amounted to meaningful consultations.[66]

Upon introducing the bill on April 8, Prime Minister Trudeau said that the Arctic pollution controls would be developed by regulations to be adopted only after Canada had consulted other nations, such as the United States, with navigational interests in the area.[67] Other official statements of intent to consult were made, and consultations with interested governments were held for more than two years before the regulations were promulgated and the Act proclaimed.[68]

It has been suggested that the consultations simply served Canada's own interests, since the proposed regulations could not be enforced without foreign acquiescence.[69] Actually, they

[64] 18 & 19 Eliz. 2, ch. 47 (1970), *reprinted in* 9 INT'L LEGAL MATERIALS 543 (1970). The Act received the Royal Assent on June 26, 1970, but was not proclaimed until Aug. 2, 1972. At the same time the Arctic Waters bill was introduced, 12-mile territorial sea legislation also was introduced. The latter bill was enacted in December 1970. It is likely, though not entirely clear from published sources, that at least some of the consultations on the Arctic Waters bill also touched on the proposed territorial sea extension.

[65] *See* Dosman, The *Northern Sovereignty Crisis*, in THE ARCTIC IN QUESTION 34, 53–54 (E. Dosman ed. 1976); McConchie & Reid, *supra* note 47, at 171.

[66] *Compare* Dosman, *supra* note 65, (no indication of real give and take), *with* the statement of the Canadian Secretary of State for External Affairs, in 6 CAN. PARL. DEB., H.C., 28th Parl., 2d Sess. 5952–53 (1970) (frank and friendly discussions).

[67] Remarks to the press, Apr. 8, 1970, in 9 INT'L LEGAL MATERIALS 600, 601 (1970). A more elaborate approach, involving consultation with interested states, and consideration by "the competent international organization," before going forward with vessel-source pollution controls in ecologically fragile offshore areas, appears in the Third Law of the Sea Conference's Convention on the Law of the Sea, Dec. 10, 1982, art. 211(6), U.N. Doc. A/CONF.62/122 (1982).

[68] *See* 6 CAN. PARL. DEB., H.C., 28th Parl., 2d Sess. 5949, 5952 (1970); *id.* 6029; Beesley, *The Canadian Approach to International Environmental Law*, 1973 CAN. Y.B. INT'L L. 3, 6.

[69] M'Gonigle & Zacher, *Canadian Foreign Policy and the Control of Marine Pollution*, in CANADIAN FOREIGN POLICY AND THE LAW OF THE SEA 100, 119–20 (B. Johnson & M. Zacher eds. 1977).

could have been enforced, though at considerable cost. The fact that consultations could help to reduce that cost does diminish the normative significance of the consultations. It does not eliminate their significance, however, since responsible Canadian government officials have said they sought to ascertain and take account of other states' interests—not just to obtain their acquiescence—and the highest ranking government legal adviser has said that Canadian conduct in enacting the Arctic Waters Pollution Prevention Act acknowledged "the duty to consult and give notice before taking action that might have a harmful effect on other States."[70] Moreover, at least one United States negotiator clearly contemplated that the negotiations were capable of influencing the ultimate Canadian decision as to whether to implement the Act.[71] One must conclude that there were meaningful consultations even as to the basic decision to go ahead, but that they did not occur until after the Canadian government had made a preliminary decision to act unilaterally.[72] Even if the consultations were unlikely to deter the government from taking any unilateral action, they apparently did affect the extent of the burden on shipping imposed by the pollution control zones.

At about the same time that the Canadian pollution control measures were under consideration, the U.S. Congress was considering a bill that became the Marine Protection, Research,

[70]Statement by J. Alan Beesley, in U.N. Doc. A/AC.138/SC.III/SR.34, at 11 (1973).

[71]Statement of the Under Secretary of State for Political Affairs, in *Conventions and Amendments Relating to Pollution of the Sea by Oil: Hearings Before a Subcomm. of the Senate Comm. on Foreign Relations*, 92d Cong., 1st Sess. 171 (1971).

[72]There have been other instances in which states have made assertions of a right to establish extended maritime zones like Canada's—apparently without consulting those states affected—but have not immediately established the regulations necessary to make them effective. It is not always apparent whether the acting government has recognized a need to consult before enacting the regulations, or whether such consultations actually have occurred. An example is the Soviet Statute of the Administration of the North Sea Route, Sept. 16, 1971, 11 INT'L LEGAL MATERIALS 645 (1972). It was inspired by the Canadian Arctic Waters Pollution Prevention Act, but simply created an institutional framework within which decisions could be made. *See* Butler, *Soviet Maritime Jurisdiction in the Arctic*, 16 THE POLAR RECORD 418 (1972). (In a 1967 incident, however, the Soviet Union informed the United States, without notice or consultation, that its icebreakers could not use the Northeast Passage. *See* Pharand, *Soviet Union Warns United States Against Use of Northeast Passage*, 62 AM. J. INT'L L. 927 (1968).) Another example of a "framework" claim, apparently without prior bilateral consultations, was the Indian Presidential Proclamation of Nov. 29, 1956, on Conservation Zones, U.N. Doc. ST/LEG/SER.B/16, at 303 (1974). This was preceded by the 1955 U.N. Rome conference on conservation, but it is not clear whether India considered discussion at the conference as a prerequisite to the validity of the claim.

and Sanctuaries Act of 1972. It includes provisions designed to control ocean dumping off U.S. coasts. When the Executive Branch initially submitted ocean-dumping legislation to the Congress, it also submitted a draft ocean-dumping convention, modeled after the domestic bill, to a pre–Stockholm Conference international working group on marine pollution. Various countries were asked to comment in the ensuing months. They did so, and the United States then submitted another draft. The Executive Branch opposed efforts in Congress to assert greater U.S. control over ocean dumping by foreign vessels than would ultimately be permitted by the convention.[73] When the Ocean Dumping Convention was finally concluded, the U.S. regulations issued by the Environmental Protection Agency under the 1972 Act were consistent with it.[74]

The 1972 Act also contains provisions empowering the Executive Branch to designate marine sanctuaries seaward to the outer edge of the continental shelf, as defined in the 1958 Convention on the Continental Shelf. If a marine sanctuary is to extend beyond the territorial jurisdiction of the United States, the Secretary of State is directed to take appropriate action to negotiate with other states and to reach agreements with them. The Act clearly implies that marine sanctuary regulations could be applied even to nonnationals if the prior negotiations have been held without reaching agreement and if the application to nonnationals would not violate international law.[75]

In separate legislative measures initially enacted in 1970, the United States began a series of steps increasing its control over polluting discharges off its coasts. In 1969, the Legal Conference on Marine Pollution Damage had been held under IMCO sponsorship. After extensive negotiations, spurred in part by the threat of unilateral action by the U.S. Congress, the Conference produced the International Convention on Civil Lia-

[73] *See International Conference on Ocean Pollution: Hearings Before a Subcomm. of the Senate Comm. on Commerce*, 92d Cong., 2d Sess. 35 (1971); *Ocean Dumping of Waste Materials: Hearings Before a Subcomm. of the House Comm. on Merchant Marine and Fisheries*, 92d Cong., 1st Sess. 463 (1971). The Executive Branch objected to a bill that would have asserted a right to control ocean dumping based on the right to explore and exploit the continental shelf.

[74] *See* Convention on the Prevention of Marine Pollution by Dumping of Wastes and Other Matter, Dec. 29, 1972, 26 U.S.T. 2403, T.I.A.S. No. 8165; E.P.A. Final Regulations, 40 C.F.R. §§ 220.1 *et seq.*

[75] Marine Protection, Research, and Sanctuaries Act of 1972, Title III, 16 U.S.C. § 1432(c) & (g) (1976).

bility for Oil Pollution Damage. The United States acted very soon thereafter, without waiting for the Convention to come into force, by prohibiting harmful oil discharge within the 12-mile combined territorial sea and contiguous zone. Civil penalties and liability for cleanup costs were imposed. Although the U.S. legislation was not restricted to damage within the land territory or the territorial sea (as was the Convention), it remained within the scope of measures discussed at the Conference. This does appear to be a case in which discussion at a multilateral conference was considered a prerequisite to unilateral action.[76]

In the Federal Water Pollution Control Act Amendments of 1972, the coverage was revised to include hazardous substances as well as oil. Hazardous substances were to be defined later by Environmental Protection Agency (EPA) regulations. At the 1969 Conference on Marine Pollution Damage, there had been discussion of extending coverage to substances other than oil, and after the 1972 legislation had been enacted, foreign governments and private interests were given an opportunity (required by U.S. law) to comment on the proposed EPA regulations before they were revised and made final.[77]

Finally, Congress extended the coverage in the Clean Water Act of 1977 to prohibit the discharge of harmful quantities of oil or hazardous substances "which may affect natural resources belonging to, appertaining to, or under the exclusive management authority of the United States (including resources under the Fishery Conservation and Management Act of 1976)."[78]

[76]The U.S. legislation, as then enacted, appears in Pub. L. No. 91–224, § 102, Apr. 3, 1970, originally codified in 33 U.S.C. § 1161(b) & (f) (1970). For the relevant discussion at the 1969 Conference, see OFFICIAL RECORDS OF THE INT'L LEGAL CONF. ON MARINE POLLUTION DAMAGE, 1969, at 101–03, 563, 761 (IMCO, 1973). *See also* R. M'GONIGLE & M. ZACHER, POLLUTION, POLITICS, AND INTERNATIONAL LAW 288–89 (1979). Although most major shipping nations were represented at the 1969 Conference, some flag-of-convenience nations were not. Nevertheless, the Conference served the same purpose as individual consultations with interested states—identification and discussion of the disparate interests affected by the proposed extension of national authority.

[77]The 1972 legislation appears in Pub. L. No. 92–500, Oct. 18, 1972. The recodified act is in 33 U.S.C. § 1321 (1976). For the discussion at the 1969 Conference, *see* OFFICIAL RECORDS, *supra* note 76, at 615–17. EPA issued proposed rules on Dec. 30, 1975, and invited comments. It received comments from (inter alia) ten foreign interests, eight of which were Soviet state-controlled shipping companies. Letter to the author from the Director, EPA Criteria and Standards Division, May 5, 1978. EPA considered the comments, and issued its final regulations in March 1978. *See* 43 Fed. Reg. 10474 (1978). The same process was used by EPA to determine harmful quantities of hazardous substances. *Id.* at 10489.

[78]Pub. L. No. 95–217, § 58, Dec. 27, 1977, *amending* 33 U.S.C. § 1321.

This measure effectively extended cleanup liability to damage occurring as far as 200 miles offshore. The Department of State was concerned about this and sought the views of several foreign governments. A number of European governments expressed considerable concern, but the Department did not have time for extensive consultations with them because the 200-mile feature of the bill had been added quite late in the legislative process.[79] The State Department took the foreign governments' views into account, and opposed the 200-mile extension when the House-Senate conference was held on the bill. The conference did soften one of the bill's features (relating to penalties for discharges beyond the 12-mile zone) that had been most disturbing to the foreign governments. Thus, the informal consultations seem to have had some effect.

In addition to the Civil Liability Convention, the 1969 IMCO Conference produced the International Convention Relating to Intervention on the High Seas in Cases of Oil Pollution Casualties.[80] It permits a coastal state party to prevent, mitigate, or eliminate a grave and imminent danger to its coastline from oil pollution following a high seas maritime casualty. Before acting, however, the coastal state must consult other states affected by the maritime casualty, particularly the flag state or states. There is an exception to the consultation requirement in cases of extreme urgency requiring immediate measures. The same consultation requirement is incorporated by reference into the 1973 Protocol Relating to Intervention on the High Seas in Cases of Marine Pollution by Substances Other Than Oil.[81] It appears also in United States legislation implementing the Convention and Protocol.[82]

Meanwhile, Latin American extended-jurisdiction practice preceding the Third U.N. Law of the Sea Conference continued to be more comprehensive than the pollution control–conser-

[79]Letter to the author dated Feb. 28, 1978, from a former member of the State Department's Office of the Law of the Sea Negotiations.

[80]Nov. 29, 1969, 26 U.S.T. 765, T.I.A.S. No. 8068. The relevant consultation provisions are in article 3.

[81]Nov. 2, 1973, art. 2(1), in 13 INT'L LEGAL MATERIALS 605 (1974). A similar, though somewhat looser, provision appears in the Protocol Concerning Regional Co-operation in Combatting Pollution by Oil and Other Harmful Substances in Cases of Emergency, Apr. 24, 1978, art. 10(d), in 17 INT'L LEGAL MATERIALS 526 (1978) (applies to Persian Gulf and Gulf of Oman).

[82]33 U.S.C. §§ 1475, 1476 (1976), *as ammended*, 92 Stat. 344 (1978).

vation practice of most other states. In March 1970, Brazil proclaimed a 200-mile territorial sea.[83] Regulations applying it to fisheries within 100 miles were issued in March 1971; they were enforced from June 1 of that year. These regulations adversely affected U.S. fishermen who had developed a lucrative shrimp fishery in that area. Brazil and the United States held informal negotiations over a period of a year before the enforcement date (both before and after the regulations were issued in March 1971), but apparently not before the proclamation was issued in March 1970.[84] Agreement was reached in May 1972. The Nicaraguan Constitution of April 5, 1965, provided for control of fishing to 200 miles, but required implementation to become effective. The Nicaraguan government indicated its willingness to discuss the matter with any interested government before any steps were taken to implement the claim.[85] On the other hand, when Uruguay proclaimed a 200-mile exclusive maritime zone in December 1969, it indicated no willingness to consult other governments and apparently had not done so already.[86] But the zone was not immediately enforced, and, in fact, the major distant-water fishing nations had no significant interest in the waters off Uruguay.

In August 1974, the Icelandic government announced its intention to extend its exclusive fishery jurisdiction to 200 miles by the end of 1975. The announcement explained the delay by referring to the pending Law of the Sea Conference negotiations, expressing the hope that they would produce agreement in 1975.[87] When the 1975 session did not produce agreement, the Icelandic government published a regulation on July 15 of that year establishing the 200-mile exclusive fishery zone as of October 15. The government announced, however, that it would

[83] Decree Law No. 1098 of Mar. 25, 1970, in U.N. Doc. ST/LEG/SER.B/16, at 3 (1974).

[84] *See Commercial Fisheries: Hearings Before a Subcomm. of the House Comm. on Merchant Marine and Fisheries*, 92d Cong., 1st Sess. 328–29 (1971); N.Y. Times, June 6, 1971, at 12, col. 1 (city ed.).

[85] *See* Windley, *supra* note 52, at 498.

[86] *See* Paolillo, *Uruguay*, in THE CHANGING LAW OF THE SEA: WESTERN HEMISPHERE PERSPECTIVES, *supra* note 52, at 151, 156–57; U.N. Doc. A/C.1/PV.1773, at 9 (1970). Similarly, Panama apparently did not consult interested nations before claiming a 200-mile territorial sea in 1967, and made no provision for traditional fishing rights to continue. *See* Windley, *supra* note 52, at 499; U.N. Doc. ST/LEG/SER.B/15, at 105 (1970).

[87] The Times (London), Aug. 30, 1974, p. 5, col. 4.

enter into discussions with other states in order (inter alia) to mitigate their hardships.[88] Negotiations were held with the United Kingdom and West Germany, though agreements were not reached by the October 15 deadline.[89]

Discussions in 1974 at the first substantive session of the Third Law of the Sea Conference, as well as at previous preparatory meetings of the U.N. Seabeds Committee, focused in part on extended maritime zones. The Icelandic claim, like Norway's contemporaneous decision to claim an extended (50-mile) fishery zone,[90] and like later 200-mile fishery zone claims, reflected the substance of the Conference discussions.[91] There are published records indicating that some governments, in addition to Iceland, asserted extended territorial sea or fishery zone claims only after satisfying themselves, first, that substantial efforts to reach formal agreement had been made at the Conference, and second, that their claims were consistent with the emerging consensus.[92] In all cases since 1976, one could infer the same thing. In a few cases, such as the United States and

[88] *See* Regulations Concerning the Fishery Limits Off Iceland, July 15, 1975, art. 2, in ICELANDIC MINISTRY FOR FOREIGN AFFAIRS, THE FISHERY LIMITS OFF ICELAND: 200 NAUTICAL MILES 13 (1975); *see also id.* at 17, 32.

[89] *See* Financial Times, Oct. 30, 1975, p. 9, col. 1. The October 15 deadline did not immediately affect British fishing interests, since its fishing agreement with Iceland ran until November 13.

[90] *See* chapter III at note 49 *supra.*

[91] *See* the Working Paper of the Second Committee on main trends of the Conference, Oct. 17, 1974, para. 99, in Third U.N. CONF. ON THE LAW OF THE SEA, OR, vol. 3, at 122 (1975).

The earlier Pakistani 50-mile fishery zone claim (Mar. 20, 1973), U.N. Doc. ST/LEG/SER.B/18, at 344 (1976), came after extended maritime zones had been discussed in the Seabeds Committee, but before the Third Law of the Sea Conference began. The Nigerian 50-mile territorial sea claim in November 1974 apparently was intended primarily to protect fishing interests. It was made after the first Conference negotiating session, and apparently after specific discussions had been held at the Conference regarding Nigeria's intentions. *See* WEST AFRICA, Sept. 23, 1974, at 1176. On the other hand, when Nigeria extended its territorial sea claim from 12 to 30 miles in 1971, there were no prior consultations. That extension (like the later extension to 50 miles, if it was a true territorial sea claim) violated international law. *See* Akinsanya, *The Nigerian Territorial Waters Decress of 1967 and 1971*, 16 INDIAN J. INT'L L. 276, 279–80 (1976); *but see* Ajomo, *The Nigerian Territorial Waters (Amendment) Decree 1971*, 3 NIGERIAN J. CONTEMP. L. 68 (1972).

[92] *See, e.g.*, the statements of the Canadian Secretary of State for External Affairs in March and June 1976, in 1977 CAN. Y.B. INT'L L. 353, 356; U.S. Secretary of State Kissinger's news conference, Oct. 18, 1975, in 73 DEP'T ST. BULL. 686 (1975); Szekely, *Mexico's Unilateral Claim to a 200-mile Exclusive Economic Zone: Its International Significance*, 4 OCEAN DEVELOPMENT & INT'L L. 195, 196–201 (1977); Yanai & Asomura, *Japan and the Emerging Order of the Sea—Two Maritime Laws of Japan*, 1977 JAPANESE ANN INT'L L. 48, 50, 65–66.

Canadian 200-mile fishery claims in 1976, there are published reports of bilateral consultations with specially interested states at the Conference.[93]

These consultations—multilateral, in the context of the Conference negotiations, and bilateral, as pressures developed to act before formal agreement could be reached—came after the prospect of unilaterally claimed 200-mile zones was a reality for many states, but in most cases, before a definitive decision to act unilaterally was made. They served the essential consultative purpose of injecting into the decision-making process the views of states with varying interests likely to be affected. Nevertheless, it can no more be said here than it could in connection with the 1958 and 1960 Law of the Sea Conferences that most governments felt *obliged* to consult at the Third Conference before deciding to act. That Conference provided a convenient sounding board and a forum for the development of the law of the sea to accommodate new maritime zones, but the participants did not perceive the Conference as satisfying a procedural requirement for unilateral action.

Greater normative significance attaches to the specific bilateral negotiations that fishery-zone states held with interested governments before they enforced their new zones against foreign fishing vessels.[94] These negotiations took for granted that

[93] While various bills calling for a 200-mile fishery zone were pending before the U.S. Congress, State Department representatives discussed them informally at the Conference with Soviet and Japanese representatives, and more formally with Canada. *See Emergency Marine Fisheries Protection Act of 1974*: Hearing Before the Senate Comm. on Foreign Relations, 93d Cong., 2d Sess. 55 (1974); 73 DEP'T ST. BULL. 642 (1975). There also may have been formal consultations with the Soviet Union outside the Conference in early 1976. *See* Joint U.S.-U.S.S.R. Communique, Mar. 1, 1976, 74 DEP'T ST. BULL. 498 (1976). Canada's bilateral negotiations (before its fishing zone was announced) with five states having the principal fishing interests off its coasts are discussed in Buzan & Johnson, *Canada at the Third Law of the Sea Conference: Strategy, Tactics and Policy*, in CANADIAN FOREIGN POLICY AND THE LAW OF THE SEA, *supra* note 47, at 255, 288–89.

[94] For example, the U.S. legislation delayed the effective date six months from the date of enactment in order to give time for negotiations. A Congressional Research Service memorandum took the position that this met the prior consultation requirement for unilateral conservation measures under the Geneva Convention on Fishing and Conservation of the Living Resources of the High Seas, *supra* note 30. *See* STAFF OF SENATE COMM. ON COMMERCE, 94TH CONG., 2D SESS., A LEGISLATIVE HISTORY OF THE FISHERY CONSERVATION AND MANAGEMENT ACT OF 1976 847, 851 (Comm. Print 1976). Australia delayed the planned effective date of its 200-mile zone pending fisheries negotiations with both Korea and Japan. Financial Times, Apr. 5, 1979, p. 22, col. 6. Canada conducted extensive negotiations with countries accounting for more than 88 percent of the foreign catch off its coasts. 1977 CAN. Y.B. INT'L L. 355, 358.

the contemplated 200-mile zones would go into force and that they would involve preferences for local fishing interests, but within those constraints, the negotiations gave foreign interests some opportunity to protect themselves. In almost every case, the claimant state seems to have regarded the negotiations as essential, and representatives of foreign fishing interests clearly have regarded them as such.[95] Like the Canadian Arctic waters negotiations in 1970, they were useful to the enacting states, but that did not extinguish their normative significance.

Another form of jurisdictional extension enjoying considerable popularity among coastal states is that resulting from the drawing of new baselines across bays and other partially enclosed areas. There is no evidence that states have engaged in any practice of prior international consultation regarding such basics as the location and length of closing lines. With few exceptions, state practice seems at most to call for consultation with interested states to phase out their interests—usually involving fishing activities.[96] One exception involved Canada's negotiations with the United States, resulting in an agreement preserving U.S. fishing interests, before Canada drew fisheries closing lines across the entrances to the Gulf of Saint Lawrence, Bay of Fundy, Queen Charlotte Sound, and Dixon Entrance–

[95] The 200-mile zones of European Community member states have presented unique problems. At the direction of the Council of Ministers, each member state adopted a 200-mile zone against nonmenbers in early 1977. These zones were not to be applied against other member states, although the United Kingdom and Ireland argued in favor of exclusive zones of as much as 50 miles within the Community. As an interim measure, member states were allowed to enact unilateral conservation measures if they first sought the Commission's approval. When the U.K. on three occasions established conservation zones without sufficient consultation, the Commission objected and challenged the failure to consult in proceedings before the European Court of Justice. *See* chapter III at notes 52–56. Ireland imposed a 50-mile exclusive fishing zone in April 1977, even against other member states, but it acted only after negotiations in the Council failed to produce agreement. Financial Times, April 7, 1977, at 4, col. 5; N.Y. Times, May 5, 1977, at A8, col. 1 (city ed.).

[96] For example, when Ireland drew straight baselines in 1959, effective Jan. 1, 1960, there apparently had been no prior consultations. *Cf.* O'Higgins, *The Irish Maritime Jurisdiction Act, 1959, in* 9 INT'L COMP. L.Q. 325, 327–31 (1960). The same may be said of the Kenyan Proclamation of June 6, 1969, U.N. Doc. ST/LEG/SER.B/15, at 95, 96 (1970), declaring Ungwana Bay to be internal waters. When Libya in 1973 claimed the Gulf of Sirte as internal or territorial waters, it consulted neither the United States nor (apparently) any other interested government. For the U.S. protest, see 68 AM. J. INT'L L. 510 (1974). The lack of consultation with the United States was confirmed in a letter dated September 30, 1974, from a member of the State Department Office of the Legal Adviser to the author. The Soviet Union did not consult Japan before drawing a 108-mile closing line across the Bay of Peter the Great in 1957. *See* chapter III at note 88 *supra*.

Hecate Strait.[97] This exception was based on a number of factors, including prior treaty rights, geographical proximity, and the close political ties between the two nations.

Finally, there is the type of ocean jurisdictional claim designed for military security purposes. An example is the air-defense identification zone, which may extend as much as 300 miles offshore. Aircraft entering the zone must identify themselves or run the risk of interception. Another example is the missile testing area over the high seas. As in the case of nuclear weapons testing discussed later in this chapter, there is no apparent practice of consulting interested states before a national security decision is made to assert such authority over airspace above the high seas.[98]

2. Claims Not Involving New Extensions

In a number of instances, new ocean-related rights have been claimed without any assertion of a right to extend coastal jurisdiction. These include assertions of new distributive, conservation, or enforcement authority within previously established jurisdictional zones and assertion of new or controversial high seas rights. As in the preceding section, the question is whether there is a duty to consult at all, and, if so, whether that duty arises before a basic decision is made or simply before it is implemented.

The Third Law of the Sea Conference's Convention on the Law of the Sea contains an express prior-consultation provision concerning conservation of such anadromous stocks as salmon. The provision says that the state of origin is to establish the appropriate regulatory measures (which would not necessarily be limited to its exclusive economic zone) and "may, after con-

[97]Other states with traditional fishing interests in those areas were consulted only for purposes of phasing them out; states with interests but no traditional fishing apparently were not consulted at all. *See* Statements of the Canadian Minister of Fisheries and Forestry, 6 CAN. PARL. DEB., H.C., 28th Parl., 2d Sess. 6183–85 (1970); 2 *id.*, 3d Sess. 2189–90 (1970); *cf.* Legault, *supra* note 42, at 386.

For a treaty obligation to consult between Spain and Portugal, *see* chapter III note 61 *supra.*

[98]Existing air defense zones are discussed, without mention of prior consultation, in J. MURCHISON, THE CONTIGUOUS AIR SPACE ZONE IN INTERNATIONAL LAW 7–9 (1955); Hayton, *Jurisdiction of the Littoral State in the "Air Frontier,"* 3 PHIL. INT'L L. J. 369, 384–89 (1964); Note, *Air Defense Identification Zones: Creeping Jurisdiction in the Airspace,* 18 VA. J. INT'L L. 485 (1978). For discussion of the establishment of missile testing areas, see 4 M. WHITEMAN, *supra* note 2, at 619–23.

sultation with other States . . . fishing these stocks, establish total allowable catches for stocks originating in its rivers."[99] Bilateral United States agreements signed in 1977 with Japan and Canada regarding salmon conservation contained prior consultation provisions.[100]

For coastal fisheries within the 200-mile economic zone, the Convention requires the coastal state to give other states access to the surplus allowable catch beyond the former's harvesting capacity. In allocating the surplus, the coastal state is to consider such factors as the interests of states without their own full economic zones, developing states in the region, and states traditionally fishing in the zone.[101] Although the Convention does not expressly mention consultation in this regard, the *Fisheries Jurisdiction* Cases suggest that when noncoastal states have significant fishing interests that may not be extinguished arbitrarily by the coastal state, the latter must negotiate—or at least consult—with them rather than simply establishing a unilateral regime governing their interests.[102] In the current economic zone context, the effect of these cases would be that the coastal state may unilaterally determine (without consultation) the total allowable catch and the available surplus, but would have to consult the significantly interested states before allocating the surplus among them. This arrangement is reflected in many bilateral fishery agreements.[103]

[99] Convention on the Law of the Sea, *supra* note 67, art. 66(2).

[100] U.S.-Japan, Mar. 18, 1977, art. 6, 28 U.S.T. 7507, T.I.A.S. No. 8728, 16 INT'L LEGAL MATERIALS 289 (1977), requires bilateral consultations regarding conservation measures in waters where U.S.-origin anadromous species mingle with those of other origins. U.S.-Canada, Feb. 24, 1977, art. 6, 16 INT'L LEGAL MATERIALS 590 (1977), permitted Canada to designate open fishing days for chinook and chum salmon, after consultation with the United States. The agreement with Canada terminated on December 31, 1977.

[101] Convention on the Law of the Sea, *supra* note 67, art. 62(2) & (3).

[102] *See* text at note 39 *supra*.

[103] For U.S. agreements, see notes 104 and 105 *infra*. Other states' bilateral agreements containing prior consultation duties for allotment of any fishery surplus include (*1*) Canada-Norway, Dec. 2, 1975, art. 2(2)(c), in 21 INTERNATIONAL PROTECTION OF THE ENVIRONMENT 244 (B. Rüster, B. Simma, & M. Bock eds. 1981); (*2*) Canada-Poland, May 14, 1976, art. 2(2)(c), *id.* at 294; (*3*) Canada-U.S.S.R., May 19, 1976, art. 2(2)(c), *id.* at 297; (*4*) Canada-Spain, June 10, 1976, art. 2(2)(c), *id.* at 305; (*5*) Mexico-Cuba, July 26, 1976, art. 2(1)(c), *id.* at 319; (*6*) Canada-Portugal, July 29, 1976, art. 2(2)(c), *id.* at 324; (7) Norway-U.S.S.R., Oct. 15, 1976, art. 2(b), *id.* at 373; (*8*) European Economic Community (EEC)–Denmark (in respect of Faroe Islands), Mar. 15, 1977, art. 2(b), 22 *id.* at 21; (*9*) EEC-Sweden, Mar. 21, 1977, art. 2(1)(b), 22 *id.* at 41; (*10*) Norway-Poland, Mar. 28, 1977, arts. 3 & 4, 22 *id.* at 47; (*11*) Japan–South Africa, Dec. 6, 1977, art. 2(1)(c), 22 *id.* at 89; (*12*) Sweden-Poland, Feb. 1, 1978, arts. 3(1) & 4, 22

United States bilateral fishery agreements fall into two categories. The agreements negotiated with Canada and Japan, the two states with the most significant fishing interests in the United States' 200-mile zone, contained prior consultation requirements.[104] United States agreements with countries having lesser fishing interests in the zone have contained only an obligation to conduct periodic consultations.[105] These latter agreements reflect the principle that specific, prior consultation is not required when the interests affected are not truly substantial.

There is one particularly interesting instance of preeconomic-zone conservation practice involving an area under U.S. control. In 1971 a bill was introduced in Congress that would have limited the Canadian and Japanese haul of fur-seal skins from the Pribilof Islands. The Interim Convention on Conservation of North Pacific Fur Seals, to which the United States, Canada, and Japan were parties, provided for recommendations by the North Pacific Fur Seal Commission concerning the size of the seasonal kill.[106] The State Department took the position that the proposed unilateral sealing restriction, if enacted

id. at 94; (*13*) Spain-Portugal, Sept. 22, 1978, art. 2(c), 22 *id.* at 100; (*14*) EEC-Norway, undated (1980), art. 2(1)(b), 22 *id.* at 173; (*15*) EEC-Canada, Dec. 30, 1981, art. 2(2)(c), 21 INT'L LEGAL MATERIALS 34 (1982).

[104]The agreement with Canada on East Coast Fishery Resources, Mar. 29, 1979, art. 16(1), Senate Exec. V, 96th Cong., 1st Sess. 13 (1979), would have set forth catch quotas for each party in designated zones, but provided that if a portion of a quota was surplus to the party's needs, it must consider a request by the other party for an allocation from the surplus. There also would have been a prior consultation provision if jointly managed stocks from one party's exclusive fishery zone were to be made available to third states. *Id.*, Annex A, para. 1(e). President Reagan withdrew the agreement from the Senate when it appeared that Senate objections to the quotas would preclude its approval. *See* President Reagan's message to the Senate, Apr. 21, 1981, in 81 DEP'T ST. BULL., June 1981, at 32–33.

The agreement with Japan, Mar. 18, 1977, arts. 3 and 4(1), 28 U.S.T. 7507, T.I.A.S. No. 8728, 16 INT'L LEGAL MATERIALS 289 (1977), requires the United States to take into account, "as appropriate," the periodic bilateral consultations with Japan in determining the total allowable catch and the portion that will not be harvested by U.S. vessels.

There were extensive U.S.-Canadian consultations before Canada closed its fishing zones to U.S. commercial fishing in June 1978. (The U.S. retaliated in kind.)

[105]Typical is the agreement with Poland, Aug. 2, 1976, 28 U.S.T. 1681, T.I.A.S. No. 8524, which calls for periodic bilateral consultations but requires only notification to Poland of decisions affecting the Polish catch. Similar agreements with Mexico, Nov. 24, 1976, 29 U.S.T. 823, T.I.A.S. No. 8853, and Aug. 26, 1977, 29 U.S.T. 781, T.I.A.S. No. 8852, were terminated in 1981 at the instigation of Mexico. *See* 81 DEP'T ST. BULL., Mar. 1981, at 31.

[106]Art. 5, para. 2(d), 8 U.S.T. 2283, T.I.A.S. No. 3948, 314 U.N.T.S. 105.

without reference to the Commission's issued findings and recommendations, and "without, at the least, consultation with the other parties to the Convention, would not be consistent with United States treaty obligations."[107] The offending section was dropped from the bill.

The State Department's position was significant on two counts. First, it equated discussions among representatives of the interested parties in the Commission with prior consultations; and second, it suggested that if a duly constituted conservation organization makes a recommendation that is within its authority and is directed to a specific member state, that state should consult the other states affected by the recommendation if it plans not to follow the organization's advice. Although consultation could be within the organization, it would have to deal specifically with the state's contemplated course of action.

Canada acted consistently with these principles when it moved unilaterally in 1972 to ban commercial salmon fishing off New Brunswick and Quebec after unsuccessfully urging a general ban within the International Commission for the Northwest Atlantic Fisheries.[108] On the other hand, when the Soviet Union declared a limited ban on fur sealing around the Komandorskiye Islands in 1970, it apparently did not consult within the North Pacific Fur Seal Commission.[109]

There have been a number of instances in which coastal states have declared marginally sedentary species to be sedentary for purposes of exclusive continental shelf exploitation rights. Often this has occurred as a result of extensive harvesting by nationals of one or two foreign states. There appears to be no established practice of consulting those states before legislation is enacted designating (or authorizing an official to designate) species as sedentary, but there normally has been consultation, or at least an effort to consult, before the legislation enters into force.

For example:

(*a*) When Australia enacted its Pearl Fisheries Act in 1952, providing for the exclusion of Japanese pearl fishermen from

[107] State Department letter, Sept. 9, 1971, in *Marine Mammals: Hearings Before a Subcomm. of the House Comm. on Merchant Marine and Fisheries*, 92d Cong., 1st Sess. 49, 50 (1971).

[108] *See Recent Developments in the Law of the Sea IV: A Synopsis*, 10 San Diego L. Rev. 559, 561 (1973).

[109] Dehner, *Creeping Jurisdiction in the Arctic: Has the Soviet Union Joined Canada?*, 13 Harv. Int'l L.J. 271, 277 (1972).

the Arafura Sea and adjacent waters, Japan apparently had not been consulted. However, Australia subsequently held extensive negotiations with Japan, and the Act was proclaimed (in September 1953) only after the negotiations had failed to produce agreement.[110]

(*b*) In 1964, the United States Congress authorized the Interior Department to define sedentary species. The Department did so only in 1968, after four years of study and negotiations with Japan and the Soviet Union, the two nations primarily interested in the important Alaskan king crab fishery.[111]

(*c*) The Soviet Union consulted Japan before declaring the king crab a creature of the Soviet continental shelf.[112]

(*d*) The Bahamas declared on July 9, 1975, that as of August 1 the spiny lobster would be considered a sedentary resource of its continental shelf. The Bahamas did not consult the United States before July 9 regarding the substantial U.S. fishing interest in the Bahamian lobster banks, nor did the U.S. State Department expect to have its views solicited at that point.[113] Nevertheless, the Bahamian government was willing to consult with the United States government before August 1, and a number of attempts were made by

[110] *See* Oda, *A Consideration of the Problems of Conservation and Distribution of Marine Resources*, 18 ZEITSCHRIFT FÜR AUSLÄNDISCHES OFFENTLICHES RECHT UND VÖLKERRECHT 61, 84–85 (1957); Leyser, *Fisheries Zones in the South-West Pacific*, 14 ARCHIV DES VÖLKERRECHTS 145, 151 (1969).

[111] *See* L. JUDA, OCEAN SPACE RIGHTS: DEVELOPING U.S. POLICY 73 (1975); Fidell, *Ten Years Under the Bartlett Act: A Status Report on the Prohibition on Foreign Fishing*, 54 BOSTON U.L. REV. 703, 727 (1974).

When the United States designated the lobster a continental shelf resource (by legislation) in 1974, it had not engaged in specific consultations regarding its intention. But it did not immediately enforce its rights against the state (Canada) with the principal interest in the lobster fishery. *See U.S. Practice in Int'l Law*, 68 AM. J. INTL L. 511–12 (1974). Because of the delay, one may infer that there were consultations with Canada before enforcement was contemplated against Canadian vessels.

[112] *See* W. BUTLER, THE SOVIET UNION AND THE LAW OF THE SEA 148–49 (1971). When the Soviet Union declared the scallop sedentary, it did not immediately apply its regulation against foreign fishermen. *Territorial Seas: Hearings Before a Subcomm. of the House Comm. on Merchant Marine and Fisheries*, 93d Cong., 1st Sess. 56, 61 (1973). The Japanese were interested in the fishery, and presumably were consulted after the declaration but before enforcement.

[113] Letters to the author from officials in the State Department's Office of Oceans and Fisheries Affairs, Oct. 24, 1975, and Jan. 9, 1976.

both governments to do so. They did not actually get together until August 13.[114]

(*e*) On the other hand, Brazil apparently enforced against France (and then announced) its claim to the lobsters of its continental shelf, without having consulted or having offered to consult the French.[115]

When new measures are taken to enforce existing continental shelf or fishery zone claims (not involving any new designation of sedentary species), there appears to be no more than a preenforcement duty to consult any close ally that is greatly interested in the affected resource. Thus, when the United States enacted the Bartlett Act in 1964, authorizing enforcement of U.S. continental shelf regulations on the high seas, both the President and the State Department assured Japan that it would be fully consulted before any enforcement that might affect its longstanding king crab fishery.[116] Apparently, no similar assurances were given to other governments.

More recently, when the State Department announced on September 5, 1974, that as of December 5 the Coast Guard would begin to board foreign vessels on the high seas to arrest crews suspected of bottom trawling on the continental shelf, it apparently contemplated meaningful consultations only with Canada before enforcement. The 90-day grace period was to be used for negotiations with a number of governments, but the discussions with all except Canada were strictly to get their cooperation in enforcing the measures proposed by the United States. The new enforcement procedure, however, was not to be applied to Canadian vessels as of December 5, and the State Department announced its intention to discuss the matter with the appropriate Canadian authorities.[117]

A coastal state's authority over the continental shelf and the economic zone implies certain rights when scientific research in those areas is proposed by other states. The precise nature

[114] Letter of Oct. 24, 1975, *supra* note 113.

[115] The incident is discussed, without mention of prior consultation, in 1 A. Szekely, *supra* note 12, at 185–87; Azzam, *The Dispute Between France and Brazil over Lobster Fishing in the Atlantic*, 13 Int'l & Comp. L.Q. 1453 (1964).

[116] *See* 50 Dep't St. Bull. 936 (1964).

[117] *See Emergency Marine Fisheries Protection Act of 1974: Hearing Before the Senate Comm. on Foreign Relations*, 93d Cong., 2d Sess. 24 (1974); 1974 Digest of U.S. Practice in Int'l Law 321–26.

of those rights was a matter of considerable debate at the Third Law of the Sea Conference, relating primarily to whether the coastal state's consent must be obtained, and if so, under what conditions it may be withheld. Usually, these questions are discussed from the perspective of the researching state. That is, one asks what conditions a state proposing to conduct research must meet in order to proceed. Under the Convention on the Continental Shelf, it must obtain the coastal state's consent for continental shelf research, but the consent should not normally be withheld if the request is for "pure" scientific research.[118] Under the Convention on the Law of the Sea, the distinction between pure and applied research is spelled out in detail. Normally, the coastal state is to grant consent for pure research projects on the shelf or in the economic zone (beyond territorial waters), subject to certain exceptions having to do with such things as disturbance to the shelf or the marine environment, or the supplying of inaccurate information by the researching state. It "may however in [its] discretion withhold [its] consent to the conduct of a marine scientific research project of another State or competent international organization" if the project involves applied research having direct significance to the exploration and exploitation of resources.[119] In all cases, the researching state is to supply essential information regarding the proposed project to the coastal state.[120]

For purposes of this study, it is useful to examine the situation posed by these norms from the perspective of the coastal state. Clearly, under the regime stemming from the Third Law of the Sea Conference, a coastal state could not lawfully issue a blanket prohibition against all scientific research on its continental shelf or in its economic zone without any possibility of an exception; it could not even do so as to all applied research in those areas. Although it could make an initial decision that it does not favor applied research by some or all nonnationals in those areas, it must ultimately act on a case-by-case basis. Since a coastal state must act in good faith in deciding whether to grant or withhold consent, it could not ignore information supplied to it by the researching state. In other words, it must

[118]Convention on the Continental Shelf, Apr. 29, 1958, art. 5(8), 15 U.S.T. 471, T.I.A.S. No. 5578, 499 U.N.T.S. 311.

[119]Convention on the Law of the Sea, *supra* note 67, art. 246(5). There is a special regime for certain continental shelf areas beyond 200 miles.

[120]*Id.* art. 248.

make its operative decision after receiving significant input from the state to be affected by the decision. Whether or not that input includes face-to-face discussion, the applicant state will have had the opportunity to consult, in the sense that it will have injected its interest into the ultimate decision-making process.

There are other cases in which a coastal or port state may want to deny access to foreigners. For example, in a number of instances, a port state has threatened to close its ports or deny access to its navigable waters if consultations in an international forum did not produce desired safety or environmental results. In some of these instances, the threatened action was ultimately taken. For example, when the United States government wished to tighten fire safety standards for cruise ships (including foreign ships) leaving U.S. ports, it first conducted negotiations within the Inter-Governmental Maritime Consultative Organization (IMCO) for amendments to the International Convention for the Safety of Life at Sea, holding open the prospect of unilateral action if the negotiations failed to produce acceptable amendments. When the ensuing amendments had not gone into force by November 1968, unilateral U.S. standards were imposed.[121]

Similarly, in 1972 the United States began trying to induce other states within IMCO to strengthen international design standards for oil tankers to prevent massive spills from accidents. The United States has enacted legislation since then providing regulatory authority for navigation in waters under U.S. jurisdiction and authorizing unilateral design regulations for tankers entering U.S. navigable waters.[122] More recently, other nations have threatened unilateral action if effective international standards could not be negotiated.[123] Once the new international standards had been negotiated, the United States and some other nations felt justified in implementing them

[121]*See* 46 U.S.C. § 362(c) (1976); 112 CONG. REC. 27282 (1966); *Safety of Life at Sea: Hearings Before a Subcomm. of the Senate Comm. on Commerce*, 89th Cong., 2d Sess. 118–19 (1966); *Passenger Vessel Legislation: Hearing Before a Subcomm. of the House Comm. on Merchant Marine and Fisheries*, 91st Cong., 1st Sess. 6–7 (1969).

[122]*See* 33 U.S.C. §§ 1221–27; 46 U.S.C. § 391a (1976), *as amended*, Pub. L. No. 95–474, 95th Cong., 2d Sess. (1978). Tanker regulation actually began with the Tank Vessel Act of 1936, but the standards were tightened in 1972 and again in 1978. *See* H.R. REP. NO. 95–1384, pt.I, 95th Cong., 2d Sess., *reprinted in* 1978 U.S. CODE CONG. & ADMIN. NEWS 5032, 5035–42.

[123]Los Angeles Times, Jan. 19, 1978, pt. I, p. 2, col. 5.

without waiting for the protocols incorporating the standards to go into force.[124]

The enactments mentioned in the two preceding paragraphs followed international negotiations, as did the U.S. offshore pollution-control legislation discussed earlier. In each of these cases, the United States, acting as the protagonist, negotiated with a specific regulatory scheme in mind. It withheld action until the negotiations had been conducted. Because of this direct, narrow focus, these negotiations may be regarded more convincingly as evincing the necessary subjective intent for a prior consultation norm than the wide-ranging Law of the Sea Conference negotiations.

The practice just considered is reinforced, in large measure, by the normative scheme from the Third Law of the Sea Conference relating to coastal states' authority to impose standards for foreign vessels in the territorial sea. Coastal states may establish national regulations to prevent vessel-source pollution in their territorial seas, but their regulations may not apply to the design, construction, staffing, or equipment of foreign vessels unless they are giving effect to generally accepted international rules or standards. In other words, the kind of authority asserted by the United States in 1972 over oil tankers in territorial waters would have to be preceded by and consistent with international negotiations that achieve some degree of consensus. In the case of vessels using port facilities or entering internal waters, however, there would be no prior consultation duty even as to design standards.[125]

The Convention on the Law of the Sea deals with another variety of unilateral preventive measure by permitting states bordering straits used for international navigation to designate sea-lanes and to prescribe traffic separation schemes. Before doing so, however, such states must refer their proposals to "the competent international organization" with a view to their adoption.[126] The intent is to give a voice to states with significant navigational interests in the straits.[127]

[124] *See* 8 ENVIR. REP. 1696, 1697 (1978).

[125] Convention on the Law of the Sea, *supra* note 67, arts. 21(2) and 211(1) & (3).

[126] *Id.* art. 41(4).

[127] This would include not only states whose ships often pass through the straits but also those who rely on the shipping that passes through them. *Cf.* Agreement Between Australia and Papua–New Guinea, Dec. 18, 1978, art. 7(6), 18 INT'L LEGAL MATERIALS 291 (1979).

Beyond the limits of national jurisdiction, a prior consultation norm has been developing for certain activities involving the seabed in the absence of a functioning international regulatory regime. The Convention on the Law of the Sea calls for prior consultation when proposed seabed activities might affect the interests of a coastal state across whose jurisdiction seabed resources lie and would require its prior consent when the activity may result in exploitation of resources within the coastal state's jurisdiction.[128]

These provisions grew out of the General Assembly's 1970 Declaration of Principles Governing the Sea-Bed. It provides that states conducting activities in the seabed area "shall pay due regard to the rights and legitimate interests of coastal States in the region of such activities, as well as of all other States which may be affected by such activities. Consultations shall be maintained with the coastal States concerned with respect to activities relating to the exploration of the area and the exploitation of its resources with a view to avoiding infringement of such rights and interests."[129] The primary concern was to give the coastal state a voice in protecting its special fishery conservation interest in the area of the high seas adjacent to its territorial sea.[130] Although the 200-mile fishery or economic zone has now supplanted the fishery conservation regime adjacent to the territorial sea, this change would not supersede the principle established by the 1970 Declaration. The principle is that when seabed activities pose a risk to a special interest of a coastal state, there is a duty to consult it. The duty would not necessarily extend to states with less clearly defined interests—the "other States which may be affected by such activities" mentioned in the 1970 Declaration.

When the United States seriously began to contemplate unilateral exploitation of the deep seabed in 1972, the State Department's Legal Adviser said, "We must consult with other

[128]Convention on the Law of the Sea, *supra* note 67, art. 142(2). Although many of the Convention's deep seabed provisions are too controversial to reflect custom, there is no serious controversy over article 142(2).

[129]General Assembly Declaration of Principles Governing the Sea-Bed and the Ocean Floor and the Subsoil Thereof, Beyond the Limits of National Jurisdiction, G.A. Res. 2749, para. 12, 25 U.N. GAOR, Supp. (No. 28) at 24, U.N. Doc. A/8028 (1970).

[130]*See* the Report of the Seabed Committee, 24 U.N. GAOR Supp. (No. 22) at 24, 25, U.N. Doc. A/7622 (1969). The fishery conservation interest had been recognized in article 6 of the 1958 Geneva Convention on Fishing and Conservation of the Living Resources of the High Seas.

countries—those whose [nationals,] like ours, are beginning to pay serious attention to the commercial possibilities of seabed mining—and those countries whose long-range Law of the Sea objectives might be deleteriously affected if deep ocean mining begins under a unilaterally established regime."[131] As the Third Law of the Sea Conference progressed, one of the chief U.S. negotiators made it clear that the United States would not unilaterally begin seabed exploitation unless negotiations at the Conference became deadlocked or unduly prolonged.[132] The U.S. Congress enacted a unilateral interim procedure for seabed mining in 1980 (authorizing U.S. companies to begin exploitation no sooner than January 1, 1988), but it did so only after extensive exchanges at the Conference about the permissibility of such unilateral action.[133]

The U.S. legislation is based on the proposition that, in the absence of an agreed international regulatory regime for the deep seabed, the right to exploit minerals beyond national jurisdiction is essentially a freedom of the high seas. When the exercise of this or any other freedom of the high seas would affect adversely the interests of readily identifiable states in their exercise of high seas freedoms, the combination of article 2 of the Geneva Convention on the High Seas and the *Fisheries Jurisdiction* Cases would impose a duty to consult those states. Article 2 of the High Seas Convention, which represents custom, provides that the freedoms of the high seas "shall be exercised by all States with reasonable regard to the interests of other States in their exercise of the freedom of the high seas."[134] The *Fisheries Jurisdiction* Cases establish that a duty to take ac-

[131]Letter from John R. Stevenson in *Law of the Sea and Peaceful Uses of the Seabeds: Hearings Before a Subcomm. of the House Comm. on Foreign Affairs*, 92d Cong., 2d Sess. 25 (1972). *See also Mineral Resources of the Deep Seabed: Hearings Before a Subcomm. of the Senate Comm. on Interior and Insular Affairs*, 93d Cong., 1st Sess. 20, 25 (1973).

[132]Statement of Ambassador Elliot L. Richardson, 78 DEP'T ST. BULL., April 1978, at 54, 56.

[133]The U.S. enactment is the Deep Seabed Hard Minerals Act of 1980, 30 U.S.C. §§ 1401–73 (Supp. IV 1980). For discussion of the Conference exchanges concerning the proposed legislation, see Oxman, *The Third United Nations Conference on the Law of the Sea: The Seventh Session (1978)*, 73 AM.J.INT'L L. 1, 30–38 (1979); Oxman, *The Third United Nations Conference on the Law of the Sea: The Eighth Session (1979)*, 74 *id.* at 1, 8–9 (1980).

[134]Convention on the High Seas, Apr. 29, 1958, art. 2, 13 U.S.T. 2312, T.I.A.S. No. 5200, 450 U.N.T.S. 82. This language was drafted with nuclear weapons tests primarily in mind. *See Industrial Radioactive Waste Disposal: Hearings Before a Subcomm. of the Joint Comm. on Atomic Energy*, 86th Cong., 1st Sess. 2875–77 (1959). Nevertheless, it clearly is broad enough to cover all freedoms of the high seas.

count of other states' interests implies a duty to negotiate with them (and thus to consult them) when those interests are at stake.[135] Thus, if a maritime right is not absolute, its exercise in a way that raises issues not theretofore settled must be pursuant to negotiations with those whose interests are involved. This duty would apply not only in favor of states with particularly important, historic interests (such as the U.K. and German fishing interests in the *Fisheries Jurisdiction* Cases), but to other affected states as well, since the Court did not restrict the scope of its principle to states with interests as compelling as those of the United Kingdom and West Germany. For example, if a state wished to lay a submarine cable across a deep seabed area in which other identifiable states had lawful, reasonably well-defined prospective mining interests, it would be implicit in the qualified right to lay the cable that negotiations be held with those states.

The right to dispose of certain wastes may well be another qualified freedom of the high seas, subject to the implied consultation norm described above. No state has disposed of high-level radioactive wastes at sea, and custom undoubtedly now prohibits any such practice—at least in the absence of extraordinary protective measures using advanced technology.[136] But low-level radioactive wastes have been dumped at sea, as have nonradioactive pollutants. Article 25(1) of the Geneva Convention on the High Seas requires states to take measures to prevent ocean pollution from radioactive waste dumping and to consider any standards and regulations formulated by competent international organizations. Article 25(2) requires states to cooperate with the competent international organizations to prevent pollution of the seas or airspace above from radioactive materials "or other harmful agents."[137] These provisions are

[135]*See* 1974 I.C.J. 3, 27–28, 32, and 175, 196–97, 201, analyzed in chapter VII, section C, of this book.

[136]Subseabed emplacement in geologically stable formations may now be feasible. *See* text at note 142 *infra*. An IAEA advisory group has also suggested that high-level radioactive wastes might be dumped safely at sea in circumstances that assure strictly controlled release rates. This would require revision of an Annex to the London Ocean Dumping Convention. The advisory group "recognized, however, that such an approach would require the establishment of a system of notification and prior consultation." *See* Report of the Third Consultative Meeting of the Contracting Parties to the [Ocean Dumping Convention], Annex 8, para. 6, IMCO Doc. LDC III / 12 (1978), in 18 INT'L LEGAL MATERIALS 817, 824 (1979).

[137]Convention on the High Seas, *supra* note 134.

significant in connection with the OECD consultation procedure regarding radioactive waste disposal, discussed below.

The United States suspended its low-level radioactive waste disposals at sea in 1970, after restricting its disposal practices in 1962.[138] The Soviet Union has not disposed of radioactive waste at sea. Japan has conducted limited disposals at sea, and has consulted the Pacific island nations.[139] Some Western European states have disposed of low-level wastes about 1,000 kilometers at sea for several years. From 1967 until 1977, this was done in consultation with the OECD's Nuclear Energy Agency (NEA). More recently, it has been done under a 1977 OECD decision establishing a procedure by which participating member states notify the NEA of planned disposals well in advance; the NEA circulates the information to all participating states; under designated circumstances (which would cover virtually every case in which any new pollution risk exists), the NEA seeks the advice of specialists; and the country planning the disposal must take account of their advice.[140] The OECD decision is binding on participating member states.[141] It would apply to the United States if the U.S. decides to resume low-level radioactive waste disposal at sea.

With the development of deep seabed drilling and emplacement technology, it has become feasible to consider embedding high-level radioactive wastes beneath the seabed. The United States has made its own investigation of this technique's scientific, environmental, and economic feasibility and has discussed its progress with an NEA seabed working group consisting

[138] *Radiological Contamination of the Oceans: Hearings Before a Subcomm. of the House Comm. on Interior and Insular Affairs*, 94th Cong., 2d Sess. 3 (1976). During the period of active U.S. radioactive waste disposal, foreign governments apparently were not regularly consulted—although licensing procedures for disposals by private firms did include provisions for public notice and hearing. *See Industrial Radioactive Waste Disposal Hearings, supra* note 134, at 3091–97, 3109–10.

[139] *See Oceanography Miscellaneous: Hearings Before a Subcomm. of the House Comm. on Merchant Marine and Fisheries*, 96th Cong., 1st & 2d Sess., pt. 2, at 263–64 (1980).

[140] Decision of the OECD Council Establishing a Multilateral Consultation and Surveillance Mechanism for Sea Dumping of Radioactive Waste, Aug. 4, 1977, arts. 3 & 4, OECD Doc. C(77) 115 (Final), 17 INT'L LEGAL MATERIALS 445 (1978). The participating OECD states are the European members (except Austria), plus the United States and Japan. This covers almost all states with active interests in disposing of nuclear waste at sea. *See* Handl, *Managing Nuclear Wastes: The International Connection*, 21 NAT RES J. 267, 308 (1981); 28 Nuclear L. Bull., Dec. 1981, at 36.

[141] Convention on the Organisation for Economic Cooperation and Development, Dec. 14, 1960, art. 5(a), 12 U.S.T. 1728, T.I.A.S. No. 4891. The binding intent is made clear in OECD Doc. ENV(79)12, at 6 (1979).

of Canada, Japan, France, the Netherlands, and the U.K. as well as the United States. It is clear that the views of NEA governments, as well as those of the International Atomic Energy Agency, will be considered before any significant decisions are made.[142]

Remote South Pacific islands provide other tempting radioactive waste disposal sites. When the United States in 1979 began to consider a plan to store spent nuclear fuel on Palmyra Island (and possibly on Wake and Midway islands), it consulted the South Pacific island governments, as well as Australia and New Zealand. Nevertheless, the twelve nations comprising the South Pacific Forum issued a formal expression of "grave concern"; the United States then undertook to consult them further, and to consider their views, throughout the U.S. feasibility study. The consultations were held as promised.[143]

Until the advent of the London Ocean Dumping Convention (signed in December 1972), there was no consistent consultation practice regarding the dumping of nonradioactive chemical wastes. In a notorious incident in 1970, the United States dumped chemical munitions (nerve gas) in the Atlantic. Interested countries were given less than two weeks' notice before the disposal operation was to begin. The decision to proceed had already firmly been made. Although the State Department said it would consider seriously any protest from foreign governments based on new information, it made clear that the notice was given simply as a briefing and not with a view to eliciting any response from the notified governments.[144] Several years earlier, the United Kingdom had disposed of about sixty-seven tons of captured

[142]*See Ocean Dumping and Pollution: Hearings Before a Subcomm. of the House Comm. on Merchant Marine and Fisheries,* 95th Cong., 1st & 2d Sess. 200, 246–48 (1978); *Oceanography Miscellaneous Hearings, supra* note 139, at 258.

[143]Washington Post, July 10, 1979, at A18, col. 1; *id.*, May 22, 1980, at A48, col. 4; letter to the author from the Director, Pacific Island Affairs, U.S. Dep't of State, Nov. 19, 1979; *Oceanography Miscellaneous Hearings, supra* note 139, at 264.

[144]*See Ocean Disposal of Unserviceable Chemical Munitions: Hearings Before a Subcomm. of the House Comm. on Merchant Marine and Fisheries,* 91st Cong., 2d Sess. 106–07, 111 (1970). The states notified were all the NATO countries, Ireland, and the Soviet Union. The government of the Bahamas was also notified. *Id.* at 95.

It is arguable that the procedure followed by the United States was inconsistent with the position embodied in its earlier proposal to the U.N. Seabeds Committee, calling for timely announcement of such an activity, with amplifying information, and with an opportunity for interested states to request consultations. *See* Brown, *The Ocean Dumping of Nerve Gas: A Case Study of "Operation Chase,"* 11 NAT. RESOURCES J. 249, 250–53 (1971).

German World War II nerve gas in the Atlantic, about 250 miles west of Scotland. Apparently no prior consultations were held.[145]

In two recent instances, European governments have canceled proposed chemical waste disposals at the last minute in response to protests from other governments. In 1971, a Dutch ship under private control was about to dump chemical wastes, but after representations from concerned states, notably Iceland, Ireland, Norway, and the United Kingdom, the Dutch government requested the firm to recall the ship. It did so, and the waste was stored on land.[146] Similarly, in 1975 when a tanker belonging to the Finnish state-owned oil company was proceeding to the South Atlantic to dispose of arsenic wastes, Brazil, Uruguay, and Argentina jointly protested to the Finnish government; after an emergency meeting, the government announced that the tanker had been denied permission to dump its cargo.[147] In neither of these cases was there prior consultation in the usual sense. The Dutch and Finnish governments did not sit down to discuss ocean dumping plans with other governments before the operations began. In fact, they may not have even considered the plans before the protests were received. But they did pay attention to communications presented by concerned foreign governments and responded in time to prevent the perceived harm. This suggests that prior consultations can be effective in the waste disposal context, but it does not suggest that the governments felt obliged to consult.

The London Ocean Dumping Convention prohibits the ocean disposal of certain particularly hazardous pollutants and requires national regulation of others. The prohibition would now preclude a state party from dumping chemical munitions, unless it could come within the force majeure clause or the escape clause that permits the dumping of otherwise-prohibited substances "in emergencies posing unacceptable risk relating to human health and admitting no other feasible solution."[148] To

[145] *See* Washington Post, Aug. 12, 1970, at 19, col. 3. The disposal occurred between 1955 and 1957.

[146] *Netherlands State Practice*, 3 NETH. Y.B. INT'L L. 226–27 (1972).

[147] *See* Bilder, *The Settlement of Disputes in the Field of the International Law of the Environment*, 144 HAGUE ACADEMY, RECUEIL DES COURS 139, 190–92 (1975). The Finnish government thought the arsenic disposal might violate the London Ocean Dumping Convention, which it had signed but had not yet ratified.

[148] Convention on the Prevention of Marine Pollution by Dumping of Wastes and Other Matter, Dec. 29, 1972, art. 5(2), 26 U.S.T. 2403, T.I.A.S. No. 8165, 11 INT'L

take advantage of the "unacceptable risk" escape clause, a state party must consult beforehand with other states likely to be affected (even if they are nonparties to the Convention) and with the International Maritime Organization (IMO).[149] The consultation procedure was devised as a practical and necessary means of limiting any unreasonable use of the escape clause.[150]

Under IMO procedures implementing the Ocean Dumping Convention, when a state determines that the only feasible means of disposing of a prohibited substance is at sea, it should provide other states and IMO with detailed information regarding the factors entering into its determination, the quantity of material to be dumped, and the time and place of the proposed dumping. IMO also should be informed of the other states' recommendations and the extent to which the proposing state has complied with them. IMO may then recommend appropriate disposal procedures. The Organization's recommendations are to be followed to the extent practicable.[151]

The Ocean Dumping Convention also permits the disposal of otherwise prohibited substances if they are rapidly rendered harmless by natural ocean processes, or if they are essentially harmless trace contaminants in other wastes. If the disposing party has any doubt about the harmlessness of the substance, it "should" consult IMO before dumping.[152] Although this is couched in nonmandatory language, the clear expectation is

LEGAL MATERIALS 1294 (1972). The force majeure clause, article 5(1), applies in dire emergencies and does not require prior consultation.

[149] IMO was formerly known as the Intergovernmental Maritime Consultative Organization (IMCO). The procedures implementing the Ocean Dumping Convention were issued as IMCO documents.

[150] *See* the *Report of the U.S. Delegation to the Intergovernmental Conference on the Convention on the Dumping of Wastes at Sea, Oct. 30–Nov. 13, 1972, in Ocean Dumping: Hearing Before a Subcomm. of the House Comm. on Merchant Marine and Fisheries*, 93rd Cong., 1st Sess. 24 (1973).

[151] *Report of the Fifth Consultative Meeting of the Contracting Parties to the [Ocean Dumping Convention], Annex* 5, IMCO Doc. LDC V/12 (1980). *See also Report of the U.S. Delegation, supra* note 150, at 24.

Prior consultation procedures for emergency ocean dumping also have been developed under the Oslo Convention and the Mediterranean Dumping Protocol, chapter III, note 37, *supra*. For these procedures, see IMCO Doc. LDC IV/8, at 1–2 and Annexes 1 and 2 (1979).

[152] Ocean Dumping Convention, Annex I, para. 8, *supra* note 148. *See* the Interim Guidelines for the Implementation of Paragraphs 8 and 9 of Annex I to the London Dumping Convention, IMCO Doc. LDC IV/12, Annex 5, pt. D (1979). *See also* IMCO Doc. LDC IV/8, *supra* note 151, regarding a comparable interim procedure and a proposal under the Oslo Convention and the Mediterranean Dumping Protocol, respectively.

that the consultation procedure will be utilized in all appropriate cases.

Under the Convention on the Law of the Sea, dumping of any substance within a coastal state's territorial sea or economic zone, or on its continental shelf, requires its consent. Subject to the requirements of the Ocean Dumping Convention, the coastal state may "permit, regulate and control such dumping after due consideration of the matter with other States which by reason of their geographical situation may be adversely affected thereby."[153] This duty would apply even if the coastal state proposes to do the dumping, and even if the substance is not on the Ocean Dumping Convention's prohibited list. If it is on the prohibited list, and if the coastal state is a party to the Ocean Dumping Convention, the procedure under that Convention would have to be followed.

The consultation norm relating to dumping at sea does not necessarily apply to all potentially polluting uses of the oceans. The norm does seem to be developing with respect to mineral exploitation within a coastal state's offshore jurisdiction, when the operations could have significant adverse effects on the environment of other states or of areas beyond national jurisdiction.[154] But intergovernmental consultation on environmental consequences apparently is not required before a permit is issued for toxic waste incineration at sea.[155] Nor are such consultations normally held before a nuclear-powered vessel program is begun, or before a nuclear-powered ship is launched. Similarly, when the U.S. Nuclear Regulatory Commission (NRC) in 1976 was considering the feasibility of eight proposed NRC-licensed floating nuclear-power plants in coastal regions of the Atlantic and the Gulf of Mexico, there apparently were no consultations with the government of Mexico or of any other nation. Nevertheless, an environmental impact statement was prepared, giving any foreign governmental or private interests

[153] Convention on the Law of the Sea, *supra* note 67, arts. 210(5) and 237(1).

[154] *See Report of the UNEP Working Group of Experts on Environmental Law*, Feb. 13, 1981, paras. 17–19, in 7 ENVT'L POL'Y & L. 50, 51 (1981).

[155] *The Report of the Third Consultative Meeting of the Contracting Parties to the [Ocean Dumping Convention], Annex* 2, IMCO Doc. LDC III/12 (1978), in 18 INT'L LEGAL MATERIALS 499, 507 (1979), requires only notification to IMO following issuance of a special permit to incinerate wastes at sea. As in the case of ocean dumping, however, if a party has doubts about the harmlessness of the proposed incineration, it "should" consult IMO. *See* IMCO Doc. LDC IV/12, Annex 9, para. 3 (1979). The consultative meetings themselves have amounted to a form of prior consultation.

an opportunity to make their views known.[156] The Convention on the Law of the Sea calls for environmental assessment, "as far as practicable," when states have reasonable grounds to expect that planned activities under their jurisdiction or control may cause substantial pollution or significant harm to the marine environment.[157]

A prior consultation norm has arisen in Antarctica regarding significant mineral exploration and exploitation, but probably not as to harvesting most marine living resources. The 1959 Antarctic Treaty provided for periodic meetings of the parties, held every two or three years.[158] As interest in exploration and exploitation of Antarctic mineral and living resources began to develop in the 1970s, these issues were placed on the agendas of the regular meetings, and special, interim meetings were also held. Attention was paid to mineral resources throughout the decade, but discussion of large-scale fishing for krill—commercially the most important Antarctic living resource—began only in 1977. The decade was a period of preliminary mineral exploration and modest fishing efforts by some countries, while commercial exploitation was insignificant and was limited to fishing. Although no formal moratorium on mineral exploitation existed, the representatives of the Treaty parties recommended intensified consultation on exploration and exploitation, while urging their nationals and other (nonparty) states: "to refrain from all exploration and exploitation of Antarctic mineral resources while making progress towards the timely adop-

[156] *Radiological Contamination Hearings*, *supra* note 138, at 714–17. The United States later adopted a policy of preparing environmental impact statements in such cases. *See* chapter III, text at note 127, for the relevant U.S. Executive Order. Before nuclear exports from the United States are licensed, the impact on the global commons is assessed and foreign nations are permitted to comment. *See In re* Westinghouse Elec. Corp., 11 N.R.C. 631, 651–62, 657 (1980), *aff'd sub. nom.* Natural Resources Defense Council v. Nuclear Regulatory Comm'n, 647 F.2d 1345 (D.C. Cir. 1981).

[157] *See* Convention on the Law of the Sea, *supra* note 67, art. 206.

[158] Antarctic Treaty, Dec. 1, 1959, art. 9, 12 U.S.T. 794, T.I.A.S. No. 4780, 402 U.N.T.S. 71. The consultative parties are Argentina, Australia, Belgium, Chile, France, Federal Republic of Germany, Japan, New Zealand, Norway, Poland, South Africa, U.S.S.R., U.K., and U.S.A.

The meetings are not open to nonparties, even as observers, and no official records are kept. Thus, the meetings do not necessarily amount to consultative sessions among all interested entities. *See* F. AUBURN, ANTARCTIC LAW AND POLITICS 156–59 (1982); International Union for the Conservation of Nature and Natural Resources, Antarctica and the Southern Ocean, 8 ENVT'L POL'Y & L. 65, 67 (1982).

tion of an agreed regime concerning Antarctic mineral resource activities. They will thus endeavour to ensure that, pending the timely adoption of agreed solutions pertaining to exploration and exploitation of mineral resources, no activity shall be conducted to explore or exploit such resources."[159]

This recommendation does not have legislative effect for the Antarctic Treaty parties unless and until ratified by them, and even then, it would not of itself bind nonparties. Moreover, the only *states* urged to refrain from exploration and exploitation are states not parties to the Treaty. Nevertheless, states (including parties) have treated the recommendation as setting forth a standard to be obeyed. It thus has taken on a legal significance it may not have had originally.[160]

Probably the same may be said of abstention from commercial exploitation of native mammals, birds and specially protected fish and plant species, because of conservation measures agreed upon at the 1964 and 1966 meetings of the parties.[161] However, this was not the case regarding the restrained exploitation of other living marine resources (notably krill), since no collective statements have been made disapproving their exploitation. On the contrary, there have been statements asserting that the right to fish in Antarctic waters is a recognized freedom of the sea even absent an agreed conservation regime and that a fishing moratorium is unobtainable.[162] The Convention on the Con-

[159]Recommendation IX-1, in *Report of the Ninth Consultative Meeting [of the Antarctic Treaty parties]* 11, 13 (1977). *See also* Recommendation X-1, para. 4, in *Report of the Tenth Consultative Meeting* 11, 12 (1979) (contemplates a negotiated regime to protect environment before mineral resource activities undertaken); Recommendation XI-1, paras. 1–7, in *Final Report of the Eleventh Consultative Meeting, reprinted in* 20 INT'L LEGAL MATERIALS 1265 (1981) (same). The governments represented at the Eighth Consultative Meeting, in 1975, urged "states and persons to refrain from actions of commercial exploration and exploitation while, acting as Contracting Parties, they seek timely agreed solutions to the problems raised by the possible presence of valuable mineral resources in the Antarctic Treaty Area." 1975 DIGEST OF UNITED STATES PRACTICE IN INT'L LAW 107.

[160]F. AUBURN, *supra* note 158, at 262, says that the recommendation has not been followed by the Consultative Parties. He cites only one instance of potential noncompliance, however, involving seismic exploration. *Id.* at 246, 260, 262. Even if the noncomplying instance has actually occurred, the seismic tests would not pose significant environmental risks. See Zumberge, *Potential Mineral Resource Availability and Possible Environmental Problems in Antarctica*, in THE NEW NATIONALISM AND THE USE OF COMMON SPACES 115, 131–33, 145 (J. Charney ed. 1982).

[161]*See Exploitation of Antarctic Resources: Hearing Before a Subcomm. of the Senate Comm. on Foreign Relations*, 95th Cong., 2d Sess. 30–31 (1978).

[162]The Ninth Consultative Meeting adopted a recommendation on living resources, but it omitted the abstention language found in the mineral resources recommendation.

servation of Antarctic Marine Resources does not contain prior consultation provisions.[163]

Finally, it is worth noting that there is no general custom requiring prior consultation when activities are conducted for national security purposes, even though such activities may threaten the high seas environment. The obvious example is the testing of nuclear weapons on remote islands. On some occasions when such tests have been announced in advance, potentially affected nations have made protests that usually have been answered by the testing state. These answers have taken one of three forms, none suggesting that the protests have influenced the decision-making process: rejection of the protest, justification of the proposed test, or an attempt to obtain needed cooperation from the other government.[164] Insofar as attempts

See Report of the Ninth Consultative Meeting, supra note 159, at 13–16 *See also Exploitation of Antarctic Resources, supra* note 161, at 34; *Antarctic Living Marine Resources Negotiations: Hearing Before the Senate Comm. on Commerce, Science and Transportation*, 95th Cong., 2d Sess. 10 (1978). The Antarctic Consultative Parties did agree in 1977 to negotiate a new marine living resources convention and to take care in the interim to avoid depletion of stocks or damage to the ecosystem, but this did not amount to a commitment to refrain from acting without consultation.

[163]The Convention, which entered into force on April 7, 1982, is in 19 INT'L LEGAL MATERIALS 841 (1980).

[164]Japan repeatedly protested prospective U.S. and Soviet tests in the Pacific and Soviet Asia in the 1950s, without much discernable effect until the U.S. and Soviet Union decided, for reasons of their own, to suspend testing. *See* the chronologies *in* 1 JAPANESE ANN. INT'L L. 78–84 (1957); 2 *id.* at 159–62 (1958); 3 *id.* at 144–46 (1959); *see also* Maebara, *Basic Principles of Japanese Foreign Policy and Prohibition of Nuclear Weapon Tests*, 2 *id.* at 104, 107–08; Pender, The International Validity of Establishment and Operation of the Pacific Atomic Proving Grounds (unpublished State Dept. memorandum, 1956). Japanese protests before the British Christmas Island tests in 1957–58 met a similar fate, although at one point a Japanese envoy spoke with the British Prime Minister to urge suspension of the tests. Maebara, *supra*, at 107; chronologies in 2 JAPANESE ANN. INT'L L. 159–63 (1958); 3 *id.* at 103–08 (1959); *see also* 580 PARL. DEB., H.C. (5th ser.) 139 (1958). The British government consulted the government of New Zealand, in part to give safety assurances but also because it needed the latter's assistance. 18 U.N. TCOR. Annexes (Agenda item 5) 75 (1956). When the French government was planning its Sahara tests in the late 1950s, it appears to have been inflexible in response to Moroccan protests. *See* U.N. Doc. A/823, at 26–27 (1959). French testing in the South Pacific has been punctuated by protests in advance of the tests by New Zealand and Australia, and by some face-to-face discussions with representatives of those nations, but without any apparent French willingness to reconsider or even to provide information about the expected size and yield of the explosions. *See, e.g.*, 22 N.Z. FOREIGN AFF. REV., Jan. 1972, at 49; *id.* Mar. 1972, at 32; *id.* Oct. 1972, at 70–71; *id.* Dec. 1972, at 9; 23 *id.* Apr. 1973, at 69; 43 CURRENT NOTES ON INT'L AFF. (AUSTR.) 131, 412 (1972); 44 AUSTR. FOREIGN AFF. REC. 322, 324–26 (1973). The Soviet resumption of testing in 1961 was not announced until after the fact. N.Y. Times, Aug. 31, 1961, at 1, col. 4; *id.* at 6, col. 2; *id.*, Sept. 1, 1961, at 1, cols. 6–7. China and India have conducted their tests in secrecy. In 1977, however, Indian Prime

have been made to impose a procedural duty in connection with national security nuclear testing, they have focused only on prior notification for safety purposes.[165] The only reported instance of meaningful consultations before nuclear testing for national security purposes involved the U.S. test at Amchitka Island (Project Cannikin) in 1971.[166]

C. Outer Space

During the first two decades of space exploration, experimental uses predominated over operational ones. Basic procedural constraints grew out of those experimental uses, though they were ultimately framed broadly enough to apply to some aspects of operational activities. Recently, these activities have increased in relative importance as comprehensive space telecommunications systems have been placed in orbit, military intelligence satellites have been launched, remote sensing has developed, and direct satellite broadcasting to home receivers has become technologically feasible. Consequently, some procedural constraints relating specifically to operational satellites now can be identified. The discussion below begins, however, with the early experimental activities.

1. Space Activities Potentially Affecting Other Uses of Outer Space

In 1958 and 1962, the United States exploded nuclear devices

Minister Desai said any further tests would be conducted in consultation with others. Seth, *Trends in India's Foreign Policy*, 9 Pac. Community 232, 245 (1978).

[165] *See* the Western Working Paper Submitted to the Disarmament Subcomm., *Proposals for Partial Measures of Disarmament*, U.N. Doc. DC/SC.1/66 (1957), in Documents on Disarmament 1945–1959, at 868, 871 (U.S. State Dept. 1960). When the White House issued a justification of U.S. nuclear tests in 1956, it was careful to mention that each test series was publicly announced in advance. No mention was made of any consultations. White House lemorandum, *Weapons Tests and Peaceful Uses of the Atom*, *id.* 702, 703.

There may be an exception when the proposed test or other use of weaponry would be so close to another state's land territory as to pose obvious safety hazards. When the Soviet Union announced in March 1970 that it would hold bombardment exercises (not involving nuclear explosives) off the Noto Peninsula and Tosa, both Japanese territories, the Japanese government protested, and the Soviet government then told the Japanese ambassador that the exercises would be canceled. 19 Japanese Ann. Int'l L. 126 (1975).

[166] The U.S. Government took into account the representations of Canada and Japan. *See* N.Y. Times, Sept. 9, 1971, at 1, col. 4; *id.* Nov. 6, 1971, at 62, col. 2; 8 Can. Parl. Deb., H.C., 26th Parl., 3d Sess. 8512–13 (1971); *id.* at 8735–36; 9 *id.* at 9311–12. Project Cannikin was conducted underground.

in outer space under the code names Argus and Starfish. The tests had scientific as well as military significance, since they were designed to emulate the natural Van Allen radiation belt. They risked disturbing the Van Allen belt (the 1962 explosion did disturb it), interfering with radio astronomy, and creating hazards for manned space explorations. The United States held no prior consultations with foreign scientists or governments.[167] The Soviet Union also failed to consult in advance of its high altitude nuclear tests in 1961 and 1962.[168]

Far more significant to the developing procedural law of outer space was the U.S. West Ford project that involved dispersing 350 million tiny needles in a short-lived orbit to test them as relayers of earth-to-earth communications. After the Space Science Board of the [U.S.] National Academy of Sciences concluded that the proposed project would not adversely affect other scientific uses, the plan was publicly announced in August 1960. The international scientific community expressed concern about the project's possible effect on optical and radio astronomy, and the International Astronomical Union in August 1961 appealed to all governments to consult it before undertaking space experiments that possibly could affect astronomical research. The "space needle" package was launched in October 1961, but the needles did not disperse into orbit. A second launch was made in May 1963 and went as planned. No harmful effects were observed.[169] The COSPAR Consultative Group on Potentially Harmful Effects of Space Experiments responded by recommending that "any future experiments with this general character be given the benefit of a thorough evaluation by the international scientific community and notably by the International Astronomical Union in order to check in advance their harmlessness to other scientific research."[170]

[167] *See* Lear, *The Facts About the 1962 Space Bomb,* SAT. REV., Apr. 6, 1963, at 45–48; CMD. NO. 2029, at 6–7 (1963); A. HALEY, SPACE LAW AND GOVERNMENT 267–69 (1963).

[168] *See* U.N. Doc. A/AC.105/15, at 1–2 (1963) (U.S. letter to the Secretary-General). Nuclear explosions in outer space are now illegal, at least for parties to the partial test ban treaty.

[169] For further details, see Johnson, *Pollution and Contamination in Space,* in LAW AND POLITICS IN SPACE 37, 46–48 (M. Cohen ed. 1964); S. Doc. No. 56, 89th Cong., 1st Sess. 390, 396, 407–10 (1965); U.N. Doc. A/AC.105/15, at 4–7 (1963) (U.S. government statement).

[170] U.N. Doc. A/5785, Annex III, at 9, 10 (1964). COSPAR is the Committee on Space Research of the International Council of Scientific Unions. Its Consultative Group on Potentially Harmful Effects of Space Experiments was established in response to the first (abortive) West Ford launch. *See* S. Doc. No. 56, *supra* note 169, at 390.

A responsible State Department official asserted about the time of the second West Ford launch that the experiment not only had been reviewed in advance by U.S. scientists, but "was also discussed thoroughly in advance with a broad range of scientists from other countries. While some of these expressed concern, there was an over-all consensus that the experiment would not impede radio astronomy or other scientific research."[171] The reported facts, however, suggest that although U.S. scientists published and otherwise disseminated to colleagues abroad technical data regarding the proposed experiment and there were discussions among scientists at some international meetings, the U.S. government did not undertake as a matter of policy to consult either scientists abroad or foreign governments.[172]

Even though the United States apparently did not engage in meaningful international consultations before West Ford, it did acquiesce in the assertions by the international scientific community and some governments that it should consult in the future. The State Department official who had defended the government's West Ford policy declared, "We are prepared to support the principle that a state should undertake appropriate international consultations before proceeding with a space activity if it has reason to believe that its activity may create a significant risk of harm."[173] The U.S. representative to the First Committee of the General Assembly, also responding to international concern over West Ford, said, "We encourage prior international discussion concerning experimental activities in space which may have undesirable effects, and we are prepared in the future, as in the past, to consult with scientists of other countries as well as United States scientists wherever practicable and consistent with our national security."[174] Although these

[171]Gardner, *Cooperation in Outer Space*, 41 FOREIGN AFF. 344, 346 (1963). *See also* U.N. Doc. A/AC.105/15, at 1 (1963) (U.S. assertion that "Nothing could be further from the truth" than a Soviet insinuation that the West Ford experiment was undertaken without consulting the world scientific community).

[172]*See* the U.S. statement of the facts surrounding West Ford, U.N. Doc. A/AC.105/15, at 5–7 (1963); *Report on Project West Ford by the Space Science Board of the National Academy of Sciences*, in S. Doc. No. 56, *supra* note 169, at 407–08. *See also* E. SKOLNIKOFF, SCIENCE, TECHNOLOGY, AND AMERICAN FOREIGN POLICY 85–87 (1967).

[173]Gardner, *Outer Space: Problems of Law and Power*, 49 DEP'T ST. BULL. 367, 369 (1963). He asserted that this principle would be in accord with existing U.S. practice, as reflected in West Ford.

[174]Senator Gore, in U.N. Doc. A/C.1/PV.1289, at 17 (1962). *See also* U.N. Doc. A/AC.105/15, at 7 (1963).

statements contained some self-judging caveats, they nevertheless expressed a good faith intention to consult. Moreover, they were particularly significant in the normative sense because they amounted to acquiescences in assertions of principle by those likely to be affected by future U.S. experiments.

The process of fashioning a consultation principle, set in motion by West Ford, did not stop with unilateral U.S. declarations of intent. In the United Nations, the Soviet Union presented a draft declaration of principles calling for the consent of all parties concerned before a state carried out space activities that might interfere with the exploration or use of space by other states.[175] Such a veto was unacceptable to the United States, and a compromise was reached embodying the principle of prior consultation. That principle was incorporated into the General Assembly's 1963 Declaration of Legal Principles Governing the Activities of States in the Exploration and Use of Outer Space.[176] Article 9 of the Outer Space Treaty was taken in part from the General Assembly Declaration. The last two sentences of article 9 provide:

> If a State Party to the Treaty has reason to believe that an activity or experiment planned by it or its nationals in outer space, including the Moon and other celestial bodies, would cause potentially harmful interference with activities of other States Parties in the peaceful exploration and use of outer space, including the Moon and other celestial bodies, it shall undertake appropriate international consultations before proceeding with any such activity or experiment. A State Party to the Treaty which has reason to believe that an activity or experiment planned by another State Party in outer space, including the Moon and other celestial bodies, would cause potentially harmful interference with activities in the peaceful exploration and use of outer space, including the Moon and other celestial bodies, may request consultation concerning the activity or experiment.[177]

These two sentences raise a number of significant questions, all of which have been discussed in international fora or in the legal literature. The most important, for purposes of the present discussion, are:

[175] *See* U.N. Docs. A/AC.105/13, at 4 (1963), and A/5549, Annex III (1963).

[176] G.A. Res. 1962, 18 U.N. GAOR, Supp. (No. 15), at 15, U.N. Doc. A/5515 (1963).

[177] Treaty on Principles Governing the Activities of States in the Exploration and Use of Outer Space, Including the Moon and Other Celestial Bodies, Jan. 27, 1967, art. 9, 18 U.S.T. 2410, T.I.A.S. No. 6347, 610 U.N.T.S. 205.

(*a*) How much discretion is vested in the acting state under the first sentence above?

(*b*) Does that sentence apply to activities or experiments that would cause potential harm to the earth's environment, or just to those potentially interfering with other space activities?

(*c*) What are "appropriate international consultations"?

(*d*) Is the second sentence purely precatory, in the sense that a state may request consultation but the requested state need not respond?

(*e*) Do the same rights and duties apply to nonparties to the Treaty?

The first sentence imposes a consultation duty only if the acting state party "has reason to believe" that its activity or experiment would cause the potential harm specified. Some commentators suggest that this gives unfettered discretion to the acting state.[178] But an acting state clearly would have to exercise good faith in finding no reason to believe there would be potential harm in a given case. If there is substantial scientific opinion to the contrary, it could hardly make such a determination.[179] Moreover, the Lake Lanoux tribunal, speaking in the context of river law but in terms equally applicable here, indicated that the acting state does not have the exclusive discretion to determine whether the interests of other states are likely to be affected by a proposed measure affecting common resources.[180] In the outer space context, this principle is buttressed

[178] *See* N. MATTE, AEROSPACE LAW 315 (1969); Gorove, *Pollution and Outer Space: A Legal Analysis and Appraisal,* 5 N.Y.U. J. INT'L L. & POL. 53, 63 (1972); Vlasic, *The Space Treaty: A Preliminary Evaluation,* 55 CALIF. L. REV. 507, 518 (1967).

[179] The Soviet representative to the Legal Subcommittee of the Outer Space Committee, referring to the "reason to believe" language of the Soviet draft that became the basis for the final Treaty, said it would require the acting state to contact other parties if the proposed activity or experiment "might interfere" with their activities. U.N. Doc. A/AC.105/C.2/SR.68, at 8 (1966). The Soviet draft is in U.N. Doc. A/AC.105/35, at 12, 14 (1966).

[180] *See* chapter II text at note 67 *supra.* Articles 3 and 13 of the outer space treaty, taken together, extend terrestrial international law to outer space activities insofar as it is not clearly superseded by the Treaty itself. *See* Valladao, *South American Contributions to Solution of the Juridical Problems of Telecommunications and Direct Satellite Broadcasting,* in THE INTERNATIONAL LAW OF COMMUNICATIONS 138, 141–42 (E. McWhinney ed. 1971).

by the express duty in an earlier part of article 9 to conduct all activities in outer space "with due regard to the corresponding interests of all other States Parties to the Treaty." Thus, if a state party notifies the acting state that its interests (as defined in article 9) are likely to be harmed, the acting state at least would have to take that representation into account in good faith when it determines whether it has reason to believe its activity or experiment would cause the potential harm covered by that article.[181]

Some commentators have concluded that the consultation duty could be construed to extend to activities potentially harmful to the earth's environment.[182] That interpretation, however, is difficult to reconcile with the language, context, preparatory work, and practical construction of article 9. The language speaks only of potentially harmful interference "with activities of other States Parties in the peaceful exploration and use of outer space." That language was drafted in reaction to the U.S. Starfish and West Ford experiments, both of which posed possible risks to such outer space uses as radio astronomy, rather than to the earth's environment. The preparatory work for the provision in the General Assembly's 1963 Declaration that became the consultation provision in the Treaty referred to changes in the *space* environment and adverse effects on other space experiments; it also contemplated, as one possible option, consultation with COSPAR's Consultative Group on Potentially Harmful Effects of Space Experiments—a scientific body concerned only with effects on the outer space environment.[183] Finally, as noted in the most thorough study to date on article 9, some outer space activities by parties to the Treaty that might have adversely affected the earth's environment have not been sub-

[181]It may have a greater duty under the last sentence of article 9. *See* text at note 190 *infra*.

[182]*See* Christol, *The International Legal and Institutional Aspects of the Stratospheric Ozone Problem* 101 (Senate Comm. on Aeronautical and Space Sciences Print, 94th Cong., 1st Sess. 1975); Herczeg, *Provisions of the Space Treaties on Consultation*, in PROC. OF THE 17TH COLLOQ. ON THE LAW OF OUTER SPACE 141, 144 (M. Schwartz ed. 1975). Herczeg relied in part on a sentence of article 9 requiring parties to avoid adverse changes in the earth's environment. That sentence, however, says nothing about consultation.

[183]*See Report of the Outer Space Committee*, U.N. Doc. A/5549, at 8, and Annex II at 3 (1963); U.N. Doc. A/AC.105/13, at 4 (1963). For the COSPAR Consultative Group's purposes and activities, see 18 U.N. GAOR, C.1 (1345th mtg.), 181 (1963). For an ambiguous statement in the preparatory work that could be taken to run counter to the position taken in the text above, see the Canadian representative's comments in U.N. Doc. A/5549/Add.l, Annex, at 10 (1963).

mitted to international consultations and have not drawn protests based on article 9.[184] One must conclude that the article 9 consultation duty is limited to potentially harmful interference with outer space activities, which could include potential interference with their ground segments.[185]

As indicated above, there is evidence that "appropriate international consultations" may have been intended to mean consultations with scientists able to evaluate the risks to other uses of outer space, rather than diplomatic consultations.[186] This view is arguably consistent with the thrust of the consultation provision, since direct scientific consultations would be a more efficient means of calculating possible effects on the space environment than would diplomatic consultations. On the other hand, if the scientists consulted are not privy to all existing and planned space uses of interested governments, purely scientific consultations would not bring to light all potentially harmful interference with activities of other states parties in outer space. Thus, it is not surprising to find statements by representatives of the United States and the Soviet Union suggesting that diplomatic consultations were intended.[187] In light of this and the declining activity of the COSPAR Consultative Group in recent

[184] *See* Sztucki, *International Consultations and Space Treaties*, in PROC. OF THE 18TH COLLOQ ON THE LAW OF OUTER SPACE 166, 177 (M. Schwartz ed. 1976). A prominent example was the U.S. decision to eliminate the quarantine requirement for astronauts returning from the moon. *See* Sand, *Space Programmes and International Environment Protection*, 21 INT'L & COMP. L. Q. 43, 50, 56–57 (1972).

[185] *See* Sztucki, *supra* note 184, at 178. Sztucki notes at page 177 that the second sentence of article 9 calls for "appropriate measures" to avoid adverse changes in the earth's environment, and that these could encompass consultations. But it does not expressly mention consultations, and it provides no standard to determine when they would be the "appropriate measures." Moreover, the fact that the last two sentences of article 9 expressly deal with consultations casts doubt on any attempt to infer a different consultation duty from other language in article 9. This would be true also of the first sentence, which speaks of conducting activities in outer space "with due regard to the corresponding interests of all other States Parties to the Treaty." Were it not for the express consultation provisions, such language probably would imply a duty to consult, but only as to "corresponding" (i.e., space activity) interests. As to an implied consultation duty from such language, see chapter VII, section C, *infra*.

[186] *See*, in addition to the preparatory work cited in note 183 *supra*, the remarks of Senator Gore in the text at note 174 *supra*. *Accord*, J. FAWCETT, INTERNATIONAL LAW AND THE USES OF OUTER SPACE 54 (1968); A. FRUTKIN, INTERNATIONAL COOPERATION IN SPACE 146 (1965); A. LEVIN, PROTECTING THE HUMAN ENVIRONMENT: PROCEDURES AND PRINCIPLES FOR PREVENTING AND RESOLVING INTERNATIONAL CONTROVERSIES 2 (UNITAR Study 1977).

[187] *See* the statement of U.S. Ambassador Goldberg in *Outer Space: Hearings Before the Senate Comm. on Foreign Relations*, 90th Cong., 1st Sess. 71 (1967), and the remarks of the Soviet representative in U.N. Doc. A/AC.105/C.2/SR.68, at 7–8 (1966).

years, it is reasonable to conclude that "appropriate international consultations" should now extend to diplomatic consultations whenever potential harm to space activities beyond purely technical interference (such as unintended radio frequency interference) is involved.[188] To be "appropriate" for the purpose specified in article 9, the consultations would have to precede a final decision to go ahead and could not simply be concerned with details of an inexorable experiment.

The last sentence of article 9, authorizing states parties to request consultations, could be either an important safety valve to insure that acting states do not abuse the discretion left by the "reason to believe" language in the preceding sentence or a virtually meaningless provision requiring nothing of the state receiving the request. At least one commentator apparently relegates it to the latter category.[189] There is support, however, for the former view. In 1966 the Soviet representative to the Outer Space Committee, after submitting the draft treaty containing what became the last sentence of article 9, responded to a request for clarification by saying that the text being drafted was "a treaty having compulsory force and . . . it would therefore be compulsory to comply with the requests for which it provided. Article [9] offered, in a sense, a double guarantee" (in the form of the two sentences on consultation).[190] That explanation seems to have been acceptable to the others present. Even if one were to treat this as inconclusive, it would be clear that a request would have to be considered in good faith by the requested state and might well give that state "reason to believe" that its activity or experiment would cause potentially harmful interference with activities of other states parties.

The duty to consult under the "reason to believe" sentence of article 9 applies only when the potential harm is to activities of other states parties. In view of the widespread adoption of the Treaty, it would be a rare case in which an activity potentially harmful to any other state would not be harmful to a state party. If such a case should arise, there remain two possible sources

[188] *See* Sztucki, *supra* note 184, at 182–83. The International Telecommunication Union (ITU) notification-consultation procedure on radio-frequency interference is discussed in the text at note 194 *infra*.

[189] Gorove, *supra* note 178, at 64, says, "One party may request consultation and the other party may simply turn it down."

[190] U.N. Doc. A/AC.105/C.2/SR.68, at 9 (1966). *See also* G. Zhukov, E. Vasilevskaya, & P. Lukin, Legal Aspects of the Utilization of Artificial Satellites for Meteorological and Radio Communication Purposes 35 (1970: NASA translation, 1972).

of a duty to consult: the last sentence of article 9, which is not limited to harmful interference with activities of states parties, and the 1963 General Assembly Declaration, which, of course, does not refer to "states parties" in its "reason to believe" provision.[191] The Declaration was adopted unanimously; all participating states recognized that it involved legal principles; some of them viewed it as either lawmaking or a codification of existing law.[192] Whatever may have been the effect of the Declaration in 1963, it probably represents custom today.

In 1971 the International Telecommunication Union (ITU) adopted a prior notification-consultation procedure complementing article 9 of the Outer Space Treaty. Under that procedure, which entered into force in 1973, the ITU has maintained a frequency registration system that gives notice to all members of frequencies being used by satellites for their radio astronomy and radiocommunication transmissions, but does not strictly preclude members from encroaching on registered frequencies. To minimize interference, a member state planning to launch a radio astronomy or radiocommunication satellite has been required to notify the ITU's International Frequency Registration Board of the details of the proposed launch. The Board has published the information, and any "administration"[193] fearing interference with its existing or planned space radio communications could send its comments to the notifying administration and to the Board. When no comments have been received within a prescribed period, the Board has registered the notified frequency. If comments have been received, the administration receiving them could proceed only after trying to resolve the difficulties through consultations.[194]

[191] On the legal effect of General Assembly resolutions, see chapter I, note 17, and accompanying text *supra*.

[192] *See, e.g.*, U.N. Doc. A / 5549 / Add.1, Annex, at 3–5 (1963) (Chairman of the Legal Subcomm., Manfred Lachs); *id.* at 5–6 (U.S.); *cf. id.* at 15 (Austrl.) and at 32–34 (U.S.S.R.).

[193] An "administration," in ITU parlance, is any governmental department or service responsible for meeting a member state's ITU obligations. *See* D. LEIVE, INTERNATIONAL TELECOMMUNICATIONS AND INTERNATIONAL LAW: THE REGULATION OF THE RADIO SPECTRUM 355 (1970).

[194] *See* ITU Radio Regulations, July 17, 1971, art. 9A, in 23 U.S.T. 1527, 1684, T.I.A.S. 7435 (applicable to radio astronomy and space radiocommunication stations except stations in the broadcasting-satellite service). Some of the details of article 9A were revised, and the article was renumbered as N12, at the World Administrative Radio Conference in 1979, but the basic procedure described in the text remains unchanged. The results of the Conference are summarized in 47 TELECOM. J. 4 (1980).

In 1977 the ITU World Broadcasting-Satellite Administrative Radio Conference devised a somewhat tighter system for broadcast satellite frequency allocations. A plan has been drawn up for two of the three ITU-designated regions of the world, with broadcasting channels assigned to states or subregions. A proposal to use an assigned channel simply requires a check by the Board for compliance with the International Telecommunication Convention, the radio regulations, and the plan; any proposal involving broadcast spillover not expressly contemplated by the plan requires not only prior consultation with affected administrations but their prior agreement.[195] Prior coordination with affected administrations is required for frequency assignments to ground stations or nonbroadcast space stations when broadcasting-satellite frequency allocations would be affected.[196]

The remaining ITU region (region two), which includes the United States, has continued to use a prior coordination procedure for broadcasting-satellite frequency allocations, much like that described above for radio astronomy and radiocommunication, until the regional conference scheduled for 1983 could devise a regional plan.[197] The United States has been the leader in espousing this evolutionary approach to the development of detailed broadcasting-satellite allocation rules and has acknowledged the need for prior consultation in the interim.[198]

The ITU coordination procedures are designed to deal with essentially technical matters, while the Outer Space Treaty obligation, as noted above, seems to contemplate broader political consultations when they would be appropriate. Nevertheless, there are many instances in which the only potentially harmful space activity interference would be with frequency-band use. In such cases, compliance with the ITU consultation procedure should qualify as compliance with article 9 of the Outer Space Treaty. This seems to be the understanding of the United States.[199]

[195] Final Acts of the World Broadcasting-Satellite Administrative Radio Conference, arts. 4, 5 (Geneva, 1977).

[196] *Id.* arts. 6, 7.

[197] *Id.* art. 12, para 12.8; Resolution No. Spa2–3 of the World Administrative Radio Conference for Space Telecommunications, Geneva 1971, in 23 U.S.T. 1822, T.I.A.S. No. 7435.

[198] *See* Lonberg, *The Broadcasting-Satellite Conference*, 44 TELECOM. J. 482, 487 (1977).

[199] For example, when the United States launched its ATS-6 and SMS-1 satellites in May 1974, it complied with the ITU notification procedure without proposing broader

A significant number of satellites have been launched into geostationary orbit and synchronized with the earth's rotation at the equator, so that the satellite appears from the earth to be stationary.[200] There is an absolute limit to the number of satellites, as well as to the number of frequencies, that can be in geostationary orbit at any given time.[201] The ITU procedures apply to potential frequency conflicts, but not to allocation of space for the satellites themselves (except insofar as the location of a geostationary satellite causes the potential frequency interference). As the geostationary "slots" have become increasingly occupied, any new launches into geostationary orbit might cause potentially harmful interference with activities of other states desiring eventually to use a geostationary orbit. If so, arguably there should be consultation before launch under article 9 of the Outer Space Treaty. There appears to be no established consultation practice on this point and the legal debate has centered, not on procedural questions, but on whether use of a geostationary orbit is an appropriation rendered unlawful by article 2 of the Outer Space Treaty.[202] The absence of consultation practice reflects a tacit understanding that the "activities of other States Parties in the peaceful exploration and use of outer space" are present or currently-planned activities rather than those simply expected in the future.

Like the ITU, the two international satellite-operating agencies have specialized consultation procedures covering some activities encompassed by article 9 of the Outer Space Treaty.

diplomatic consultations. This apparently provoked no protests from other governments. Letter from NASA General Counsel to the author, Nov. 25, 1974.

An earlier ATS launch, before adoption of the 1971 ITU rules and before the U.S. became a party to the Outer Space Treaty, was preceded by consultations with scientists regarding possible interference with an important Australian radio telescope. It appears, however, that the consultations occurred only because the scientists learned of the potential problem almost by accident. As a result of the consultations, the U.S. rendered inoperative the potentially harmful experiment. *See* Swenson & Bracewell, *Radio Astronomy: Conflict of Frequencies*, 155 SCIENCE 518 (1967).

[200] As of May 1979, there were well over 100 objects in the geostationary orbit. *See* U.N. Doc. A/AC.105/203/Add.3, Annex II (1979).

[201] *See* Goedhuis, *The Present State of Space Law*, in THE PRESENT STATE OF INTERNATIONAL LAW AND OTHER ESSAYS 201, 227 (M. Bos ed. 1973); Moore, *Direct Broadcast Satellites by Treaty or Regulation: The Committee on Peaceful Uses of Outer Space v. the ITU*, PRO. OF THE 19TH COLLOQ. ON THE LAW OF OUTER SPACE 341, 342 (M. Schwartz ed. 1977).

[202] *See* Goedhuis, *supra* note 201, at 227–30; Haanappel, *Article II of the Outer Space Treaty and the Status of the Geostationary Orbit*, in PROC. OF THE 21ST COLLOQ. ON THE LAW OF OUTER *Space* 28 (M. Schwartz ed. 1979).

The International Telecommunications Satellite Organization (INTELSAT) develops and operates the space segment of the global commercial telecommunications satellite system. It has about 105 members, not including the Soviet Union or other Eastern European states. Its constituent instrument requires any party, or communications entity designated by a party, to consult the INTELSAT Board of Governors before establishing space segment facilities to meet its public telecommunications services requirements. In the case of a planned domestic system, the consultations relate only to technical compatibility with the use of the radio frequency spectrum and orbital space by INTELSAT; in the case of a planned international system, the consultations cover technical compatibility plus avoidance of significant economic harm to INTELSAT's global system.[203] The International Maritime Satellite Organization (INMARSAT) has a consultation procedure like INTELSAT's international scheme.[204]

The INTELSAT Board of Governors has decided that the INTELSAT consultation procedure does not apply to experimental satellites. Nevertheless, in several instances those planning experimental satellite systems have voluntarily coordinated them in advance with INTELSAT.[205] States and communications entities have complied with their consultation obligations regarding operational satellites, and INTELSAT has coordinated its own satellite launches under the ITU notification-consultation procedure.[206]

[203] Agreement Relating to the International Telecommunications Satellite Organization, Aug. 20, 1971, art. 14(c) & (d), 23 U.S.T. 3813, T.I.A.S. 7532. Article 14(e) contains only a prior notification requirement regarding "specialized telecommunications services," but consultations appear likely under that provision. For a description of the procedure under article 14, see Colino, *International Cooperation Between Communications Satellite Systems: An Overview of Current Practices and Future Prospects*, 5 J. Space L. 65, 76–81 (1977).

If the consultations relating to international systems are to serve their designated purpose, they would have to precede a final decision to launch the space segment. In the case of domestic systems, the consultations might cover only operational details.

[204] Convention on the International Maritime Satellite Organization, Sept. 3, 1976, art. 8, 31 U.S.T. 135, T.I.A.S. No. 9605, 15 Int'l Legal Materials 1052 (1976). INMARSAT has about 35 members, including the Soviet Union and some other Eastern European states.

[205] *See* Colino, *supra* note 203, at 79–80.

[206] *Id.* at 72, 76, 83–87. In addition, the Soviet Union (not an INTELSAT member) has coordinated its STATSIONAR satellite system with the INTELSAT system under the ITU procedures. *Id.* at 82. Apparently, INMARSAT will also coordinate its satellite system under the ITU procedures. INMARSAT Convention, art. 28, note 204 *supra*.

Outside the communication field, article 12 of the Outer Space Treaty permits representatives of states parties to visit stations, installations, equipment, and space vehicles of other states parties on the moon and other celestial bodies on a basis of reciprocity, subject to advance notification and consultation. A similar provision appears in article 15 of the Agreement Governing the Activities of States on the Moon and Other Celestial Bodies.[207] The Agreement also contains a broader consultation duty that applies whenever activities of states parties on the moon may interfere with activities of other states parties.[208]

The United States, with support from a number of other nations, had proposed another relevant provision for the Agreement. It would have required states parties to notify in advance the U.N. Secretary-General, the public, and the international scientific community of the details of proposed missions to the moon or other celestial bodies.[209] This would have been more than a simple prior notification procedure, since the purposes were to promote safety, avoid interference with other missions, avoid duplication of experiments, and avoid environmental harm to celestial bodies.[210] Few of these purposes could have been met without implying an obligation to consult if requested. Several governments were cool to this proposal, since it might have forced them to reveal information of military significance.[211] When the draft Agreement finally emerged from the Outer Space Committee, it simply required that information on the time, purposes, locations, orbital parameters, and duration be given "as soon as possible after launching."[212] This, of course, implies no prior consultation duty.

2. Space Activities Potentially Affecting Terrestrial Interests

Although article 9 of the Outer Space Treaty probably does

[207] G.A. Res. 34/68, Annex, 34 U.N. GAOR Supp. (No. 46) at 77, U.N. Doc. A/34/46 (1979). The consultation duty relates to the details of the visit, rather than to its permissibility. *See* Sztucki, *supra* note 184, at 179. It is questionable whether there would be a right to visit, in the absence of an applicable treaty provision. The point is that such a right has been tied to a prior consultation requirement intended to insure that exercise of the right will not unduly interfere with the visited state's activities.

[208] *See* Agreement art. 8(3), in G.A. Res. 34/68, Annex, *supra* note 207.

[209] *See* U.N. Doc. A/AC.105/C.2(XI)/Working paper 3 (1972), *reprinted in* U.N. Doc. A/AC.105/196, Annex I, at 36 (1977).

[210] *See* U.N. Doc. A/AC.105/C.2/SR.205, at 114–15 (1973).

[211] *See* Goedhuis, *supra* note 201, at 217.

[212] Art. 5(1), in G.A. Res. 34/68, Annex, *supra* note 207.

not apply to potential interference with the earth's environment, it remains to be seen whether there are other sources from which consultation duties arise when the effect of a space activity would be felt wholly or primarily on earth or in the earth's atmosphere.[213]

No general norm to that effect can be found. For example, when the United States eliminated the quarantine of astronauts returning from the moon, it did so without international consultation and without drawing protests from other governments.[214] Similarly, there is no established practice of consulting before conducting high-altitude chemical tests in the earth's atmosphere, or before a nuclear-powered satellite is launched.[215] Proposals for broad prior consultation or consent requirements relating to space activities that could affect the human environment are, at present, de lege ferenda.[216] On the other hand, space-related activities that pose a substantial risk of appreciable harm to an identifiable, relatively contained area of the earth's environment (a specific river system, air shed, or partially enclosed sea) would be subject to a present prior consultation norm benefiting the states peculiarly interested in that area. This would simply be one application of the environmental prior consultation norms discussed in chapters II and III.

There has been considerable talk and some action relating to prior consultation or consent norms in connection with direct satellite broadcasting and remote sensing—two space activities

[213]As pointed out in the text at note 185 *supra*, article 9 would reach ground activities integrated with space systems. The present discussion deals with other earthbound interests.

[214]Sand, *supra* note 184, at 50, 56–57. *See also* Dembling & Kalsi, *Pollution of Man's Last Frontier: Adequacy of Present Space Environmental Law in Preserving the Resource of Outer Space*, 20 NETH. INT'L L. REV. 125, 141–42 (1973), suggesting that there should have been prior consultation.

[215]As to chemical experiments, see Sand, *supra* note 184, at 53. A 1964 COSPAR report concluded that chemical experiments until then had resulted in nothing more than harmless, short-term alterations of the upper atmosphere. *Statement on Upper Atmospheric Pollution by Rocket Exhaust and Chemical Injection Experiments by the COSPAR Consultative Group on Potentially Harmful Effects of Space Experiments*, in S. Doc. No. 56, *supra* note 169, at 394.

As to nuclear-powered satellites, see the remarks of the Chairman of the U.N. Outer Space Committee, in U.N. CHRON., Apr. 1978, at 52. It is apparent from the Canadian reaction to the reentry and impact in Canada in 1978 of a Soviet nuclear-powered satellite that the international community had little knowledge of any precautions taken by the U.S.S.R. and the U.S.A. *Id.* at 52–53.

[216]Sand, *supra* note 184, at 59, makes such a proposal. *See also* DAVID DAVIES MEMORIAL INSTITUTE OF INTERNATIONAL STUDIES, DRAFT CODE OF RULES ON THE EXPLORATION AND USES OF OUTER SPACE, rule 2.4 (1962).

affecting sensitive terrestrial interests.[217] The United States originally opposed any procedural constraints on direct broadcasting and on the remote sensing process (including opposition to constraints on the dissemination of sensed data), while the Soviet Union and most other nations have favored a prior consent regime for direct broadcasting and for dissemination of detailed sensed information. A few countries object not only to dissemination but to any sensing of their territories unless they have given their consent.

In 1975 the United States retreated from its opposition to all procedural constraints on direct broadcasting and espoused a prior notification-consultation regime. Under its proposal, states within the reception area would be notified of the intention to conduct direct satellite broadcasting and could insist on prior consultation without requiring prior approval.[218] Although this has received some support as a compromise solution and represents the minimum procedural norm acceptable to all interested states,[219] most governments except the United States favor something closer to a prior consent regime. In December 1982, the U.N. General Assembly adopted principles that would permit international direct satellite broadcasting to be established only when there has been prior notice to the proposed receiving state and consultation with it on request; in addition, the broadcasting service would have to be "on the basis of agreements and/or arrangements in conformity with the relevant instruments of" the ITU.[220] A prior consent formulation for intentional international satellite broadcasting is embodied in decisions taken at ITU Administrative Confer-

[217]Direct satellite broadcasts are those picked up by home receivers without the aid of ground stations. Thus, the receiving state cannot censor the programs, except by jamming. Remote sensing provides images of the earth's surface, and can be used, inter alia, to identify exploitable natural resources.

[218]*See* the statements by U.S. representatives in 73 DEP'T ST. BULL. 673, 675 (1975), and in U.N. Doc. A/AC.105/C.2/SR.304, at 8 (1979).

[219]*See, e.g.*, REPORT OF THE 57TH CONF. OF THE INT'L LAW ASS'N, 1976, at 270–71, 274, 283–84 (1978); U.N. Doc. A/AC.105/240, Annex II, at 6 (1979).

[220]*See* G.A. Res. 37/92, Annex, paras. 13, 14 (1982). The vote was 108–13–13, with the United States opposed. The formulation is a compromise between the strict prior consultation and prior consent views. *See* Jiménez de Aréchaga, *International Law in the Past Third of a Century*, 159 HAGUE ACADEMY, RECUEIL DES COURS 1, 266 (1978). The 1972 UNESCO Declaration on the Use of Satellite Broadcasting, art. 9, in 11 INT'L LEGAL MATERIALS 1476 (1972), is more equivocal on the need for prior agreement, but clearly calls for prior consultation. It says states should "reach *or promote* prior agreements" (emphasis added).

ences.[221] Since the General Assembly formulation defers to the stricter ITU standard, the latter would seem to supply the norm for direct broadcasting aimed at another state's receivers. Once direct television broadcasting satellite service has been established, consultations are to be undertaken on request.[222]

There appears to be no consent requirement before a state's resources are sensed from outer space, despite the opposing view of Argentina, Brazil, and a few others.[223] There is considerable support for a prior consent requirement relating to dissemination of sensed data, at least when relatively sensitive data are concerned.[224] In practice, the United States appears to have recognized a need to consult internationally before proceeding with a fully operational remote sensing program, although it continues to hold out against a consent requirement.[225] The U.S. Landsat remote sensing program was regarded as purely

[221] ITU Radio Regulation 428A, July 17, 1971, 23 U.S.T. 1527, 1648, T.I.A.S. 7435, provides: "In devising the characteristics of a space station in the broadcasting-satellite service, all technical means available shall be used to reduce, to the maximum extent practicable, the radiation over the territory of other countries unless an agreement has been previously reached with such countries." *See* A. Chayes & P. Laskin, Direct Broadcasting from Satellites: Policies and Problems 20–22 (Report of Am. Soc'y of Int'l L. Panel on International Telecommunications Policy, 1975), noting that Regulation 428A "would seem to mean that a broadcaster may not establish a system that transmits beyond the range of 'unavoidable' spillover without the recipient's consent." The practical effect of the broadcast frequency allocations made by ITU World Administrative Radio Conferences appears to preclude deliberate state-to-state satellite broadcasting without the consent of the receiving country. *See* U.N. Doc. A/AC.105/196, Annex IV, at 1–4 (1977) (Working paper submitted by U.K.). At the 1979 World Administrative Radio Conference, Regulation 428A was renumbered as 6222, without any change in language.

[222] G.A. Res. 37/92, Annex, para. 10 (1982).

[223] *See* the U.N. Secretary-General's background paper on remote sensing, U.N. Doc. A/AC.105/118, at 52 (1973); Stowe, *The Development of International Law Relating to Remote Sensing of the Earth from Outer Space*, in Proc. of the 19th Colloq. on the Law of Outer Space 92, 94 (1977); Christol, *International Space Law and the Less Developed Countries*, *id.* 243, 249–50. The Argentina-Brazil position appeared in their draft treaty on remote sensing, U.N. Doc. A/C.1/1047, art. 5 (1974).

[224] *See* not only the Argentina-Brazil draft treaty, *supra* note 223, art. 9, but also the France-U.S.S.R. working paper, U.N. Doc. A/AC.105/C.2/L.99, para. 5 (1974), and the draft text submitted by Chile, Nigeria, and Sierra Leone, U.N. Doc. A/AC.105/218, para. 16 (1978). The French-Soviet proposal would have required prior consent for all dissemination except information on natural disasters and phenomena that can be detrimental to the environment in general. Later, the Soviet Union advocated a prior consent requirement only for dissemination of high-resolution data. *See* U.N. Doc. A/AC.105/240, Annex I, at 5, 12 (1979). Colombia, Mexico, and some others have advocated a prior consent duty if data on natural resources are to be disseminated. See U.N. Doc. A/AC.105/288, Annex I, at 4–5, 12–14 (1981).

[225] *See U.N. Doc.* A/AC.105/C.2/SR.304, at 8–9 (1979).

experimental for several years, though it did involve dissemination, at cost, of the data obtained.[226] The Executive Branch resisted pressure from some members of Congress to convert it to an operational program, with an extensive network of ground stations and a comprehensive space segment, until the U.S. government could take other governments' views into account.[227] These consultations preceded not only actual dissemination of sensed data on a systematic basis but fully operational sensing itself. Because the principal proponent of unimpeded remote sensing activities has felt constrained to consult before establishing a program capable of systematic dissemination, while others advocate a more stringent norm, one must conclude that consultation is the minimum applicable predissemination requirement. Support for a predissemination consent norm is less extensive than in the case of direct satellite broadcasting.

In at least two other situations where space-related activities could affect peculiarly another state or a few identifiable states, consultation is required before a decision is implemented—although probably not before it is made. First, the Agreement

[226]The first Landsat (then called ERTS-1) launch in July 1972 was coordinated with foreign scientists, and was preceded by a discussion in the First Committee of the General Assembly that raised the question of sovereign rights to remotely sensed data. *See* 26 U.N. GAOR, C.1 (1821st mtg.) at 5, 13; (1822nd mtg.) at 2; (1823rd mtg.) at 1-2, 13; (1824th mtg.) at 5, 8; (1825th mtg.) at 3, 5, 7 (1971). Although the First Committee discussion did not consider the proposed ERTS-1 launch in any detail, it was conducted with that launch in mind.

The Soviet Union operates an experimental remote sensing program, but apparently disseminates the data internationally only with the consent of the sensed states. *See* U.N. Doc. A/AC.105/216, at 10 (1978).

[227]*See* the statement of the Acting Director, Bureau of International Scientific and Technological Affairs, U.S. State Dep't, in *Earth Resources Satellites: Hearings Before the Senate Comm. on Aeronautical and Space Sciences*, 93d Cong., 2d Sess. 282–83, 292–93 (1974). When the National Oceanic and Atmospheric Administration (NOAA) began seriously to contemplate a fully operational system, it prepared a report identifying the relevant issues, including those with international implications, and distributed the report to foreign governments (among others). *See* Aeronautics and Space Report of the President: 1980 Activities 49, *reprinted in* 1 UNITED STATES SPACE LAW: NATIONAL AND INTERNATIONAL REGULATION pt. I.A.6 (S. Gorove ed. 1982).

There have been a number of internationally coordinated space efforts with remote-sensing significance. *See, e.g.,* Convention for the Establishment of a European Space Agency, May 30, 1975, arts. 2(c) & 5(3), and Annex IV, art. 1, in 14 INT'L LEGAL MATERIALS 864 (1975); Agreement for a Cooperative Program Concerning the Development, Procurement and Use of a Space Laboratory, in Conjunction with the Space Shuttle System, Aug. 14, 1973, art. 9(B), 24 U.S.T. 2049, T.I.A.S. 7722; [U.S.] Act of June 19, 1975, 89 Stat. 223, 42 U.S.C. § 2484 (1976). These measures involve prior consultation, but the consultation is not intended primarily to consider the adverse interests of other states.

on the Rescue of Astronauts states that if its assistance would help rescue operations, the launching party is to cooperate with the state party on whose territory the spacecraft has landed; the latter party may control the search and rescue operations, but it "shall act in close and continuing consultation with the launching authority."[228] Second, the U.S.-European agreement on the use of a European Space Laboratory in connection with the U.S. Space Shuttle program provides that the U.S. government will consult with its European partners on the appropriate measures to be taken if the Space Shuttle program is not continued.[229]

D. Synthesis: Oceans and Outer Space

This chapter has considered measures taken in areas usually regarded as res communis. In a well-developed world-ordering system, one might expect to find that any procedural duties of states proposing to act in those areas would be owed to an appropriate international organization or other representative group acting on behalf of the larger world community, as well as to individual states peculiarly affected. The system has not yet reached that point. With a few exceptions (such as ocean dumping, under either the London Ocean Dumping Convention or the OECD radioactive waste disposal procedure), any prior consultation duty is owed primarily or exclusively to individual states. Even as to them, it cannot be said that there is an across-the-board duty to consult before a government makes an initial decision to act unilaterally in a way that might adversely affect the ocean or outer space environment.

Bilateral consultations with affected governments have been episodic, at best, before relatively firm decisions have been made to assert new claims to territorial or exclusive jurisdiction in the oceans. In some cases, multilateral negotiations at the Law of the Sea Conferences have antedated such decisions, but in other

[228] Agreement on the Rescue of Astronauts, the Return of Astronauts and the Return of Objects Launched into Outer Space, Apr. 22, 1968, art. 2, 19 U.S.T. 7570, T.I.A.S. No. 6599, 672 U.N.T.S. 119. Sztucki, *supra* note 184, at 166, says this provision also implies that there will be a preliminary consultation to decide whether participation by the launching authority is needed.

[229] Agreement for a Cooperative Program Concerning the Development, Procurement and Use of a Space Laboratory, in Conjunction with the Space Shuttle System, Aug. 14, 1973, art. 9(C), 24 U.S.T. 2049, T.I.A.S. 7722.

cases those negotiations have followed a basic, unilateral decision to assert a claim at some point in the future. Even when there have been prior negotiations at Law of the Sea Conferences, there is little evidence of the necessary opinio juris. Nevertheless, in almost all recent instances other than those involving defense-related claims or baselines across partially enclosed sea areas, there have been multilateral and / or bilateral negotiations with interested states before territorial or exclusive jurisdictional claims are put into effect,[230] and these negotiations seem to be regarded as essential. This is in part because the affected states' cooperation is desired, but it is also because their equities are recognized. These consultations do not regularly deal with such basic elements of the decision as the nature of the claim, its precise boundaries, or its effective date, but they do consider such matters as the magnitude and conditions of allowable foreign use in the area, length of any phase-out period, and so forth.

The normative framework is similar when new unilateral measures are proposed within existing areas of territorial sea or exclusive maritime jurisdiction. Thus, for example, there is no generally applicable norm requiring consultation before legislation either designates new species as creatures of the continental shelf or empowers a government official to do so. But there is an expectation that states traditionally fishing for those creatures will be consulted before the new regulation is put into force. The same principle applies to allocation of fishery quotas for years following that in which a new fishery zone claim is implemented: The coastal state may make the basic decision as to the amount it can harvest, without prior consultation, but must consult states with substantial fishing interests in the zone before allocating the surplus. Similarly, a coastal state may decide, without consultation, that it will look with disfavor on oceanographic research conducted by others on its continental

[230]The early claims of Ecuador and Peru are exceptions. *See* text at note 17 *supra*. Later claims of Uruguay and Panama may also be exceptions. *See* note 86 and accompanying text *supra*. Although some Latin American practice is consistent with the norm stated in the text (e.g., the Brazilian territorial sea claim in 1970–71 and the Nicaraguan fisheries claim in 1965), it is arguable that regional custom in Latin America does not require consultation before implementation of an exclusive maritime claim.

The statement in the text does not apply to claims of the right to explore and exploit a state's own continental shelf. That has been considered an inherent right, not subject to consultation, so long as the claim does not overlap another state's reasonable claim and does not extend beyond the natural prolongation of the land territory.

shelf or in its economic zone; but it must nevertheless consider any requests to conduct research on a case-by-case basis and take account of the position put forward by the requesting state.

When the only ocean-related right that lawfully could be asserted relates, not to the establishment or administration of a territorial sea or exclusive maritime area, but to a preferential or shared use, the prior consultation duty applies to all essential elements of the basic decision except the determination in principle to go ahead. It similarly applies to decisions on details of implementation.

This consultation duty in shared-use situations stems in part from the *Fisheries Jurisdiction* Cases. It extends to any state with an interest of a magnitude greater than that shared by all states interested in the res communis, and is not limited to states with as much to lose as the United Kingdom or the Federal Republic of Germany had in those cases. The duty is buttressed by treaty and nontreaty practice. The former includes article 7 of the Geneva Convention on Fishing and Conservation, the European Fisheries Convention, and (indirectly) article 2 of the Geneva Convention on the High Seas. Examples of nontreaty practice include the creation of the Canadian Arctic pollution control zones (involving extensive consultations after the relevant legislation was introduced in Parliament, but before it had gone through the legislative process), the U.S. State Department's alacrity in consulting foreign governments when the Congress was considering the extension of liability for oil pollution damage to 200 miles offshore, the General Assembly's 1970 Declaration of Principles Governing the Sea-Bed, and United States practice involving deep seabed mining while the Third Law of the Sea Conference was being held.

When unilateral action is permissible on the high seas because of special circumstances justifying what otherwise would be a violation of international law, a prior consultation norm applies unless there is an immediate emergency permitting no time for discussion. This force majeure exception seems inherent in any prior consultation norm that applies to situations in which major harm may result from any delay.

The Ocean Dumping Convention and state ocean dumping practice outside the Convention's regime also support the norm suggested by practice involving international watercourses and partially enclosed areas—requiring consultation with affected states, or with a body representing the international community, before a government executes a decision posing a significant risk of appreciable environmental harm beyond its own territory.

In addition, ocean-related practice arguably establishes a prior consultation norm when a competent international body has made a nonbinding recommendation concerning a proposed course of action by member states, but a member elects not to comply with the recommendation. The fact of membership raises a good-faith duty to consult the other members (or at least those specially affected) before departing from the recommendation, unless the discussion leading to the recommendation has served the same purpose. A leading example is found in the U.S. State Department's position when Congress was considering legislation regarding the fur seal harvest on the Pribilof Islands.[231] A fortiori, there would be a duty to refrain from unilateral action on a matter within the international body's competence unless there has been a submission of the matter for the body's consideration.[232]

The principal normative expectation emerging from practice related to outer space is that consultation will occur with interested states before a firm decision is made to undertake a space activity involving a serious risk of harm to the special interests of an identifiable state or group of states. Article 9 of the Outer Space Treaty supports this expectation when the effect is on other space activities; the expectation similarly is embodied (even as to effects on terrestrial interests) in the ITU, INTELSAT, and INMARSAT procedures. It also appears in the evolving law relating to direct satellite broadcasting and remote sensing (which may in some respects go further, by imposing prior consent obligations).

When the proposed space-related act posing the risk does not involve a space launch or a long-term use of outer space, any consultation duty applies to the manner in which the act is to be executed rather than to the basic decision whether or not to act. Examples include proposed visits to existing moon installations, rescues of astronauts, and elimination of joint space programs.

Finally, when a proposed space-related activity poses a risk

[231] *See* text at and following notes 106–07 *supra*.

[232] The principle is the same as that discussed in chapter II, text at notes 22–24 and 32–33 *supra*, relating to international lake and river commissions.

only to interests held in common by many or all states, as in the case of removal of quarantine for returning astronauts, prior consultation practice has not evolved. It may be questioned, however, whether the evolution will be long delayed when a serious environmental risk is involved. The ocean dumping analogy is a strong one and may lead to similar practice, at least when the risk from a particular outer space activity is thought to be greater than it was when the astronaut quarantine was removed. Perhaps all that is needed is agreement on an international agency competent to represent the common interest.

CHAPTER V

Alliances and International Organizations

A. INTRODUCTION

This chapter examines prior consultation practice regarding matters in which groups of nations have formally expressed their common interest (by adhering to the constituent instrument of an alliance or organization) and for which potentially useful multilateral consultative structures exist within the alliance or organization. The bodies selected for study include two comprised of states with widely shared values and common (though not necessarily uniform) apprehensions about possible external threats to those values. One of these bodies—the North Atlantic Treaty Organization (NATO)—is political-military in character, and the other—the European Community—is political-economic. These will be contrasted with the United Nations, the "universal" political-economic-social organization bringing together more than one hundred fifty nations with widely differing values and perceptions of world order.

In each case, the focus will be on consultations in the organizational context, rather than on consultation practice among individual member states. In other words, the study will concentrate on matters directly relevant to the achievement of each body's primary goals, as defined in its constituent instrument and its other basic documents.

B. A POLITICAL-MILITARY ALLIANCE: NATO

1. The Role of Consultation

The North Atlantic Alliance's stated purposes include safeguarding the freedom and democratic heritage of the members through collective self-defense, and promoting stability and well-being in the North Atlantic area.[1] The political consultation concept is important enough to the achievement of these purposes to be woven into the North Atlantic Treaty and stressed in all major NATO pronouncements on cooperation within the Alliance. Every NATO Secretary General has called upon the member states to conduct timely consultations when they formulate decisions affecting the Alliance.[2] Implicit in these assertions are the notions that a political alliance must reflect and generate mutual trust, and that the degree of trust is gauged by the extent to which national decision makers take the interests of other members into account when they act on matters within the ambit of the alliance. These notions prompted NATO's "three wise men," appointed in 1956, to assert, "Consultation within an alliance means more than exchange of information, though that is necessary. It means more than letting the NATO Council know about national decisions that have already been taken; or trying to enlist support for those decisions. It means the discussion of problems collectively, in the early stages of policy formulation, and before national positions become fixed."[3]

Consultation norms within the Alliance are not necessarily

The research for section B was supported by a NATO Research Fellowship. NATO is not responsible for anything said herein.

An earlier version of this section was published as an article, Kirgis, *NATO Consultations as a Component of National Decisionmaking,* 73 Am. J. Int'l L. 372 (1979). It is printed here by permission of the American Journal of International Law, which is published by the American Society of International Law.

[1]North Atlantic Treaty, Apr. 4, 1949, preamble, 63 Stat. 2241, T.I.A.S. No. 1964, 34 U.N.T.S. 243. NATO members are Belgium, Canada, Denmark, France, Federal Republic of Germany, Greece, Iceland, Italy, Luxembourg, the Netherlands, Norway, Portugal, Spain, Turkey, the United Kingdom, and the United States.

[2]Paul-Henri Spaak and Joseph Luns have been particularly emphatic. *See, e.g.*, Spaak, *The Political Future of NATO,* 7 NATO Letter, No. 12, at 1, 4–5 (1959); Luns, *Introduction,* in Transatlantic Crisis: Europe and America in the '70's 9, 12 (J. Godson ed. 1974). The efforts of the first four Secretaries-General are outlined in F. Beer, Integration and Disintegration in NATO 30–37 (1969). For the relevant Treaty provisions and collective pronouncements, see subsection 2 *infra*.

For the view that the process of consultation should be NATO's central function, see Holmes, *Fearful Symmetry: The Dilemmas of Consultation and Coordination in the North Atlantic Treaty Organization,* 22 Int'l Org. 821 (1968).

[3]Report of the Committee of Three on Non-military Co-operation in NATO, Dec. 13, 1956, in NATO Information Service, NATO Facts and Figures 308, 316 (1976). The three were Gaetano Martino (Italy), Halvard Lange (Norway), and Lester M. Pearson (Canada), all foreign ministers of their countries.

For the various possible meanings of "consultation" in the Alliance, see H. Cleveland, NATO: The Transatlantic Bargain 19 (1970).

limited to those embodied in the North Atlantic Treaty or other formal document. Insofar as NATO consultation practice has engendered expectations among Alliance decision makers that member governments will consult the others before they make decisions in definable circumstances, the practice can create legal norms within the Alliance. In traditional international law terms, a special custom within the Alliance is established if the nontreaty expectations are firm and are very widely shared among Alliance decision makers.

Some decisions by Alliance members must be made collectively if they are to be effective. This was true, for example, of decisions relating to the Conference on Security and Cooperation in Europe, where no individual state or small group of NATO states could hope to gain much by taking independent positions. It was also true of the U.S. nonmilitary responses to the Soviet invasion of Afghanistan in the winter of 1979–80.[4] Because there is little incentive to eschew allied consultation in such cases, the consultations do not normally reflect any perceived unwritten obligation and are of marginal significance to a normative study. This discussion will therefore concentrate on situations in which individual allies, or a small coterie of allies, might stand to gain—at least in the short run—by acting alone. Such cases test the extent of allied cooperation and make it possible to gauge a political alliance's capability to influence member governments' conduct through the growth of procedural legal norms.

We are concerned with the role of the Alliance as a means for bringing the collective interests of the membership into the decision-making process of each member. For example, if the U.S. government were considering a decision that could affect the capacity of the Alliance to serve its essential purposes, the question would be whether the United States is expected to (and does) consult the North Atlantic Council or in some other manner reaches all the NATO allies, not whether it consults one or a few allies with which it may have a special relationship.

Not all NATO consultations appear in published or unclassified records. The North Atlantic Council, the plenary body composed of representatives of all member states, holds meet-

[4]Some allies nevertheless thought the U.S. consultations were too hurried before it announced sanctions against the Soviet Union. *See* Financial Times, Apr. 18, 1980, at 18, col. 4.

ings of the permanent representatives (ambassadors) at least weekly and of the foreign ministers twice a year, but the proceedings are not public and the communiques issued after each ministerial meeting are so general as to reveal little more than the broad subjects discussed. In addition to the Council meetings, there are weekly luncheons at NATO headquarters attended by the member states' permanent representatives, but those discussions are strictly off the record. There are also informal, unrecorded consultations outside the Brussels headquarters, particularly in Washington, where diplomats at subambassadorial level stay in contact with their counterparts among the member countries' embassies. To avoid inaccuracies stemming from the lack of complete records, the discussion to follow deals only with those instances for which prior consultation or the lack thereof has been documented or may reasonably be inferred through published materials, unclassified NATO documents, or personal interviews.

2. The NATO Consultation Framework

a. North Atlantic Treaty Provisions. The North Atlantic Treaty provides, "The Parties will consult together whenever, in the opinion of any of them, the territorial integrity, political independence or security of any of the Parties is threatened."[5] This not only requires the allies to consult when one of them perceives such a threat, but implies that no party will respond unilaterally without first calling for consultation with the others. This implied duty can reasonably be inferred on a number of grounds. The consultation provision immediately precedes the article contemplating individual, as well as collective, self-defense in case of an armed attack against any party. Since any unilateral response could endanger all the allies, the consultation provision should be construed broadly to enable them to air their interests before the response is taken. Moreover, provisions in the constituent instrument of a political alliance should be construed, if it is reasonable in light of their language and context, in a manner most likely to promote cooperative effort.

This duty applies only when the territory, independence, or

[5]North Atlantic Treaty, *supra*, note 1, art. 4. The Warsaw Treaty, May 14, 1955, art. 3, in A SOURCE BOOK ON SOCIALIST INTERNATIONAL ORGANIZATIONS 1136 (W. Butler ed. 1978), contains a comparable provision. *See also id.* art. 4.

security of a party is "threatened." If there is more than a threat—for example, an actual armed attack without warning—nothing would require the attacked ally to delay its initial defensive measures for NATO consultations.

The Treaty's only other consultation provision requires the parties to consult, at the request of any of them, to review the Treaty after it has been in force for ten years or more. This implies that no party may denounce the Treaty or radically alter its commitments under it—moves that would have obvious effects on the security interests of the other allies—without consulting them. In other words, this provision qualifies the implied right of withdrawal that is generally thought to be inherent in a political alliance.[6]

In practice, the consultation issue has arisen in a variety of situations not involving immediate threats to the territorial integrity of member states or full-scale denunciations of the Treaty. One question, to which we shall return later, is whether the practice establishes broader norms of which those Treaty provisions are specific applications.

b. Recommendations and Declarations. When NATO's "three wise men" considered the role of consultations in fostering political cooperation within the Alliance in 1956, they recommended (inter alia):

> A member government should not, without adequate advance consultation, adopt firm policies or make major political pronouncements on matters which significantly affect the Alliance or any of its members, unless circumstances make such prior consultation obviously and demonstrably impossible; in developing their national policies, members should take into consideration the interest and views of other governments, particularly those most directly concerned, as expressed in NATO consultation, even where no community of views or consensus has been reached in the Council; where a consensus has been reached, it should be reflected in the formation of national policies.[7]

[6]The provision appears in North Atlantic Treaty, *supra,* note 1, art. 12. A right of withdrawal, implied by the nature of a treaty, is recognized in Vienna Convention on the Law of Treaties, art. 56(1)(b), U.N. Doc.A/CONF.39/27, 8 INT'L LEGAL MATERIALS 679 (1969). On its applicability to political alliances, see Fitzmaurice, *Second Report on the Law of Treaties* [1957] 2 Y.B. INT'L L. COMM'N 16, 38–39; T. ELIAS, THE MODERN LAW OF TREATIES 106 (1974); *cf. Int'l L. Comm'n Commentary to draft art.* 53, [1966] 2 Y.B. INT'L L. COMM'N 251, 61 AM. J. INT'L L. 417 (1967).

[7]Report of the Committee of Three, *supra,* note 3, at 318–19. The report drew in part on a 1951 report of another three-person NATO committee.

In addition, the 1956 report recommended "NATO consultation whenever economic issues of special interest to the Alliance are involved, particularly those which have political or defence implications or affect the economic health of the Atlantic Community as a whole."[8] The North Atlantic Council formally approved these recommendations.[9]

After reviewing a series of studies in 1967 on the future of the Alliance, the Council stated that "As sovereign states the Allies are not obligated to subordinate their policies to collective decision. The Alliance affords an effective forum and clearing house for the exchange of information and views; thus, each Ally can decide its policy in the light of close knowledge of the problems and objectives of the others. To this end the practice of frank and timely consultations needs to be deepened and improved."[10] The Council also made the highly equivocal statement: "In accordance with established usage the Allies, or such of them as wish to do so, will also continue to consult on [problems arising outside the North Atlantic Treaty area] without commitment and as the case may demand."[11]

In 1974 the NATO Heads of Government agreed to the Declaration on Atlantic Relations. During the previous year, Secretary of State Kissinger's tumultuous "Year of Europe," attempts to define the principles of transatlantic cooperation had created more discord than harmony. The consultation issue was particularly troublesome. In the end, the Declaration had this to say:

> The Allies are convinced that the fulfilment of their common aims requires the maintenance of close consultation, co-operation, and mutual trust, thus fostering the conditions necessary for defence and favourable for détente, which are complementary. In the spirit of the friendship, equality and solidarity which characterize their relationship, they are firmly resolved to keep each other fully informed and to strengthen the practice of frank and timely consultations by all means which may be appropriate on matters relating to their common interests as members of the Alliance, bearing in mind that these interests can be affected by events in other areas

[8] *Id.* at 323.

[9] Resolution on the Report of the Committee of Three on Non-military Co-operation in NATO, Dec. 13, 1956, *id.* at 335.

[10] Report of the Council for the Future Tasks of the Alliance (the Harmel Report), Dec. 14, 1967, *id.* at 336, 337.

[11] *Id.* at 339.

of the world. They wish also to ensure that their essential security relationship is supported by harmonious political and economic relations. In particular they will work to remove sources of conflict between their economic policies and to encourage economic cooperation with one another.[12]

The clear purport of the 1956, 1967, and 1974 pronouncements is that allied consultation should be informative and should precede important decisions, although it is not clear which decisions would be of the requisite magnitude. The assertion that consultation should *precede* decision was made explicit in the 1956 report and was retained in shorthand form in the 1967 and 1974 references to "frank and timely consultations." The 1956 and 1967 pronouncements left unclear whether the allies actually expected to be consulted regarding problems outside, as well as within, the North Atlantic Treaty area. The 1974 declaration is less equivocal on that point, noting that the allies' common interests can be affected by events in other areas of the world. Thus, even though the 1974 declaration does not define the circumstances in which common interests would be affected, it shows that prior consultation expectations may arise even as to events outside Europe and North America.

Do these pronouncements create a legal obligation to consult when "common interests" would be affected? The leading study on the legal effect of North Atlantic Council decisions concluded that, "To the extent that a resolution *purported* to impose an obligation, member states in principle have acted as if they were bound by reason of their concurrence. . . . [E]ven if one takes the view that the NATO Council . . . is nothing more than a conference of member states and has no power to make authoritative decisions, there can be no question . . . that certain resolutions agreed upon unanimously by the national representatives in the Council would constitute *international agreements* creating international obligations for the member states."[13] That would be so, a fortiori, when the heads of government issue a declaration. But none of the major pronouncements on consultation was couched in clearly obligatory terms, and all are rather vague as to just what types of decision call for consul-

[12]Declaration on Atlantic Relations, June 26, 1974, para. 11, *id.* at 340, 342, *reprinted in* 71 DEP'T ST. BULL. 42, 44 (1974).

[13]Stein and Carreau, *Law and Peaceful Change in a Subsystem: "Withdrawal" of France from the North Atlantic Treaty Organization*, 62 AM. J. INT'L L. 577, 608, 613 (1968) (emphasis in the original).

tation.[14] Even the 1974 declaration said only that the parties "are firmly resolved" to strengthen the "practice" of prior consultation. This suggests that existing practice had not been extensive or consistent enough to establish a prior consultation norm on all matters of common interest to the Alliance; certainly, words such as "firm resolve" do not convey an intent to create a binding norm then and there.

In fact, the declaration deliberately fell short of a normative assertion, but only because the French government would have dissented if it had stated the prior consultation principle in clearly obligatory terms. After the declaration had been signed, Secretary of State Kissinger told the press that the problem was whether the consultation principle "was intended to be a legal obligation or a practice reflecting the spirit of the alliance."[15] He also said that it had always been the American view that a declaration does not represent a set of legal obligations, but this appears to have been partly another bow to the French antipathy and partly an expression of the Austinian notion that there can be no truly "legal" obligation without the means to compel compliance.[16] At the same news conference, Secretary Kissinger described United States intentions in terms that very nearly promised to consult: "As the country which has the most interests outside of the treaty area of any of our allies, we will meticulously implement the principle of consultation . . . ." He added that although emergencies might arise in which the United States would have to act without consulting the allies, "[I]n all situations which are not emergency situations, the United States feels an obligation to concert its general policies with those of its allies."[17] NATO officials viewed the declaration as a commitment,[18] though it is not clear whether they considered it a

[14] In addition to the 1956, 1967, and 1974 pronouncements, the North Atlantic Council has endorsed the principle of intensified consultations on several occasions. *See, e.g.*, the Council's communiques of May 10, 1961, para. 10, in NATO, TEXTS OF FINAL COMMUNIQUES 1949–74, at 136, 137–38 (1975); Dec. 15, 1962, para. 7, *id.* at 147, 148; May 24, 1963, para. 7, *id.* at 150, 151. Nonmandatory language was used.

[15] Kissinger News Conference, 71 DEP'T ST. BULL. 37, 39 (1974).

[16] Kissinger's disclaimer regarding the legal effect of a declaration is in *id.* at 37. The French position is reported in Atlantic News, June 19, 1974, at 1, and June 20, 1974, at 2. *See also* the remarks of U.S. Press Secretary Ronald Ziegler, 71 DEP'T ST. BULL. 171, 172 (1974) ("consultation should not be viewed as a legally binding obligation"), and of Kissinger in *id.* at 629, 632 ("you can't wave a paper at somebody and tell him he's obliged to consult if he doesn't want to consult").

[17] *Id.* at 37, 38.

[18] *See* Neff, *NATO Political Consultation: Fact or Myth?*, 23 NATO REV., No. 1, at 7 (1975).

legal commitment in the sense that a failure to consult would violate an obligatory norm of the organization. Nor is it clear whether they thought it applied to all matters of common interest to the Alliance. Perhaps the declaration might best be put in the "twilight zone" between formally binding instruments and those of no legal significance.[19]

Several presidents of the United States have affirmed their intention to consult the NATO allies on decisions of particular interest to them. For example, when General de Gaulle proposed that France, the United Kingdom, and the United States form a tripartite "directorate" for closer political coordination, President Eisenhower replied, "We cannot afford to adopt any system which would give to our other allies, or other free world countries, the impression that basic decisions affecting their own vital interests are being made without their participation."[20] This is significant because of its context. The President declined a tempting opportunity to limit consultations on important matters to those allies having the most to contribute, in favor of a continuing commitment to the more cumbersome process of NATO consultations.

Although the President did not use the language of legal obligation, the necessary inference from what he said—that basic decisions affecting the allies' vital interests would not be made without their participation—must have created expectations that the United States, at least, would act accordingly. That kind of expectation, if reinforced in practice and through affirmation over time by the appropriate decision makers, can create a norm having the force of law, even though—as in most international law situations—unwilling governments cannot be coerced into compliance.

Presidents Nixon, Ford, and Carter all reaffirmed the American intention to consult. On his thirty-sixth day in office, President Nixon pledged to the North Atlantic Council that there would be full and genuine consultations before and during U.S. arms control negotiations with the Soviet Union, and added: "Beyond consulting on those negotiations, and beyond consulting on other policies that directly affect the NATO nations

[19] *Cf.* Schachter, *The Twilight Existence of Nonbinding International Agreements,* 71 Am. J. Int'l L. 296 (1977).

[20] *The Atlantic Alliance: Hearings Before a Subcomm. of the Senate Comm. on Government Operations,* 89th Cong., 2d Sess., pt. 7, at 230 (1966) [hereinafter cited as *Hearings on the Atlantic Alliance*].

themselves, I intend to consult on a broad range of other matters. I shall not only welcome but actively seek the counsel of America's NATO partners on the questions that may affect the peace and stability of the world, whatever the part of the world in which they arise."[21] President Ford, addressing the North Atlantic Council in 1975, called for improving the process of political consultation, and concluded, "We should further cultivate the habit of discussing our approaches to those matters which touch the interests of all so that we can develop common policies to deal with common problems."[22] President Carter, within the same forum in 1978, said, "We have set an excellent record of consulting with one another on a wide range of issues. That can and should continue, and the United States will increasingly draw the NATO allies into its counsels."[23]

The pronouncements discussed in this subsection all assert or imply that consultations will precede decision making and will not be limited to decisions regarding events within the North Atlantic geographic area. They would raise expectations that the allies will be consulted before decisions affecting their vital interests are made, at least to the extent that actual practice defines the decisions and allied interests sufficiently to guide those responsible for conducting consultations or for evaluating the adequacy of others' consultations. To this the discussion now turns.

3. Action Within the Alliance Affecting NATO Defenses in Europe

a. Decisions to Limit Military Commitments. If there are obligatory NATO consultation norms not stemming directly from North Atlantic Treaty provisions, one would expect them to be most evident when significant changes in military commitments to the Alliance are at stake. That is, in fact, the case.

The NATO allies annually make and revise rolling five-year defense plans under a system that involves detailed consultations by each member government in the preparation of its annual defense budget. In its current form, the rather elaborate process essentially involves an annual comparison between the

[21] 60 DEP'T ST. BULL. 250, 252 (1969).
[22] 72 *id.* at 886, 888 (1975).
[23] 78 *id.*, Feb. 1978, at 16.

proposed five-year defense plans of those allies participating in the integrated NATO defense system (all member states except France, Greece, and Iceland) and the force goals approved by the NATO Defence Planning Committee, which consists of representatives of the same member states. When a member state's proposed defense plan falls short of the goals set for it by the Defence Planning Committee, the NATO staff and representatives of other allied governments attempt to persuade the member to come closer to the goals. Nevertheless, each member government retains the final authority to determine the size of its military budget,[24] and the combined NATO five-year Force Plan emerges each year as the sum of those national decisions. Each government is committed to supply the forces designated in the Plan for the first year only.[25]

Although this process has evolved over the years, some form of review has been held before national defense budgets have been adopted each year since 1952.[26] The allies participating in the integrated defense system do not consider themselves free to bypass this consultation process. Thus, at least for member states that have not opted out of fully integrated NATO defense, this procedure amounts to a legal duty supported by consistent practice under the conviction that the practice is required—the essence of custom in international law.

There have been several occasions when individual member states have wished to withdraw substantial force commitments from NATO, apart from the normal fluctuations reflecting annual budget revisions. In 1955 the North Atlantic Council adopted a resolution setting forth the procedures for such cases. The resolution said that the Council:

> RECOGNISING that important quantitative or qualitative changes in member countries' contributions to NATO defence are of concern to the Alliance as a whole and that any such change is therefore properly the subject of multilateral consideration within NATO; . . .
>
> RECOGNISING also that, while the procedures of the Annual Review are the normal method adopted in the Alliance for mul-

[24] *See* L. Sloss, NATO Reform: Prospects and Priorities 6 (3 The Washington Papers, 1975).

[25] This simplified outline of the military budget consultation procedure is based on NATO Facts and Figures, *supra* note 3, at 113–15, and on an interview with the Head of the NATO Press Service, July 5, 1978.

[26] NATO Facts and Figures, *supra* note 3, at 112.

tilateral consideration of national contributions to NATO defence, provision should be made for circumstances in which a member government feels compelled to make important qualitative or quantitative changes in its current or prospective force contributions to NATO, at a time of year, or with a degree of urgency, which render impracticable their consideration under the normal procedure;

AGREES therefore that in the circumstances described above:

(*a*) The government concerned shall inform the Council and the appropriate NATO military authorities of the changes contemplated. This shall be done, whenever possible, in time for the Council's views to be fully considered by the government concerned before the execution of decisions on the matters in question.

(*b*) If a government feels compelled to withdraw units from the area of NATO command to which they are assigned or earmarked in order to meet an emergency elsewhere, it shall at once inform the appropriate NATO military authorities, and the Council, at the first possible opportunity.[27]

This resolution uses legislative language calling upon member states to consult "before the execution" of pertinent decisions in the absence of an emergency. It would create a legal obligation unless the parties' practice demonstrates that they do not view it as such.[28]

At various times the United States, France, Canada, Greece, the United Kingdom, the Netherlands, and Italy have reduced their NATO military commitments in ways that would arguably fall within the resolution's compass. Because the French and Greek reductions were special cases, they will be examined after the others.

In the spring of 1966, the United States withdrew 30,000 trained troops from Europe for use in Viet Nam, replacing them with 15,000 inexperienced troops. The remaining 15,000 replacements were to be supplied by the end of the year. There appears to have been no prior consultation.[29] One could argue, however, that the temporary nature of the reduction in strength removed the incident from the resolution's purview, or that the

[27]North Atlantic Council Resolution on Important Changes in National Defence Efforts, Oct. 5, 1955, paras. 3, 7, 8, NATO Doc. C-M(55) 82(Final) (unclassified). The consultations actually are conducted by NATO's Defence Planning Committee.

[28]On the legal effect of "legislative" Council resolutions, see text at note 13 *supra.*

[29]*See Hearings on the Atlantic Alliance, supra* note 20, pt. 1, at 26; pt. 4, at 146, 147; pt. 6, at 194 (1966).

situation in Viet Nam amounted to an emergency in which only prompt notification was required. Consequently, this was not a clear case of failure to comply with the consultation procedure.

Another indeterminate case occurred in 1967, when a coordinated effort by the United States and United Kingdom to reduce the foreign exchange costs of stationing forces in West Germany resulted in the removal of 33,000 troops and four air squadrons to the United States and of 5,000 troops to the United Kingdom. All of the troops and equipment remained committed to NATO. Consultations were held with the West German government and apparently with some other allies before the decisions were made, but the discussions within NATO itself—which were held before the removals—seem essentially to have consisted of efforts by the U.S. and U.K. to convince the allies to acquiesce.[30] Since technically there was no change in the American and British force contributions to NATO, the consultation procedure arguably did not apply. One could also argue that even if it did apply, the U.S. and U.K. complied with it by discussing the matter within NATO before they removed the troops and equipment. But it is conceivable that the decisions involved "important qualitative changes" in force contributions, which would have brought the consultation procedure into play; if so, the presentations to the allies would not have satisfied its requirements unless there was some realistic chance that the final decisions—or at least the manner in which they were to be executed—could have been affected by the allies' responses.

When the United States later contemplated a troop reduction that clearly would have come within the consultation procedure, it did discuss the matter with its NATO allies. In 1970–71, the Nixon administration considered reducing U.S. troop strength in Europe, conducted a study, consulted within NATO, and finally decided against any such cuts.[31]

The Canadian government carried out a comprehensive defense review in the spring of 1969. By early April it had decided

[30] *See* H. CLEVELAND, *supra* note 3, at 113–16; 16 KEESING'S CONTEMP. ARCHIVES 22176–77 (1967).

[31] *See* Yochelson, *The American Military Presence in Europe: Current Debate in the United States*, 15 ORBIS 784, 788 (1971); Kohl, *The Nixon-Kissinger Foreign Policy System and U.S.-European Relations: Patterns of Policy-Making*, 28 WORLD POLITICS 1, 27–30 (1975). At various times the United States has pledged to its NATO allies that it would not reduce its NATO troop commitment unilaterally. See *U.S. Forces in NATO: Hearings Before a Subcomm. of the House Comm. on Foreign Affairs*, 93d Cong., 1st Sess. 335 (1973).

to remain within the integrated military command but to conduct a phased reduction of Canadian forces in Europe. In announcing its intention, the government expressly recognized an obligation to follow the NATO consultation procedure to determine the magnitude of the reduction and details concerning it, but rejected any duty to consult regarding the basic decision to reduce the forces.[32] When some of the allies suspected that Canada might not follow the procedure exactly, they objected; the Canadian government reiterated its intention to comply, though it insisted that the initial decision to reduce forces was not subject to the procedure.[33] Clearly, Canada acquiesced in a legal duty to consult the allies regarding execution of the basic decision.

A similar defense review was conducted by the British government in 1974. A decision was reached in December to reduce the portion of gross national product committed to defense by a total of 1 percent over the next ten years, and a tentative blueprint was drawn up showing how this would be carried out. It included, among other things, withdrawal of British regular forces in the Mediterranean from NATO command. The British government stated its intention to consult the NATO allies before making its final decisions.[34] In the end, some changes were made in response to the consultations, though they were not of major significance. The British Defence White Paper on the cutbacks reveals the scope and effect of the consultations:

> During our consultations with our NATO Allies they have asked us to reconsider those features of the reductions which they consider most damaging and to study the possibility of undertaking certain compensatory measures. We have undertaken to study such measures on the clear understanding that all of Britain's defence commitments and capabilities must be met from within the total of resources which the Government decided last December it could in future allocate to defence.[35]

In December 1976 the United Kingdom announced another substantial reduction in planned defense expenditures, amounting to about £230 million. Again, consultations were

[32] *See* 7 CAN. PARL. DEB., H.C., 28th Parl., 1st Sess. 7724, 7905–06 (1969); 9 *id.* at 9306.

[33] *Id.* at 9327, 9382.

[34] See 22 NATO REV., No. 4, at 13, 14 (1974); 882 PARL. DEB., H.C. (5th ser.) 1352–53 (1974).

[35] STATEMENT ON THE DEFENCE ESTIMATES 1975, Cmd. No. 5976, at 13 (1975).

held before the final decision, but without any prospect of inducing a reconsideration of the size of the net reduction.[36] Similarly, when the British government decided in June 1981 that it would phase out a substantial number of the Royal Navy's large warships over a period of years, it delayed any decision on the details of the plan pending discussions with the NATO allies.[37]

In May 1974 the Netherlands proposed a large reduction in its military manpower assigned to NATO. The government then went through the established consultation procedure and modified some aspects of its proposal in response to allied criticisms. Nevertheless, the final reduction was quite substantial.[38] When the Dutch government in August 1975 proposed another reduction, this time affecting only its naval forces and equipment, further NATO consultations were held. The allies asked the government to reconsider, but its final decision remained unchanged.[39]

Italy devised a plan to reduce its armed forces by 20 percent in early 1976 and initiated NATO consultations. Because the reduction actually would increase the efficiency of the Italian armed services, the NATO allies contented themselves with a token statement of concern. No change was made in the Italian plan.[40]

The French measures of March 1966 were of a nature and magnitude quite different from those discussed above. Without prior consultation, General de Gaulle announced that France was going to withdraw all its army and air forces then under NATO command[41] and demand that NATO military headquarters and individual allied military installations be removed from French territory.[42] The French notes to the allied gov-

[36]*See* Atlantic News, Sept. 21, 1977, at 1–2.

[37]*See* Washington Post, June 20, 1981, p. A11, col. 2.

[38]*See* Atlantic News, July 10, 1974, at 1–2. The Dutch NATO commitment was reduced by 20,000 men.

[39]NATO Press Release (75) 16, Sept. 26, 1975; interview with the Head of the NATO Press Service, July 7, 1978.

[40]Interview with the Head of the NATO Press Service, *supra* note 25; *see also* 26 NATO Rev., No. 1, at 17 (1978).

[41]French naval forces already had been withdrawn.

[42]Individual allies could have kept their military facilities in France if they had agreed to place them under French operational control.

Although there was no consultation, de Gaulle had warned as early as September 1965 that France planned eventually to withdraw from the integrated NATO command. *See* R. Jordan, Political Leadership in NATO: A Study in Multinational Diplomacy 192–95 (1979).

ernments expressly rejected negotiations over anything other than problems caused by the decision.[43] Not only did France fail to comply with the Council's consultation procedure, but it arguably breached the implied North Atlantic Treaty obligation to consult by means of a review conference if it wished radically to alter its Treaty commitment.[44]

Greece followed the French lead in 1974, albeit on a much smaller scale. It withdrew from the NATO integrated military command, which involved little more than the removal of Greek officers from NATO facilities in Turkey. It also withdrew from the NATO Defence Planning Committee, but kept its representatives in the Supreme Headquarters Allied Powers Europe (SHAPE) and in some other military coordinating bodies. There was no consultation before the Greek decision.[45]

Despite the French and Greek failures to consult, the overall NATO practice of compliance with the Council's consultation procedure adequately supports it as the law of the organization. Canada, the United Kingdom, the Netherlands, and Italy demonstrated that they felt obliged to consult, but by their practice they established that the consultations need not precede a firm decision to reduce forces. They need only precede decisions regarding such matters as the magnitude and timing of the reduction—"the execution of decisions on the matters in question," to use the terms of the Council resolution. The one case in which the United States consulted even as to the basic decision cannot by itself establish a precedent.

The other cases were borderline as to whether they fit within the resolution (the 1966 and 1967 cases involving the United States), or involved aberrational conduct (de Gaulle's highly

[43] *See, e.g.*, the French Aide-Mémoire to Canada, in 3 CAN. PARL. DEB., H.C., 27th Parl., 1st Sess. 2917–18 (1966); French Aide-Mémoire to the U.S., 54 DEP'T ST. BULL. 617–18 (1966), and the U.S. response, *id.* at 617. *See also* the statement by Secretary of State Dean Rusk, *id.* at 695.

The French did not ask NATO to remove its political headquarters, though the allies ultimately decided that the civilian headquarters should follow the military to Belgium. France did continue to participate not only in NATO political activities, but in some defense matters. *See* H. CLEVELAND, *supra* note 3, at 102–03.

[44] *See* text at note 6 *supra*. Stein & Carreau, *supra* note 13, at 620, 639, conclude that even if France was entitled to withdraw its military cooperation under the doctrine of changed circumstances, it had a good-faith duty to submit a reorganization proposal to the Council.

[45] Interview with the Head of the NATO Press Service, *supra* note 25; *see also* R. HILL, POLITICAL CONSULTATION IN NATO: PARLIAMENTARY AND POLICY ASPECTS 79 (Canadian Dep't of Nat'l Defence ORAE Mem. No. M72, 1975).

nationalistic decision, of which only three members of his own cabinet were informed in advance,[46] and Greece's decision, made virtually overnight in reaction to the Turkish invasion of Cyprus). The allied responses to the manner in which France and Greece acted, though diplomatic in tone, clearly did not acquiesce in the failures to consult.[47] The resolution's normative character thus seems to have been preserved.

b. Use or Production of Tactical Nuclear Weapons. Another formal NATO consultation procedure is in the guidelines on the use of tactical nuclear weapons in Europe. Originally devised at the 1962 NATO ministerial meeting in Athens and since revised, these guidelines require (subject to a caveat mentioned below) that a member considering the use of nuclear weapons in Europe consult all member governments. The latter would transmit their views through the North Atlantic Council or the NATO Defence Planning Committee to the government of the nuclear power, which retains the final decision-making authority. The caveat is that the full procedure need not be used if time and circumstances do not permit. It is apparently understood that time and circumstances would not permit during either a nuclear or a full-scale conventional attack on Western Europe. But even in those cases, consultation apparently would be required with those NATO states on whose territories the weapons are based or would fall and with those providing the nuclear warheads and / or delivery systems.[48] Consultation with these states has been called an "obligation" in a report issued by a committee of the Western European Union.[49] The implication is not that full-scale NATO consultation is never an ob-

[46]*See* Rousseau, *Chronique des Faits Internationaux,* 70 REVUE GÉNÉRALE DE DROIT INT'L PUBLIC 736, 760–61 (1966).

[47]*See* the declaration by the NATO allies other than France, stressing the need to consult and act together, 3 CAN. PARL. DEB., H.C., 27th Parl., 1st Sess. 2875 (1966). *See also* the statement by U.S. Under Secretary of State George Ball regarding French unilateralism, 54 DEP'T ST. BULL. 613, 616 (1966).

[48]*See* STAFF OF SENATE COMM. ON FOREIGN RELATIONS, 93D CONG., 1ST SESS., U.S. SECURITY ISSUES IN EUROPE: BURDEN SHARING AND OFFSET, MBFR AND NUCLEAR WEAPONS 19–20 (Comm. Print 1973); *Nuclear Weapons and Foreign Policy: Hearings Before Subcomms. of the Senate Comm. on Foreign Relations,* 93d Cong., 2d Sess. 156–57 (1974) (statement of Secretary of Defense James R. Schlesinger); COMM. ON DEFENCE QUESTIONS AND ARMAMENTS OF THE WESTERN EUROPEAN UNION ASSEMBLY, COMMUNICATIONS AND CRISIS MANAGEMENT IN THE ALLIANCE 20 (1977) [hereinafter cited as REPORT OF THE COMM. on DEFENCE QUESTIONS AND ARMAMENTS].

[49]REPORT OF THE COMM. on DEFENCE QUESTIONS AND ARMAMENTS, *supra* note 48.

ligation, but that the obligation is qualified by the need to act quickly in extreme circumstances—provided that the governments primarily involved are consulted.

The Athens guidelines concern the use of nuclear weapons once they have been deployed in Europe. In the late 1970s the United States consulted its European allies intensively regarding another nuclear weapons issue: whether to produce an enhanced radiation warhead, or "neutron weapon."[50] The case, however, was not one in which the United States had a substantial incentive to make its decision unilaterally, since the warhead was to be produced primarily for use in Europe. There would have been little point in producing it without some assurances from the European states that they would ultimately allow it to be deployed on their territories. When the United States finally decided in 1981 to produce the warhead, it did so without further consultations, but with the acknowledgement that it would have to consult the countries involved before deploying the warhead on their territories.[51]

c. Appointment of SACEUR. There is greater normative significance in the U.S. practice of consulting its NATO allies before appointing a new Supreme Allied Commander, Europe (SACEUR). Although it would be shortsighted not to consult fully, the importance of the position to the United States and its practical ability to place its preferred designee in the job could induce it to hold only pro forma consultations. It appears, however, that the U.S. government has taken the consultations seriously.[52]

d. Disputes Among Member States. On a few well-known occasions, a NATO member state has attempted to resolve a dispute with another member by using force or taking other action that would adversely affect the other member's military capability

[50]The enhanced radiation warhead would kill enemy troops without causing extensive damage to inanimate objects. On the NATO consultations, see Atlantic News, Sept. 28, 1977, at 4; *id.*, Oct. 14, 1977, at 1; *id.*, Dec. 10, 1977, at 2; *id.*, Mar. 22, 1978, at 4; *id.*, Mar. 24, 1978, at 1.

[51]*See* Washington Post, Aug. 10, 1981, at A6, cols. 3–4.

[52]U.S. consultations appear in H. CLEVELAND, *supra* note 3, at 128; R. JORDAN, *supra* note 42, at 44, 143; N.Y. Times, Sept. 6, 1974, at 1, col. 5; *id.*, Mar. 1, 1979, at A13, col. 6.

in the European area. The issue is not whether there are prior consultations between the disputants in such cases, but whether there are prior consultations within NATO in order to bring the collective interests of the Alliance into the decision-making process.

The most notorious nonamicable attempts to resolve disputes have been the Anglo-Icelandic "cod wars" and the Cyprus hostilities involving Greece and Turkey. The first cod war occurred in 1958, when Iceland extended its exclusive fisheries jurisdiction to twelve miles. This cut heavily into long-established British fishing interests off Iceland's coasts. Just before the decree's September 1 effective date, fishery experts of the NATO states (including Iceland and the U.K.) met to try to find a solution. When no solution was reached, Iceland put the new fishing zone into effect, and the British government promptly sent in destroyers to protect the British trawlers. Although there is no public record of what was said at the NATO meeting, it is reasonable to assume not only that Iceland discussed its plans to go ahead as scheduled, but that the U.K. revealed its proposed response.[53]

Iceland again extended its exclusive fishery zone (to fifty miles) on September 1, 1972, but the U.K. refrained from sending in destroyers until May 1973, after incidents had occurred between the Icelandic Coast Guard and British trawlers. The British government did not consult its NATO allies before acting. It simply told the North Atlantic Council what it was doing.[54]

In July 1974 a faction of the Greek Cypriot National Guard, supported by the military junta in Greece, ousted Archbishop Makarios as President of Cyprus and installed a firm advocate of union with Greece. Five days later, Turkey invaded Cyprus and set up a Turkish Cypriot administration in northern Cyprus. Turkey later widened its area of control. Although high-level representatives of the United States and United Kingdom were in urgent telephone and personal contact with their Turkish and Greek counterparts during the five days before the original Turkish invasion, there is no indication that the Turks

[53] *See* 11 KEESING'S CONTEMP. ARCHIVES 16479 (1958). The British government already had warned that it would send in destroyers if necessary.

[54] *See* 19 *id.* at 26028, 26030 (1973); Atlantic News, May 23, 1973, at 1.

or Greeks felt obliged to consult anyone.[55] Rather, the contacts amounted to last-minute peacekeeping efforts by two vitally concerned allies, and in any event they did not encompass the Alliance as a whole.

Greek-Turkish animosities over Cyprus have also raised a NATO consultation issue in a somewhat different form. When violence between Greek and Turkish Cypriots threatened to escalate into war between Greece and Turkey in November 1967, the President of the United States hurriedly dispatched Cyrus Vance to Ankara to mediate the dispute, without consulting NATO. Nevertheless, the NATO Secretary-General, Manlio Brosio, quickly joined Vance and worked with him to quell the crisis.[56] In effect, the United States acted without consultation in its initial reaction to a perceived emergency, but did consult fully with the authorized NATO representative in resolving the matter.

When measures adversely affecting an ally's military capabilities have fallen short of threatened or actual hostilities, there are instances of consultation within the Alliance. For example, after the 1971 Icelandic elections, the new government announced that it would invoke the consultative procedure in the 1951 agreement with the United States with a view to possible termination of their mutual defense arrangement. Under the procedure, Iceland could have closed the U.S. air base at Keflavik after allowing six months for consultations within the North Atlantic Council and a further twelve months for readjustment if the consultations failed to produce an agreed solution.[57] Council consultations were held, and a settlement permitting continued U.S. operation of the base was reached in 1974 (following a change of government in Iceland).[58]

[55] *See* Stern, *Bitter Lessons: How We Failed in Cyprus,* FOREIGN POL'Y, No. 19, at 34, 62–64 (1975); Rudnick, *NATO and the Cyprus Crisis,* THE ROUND TABLE, No. 266, at 182, 187 (1977). For a report of postinvasion NATO consultations, *see* R. HILL, POLITICAL CONSULTATIONS IN NATO 27 (6 Wellesley Papers 1978).

When Turkey sent the Sismick I into the Aegean Sea for geologic soundings in July 1976, serious tension with Greece again resulted. There were no North Atlantic Council consultations because the matter was considered essentially a bilateral affair. Atlantic News, July 20, 1976, at 3.

[56] *See* R. JORDAN, *supra* note 42, at 210–12.

[57] *See* Defense Agreement with Iceland Pursuant to the North Atlantic Treaty, May 5, 1951, art. 7, 2 U.S.T. 1195, T.I.A.S. No. 2266, 205 U.N.T.S. 173.

[58] *See* Bjarnason, *Iceland's Position in NATO,* 15 ATLANTIC COMMUNITY Q. 393, 400–401 (1977).

Similar situations have occurred in Portugal and in Greece. Both have considered closing U.S. bases. In 1975 the Portuguese government discussed closing U.S. air bases in the Azores with the United States and in the North Atlantic Council; in 1982 the socialist Greek government affirmed that it would not act unilaterally when it contemplated closing all U.S. bases in Greece.[59]

After the Turkish invasion of Cyprus in 1974, the U.S. Congress legislated an embargo on arms transfers to Turkey. The legislation was discussed in the North Atlantic Council before it went into force, but not with much hope of influencing the outcome.[60] Later, when the House of Representatives rejected a proposal for a partial lifting of the embargo, Turkey retaliated by closing American bases. The NATO allies knew beforehand of the Turkish threat to close the bases, but the decision to do so apparently was not discussed in the North Atlantic Council until after it had been made.[61] The element of retaliation sets this case apart.

Not all policy decisions directly affecting an ally's military capability have involved arms embargoes or the closing of bases. For example, in the fall of 1962 the United States decided not to proceed with the development of Skybolt, a missile the United Kingdom had relied upon to give new life to its strategic bomber force. Before President Kennedy and Prime Minister MacMillan formally announced the demise of Skybolt at their December 1962 summit meeting in the Bahamas, Secretary of Defense McNamara had flown to London to discuss the decision and had then attended a North Atlantic Council Ministerial

[59] 35 Facts on File 387 (1975) refers to Portuguese willingness to resume talks with the U.S. on the Azores issue. R. Hill, *supra* note 55, at 95, poses the North Atlantic Council discussion hypothetically. The author, however, was in a position to know whether the discussion occurred, and presumably stated it hypothetically to avoid public confirmation of matters not officially on the public record. The Greek intention to consult appears in Washington Post, May 15, 1982, at A26, col. 4.

[60] André de Staercke, who was the Belgian Permanent Representative to NATO at that time and dean of the NATO ambassadorial corps, characterized the discussion as notification rather than consultation. Interview with Ambassador de Staercke, July 6, 1978. To the same effect: interview with a political officer in the U.S. delegation to NATO, July 14, 1978.

[61] Interview with U.S. political officer, *supra* note 60; Atlantic News, July 11, 1975, at 3; *id.*, July 30, 1975, at 1–2.

It will be recalled that the French measures of March 1966 included the closing of allied military installations. There were no prior consultations. *See* text at note 42 *supra*. That case, however, involved a violation of an explicit procedural norm.

meeting at which the allies undoubtedly explored the matter.[62] Despite assertions to the contrary by Secretary McNamara and Prime Minister MacMillan, the U.S. decision seems to have been made before the London and NATO discussions. The only questions left open had to do with the alternatives to Skybolt to be offered the United Kingdom.[63]

Another decision affecting an ally's military capability, though less directly than in the case of Skybolt, was that of the U.S. and U.K. to supply arms to Tunisia during Algeria's war of independence from France. There was no prior NATO consultation. Since the arms could well have found their way to Algeria or could have freed other weapons for that purpose, the Anglo-American decision precipitated a minor NATO crisis. France charged that the two allies had violated the consultation principles set forth by the three wise men in 1956.[64]

The occasional instances of Council consultation are not sufficient to establish a duty to consult the allies before taking any action weakening the ability of another ally to participate in the common defense. Measures of this sort are to be distinguished from those that directly weaken the Alliance as a body. In such cases, usually involving troop reductions or military budget cuts, consultations before final decisions are the norm.

4. Détente with Eastern Europe and the German Question

a. Arms Control Negotiations. Post–World War II arms control negotiations began in earnest in the early 1960s and have continued in various forms ever since. With a few exceptions, such as the Conference on Security and Cooperation in Europe (CSCE) and the Mutual and Balanced Force Reductions (MBFR) talks, these negotiations have not involved formally coordinated NATO

[62] *See* The Times (London), Dec. 8, 1962, at 8, col. 3; *id.*, Dec. 14, 1962, at 8, col. 4, and 12, col. 1. The Final Communique of the North Atlantic Council Ministerial session, Dec. 15, 1962, in NATO, TEXTS OF FINAL COMMUNIQUES 1949–1974, at 147, 148 (1975), refers to a discussion of adequate and balanced forces, nuclear and conventional, and to a need for closer alignment between NATO military requirements and national force plans.

[63] *See* H. TREWHITT, MCNAMARA 175 (1971).

[64] *See* F. Beer, *supra* note 2, at 16; M. BALL, NATO AND THE EUROPEAN MOVEMENT 140 (1959); G. LISKA, NATIONS IN ALLIANCE: THE LIMITS OF INTERDEPENDENCE 79 (1962). For the recommendations of the three wise men, see text at note 7 *supra*.

positions.[65] Instead, one or a few member states have carried on negotiations with the Eastern bloc; in a few cases, such as the seabed arms-control negotiations, all NATO states have been free to participate without any commitment to present a united front. Whenever there is no commitment to coordinate among all NATO members, the issue of prior consultation tends to arise between the negotiating and the nonparticipating members.

In most cases the United States has been either the leading or the sole negotiator from the Alliance. A number of instances can be found in which high-ranking U.S. officials have said that their government consults within NATO before presenting a new position in arms control negotiations, or have pledged that it will do so.[66] The record suggests, however, that the U.S. "consultations" are sometimes mere notifications or briefings.

One of the first examples involved the 1963 partial test ban treaty.[67] At most, the United States informed several of its major European allies of the treaty's details just before the Moscow signing.[68] The Assembly of the Western European Union (WEU) adopted a resolution regretting "the absence of sufficient and previous consultations and [requesting] that in the future the conclusion of treaties affecting the vital interests of member States of NATO and WEU be preceded by consultations in the spirit of the treaties."[69] This very nearly asserted a duty to con-

[65]On NATO consultations relating to CSCE and MBFR, see M. SAULLE, NATO AND ITS ACTIVITIES 92–98, 121–24 (1979). As noted earlier, efforts such as CSCE and MBFR that require detailed coordination in order to be effective are not particularly significant to a normative study of prior consultations. Consequently, they are mentioned only briefly in this section. In the same category are the U.S.-Soviet and U.S.-Eastern European negotiations on restraining conventional arms transfers and on intermediate-range nuclear forces (INF). U.S. consultations within NATO on impending INF talks are reported in 82 DEP'T ST. BULL., Jan. 1982, at 31.

[66]*See* Secretary of State Dean Rusk's statement in *Hearings on The Atlantic Alliance, supra* note 20, pt. 5, at 161 (1966); H. CLEVELAND, *supra* note 3, at 70 (reporting President Nixon's pledge to consult) and at 177; statement by President Carter, 78 DEP'T ST. BULL., May 1978, at 31.

[67]Treaty Banning Nuclear Weapon Tests in the Atmosphere, in Outer Space and Under Water, Aug. 5, 1963, 14 U.S.T. 1313, T.I.A.S. No. 5433, 480 U.N.T.S. 43.

[68]*See* Report of the Comm. on Defence Questions and Armaments, The Moscow Test Ban Treaty and Its Effects on the Western Alliance, Assembly of the Western European Union Doc. 288, in Proc. of the 9th Ordinary Sess., pt. 2, vol. 3, at 79, 88 (1963).

[69]Assembly of the Western European Union, Collected Texts Adopted and Replies of the Council, 9TH Ordinary Sess., at 15 (1963).

sult, and within a few years the United States began acknowledging an intention to do so.

The European allies were not vitally interested in some of the other arms control negotiations of that era. These included the negotiations leading to the Antarctic treaty and the outer space treaty, both of which contain arms control provisions. In these instances, allied consultations were desultory.[70]

On the other hand, the European allies were quite interested in the nuclear nonproliferation treaty. After the negotiations had dragged on for some time, the United States–Soviet talks suddenly became serious in late 1966. Without consulting its NATO allies, the United States worked out with the Soviet Union the arrangement that eventually became the core of the treaty.[71] It involved a promise by nuclear-weapon states not to transfer nuclear weapons to nonnuclear states or to assist them in their manufacture, and a promise by the latter not to receive or manufacture nuclear weapons. This meant, of course, that the North Atlantic Alliance would be limited to three nuclear powers, at least if those three all became parties to the nonproliferation treaty. The allies let the United States know of their disenchantment with the failure to consult. The result was close consultation in the North Atlantic Council from April 1967 until the drafting was completed and the treaty signed on July 1, 1968.[72]

A similar scenario unfolded in the fall of 1967, when the United States government was considering its options regarding development and deployment of antiballistic missile (ABM) systems. Without consulting the NATO allies, Secretary of Defense Robert McNamara announced that the United States had decided to go ahead with a "thin" ABM system to defend against a possible Chinese attack, rather than a more ambitious system capable of defending against an all-out Soviet attack. Although

[70]*See* H. Cleveland, *supra* note 3, at 67.

[71]*Id.* at 68, noting that the allies were brought up to date several weeks later.

[72]Treaty on the Non-Proliferation of Nuclear Weapons, July 1, 1968, 21 U.S.T. 483, T.I.A.S. No. 6839, 729 U.N.T.S. 161. On the consultations, see H. Cleveland, *supra* note 3, at 68–69; R. Jordan, *supra* note 42, at 215–16; F. Beer, *supra* note 2, at 24–25; Lyon, *Beyond NATO?,* 24 Int'l J. (Canada) 268, 271 (1974).

E. Goodman, The Fate of the Atlantic Community 383 (1975), says that the "allied consultation was in the nature of a tardy effort to make amends for oversights in a deal originally struck by the superpowers." But, given the forceful objections by the allies after they had been bypassed in 1966, this is tantamount to saying that the United States was acquiescing in an assertion by the allies of a right to be consulted. Customary international law is created by just such a process.

selection of the "Chinese option" arguably put the decision outside the area of NATO concern, the NATO allies did not agree. A week after Secretary McNamara's announcement, he was openly challenged at a meeting of the NATO Nuclear Planning Group for having failed to consult. It was noted that even a "thin" system could be used against a Soviet attack, and the question was raised whether the United States planned to protect itself at least partly from Soviet attack while leaving Europe vulnerable. Secretary McNamara responded that the ABM issue had not really been decided yet and that European views would be taken into account before the decision was made.[73] As it turned out, the U.S. decision was not final, and the ABM's fate became tied to the U.S.-Soviet strategic arms limitation talks (SALT).

The SALT negotiations were bilateral between the two superpowers. They began in 1968, near the end of the Johnson administration, and have produced an interim (SALT I) agreement in May 1972, an acceptance of limits on strategic delivery vehicles in 1974, the signing of a SALT II agreement in 1979, and preliminary progress toward strategic arms reduction talks (START). Throughout these negotiations, the United States has been in frequent contact with its NATO allies. In 1968, the NATO Secretary General, Manlio Brosio, asserted in diplomatically veiled terms that the allies expected to be consulted.[74] He later cited the U.S.-NATO contacts on SALT as examples of trustful and complete consultations, an assessment shared by the former dean of the NATO corps of permanent representatives.[75] As will be seen, however, not all European governments joined in that assessment—at least with respect to SALT I.

In January 1969 the U.S. permanent representative briefed the North Atlantic Council on the outgoing Johnson administration's SALT objectives and negotiating principles. The briefing occurred after the initial American proposal had been prepared, and would have followed its presentation to the So-

[73] *See* H. Cleveland, *supra* note 3, at 59; J. Newhouse, Cold Dawn: The Story of SALT 96–99 (1973).

A rather different version, indicating that the United States held NATO consultations beginning in March 1967, appears in R. Jordan, *supra* note 42, at 216.

[74] R. Jordan, *supra* note 42, at 219.

[75] Brosio, *Consultation and the Atlantic Alliance,* 16 Survival 115, 117 (1974) (referring also to the multilateral CSCE and MBFR negotiations); interview with André de Staercke, *supra* note 60.

viet Union if the 1968 invasion of Czechoslovakia had not led the United States to postpone the first SALT meeting.[76]

When the Nixon administration took office, it began to prepare its own proposals. President Nixon told the Soviet ambassador that negotiations could not begin until his review was completed and consultations had been held with the allies.[77] During the ensuing three years of negotiations leading to the SALT I agreement, United States officials routinely briefed the allies in Brussels before and after each of the seven negotiating rounds. It appears, however, that the actual proposals were developed almost entirely within the administration, at times even without the participation of the U.S. arms control bureaucracy. The most crucial negotiations in the spring of 1972 were prepared in total secrecy and were then conducted equally secretly by Secretary of State Kissinger in Moscow while the seventh round was following its own course in Helsinki.[78] In the eyes of at least some European allies, the "consultations" were little more than notifications of what the United States already had decided to do or had done.[79] Nevertheless, the allies raised no strong objections to the procedure, probably because the substance of the SALT I agreement did not seriously affect Western European security and because the regular briefings did provide some assurance of that.[80]

Some other bilateral U.S.-Soviet negotiations at about the same time were conducted with little or no prior NATO consultation. In 1972 the two superpowers signed their nonbinding

[76] J. NEWHOUSE, *supra* note 73, at 120–30, 137–38. The Newhouse book is an insider's account of the SALT I negotiations.

[77] *Id.* at 141.

[78] *Id.* at 176–86, 203, 214–18, 223–24, 234–56.

[79] *See* Smart, *Perspectives from Europe*, in SALT: THE MOSCOW AGREEMENTS AND BEYOND 185, 190 (M. Willrich & J. Rhinelander eds. 1974). The reasons for imperfections in SALT I consultations are explained in Makins, *Bringing in the Allies*, FOREIGN POLICY No. 35, at 91, 98–99 (1979).

[80] *See* SMART, *supra* note 79; Buchan, *The United States and the Security of Europe*, in 8 CRITICAL CHOICES FOR AMERICANS, WESTERN EUROPE: THE TRIALS OF PARTNERSHIP 297, 305 (D. Landes ed. 1977). The SALT I agreement was the Interim Agreement on Certain Measures with Respect to the Limitation of Strategic Offensive Arms, with Protocol, May 26, 1972, 23 U.S.T. 3462, T.I.A.S. No. 7504 (no longer in force).

The initial ABM agreement, negotiated in tandem with SALT I, is the Treaty on the Limitation of Anti-Ballistic Missile Systems, May 26, 1972, 23 U.S.T. 3435, T.I.A.S. No. 7503.

Basic Principles of Relations—the forerunner of the Helsinki Accords eventually reached in the Conference on Security and Cooperation in Europe. The Basic Principles did not include some points, important to the West, that were later incorporated in the Helsinki Accords and did include "peaceful coexistence" language that was open to Soviet interpretation as legitimating ideological warfare. The United States did not consult its NATO allies in advance.[81] Similarly, the U.S.-Soviet Agreement on the Prevention of Nuclear War[82] was signed in 1973 without any meaningful prior NATO consultation. In general, the Agreement commits each party to avoid the threat or use of force against the other except in self-defense and states that if a risk of nuclear conflict arises, the parties will consult each other and make every effort to avert the risk. Several commentators have noted that this was almost certain to raise fears among the United States' NATO allies about the credibility of the U.S. nuclear deterrent to an attack on Western Europe.[83]

The record is less clear as to meaningful NATO consultation before President Nixon's visit to Moscow in early July 1974, when two bilateral agreements were signed: a protocol reducing from two to one the number of ABM deployment areas permitted under the 1972 ABM treaty[84] and an agreement (which has never entered into force) limiting the strength of underground nuclear weapon tests. On June 18 and 19, Secretary of State Kissinger briefed the North Atlantic Council on the President's imminent trip. He assured the Council that no allied interests would be compromised. President Nixon then stopped in Brussels on his way to Moscow, explaining in general terms the objectives of his trip. Nowhere does it appear, however, that the allies were given the opportunity at either the Kissinger or

[81] *See* E. GOODMAN, *supra* note 72, at 389.

[82] June 22, 1973, 24 U.S.T. 1478, T.I.A.S. No. 7654.

[83] *See* E. GOODMAN, *supra* note 72, at 390; R. HILL, *supra* note 55 at 23; Hassner, *How Troubled a Partnership,* 24 INT'L J. (Canada) 166, 178 (1974). Shortly before the agreement was signed, Henry Kissinger said that when the interests of the European allies were directly affected by U.S. bilateral negotiations with other superpowers, the United States had been consulting them scrupulously. Kissinger, *The Year of Europe,* 68 DEP'T ST. BULL. 593, 597 (1973). His definition of consultation, however, did not always coincide with that of the European allies.

[84] Protocol to the Treaty of May 26, 1972, on the Limitation of Anti-Ballistic Missile Systems, July 3, 1974, 27 U.S.T. 1645, T.I.A.S. No. 8276.

the Nixon briefing to contribute to the positions being adopted by the United States.[85]

In July 1977 the United States, the United Kingdom, and the Soviet Union began negotiations pointing toward a comprehensive nuclear test ban treaty that would include a ban on underground tests. Although the negotiations have been discussed in the North Atlantic Council, the discussions—like most relating to U.S.-Soviet bilateral negotiations—appear to have been more in the nature of briefings than real consultations.[86]

All of the U.S.-Soviet negotiations mentioned to this point have had potential, but indirect, effects on Western Europe. The SALT II and START negotiations have posed issues of much more direct concern to the European allies. These encompass limitations on forward based systems (aircraft and missiles based in Western Europe) and on deployment of cruise missiles, as well as reductions in strategic weaponry. As the issues have moved closer to home for the European NATO members, they have increasingly expected to participate in the U.S. decision-making process. The Carter administration therefore undertook much closer consultations than had occurred during the SALT I and early SALT II negotiations, giving the European allies the opportunity to air their views while negotiating positions were being formed, and the Reagan administration continued the trend in connection with START.[87] The

[85]The Kissinger-Nixon briefings are reported in Atlantic News, June 18, 1974, at 3; *id.*, June 20, 1974, at 1; *id.*, June 21, 1974, at 1; *id.*, June 26, 1974, at 1; *id.*, June 27, 1974, at 2. The Moscow visit involved broad strategic arms limitation discussions as well as the signing of the two agreements.

[86]Interview with the Director, Office of NATO and Atlantic Political-Military Affairs, U.S. Dep't of State, Aug. 2, 1978.

The bilateral U.S.-Soviet talks on a proposed agreement prohibiting chemical weapons have involved some coordination between the United States and those allies represented at the Geneva disarmament conference, but no political consultations at NATO Headquarters in Brussels. *Id.*

[87]*See, e.g.*, Vance, *Comment*, in THE NEW ATLANTIC CHALLENGE 366, 367 (R. Mayne ed. 1975); *Western Security Issues: European Perspectives: Hearing Before Subcomms. of the House Comm. on Foreign Affairs*, 96th Cong., 1st Sess. 7–8, 17–18, 25, 27–28 (1979). As to the closer consultations, see statement of President Carter, 78 DEP'T ST. BULL., Feb. 1978, at 16, 17, *reprinted in* 26 NATO REV., No. 1, at 29 (1978); statement of the Ass't Secretary of State for European Affairs, in 78 DEP'T ST. BULL., Mar. 1978, at 27, 29; S. TALBOTT, ENDGAME: THE INSIDE STORY OF SALT II 141–42 (1979).

The Guadeloupe four-power summit in January 1979 stemmed from President Carter's inclination to draw into his counsels at an early stage those NATO allies that would be most acutely affected by the impending SALT III negotiations, but it excluded all other NATO allies. The departure from pan-NATO consultation was temporary. The NATO Nuclear Planning Group discussed SALT III issues in April, and they

need to prevent leaks regarding such matters as fallback positions serves, however, to circumscribe the revelations U.S. representatives can make to their NATO colleagues. Sometimes the U.S. representatives do not themselves know fully their superiors' bargaining intentions.[88]

The allies have systematically consulted one another before taking positions in a number of multilateral arms control negotiations. In the MBFR negotiations, the NATO allies have presented coordinated positions. The United States has been tempted to try to settle the MBFR issues bilaterally with the Soviet Union, but it has consistently referred Soviet proposals to its NATO allies before taking any position.[89] Similarly, during the negotiations from 1967 until 1971 on seabed arms control, when a NATO member wanted to make a new proposal, it would normally consult the others before putting the proposal into final form.[90] The same was true during the contemporaneous Geneva negotiations on banning biological weapons.[91] Before each session of the Third U.N. Law of the Sea Conference, the North Atlantic Council met to discuss the outstanding issues and the responses of individual allies.[92]

were considered at some length by the NATO foreign ministers in May. *See* N.Y. Times, May 31, 1979, at A3, col. 3 (city ed.).

With the advent of the Reagan administration, START replaced SALT III. The Final Communique of the North Atlantic Council Special Ministerial Session, Jan. 11, 1982, in 30 NATO Rev., No. 1, at 29, 30 (1982), welcomed START and said, "The Allies look forward to continued close consultations with the United States in the Council on [START and intermediate nuclear forces negotiations]." The NATO foreign ministers discussed START in May 1982. *See* N.Y. Times, May 19, 1982, at A8, col. 6. President Reagan discussed it within the North Atlantic Council in June 1982. *Id.*, June 11, 1982, at A1, col. 3. *See also* Burt, *The Evolution of the US START Approach*, 30 NATO Rev., No. 4, at 1, 7 (1982).

[88] *See, e.g.*, S. Talbott, *supra* note 87, at 63.

[89] *See* E. Goodman, *supra* note 72, at 376; R. Hill, *supra* note 55, at 95; Washington Post, Nov. 6, 1979, at A10, col. 1.

[90] *See* R. Hill, *supra* note 55, at 73 (giving Canadian practice as an example).

The negotiations produced the Treaty on the Prohibition of the Employment of Nuclear Weapons and Other Weapons of Mass Destruction on the Seabed and the Ocean Floor and the Subsoil Thereof, Feb. 11, 1971, 23 U.S.T. 701, T.I.A.S. No. 7337.

[91] *See* Fabiani, *Biological Weapons Ban Near After Years of East-West Effort*, 20 NATO Rev., Nos. 1 & 2, at 20–23 (1972). The neogtiations produced the Convention on the Prohibition of the Development, Production and Stockpiling of Bacteriological (Biological) and Toxin Weapons and on Their Destruction, Apr. 10, 1972, 26 U.S.T. 583, T.I.A.S. No. 8062.

[92] *See* Fabiani, *The Caracas Conference on the Law of the Sea, June-August 1974*, 22 NATO Rev., No. 3, at 22, 23; Atlantic News, Mar. 8, 1978, at 1.

When the Reagan administration decided to reevaluate the U.S. position after seven years of negotiations under previous administrations, it acknowledged the need to

In all of these multilateral negotiations, the European NATO allies have had particular interests to protect. The MBFR negotiations are the most obvious example, since they deal with East-West force reductions in Central Europe. The seabed arms control negotiations and the Law of the Sea Conference involved defense-related issues of considerable interest to the NATO maritime states—all except Luxembourg. The biological weapons negotiations were significant not only because they led to a ban on production and use of a specific type of weapon, but because they were closely related to the 1925 Geneva Protocol prohibiting gas warfare to which all NATO states except the United States were already parties.[93]

b. Other Policies Toward Eastern Europe. Some significant policy decisions on relations with potential adversaries in Eastern Europe have been made outside the arms control context. These have included decisions on Berlin and German reunification, steps toward rapprochement with the Soviet Union by individual NATO members, responses to dramatic developments within the Eastern bloc, and development of strategic defense plans by the nuclear powers in the Alliance. Some of these decisions have greater normative significance than others. For example, U.S. consultations with the allies lacked a sense of legal duty when the United States was developing its response to the imposition of martial law in Poland in December 1981,[94] because the thrust was to persuade rather than to listen. Clearly, the intended action would be more effective with the participation of the other allies than without it.

On matters concerning Berlin and the "German question," the United States, the United Kingdom, France, and the Federal Republic of Germany have borne special responsibilities. The former three consistently have consulted each other before taking positions and they have included Bonn in the consultations since West German accession to NATO. Prior consultations with

consult its allies before formulating a new position. *See U.S. Policy and the Third United Nations Conference on the Law of the Sea: Hearings Before the House Comm. on Foreign Affairs*, 97th Cong., 1st Sess. 5, 9 (1981).

[93] *See* Protocol for the Prohibition of the Use in War of Asphyxiating, Poisonous or Other Gases, and of Bacteriological Methods of Warfare, June 17, 1925, 26 U.S.T. 571, T.I.A.S. No. 8061, 94 L.N.T.S. 65. The United States became a party at the same time it ratified the biological weapons treaty.

[94] *See* Washington Post, Dec. 25, 1981, at A30, col. 1; *id.*, Dec. 30, 1981, at A14, col. 1.

the other members of the Alliance, however, generally have occurred only before relatively formal contacts have been made with the Eastern bloc on specific issues, such as sending a diplomatic note in response to a Soviet initiative or signing an agreement, and then only when the contacts have not been in response to an immediate crisis. Individual members ordinarily have not held consultations with the entire Alliance at each step in the development of their policies toward Eastern Europe.

For example, during the period of heightening tension over Berlin but before the serious problems of 1958–61, the three allied powers responsible for the city developed the practice of discussing proposed political communications to the Soviet Union with the North Atlantic Council. These appear to have been genuine consultations rather than mere briefings.[95] Similarly, there were NATO consultations before the 1955 summit and foreign ministers conferences at which the United States, the United Kingdom, and France met with the Soviet Union to try to resolve the question of German reunification.[96]

The Berlin "crises"—an overstatement for the most part—began on November 27, 1958, when the Soviet government sent notes to the United States, the United Kingdom, France, and the Federal Republic of Germany asserting that the 1944 and 1945 four-power agreements relating to Germany were void and that the Soviet Union would give the German Democratic Republic control over access to Berlin. The foreign ministers of the four Western allies met just before a North Atlantic Council meeting and agreed on the issues to be covered in their replies. They issued a statement to that effect, adding that "They will consult their allies in the Atlantic Council, following which the four Governments will formulate their replies."[97] They did so. Another Soviet note was delivered on January 10, 1959. The four allies cleared their responses with the Council before delivering them to the Soviet government.[98] They proposed a conference among the United States, the United Kingdom, France, and the Soviet Union, to which the latter eventually

[95] *See* Luns, *Progress Report on NATO,* 6 NATO LETTER, NO. 12, at 3, 8 (1958); P.-H. SPAAK, WHY NATO? 35 (1959).

[96] *See* R. HILL, *supra* note 55, at 17; M. SAULLE, *supra* note 65, at 82–83. For a discussion of NATO consultations on relations with Eastern Europe generally, *see id.* at 63–64, 71–90.

[97] 7 NATO LETTER, NO. 1, at 11 (1959).

[98] *Id.,* NO. 3, at 6–7 (1959).

agreed. A month before the conference, the allied negotiating position was discussed extensively in a North Atlantic Council ministerial meeting.[99] Nevertheless, specific negotiating proposals apparently were adopted just before and during the conference's two sessions by the three Western participants plus the Federal Republic of Germany; the North Atlantic Council was simply being kept apprised of the proceedings.[100] The conference proved inconclusive.

On June 15, 1961, Soviet Premier Khrushchev announced that if all states formerly at war with Germany did not sign a peace treaty by the end of the year, the Soviet Union would sign a separate peace treaty with East Germany. The United States, the United Kingdom, and France rejected this position in notes delivered to the Soviet Union on July 17 after they had obtained the approval of the North Atlantic Council.[101] On August 13, the true crisis developed when East German authorities sealed the border between East and West Berlin. The Berlin wall soon followed. At the height of the crisis, the three Western allies apparently acted without consulting the others (except, eventually, West Germany), although they were kept informed. The actions included the delivery of protest notes to the Soviet Union, the call-up of more than 75,000 U.S. reservists, and the transit of 1500 U.S. troops in armored trucks on the autobahn to West Berlin.[102] These measures required a series of prompt decisions that probably could not have been effectively coordinated beyond the inner circle of allies. Eventually, when the discussions among the four Western allies disintegrated, the others were brought in.[103] The crisis cooled in October.

Allied handling of relations with Eastern Europe since 1961 has followed much the same pattern: Council consultations before formal contacts and foreseeable events important to West European security, but not necessarily before steps in the gradual development of policy, or before responses to genuine crises. For example, before the Federal Republic of Germany con-

[99] *Id.*, No. 4, at 13 (1959).

[100] *Id.*, No. 6, at 15 (1959); *id.*, No. 8, at 9 (1959).

[101] *See* 13 KEESING'S CONTEMP. ARCHIVES 18163, 18223 (1961).

[102] These events are recounted, without mention of prior NATO consultations, in *id.* 18274–75, 18277–78, 18307–10; A. SCHLESINGER, A THOUSAND DAYS 393–400 (1965); T. SORENSON, KENNEDY 593–96 (1965). *See also* A. BUCHAN, CRISIS MANAGEMENT 36–39 (The Atlantic Papers, NATO Series, No. 2, 1966).

[103] *See* F. Beer, *supra* note 2, at 18–19.

cluded its normalization treaty with the German Democratic Republic in 1972, it consulted its NATO allies.[104] When the latter government restricted foreign access to East Berlin in 1977, the three allies responsible for Berlin consulted within NATO before sending a written protest to the Soviet Union.[105] When the Prime Minister of Turkey planned to go to the Soviet Union in 1978 to sign a "political document" of good will, he discussed the matter before any specific language had been drafted—though apparently without much give and take—in the NATO summit meeting of May 1978.[106] Chancellor Schmidt of the Federal Republic of Germany consulted the allies before his official state visit to Moscow in the summer of 1980, but French President Giscard d'Estaing did not do so before his less formal meeting in Warsaw, a few weeks earlier than Schmidt's, with Soviet President Brezhnev.[107]

There were only minimal consultations in the North Atlantic Council while the West German Ostpolitik policy was evolving toward normalization with East Germany and while some other members were pursuing détente with Eastern Europe in the 1960s.[108] And in the crisis situation sparked by the Soviet invasion of Czechoslovakia in 1968, the United States did not

[104] *See* the Final Communiques of North Atlantic Council Ministerial sessions, Dec. 10, 1971, and May 31, 1972, in NATO, TEXTS OF FINAL COMMUNIQUES 1949–1974, at 266 and 276 (1975).

[105] *See* Atlantic News, Jan. 12, 1977, at 3.

[106] Interviews with political affairs counselor, U.S. delegation to NATO, July 10, 1978, and with public affairs adviser, Bureau of European Affairs, U.S. Dep't of State, Aug. 1, 1978. *See also* N.Y. Times, May 30, 1978, at A1, col. 5 (city ed.).

[107] *See* Financial Times, May 20, 1980, at 2, col. 1; *id.*, May 28, 1980, at 1, col. 3; Washington Post, May 21, 1980, at A18, col. 1. Although the United States was piqued at the French, it did not consider the failure to consult a breach of duty. *See* Newsweek, June 2, 1980, at 21.

[108] *See* H. CLEVELAND, *supra* note 3, at 133, 136, 140; R. HILL, *supra* note 55 at 92–93. Hill notes that the allies did not expect extensive consultations from West Germany during its Ostpolitik phase. R. JORDAN, *supra* note 42, at 221, refers to Alliance consultations throughout the Ostpolitik period, but the reference is apparently to these briefings.

See also Secretary of State Dean Rusk's statement in *Hearings on The Atlantic Alliance*, *supra* note 20, pt. 5, at 161 (1966), mentioning discussions among the four major allies during the post–Berlin crisis period, but indicating that the other allies were merely briefed.

The West German government failed to consult all the allies before deciding to hold a presidential election in Berlin. *See* H. CLEVELAND, *supra* note 3, at 22. And on at least one occasion, then-Chancellor Adenauer proposed a long-term German reunification plan to the Soviet ambassador, without consulting any ally. *See* W. GRIFFITH, THE OSTPOLITIK OF THE FEDERAL REPUBLIC OF GERMANY 94–95 (1978).

consult its allies before sending two destroyers into the Black Sea. Some of the allies questioned that lack of consultation.[109]

A final class of cases involving policies toward potential adversaries is represented by changes in U.S. strategic defense plans. Since NATO defenses rely heavily on the retaliatory capability of the United States on a global scale, as well as within Europe, significant changes in the U.S. strategic defense policy are of vital interest to the Alliance. Nevertheless, when Secretary of State Dulles announced the U.S. massive retaliation policy in January 1954, he simply notified, but did not consult, the NATO allies beforehand.[110] In 1962 the Kennedy administration abruptly switched to a strategy of flexible response. There was little or no consultation with the NATO allies, who were left confused about the countermeasures the United States was planning in the event of a Soviet attack on Western Europe.[111] When the United States modified its nuclear defense strategy in 1980 to include possible retaliation against Soviet military targets, it characterized the change as evolutionary and noted that the allies had been briefed earlier—though the actual announcement took them by surprise.[112]

In sum, the following pattern has emerged. The European NATO allies have strenuously asserted that the United States has a duty to consult them before making decisions on arms control negotiations only when the decisions directly and significantly could weaken the defense of Western Europe. The

[109] *See* H. CLEVELAND, *supra* note 3, at 20–21. It had been routine for the United States to send warships occasionally through the Dardanelles in order to show that the Black Sea is an international body of water. The State Department wished to assert that this was just another routine visit, which NATO consultations would belie. *Id.*

[110] Interview with André de Staercke, *supra* note 60. The United States already had announced a massive retaliation policy relating to any Soviet attack on Western Europe. The 1954 announcement applied to a Communist attack anywhere, if the attack could start a general war.

Secretary Dulles did acknowledge that the United States would consult its NATO allies if it actually had to retaliate massively. *See* R. OSGOOD, LIMITED WAR 208–13 (1957). This appears to have been a recognition of the U.S. obligation under article 4 of the North Atlantic Treaty. *See* text at note 5 *supra.*

A similar pledge to the NATO allies, relating to the use of nuclear weapons anywhere in the world, was made by the United States and the United Kingdom in 1962. *See* H. CLEVELAND, *supra* note 3, at 15–16.

[111] Staff of Senate Comm. on Government Operations, *Basic Issues,* in THE ATLANTIC ALLIANCE 7, 21 (H. Jackson ed. 1967). *See also* H. CLEVELAND, *supra* note 3, at 47.

[112] *See, e.g.,* Financial Times, Aug. 12, 1980, at 4, col. 5.

When the United States decided in 1965 to produce multiple independently targeted reentry vehicles, it had not consulted its allies. *See* J. NEWHOUSE, *supra* note 73, at 91.

United States has acquiesced in that relatively narrow assertion. Otherwise, the European allies themselves engage in prior consultations only in the case of a significant, foreseeable event involving Eastern Europe, or when a specific, rather formal contact with Eastern Europe is contemplated, and then only if the situation is not a true emergency.

5. Developments Outside the North Atlantic Treaty Area

a. Confrontations. The North Atlantic Alliance was established to defend a relatively well-defined area encompassing North America and Western Europe. The defense is directed against a possible attack from Eastern Europe. A working hypothesis—at least in the early years of NATO—was that events outside these areas were of little concern to the Alliance. Under that hypothesis, a member would not be expected to consult the others before acting outside the Treaty area, even if a confrontation were involved. In practice, however, several cross-currents have influenced the expectation and likelihood of prior consultation. These include such factors as the need to act quickly in a crisis, the importance to the mission of surprise, the likelihood of Soviet military involvement, the prospect of escalation, the geographic proximity of the events to the Treaty area, the desire of individual allies to be associated with or disassociated from the policy of the acting ally, and the desire of that ally to have the active support or participation of the others.

The United States consulted its allies in late 1979 and early 1980 regarding appropriate responses to the Soviet intervention in Afghanistan and to Iran's detention of American hostages in Teheran—until the U.S., without prior consultation, staged a paramilitary attempt to free the hostages in April 1980. It explained in the latter case that the need for surprise precluded consultations, but indicated that the allies would be consulted if any punitive military measures were contemplated against Iran.[113] The earlier consultations regarding events in Afghanistan and Iran had marginal normative significance for the same reason that the consultations on the response to martial law in Poland did. The United States was trying to obtain the allies' participation.

[113]*See* the statements by the U.S. Secretary of Defense, in 80 DEP'T ST. BULL., June 1980, at 42, 46 (allies understood why they were not consulted, but expected to be consulted before such military action as blockading or mining Iranian harbors).

In the 1950s Secretary of State John Foster Dulles made clear that the United States, as a nation with worldwide responsibilities, might have to respond on occasion to a crisis outside the Treaty area without waiting to consult its NATO allies. He gave a specific example: the protection of Taiwan in the event of an attack from the Chinese mainland. This principle, at least as it applied to an area half a globe away, does not seem to have aroused substantial NATO opposition; nevertheless the Secretary-General, Lord Ismay, tried for a time to persuade the United States to conduct joint military planning with its NATO allies on a global basis.[114]

It was another story, however, when Great Britain and France intervened militarily after President Nasser of Egypt nationalized the Suez Canal Company in 1956. They acted without consulting their NATO allies, who objected sharply not only to the lack of consultation but to what some viewed as attempts to deceive them.[115]

Another Middle Eastern incursion by NATO members occurred in 1958, when the United States and Great Britain landed forces in Lebanon and Jordan, respectively. They acted at the invitation of those governments and in response to a volatile situation sparked by the overthrow of the Iraqi government under circumstances that could have led to insurrection in Lebanon and Jordan. It appears that the United States and the United Kingdom did consult their allies in the North Atlantic Council before matters came to a head, advising that they would respond to requests for help in a crisis. A number of the allies preferred not to become involved and, accordingly, remained silent. Apparently, there was no consultation immediately preceding the decision to land forces.[116]

The European allies made various decolonialization decisions without significant NATO consultation during the most tur-

[114] *See* Dulles, *Developing NATO in Peace,* 34 DEP'T ST. BULL. 706, 709–10 (1956); R. JORDAN, *supra* note 42, at 38, 45–46.

[115] Interview with André de Staercke, *supra* note 60. *See* F. Beer, *supra* note 2, at 13; Brosio, *supra* note 75, at 115, noting President Eisenhower's outburst at the British-French conduct.

[116] *See* Prime Minister MacMillan's statement of July 17, 1958, in 6 NATO LETTER, No. 8, at 10–11 (1958); Luns, *supra* note 95, at 8–9; F. Beer, *supra* note 2, at 29; Jordan & Newman, *The Secretary-General of NATO and Multinational Political Leadership,* 30 INT'L J. (Canada) 732, 754 n.55 (1975). Paul-Henri Spaak, then the Secretary-General of NATO, said that the U.S. and the U.K. "acted after full consultation with their Atlantic partners in the NATO Council." R. JORDAN, *supra* note 42, at 69–70.

bulent self-determination period, running from the independence of India and Indonesia shortly after World War II through the hostilities in the former Belgian Congo beginning in 1960. That period saw a number of decolonization crises for the European states involved, sometimes with important implications for other members of the Alliance. This was true not only in the Congo but in such places as Algeria and Indochina as well. Nevertheless, it took the United Nations' involvement in the Congo and the superpowers' jockeying for position there to generate any real interest among the allies in being consulted collectively before controversial decolonization decisions were made.[117]

In the 1960s and early 1970s the United States took or threatened military action in several situations arising outside the Treaty area. In at least one case the United States attempted to consult but was largely rebuffed; in other cases it neither attempted nor was expected to consult; and in two cases it consulted the other allies so hurriedly that they were dissatisfied with their meager opportunity for input.

The first case grew out of the U.S. involvement in Vietnam. Although the Johnson administration insisted that the war was a NATO concern, the allies preferred not to become involved so long as there was no direct U.S.-Soviet confrontation.[118] Even when there was a dramatic escalation, as when the United States sent ground troops into Cambodia, the allies did not make consultation an issue.[119]

Other instances in which the United States neither consulted NATO nor was criticized for the omission included the Bay of Pigs invasion in 1961,[120] intervention in the Dominican Republic in 1965,[121] and the *Mayaguez* incident in 1975.[122] Despite the possible spillover from all these situations to relations between the Alliance and Eastern Europe, the allies simply regarded them as too remote for concern.

[117]*See* A. BUCHAN, *supra* note 102, at 24; F. Beer, *supra* note 2, at 16, 22.

[118]*See* Neff, *supra* note 18, at 8; R. HILL, *supra* note 55, at 89.

[119]For an account of the U.S. decision-making process regarding the Cambodian incursion, see M. & B. KALB, KISSINGER 154–64 (1974).

[120]*See* A. BUCHAN, NATO IN THE 1960S, at 119 (rev. ed. 1963).

[121]*See* A. BUCHAN, *supra* note 102, at 34–35

[122]*See* R. HILL, *supra* note 55, at 71, putting the situation hypothetically but in such a manner as to suggest that there was no consultation. *See also* R. ROWAN, THE FOUR DAYS OF MAYAGUEZ 66–70, 88–92, 140–44, 172–80 (1975), discussing U.S. decision making without mentioning NATO consultation.

In quite another category were the Cuban missile crisis in 1962 and the U.S. worldwide military alert during the 1973 Middle Eastern war. Because of the element of Soviet-U.S. confrontation, the allies were vitally concerned. The problem was time.

It would have taken about ten days from the United States' discovery of Cuban launching pads and missile-designed buildings until the missiles could be on the pads ready for firing. President Kennedy had to consult his own experts and senior political-military advisers before deciding what to do. He apparently felt that he could not afford the luxury of seeking another set of opinions from another set of potential advisers, his NATO partners.[123] Just before announcing his decision, he sent Dean Acheson hurriedly to Europe to notify the allies. Although Acheson is reported to have told General de Gaulle that he was there merely to inform, not to consult, the then-dean of the NATO ambassadorial corps, Belgian Permanent Representative André de Staercke, recalls that Acheson actually asked him whether the allies had any objection to the U.S. plan. Ambassador de Staercke called the NATO Secretary-General and told him they had only a few minutes to decide whether to raise any objection. They did not, and undoubtedly would not have done so under the circumstances, even if they had disagreed with the American plan.[124] At the next North Atlantic Council Ministerial meeting, some questions were raised regarding consultation in such crises, "but no real complaint was made against the United States for the manner in which the allies were consulted or informed."[125]

The 1973 worldwide military alert was called in response to a message from General Secretary Brezhnev to President Nixon complaining about alleged Israeli violations of an agreed ceasefire after Israeli forces had crossed the Suez Canal. Brezhnev's message proposed that the United States and the Soviet Union urgently dispatch peacekeeping contingents to Egypt—a pro-

[123] *See* A. Schlesinger, *supra* note 102, at 803; A. Buchan, *supra* note 102, at 33–34, 41. Nevertheless, the President did consider the effects on NATO of the decisions he was making. *See* R. Kennedy, Thirteen Days 98–99 (1969).

[124] Interview with André de Staercke, *supra* note 60. The exchange between Acheson and de Gaulle is set forth in E. Abel, The Missile Crisis 112 (1966).

[125] Statement of the Canadian Secretary of State for External Affairs, in 3 Can. Parl. Deb., H.C., 25th Parl., 1st Sess. 2699 (1962).

posal the United States had already firmly rejected—and said that if the United States did not do so, the Soviet Union "should be faced with the necessity urgently to consider the question of taking appropriate steps unilaterally. Israel cannot be allowed to get away with the violations."[126] A hastily assembled group of U.S. governmental experts, led by Secretary of State Kissinger, concluded that there was a high probability of some kind of unilateral Soviet move. Informed of this, the President called the first stage of the worldwide military alert within two hours of the receipt of Brezhnev's message. Although Kissinger telephoned the NATO military commander in Europe, he simply sent a middle-of-the-night cable to the U.S. political delegation at NATO headquarters in Brussels, telling the delegation to inform the allies. Because of technical problems in the NATO communications system, the allies were not actually informed until a few hours later.[127]

Ambassador de Staercke, then still dean of the NATO ambassadorial corps, protested that if the Secretary of State could call the NATO military commander, he also could have called the NATO Secretary-General and the dean of the ambassadors.[128] Other NATO allies made it clear that they expected such prior consultation as was practicable under the circumstances, though they recognized that full consultations would not have been possible—at least if the Soviet threat was as serious as the U.S. decision makers had thought.[129] Publicly and privately, the United States conceded that it had not consulted adequately at the height of the crisis and that it would be willing to review its consultation procedures, although it reserved the right to proceed without extensive consultations in an emergency.[130] As a result of the procedural review, the United States

[126] *Quoted in* M. & B. KALB, *supra* note 119, at 490.

[127] *Id.* at 490–93; interview with André de Staercke, *supra* note 60.

[128] Interview with André de Staercke, *supra* note 60.

[129] *See* Neff, *supra* note 18, at 7–8; M. & B. KALB, *supra* note 119, at 497. Some responsible U.S. government officials assessed the Soviet threat somewhat differently than did the Secretary of State—who assessed it differently from the President. *See id.* at 497–98.

[130] Interview with André de Staercke, *supra* note 60; M. &. B. KALB, *supra* note 119, at 499; Kissinger, *The United States and a Unifying Europe: The Necessity for Partnership,* 69 DEP'T ST. BULL. 777, 779 (1973); *United States–Europe Relations and the 1973 Middle East War: Hearings Before Subcomms. of the House Comm. on Foreign Affairs,* 93d Cong., 1st & 2d Sess. 31–32, 48–49, 57 (1974) (statement of the Assistant Secretary of State for European Affairs). *See also* R. HILL, *supra* note 55, at 26–27.

pledged to consult any NATO ally before U.S. forces on the ally's territory are alerted.[131]

The consultation issue arose again with the creation of the United States Rapid Deployment Force during the Carter administration. The force, designed to respond to crises outside the NATO area, engendered concern about its possible effect on U.S. forces assigned to NATO. To deal with this, the NATO Defense Ministers agreed in 1981 that when a member considers out-of-area deployment of forces to resist aggression or threats to other nations' security, it "should be prepared to participate fully in consultations within the Alliance."[132] This statement has a quasi-legislative quality, expressing a procedural norm for future conduct. It explains why the British government felt duty-bound to consult in an emergency session of the North Atlantic Council before deploying forces in response to the Argentine invasion of the Falkland Islands in 1982.[133]

b. Political Developments. Some decisions relating to events outside the Treaty area are significant to the Alliance even though they do not involve immediate crises. To the extent that they do not, any expectation of prior consultation is weakened. For example, the United States, the United Kingdom, France, Belgium, and the Federal Republic of Germany failed to consult the smaller NATO states before deciding to meet in Paris in June 1978 to consider playing a larger role in Africa following the abortive Shaba invasion earlier that year. However, once they had decided to meet (and thus had taken the first step toward more active involvement in Zaire and perhaps in all of Africa), they did discuss their plans at the May 1978 NATO summit meeting.[134] Later that summer, the United States did

[131] Interview with the Director, Office of NATO and Atlantic Political-Military Affairs, U.S. Dep't of State, Aug. 2, 1978.

[132] NATO Defence Planning Committee, Final Communique, May 13, 1981, in 29 NATO Rev., No. 3, at 29, 30 (1981). *See also* Document on Integrated NATO Defence, June 10, 1982, and Defence Planning Committee, Final Communique, May 7, 1982, in 30 NATO Rev., No. 3, at 27, 30, 31 (1982).

[133] *See* The Times (London), Apr. 3, 1982, at 3, col. 5.

[134] The Netherlands and Norway first were informed of the impending Paris meeting at the May NATO summit meeting in Washington. Het Parool, June 16, 1978 (translation by U.S. mission to NATO). Secretary of State Cyrus Vance, in his press briefing on May 30, 1978, 78 Dep't St. Bull., July 1978, at 5, mentioned the discussion at the May 1978 summit meeting.

not consult its NATO allies before President Carter decided to invite Egyptian President Sadat and Israeli Prime Minister Begin to the important Camp David summit meeting at which a framework leading to an Egyptian-Israeli peace treaty was worked out. The allies did not expect to be consulted.[135]

In a significant series of decisions focused outside the Treaty area, the NATO allies have made overtures to the People's Republic of China, which led to its recognition as the government of China. Consultation practice within NATO has been inconsistent. Thus, although the Canadian government at one point thought it was required to (and did) consult its NATO allies before recognizing the People's Republic, France did not consult them before it extended recognition.[136] The United States bypassed NATO on Henry Kissinger's first, secret trip to Peking and was taken to task for forgetting its alleged NATO obligation to consult.[137] Nevertheless, when the United States formally recognized the People's Republic on January 1, 1979, it felt no greater duty to its NATO allies than to give them prior notification of its intent, and the allies expected no more.[138]

These inconsistencies suggest that there is no NATO prior consultation norm relating to politically sensitive acts outside the Treaty area, at least insofar as the acts do not raise the specter of armed confrontation with the Soviet Union or of increased NATO vulnerability to attack.[139] When that specter

[135]The Carter decision was made immediately after President Sadat announced that he would not resume direct peace talks with Israel, and it involved little or no input even from President Carter's own foreign policy advisers. *See* 38 FACTS ON FILE 581, 601–02 (1978); Washington Post, Aug. 18, 1978, at A6, cols. 3–4. The allies expected only to be informed of developments in Middle East talks. *See* Atlantic News, July 26, 1978, at 4.

[136]See statements of the Canadian Secretary of State for Foreign Affairs, in 3 CAN. PARL. DEB., H.C., 26th Parl., 2d Sess. 3307, and 4 *id.* at 3479–80 (1964). France recognized the People's Republic in 1964, but Canada did not do so until 1970.

[137]*See* Brosio, *supra* note 75, at 116.

[138]Interview with political affairs counselor, *supra* note 106; R. HILL, *supra* note 45, at 40. *See also* Remarks of President Carter, 79 DEP'T ST. BULL., Jan. 1979, at 25, 26, *reprinted in* 18 INT'L LEGAL MATERIALS 443, 444 (1979).

[139]This may also be true regarding acts closer to home than those discussed in the text. On a number of occasions the desire to be disassociated from any contacts with Franco's Spain overrode any desires the allies may have had to be consulted before an individual ally took a step involving Spain. For example, the United States, without protest, simply kept its allies informed as it negotiated a friendship and cooperation treaty with Spain. *See Spanish Base Treaty: Hearings Before the Senate Comm. on Foreign Relations*, 94th Cong., 2d Sess. 7, 9 (1976); *Final Communique of the Defence Planning Comm.*, May 23, 1975, para. 5, in NATO FINAL COMMUNIQUES 1975, at 11, 12. When the Federal Republic of Germany explored the possibility of establishing Spanish bases in 1959, it consulted only the major allies. *See* G. LISKA, *supra* note 64, at 74–75. The

does exist, however, the allies expect prior consultation to the extent feasible under the circumstances. Although U.S. practice during the Cuban missile crisis was inconclusive on this point, the assertion-acquiescence processes set in motion by the 1956 British-French Suez intervention and the 1973 U.S. worldwide military alert support the norm. In both cases, the allies protested what they considered to be inadequate prior consultation, and the states precipitating the protests acquiesced by joining in the ensuing Alliance declarations calling for effective prior consultations: the three wise men's Council-approved report of 1956 and the 1974 Declaration on Atlantic Relations. The 1956 prescription lends normative significance to the 1958 NATO consultations on American and British intentions regarding Lebanon and Jordan. The 1981 Defense Ministers agreement lends similar significance to the 1982 consultations on the British response to the Falkland Islands crisis.

It is perhaps debatable whether this record of state practice is sufficient to establish a binding procedural norm requiring prior consultation when a NATO ally faces a decision on events outside the Treaty area that could lead to an armed confrontation with the Eastern European bloc or that could render the Alliance vulnerable to attack. The better view is that the record does establish the duty to consult, insofar as the risk is substantial and if consultation is feasible under the circumstances. When the occasions for state practice are few and the assertion-acquiescence record is both reasonably clear in those few instances and consistent with the shared goals of the interested states, a special custom can arise. It has arisen in this instance.

6. Economic and Environmental Policies

Article 2 of the North Atlantic Treaty provides in part that the allies "will seek to eliminate conflict in their international economic policies and will encourage economic collaboration between any or all of them."[140] This does not expressly require prior consultations, but as noted earlier, the North Atlantic Council approved the three wise men's 1956 recommendation that NATO consultations be held whenever economic issues

U.K. would not normally consult the allies before drafting a note to Spain concerning Gibraltar. R. HILL., *supra* note 55, at 97.

[140] North Atlantic Treaty, *supra* note 1, art. 2.

arise with political or defense implications or with consequences for the economic health of the Atlantic community as a whole.[141] The latter part of this advice has not always been followed. It was ignored in August 1971 when the United States imposed its 10 percent import surcharge and closed the "gold window" backing the U.S. dollar—actions with obvious consequences for the economic health of the Atlantic community.[142] In fact, attempts to coordinate economic policies within the Alliance have been largely unsuccessful from the beginning.[143]

On the other hand, there is a long record of prior consultation regarding decisions to supply military useful goods or technology to Communist countries. The consultations do not actually take place in a NATO forum, but in the Coordinating Committee (COCOM), a loosely structured but security-conscious group based in Paris. COCOM consists of Japan and all NATO states except Iceland. Formed in 1949, it maintains periodically changing, unanimously adopted lists of items that member states normally will not send to Communist countries unless an exception has been granted by unanimous consent.

The exception procedure amounts to a prior consultation arrangement rather than a formal veto power, because COCOM decisions, given after confidential discussions in Paris, are recommendatory only. Each member retains the power of final decision, although it is very unusual for a member not to accept a COCOM recommendation.[144] It is also very unusual for a member to try to circumvent COCOM by selling a listed item to a Communist country without submitting the matter for discussion in Paris.[145] Nevertheless, there has been some concern—

[141] *See* text at notes 8–9 *supra*. The 1974 Declaration on Atlantic Relations, *supra* note 12, says that the allies "will work to remove sources of conflict between their economic policies and to encourage economic co-operation with one another."

[142] *See* Brosio, *supra* note 75, at 116.

[143] *See* G. Wright, *NATO in the New International Order*, 36 BEHIND THE HEADLINES, No. 4, at 5 (1978).

[144] *See Export Licensing of Advanced Technology: A Review: Hearings Before a Subcomm. of the House Comm. on International Relations*, 94th Cong., 2d Sess., pt. 1, at 50–51, 61 (1976); *Extension of the Export Administration Act: Hearings Before a Subcomm. of the Senate Comm. on Banking, Housing and Urban Affairs*, 94th Cong., 2d Sess. 174–75 (1976).

[145] One instance in which there may have been circumvention was the license granted in 1975 by Rolls Royce to the People's Republic of China for the manufacture of Spey jet engines. The license may have accelerated substantially the development of Chinese propulsion design and production technology, according to a CIA statement in *Export Licensing of Advanced Technology: A Review: Hearings Before a Subcomm. of the House Comm. on International Relations*, 94th Cong., 2d Sess., pt. 2, at 8 (1976). The proposed deal had been submitted to COCOM in 1973, but had been withdrawn after some members

particularly in the United States—that the controls became too relaxed as economic pressures to export high-technology goods increased. Thus, at the Ottawa summit in July 1981, the heads of state of the seven major "Western" countries (including Japan) acknowledged a need for improved consultation and undertook to try to strengthen the control system.[146] Consequently, although there is no treaty obligation to submit any matter to COCOM or to abide by its recommendations, the "Western" nations, including NATO members, appear to have recognized a customary norm to consult before sending listed items to the Eastern bloc, and they are making some effort to insure that the system is effective.

NATO's concern with the environment is expressed through its Committee on the Challenges of Modern Society (CCMS), created in 1969 at the urging of the United States. The primary focus of CCMS is on pilot environmental studies conducted by individual member states. CCMS meets twice a year, once to discuss the pilot studies and once to conduct round-table discussions on matters of mutual interest. The round-table discussions have sometimes been occasions for consultation regarding such proposed U.S. measures as toxic substances controls, a fluorocarbon ban, and aircraft noise regulations.[147] However, the one-year hiatus between round tables and the practice of discussing only one issue at each meeting combine to prevent CCMS from becoming a forum in which member states could consult the others routinely before taking any environmentally related action that could adversely affect them.[148]

7. Synthesis of NATO Practice

NATO practice has established a norm requiring consultation within the Alliance before a member government makes a final decision on a course of action that (*a*) could have a direct,

expressed reservations. It was not resubmitted, but the U.K. did consult at least some of the allies bilaterally. *See Rolls-Royce Deal: Its Political and Military Meaning, excerpted from* Business China, Feb. 6, 1976, *id.* at 26–27; Financial Times, Dec. 23, 1975, at 4, col. 5.

[146]Ottawa Declaration, July 21, 1981, 17 WEEKLY COMP. of PRES. DOC. 791, 795 (July 27, 1981).

[147]Ward, Kendall, & Bresee, *Ten Years of CCMS: The Record and the Future,* 27 NATO REV., No. 6, at 12, 16 (1979); interview with CCMS Project Officer, July 5, 1978.

[148]On the limitations of CCMS, see Kyba, *Environmental Co-operation To Meet Political Objectives,* INTERNATIONAL PERSPECTIVES, July-Aug. 1977, at 11.

long-term, adverse effect on the Alliance's collective ability to defend against an attack from outside the Treaty area, or (*b*) could significantly enhance the military capability of those states presumed most likely to attack, i.e., those controlled by Communist governments. These two cases, of course, are opposite sides of the same coin.

This norm is supported not only by the implied duty of parties to the North Atlantic Treaty to consult before denouncing it, but also by the regular defense-budget consultation procedure, the Council's 1955 consultation procedure for extraordinary force reductions, the U.S. practice of consulting before appointing SACEUR, and the evolving practice of consulting before undertaking arms control negotiations that are particularly likely to affect means of defense relied upon by the European allies. As for the other side of the coin, the well-established COCOM procedure supports the norm.

There are some limitations. The norm does not require consultations before an initial decision is made, even if the decision establishes a general course of action that is irreversible for all practical purposes. An example would be the decisions by several allies to reduce their forces assigned to NATO. The duty arises, in other words, only before a final decision is made establishing just what is to be done. Even that norm does not extend to decisions by one NATO member to take action that could weaken the ability of another to participate in the common defense. Those decisions usually are made in an atmosphere of such tension between the allies directly involved that consultations within the Alliance have not occurred and could not reasonably be expected.

A second obligatory norm requires such NATO consultations as are feasible when an ally contemplates action within or outside the Treaty area that could lead, in the short run, to armed confrontation with the Soviet Union or could seriously exacerbate an existing confrontation with it. Support for this norm is found in the Treaty's implied duty to consult before countering a threat to the territory, independence, or security of any party; it also is found in the NATO procedure on the use of tactical nuclear weapons, as well as in the assertions and acquiescences when individual allies have acted in crises. The norm extends also to deployment of forces outside the Treaty area, when the deployment could appreciably increase the allies' vulnerability to attack from Eastern Europe.

No NATO member is required to consult if the consultation could cause it to lose such control over events as to threaten seriously its own perceived defense interests. Thus, the United States has not been expected to reveal its secret fallback positions before SALT bargaining sessions with the Soviet Union. Nor is an ally required to consult before responding to an immediate military crisis. Nevertheless, as the allied response to the 1973 U.S. worldwide alert shows, the duty is not excused simply because the acting state believes it should make a quick decision. Nor is the duty, as it applies to confrontation situations, simply a duty to consult after an initial decision but before a final one. The expectation is that the allies will be taken into the basic decision-making process insofar as is practicable under the prevailing circumstances.

There have been a number of nonconfrontation situations outside the Treaty area in which the decisions of individual allies could have affected the interests of others. Sometimes there have been prior consultations in these cases, but not with such consistency as to establish an obligation.

Normative expectations have arisen in the Alliance beyond the narrow ones found strictly in the North Atlantic Treaty. The expectations have arisen partly from provisions in the Treaty itself, partly from Council declarations, and partly from statements by NATO secretaries-general and U.S. presidents, but also from less formal practice. As a result, prior consultations are required in the two categories discussed above. But, despite sweeping language sometimes found in the declarations and statements, there is no all-encompassing duty to consult whenever an individual government's decision might affect the interests of its NATO allies. The political-military Alliance has not yet reached that stage of shared decision making.

C. A Regional, Multilateral Political-Economic Organization: The European Communities

1. The Distinctiveness of the European Communities

In economic terms, the European Communities together constitute a customs union—an organization of states without tariff barriers to trade among themselves, but with a common tariff against imports from nonmember states.[149] The customs union was to be created in stages during a twelve-year transitional period ending on December 31, 1969. It was actually created by July 1, 1968, although several transitional provisions in the European Economic Community (EEC) Treaty remained operative until the end of 1969. Economic and monetary union was set as a further goal at the Hague European summit in December 1969. That goal has proved elusive, although a step in its direction was finally taken with the establishment of the European Monetary System in March 1979. The common commercial policy encompasses trade relations with nonmember states going beyond mere tariff policy. It was supposed to be in force after the transitional period, but it still had not fully evolved as of mid-1982.

In political terms, the three European Communities, unlike NATO, are commonly described collectively as a supranational organization ("the Community"). Just what that means has been the subject of academic debate. One might be content to say that the supranational organization stands somewhere between the traditional international organization, with its heavy reliance on the independent wills of its constituent governments, and the federal state, with its greater concentration of power in a central government. More ambitious definitions would stress the supranational organization's authority to legislate with direct effect on individuals and entities in member states, or would characterize it as an organization in which significant policy-making functions are delegated to persons and institutions not directly accountable to the member governments for their decisions.[150] One might also stress the organization's authority to

[149]The three Communities are the European Coal and Steel Community (ECSC), the European Economic Community (EEC), and the European Atomic Energy Community (Euratom). Since July 1, 1967, they have had common institutions: the Commission, the Council, and the Assembly (or European Parliament). Each Community still has its own governing treaty and thus is still technically separate from the others, although for most purposes the three may be treated as a single organization. They are so treated here, even though they are sometimes called "the Communities."

In 1982, the member states were Belgium, Denmark, the Federal Republic of Germany, France, Greece, Ireland, Italy, Luxembourg, the Netherlands, and the United Kingdom. As of mid-1982, Portugal and Spain were negotiating terms of eventual membership. In 1972, Norway rejected membership in a national referendum.

[150]*Compare* Robertson, *Legal Problems of European Integration*, 91 HAGUE ACADEMY, RECUEIL DES COURS 105, 143–48 (1957), *with* I. CLAUDE, SWORDS INTO PLOWSHARES: THE PROBLEMS AND PROGRESS OF INTERNATIONAL ORGANIZATION 109–12 (4th ed. 1971), *reprinted in* EUROPEAN COMMUNITY LAW AND INSTITUTIONS IN PERSPECTIVE 20, 25 (E. Stein, P. Hay & M. Waelbroeck eds. 1976).

conduct relatively limited external relations for its members.

Whatever definition one uses, the European Community is clearly distinguishable from an organization such as NATO by its more centralized decision-making authority. The Council of the European Communities, composed of representatives of the member states, has express legislative powers. So does the Commission, which is composed of individuals acting independently from their governments. The Commission's autonomous legislative power applies primarily to measures implementing policies adopted by the Council. Nevertheless, the Commission plays an important role in shaping those policies by proposing them in the first instance to the Council, which often can act only after receiving such a proposal and after obtaining the opinion of the Assembly (the European Parliament, a representative body of persons directly elected by the voters in the member states). The legislative output of the Council and Commission consists of regulations (binding legislation directly applicable in all member states), directives, and decisions (binding upon addressees).[151]

In an organization with centralized decision-making capability, one would expect to find less emphasis on consultation as a harmonizing norm than in a looser alliance. In one sense that is so. In the Community, the governing treaties and the legislative decisions made pursuant to them call upon member states to take coordinated action in many instances; when they do not, they sometimes go further than a mere consultation requirement and call for Commission consent (or authorization) before national governments may act. On the other hand, there have been a great many instances in which the treaties and legislative enactments have not gone so far, but have instead imposed a prior consultation norm on member governments. As the discussion below will indicate, the consultation norm applies to a greater variety and proportion of national decisions within the European Community's political-economic frame of reference than in the political-military context of NATO.

Legal norms in a supranational organization such as the Community stem primarily from formally binding, explicit commands—provisions in the relevant treaties and the legislative

[151]*See* EEC Treaty art. 189. The Council and Commission also can adopt nonbinding recommendations and opinions. *Id.* The Assembly's powers, for the most part, are advisory.

acts of the Council and Commission—rather than from relatively unstructured assertion and acquiescence. Thus, the discussion will focus on formal Community obligations, examining individual state practice to see if it comports with the formal obligations.

2. Institutional Provisions

Community institutions must follow some form of consultation procedure before acting on a variety of matters of particular importance. This appears most prominently in the EEC Treaty procedure for adoption of significant Community legislation. Because those who conceived and negotiated the Community treaties were not ready to create a federal parliamentary democracy, the European Parliament is not a full partner in the legislative process. Nevertheless, it was recognized that attention should be paid to the views of the body with the strongest claim to popular representation. Thus, for many important Community decisions, the Council is empowered to act only after consulting the Parliament, and for one important annual decision—adoption of the budget—the Parliament's approval is required.[152] In practice, the Council consults the Parliament

[152] *See, e.g.*, EEC Treaty arts. 43(2) (common agricultural policy), 54 (freedom of establishment), 75(1) (common transport policy), 87(1) (competition policy), 100 (approximation of certain laws), 127 (European Social Fund), 235 ("necessary and proper" clause), and 236 (amendments to the Treaty). The European Parliament's budgetary powers are set forth in article 203, and its current budgetary role is outlined in the Joint Declaration of June 30, 1982, in 25 O. J. EUR. COMM. (No. C 194) 1 (1982).

When consultation is required by the treaties, failure to wait for Parliament's opinion will nullify a Council regulation. Roquette Frères v. Council, 1980 E. Comm. Ct. J. Rep. 3333; Maizena v. Council, *id.* at 3393.

There is a "conciliation procedure" created by agreement among the Parliament, Council, and Commission, by which the Parliament and Council must try to work out their differences regarding proposed Community acts having appreciable financial implications, unless the proposed act simply would implement an existing one. *See* Joint Declaration of the European Parliament, the Council and the Commission, Mar. 4, 1975, in 18 O.J. EUR. COMM. (No. C 89) 1 (1975). In practice, the conciliation procedure has been expanded to include any act affecting the Parliament's institutional position within the Community. *See* 1981–82 EUR. PARL. DOC. (No. 1–216/81) 25–26 (1981). The Commission has proposed that the procedure be changed to reflect this practice. *See* 14 BULL. EUR. COMM., No. 12, at 10–11 (1981).

Sometimes Parliament has asserted a right to be consulted even though the Treaty does not clearly require it. *See, e.g.*, Parliament's Opinion on the Proposed Regulation on Community Aid for Industrial Restructuring and Conversion Operations, Apr. 26, 1979, para. 13, in 22 O.J. EUR. COMM. (No. C 127) 52 (1979). The Commission acquiesced. *See* 13 BULL. EUR. COMM., No. 2, at 85 (1980).

not only when required by the treaties but also before it adopts any significant legislative act.[153] In a number of instances, the Council may act only after consulting another broadly representative body, the Economic and Social Committee.[154]

A crisis developed in 1965 concerning the powers of the Commission and voting procedure in the Council. When it was resolved in early 1966, the members of the Council declared, "Before adopting any particularly important proposal, it is desirable that the Commission should take up the appropriate contacts with the Governments of the Member States."[155] Although some have viewed this as creating a consultation duty,[156] it is carefully couched in nonmandatory terms that would not create firm expectations of compliance in any ascertainable class of cases. Thus, it does not rise to the level of a procedural duty imposed on the legislative function.

In one important transitional situation, prior consultation by Community institutions has been thought essential. During the period from the close of accession negotiations with Denmark, Ireland, Norway, and the United Kingdom to the entry into force of the Accession Treaty, the Council and Commission promised to consult them before adopting any decision likely to affect them as future members of the Community. A reciprocal obligation was undertaken by the applicant states.[157] The

[153] *See* 1981–82 EUR. PARL. DOC. (NO. 1–216/81) 7 (1981).

[154] The Committee consists of representatives of producers, farmers, carriers, workers, dealers, craftsmen, professionals, and the general public. *See* EEC Treaty art. 193. For situations in which it must be consulted, *see* arts. 49 (freedom of movement for workers), 54 (freedom of establishment), 75(1) (common transport policy), 100 (approximation of certain laws), 121 (common social policy), and 127 (European Social Fund). It has a counterpart, the Consultative Committee, in the Coal and Steel Community. *See* ECSC Treaty art. 18.

In the labor policy field, Community institutions are enjoined to consult within the Standing Committee on Employment before they adopt any measures. Council Dec. 70/532/EEC, Dec. 14, 1970, art 2, in O.J. EUR. COMM. (spec. ed. 1970(III)) 863 (1972), *as amended,* Council Dec. 75/62/EEC, Jan. 20, 1975, in 18 O.J. EUR. COMM. (No. L 21) 17 (1975). The procedure is likely to be developed further, when the Communities settle on a labor market policy. *See* 13 BULL. EUR. COMM., No. 4, at 45–46 (1980).

[155] EEC COMMISSION, NINTH GENERAL REPORT ON THE ACTIVITIES OF THE COMMUNITY 31 (1966).

[156] *See* J. KUSUMOWIDAGDO, CONSULTATION CLAUSES AS MEANS OF PROVIDING FOR TREATY OBEDIENCE 194 (1981); Thompson, *The European Economic Community After the 1965 Crisis,* 16 INT'L & COMP. L.Q. 1, 6 (1967).

[157] Commission Report, *The Enlarged Community,* pt. 4 (1972) in 11 INT'L LEGAL MATERIALS 397, 398 (1972). In the case of the Council, this meant that consultations would take place before decisions were adopted. Norway did not become a member.

same procedure was applied to Greece and is contemplated for Portugal and Spain.[158]

In another longstanding transitional situation, a prior consultation scheme for Community institutions has been developed to minimize potential conflicts with member states. The Community has the power to preempt member states' competition (antitrust) laws by adopting comprehensive Community-wide rules on competition, but it has not yet fully done so. Since Community and national competition rules coexist, with Community rules prevailing in the event of a conflict, it has been necessary to devise a system for Commission consultation with representatives of member states in the early stages of Commission decision making on companies' compliance with Community competition rules. This is done through an advisory committee of national officials concerned with restrictive practices and monopolies.[159]

3. Relations Within the Common Market

The Community has devised prior consultation or prior consent requirements for a variety of national measures that could affect (*a*) the internal functioning of the common market for traded goods, (*b*) the effective integration of member states' economies, or (*c*) the achievement of monetary stability among member states. One important type of measure affecting traded

[158]*See* Commission Communication to the Council, *The Transitional Period and the Institutional Implications of Enlargement,* 11 BULL. EUR. COMM. Supp. 2/78, at 6–7 (1978). The Community consulted at least two affected states—Turkey and Israel—regarding the final terms of Greek membership. *See* Additional Protocol to the EEC-Turkey Association Agreement, Nov. 23, 1970, art. 56, in 3 COLLECTION OF THE AGREEMENTS CONCLUDED BY THE E.C. 583 (obligating the Community to consult); 12 BULL. EUR. COMM., No. 2, at 77 (1979); *id.*, No. 3, at 80. Regarding the consultations with Israel, *see* 11 *id.*, No. 12, at 90 (1978); 12 *id.*, No. 3, at 81 (1979).

Institutional consultation duties appear in the preferential trade provisions of the Lomé Conventions among the EEC and the African, Caribbean, and Pacific (ACP) countries. *See* chapter VI, at notes 96 and 180 (concerning possible EEC trade measures that could harm ACP interests).

[159]Council Reg. 17, Feb. 6, 1962, art. 10, in O.J. EUR. COMM. (spec. ed. 1959–62) 87 (1972). The relevant EEC Treaty articles are 85–89.

At least one member state, the Federal Republic of Germany, has adopted a reciprocal procedure calling for consultation with the Commission when the initiation of proceedings under national competition law might overlap with potential Community proceedings. *See* Markert, *Some Legal and Administrative Problems of the Co-Existence of Community and National Competition Law in the EEC,* 11 COMMON MKT. L. REV. 92, 100 (1974).

goods, however, is not subject to a formal consultation procedure. In some cases where a formal procedure exists, it has not been scrupulously followed. Moreover, the relevant Community instruments are dotted with escape clauses that often permit national action to be taken without consultation in "urgent" circumstances.

The drafters of the EEC Treaty recognized that while internal tariffs were being dismantled during the transitional period, individual member states might come under strong pressure to take retrogressive steps affecting the trade or commerce of other members. Some of these were permitted if authorized by the Commission. This prior consent regime applied to protective trade measures, antidumping duties, and measures adversely affecting common carriers of other member states.[160]

Prior consent requirements also have been established for certain trade-distorting government subsidies and for the use of countervailing duties to neutralize them. Thus, direct taxes may not be remitted for intra-Community exports, nor countervailing duties imposed if they are remitted, without prior approval from the Council.[161] With a few exceptions, government subsidies to industries are prohibited if they could distort competition within the common market; proposed government subsidies must be notified to the Commission in advance, and may not be granted if the Commission (or in some cases the Council) disapproves. Once granted, they must be abolished or modified if the Commission so orders, after giving the parties concerned an opportunity to be heard.[162] Special prior approval mechanisms apply to national shipbuilding aids and to specific national aids to the steel industry.[163] These veto powers are premised on the Community's strong interest in regulating the

[160] *See* EEC Treaty arts. 76 (common carriers), 91(1) (antidumping), and 226 (protective trade measures). Beyond the transitional period, protective measures can be imposed for balance-of-payments purposes if authorized by the Commission, or unilaterally in a crisis. *See* EEC Treaty arts. 108(3), 109, and text at note 187 *infra*.

[161] EEC Treaty art. 98.

[162] EEC Treaty arts. 92, 93. Instances in which this prior review procedure has been used appear in the Commission's annual REPORTS ON THE ACTIVITIES OF THE EUROPEAN COMMUNITIES. *See, e.g.*, TENTH GENERAL REPORT, 1976, at 98–100 (1977); ELEVENTH GENERAL REPORT, 1977, at 107–09 (1978). On a few occasions, member governments have adopted subsidy schemes without following the review procedure. *See, e.g.*, Financial Times, May 29, 1975, at 22, col. 3; 11 BULL. EUR. COMM., No. 3, at 40 (1978).

[163] *See* Council Directive on Aid to Shipbuilding, Apr. 28, 1981, art. 10, in 24 O.J. EUR. COMM. (No. L 137) 39 (1981); Council agreement on aids to the steel industry, 14 BULL. EUR. COMM., No. 6, at 18–19 (1981).

extent to which member governments distort competition by pouring public funds into financially weak, but politically powerful, industries. Something more than prior consultation was thought necessary.

The Community has endeavored to harmonize national value-added tax systems by setting forth what member states may and may not do, leaving them discretion in some areas. Thus, member states are for the most part told what exemptions they must allow, but they are to supply the rules to prevent the exemptions from fostering tax evasion. When members are given greater discretion—as when they are allowed to exempt certain international trade transactions and to exclude some goods from the system of tax deductions for cyclical economic reasons—their discretion is made subject to a consultation procedure.[164] Even greater discretion, permitting derogations from the Community tax system in special circumstances, requires express or tacit prior consent from the Council.[165]

Member states have retained the discretion to impose new trade-related health, safety, security, morality, and cultural standards or prohibitions, including those on trade with other member states.[166] The EEC Treaty requires the Council to harmonize these potential nontariff trade barriers[167] The Council has done this gradually by directives. A member state that has "reason to fear" that its proposed measure would create a nontariff trade barrier or otherwise "distort the conditions of competition in the common market" must consult the Commission, which may make recommendations.[168] Member states do not

[164] *See* Sixth Council Directive on the Harmonization [of] Turnover Taxes, May 17, 1977, arts. 16, 17(1), 20(5), 24(1), in 20 O.J. EUR. COMM. (No. L 145) 1 (1977). *See also* Van Paassen v. Staatssecretaris van Financiën, 1979 E. Comm. Ct. J. Rep. 2063, 2078.

See also the Commission's draft Council decision establishing a prior information and consultation procedure for tax matters, 24 O.J. EUR. COMM., (No. C 346) 6 (1981) (procedure would apply when member state intends to adopt tax measures that may have an appreciable influence on the establishment or functioning of the common market or on the implementation of a common policy or common action).

[165] Sixth Council Directive, *supra* note 164, arts. 27, 30.

[166] *See* EEC Treaty art. 36.

[167] *See* EEC Treaty art. 100. Several such directives have been issued. *See* 3 H. SMIT & P. HERZOG, THE LAW OF THE EUROPEAN ECONOMIC COMMUNITY 3–479, 3–495 to 3–503 (1976).

[168] *See* EEEC Treaty art. 102. The European Free Trade Association (EFTA) has a similar requirement. *See* EFTA SECRETARIAT, THE EUROPEAN FREE TRADE ASSOCIATION 69–70 (1976).

The Commission of the European Communities schedules meetings at which national officials responsible for standardization policy discuss their intention regarding proposed technical specifications. *See* 13 BULL. EUR. COMM., No. 1, at 14 (1980).

have unlimited discretion to determine that no trade barrier would occur. In the celebrated *Costa* case, the European Court of Justice said, "[M]ember states have unambiguously bound themselves to a prior consultation of the Commission in all those cases where their legislative projects might create a risk, no matter how feeble, of a possible distortion."[169]

There are "gentlemen's agreements" among the member governments calling for prior notification to the Council or Commission of proposed new product standards and environmental measures. These agreements, which are more specific than the EEC Treaty provisions mentioned in the preceding paragraph, call on the members to defer long enough to let the Council adopt a directive, or the Commission a recommendation, depending on the circumstances.[170] Moreover, Council directives require national authorities to submit draft rules to the Commission on the disposal of various kinds of nonradioactive waste, giving the Commission a chance to discuss them and to make recommendations, if necessary.[171] In each of these instances, the purpose is to forestall nontariff barriers to trade.[172]

The Community, of course, has attempted to go beyond the mere elimination of trade barriers and has moved by fits and starts in the direction of an economic and monetary union. Since 1964, member governments have undertaken, first informally and later through binding Council decisions, to consult within the Community before altering the exchange rates of their currencies.[173] Under the European Monetary System (EMS), which entered into force for eight Community members in March

[169]Costa v. E.N.E.L., 1964 C.J. Comm. E. Rec. 1141, 1964 Comm. Mkt. L.R. 425, 456. *See also* 3 H. Smit & P. Herzog, *supra* note 167, at 3–542, 3–543. (The *Costa* case did not involve product standards, but rather the creation of a state-controlled monopoly for the supply of electricity. Thus, the article 102 consultation procedure is not limited to measures directly affecting traded goods.)

[170]*See* the Agreement of May 28, 1969, in O. J. Eur. Comm. (spec. ed. 2d ser.) 32 (1974); Agreement of Mar. 5, 1973, in 16 O.J. Eur. Comm. (No. C 9) 1 (1973). The procedures do not apply to measures urgently required on grounds of safety or health.

[171]Council Directive 75/442/EEC, July 15, 1975, art. 3(2), in 18 O.J. Eur. Comm. (No. L 194) 39 (1975); Council Directive 78/319/EEC, Mar. 20, 1978, art. 12, in 21 O.J. Eur. Comm. (No. L 84) 43 (1978) (subject to an exception for emergencies). The Commission could act under art. 102.

[172]Environmental measures adopted for environmental purposes are examined at notes 205–08 *infra*.

[173]*See* the Declaration of May 8, 1964, in O.J. Eur. Comm. (spec. ed. 2d ser.) 16 (1974); Council Dec. 69/227/EEC, July 17, 1969, in O.J. Eur. Comm. (spec. ed. 1969(II)) 350 (1972); Council Dec. 74/120/EEC, Feb. 18, 1974, arts. 7–10, in 17 O.J. Eur. Comm. (No. L 63) 16 (1974).

1979, exchange rate adjustments among participating states require common consent; important exchange rate decisions between participating and nonparticipating states require prior EMS consultation.[174] Greece and the U.K. do not participate.

Although prior consultation has been considered an important transitional procedure as Community states move from monetary autonomy to integration,[175] compliance before 1979 was sporadic at best. For example, when France devalued the franc in August 1969, it simply notified its Community partners (and the International Monetary Fund) in advance.[176] However, when the German mark was floated in September 1969 and revalued a month later, there were prior Community consultations.[177] Similarly, there were Community consultations immediately before the German-Dutch float in May 1971.[178]

During the worldwide monetary crisis of February 1973, Italy floated the lire, apparently without prior consultation.[179] When France floated the franc in January 1974, it engaged in no more than perfunctory consultations with the President of the Commission and the Chancellor of West Germany.[180] Italy and France

[174] *See* Council Resolution on the Establishment of the European Monetary System and Related Matters, Dec. 5, 1978, in 11 BULL. EUR. COMM., No. 12, at 10, 11 (1978).

[175] *See, e.g.,* EEC Working Party, *The Establishment by Stages of Economic and Monetary Union in the Community* (the Werner Report), 3 BULL. EUR. COMM., No. 7, Supp. at 11 (1970); Commission Communication to the Council, Mar. 1976, in 9 BULL. EUR. COMM., No. 4, at 23–24 (1976).

[176] *See* Strange, *International Monetary Relations,* in 2 INTERNATIONAL ECONOMIC RELATIONS OF THE WESTERN WORLD 1959–1971, at 18, 328 (A. Shonfield ed. 1976). France argued that its participation in the Group of Ten central bankers meeting nine months earlier served as prior consultation, since the discussions had focused on the amount by which France ultimately devalued. *Id.* Of course, the earlier discussions could not have considered the immediate events leading to the 1969 devaluation. *See also* Russell, *L'Engrenage, Collegial Style and the Crisis Syndrome: Lessons from Monetary Policy in the European Community,* 13 J. COMMON MKT. STUDIES 61, 79 (1975).

The United Kingdom did consult the Community's Monetary Committee before it devalued the pound sterling in November 1967. *Id.* at 83. The U.K. was not then a member of the Community.

[177] *Id.;* Telex No. 26146, Oct. 9, 1969, from Brussels to the European Community Information Service in Washington, in the latter's files.

[178] *See* the address by Raymond Barre to the European Parliament, May 18, 1971, *reproduced in* EUROPE DOCUMENTS, No. 624, at 1–2, 5 (May 24, 1971).

[179] This may be inferred from the Commission's Communication to the Council of Apr. 30, 1973, in 6 BULL. EUR. COMM., Supp. 5/73, at 7 (1973). However, there were several Community meetings on the monetary crisis shortly before the Italian float. *See* 6 BULL. EUR. COMM., No. 2, at 25–31 (1973).

[180] *See* N.Y. Times, Jan. 23, 1974, at 50, col. 3 (city ed.); R. SOLOMON, THE INTERNATIONAL MONETARY SYSTEM, 1945–1976, at 260–61 (1977). The Monetary Committee of the European Commission discussed the French action on the day it became effective.

repeated their floating performances in January and March 1976, respectively, although the French action—which involved leaving the European currency "snake"—was preceded by consultation with the finance ministers of those countries participating in the snake.[181] There was no Community consultation before the realignment of four snake currencies in October 1976, nor before the adjustments to three snake currencies in April and August 1977.[182] The revaluations of the German mark, Belgian franc, and Dutch guilder in October 1978 were preceded by consultations with the finance ministers and central bank governors of the other snake countries, but not with those of Community members outside the snake.[183] The Commission frequently has expressed its displeasure when the full Community consultation procedure has not been followed.[184]

EMS states' consultation performance improved considerably with the advent of the 1979 procedure. Even when the prior consent aspect of the new system has not worked as contemplated, there has been prior consultation.[185]

Measures other than exchange rate variations have sometimes been used by member states in balance of payments difficulties. For example, the Italian government in March 1964 reacted to speculation against the lira by seeking large credits

7 BULL. EUR. COMM., No. 1, at 41 (1974). Shortly thereafter the Commission publicly disapproved of such action. *Id.*, at 5, 7.

[181] 9 *id.*, No. 1, at 30 (1976); 9 *id.*, No. 3, at 30 (1976). Not all Community states participated in the snake, and two nonmembers of the Community (Norway and Sweden) did. In early 1979 a modified version of the snake became the European Monetary System. Although European nonmembers of the Community, such as Norway and Sweden, were eligible to participate in the exchange rate and intervention mechanism, none did.

[182] In October 1976, the German mark was revalued, while the Danish and the Norwegian kroner and the Swedish krona were devalued. *See* EUROPEAN COMMISSION, TENTH GEN'L REP. ON THE ACTIVITIES OF THE EUROPEAN COMMUNITIES, 1976, at 116–17 (1977). Denmark, Norway, and Sweden devalued within the snake in April 1977; the former two devalued again in August, while Sweden left the snake. *See* 10 BULL. EUR. COMM., No. 4, at 23 (1977); 10 *id.*, No. 7/8, at 23–24 (1977).

[183] Washington Post, Oct. 17, 1978, at D8, col. 1; 11 BULL. EUR. COMM., No. 10, at 19 (1978).

[184] *See* the Commission's pronouncements cited in note 182 *supra*.

[185] This occurred when Denmark devalued the krone in November 1979 and when Italy devalued the lira in March 1981. *See* Financial Times, Mar. 24, 1981, at 2, col. 1. The prior consent requirement was met in September 1979, in October 1981, in February 1982, and in June 1982, when the participants joined in adjustments of the cross-rates among some of the participating currencies. *See* 12 BULL. EUR. COMM., No. 9, at 26 (1979); 14 *id.*, No. 9, at 14–15 (1981); 15 *id.*, No. 2, at 18 (1982); N.Y. Times, June 14, 1982, at A6, col. 4.

from the International Monetary Fund and the United States. The Council responded with a decision requiring consultation within the Community's Monetary Committee before a member state seeks financial resources under international agreements or participates in substantial monetary support for third countries.[186]

The EEC Treaty contemplates that the Council will provide assistance to a member state in balance-of-payments difficulties. If the Council does not give adequate assistance, the Commission may authorize the state to take protective measures; if "a sudden crisis in the balance of payments occurs," the state may take temporary protective measures without prior authorization or consultation.[187]

Whenever a member state has sought to apply protective balance-of-payments measures under a claim of sudden crisis, the Commission has responded that the urgency was not such as to preclude prior consultation. For example, following the French strikes and student unrest in the spring of 1968, the French government notified the Commission that its balance-of-payments position justified its imposition of import quotas extending beyond July 1 (when the Community's transitional period terminated), and that it would grant certain export subsidies. The Commission replied that there was no sudden crisis in the French balance of payments and joined with France to set in motion the Community mechanisms for authorized protective measures and assistance.[188] In 1974, when Italy notified the Commission of its decision to impose a six-month import deposit requirement for balance-of-payments purposes, the Commission expressed its disappointment with the Italian failure to consult, but approved the Italian fait accompli.[189] In May 1976 Italy did get prior Commission authorization before applying an even more comprehensive import deposit require-

[186] *See* Russell, *supra* note 176, at 78; Council Dec. 64/301/EEC, May 8, 1964, in O. J. EUR. COMM. (spec. ed. 1963–64) 143 (1972) (subject to an escape clause when "circumstances . . . require otherwise"); Council Dec. 71/143/EEC, Mar. 22, 1971, art. 2, in O.J. EUR. COMM. (spec. ed. 1971 (I)) 177 (1972) (consultation required before turning to sources of medium-term credit outside the Community).

[187] EEC Treaty arts. 108(3), 109.

[188] *See* 3 H. SMIT & P. HERZOG, *supra* note 167, at 3–618 to 3–620.

[189] *Id.* at 3–620 to 3–622. *See also* 7 BULL. EUR. COMM., No. 5, at 6–13 (1974); *id.*, No. 6, at 37. Restrictive Danish measures at about the same time also were taken without prior consultation. *Id.*

ment.[190] Apparently, however, Italy did not consult the Commission later in the year, when it imposed a surcharge on the purchase of foreign exchange,[191] or in May 1981, when it imposed an import deposit requirement that was somewhat milder than the 1976 scheme.[192]

In a field related to balance of payments, the EEC Treaty calls upon member states to consult on proposed measures that would affect significantly business-cycle fluctuations.[193] The Council, in a series of implementing decisions and directives beginning in 1960, has required that member states consult within the Community before adopting significant short- and medium-term economic policy measures.[194] It also has issued prior consultation directives in specific fields where national action could affect business cycles. For example, the Council has required member states to maintain designated minimum petroleum reserves and to consult the others before drawing them below that level, except in cases of particular urgency or to meet minor local needs.[195] There is some doubt, however, whether business cycle consultations in the Community amount to more than "notification of decisions already taken in national capitals."[196] For this reason, the Council has continued to try to tighten the procedures.[197]

The Community's common transport policy relies heavily on prior consultations to coordinate member states' decisions. A Council decision requires notification to the Commission, and an opportunity for it to respond, before a member state adopts

[190] *See* EUROPEAN COMMISSION, TENTH GEN'L REP. ON THE ACTIVITIES OF THE EUROPEAN COMMUNITIES, 1976, at 119–20 (1977).

[191] *Id.* at 120; Financial Times, Oct. 5, 1976, at 4, col. 5.

[192] 14 BULL. EUR. COMM., No. 6, at 24 (1981).

[193] EEC Treaty art. 103(1). Although the language of this provision sounds as though the consultation duty arises when a proposed measure is designed to counteract the business cycle, Smit and Herzog argue that the key is actual impact rather than intent. They say, for example, that developments in wage-rate policy are subject presumptively to the consultation duty because of their impact on the business cycle. 3 H. SMIT & P. HERZOG, *supra* note 167, at 3–567 to 3–568.

[194] For a summary of the measures, with citations, see *id.* at 3–564, 3–575 to 3–579. The most important is the "convergence decision," Council Dec. 74/120/EEC, Feb. 18, 1974, arts. 7–10, in 17 O.J. EUR. COMM. (No. L 63) 16 (1974).

[195] *See* Council Directive 68/414/EEC, Dec. 20, 1968, in O.J. EUR. COMM. (spec. ed. 1968(II)) 586 (1972), *as amended,* Council Directive 72/425/EEC, Dec. 19, 1972, in O.J. EUR. COMM. (spec. ed. Dec. 28–30, 1972) 69 (1972).

[196] Barattieri & Thomas, *Monetary and Economic Co-operation in the EEC,* 51 INT'L AFFAIRS 499, 503–04 (1975).

[197] *See* 12 BULL. EUR. COMM., No. 6, at 31 (1979).

"any law, regulation or administrative provision concerning transport by rail, road or inland waterway liable to interfere substantially with the implementation of the common transport policy."[198] There is an exception for cases of "extreme urgency." Consultations under this procedure have covered a wide variety of measures, including the 1967 proposed German transport reform program; proposals for new freight tariffs, highway tolls, and maximum truck weights; and subsidies for various types of transportation.[199]

The Council's prior consultation procedure has been less successful for major transportation infrastructure projects. Although it has been used in connection with some major international waterways, railways, and highways, this procedure appears to have prompted little more than exchanges of information unless active cooperation was needed to make a project feasible.[200]

Where the common transport policy has left regulatory details to the member governments, it has done so subject to prior consultation. Thus, a 1966 Council regulation provides a framework for common rules relating to bus services between member states, and authorizes individual member states to impelment the regulation after consulting the Commission.[201] A 1969 Council regulation sets out required minimum ages for freight and passenger drivers, maximum driving periods, and minimum rest periods, leaving it to member states—after they consult the Commission—to adopt the means of control and the penalties

[198]Council Dec. of Mar. 21, 1962, in O.J. EUR. COMM. (spec. ed. 1959–62) 96 (1972), *amended by* Council Dec. 73/402/EEC, Nov. 22, 1973, in 16 O.J. EUR. COMM. (No. L 347) 48 (1973).

[199]*See* STABENOW, EVOLUTION OF TRANSPORT POLICY IN THE EUROPEAN COMMUNITY 13–14 (Report to the Conf. on Canadian Nat'l Transportation Policy 1972); 2 H. SMIT & P. HERZOG, *supra* note 167, at 2–784 to 2–785.

[200]The procedure was established by Council Dec. 66/161/EEC, Feb. 28, 1966, in O.J. EUR. COMM. (spec. ed. 1965–66) 92 (1972), *superseded by* Council Dec. 78/174/EEC, Feb. 20, 1978, in 21 O.J. EUR. COMM. (No. L 54) 16 (1978). The 1978 decision, like the earlier one, sets forth a consultation procedure. Regarding the difficulties in implementing the earlier procedure, see 2 H. SMIT & P. HERZOG, *supra* note 167, at 2–785 to 2–786; STABENOW, *supra* note 199, at 34; Commission Communication to the Council, Oct. 25, 1973, in 6 BULL. EUR. COMM., Supp. 16/73, at 20 (1973).

[201]Council Reg. 117/66/EEC, July 28, 1966, art. 10, in O.J. EUR. COMM. (spec. ed. 1965–66) 177 (1972). Common rules concerning shuttle services and coach services were adopted in 1972. In each instance, member states were authorized to implement the rules after consulting the Commission. *See* Council Reg. 516/72/EEC, Feb. 28, 1972, art. 24, in O.J. EUR. COMM. (spec. ed. 1972(I)) 137 (1972); Council Reg. 517/72/EEC, Feb. 28, 1972, art. 22, in *id.* at 143.

for breach.[202] Similar consultation-before-implementation provisions appear in two 1974 Council directives setting forth standards for licensing freight and passenger drivers.[203]

In the related aeronautical industry, Council members have agreed that member governments should consult each other before embarking on new programs to develop civil aircraft and engines. The purpose is to enhance the competitive position of the European industry by promoting joint ventures.[204]

Finally, as noted in chapters II and III, there is some intra-Community consultation practice regarding "pure" environmental protection and fishery conservation, as distinguished from practice concerning potential nontariff trade barriers in the form of environmental or conservation measures. The Euratom Treaty requires consultation with the Commission when member states plan nuclear power stations or industries engaged in the nuclear fuel cycle and when they plan to dispose of radioactive waste.[205] The Commission has proposed a consultation procedure for conventional power stations that are likely to affect the territory of another member state.[206] A Council directive contemplates consultations, with Commission advisory participation, when member states propose to issue permits for significant (but nonprohibited) discharges that could pollute groundwaters.[207] Consultations directed in part to environmental issues are required when member states plan regional development programs, though the consultations often come late in the planning stages.[208]

On fishery conservation, an interim scheme was adopted in 1976, pending agreement on a definitive common fisheries pol-

[202]Council Reg. 543/69/EEC, Mar. 25, 1969, art. 18(1), in O.J. EUR. COMM. (spec. ed. 1969(I)) 170 (1972), *amended by* Council Regs. 514/72/EEC and 515/72/EEC, Feb. 28, 1972, in O.J. EUR. COMM. (spec. ed. 1972(I)) 124 & 134 (1972). For an example of compliance (by the Netherlands), see 11 BULL. EUR. COMM., No. 1, at 39 (1978).

[203]Council Directive 74/561/EEC, Nov. 12, 1974, arts. 2(2), 7(1), in 17 O.J. EUR. COMM. (No. L 308) 18 (1974); Council Directive 74/562/EEC, Nov. 12, 1974, arts. 1(3), 6(1), *id.* at 23. For examples of compliance (by Ireland and West Germany), see 11 BULL. EUR. COMM., No. 5, at 53 (1978); 12 *id.*, No. 7/8, at 47 (1979).

[204]*See* Council Res. of Mar. 4, 1975, preamble and art. I(1)(b), in 18 O.J. EUR. COMM. (No. C 59) 1 (1975). The resolution also urges member states to grant and harmonize aid to the industry, subject to the Community's (prior consent) regime for state aids. As to the latter, see text at note 161 *supra*.

[205]Euratom Treaty arts. 37, 41, 43.

[206]*See* chapter II at note 39 *supra*; chapter III at note 30 *supra*.

[207]*See* chapter II at note 37 *supra;* chapter III at note 40 *supra*. Note also the procedure for titanium dioxide discharges, chapter III at notes 41–42 *supra*.

[208]*See* chapter III at notes 12–13 *supra*.

icy. Temporary conservation measures may be enacted by member states if they seek the Commission's approval first and consult it "at all stages of the procedures."[209]

4. External Relations

The EEC Treaty contains transitional consultation provisions designed to assist in developing the common commercial policy by which Community institutions now conduct trade relations with the outside world. During the transitional period the member states, in consultation with the Commission, were to adjust their tariff agreements with nonmembers to avoid delaying progress toward the common customs tariff.[210] In 1961 the Council required member states to consult the Commission before negotiating any major new or revised trade agreement.[211] Although compliance with this procedure seems generally to have been good, France in 1969 negotiated a trade agreement with the Soviet Union without consulting the Commission.[212] This prompted the Council to adopt a new decision acknowledging that member states might extend existing trade agreements beyond the transitional period (subject to prior consultation) and permitting them to negotiate new trade agreements with state-trading countries (subject to prior consultation plus authorization from the Council).[213]

The ECSC and Euratom Treaties do not delegate external commercial relations authority to the Community, as does the

[209]Council Res. of Nov. 3, 1976, Annex VI, *quoted in* 1977 E. Comm. Ct. J. Rep. 945. *See* chapter III at notes 52–56 *supra*.

[210]EEC Treaty art. 111(4). Import quotas could be liberalized without prior consultation. *Id.* art. 111(5).

Member states were also required to consult each other regarding coordinated action in international economic organizations such as the General Agreement on Tariffs and Trade. *Id.* art. 116.

[211]Council Dec. of Oct. 9, 1961, arts. 1–2, in O.J. EUR. COMM. (spec. ed. 1959–62) 84 (1972). As usual, there was an escape clause for "exceptional cases." *Id.* art. 3. The decision implemented EEC Treaty art. 111(4).

[212]On the positive results under the 1961 decision, *see* European Parliament Comm. on External Economic Relations, *Report Concerning Cooperation Agreements Between Member States and Third Countries,* Feb. 11, 1974, 13 INT'L LEGAL MATERIALS 1235, 1240 (1974). On the French action in 1969, see Leopold, *External Relations Power of EEC in Theory and in Practice,* 26 INT'L & COMP. L.Q. 54, 67 (1977).

[213]Council Dec. 69/494/EEC, Dec. 16, 1969, arts. 1–2, 5–6, 9–13, on O.J. EUR. COMM. (spec. ed. 1969(II)), 603 (1972). The Eastern European states did not recognize Community institutions; hence the authorization for individual member states to enter into new trade agreements with them.

EEC Treaty. Each of those treaties contains a provision contemplating commercial agreements between member states and third states, subject to prior notification and consultation.[214]

Commercial policy responsibility under the EEC Treaty was transferred to the Community on January 1, 1973. At that point Community institutions assumed sole authority to conclude trade agreements with nonmember states (except with the Eastern European bloc, which still did not recognize the Community) and to establish nontreaty trade measures. When the Commission negotiates trade agreements with nonmembers, it must consult a special committee appointed by the Council.[215]

On an interim basis, the Council permitted individual member states to change their own (nontreaty) restrictions on imports from nonmembers. The Council set up a prior consultation procedure to consider either common import terms or coordinated member-state action regarding the nonmember and product in question. "In urgent cases" new or amended quotas could have been applied without prior consultation.[216] A prior consultation system also was adopted for Community surveillance and protective measures against "liberalized" imports (those not subject to any quotas) when they threatened or caused injury to Community producers. The system permitted individual member states to apply protective measures in certain cases, subject to prior consultation unless urgency precluded it.[217]

In 1975 the Council created a new procedure for "nonliberalized" imports from state-trading countries. It established annual import quotas for specified goods, while permitting member states to initiate a notification and consultation procedure within the Community that could result in a tightening of individual quotas, either by Commission acquiescence in the proposed modification or by Council decision. Again, the Council added an escape clause doing away with the prior consultation requirement "in urgent cases."[218] A similar procedure under the

[214]ECSC Treaty art. 75; Euratom Treaty art. 103.

[215]EEC Treaty art. 113(3).

[216]Council Dec. 72/455/EEC, Dec. 19, 1972, arts. 1–4, in O.J. EUR. COMM. (spec. ed. Dec. 30–31, 1972) 101 (1972). Prior Council authorization (not just consultation) was required once Community negotiations with a nonmember country began. *Id.* art. 5. This decision was superseded in 1979. *See* Council Reg. 926/79/EEC, note 220 *infra.*

[217]Council Reg. 1439/74/EEC, June 4, 1974, arts. 9, 14, in 17 O.J. EUR. COMM. (No. L 159) 1 (1974). This regulation was superseded in 1979. *See* Council Reg. 926/79/EEC, note 220 *infra.*

[218]Council Dec. 75/210/EEC, Mar. 27, 1975, in 18 O.J. EUR. COMM. (No. L 99) 7 (1975).

ECSC Treaty was applied to steel imports from state-trading countries.[219]

In 1979 the EEC took over a greater measure of control over imports from all countries, including state-trading countries. Lists of liberalized imports and mandatory prior consultation procedures were established for collective surveillance and protective measures imposed by the Community, and for individual measures imposed by member states during a trial period. These procedures permitted member states to initiate their own protective measures until December 31, 1981 (later extended until December 31, 1984). The time limit was waived in certain situations. In urgent cases, member states could apply their own protective measures after abbreviated consultations. In cases of "extreme urgency," member states could carry out surveillance (import monitoring) subject only to prior notification to the Commission. When member states were allowed to retain their own preexisting quotas on nonliberalized imports, they could change the quotas subject to the Commission's right to be consulted on request.[220]

Since the end of the transitional period, the Community (rather than individual member states) has decided upon antidumping and countervailing duties against goods imported from nonmember states. Consultations within the Community are required before the duties may be imposed, even provisionally, except "in cases of extreme urgency."[221]

[219] *See* 8 BULL. EUR. COMM., No. 4, at 51–52 (1975); 10 *id.*, No. 9, at 53–54 (1977).

[220] Council Reg. 925/79/EEC, May 8, 1979, arts 3–9, in 22 O.J. EUR. COMM. (No. L 131) 1 (1979) (imports from state-trading countries); Council Reg. 926/79/EEC, May 8, 1979, arts. 3–9, 12–14, 17, in *id.* at 15 (imports from market-economy countries). Council Reg. 926/79/EEC was superseded by Council Reg. 288/82/EEC, Feb. 5, 1982, in 25 O.J. EUR. COMM. (No. L 35) 1 (1982), which contains similar provisions for surveillance and protection in articles 3–5, 10–17 and 20.

See also Council Reg. 2532/78/EEC, Oct. 16, 1978, in 21 *id.* (No. L 306) 1 (1978) (imports from People's Republic of China); Commission Recommendation 77/328/ECSC, Apr. 15, 1977, in 20 *id.* (No. L 114) 4 (1977) (coal and steel). Commission Recommendations under the ECSC Treaty are binding as to the aim to be pursued. *See* ECSC Treaty art. 14.

Commission Dec. 80/47/EEC, Dec. 20, 1979, arts 2(1), 3(1), in 23 O.J. EUR. COMM. (No. L 16) 14 (1980), established prior authorization procedures for surveillance and protective measures affecting nonliberalized imports that could cause trade deflection within the Community.

[221] *See* Council Reg. 3017/79/EEC, Dec. 20, 1979, arts. 7, 11, in 22 O.J. EUR. COMM. (No. L 339) 1 (1979). As to coal and steel, see Commission Recommendation 3018/79/ECSC, Dec. 21, 1979, arts. 7, 11, *id.* at 15. These measures superseded similar procedures that had been in effect for several years.

During the transitional period, member states could apply their own antidumping

There is one further noteworthy procedural requirement relating to imports. The EEC Treaty permits the Commission in certain circumstances to designate protective measures a member state may take against trade originating outside the Community, to avoid deflection of imports from one member state to another. During the transitional period neither the prior authorization requirement nor any prior consultation procedure applied "in case of urgency."[222]

The Commission has the authority to adopt export controls to prevent or remedy a Community-wide shortage of essential products. Before it does so, it must consult member states. When this procedure was adopted, an interim dispensation permitted any member state to apply its own export controls to deal with a shortage in its own territory. Before doing so, it had to consult the other member states and the Commission, unless the situation was too urgent to permit consultation.[223]

Since 1962 some form of prior consultation requirement has attached to the grant or guarantee of export credits by public authorities. The requirement has evolved into Council-devised export credit norms from which member states could not depart, save in certain exceptional cases, without following a designated prior consultation procedure. In 1978 the Community adhered to the OECD Export Credit Arrangement, bringing several other OECD member states into the consultation process when significant deviations from the OECD export credit guidelines were contemplated. Not all exported products are covered by the OECD guidelines.[224] They were revised in 1982, and no longer contemplate deviations.

The common commercial policy extends only to imports and

and countervailing duties, subject to prior consultations in nonurgent cases. Council Reg. 459/68/EEC, Apr. 5, 1968, art. 26, in O.J. Eur. Comm. (spec. ed. 1968 (I)) 80 (1972).

[222]EEC Treaty Apr. 5, 1968, art. 26, in O.J. Eur. Comm. (spec. ed. 1968 (I) 80 (1972).

[223]Council Reg. 2603/69/EEC, Dec. 20, 1969, arts. 2, 3, 6, 8, in O.J. Eur. Comm. (spec. ed. 1969(II)) 590 (1972). The dispensation for individual members was to apply only until Dec. 31, 1972, when the Council was to have decided on the adjustments to be made to it. This the Council apparently did not do.

[224]*See* Council Dec. 73/391/EEC, Dec. 3, 1973. Annex, in 16 O.J. Eur. Comm. (No. L 346) 1 (1973), *as amended,* Council Dec. 76/641/EEC, in 19 O.J. Eur. Comm. (No. L 223) 25 (1976); Council Dec. of Mar. 14, 1977, on the Application of Certain Guidelines in the Field of Export Credits, E.C. Doc. I/89/1/77 (CCG rev. 1). The Community implemented the OECD guidelines in the Council Dec. of Apr 4, 1978, 11 Bull. Eur. Comm., No. 4, at 75 (1978). The OECD guidelines are discussed in chapter VI at notes 194–97 *infra.*

exports, not to agreements with nonmember states on currency arrangements, development aid, or foreign investment. These agreements, however, can have obvious trade effects and are often of broad Community interest even when their trade effects are marginal. Consequently, the Council has adopted a prior consultation requirement to be applied when a member state proposes to negotiate or renew an economic or industrial cooperation agreement with a third country, or when it proposes certain (primarily trade-related) measures pursuant to cooperation agreements.[225] Despite the consultation requirement, member states sometimes have committed themselves to specific terms to be included in cooperation agreements with Eastern European states before informing the Commission or other member states.[226] Nevertheless, the consultation requirement seems for the most part to have worked to the satisfaction of Community organs.

Prior consultation is not the invariable Community rule for trade-related arrangements between member states and third countries. In 1977 the Council rejected a Commission recommendation that bilateral ocean-shipping agreements be subject to prior consultations within the Community. The Council adopted a consultation procedure, but did not require that the consultations precede the agreements.[227] Similarly, the Council's procedure relating to air transport arrangements between member states and third countries contemplates consultations after developments have taken place.[228]

[225]*See* Council Dec. 74/393/EEC, July 22, 1974, in 17 O.J. EUR. COMM. (No. L 208) 23 (1974), *reprinted in* 13 INT'L LEGAL MATERIALS 1197 (1974). Note also the prior consultation requirements in the Council's decision on member states' extension of then-existing trade agreements and negotiation of new agreements with state-trading countries at note 213 *supra*.

[226]This apparently happened when the U.K. was negotiating its cooperation agreement of February 17, 1975, with the Soviet Union, and when the French government prepared a letter to accompany its cooperation agreement initialed with Poland in March 1975. *See* Financial Times, Mar. 7, 1975, at 36, col. 5; EUROPEAN REPORT, Mar. 22, 1975, External Relations at 2; *id.*, Mar. 28, 1975, External Relations at 1; *id.*, May 28, 1975, External Relations at 3. In each case the Commission objected informally to the lack of prior consultation.

[227]*See* Council Dec. 77/587/EEC, Sept. 13, 1977, in 20 O.J. EUR. COMM. (No. L 239) 23 (1977). The consultation procedure was to be reviewed in three years. It apparently remained in force beyond that time. Arguably, member states are obliged to consult before entering into multilateral shipping agreements. *See* EUROPE NEWSLETTER, June 30, 1977, at 6.

[228]*See* Council Dec. 80/50/EEC, Dec. 20, 1979, arts. 1(b), 3, in 23 O.J. EUR. COMM. (No. L 18) 24 (1980). The Decision does call for prior consultations on positions to be

The EEC Treaty contains seemingly inconsistent procedural provisions relating to measures affecting the movement of capital. Although the Council is to issue directives coordinating member states' exchange policies on the movement of capital to and from nonmember states, some differences in national exchange regulations still persist. When the differences could result in the movement of capital from a member state with a restrictive policy to one with a more liberal policy and thence to a nonmember state, the restrictive-policy state, after consulting the other member states and the Commission, may apply appropriate exchange restrictions or other measures.[229] Another provision, however, requires prior Commission authorization for capital movement restrictions if a member state experiences a capital "disturbance"—an excessive inflow or outflow of capital. No authorization (or consultation) is required in urgent cases or when secrecy is necessary.[230]

Finally, going beyond economic affairs, the Community's Foreign Ministers agreed in July 1973 that:

> Governments will consult each other on all important foreign policy questions and will work out priorities, observing the following criteria:
>
> the purpose of the consultation is to seek common policies on practical problems;
>
> the subjects dealt with must concern European interests whether in Europe itself or elsewhere where the adoption of a common position is necessary or desirable.
>
> On these questions each State undertakes as a general rule not to take up final positions without prior consultation with its partners within the framework of the political cooperation machinery.[231]

taken on air transport questions in international organizations. *Id.* arts. 1(a), 2.

The Commission has proposed a decision establishing a consultation procedure for relations and agreements with third countries in the field of transport by rail, road, and inland waterway. 14 BULL. EUR. COMM., No. 6, at 47–48 (1981).

[229]EEC Treaty art. 70. The Council could override these measures if they are too restrictive.

[230]EEC Treaty art. 73. Secrecy usually would be required, to prevent speculation. *See generally* 2 H. SMIT & P. HERZOG, note *supra* 167, at 2–743 to 2–747.

[231]*Second Report on European Political Cooperation on Foreign Policy,* approved by the Foreign Ministers on July 23, 1973, *quoted in* 9 BULL. EUR. COMM., Supp. 1/76, at 15 (1976).

Although this has been termed a political commitment rather than a legal obligation,[232] it—like the 1974 NATO Declaration on Atlantic Relations—fits within the "twilight zone" of quasi-legal instruments.[233] Because it articulates an agreed norm, it lends legal quality to consultations within its scope—particularly if it has been followed when the acting state's short-term interests might have been served by skipping the consultations. There have indeed been a number of consultations, including some in instances where unilateral action without consultation must have been a tempting alternative.[234] These instances tend to give the agreement legal significance, as well as defining the type of subject to which consultation expectations have attached: matters of particular interest to Europe or, more broadly, to the West; responses to significant breaches of the peace, even outside the West; and policymaking regarding important issues in the United Nations.

5. Synthesis of European Community Practice

Obligatory Community consultation norms spring almost entirely from formally binding instruments signed and ratified by the member states or issued by duly constituted legislative bodies. In a few instances, however, legally significant expectations have been created by measures that are not formally binding. Examples in this twilight zone would be the gentlemen's agreements on proposed technical trade barriers and the 1973 foreign policy agreement.[235]

It is difficult to characterize all the situations in which the consultation norm prevails. There is a temptation to say that it is the Community's transitional norm—the procedural safeguard against new national disparities during not only the for-

[232] *Id. See also* West German Chancellor Helmut Schmidt's statement of Apr. 8, 1976, in TEXTS RELATING TO THE EUROPEAN POLITICAL CO-OPERATION 161 (2d ed. 1977).

[233] *See* text at note 19 *supra.*

[234] For example, there have been consultations regarding *(a)* positions to be taken in the Conference on Security and Cooperation in Europe; *(b)* responses to U.S. Secretary of State Kissinger's "Year of Europe"; *(c)* responses to the 1973 Middle East War and the Bangladesh war of secession; *(d)* admission of the People's Republic of China to the U.N.; *(e)* Rhodesian sanctions; and *(f)* hijacking and drug traffic problems. *See* Fitzgerald, *European Political Cooperation,* 22 EUR. Y.B. 18, 29–34 (1974); Wallace & Allen, *Political Cooperation: Procedure as a Substitute for Policy,* in POLICY-MAKING IN THE EUROPEAN COMMUNITIES 227, 232–38, 241–42 (H. Wallace, W. Wallace, & C. Webb eds. 1977).

[235] *See* text at notes 170 and 231 *supra.*

mal twelve-year transitional period, but also the subsequent transition toward economic and monetary union within the Community and toward integrated decision making on relations with nonmember states. The trouble is that the "transitional" characterization is both underinclusive and overinclusive: The prior consultation norm is neither limited to situations considered transitional by the Community nor invariably applied to situations that are considered transitional.

Perhaps it would be more accurate to characterize prior consultation as the procedural hallmark of the Community's quasi-federalism. As a supranational organization of parliamentary democracies, the Community approaches, but does not attain, the status of a democratic federal union. In many instances, where power is not as centralized as in a federal union, or where power is allocated to an institution different from that which would normally have it in a democratic union, a prior consultation requirement (or, occasionally, a duty to obtain prior authorization) injects inclusive interests into decision making. As we have seen, that has been the case over a wide spectrum ranging from trade barriers to currency value modifications to business cycle decisions. It also applies in some instances at the Community institution level, most importantly in the relationship between the Council and the European Parliament.

Until 1979, insofar as the prior consultation requirement was attached to action by, or at the behest of, individual member states, the requirement was invariably excused in "urgent" cases. In 1979, the Council took a small step toward centralization of authority when it adopted a (truncated) prior consultation procedure for member states' protective measures against non-quota imports from third countries in urgent cases. It is too early to say whether this is a meaningful step away from unilateralism when member states claim an urgent need to act.

D. "Universal" Organizations: The United Nations and Related Agencies

The United Nations Charter contains only a few consultation provisions potentially relevant to this study.[236] The most prom-

[236] It also contains a few that do not relate to unilateral action (by the organization or its members) that could adversely affect the interests of others. *See, e.g.,* U.N. Charter arts. 50, 71 (first sentence).

inent is in article 33, which refers to negotiation as one of several enumerated means of settlement when a dispute is likely to endanger international peace. *Negotiation* would encompass consultation. Insofar as dispute *settlement* includes the *avoidance* of nascent disputes that could endanger peace, the reference to negotiation arguably could require prior consultation.[237]

The negotiation principle in article 33 has been cited by the International Court of Justice in the *North Sea Continental Shelf* Cases—in which Denmark and the Netherlands tried to establish against the Federal Republic of Germany a continental shelf delineation based on equidistance—as "a principle which underlies all international relations" and as a dispute settlement method having "fundamental character" in view of the restricted availability of international judicial or arbitral settlement.[238] In the *Fisheries Jurisdiction* Cases, the Court took the same approach regarding Iceland's fishery jurisdiction extension to fifty miles.[239] In each of these cases, however, there were factors in addition to article 33 upon which the court relied for the duty to negotiate. Moreover, in none of the cases did the Court focus specifically on the role of article 33 in dispute avoidance, as distinguished from dispute settlement. Thus, it would be difficult to argue that article 33, standing alone, supplies a duty to negotiate (or to consult) before a state takes any action that might be adverse to the interests of another state.

On the other hand, the Charter does contain provisions requiring the organization to consult individual member states before taking certain steps affecting them. One example is in article 44, which, although never used, is nonetheless significant for the principle it embodies. It assumes that article 43 agreements (making national armed forces available to the Security Council for enforcement action) will be in effect and states that before the Security Council calls on a member not represented on it to provide armed forces, it shall "invite that Member, if the Member so desires, to participate in the decisions of the Security Council concerning the employment of contingents of that Member's armed forces."[240] This reflects the principle that

[237]The Security Council broadly construes article 33's reference to "disputes" to mean that states are obligated to seek peaceful solutions to their problems. *See* L. GOODRICH, E. HAMBRO, & A. SIMONS, CHARTER OF THE UNITED NATIONS: COMMENTARY AND DOCUMENTS 265 (3d ed. 1969).

[238]North Sea Continental Shelf Cases, 1969 I.C.J. 3, 48.

[239]Fisheries Jurisdiction Cases (Merits), 1974 I.C.J. 3, 32 and 175, 201.

[240]*See also* article 106, which applies pending the entry into force of article 43 agreements. Like article 44, article 106 has not been used.

a member state should be heard before the organization takes permissible action of peculiar sensitivity to that member.

U.N. Charter article 32 requires the Security Council to invite a state party to a dispute to participate, without vote, in the discussion relating to the dispute if that party is not already a member of the Council. Although *dispute* has been treated as a narrow word permitting the Security Council to avoid consultation in some instances,[241] article 32 clearly does reflect the principle that before the Security Council injects itself into what the Charter drafters thought would be matters of particular sensitivity to the states involved, it should hear them out.

When sensitive, direct U.N. contact is contemplated with individuals and organizations that are subject to the jurisdiction of member states, the Charter and related instruments call for consultation with the government before the designated U.N. organ or related body makes a decision. Thus, for example, the Economic and Social Council must consult a member government before entering into a consultative arrangement with any of its national nongovernmental organizations.[242] The General Assembly and Trusteeship Council, upon accepting petitions from persons in trust territories, must examine them in consultation with the administering authority.[243] Under the U.N. system for petitions from individuals alleging a consistent pattern of gross human rights violations, each petition is furnished to the respondent government, and its reply, if any, is considered before a preliminary decision on its admissibility is made.[244] Comparable procedures for ascertaining the views of governments allegedly violating human rights appear in U.N.-sponsored human rights conventions setting up review machinery.[245]

[241] The Security Council has distinguished "disputes" from "situations which might lead to international friction or give rise to a dispute" (article 34). The article 32 procedural requirement does not apply to such "situations." *See generally* L. GOODRICH, E. HAMBRO, & A. SIMONS, *supra* note 237, at 252–53.

[242] U.N. CHARTER art. 71.

[243] *Id.*, art. 87.

[244] *See* ECOSOC Res. 728F, para 2(e) & (f), 28 U.N. ESCOR, Supp. (No. 1) 19, U.N. Doc. E/3290 (1959); ECOSOC Res. 1503, paras. 1, 4(a), 5, 48 U.N. ESCOR, Supp. (No. 1A) 8, U.N. Doc. E/4832/Add.1 (1970); Subcomm. on Prevention of Discrimination and Protection of Minorities Res. 1 (XXIV), para. 1(b), U.N. Doc. E/CN.4/1070, at 50 (1971).

[245] *See* International Convention on the Elimination of all Forms of Racial Discrimination, Dec. 21, 1965, arts. 11(1), 14(6) & (7), 660 U.N.T.S. 195; International Covenant on Civil and Political Rights, Dec. 16, 1966, art. 41(1), and Optional Protocol, arts. 4, 5, in UNITED NATIONS, HUMAN RIGHTS: A COMPILATION OF INTERNATIONAL INSTRUMENTS, U.N. Doc. ST/HR/1/Rev.1, at 8 & 16 (1978).

These human rights procedures may be characterized as reflections of the due process principle that a respondent should be heard before its conduct is judged, but given the context in which U.N. judgments on human rights are made—involving a heavy element of discretion, with political considerations inevitably playing a greater role than in a more juridical setting—the hearing (or written submission) takes on the flavor of prior consultation, as that concept is used in this study.

Another delicate set of issues surrounds the activities of U.N. peacekeeping forces invited by a government into its own territory to assist in quelling an externally supported internal disturbance. The forces must be under U.N. command, yet what they do may ordain the continuing existence or extinction of the inviting government. The principal examples have been in Lebanon and Zaire (then the Congo). These are to be distinguished from U.N. peacekeeping efforts designed primarily to prevent open hostilities between two or more member states, where the U.N., though acting with the initial consent of a territorial government, does not assume quite the same supportive role.[246] In Lebanon, the organization and activities of the U.N. Observer Group in 1958 were planned and executed in close consultation with the government. Although not expressly required by the enabling Security Council resolution, the consultation principle seems to have been regarded by the Secretary-General as virtually inherent in his mandate. The Lebanese government clearly took that view.[247] A similar unwritten understanding existed when the U.N. Interim Force in Lebanon(UNIFIL) was created in 1978 to help restore effective Lebanese governmental control over its own territory after the hostilities of 1977 and early 1978.[248]

In the Congo, the enabling Security Council resolution au-

[246] There are national sensitivities in such cases as well. This explains not only the consent requirement for stationing peacekeeping forces but the practice of consulting the territorial state(s) regarding the composition of the forces. As to the Middle East, *see* Report of the Secretary-General on UNEF Experience, Oct. 9, 1958, paras. 15–16, 155–161, 13 U.N. GAOR, Annexes (Agenda Item 65) 8 at 10–11, 28–29, U.N. Doc. A/3943 (1958). On consultations on composing the U.N. Emergency Force (UNEF) after the 1973 Yom Kippur war, see the Secretary-General's report of Oct. 27, 1973, paras. 3, 4, U.N. Doc. S/11052 and Rev. 1 (1973), *approved in* S.C. Res. 341 (1973). As to Cyprus, see S.C. Res. 186, para. 4, U.N. Doc. S/5575 (1964).

[247] *See* 1 R. Higgins, United Nations Peacekeeping 1946–1967, at 546–47, 552, 558–59 (1969).

[248] *See* U.N. Docs. S/12611, at 3 (1978); S/12620, at 1, 2 (1978); *id.* Add. 1, at 2–3; *id.* Add 2, at 3; *id.* Add. 3, at 3.

thorized the Secretary-General "to take the necessary steps, in consultation with the Government of the Republic of the Congo, to provide the Government with such military assistance as may be necessary until . . . the national security forces may be able, in the opinion of the Government, to meet fully their tasks."[249] Although the Secretary-General's representative was later criticized for ordering military intervention in the constitutional crisis between President Kasavubu and Prime Minister Lumumba without consulting the government, he in fact acted at the invitation of Kasavubu, who had at least as strong a claim as Lumumba had to represent the government.[250]

The "sensitivity principle" also is written into the Headquarters Agreement between the United Nations and the United States, requiring consultation in one instance by the U.N. and in a related instance by the United States. The Agreement designates six groups of people requiring access to the U.N. headquarters district in New York City. These include officials representing member governments and the U.N. itself or its specialized agencies. Also included are some quasi-official individuals: experts in the service of, or persons on official business with, the U.N. or the specialized agencies, and representatives of nongovernmental organizations recognized under article 71 of the Charter. A final category, of particular sensitivity to the United States because its members are entitled to special Constitutional liberties and are not subject to the usual norms of conduct associated with the U.N., comprises members of the foreign press and other information agencies. They are entitled to unimpeded access to the headquarters district only if they have been accredited by the U.N. or specialized agencies after consultation with the United States.[251]

Under the Headquarters Agreement, the United States may deport individuals in any of the six privileged categories if they abuse their privileges in activities outside their official capacities, but only "after consultation with the appropriate Member in

[249]S.C. Res. of July 13, 1960, para. 2, U.N. Doc. S/4387 (1960). The language was proposed by the Secretary-General.

[250]*See* G. Abi-Saab, The United Nations Operation in the Congo 1960–1964, at 59–64 (1978).

[251]Agreement Between the United Nations and the United States of America Regarding the Headquarters of the United Nations, June 26, 1947, § 11, 61 Stat. 3416, 12 Bevans 956, 11 U.N.T.S. 11. The consultation provision does not apply to persons in the other categories.

the case of a representative of a Member (or a member of his family) or with the Secretary-General or the principal executive officer of the appropriate specialized agency in the case of any other [privileged] person."[252] When the United States requested the departure of the Permanent Representative of Viet Nam in 1978, a controversy arose over whether the consultation requirement had been met. The United States acknowledged that consultation was a condition precedent, but asserted that it had complied insofar as that was possible under the circumstances.[253] Although the dispute went unresolved, the consultation requirement remained intact.

Yet another prior consultation procedure involves international claims by the organization for injuries suffered by its agents. After the *U.N. Reparations* Case had upheld the organization's capacity to assert claims, the Secretary-General proposed (and the General Assembly approved) a procedure involving consultation with the victim's government to determine whether it has any objection to the claim or wishes to join in its submission.[254]

Each of these U.N. procedures fits within the sensitivity principle. One can also find examples involving the specialized agencies. Some examples involve consultation by member states, some by the agencies. The Convention on the Privileges and Immunities of the Specialized Agencies contains consultation provisions modeled on those of the U.N. Headquarters Agreement regarding expulsion of representatives and officials, and also requires consultation before a state party responds to any asserted abuse by a specialized agency of its privileges or im-

[252] *Id.* § 13. The preparatory work stresses the consultation requirement's importance, and indicates that it applies to all six categories despite some confusing language in § 13(b)(3) regarding persons entitled to diplomatic privileges and immunities. *See* 2 U.N. GAOR, C.6 Annex (Agenda Item 11) 326 at 330–31, U.N. Doc. A/371 (1947); 2 U.N. GAOR, Annexes 1519 at 1521, U.N. Doc. A/427 (1947); Gross, *Immunities and Privileges of Delegations to the United Nations,* 16 INT'L ORG. 483, 509 (1962). Consultation is not required when a receiving state declares a normal diplomatic envoy persona non grata. *See* Vienna Conv. on Diplomatic Relations, Apr. 18, 1961, art. 9(1), 23 U.S.T. 3227, 500 U.N.T.S. 95.

[253] The debate is summarized in U.N. Docs. A/AC.154/SR.69, at 2–7; SR.70, at 4–5; SR.71, at 2–6; SR.72, at 3–5 (1978). For an earlier case in which the United States failed to consult, see Gross, *supra* note 252, at 512–14.

[254] Report of the Secretary-General, 4 U.N. GAOR, C.6 Annex (Agenda Item 51) 18 at 20, U.N. Doc. A/955 (1949); G.A. Res. 365 (IV), 4 U.N. GAOR, Resolutions, U.N. Doc. A/1251, at 64 (1949).

munities.[255] The same principle explains the consultation procedures surrounding the International Monetary Fund's use of members' currencies.[256] It also underlies the World Court's opinion that the mutual obligations of cooperation and good faith between a host state and a specialized agency require consultation before the agency removes its long-established office from the host state.[257]

There is a significant prior consultation network among organizations in the U.N. family. Consultations on proposed budgets are required by the relationship agreements between the U.N. and all specialized agencies (including the International Atomic Energy Agency [IAEA], which is not technically a specialized agency) except the International Telecommunication Union (ITU) and the Universal Postal Union (UPU) (very general agreements) and the financial organizations (which do not rely on annual contributions from members, except in the case of the International Development Association, and which are required to exercise independent judgment based solely on economic factors).[258] These consultations, however, do not always take place before budgets are approved, and seem to be concerned primarily with matters of form.[259]

Aside from budgetary matters, there is a network consisting of relationship agreements, rules of procedure, memoranda of understanding, and practice apart from written instruments by which the United Nations—particularly the Economic and Social Council (ECOSOC)—and the U.N.-related organizations

[255] Convention on the Privileges and Immunities of the Specialized Agencies, Nov. 21, 1947, §§ 24, 25, 33 U.N.T.S. 261. The provision on abuse by a specialized agency (§ 24) also requires submission of any dispute to the I.C.J.

For a consultation provision relating to measures by a host state to protect itself against abuses by representatives or missions to "universal" international organizations, see the Vienna Convention on the Representation of States in Their Relations with International Organizations of a Universal Character, Mar. 14, 1975, art. 77(4), U.N. Doc. A/CONF.67/16, *reprinted in* 69 AM. J. INT'L L. 730 (1975). *See also* 1975 U.N. JURIDICAL Y.B. 155, n.13.

[256] *See* chapter VI at notes 35–43 *infra*.

[257] *See* Advisory Opinion on Interpretation of the Agreement of 25 March 1951 Between the WHO and Egypt, 1980 I.C.J. 73, 93–96.

[258] *See* U.N. Charter art. 17(3); L. GOODRICH, E. HAMBRO, & A. SIMONS, *supra* note 237, at 424. *See, e.g.*, these agreements: U.N.–ILO, Dec. 19, 1946, art. 14(3), 1 U.N.T.S. 186; U.N.–FAO, Feb. 3, 1947, art. 14(3), 1 U.N.T.S. 212; U.N.–UNESCO, Feb. 3, 1947, art. 16(3), 1 U.N.T.S. 238; U.N.–IAEA, Nov. 14, 1957, art. 16(3), 281 U.N.T.S. 370.

[259] *See* M. HILL, THE UNITED NATIONS SYSTEM: COORDINATING ITS ECONOMIC AND SOCIAL WORK 43–44, 120 (1978).

consult each other before taking action that would encroach on each other's areas of interest. In part this reflects the general consultation-coordination authority of ECOSOC under article 63(2) of the Charter, but the network encompasses consultations not directly involving ECOSOC as well as those that do.[260]

For example, the ECOSOC Rules of Procedure require the Secretary-General to consult any specialized agency and to report on the consultations before ECOSOC takes up an agenda item proposing new U.N. activities in an area of direct concern to the specialized agency.[261] The Standing Orders of the International Labor Conference contain a provision calling for consultation with the United Nations or with any specialized agency when a proposal submitted to the Conference involves new activities of direct concern to the U.N. or to the agency.[262] Some U.N.-related agencies and organs—notably the International Labor Organization (ILO) and the U.N. Environment Program (UNEP)—have entered into a series of arrangements with other agencies and organs having overlapping interests, calling for prior consultations on matters within the overlapping areas.[263]

[260] Article 63(2) empowers ECOSOC to coordinate the activities of the specialized agencies through (inter alia) consultation with and recommendations to them.

[261] ECOSOC Rules of Procedure, Rule 77, U.N. Doc. E/5715 (1975). *Id.* Rule 78 requires prior consultation when ECOSOC is to consider a proposed convention that may affect the activities of specialized agencies. *See also* Rules of Procedure of the Functional Commissions of ECOSOC, Rule 73, U.N. Doc. E/5975 (1977).

[262] Article 17*bis*, in CONSTITUTION OF THE INTERNATIONAL LABOUR ORGANISATION AND STANDING ORDERS OF THE INTERNATIONAL LABOUR CONFERENCE 39 (1980).

[263] *See, e.g.,* Understanding between the ILO and IMCO (IMO), May 22, 1974, 58 ILO OFFICIAL BULL., ser. A, No. 3, at 254 (1975); Understanding between the ILO and the United Nations Industrial Development Organization (UNIDO), Aug. 31, 1976, 60 *id.*, ser. A, No. 2, at 77 (1977); Understanding between the ILO and UNEP, July 6, 1977, 60 *id.*, ser. A, No. 4, at 282 (1977); Understanding between FAO and UNEP, *in* U.N. Doc. UNEP/GC/INFORMATION/6, at 1 (1977). The UNEP prior consultation policy appears in U.N. Doc. UNEP/GC/59, at 4 (1976). Procedures for prior consultations relating to oceanography (involving the U.N., UNESCO, FAO, WMO, IMO, UNEP, and occasionally other bodies) are outlined in U.N. Doc. E/AC.51/93, at 20 (1978).

For the FAO policy, see *Guiding Lines for Formal Relationship Agreements Between FAO and Other Intergovernmental Organizations,* Part C, *in* BASIC TEXTS OF THE FOOD AND AGRICULTURE ORGANIZATION OF THE UNITED NATIONS 165 (1978).

The GATT CONTRACTING PARTIES are required to consult the IMF before deciding what to do about members' trade restrictions taken for balance-of-payments purposes. *See* GATT art. 15(2); GATT-IMF exchange of letters, IMF 1949 ANN. REP. 75. There is no reciprocal IMF duty to consult the GATT CONTRACTING PARTIES, primarily because of the unwieldy GATT consultative mechanisms. *See* Roessler, *Selective Balance-of-Payments Adjustment Measures Affecting Trade: The Roles of the GATT and the IMF,* 9 J. WORLD TRADE L. 622, 644–45 (1975).

Note also the arrangements between the U.N. and the specialized agencies, and

Moreover, the general undertaking to cooperate with the U.N., found in its relationship agreements with the specialized agencies, implies a duty to consult before an agency does something that would hinder coordination of activities among the U.N. and its specialized agencies.[264] In other instances, prior consultations have occurred pursuant to resolutions and inter-agency understandings that do not explicitly require consultations before matters of overlapping interest are considered.[265]

There is another revealing, if less general, example of prior consultation practice within the United Nations family. Most relationship agreements between the U.N. and the specialized agencies call upon the latter to consider U.N. recommendations directed to them, without any requirement that the agencies be consulted before the recommendations are made. The exceptions are the agreements with the International Monetary Fund and the World Bank Group. In order to ensure the exercise of independent economic judgment by those agencies, their relationship agreements require consultations before U.N. recommendations are made, and thus before they must consider such recommendations.[266] The prior consultation requirement

between several of the latter among themselves, to participate in each other's meetings. *See* Suy, *The Status of Observers in International Organizations,* 160 HAGUE ACAD., RECUEIL DES COURS 75, 97–98 (1978).

[264] *Cf.* Advisory Opinion on Interpretation of the Agreement of 25 March 1951 Between the WHO and Egypt, *supra* note 257.

[265] *See, e.g.,* M. HILL, *supra* note 259, at 53–54; F. WOLF, BUILDING THE LAW OF THE WORLD: A LOOK AT THE PROCESS 7–10 (1976); J. Dobbert, commenting on FAO's World Food Program, in THE EFFECTIVENESS OF INTERNATIONAL DECISIONS 457 (S. Schwebel ed. 1971). For a typical procedure, *see* ITU Res. on Relations Between the Union and Other Specialized Agencies Having a Substantive Interest in Telecommunication Services, Admin. Council Res. 196 (amended), 1973, in G. WALLENSTEIN, INTERNATIONAL TELECOMMUNICATION AGREEMENTS, pt. 4, § 7, at 14 (1979). *See also* the working arrangements between the World Meteorological Organization (WMO) and the World Health Organization (WHO), in WMO, AGREEMENTS AND WORKING ARRANGEMENTS WITH OTHER INTERNATIONAL ORGANIZATIONS 31 (WMO Basic Docs. No. 3, 1973); WMO-International Civil Aviation Organization (ICAO), *id.* at 37; WMO-United Nations Educational, Scientific and Cultural Organization (UNESCO), *id.* at 45.

I. DETTER, LAW MAKING BY INTERNATIONAL ORGANIZATIONS 152–53 (1965), points out that the WMO-WHO understanding does not set forth a legal obligation to consult under ascertainable circumstances. She would presumably make the same point about the other WMO understandings and about the ITU procedure.

[266] *See* Agreement between the U.N. and the IMF, Nov. 15, 1947, art. 4(2), 16 U.N.T.S. 326; Agreement between the U.N. and the International Bank for Reconstruction and Development (IBRD), Nov. 15, 1947, art. 4(2), 16 U.N.T.S. 346. This provision is incorporated by reference into the Agreement between the U.N. and the International Finance Corp., Feb. 20, 1957, 265 U.N.T.S. 314, and the Agreement between the U.N. and the International Development Association, Mar. 27, 1961, 394 U.N.T.S. 221.

operates as a safeguard against political encroachment on that portion of the U.N. system designed to be apolitical.

E. Synthesis: Alliances and International Organizations

Prior consultation practice in an alliance or international organization is most likely to rise to the level of a legal norm under either of two circumstances: (*a*) the proposed unilateral action, though not so clearly antithetical to attainment of the organization's goals as to be prohibited or tightly regulated, could seriously interfere (if taken without consideration of the collective interest) with the means or timetable by which the organization seeks to attain its primary goals; or (*b*) the proposed action is by a collective organ and would affect the special interests or sensitivities of another organ, entity, or constituency that is within the "family." At least as to the former category, an exception is generally allowed for a response to a true emergency—but watchdogs in the alliance or organization tend toward skepticism regarding the existence of any given emergency.

Examples of the consultation norm in the former category include NATO expectations regarding significant arms control agreements and potential armed confrontations with the Soviet Union; and European Community norms regarding nonprohibited trade, monetary, or fiscal measures that might interfere with progress toward economic and monetary union. In the United Nations, the activity most clearly antithetical to the attainment of the organization's purposes—the offensive use of armed force—is rendered unlawful.

The category relating to action by a collective organ does not apply to NATO, since its organs do not have international personality apart from member states, but it does apply to the European Communities, where (for example) the Council can act on most important matters only after consulting a more representative body, such as the European Parliament or the Economic and Social Committee, and in the United Nations, where U.N. organs and specialized agencies have developed a network of consultation practice relating to proposed action affecting more than one of them.

The more structured the organization, the less one can infer unwritten prior consultation norms. Thus, the European Communities, with their quasi-federal structure and their complex series of formal procedural enactments, cannot be said to have a "common law" of prior consultation. The duty appears in a formally adopted instrument—or at least in a written understanding—or it does not exist.[267] In the loosely structured North Atlantic Alliance, however, the few formal consultation requirements are supplemented by sufficient state practice to establish important unwritten consultation norms. In the United Nations, most procedural rules appear in formal agreements or in other instruments tailored to the specific case, but one cannot rule out the possibility of less formalized norms stemming from consistent practice. Such a practice-generated consultation norm probably exists when one U.N. organ or agency proposes significant action in a field in which another clearly has concurrent jurisdiction.

[267] There are occasional signs that Community institutions may consider prior consultation to be the accepted standard of behavior for member states even in the absence of formal legislation. For example, when asked why two member states rescheduled the debts of some thirty least-developed countries without consulting the other members, the Commission and Council seemed to assume that consultations were expected. They replied, in effect, that informal consultations had been held. *See* 22 O.J. EUR. COMM. (No. C 15) 12 (1979); *id.* (No. C 28) 26. Such instances are insufficient to establish an unwritten legal norm.

Chapter VI

Economic Relations

A. Introduction

This chapter considers economic relations among nations not as closely bound to each other as those in the European Community, though in many instances the consultation issue does arise among nations that have attempted to order their mutual economic relations through some form of treaty—the International Monetary Fund Agreement (the Fund Agreement), the General Agreement on Tariffs and Trade (GATT), bilateral trade agreements, and so forth. Recurring questions have to do not only with the extent to which those agreements require prior consultations, but the extent to which the treaty obligations are honored in practice.

Uncertainties abound in prior consultation practice involving economic relations. Although a remarkable array of treaty norms calling for prior consultation can be found, some of them have been less than scrupulously observed. The question then arises whether state practice has effectively superseded the treaty norm or, if not, has severely restricted its effectiveness. In some other instances, there is extensive consultation practice without the benefit of a treaty norm, but it is not always clear whether this practice reflects the opinio juris required for the development of customary international law. Sometimes state practice seems to establish a prior consultation norm among states in a relationship of mutual or one-way economic dependence, yet in other instances state practice seems not to recognize such a rule.

These uncertainties counsel caution before one finds binding consultation norms. Yet there do seem to be some norms, as indicated in the following sections. Each section deals with measures reflecting a particular kind of economic activity or policy, such as measures taken primarily for balance-of-payments purposes, those aimed at protecting or stimulating certain sectors of the economy, and those directed at internationally mobile capital.

I am grateful for the research assistance of Bruce Barsook, then a UCLA law student, in the preparation of parts of this chapter.

B. Balance-of-Payments Measures

1. Monetary Measures

The most direct way to deal with a persistent balance-of-payments problem is to change the value of the currency, either by repegging it at a new level or by letting it float in value against other currencies. Under the postwar monetary system in force until 1978, however, the International Monetary Fund Agreement—encompassing virtually all nations other than the People's Republic of China and most of the Eastern European bloc—directed members not to repeg or float their currencies according to their own dictates. They were obliged to maintain par values of their currencies based on gold or the U.S. dollar as the common denominator. Each currency could fluctuate within a very narrow band around its par value, but for any greater deviation the member was supposed to propose a new par value that could be given effect "only after consultation with the Fund."[1] In most cases the Fund was entitled to object, and if the member made the change despite the objection it would be ineligible to use the Fund's monetary resources. The Fund thus represented not only the major trading partners of a devaluing country and others who might be directly affected by a change in a currency's value but the world monetary order as a stable system designed to promote global prosperity.

Early in the Fund's history, postwar reconstruction put significant strains on European currencies. The French franc was the first of the Fund's major currencies to deviate from the system. In January 1948 the French government proposed a multiple exchange rate for the franc. The Fund's Board of Governors met thirteen times within a week to discuss the proposal and to try to reach a compromise that would remain within the single-par-value concept. The Fund's Managing Director

[1]Fund Agreement, Dec. 27, 1945, art. IV(5)(b), 60 Stat. 1401, 2 U.N.T.S. 39, 3 Bevans 1351. For members with established par values, this was an "absolute" duty. *See* Gold, *The Legal Structure of the Par Value System,* 5 L. & Pol'y in Int'l Bus. 155, 159–60 (1973).

Some members did not immediately establish par values, but even they were obliged "to collaborate with the Fund to promote exchange stability." Fund Agreement art. IV(4)(a). The Fund's Board of Governors prescribed as a term of membership the duty to obtain the Fund's agreement before changing the exchange rates of their currencies. *See* J. Gold. A Second Report on Some Recent Legal Developments in the International Monetary Fund 8 (1977).

appealed to the French Premier not to adopt a multiple rate, but the French went ahead anyway on January 25. The Fund simultaneously announced that it did not concur.[2]

The first major Fund-approved devaluation occurred in September 1949, when the United Kingdom devalued the pound sterling from $4.03 to $2.80. Within a month, twenty-eight other countries devalued their currencies. The British decision had been contemplated at least since the fall of 1948, when there were discussions within the Fund of the need for European devaluations and of the fact that their magnitude would depend on the amount by which the pound—Europe's major currency—was to be devalued. Intensive discussions were held in the summer of 1949. Finally, during the Fund's annual meeting in September, the British Chancellor of the Exchequer told the Fund's Managing Director that his government proposed to devalue the pound. He also notified the Fund's Governors representing the other sterling area countries, seeking a simultaneous devaluation. Two days later the British representative argued the case for the devaluation before the Board of Governors. The board debated the need for a devaluation and its proposed magnitude before approving the British proposal. It appears, however, that the board's only practical choice was to accept the British decision.[3]

Immediately after the British devaluation, Belgium proposed to the Fund that the Belgian franc float against other currencies. The Executive Directors discussed the proposal, finally approving it on the understanding that a new par value would be established as soon as possible. Two days later the Belgian government recanted and proposed a straight devaluation, which the board approved.[4] A year later, however, when Canada proposed a floating rate for its dollar and presented its case to the board, it withstood the disapproval of some board members and floated the dollar anyway.[5]

[2] *See* J. Horsefield, 1 The International Monetary Fund 1945–1965, at 200–02 (1969). A multiple exchange rate, or multiple currency practice, produces more than one exchange rate against all other currencies, with each rate normally tied to the use for which a foreign currency is to be put in a particular transaction.

[3] *Id.* at 234–40; F. Southard, The Evolution of the International Monetary Fund 25–26 (Princeton Essays in Int'l Fin. No. 135, 1979). It appears that the final British decision to propose a devaluation was made in July or August 1949, sandwiched between tripartite conferences with U.S. and Canadian officials. *See* 35 Fed. Res. Bull. 1169 (1949).

[4] *See* J. Horsefield, *supra* note 2, at 240–41.

[5] *Id.* at 273–74.

Because impending devaluations encourage currency speculators and discourage traders in goods, decisions have to be made quickly and quietly. Extended consultations are impracticable. Consequently, one must conclude that in all of the cases just outlined there were adequate prior consultations. In the Belgian case the consultations clearly influenced the result, but even in the others there was give and take before the proposing government made an irrevocable decision. These cases thus could well be taken to supply a standard for feasible prior consultations in later cases—unless circumstances subsequently changed so much that they rendered even such compressed consultations impracticable.[6]

In the 1950s there were a number of devaluations not directly involving the major reserve currencies. The practice developed of submitting a proposed devaluation on very short notice (sometimes only a few hours) to forestall speculation. In 1953 the French Executive Director proposed that the board disapprove this practice; the board's consensus, however, was that some emergencies required immediate action and that the matter consequently had to be considered case by case.[7] From that point, it was only a short step to the practice of giving pro forma notice of decisions already firmly taken.

Devaluations continued in the 1960s. In some cases, particularly those involving nonreserve currencies, there appear to have been meaningful prior consultations with the Fund's staff, the Executive Directors, or both. In these cases the consultations often went on for weeks without necessarily involving any specific devaluation proposal until the last minute. But in other cases the only consultations consisted of a cable late Friday afternoon to the Fund, a staff report prepared on Saturday, and Executive Directors' approval on Sunday afternoon or Monday morning.[8]

The United Kingdom devalued the pound sterling from $2.80

[6]Fundamentally changed circumstances could justify the suspension or termination of particular clauses of a treaty. *See* Vienna Convention on the Law of Treaties, May 23, 1969, arts. 44, 62, U.N. Doc. A/CONF.39/27, *reprinted in* 8 INT'L LEGAL MATERIALS 679 (1969).

[7]J. HORSEFIELD, *supra* note 2, at 383.

[8]*See M.* DE VRIES, 1 THE INTERNATIONAL MONETARY FUND 1966–1971, at 468–76 (1976), for a discussion of devaluations by India, Ghana, Finland, Iceland, Turkey, and Ecuador. The typical weekend devaluation practice is summarized in de Vries, *The Par Value System: An Overview,* in 2 THE INTERNATIONAL MONETARY FUND 1945–1965, at 39, 46 (J. Horsefield ed. 1969).

to $2.40 in November 1967. This followed intensive discussions earlier in the month with the Fund's management and came on the heels of a series of OECD meetings at which French and German officials discussed with the British the extent to which sterling would have to be devalued if they were to make a balance-of-payments loan.[9] After the devaluation decision had been made, but before it was announced, there were hurried contacts—more in the nature of notifications than consultations—with the sterling area countries, Britain's partners in the European Free Trade Association, the European Community countries and the United States, as well as last minute discussion by the Fund's Executive Directors.[10] As had occured in 1949, the 1967 British devaluation triggered others, though this time they accounted for only a relatively minor share of world trade. There were the usual rushed Fund consultations.[11]

The French franc was devalued in August 1969. At the November 1968 meeting of the Group of Ten (finance ministers and central bank governors of the ten principal industrial members of the Fund), the participants discussed devaluing the franc and bargained about the size of the prospective devaluation. It was widely assumed that France would propose an 11.1 percent devaluation shortly after the meeting, but instead President de Gaulle announced that there would be no devaluation.[12] Although France took other measures, the drain on French reserves resumed in the spring and summer of 1969. Quite unexpectedly, the French government cabled the Fund on Saturday, August 9, requesting concurrence in an 11.11 percent devaluation, effective August 10. Before the Executive Board could meet, the French government publicly announced the devaluation. The Executive Directors acknowledged that the timing avoided further speculation against the franc, but "very much regretted" that France had presented them with a fait accompli.[13] Nevertheless, they concurred in the devaluation. Subsequent changes in the Fund's rules and in the international

[9]M. de Vries, *supra* note 8, at 432–33; Strange, *International Monetary Relations,* in 2 International Economic Relations of the Western World 1959–1971, at 18, 139–40 (A. Shonfield ed. 1976).

[10]754 Parl. Deb., H.C. (5th ser.) 1140–47, 1153–62, 1434–44 (1967).

[11]M. de Vries, *supra* note 8, at 437–40.

[12]*See* The Times (London), Nov. 23, 1968, at 11, col. 3; M. de Vries, *supra* note 8, at 450–53.

[13]M. de Vries, *supra* note 8, at 454–56. The French did no better by their European Community partners. *See* chapter V at note 176 *supra*.

monetary system render it rather academic to ask whether this concurrence, coupled with the mild "regret" expressed by the Executive Directors, amounted to an acquiescence in the unilateral procedure adopted by France. At the time, the Fund did not think it had acquiesced in any changed procedure, and continued to take the prior consultation requirement seriously.

The weakness of the pound sterling and the French franc in the late 1960s largely reflected the strength of the German mark. As speculative capital flowed into West Germany in 1969, it became increasingly apparent that the mark's exchange rate would have to increase. On the weekend of September 27–28, the West German authorities notified the Fund's Managing Director that they were likely to let the mark float. On Monday, September 29, they notified the Managing Director that the mark would indeed float, effective immediately.[14] There was no prior consultation, nor did the Fund effectively protest the lack of consultation. When the West German authorities revalued the mark at a new par value shortly thereafter, they went through the process that had become standard for devaluations: a cable on Friday afternoon proposing a new par value effective at the beginning of business Monday morning. The Fund concurred.[15]

Canada floated its dollar in 1970 after hurried, but genuine, consultations with the Fund's Managing Director. The Executive Directors, however, were not given a chance to discuss the decision before it was made. They criticized Canada's failure to consult, but refrained from formal disapproval of the Canadian action.[16]

When West Germany (this time joined by the Dutch) again floated its currency in May 1971, German officials simply notified the Fund on a Sunday that as of Monday morning they would no longer maintain a fixed exchange rate. This caused some concern among the Executive Directors, but they did not effectively object.[17]

It remained for the United States, on August 15, 1971, to

[14]M. de Vries, *supra* note 8, at 458–59. Technically, the duty to consult under the original Fund Agreement applied only to changes in par value, not to abrogations of the duty to see that transactions corresponded to the officially unchanged par value. A decision to float was of the latter variety.

[15]*Id.* at 460–62.

[16]*See* F. Southard, *supra* note 3, at 34–36.

[17]M. de Vries, *supra* note 8, at 522–24.

deliver the lethal blow not only to the fixed exchange rate system, but to the practice of consulting the Fund even at the last minute. When the United States announced that it would no longer convert dollars to gold, it had only notified the Fund's Managing Director a few hours in advance and had not consulted either the Executive Directors as a group or any individual trading partners. Not even Canada—the country most intimately affected—was consulted.[18]

The U.S. action triggered a string of devaluations and currency floats too long to be chronicled here. Bare notification to the Fund, not consultation, became the rule.[19] This was so even though the prior consultation requirement in the Fund Agreement was not formally terminated until 1978, and even though the Executive Directors adopted a decision in 1974 calling upon members with floating exchange rates to consult with the Fund before acting to depress the falling values or enhance the rising values of their own currencies.[20] The Fund's Managing Director, referring to the period beginning in the mid-1960s, wrote this epitaph: "In practice, the ability of the Fund to influence, or even discuss, exchange rates under the par value system was seriously impeded by the very nature of changes in par values. There was the need for complete confidentiality, and considerable diplomacy, in dealing with what were usually large, discrete changes in exchange rates."[21]

It is arguable that between World War II and the mid-1960s such a fundamental change of circumstances had occurred that members were excused from fulfilling the consultation duty.

[18] *Id.* at 529–30; *see also* R. SOLOMON, THE INTERNATIONAL MONETARY SYSTEM 1945–1976, at 189 (1977); *The International Implications of the New Economic Policy: Hearings Before a Subcomm. of the House Comm. on Foreign Affairs,* 92d Cong., 1st Sess. 81 (1972) (other nations were informed of the decision immediately after it was made); *United States–Canadian Relations: Hearings Before a Subcomm. of the House Comm. on Int'l Relations,* 94th Cong., 2d Sess. 5 (1976).

Similarly, when New Zealand devalued its dollar in August 1975, it did not consult its major trading partner, Australia. Financial Times, Aug. 11, 1975, at 7, cols. 4–5. Australia reciprocated in November 1976. *Id.,* Nov. 30, 1976, at 9, col. 5 (at col. 6).

[19] To take just the U.K. and France as examples, the British floated sterling in June 1972 and in November 1977 without consulting the Fund, and the French followed suit with the franc in January 1974. *See* 1972 I.M.F. ANN. REP. 39–40; GUARDIAN WEEKLY, Nov. 6, 1977, at 3, col. 3; R. SOLOMON, *supra* note 18, at 260–61.

[20] *See* Executive Board Dec. No. 4232–(74/67), June 13, 1974, para. 3(a), in SELECTED DECISIONS OF THE INT'L MONETARY FUND AND SELECTED DOCUMENTS 21 (8th issue 1976) (hereinafter cited as SELECTED DECISIONS (8th issue)).

[21] Witteveen, *The Emerging International Monetary System,* 5 IMF SURVEY 177, 181 (1976).

The drafters of the Fund Agreement at the Bretton Woods Conference in 1944 did not foresee the tremendous capital mobility that by the mid-1960s fostered quick, speculative inflows and outflows too massive to be covered by central banks trying to hold a fixed exchange rate, even with the aid of IMF financing. Probably the existence of a world without such capital mobility constituted an essential basis of the consent of parties to engage in meaningful international consultations (which could not be kept secret for long) before altering their exchange rates. The change to a world in which ruinous reserve outflows were likely to occur when a devaluation was rumored would radically transform the extent of the obligation to consult, so long as there was no foolproof way to keep the very existence of the consultations absolutely confidential. Thus, all the conditions for termination or suspension of the Fund Agreement's par value consultation duty probably were met.[22]

This is of more than historical interest, even though the Fund Agreement as revised in 1978 is no longer based on par values and no longer expressly requires consultation with the Fund before an exchange rate is altered. The revised Fund Agreement does impose on each member a duty to provide the Fund with the information necessary for it to exercise "firm surveillance" over the member's exchange rate policies and to consult with it, on request, regarding those policies.[23] In the absence of justifiably inconsistent practice under the former Agreement, this might imply a duty to notify the Fund in advance of any member's decision that would significantly affect the exchange rate of its currency, so the Fund could make a timely request for consultation.[24] But the practice of the 1960s and 1970s, considered in light of the prevailing circumstances, militates against finding any such implied duty.[25]

[22] *See* Vienna Convention on the Law of Treaties, *supra* note 6, art. 62.

[23] Fund Agreement, *as revised effective* Apr. 1, 1978, art. IV(3)(b), 29 U.S.T. 2203, T.I.A.S. No. 8937, *reprinted in* 15 INT'L LEGAL MATERIALS 546 (1976).

[24] Under the original Fund Agreement, the Executive Directors found a prior consultation duty regarding the adaptation of exchange restrictions in the language of art. IV(4)(a): "Each member undertakes to collaborate with the Fund to promote exchange stability, to maintain orderly exchange arrangements with other members, and to avoid competitive exchange alterations." *See* Executive Board Dec. No. 237–2, Dec. 18, 1947, attached memorandum para. II(B)(5), in SELECTED DECISIONS OF THE INT'L MONETARY FUND AND SELECTED DOCUMENTS 215 (9th issue 1981) (hereinafter cited as SELECTED DECISIONS (9th issue)).

[25] When the revised Agreement went into force, the Fund's General Counsel said that members would not be required to consult before making changes in exchange

While the Fund has retreated from a formal duty to consult before an exchange rate alteration, eight European Community members undertook in 1979 to consult among themselves. From the date of that undertaking through June 1982, six exchange rate adjustments occurred among them; on all six occasions there were prior consultations.[26]

Since its inception, the International Monetary Fund has been concerned not only with exchange rate policies, but with eliminating, or at least minimizing, the use of governmental restrictions on the making of payments and transfers for current international transactions—"exchange restrictions" on transactions other than capital movements. Exchange restrictions have often been used as a substitute for, or a prelude to, devaluation. They limit the availability or use of foreign exchange and thus help prevent a drain on reserves when a country's balance-of-payments situation is deteriorating. Under a provision in the original Fund Agreement, retained in the 1978 revision, the Fund must approve a member's new exchange restriction.[27] Although the provision does not make it clear that the approval must precede the restriction, the Fund's Executive Directors so decided as long ago as 1947.[28] Certain nonindustrialized members deemed still to be in a transitional period may maintain any exchange restrictions they had when they joined the Fund and may adapt them after consultation with (and perhaps only after approval from) the Fund.[29] A fortiori, members not in the transitional period must obtain Fund approval before adapting previously approved exchange restrictions.

These rules have not been without some problems. One has been in defining "exchange restrictions." The Fund's definition—direct governmental limitations on the availability or use

arrangements or exchange rate policies, although the Managing Director would be available for that purpose. J. Gold, A Third Report on Some Recent Legal Developments in the International Monetary Fund 12 (1978).

[26] *See* chapter V note 185 *supra*.

[27] Art. VIII(2)(a) of both the original and the revised Fund Agreement, *supra* notes 1 and 23. There is an exception if the Fund formally declares a currency scarce. A member may impose new restrictions on the availability or use of such a currency after mere consultation with the Fund. *Id.* arts. VII(3)(b) and VIII(2)(a).

[28] Executive Board Dec. No. 237–2, *supra* note 24, para.. II(A).

[29] Art. XIV(2) of the original and revised Fund Agreement. On the duty to consult, and perhaps to obtain approval, before a member in the transitional period adapts an existing restriction, see Executive Board Dec. No. 237–2, *supra* note 24, paras. I(A)(1) and II(B)(5).

of exchange as such[30]—clearly covers such measures as restrictions on the use of foreign exchange for certain types of imports or certain foreign travel, and clearly does not cover such measures as direct quotas on the imports of goods, but it leaves some grey areas. The Fund has interpreted it to apply to multiple currency practices and governmentally induced delays in making foreign exchange available for current payments.[31]

There have been "numerous failures" by members to seek the prior approval of the Fund even for measures that clearly were exchange restrictions.[32] Particularly notorious examples involved the United Kingdom in 1968 and France in 1969,[33] but these do not stand alone. The question then is whether the prior consultation–prior approval requirement for exchange restrictions has been eclipsed in the same manner as was the prior consultation requirement for exchange rate alterations. Several factors suggest a negative answer. The revised Fund Agreement has eliminated the express requirement only as to exchange rate alterations, not as to exchange restrictions. Moreover, restrictions on payments for current transactions are less justifiable now than before the 1978 revision, since fluctuations in the exchange rate can now take care of a good many balance-of-payments problems. Thus, prior Fund scrutiny of exchange restrictions is more important now than before. In addition, the major circumstance calling for secrecy and quick execution regarding a decision to change an exchange rate—the great mobility of capital—has little or no relevance to changes in exchange restrictions on noncapital transactions. Consequently, the impracticability argument against prior consultation is not nearly as strong when applied to exchange restrictions as when applied to exchange rate alterations.[34]

[30]Executive Board Dec. No. 1034–(60/27), June 1, 1960, para. 1, in SELECTED DECISIONS (9th issue), *supra* note 24, at 209.

[31]*See* Executive Board Dec. No. 237–2, *supra* note 24, para. II; Executive Board Dec. No. 3153–(70/95), Oct. 26, 1970, in SELECTED DECISIONS (9th issue), *supra* note 24, at 211. Multiple currency practices are explained in note 2 *supra.*

[32]Gold, *Some Characteristics of Operation, in* 2 THE INTERNATIONAL MONETARY FUND 1945–1965, at 582, 584 (J. Horsefield ed. 1969).

[33]*See* M. DE VRIES, *supra* note 8, at 357 (France) and 441–42 (U.K.). The situation did not change in the 1970s. *See* Gold, *Recent International Decisions to Prevent Restrictions on Trade and Payments,* 9 J. WORLD TRADE L. 63, 70 (1975).

[34]Prior consultation and approval objectives could be met if a member notifies the Fund of a proposed change in time for adequate Fund discussion, even if the Executive Board does not take up the matter as soon as it reasonably could. The Fund has such a tacit approval procedure for relatively minor changes in multiple currency practices.

A major goal of the Fund, of course, is to obviate the need for harmful devaluations and exchange restrictions by providing international liquidity for members in balance-of-payments difficulties. Thus, members may draw on the Fund's resources, but must eventually repay the Fund.[35] The Fund also augments members' reserves by distributing and facilitating the use of special drawing rights (SDRs) that a member may sell to certain other members for currencies usable in discharging its international obligations.

In all these transactions, the Fund (and, at least indirectly, the member seeking usable currencies) is required to consider the interests of the members whose currencies are to be used. The method of doing this has evolved over time. First, under a procedure gradually developed over the years and then codified in 1962, before a member state drew resources from the Fund, the Managing Director contacted the states whose currencies might be drawn. This was done even when speed in arranging the drawing was essential. The same practice was followed before the "borrowing" member repaid by using another member's currency to repurchase its own. With the 1978 revision of the Fund Agreement, the case-by-case consultation procedure disappeared as the Fund adopted policies and procedures on selection of currencies that took into account, "in consultation with members," such things as their balance of payments and reserve positions.[36]

Under the revised Fund Agreement, the Fund is to determine which members' currencies are "freely usable currencies," the effect being that they may be used (without the consent of

See J. Horseeld, *supra* note 2, at 407–08.

[35]Technically, the Fund does not lend. It sells convertible currencies in exchange for the member's own currency, with the member being obligated to repurchase its own by a specified future date.

[36]*See* revised Fund Agreement, *supra* note 23, art. V(3)(d), which includes the language quoted in the text. For the Fund's policy on selection of currencies under the revised Fund Agreement, see Executive Board Dec. No. 6774–(81/35), Mar. 5, 1981, in Selected Decisions (9th issue), *supra* note 24, at 85. For the earlier procedure, see the Fund's Statement on Currencies to Be Drawn and to Be Used in Repurchases, in Selected Decisions (8th issue), *supra* note 20, at 56, 57–58.

When the Fund enters into a Standby Arrangement obligating it to sell currencies to a member in the future if certain conditions are met, it obtains a letter of intent from the member supplementing the terms of the Arrangement and promising that the member will consult the Fund as to the currencies it wishes to purchase. *See* the Model Standby and Extended Arrangements, paras. 3 & 5, in J. Gold, Financial Assistance by the International Monetary Fund: Law and Practice 46–49 (IMF Pamphlet No. 27, 1979).

the issuing member) for a number of Fund-related transactions. The Fund is required to consult a member before placing its currency on, or removing it from, the list of freely usable currencies. Moreover, the Fund must consult each member, even if its currency is not freely usable, on the procedures to be used in making exchanges involving its currency.[37]

The Fund facilitates the use of SDRs by designating, from among members participating in the SDR facility, those to provide currencies (not necessarily their own) in exchange for SDRs from another participant that needs the currencies to improve its balance of payments or to bolster depleted foreign exchange reserves. From the SDR facility's inception in 1969, it has been recognized that the Executive Directors representing eligible designees should be consulted before the Fund makes a designation. The problem is that members must be able to rely on SDR availability, yet they cannot be expected to give much advance notice in their times of need. This makes it impracticable to wait until the eve of a transaction to discover whether a potential designee would resist the honor. The solution has been that the Executive Board adopts quarterly plans consisting of lists of eligible designees and the maximum amounts for which each could be designated without further consultation during the quarter.[38] Since each member is represented by someone on the Executive Board, there is prior consultation on a quarterly basis. This is in addition to the prior consultation with each participant concerning the procedure by which it will provide currencies.

From time to time, the Fund needs to replenish its holdings of certain members' currencies. When this happens, it can ask the member to lend the Fund its currency or to let the Fund borrow it from another source, or it can require the member to provide its currency for SDRs up to a stated limit.[39] The

[37] Fund Rules o–3(b) and o–4(a), in J. Gold, USE, CONVERSION, AND EXCHANGE OF CURRENCY UNDER THE SECOND AMENDMENT OF THE FUND'S ARTICLES, app. C, at 114 (IMF Pamphlet No. 23, 1978). Rule o–4(a) is paraphrased, in terms more clear than in the rule itself, *id.* at 88. As of June 15, 1981, the Fund has designated the West German mark, French franc, Japanese yen, pound sterling, and U.S. dollar as freely usable currencies. Executive Board Dec. No. 5719–(78/46), in SELECTED DECISIONS (9th issue), *supra* note 24, at 268.

[38] *See* M. DE VRIES, *supra* note 8, at 227; Fund Rule P–5, in J. GOLD, *supra* note 37, app. C, at 116. The authority to designate SDR recipients is in art. XIX(5) of the revised Fund Agreement, *supra* note 23.

[39] *Id.* art. VII(1).

former alternative obviously requires not only prior consultation but concurrence by the member; the latter requires a decision by the Fund's Executive Board, which—as noted above—will always include one director charged with representing the interests of the member whose currency is sought.

Whenever a participant exchanges its currency or another's for SDRs, whether with the Fund or with another participant, there has to be a way to determine how many SDRs the exchanged currency is worth. If the currency has a floating rate or any rate not pegged to the SDR, the exchange value may not be certain. Thus, the Fund has authority to adopt regulations determining the exchange rate between each participant's currency and the SDR, but it may do so only after consulting the participant on the procedure for making the determination.[40]

The revised Fund Agreement seeks to substitute SDRs for gold as the ultimate monetary reserve. Under the former system, the Fund had amassed a substantial gold stock that became something of an embarrassment when it decided to deemphasize gold. Consequently, the revised Agreement authorizes it to sell gold for the currency of any member, but only after consulting the member. If this would increase the Fund's holdings of the member's currency above the amount at which the Fund Agreement requires a surcharge, the member may require the Fund to exchange the excess for another member's currency—provided that the other member has been consulted and the exchange would not increase the holdings of its currency above the surcharge point.[41]

Another consultation requirement relating to the use of members' currencies applies to the Supplementary Financing Facility, created in 1977 to provide extraordinary financing for members with serious balance-of-payments imbalances in relation to their Fund quotas. To operate the Facility, the Fund had to borrow currencies from members. The Fund entered into a letter agreement with each member willing to lend its currency or another freely usable currency in its reserves, permitting the Fund to make calls over a five-year period. The agreement obligates the Fund to give the member notice of its intent to make a call and to consult if the member represents

[40] *Id.* art. XIX(7).
[41] *Id.* art. V(12)(c).

that its balance-of-payments and reserve positions do not justify the call. The Fund is to give the member the overwhelming benefit of any doubt, but it is not strictly bound to accept the member's representations.[42]

Finally, the Fund may require a "borrowing" member to repurchase its own currency before it would normally be obligated to do so if the Fund determines, after consulting the member, that the latter's balance-of-payments and reserve positions have improved sufficiently to warrant the early repurchase.[43]

This impressive list of consultation requirements provides the procedural mechanism enabling member states to delegate significant quasi-governmental authority (in the form of "international central banking" functions) to an international institution without abandoning all sovereign prerogatives. It also provides the mechanism by which the organization can take action affecting the sensitive interests of individual members (concerning the international use of their currencies) without losing their support. As chapter V demonstrates, the consultation principle serves similar purposes in the European Communities and, at least theoretically, in the United Nations.

Because of its institutional function, the Fund's prior consultation practice does not necessarily apply to decisions by individual states to use the currencies of other states in transactions not involving the Fund. To find a customary duty in such cases, one would have to find consistent practice by the states themselves. The finance ministers and central bankers of the major Western trading nations do consult frequently, though they do not generally publicize any discussions they may have as to their intent to buy or sell a particular foreign currency at a particular time. Thus, even though one can discover some pledges to consult before using a foreign currency,[44] available sources do

[42]Executive Board Dec. No. 5509–(77/127), Aug. 29, 1977, Annex, in SELECTED DECISIONS (9th issue), *supra* note 24, at 133. By 1981 the resources of the Supplementary Financing Facility were fully committed. The Fund then replaced that Facility with its "enlarged access policy," relying on a commitment by the Saudi Arabian Monetary Agency to lend it substantial resources. *See* 1981 I.M.F. ANN. REP. 91–92, 153–55.

[43]Revised Fund Agreement, art. V(7)(b), *supra* note 23. The Fund's procedures for early repurchase are in SELECTED DECISIONS (9th issue), *supra* note 24, at 91.

[44]The United States made such a pledge to France and (less specifically) to five other states at the Rambouillet summit in 1975. *See* Financial Times, Nov. 18, 1975, at 7, col. 1; *id.*, Nov. 19, 1975, at 40, col. 2. The U.S. later made substantial foreign exchange purchases and sales in an effort to stabilize the market. These interventions were preceded by consultations with the countries whose currencies were bought and sold. *Id.*, Mar. 19, 1976, at 6, col. 1. *See also* R. MIKESELL & H. GOLDSTEIN, RULES FOR A

not reveal consistent practice. Had there been consistent, norm-creating practice by the mid-seventies, one would expect to find it codified in the thorough revision of the Fund Agreement that went into force in 1978. No such codification appears. It is most unlikely, therefore, that custom requires one nation to consult another before using its currency in the foreign exchange market. Nor does it appear that governments regularly consult each other before adopting domestic monetary measures that affect their balance of payments.[45]

2. Trade Measures for Balance-of-Payments Purposes

The General Agreement on Tariffs and Trade provides the basic legal framework for trade measures, since GATT contracting parties account for more than 85 percent of world trade. GATT article XI prohibits them from imposing quantitative restrictions (quotas) on imports from, or exports to, other contracting parties, subject to some exceptions.[46] The exception in article XII permits temporary import quotas when necessary for balance-of-payments purposes. It contains a consultation requirement:

> Any contracting party applying new restrictions or raising the general level of its existing restrictions by a substantial intensification of the measures applied under this Article shall immediately after instituting or intensifying such restrictions (or, in circumstances in which prior consultation is practicable, before doing so) consult with the CONTRACTING PARTIES as to the nature of its balance of payments difficulties, alternative corrective measures which may be available, and the possible effect of the restrictions on the economies of other contracting parties.[47]

The same provision appears in article XVIII(12)(a), dealing with the trade and balance-of-payments problems of developing

FLOATING RATE REGIME 6–7 (Princeton Essays in Int'l Fin. No. 109, 1975), referring to U.S. market interventions since March 1973.

[45]The U.S. Federal Reserve Board, like its counterparts elsewhere, normally makes decisions in secret affecting the domestic money supply. Such was the case in October 1979, for example, when the Fed dramatically raised the rediscount rate and increased member-bank reserve requirements. *See* Financial Times, Oct. 8, 1979, at 2, col. 2.

[46]The current text of GATT appears in IV GATT, BASIC INSTRUMENTS AND SELECTED DOCUMENTS 1 (1969) (hereinafter cited as BISD).

[47]GATT art. XII(4)(a). In GATT, references to CONTRACTING PARTIES are to the parties acting collectively as the GATT plenary body; references to contracting parties are to individual parties. *See* GATT art. XXV(1).

countries. It is interesting to compare this provision with the article XII language in force until changed in 1955 to read as set forth above. The original language was: "Any contracting party which is not applying restrictions under this Article, but is considering the need to do so, shall, before instituting such restrictions (or, in circumstances in which prior consultation is impracticable, immediately after doing so), consult with the CONTRACTING PARTIES."[48]

Although a GATT working party said at the time that the language had been redrafted simply for the sake of brevity and without any change of intent,[49] there was a clear shift of emphasis from prior to subsequent consultation. This responded to the perception by another GATT working party that secrecy is needed in such cases in order to prevent imports from streaming in just ahead of the quotas.[50] The 1955 amendment simply recognized that secrecy would be difficult to maintain and that prior consultation therefore would be the exception rather than the rule—as was already occurring in the International Monetary Fund when devaluations were planned. It has indeed been the exception in GATT.[51]

The prior consultation principle is further diluted in the GATT Protocol Relating to Trade Negotiations Among Developing Countries,[52] which provides for special trade concessions among the parties. It permits quantitative restrictions for balance-of-payments purposes, even on products subject to concessions, but when restrictions are imposed or intensified on these products, "immediate notice of such action must be given to the Committee [of participating countries] and such action may be the subject of consultations as provided for" in a subsequent provision that requires consultations when representations are made by a party on any matter covered by the

[48]GATT, Oct. 30, 1947, art. XII(4)(a), 61 Stat. pt. 5, at A3 (1947), 55 U.N.T.S. 194, 4 BEVANS 639.

[49]GATT Working Party Report on Quantitative Restrictions, BISD 3d Supp. 170, 171 (1955).

[50]*See* GATT Working Party Report on Consultation Procedure Under Article XII:4(a), II BISD 89, 90–92 (1952).

[51]*See* J. JACKSON, WORLD TRADE AND THE LAW OF GATT 698 (1969). Prior consultations with individual governments or importers are not as rare as they are with the GATT plenary body. *See, e.g.*, Financial Times, Aug. 22, 1979, at 4, col. 6 (consultations by Malta with importers).

[52]Dec. 8, 1971, BISD 18th Supp. 11 (1972), *reprinted in* 11 INT'L LEGAL MATERIALS 737 (1972).

Protocol.[53] Thus, even if consultations are mandatory when representations are made (despite the equivocal language in the provision), there is no suggestion that they would normally precede the action.

The GATT Declaration on Trade Measures Taken for Balance-of-Payments Purposes does not require prior consultation. It simply requires parties to notify GATT promptly when they introduce or intensify such measures and to be ready to consult in the GATT Committee on Balance-of-Payments Restrictions.[54]

Quantitative restrictions for balance-of-payments purposes may be imposed on trade among members of some regional economic organizations, subject to the rules of each organization. As noted in chapter V, the European Economic Community Treaty contemplates trade restrictions only if Community assistance is inadequate to stem the balance-of-payments problem, and then only if authorized by the European Commission—unless "a sudden crisis in the balance of payments occurs," in which case the member state may take temporary action without prior authorization or consultation.[55] The European Free Trade Association Convention says that a member state applying quotas for balance-of-payments purposes "shall notify them to the Council, if possible before they come into force."[56] The Council may recommend changes in the quotas, but the recommendation would inevitably come after the quotas had been introduced. Essentially the same provisions appear in the Caribbean Community Treaty, and appeared in the former Caribbean Free Trade Association Agreement.[57]

[53] *Id.*, para. 11. Virtually the same provision appears in the Agreement on ASEAN Preferential Trading Arrangements, Feb. 24, 1977, art. 12(2) & (3), in 6 BASIC DOCUMENTS OF ASIAN REGIONAL ORGANIZATIONS 354 (M. Haas ed. 1979).

[54] BISD 26th Supp. 205 (1980). The Declaration was proposed by the "Framework" group in the GATT-sponsored Tokyo Round trade negotiations, which ended in 1979 with widespread agreement on tariff reductions and agreement among some states on a number of trade agreements, or codes, designed to pare down some prominent nontariff barriers to trade. The texts drafted in the "Framework" group affect provisions in the GATT itself, and thus will ultimately take the form of GATT amendments. *See* the Statement by the GATT Director-General, Apr. 12, 1979, in 18 INT'L LEGAL MATERIALS 553, 555 (1979).

[55] EEC Treaty arts. 108, 109. *See* chapter V at note 187 *supra*.

[56] Convention Establishing the European Free Trade Ass'n, Jan. 4, 1960, art. 19(2), 370 U.N.T.S. 3.

[57] *See* Treaty Establishing the Caribbean Community, July 4, 1973, art. 28(2), 12 INT'L LEGAL MATERIALS 1033 (1973); Agreement Establishing the Caribbean Free Trade Ass'n, Apr. 30, 1968, 7 INT'L LEGAL MATERIALS 935 (1968).

There is one other legal framework in which quotas for balance-of-payments purposes raise the prior consultation issue. Each time the International Monetary Fund in recent years has entered into an arrangement with a member in balance-of-payments difficulties to sell it currencies in the future, the member's accompanying letter of intent has promised (somewhat obliquely) to consult the Fund before introducing or intensifying import restrictions for balance-of-payments purposes while the arrangement lasts.[58] The Fund's General Counsel has said that the arrangement and letter do not comprise a contract obligating the member to meet the economic performance criteria set out in them,[59] but that does not mean that the prior consultation pledge—which, unlike the economic performance criteria, concerns a matter wholly within the control of the government—imposes no obligation. More damaging to the argument for a legal duty, perhaps, is the fact that a comparable prior consultation provision was discussed when the most recent Fund Agreement revision was being drafted, but a consensus could not be reached and the provision was left out.[60] Nevertheless, if individual member states continue to make the pledge in their letters of intent, they would seem to be bound by it. But so long as unequivocal promises appear only in letters of intent to the Fund, and so long as prior consultation practice remains sporadic at best when letters of intent are not involved, there will be no customary duty to consult before restricting imports for balance-of-payments purposes.

In recent years, temporary import surcharges have supplanted quotas as the favorite balance-of-payments trade measure, even though the General Agreement authorizes only quotas

[58]The prior consultation pledge apparently has been used consistently in connection with the Fund's standby arrangements since February 1975, and was used some of the time from 1968 until then. Financial Times, Oct. 1, 1976, at 40, col. 1. *See also* J. Gold, *supra* note 36, at 46–56 (sample standby and extended arrangements); British letter of intent to the Fund, Financial Times, Dec. 16, 1976, at 9, col. 1 (at col. 8).

As a result of the oil crisis of 1973–74, the Fund established an "oil facility" to supply special assistance to members in particular balance-of-payments difficulty from their reliance on oil imports. Members' letters of intent in connection with purchases from the oil facility represented that they would not introduce or intensify import restrictions without consulting the Fund. Letter from J. Gold to the author, Jan. 23, 1976, and *see* J. Gold, *Recent International Decisions to Prevent Restrictions on Trade and Payments,* 9 J. World Trade L. 63, 66 (1975).

[59]J. Gold,, *supra* note 36, at 17.

[60]*See* Gold, *The Second Amendment of the Fund's Articles of Agreement: A General View (I),* in 15 Finance & Development, Mar. 1978, at 10, 12.

for this purpose. As in the case of quotas, the practice is to notify and consult after the fact, not before.[61] This occurred in such prominent instances as the imposition of import surcharges by the United Kingdom in 1964 and the United States in 1971, and in many other cases as well.[62] The lack of prior consultation in such cases has sometimes drawn protests from the surcharging state's principal trading partners, especially from those with which a special trade relationship exists.[63] Nevertheless, it has been defended on grounds identical to those used when a devaluation occurs: the need for secrecy and quick action does not permit the luxury of meaningful prior consultation.[64] This explains the fate of a 1974 draft International Monetary Fund declaration calling for prior consultation when balance-of-payments trade measures are contemplated: It never gained enough adherents to enter into force.[65] There clearly is no unwritten prior consultation norm.

Yet another trade-related measure designed to alleviate balance-of-payments pressures is the import deposit scheme requiring importers to deposit a percentage of the value of certain imports for a stated period, usually without interest. In a celebrated case in 1968, the United Kingdom imposed an import deposit requirement covering about one-third of its imports. The British government notified GATT and the International Monetary Fund's Group of Ten a few days before the scheme

[61] *See* Roessler, *Selective Balance-of-Payments Adjustment Measures Affecting Trade: The Roles of the GATT and the IMF*, 9 J. WORLD TRADE L. 622, 630 (1975).

[62] *See* 14 KEESING'S CONTEMP. ARCHIVES 20396–97 (1964) (U.K. surcharge); sources cited, *supra* note 18 (U.S. surcharge). It is virtually impossible to find an instance in which prior consultation has been recorded, though it is likely that prospective import surcharges have been mentioned to IMF officials on some occasions when they were discussing balance-of-payments financing with member states.

[63] The United Kingdom's partners in the European Free Trade Association were "shocked and angry" because they were not consulted in 1964. *See* G. & V. Curzon, *The Management of Trade Relations in the GATT*, in 1 INTERNATIONAL ECONOMIC RELATIONS OF THE WESTERN WORLD 1959–1971, at 143, 217–18 (A. Shonfield ed. 1976); *see also* EFTA, 5TH ANN. REP. 7, 37–38 (1965). The EFTA Convention, *supra* note 56, does not expressly require prior consultation in such cases, but does recognize the economic interdependence of the member states and requires periodic exchanges of views on members' economic and financial policies. *Id.* art. 30.

[64] For a particularly forceful presentation of this argument by the British government, see 701 PARL. DEB., H.C. (5th ser.) 341–42 (1964).

[65] *See* the proposed Declaration on Trade Measures, June 13, 1974, 3 IMF SURVEY 181, *reprinted in* 13 INT'L LEGAL MATERIALS 1003 (1974); J. GOLD, WORK PAPER ON LAW AND REFORM OF THE INTERNATIONAL MONETARY SYSTEM 54 (World Peace Through Law Center, 1975). The declaration would not have been limited to surcharges, but they seem to have been foremost in the minds of the drafters.

went into force, but apparently did not seek their views before it made the decision.[66] Similar Italian measures in 1974 and 1981 apparently were not preceded by consultations even within the European Economic Community, but when Italy imposed import deposit requirements in 1976, it did get prior authorization from the European Commission.[67] Finland adopted an import deposit scheme without prior consultation in March 1975.[68] When New Zealand imposed an import deposit requirement on certain consumer goods in early 1976, it waited until afterward to consult within the GATT and with the European Commission.[69] Apparently the only protest against the failure to consult in these cases was the European Commission's expression of disappointment at Italy's conduct in 1974, but in that case Italy either stretched or broke the express rules of the European Economic Community. Thus, it does not appear that there is any unwritten prior consultation norm for otherwise lawful import deposit schemes.

C. Trade Measures Relating to Segments of National Economies

1. Introduction

This section considers trade measures other than those adopted primarily for balance-of-payments purposes. In most cases these measures have been designed to protect or stimulate discrete segments of national economies, such as particular industries or specific agricultural interests. In a lesser number of cases, considered later in this section, the measures have been designed for other purposes, such as conserving resources, earn-

[66] Heleniak, *The United Kingdom's Import Deposit Scheme,* 3 J. World Trade L. 584 (1969), says the U.K. undertook consultations with its major trading partners before it announced the import deposit legislation. But the consultations apparently did not precede the firm decision to act. The Chancellor of the Exchequer was quoted as saying on his return from the Group of Ten meeting that the measures "were not even discussed at the conference—I had prepared them before I left London." The Times (London), Nov. 23, 1968, at 1, col. 4. The GATT working party did not meet until several days after the November 27 effective date of the legislation. BISD 17th Supp. 144 (1970).

[67] *See* chapter V at notes 189–92 *supra.*

[68] Financial Times, Mar. 25, 1975, at 4, col. 1; interviews with U.S. Treasury and State Dept. officials, June 25 & 26, 1975.

[69] *See* BISD 23d Supp. 84, 88 (1977); European Commission, Tenth Gen'l Rep. on the Activities of the European Communities, 1976, at 280 (1977).

ing oligopolistic profits for the national treasury, or withholding strategic goods from a potential adversary. In order to remain on the path set out in chapter I, no attention will be given to retaliatory trade measures.

2. Protective Measures Against Imports

GATT contracting parties are bound by certain tariff reductions and other obligations to which they have agreed at the various GATT negotiating rounds. GATT article XIX(1), however, is an escape clause permitting them to deviate from their obligations when particular imports cause or threaten serious, unforeseen injury to domestic producers. Article XIX(2) sets forth the procedure if a party wishes to invoke the escape clause:

> Before any contracting party shall take action pursuant to the provisions of paragraph 1 of this Article, it shall give notice in writing to the CONTRACTING PARTIES as far in advance as may be practicable and shall afford the CONTRACTING PARTIES and those contracting parties having a substantial interest as exporters of the product concerned an opportunity to consult with it in respect of the proposed action. . . . In critical circumstances, where delay would cause damage which it would be difficult to repair, action under paragraph 1 of this Article may be taken provisionally without prior consultation, on the condition that consultation shall be effected immediately after taking such action.[70]

This language, unlike the GATT language discussed earlier on quotas for balance-of-payments purposes, clearly treats prior consultation as the norm, rather than the exception. That was the understanding of the contracting parties from the start.[71] In recent years, however, the "critical circumstances" exception has nearly overwhelmed the norm, with intergovernmental consultation following action rather than preceding it in the great majority of cases.[72] It may be doubted whether time constraints

[70]GATT, *supra* note 46, art. XIX(2). Article XIX(1) limits parties' freedom to raise duties only when the increase would derogate from a GATT obligation (including derogation from a bound tariff rate). When a tariff increase would not derogate from a GATT obligation, the Agreement does not impose a prior consultation requirement.

GATT art. XIX is concerned with the effect on exporters. But one state's protective measure against imports can also affect other importing states to which the trade may be diverted. Their interest in prior consultation is considered in subsection 6 *infra*.

[71]*See* GATT Analytical Index 108 (3d rev. 1970); G. Curzon, Multilateral Commercial Diplomacy 118 (1966).

[72]*See* OECD High Level Group on Trade and Related Problems, Policy Per-

truly precluded consultation in many of these cases. The United States, which accounts for almost 50 percent of the escape clause investigations worldwide, has consistently found time to comply with its statutory notice and hearing requirement (a partial substitute for intergovernmental consultation).[73]

GATT's general consultation clauses, articles XXII and XXIII, relate primarily to the settlement of matured disputes and have not been interpreted to require prior consultation.[74] If these clauses are combined with a prior notification norm, as is rather gingerly suggested by one of the "Framework" understandings reached in the Tokyo Round trade negotiations, the effect would be a general trade norm calling for prior consultation on request.[75] The trouble is that the prior notification norm is not firmly established.

Article XVIII of the General Agreement contains provisions allowing developing countries to protect infant industries under less stringent circumstances than those spelled out in article XIX(1). If the import restriction would affect goods bound under a GATT concession, the party proposing it must enter into negotiations with any contracting party with which the concession was originally negotiated and with any other contracting party determined by the contracting parties to have a

SPECTIVES FOR INTERNATIONAL TRADE AND ECONOMIC RELATIONS 83–84 (1972); EXECUTIVE BRANCH GATT STUDY NO. 11, THE GATT PROVISIONS ON COMPENSATION AND RETALIATION 2 (Senate Finance Comm. Print, 93d Cong., 1st Sess. 1973). During the years 1974–76, prior intergovernmental consultation occurred in only five of the twenty-six article XIX cases. *See* Meier, *Externality Law and Market Safeguards: Applications in the GATT Multilateral Trade Negotiations*, 18 HARV. INT'L L.J. 491, 496 n.20 (1977).

[73] Interview with State Dep't official, June 26, 1975. The hearings are mandated by the Trade Act of 1974, 19 U.S.C. § 2251(c) (1976).

[74] *See* G. & V. Curzon, *GATT: Traders' Club,* in THE ANATOMY OF INFLUENCE: DECISION MAKING IN INTERNATIONAL ORGANIZATION 298, 315 (R. Cox & H. Jacobson eds. 1973); Shihata, *Destination Embargo of Arab Oil: Its Legality under International Law,* 68 AM. J. INT'L L. 591, 623 (1974).

In 1958 a GATT working party recommended, in a report adopted by the CONTRACTING PARTIES, that GATT parties, "when contemplating action on problems arising in commodity trade, should consider the possibility of initiating consultations under Article XXII with a view to arriving at mutually acceptable solutions, thus avoiding the need for unilateral action." BISD 7th Supp. 42, 45 (1959). This did not assert a duty to consult under article XXII, but rather held it out as a desirable possibility.

[75] *See* BISD 26th Supp. 210 (1980). This Understanding Regarding Notification, Consultation, Dispute Settlement and Surveillance says, "Contracting parties should endeavour to notify [trade measures affecting the operation of the General Agreement] in advance of implementation," and they should undertake to strengthen their consultative procedures. In any event, this contemplates notification only before implementation, not before basic decision making, and does not say when consultation should occur.

substantial interest. In some circumstances, further consultations with the contracting parties must be held. It appears, however, that the practice of consulting before acting is no more prevalent here than it is under article XIX.[76] Moreover, one of the "Framework" decisions negotiated in the Tokyo Round contemplates that in "unusual circumstances," developing countries may provisionally apply safeguard measures immediately after notification.[77]

GATT article XXVIII permits developed as well as developing countries to increase bound duties at three-year intervals, if there has been prior notification to, and agreement or an attempt to reach agreement with, the contracting parties primarily concerned.[78] In practice, attempts to reach agreement have generally preceded action, but not always.[79]

In some circumstances involving "market disruption," importing countries tend to protect their domestic industries without paying scrupulous attention to such GATT standards as the injury and causation tests in article XIX, or the generally accepted notion that the GATT most-favored-nation clause requires article XIX action to be taken equally against all exporting contracting parties.[80] In recognition of this fact of life, suggestions have been made that the importing state in "market disruption" cases should take exporting states' interests into account by consulting them before taking unilateral action.[81] So

[76] For example, the Indian government notified GATT after it decided, under article XVIII, to apply temporary auxiliary duties to certain bound items in 1973. *See* BISD 20th Supp. 26 (1974).

[77] *See* BISD 26th Supp. 209 (1980).

[78] GATT art. XXVIII(1)&(3). The drafters clearly intended that the negotiations would precede withdrawal of any bound duties. *See* GATT ANALYTICAL INDEX 157 (3d rev. 1970).

GATT art. XXVIII(4) permits withdrawal of tariff concessions whenever the CONTRACTING PARTIES authorize negotiations with the contracting parties primarily concerned. It is to be used only "in special circumstances."

[79] *See* J. JACKSON, *supra* note 51, at 231–33. For two instances in which negotiations followed withdrawal of concessions under article XXVIII, see BISD 20th Supp. 26 & 28 (1974) (India and Indonesia).

[80] The article XIX tests are *(a)* actual or threatened serious injury to domestic producers, *(b)* caused by increased imports of like or competitive products, *(c)* which are, in turn, caused by *(i)* unforeseen developments and *(ii)* the effect of obligations (such as tariff concessions) incurred under the GATT. The equal-treatment notion may be found in GATT Secretariat, Modalities of Application of Article XIX, GATT Doc. L/4679 (1978).

[81] *See* Decision of the GATT CONTRACTING PARTIES, Nov. 19, 1960, in BISD 9th Supp. 26, 27 (1961); Metzger, *Injury and Market Disruption from Imports, in* 1 COMM'N ON INT'L TRADE AND INVESTMENT POLICY, UNITED STATES INTERNATIONAL ECONOMIC

far, these suggestions have not produced any widely adopted, formal agreement beyond the textile field, although a strenuous attempt was made to negotiate a broad "safeguards code" in the Tokyo Round GATT negotiations ending in 1979. In the form proposed by its principal proponent, the European Communities, it would have permitted import restraints under a looser injury test than found in article XIX and would have permitted selective measures against goods from exporting countries primarily responsible for the "injurious" imports. The developing countries would not accept selective application without prior authorization in each case by a committee of signatories. The European Communities would accept nothing more stringent than a prior consultation requirement, which would be excused in an emergency.[82] Thus, prior consultation was a common denominator acceptable to both sides, at least in the absence of an emergency. The real procedural argument was over prior authorization.

Before any prospective safeguards code appeared on the horizon, agreements were negotiated to deal with perceived or prognosticated market disruption. These include the GATT Protocol Relating to Trade Negotiations Among Developing Countries, which contains prior consultation provisions corresponding to GATT articles XIX(2) and XXVIII(4).[83] Other relevant agreements include the GATT-related multilateral textile arrangements, bilateral trade agreements, regional economic integration arrangements, and orderly marketing agreements. These are discussed seriatim below.

Each of the textile agreements—the Short-Term Arrangement on cotton textiles, in force from October 1, 1961, until September 30, 1962; the Long-Term Arrangement on cotton textiles, in force from October 1, 1962, until December 31,

POLICY IN AN INTERDEPENDENT WORLD 187 (1971); OECD HIGH LEVEL GROUP ON TRADE AND RELATED PROBLEMS, REPORT ON POLICY PERSPECTIVES FOR INTERNATIONAL TRADE AND ECONOMIC RELATIONS 83 (1972).

These suggestions appear to have had some impact. For example, in August 1980 the United States government—under heavy domestic industry pressure—reclassified partially unassembled truck cabs and chassis in such a way as to increase substantially the import duties on them. The Japanese, who were uniquely affected by the increase, had been consulted at some length beforehand. *See* Financial Times, Aug. 22, 1980, at 1, col. 3.

[82] *See* 12 BULL. EUR. COMM., No. 4, at 13 (1979); Financial Times, July 3, 1979, at 4, col. 6.

[83] GATT Protocol, *supra* note 52, paras. 8–9, 13. GATT art. XIX(2) is discussed in the text at note 70 *supra*; art. XXVIII(4) is discussed in note 78 *supra*.

1973; and the Multifiber Arrangement, in force from January 1, 1974, until July 31, 1986 (as renewed in December 1981)—has contained a safeguard provision permitting importing countries to apply unilateral import restrictions to protect injured domestic producers, subject to prior notification and prior consultation if requested. Provisional action could be taken "in critical circumstances" without consultation.[84] The Long-Term and the Multifiber Arrangements have expressly contemplated bilateral trade-restricting agreements as well as unilateral action.[85]

Until about the end of September 1964, unilateral restraints on textiles predominated over bilateral agreements, but since then the order has been reversed.[86] The agreements, of course, stem from consultations and are actually extensions of the consultation requirement for unilateral restraints. The importing state enters into consultations with the aim of reaching a favorable agreement, retaining the option of unilateral action if no agreement is reached. When agreements have been reached, they typically set import quotas for some products and establish a prior consultation procedure if imports of others reach too high a level.[87]

When unilateral restraints actually have been imposed, exporting states sometimes have asserted that the prior consul-

[84]Short-Term Arrangement, July 21, 1961, para. A, 12 U.S.T. 1675, T.I.A.S. No. 4884; Long-Term Arrangement, Oct. 1, 1962, art. 3, 13 U.S.T. 2673, T.I.A.S. No. 5240, 471 U.N.T.S. 296; Arrangement Regarding International Trade in Textiles (Multifiber Arrangement), Dec. 20, 1973, art. 3, 25 U.S.T. 1001, T.I.A.S. No. 7840.

The "critical circumstances" exception has gotten narrower with each Arrangement, but importing states have sometimes avoided it by invoking the broader "emergency" exception in GATT article XIX. When the Arrangement was renewed in December 1981, it was agreed that all parties should refrain from resorting to measures outside the Arrangement that would affect textiles covered by it, until relief measures under the Arrangement have been exhausted. Conclusions of the Textiles Committee, Dec. 22, 1981, in 25 O.J. EUR. COMM. (No. L 83) 10, 12 (1982).

As of Jan. 1, 1982, there were forty-four parties to the Multifiber Arrangement, including the European Economic Community, representing its ten member states.

[85]*See* art. 4 of each, *supra* note 84.

[86]*See* Metzger, *supra* note 81, at 167, 179. As of February 1978, there were 105 bilateral agreements in force; 21 unilateral import restraints had been imposed under the Multifiber Arrangement. THE RISE IN PROTECTIONISM 91 (IMF Pamphlet No. 24, 1978).

[87]The U.S. agreements to this effect are summarized in THE HISTORY AND CURRENT STATUS OF THE MULTIFIBER ARRANGEMENT 38–55 (U.S. Int'l Trade Comm'n Pub. 850, 1978). The European Economic Community's agreements are summarized in 1 L. LAZAR, TRANSNATIONAL ECONOMIC AND MONETARY LAW 2.17.013–.016 (1978).

tation duty was ignored.[88] A review undertaken in the third year of the Multifiber Arrangement by the GATT Textile Committee suggested, however, that the prior consultation requirement had generally been met, although there were some claims by importing states of critical circumstances justifying immediate provisional measures.[89] In one particularly interesting case, France imposed quotas in 1977 on certain textile imports without consulting the supplier countries. The European Communities Commission objected and announced that textile imports would not be restricted until consultations had been held with those countries.[90] After the Commission took action, France agreed to rescind its quotas.[91]

The United States has entered into bilateral trade agreements, not always limited to textiles, with several Eastern European states and the People's Republic of China. Whenever a significant volume of trade is foreseen, the agreements contain safeguard clauses requiring prior consultation except in emergencies.[92] The agreement with the Soviet Union has not entered into force for reasons other than dissatisfaction with the market disruption clause.[93]

The European Economic Community has signed a great many bilateral agreements with nonmember states granting preferential access to each other's markets. They all contain safeguard clauses permitting unilateral action in the event of market dis-

[88] *See* BISD 24th Supp. 28, 35 (1978). In a particularly conspicuous case, India claimed that the European Economic Community did not adequately consult it before imposing restrictions on shirts and blouses in 1977. The Community asserted that adequate consultations were held. *See* EUROPEAN REP., Apr. 30, 1977, External Relations, at 3; Commission Reg. 561/77/EEC, Mar. 16, 1977, preamble, in 20 O. J. EUR. COMM. (No. L 71) 29 (1977); 10 BULL. EUR. COMM., No. 2, at 60 (1977). The case was complicated by the fact that a bilateral textile agreement had already been entered into by the EEC and India.

[89] GATT Doc. COM.TEX/SB/196, at 25–29 (1976).

[90] *See* 1 L. LAZAR, *supra* note 87, at 2.17.012.

[91] *See* THE RISE IN PROTECTIONISM, *supra* note 86, at 18, 94–95.

[92] *See* the trade agreements with Romania, Apr. 2, 1975, art. 3 & Annex 1, 26 U.S.T. 2305, T.I.A.S. No. 8159; Hungary, Mar. 17, 1978, art. 7 & Annex, 29 U.S.T. 2711, T.I.A.S. No. 8967, *reprinted in* 17 INT'L LEGAL MATERIALS 1475 (1978); and the People's Republic of China, July 7, 1979, art. 7, T.I.A.S. No. 9630, *reprinted in* 18 INT'L LEGAL MATERIALS 1041 (1979). *See also* the textile agreements with Yugoslavia, Jan. 14, 1976, 27 U.S.T. 1622, T.I.A.S. No. 8271; Hungary, Feb. 18, 1976, 27 U.S.T. 1619, T.I.A.S. No. 8270; and Czechoslovakia, Mar. 28, 1977, 28 U.S.T. 5463, T.I.A.S. No. 8645.

[93] The agreement as signed, Oct. 28, 1972, is in 11 INT'L LEGAL MATERIALS 1321 (1972). It was repudiated by the Soviet Union before the required notices of acceptance had been exchanged, because of dissatisfaction with the emigration provisions in the U.S. Trade Act of 1974.

ruption. All that have been signed since mid-1972 require prior consultation, usually in a joint committee, unless "exceptional circumstances" justify immediate action.[94] Similar provisions appear in preferential trade agreements not involving the Community,[95] and in the Community's association agreements with the African, Caribbean, and Pacific (ACP) states.[96] (Practice related to the first ACP agreement provides a significant insight

[94]*See* the preferential trade agreements between the EEC and the following fifteen countries: Austria, July 22, 1972, art. 27, 1 COLLECTION OF THE AGREEMENTS CONCLUDED BY THE EUROPEAN COMMUNITIES 7 (1977); Iceland, July 22, 1972, art. 27, 2 *id.* at 531 (1977); Portugal, July 22, 1972, art. 30, 1 *id.* at 749; Sweden, July 22, 1972, art. 27, 2 *id.* at 381; Switzerland, July 22, 1972, art. 27, 3 *id.* at 18 (1978); Norway, May 14, 1973, art. 27, 2 *id.* at 217; Finland, Oct. 5, 1973, art. 27, *id.* at 5; Israel, May 11, 1975, art. 16, 4 *id.* at 164 (1978); Tunisia, Apr. 25, 1976, art. 37, in 21 O.J. EUR. COMM. (No. L 265) 2 (1978); Algeria, Apr. 26, 1976, art. 36, *id.* (No. L 263) 2; Morocco, Apr. 27, 1976, art. 38, *id.* (No. L 264) 2; Egypt, Jan. 18, 1977, art. 35, *id.* (No. L 266) 2; Jordan, Jan. 18, 1977, art. 32, *id.* (No. L 268) 2; Syria, Jan. 18, 1977, art. 33, *id.* (No. L 269) 2; Lebanon, May 3, 1977, art. 33, *id.* (No. L 267) 2.

In addition, the nonpreferential agreement with the People's Republic of China, Apr. 3, 1978, art. 5, *id.* (No. L 123) 2, requires consultations before either party acts to solve any trade problems, save in exceptional cases where the situation does not admit any delay. *See also* the Cooperation Agreement between the EEC and the Association of South-East Asian Nations (ASEAN), Mar. 7, 1980, arts. 2(3)(f), 5, in 23 *id.* (No. L 144) 2 (1980). Three agreements with South American countries provide for narrow preferential treatment for certain items. As to those items, there are market disruption clauses, subject to prior consultation (except when the only protective action permitted is a return to previously established duties). *See* the agreements with Argentina, Nov. 8, 1971, Annex I, 4 COLLECTION, *supra* at 941; Uruguay, Apr. 2, 1973, Annex I, *id.* at 961; Brazil, Dec. 19, 1973, Annexes I & II, *id.* at 917.

[95]*See, e.g.,* Trade Agreement Between South Africa and Malawi, Mar. 13, 1967, arts. 12, 14, in 7 INT'L LEGAL MATERIALS 757 (1968); Trade Expansion and Economic Cooperation Agreement Among India, the United Arab Republic and Yugoslavia, Dec. 23, 1967, art. 4, *id.* at 735. *But see* Agreement on ASEAN Preferential Trading Arrangements, Feb. 24, 1977, art. 12(1), *supra* note 53 (notice and consultation not required to precede action).

[96]*See* the second EEC-ACP Convention of Lomé, Oct. 31, 1979, arts. 12, 13(1) & (3), in 19 INT'L LEGAL MATERIALS 341 (1980). *See also* the first (superseded) EEC-ACP Convention of Lomé, Feb. 28, 1975, arts. 10, 11(1) & (3), in 14 *id.* at 604 (1975). The two Lomé Conventions also provide for prior consultation when Community measures regarding common organization of the market, specific rules under the common agricultural policy, or measures for the approximation of laws would be likely to affect ACP trade with the Community. Second Lomé Convention, *supra,* arts 2(2)(c), 7; first Lomé Convention, *supra,* arts. 2(2)(b), 5.

The earlier Yaoundé Conventions required prior consultations with the associated African states only when the Community planned to restrict imports in connection with its common agricultural policy. Consultations with the Community were required when the African states wished to introduce duties for economic development purposes. *See* Convention Between the European Economic Community and Associated African States (Yaoundé I), July 20, 1963, arts. 3, 11 and Protocol No. 1, art. 4, in 2 *id.* at 971 (1963); and Yaoundé II, July 29, 1969, art. 3 and Protocols No. 1, arts. 1, 3, and No. 2, art. 3, in 9 *id.* at 484 (1969).

into consultation expectations outside the strict legal framework of a treaty regime. Before the agreement went into force, the ACP states asserted a right to be consulted before the Community took action that could affect their trade interests. The Community acquiesced, defining consultation as it has been defined in this study—discussion before a decision is made, with account being taken of the views expressed.[97])

To the extent that regional economic integration agreements permit new protective barriers against trade inter sese, they provide for some type of prior participation by an organ of the association. As noted in chapter V, the European Economic Community Treaty permitted trade protection for weak industries or regions during the transitional period, but only upon prior authorization from the Commission.[98] The European Free Trade Association Convention permits such protection without limiting it to a transitional period, upon prior authorization from the EFTA Council.[99] The Andean Pact is similar.[100] The Caribbean common market treaty is less demanding, if the protective measures are temporary quotas geared to import levels during periods specified in the treaty. In such cases the treaty provides for prior notification, if possible, to the Common Market Council, which may make recommendations. If any other protective measure is contemplated, the Council's prior authorization is required.[101]

The discussion so far has concentrated primarily on formal agreements containing escape clauses. Two varieties of understanding remain to be discussed: (*a*) declarations and resolutions adopted under the auspices of international agencies, and (*b*) orderly marketing agreements and voluntary export restraints limiting trade in specific products between two states.

A prominent example of the former variety was the 1974 OECD "Code of Good Conduct" in which the OECD states pledged to avoid unilateral protectionist measures for one year and "to consult with each other, making full use of the general procedures of consultation within OECD, in order to assure

[97] *See* European Rep., July 17, 1976, External Relations.

[98] EEC Treaty art. 226. *See* chapter V note 160 *supra*.

[99] EFTA Convention, *supra* note 56, art. 20.

[100] Agreement on Andean Subregional Integration, May 26, 1969, arts. 79–80, in 8 INT'L LEGAL MATERIALS 910 (1969). These provisions were not affected by the 1976 Lima Protocol amending the Agreement.

[101] Treaty Establishing the Caribbean Community, *supra* note 57, art. 29.

that the present Declaration is properly implemented."[102] The pledge was renewed annually for several years. It was recognized that emergency measures might be taken despite the pledge, but in such cases the consultation clause would apply. Moreover, even though the clause contained no pledge to consult nonparties, developing countries used it to argue that they should be consulted when an OECD state contemplated trade restrictions affecting them.[103] The 1980 OECD Declaration on Trade Policy, which replaced the 1974 pledge, contains a consultation promise much like that in the 1974 instrument.[104]

The developing countries have, in fact, mounted a sustained effort to persuade the industrialized world not to protect its producers from their competition without at least consulting them (or, preferably, obtaining some form of international approval) in advance. We already have seen this effort at work in the various textile arrangements and in the Tokyo Round safeguard mechanism negotiations. It has found expression also in the Agreed Conclusions of the U.N. Conference on Trade and Development (UNCTAD) Special Committee on Preferences, which was concerned that industrialized countries might unnecessarily modify or withdraw trade preferences granted to certain products imported from developing countries:

> Preference-giving countries will offer opportunities for appropriate consultations to beneficiary countries, in particular to those having a substantial trade interest in the product concerned, in connexion with the use of safeguard measures; where prior consultations are not possible, preference-giving countries will undertake for the purpose [of considering the aims of the generalized system of preferences and the interests of developing countries], to inform all beneficiary countries, through the Secretary-General of UNCTAD, with a minimum of delay, of the action taken.[105]

On a regional level, the Latin American members of the Organization of American States (OAS) have long asserted that the United States should not adopt safeguard measures against

[102]OECD Trade Declaration, May 30, 1974, 71 DEP'T ST. BULL. 32 (1974), *reprinted in* 13 INT'L LEGAL MATERIALS 998 (1974).

[103]*See* Report of the GATT Comm. on Trade and Development, BISD 21st Supp. 35, 40 (1975).

[104]OECD Declaration on Trade Policy, June 4, 1980, in OECD OBSERVER, Special Supp. 3 (1980).

[105]U.N. Doc. TD/B/332, Annex, at 3 (1970). The Special Committee included developed as well as developing countries. Ireland and New Zealand expressed reservations as to the feasibility of prior consultation. U.N. Doc. TD/B/300/Rev.1, at 40–41 (1970).

their products without prior consultation. The United States acquiesced in 1970, joining in the Inter-American Economic and Social Council resolution creating the Special Committee for Consultation and Negotiation (CECON). Among other things, the resolution directed CECON: "To conduct consultations between the United States of America and the Latin American countries prior to the adoption by the former of measures that might adversely affect imports from Latin America, [or that might adversely affect Latin American exports to third countries,] in order to seek a satisfactory solution for the interested parties, in the terms indicated in the Action Plan of Viña del Mar."[106]

This procedure was reaffirmed by the OAS General Assembly in 1975.[107] It was put to the test in November 1977, when the United States, responding to an alleged sudden crisis in the domestic sugar market, announced without prior consultation that it would increase its import duty on sugar. This led the OAS Secretary-General to condemn the United States for acting without consulting CECON.[108] When the Permanent Council of the OAS met shortly thereafter, several Latin American countries criticized the American failure to consult, and the Permanent Council adopted a declaration saying, inter alia, "The member states, before taking measures that may affect imports from other member states, should, in accordance with the commitments they have entered into, hold the prior consultations provided for in [the resolution above]."[109] The United States did not object to the norm, claiming only that the cir-

[106] Inter-American ECOSOC Res. REM-1/70, para. 7(c) (1970), in OAS Doc. OEA/Ser.X/10.5, at 7 (1976). The United States reserved its position on the bracketed phrase. At Viña del Mar the Latin American states had asserted "the necessity for the functioning of the machinery of consultation contemplated in UNCTAD and GATT prior to the adoption of measures that may mean retrogression in the treatment of imports of Latin American products." Latin American Consensus of Viña del Mar, May 17, 1969, para. 12, in 8 INT'L LEGAL MATERIALS 974 (1969).

The Australian government has given a comparable commitment to the ASEAN countries, but a subsequent Australian statement seemed to scale down the commitment to one of prior notification. *See* Barclay, *Problems in Australian Foreign Policy, July-December* 1978, in 25 AUSTL. J. POL. & HIST. 7, 15 (1979).

[107] *See* O.A.S. G.A. Res. AG/RES.201(V-0/75), May 19, 1975, para. 6, in 1975 DIGEST OF UNITED STATES PRACTICE IN INT'L LAW 513.

[108] *See* Washington Post, Nov. 14, 1977, at A4, col. 5. For analysis of negotiations involving proposed unilateral U.S. trade action, see Odell, *Latin American Trade Negotiations with the United States,* 34 INT'L ORG. 207 (1980).

[109] O.A.S. press release E-153/77, Dec. 2, 1977, at 2. *See also* O.A.S. press release E-151/77, Nov. 28, 1977, at 4.

cumstances of the case did not allow time for consultation. Subsequently, when legislative or administrative measures designed to increase barriers to sugar imports were being considered, the United States did consult interested Latin American governments.[110]

When immediate action has not seemed essential, the Western industrialized countries have turned increasingly in recent years to orderly marketing agreements and voluntary restraint arrangements. The former are binding intergovernmental agreements imposing quantitative limits on trade in sensitive products between the parties; the latter are export restraints undertaken by suppliers or their governments pursuant to nonbinding understandings with importing states. These devices have been especially popular among states importing not only textiles, but certain kinds of steel, shoes, television sets, and meats. By their nature, they reflect (successful) attempts to agree with supplier states instead of immediate imposition of unilateral import restraints, which are often threatened if the talks fail.

The real question for our purposes is whether these negotiated arrangements reflect an opinio juris on the part of the decision makers in the importing states to the effect that negotiations (or at least consultations) are required when trade restrictions are contemplated. The reasons government officials give are usually self-serving and do not proclaim any legal compulsion to negotiate. For example, in 1977 when President Carter decided to negotiate an orderly marketing agreement with Japan on color television sets instead of accepting the International Trade Commission's recommended increase in the tariff rate, he justified his action as being less inflationary than a tariff increase, less subject to circumvention, less expensive (in the sense that the United States would not have to give concessions on other imports or suffer retaliation against its exports), and more selective than a tariff increase on sets from all countries.[111] Other governments have given similar reasons when they have negotiated orderly marketing agreements.[112]

[110] O.A.S. press releases E-16/79, Feb. 22, 1979, at 1–3; E-20/79, Feb. 26, 1979, at 1–3; E-21/79, Feb. 27, 1979, at 1; telephone interview with State Department official in Office of Regional Economic Policy, Latin American Bureau, June 18, 1982.

[111] President Carter's letter to the Speaker of the House and the President of the Senate, May 19, 1977, 13 WEEKLY COMP. OF PRES. DOC. 761–62, *reprinted in* 16 INT'L LEGAL MATERIALS 588–89 (1977).

[112] *See* G. & V. CURZON, *supra* note 63, at 276–77; Sarna, *Safeguards Against Market*

One must evaluate these statements in light of domestic political realities. It would be highly impolitic for a national leader to declare in public that he has decided not to protect his constituents unilaterally, and instead will subject their economic interests to negotiations with the competitor nation, because of international law obligations. Moreover, one must consider the rise in negotiated restraints in light of the consistent pattern of prior consultation requirements (absent any "emergency") in the trade agreements and formal declarations we have been examining. The norm is so well established in those instruments, and is so consistently asserted by states with the most to lose from safeguards, that it supplies the opinio juris when states powerful enough to act unilaterally undertake instead to negotiate without expressly disclaiming any duty to do so. This is not to say, of course, that they have none of the self-serving motivations set forth in their public statements; it is simply to say that those motivations do not preempt the implicit acknowledgement that unilateral trade restrictions in a nonemergency situation cannot be justified without a good faith attempt to negotiate a solution or at least to engage in consultations.[113]

Particularly revealing in this regard is the recent history of trade restrictions on beef. In July 1974 the European Economic Community suspended the issuance of import licenses for beef and veal, except those covered by GATT quotas. In March and June it had held discussions with its principal South American beef and veal supplier states, but it had not done so with Australia, another major beef exporter.[114] Shortly thereafter, the Australian Prime Minister visited several European Community capitals. As he later reported to the Australian parliament: "In each European Community capital I took up forcefully the Community's current import restrictions on beef. I left heads of government in no doubt about our attitude to the Community's action in imposing restrictions without warning or consultation."[115] In other words, he asserted a right to be consulted.

Disruption—The Canadian View, 10 J. WORLD TRADE L. 355, 364 (1976).

[113] Even negotiated "solutions" have their drawbacks for importing states. *See* Sarna, *supra* note 112. Thus, this is not a case of finding compulsion from a course of conduct governments always would follow anyway in their own self-interest.

[114] *See* 7 BULL. EUR. COMM., No. 3, at 80 (1974); EUROPEAN COMMISSION, EIGHTH GEN'L REP. ON THE ACTIVITIES OF THE EUROPEAN COMMUNITIES, 1974, at 159–60, 255 (1975).

[115] 46 AUSTL. FOR. AFF. REC. 63 (1975).

In 1974, Japan also abruptly embargoed beef imports from Australia, setting off a response like that noted in the text. *See id.* at 674. In the aftermath, the two countries

There is no evidence that the European governments rejected the assertion. That is significant in itself. It also sheds light on the recent U.S. practice of negotiating voluntary restraints with Australia and other exporting states when beef imports approach the statutory trigger point at which Congress has mandated unilateral quotas.[116] As in the case of other bilateral restraints negotiated by the United States, the motives are mixed. Some are self-serving, but there is also a clear recognition that exporting states such as Australia expect to be consulted. There is an international mechanism for such consultations in the Arrangement Regarding Bovine Meat, negotiated in the Tokyo Round.[117]

Other revealing examples of state practice have involved U.S. import restrictions on shoes and special steels. Orderly marketing agreements on shoes were reached with South Korea and Taiwan in 1977, but not with the other major supplier, Italy. When the United States later considered unilateral restraints against Italian shoes, consultations were held with the Commission of the European Communities.[118] On the other hand, in 1976 when the United States negotiated orderly marketing agreements on special steels with major suppliers, it imposed—apparently without consultation—a basket quota on small supplier states.[119]

signed a Basic Treaty of Friendship and Cooperation, July 16, 1976, Australian Treaty Series 1977, No. 19, which contains several general cooperation and consultation clauses. These appear to have raised expectations that each will consult over any issue that significantly affects the other. *See* arts. 3(3), 4, 5(2), 12. *See also* Millar, *Japan and Australia: Partners in the Pacific,* 8 PACIFIC COMMUNITY 28, 42 (1976).

[116] *See Livestock and Poultry Price Situation: Hearings Before the House Comm. on Agriculture,* 93d Cong., 2d Sess. 131 (1974); N.Y. Times, Jan. 1, 1975, at 23, col. 3 (city ed.); 22d ANN. REP. of the PRESIDENT ON THE TRADE AGREEMENTS PROGRAM, 1977, at 59–60 (1978).

The U.S. voluntary restraint practice supplanted earlier ad hoc controls on beef and cattle. There seems to have been no consistent pattern of prior consultation by either the United States or Canada relating to ad hoc controls by each of them on their beef and cattle trade. Some of the controls were retaliatory. *See* Kindred & Biggs, *Trade and Investment Issues: Patterns of Canadian-American Economic Problems,* 1 CAN.-U.S. L.J. 114, 126–27 (1978).

While Congress was considering a potentially restrictive change in the meat quota formula in 1979 (in a bill eventually enacted as P.L. 96–177), the State Department entertained the representations of the major meat-exporting countries and then reached a compromise with the Congress, softening the bill's impact somewhat. Letter to the author from a U.S. State Department official, Jan. 22, 1980.

[117] Arrangement Regarding Bovine Meat, Apr. 12, 1979, arts. 4(5), 5(2), BISD 26th Supp. 84 (1980).

[118] *See* Financial Times, Feb. 12, 1980, at 6, col. 3.

[119] *See* Odell, *supra* note 108, at 217–18.

As the discussion has suggested, unilateral protective measures adopted without prior consultation usually have been under a claim of emergency in order to come within the recognized exception in GATT article XIX and in other trade agreements. A significant example was the French imposition of selective import quotas following internal disturbances in the spring of 1968. Although the French government attempted to justify its action to its European Community partners on balance-of-payments grounds, it argued in the GATT that it had acted to provide a respite until its economy could recover from the shock. Members of the GATT working party "expressed regret that the Government of France had not consulted in the GATT before introducing the measures that had been taken. They emphasized the particular importance which they attached to prior consultation if any additional measures were contemplated in the trade fields." The French representative replied that the urgent situation did not permit time for consultation.[120] In this case, as in others when the same claim has been made, neither a GATT working party nor any other international body will authoritatively assess the claim of emergency.[121] Consequently, the scope of the emergency exception is left to the familiar horizontal process of assertion and response, with many industrialized states attempting to broaden it as much as possible while most of the others try to restrict it.

Countervailing and antidumping duties are no less susceptible to prior consultation assertions than are many safeguard measures. Countervailing duties neutralize subsidies granted by a foreign government to its exporters or producers for export; antidumping duties erase the "margin of dumping" by increasing the price of imports offered at less than their normal value (in the usual case, less than their comparable price in the exporting country). GATT article VI permits both types of duty, subject to certain conditions. Prior consultation is not one of them, except when the importing country wishes to impose a countervailing or an antidumping duty to offset injury, not

[120]BISD 16th Supp. 57, 62, 63 (1968).

[121]This is often true even within a relatively cohesive trading association. *See* the discussion of the 1979 Icelandic import deposit scheme for furniture, introduced without warning in order "to avert the possibility of stockpiling," and notified after the event to the two European Free Trade Association Councils, 19th ANN. REP. OF THE EUROPEAN FREE TRADE ASSOCIATION 18–19 (1979).

in its own territory, but in some third country. In such third-country cases, a prior GATT waiver is required unless delay might cause damage difficult to repair.[122]

Although article VI is largely silent on prior consultation, that does not end the matter. In 1961 a GATT Group of Experts thought it "normal, and at least desirable," that a government investigating an alleged foreign subsidy enter into direct contact with the government of the exporting country.[123] The United States, which has begun far more countervailing duty proceedings than any other country, followed this procedure even before it became a party to the 1979 Subsidies / Countervailing Measures Code (discussed below). Its practice has been to notify the appropriate foreign embassy when a subsidy complaint is received, seeking help in determining the existence and magnitude of the alleged subsidy. This has had at least three purposes, two of which are self-serving. It has aided fact-finding and has permitted the U.S. government to apply some pressure toward removal of the subsidy, but it has also given the other government an opportunity to make its case. If a probable subsidy has been found and its amount tentatively determined, American officials have gone beyond talks with the embassy and have proposed the subsidy's removal. If those discussions (or pressure tactics) fail, and if U.S. statutory requirements have been met, a countervailing duty has been imposed.[124]

Prominent instances in which the United States has used essentially this procedure include the 1964–65 investigation of alleged Canadian subsidies on automotive parts, culminating in the Canadian-American Automotive Parts Agreement;[125] the 1972–73 investigation of Canadian investment incentives for

[122]GATT art. VI(6)(b)&(c).

[123]REPORT OF THE GATT GROUP OF EXPERTS, ANTIDUMPING AND COUNTERVAILING DUTIES 21 (1961).

[124]The description is based primarily on an interview with U.S. Treasury Department officials in charge of tariff affairs, June 27, 1975, though they did not characterize the talks as pressure tactics. The U.S. statutory requirements appear in 19 U.S.C. §§ 1671–1671f (Supp. III 1979).

In a few instances the United States has expressly promised to consult before taking countervailing duty action. *See* the agreements on cheese subsidies with the European Communities, Canada, Norway, and Sweden, in H.R. DOC. NO. 153, pt. 1, 96th Cong., 1st Sess. 417, 564, 572, 580 (1979). But contemporaneous U.S. agreements with other countries on cheese subsidies did not expressly promise to consult. *See id.* at 438 (Switzerland), 466 (Austria), 492 (Finland), 551 (Iceland), 556 (Portugal).

[125]*See* Butler, *Countervailing Duties and Export Subsidization: A Re-emerging Issue in International Trade,* 9 VA. J. INT'L L. 82, 131–32 (1969).

Michelin steel cord and tire plants, culminating in a countervailing duty;[126] the 1975 "cheese war" between the United States and the European Economic Community, culminating in a decision by the latter to eliminate subsidies on a range of cheeses competing with those produced in the United States and a decision by the United States not to impose countervailing duties on the remaining subsidized cheeses;[127] and investigations in 1975 and 1982 of various European aids to the steel industry, culminating in a finding in 1975 that there was no subsidy and in 1982 that a subsidy existed.[128] European export restraints forestalled the countervailing duty in 1982.

The European Communities also developed the equivalent of a prior consultation procedure before they adhered to the Subsidies / Countervailing Measures Code. Beginning in 1968, the Commission would notify representatives of the exporting country and the exporters and importers concerned whenever a countervailing duty was contemplated. They could submit information and could request a hearing. All relevant, nonconfidential information would be supplied to them. If they followed the prescribed procedure, a hearing would be held and the Commission would then decide whether a countervailing duty was warranted.[129] In politically sensitive cases, high-level consultations have been held with exporting-country officials to try to settle the issues, with countervailing duties or comparable import measures held out as last resorts.[130]

[126] Interview, *supra* note 124. *See also* Note, *The Michelin Decision: A Possible New Direction for U.S. Countervailing Duty Law,* 6 L. & POL'Y IN INT'L BUS. 237, 240 (1974). The Canadian government asserted, however, that the consultations were inadequate under GATT art. XXII(1). *See* 1973 CAN. ANN. REV. 235.

[127] *See* Financial Times, Apr. 10, 1975, at 6, col. 5; *id.,* Apr. 25, 1975, at 6, col. 2; 8 BULL. EUR. COMM., No. 4, at 60 (1975).

[128] *See* Financial Times, Oct. 7, 1975, at 6, col. 1; *id.,* Oct. 21, 1975, at 4, col. 8; N.Y. Times, June 11, 1982, at D1, col. 6; *id.,* June 12, 1982, at 1, col. 2.

[129] *See* Council Reg. 459/68/EEC, Apr. 5, 1968, arts. 10, 22, 25, in O.J. EUR. COMM. (spec. ed. 1968(I)) 80 (1972), *as amended,* Council Reg. 1681/79/EEC, Aug. 1, 1979, in 22 *id.* (No. L 196) 1 (1979); Commission Recommendation 77/329/ECSC, Apr. 15, 1977, arts. 11, 22, 25, in 20 *id.* (No. L 114) 6 (1977), *as amended, id.* (No. L 352) 13. When the Communities implemented the 1979 Subsidies/Countervailing Measures Code, these acts were superseded. *See* note 131 *infra.*

[130] For example, before the Commission authorized the U.K. to impose quotas against imports of indirectly subsidized U.S. synthetic fibers in February 1980, extensive negotiations were held with the U.S. government on the existence and possible amount of the subsidy, and on measures that might alleviate European concerns. *See* Financial Times, Oct. 19, 1979, at 20, col. 2; *id.,* Dec. 19, 1979, at 1, col. 7; *id.,* Jan. 28, 1980, at 1, col. 3; N.Y. Times, Feb. 19, 1980, at D11, col. 1 (city ed.). The U.K. ultimately acted

Drawing on these procedures, the Subsidies / Countervailing Measures Code emanating from the Tokyo Round negotiations requires states parties to afford interested exporting Code parties access to nonconfidential information and reasonable opportunities for consultation before and during any countervailing duty investigation. The consultation, however, must not prevent the investigation from proceeding expeditiously. The United States and the European Communities have implemented the Code in their countervailing duty procedures.[131]

The procedural norm for antidumping duties is similar. In 1961 the GATT Group of Experts recommended that all interested parties be given a hearing before an antidumping duty is imposed and thought it desirable that the government of the interested country be advised beforehand, whenever practicable.[132] These views were later incorporated into the 1967 International Anti-Dumping Code which, like the later Tokyo Round Anti-Dumping Code, requires governments of exporting countries and interested private parties to be notified and given nonconfidential information regarding an investigation. They are to have full opportunity to defend their interests. The importing state, however, may apply provisional antidumping duties immediately.[133]

These procedures are followed by the United States and the European Communities, which together account for most of the antidumping investigations to date. In practice, the consultations usually are held with interested importers and exporters rather than with the foreign government, unless the

under GATT art. XIX, rather than art. VI.

Similar negotiations were held regarding prospective Community-wide measures. *See* Financial Times, July 23, 1980, at 14, col. 5; 13 BULL. EUR. COMM., No. 12, at 82 (1980).

[131] *See* Agreement on Interpretation and Application of Articles VI, XVI and XXIII of the General Agreement on Tariffs and Trade, Apr. 12, 1979, art. 3, BISD 26th Supp. 56 (1980). For the relevant U.S. implementing procedures, see 19 C.F.R. §§ 355.25–355.44 (1981). For the European procedures, see Council Reg. 3017/79/EEC, Dec. 20, 1979, art. 7, in 22 O.J. EUR. COMM. (No. L 339) 1 (1979); Commission Recommendation 3018/79/ECSC, Dec. 21, 1979, art. 7, in *id.* 15.

[132] Report of the GATT Group of Experts, *supra* note 123, at 17–18.

[133] International Anti-Dumping Code, June 30, 1967, arts. 6, 10, 19 U.S.T. 4348, T.I.A.S. No. 6431, *reprinted in* 6 INT'L LEGAL MATERIALS 920 (1967). The 1979 Tokyo Round Code supersedes the 1967 Code for the 1979 Code's parties (including the multistate European Communities and most other major industrialized countries). *See* Agreement on Implementation of Article VI, Apr. 12, 1979, arts. 6, 16(5), BISD 26th Supp. 171 (1980).

investigation involves a product from a state-trading country.[134] One can find occasional instances in which the consultations have been inadequate, as when the European Commission in 1977 refused to disclose to Japanese bearing producers how it arrived at its estimated margin of dumping.[135] In the usual case, however, the dumping investigations result in no new duty, often as a result of a price undertaking on the part of the producers.[136]

In late 1977 the United States formulated a new "reference price" plan for steel imports—setting minimum reference prices for several types of steel, with antidumping duties to be levied on imports offered for sale at lower prices. This did not involve any immediate imposition of duties, but it was nevertheless preceded by discussions with Japan and the European Communities, whose exporters would be most seriously affected. In addition, U.S. officials gave assurances that the reference prices would be worked out in consultation with foreign producers.[137] The European Coal and Steel Community followed with a similar plan of its own, but applied it only on a temporary basis while orderly marketing agreements were being negotiated with foreign suppliers.[138] It is not clear that foreign interests were consulted before the European plan was adopted.

In the area of government procurement, protective measures traditionally have taken a nontariff form. For years, the Buy

[134]The U.S. procedure is set out in 19 C.F.R. §§ 353.35–353.57 (1981). If the proceeding is initiated by the administration (rather than by private parties) and involves imports from a party to the Tokyo Round Anti-Dumping Code, the regulations require an opportunity for intergovernmental consultations.

The former U.S. practice was described to the author in interviews with U.S. Treasury Department officials, June 27, 1975. In the case of Japanese products, officials from the interested government agency, the Ministry for International Trade and Industry (MITI), have normally participated in the investigation.

The EEC procedure is set out in the instruments cited, note 131 *supra*. The U.S. and EEC procedures require hearings if properly requested by an interested party.

As in countervailing duty cases, government-to-government consultations are held when political sensitivities run high. *See, e.g.,* Financial Times, Aug. 1, 1980, at 4, col. 5 (U.S.-EEC talks concerning antidumping action brought by U.S. Steel).

A somewhat different procedure appears in the Andean Pact, *supra* note 100, art. 77. It involves prior consultation with, and authorization from, the Pact's three-member Board.

[135]*See* Van Bael, *Ten Years of EEC Anti-Dumping Enforcement*, 13 J. World Trade L. 395, 404–07 (1979).

[136]*Id.* at 397.

[137]*See* N.Y. Times, Nov. 8, 1977, at 45, col. 6; Washington Post, Nov. 16, 1977, at D9, col. 1; Financial Times, Nov. 30, 1977, at 6, cols. 7–8.

[138]*See* Financial Times, Dec. 20, 1977, at 1, col. 7, and Dec. 21, 1977, at 4, col. 1.

American Act gave a preference to domestic suppliers of a wide variety of goods procured by the federal government. Other industrialized countries have followed similar practices. This formidable nontariff trade barrier now has been lowered substantially for parties to the Government Procurement Code negotiated in the Tokyo Round. The Code's basic principle is that suppliers in all states parties must be given equal opportunity with domestic suppliers to obtain major government procurement contracts. Developing countries are permitted some exemptions, and there is a provision permitting any party to modify, in exceptional circumstances, its original list of government entities subject to the Code. In these cases, however, the Code specifies a procedure amounting to prior consultation with, and / or approval by, other interested parties or the international Committee on Government Procurement.[139]

Finally, there is an interesting case study involving protective measures against "invisible" imports. In 1975 the Canadian government introduced a bill in parliament to eliminate tax deductions for Canadian companies advertising on U.S. television stations. The purpose was to boost the Canadian television industry. Consultations were held with the U.S. government while the bill was pending, but they did not produce agreement, and the bill was enacted.[140]

To summarize this section, firm expectations have been established requiring consultation with major exporting interests before an importing state adopts a measure that will adversely affect specific, identifiable imports in the short run, if the importing state somehow has led exporters to expect a continuation of the status quo (by giving a tariff commitment, by establishing a quota, or even by a previous course of action). There is an exception if an emergency requires immediate action. The norm applies to safeguard measures (whether within GATT article XIX or not), countervailing and antidumping duties, and significant changes in "buy national" practices. It may apply even to measures against invisible imports. The "emergency" exception is the Achilles' heel, with importing states taking advantage of it liberally. The exception's contours have

[139]*See* Agreement on Government Procurement, Apr. 12, 1979, art. III, paras. 4 & 5, and art. IX, para. 5, BISD 26th Supp. 33 (1980).

[140]*See* Kindred & Biggs, *supra* note 116, at 117–18. *See also id.* at 118–19, concerning repeal of Canadian tax deductions for the expense of advertising in American magazines.

yet to be well defined, but in any event a government invoking it would be under a duty to do so in good faith.

3. Measures to Encourage Exports

Sometimes governments encourage exports for balance-of-payments reasons, sometimes to assist an export sector of the economy. The encouragement can have effects unwanted by importing states and by competing exporting states, particularly if it takes the form of a subsidy. This subsection will examine the interest of the importing state in having its viewpoint considered before an export-related subsidy is granted. The interests of competing exporting states will be discussed in subsection 6, below.

GATT article XVI requires each contracting party to notify the plenary body of any subsidy that directly or indirectly increases exports of any product from, or reduces imports of any product into, its territory. If it is determined that serious prejudice to the interests of any other contracting party is caused or threatened, consultations must be held on request to discuss the possibility of limiting the subsidy.[141] But article XVI does not require the notification or the consultation to precede the subsidy.

Compliance with even the postsubsidy notification obligation has been poor.[142] As a result, the Subsidies / Countervailing Measures Code negotiated in the Tokyo Round contains strengthened provisions on subsidy notification and consultation.[143] Like article XVI, however, these do not require anything to be done before a subsidy is granted.

Despite the lack of a treaty obligation, state practice could supply a prior consultation norm. In this instance, however, it does not. For example, in 1969 and 1971 Canadian federal, provincial, and local governments granted investment incentives (production subsidies) for the construction of export-oriented Michelin steel cord and tire plants in Nova Scotia. Although the plants would market a substantial percentage of their production in the United States, where they would compete with

[141] GATT, *supra* note 46, art. XVI(1).

[142] *See* Evans, *Subsidies and Countervailing Duties in the GATT: Present Law and Future Prospects,* 3 INT'L TRADE L.J. 211, 229–31 (1977).

[143] Agreement on Interpretation and Application of Articles VI, XVI, and XXIII, *supra* note 131, arts. 7, 12.

U.S. producers, there was no prior consultation with U.S. authorities. When the Canadian Minister of Regional Economic Expansion was asked in the House of Commons about the lack of consultation, he replied, "I think it would be quite improper to ask another country whether we should go ahead with plans that we think are legitimate and in the interests of our own country."[144]

The record is the same when it comes to outright export subsidies. The United States did not consult in the GATT before its Domestic International Sales Corporation (DISC) legislation went into effect in January 1972.[145] Under the legislation, a DISC received a subsidy in the form of a special income tax deferral on export sales. Similarly, before the European Community reintroduced a suspended cheese export subsidy in February 1975, it did no more than notify the United States—a major cheese market and competing producer—that it was about to do so.[146]

4. Export Restraints

The GATT prohibits quantitative restrictions on exports, but riddles the rule with exceptions allowing export restraints related to such things as shortages of foodstuffs or other essential products, protection of national cultural property, conservation of resources, implementation of price stabilization programs, husbanding of (nonessential) products in short supply, and protection of national security.[147] It is silent as to the procedure to be followed when a party invokes an exception.

The United States occasionally has imposed export controls on items in short domestic supply. The Export Administration Act neither requires nor contemplates prior consultation with U.S. trading partners in such cases.[148] Nevertheless, the government's policy is to consult interested trading partners before short-supply export controls are imposed, unless there is a speculative market in the commodity being controlled. For example, the United States consulted interested governments when it

[144] *Canadian Practice in Int'l Law,* 1973, in 1974 CAN. Y.B. INT'L L. 304, 322.

[145] *See* Jackson, *The Jurisprudence of International Trade: The DISC Case in GATT,* 72 AM. J. INT'L L. 747, 760–61 (1978); BISD 23d Supp. 98 (1977).

[146] Interview with U.S. Treasury Department officials, June 27, 1975.

[147] GATT, *supra* note 46, arts. XI, XX, XXI.

[148] *See* 50 U.S.C. app. § 2406 (Supp. III 1979).

considered export controls on hides and skins in the early 1970s and decided not to impose the controls. It did not, however, consult Japan before it imposed controls on the export of soybeans in 1973, because of the active market in soybean futures and the consequent risk of speculation.[149] Japan, which was relying on U.S. soybeans as foodstuffs, complained about the lack of consultation.[150]

In addition, short-supply export controls are sometimes applied by the European Communities. As in the case of the United States, the governing legislation does not contemplate consultations with those whose supplies are curtailed.[151] Available records do not reveal a consultation policy akin to that of the United States.

There is little evidence of consistent consultation practice when export controls are imposed for reasons other than short supply. Clearly there is no established practice of consulting a potential adversary or a politically unstable government before deciding to withhold militarily useful goods from it. Thus, the United States apparently did not seek the official Soviet view before it decided to deny an export license for a sophisticated computer system to the Soviet Union in 1977,[152] and it kept its own counsel before it denied a Pakistani request to buy A-7 attack bombers in the same year.[153]

When the export control denies sensitive materials to political allies, the picture is less clear. In the spring of 1975, the United States Nuclear Regulatory Commission withheld export licenses for nuclear equipment and fuels while it reviewed its procedures on security in transit and in processing. At that time, the European Communities were entirely dependent on the United States for highly enriched uranium and were 60 percent dependent on it for the less enriched variety. The Commissioner responsible for energy policy immediately dispatched an aide-mémoire to the United States, complaining about the lack of consultation. The U.S. reply, which apparently did not attempt to justify the prior silence, failed to satisfy the Community.[154]

[149] Interview with U.S. State Department official, June 26, 1975.

[150] *See* J. COMMERCE, June 29, 1973, at 7, cols. 2–5.

[151] *See* Council Reg. 2603/69/EEC, Dec. 20, 1969, in O.J. EUR. COMM. (spec. ed. 1969(II)) 590 (1972).

[152] *See* N.Y. Times, June 24, 1977, at A3, col. 1.

[153] *See* L.A. Times, June 4, 1977, pt. I, at 12, col. 1.

[154] *See* Drozdiak, *US-EC Uranium Relations*, EUROPEAN COMMUNITY, June 1975, at 8–10.

In the fall of 1973 the Canadian government made two decisions affecting its export of oil to the United States (then at a level of 1.2 million barrels a day). One was a tentative decision to extend the western oil pipeline from its terminal in Toronto to Montreal, which would eventually channel to eastern Canada 50 percent of the western oil that was being exported to the United States. There was no prior consultation. Nor did the Canadian government solicit American opinions as it progressed toward a final decision, though it did on occasion receive unsolicited views.[155] At about the same time, Canada imposed the first of an escalating series of export charges on crude oil to raise revenue for OPEC oil imports to the eastern provinces. Canada notified the United States, but did not give it a chance to argue before the first charge was levied. Although there were frequent consultations in the ensuing months, some of them preceding hikes in the export charge, the Canadian government apparently felt no obligation to consult before each increase.[156]

In 1974 and 1975, Canada increased the price of natural gas exported to the United States and reduced the quantity of oil and natural gas exported. In each case there was no consultation before the initial decision, but the United States pressed for, and obtained, consultations before subsequent, implementing decisions were made. The United States particularly wanted to influence the implementing decision on the extent of the natural gas cutback, since rigidities in the gas distribution system made it difficult to deliver gas from other sources to cover a shortage from any given source. The Canadian government was sensitive to this need for consultation.[157]

In 1979 the President of the United States and the Prime Minister of Canada agreed to establish a bilateral consultative mechanism, to function at least to the end of 1979, which would "develop options for decision by each government" regarding oil supplies and oil exchanges, the possibilities for liquefied and

[155] Interview with U.S. State Department officials, June 30, 1975.

[156] *Id.;* discussion with the Canadian Deputy Minister of Energy, Mines, and Resources, Apr. 25, 1974.

[157] The information in this paragraph comes (piecemeal) from interviews with officials of the U.S. Treasuty Department and the U.S. State Department, June 25 and 26, 1975; N.Y. Times, Sept. 21, 1974, at 1, col. 5, and 36, col. 7 (city ed.); *id.*, Nov. 23, 1974, at 1, col. 2, and 48, col. 3 (city ed.); *id.*, Dec. 5, 1974, at 8, col. 1 (city ed.); *id.*, July 17, 1975, at 1, col. 7 (city ed.); Toronto Globe and Mail, July 18, 1975, at B10, cols. 7–8; *United States–Canadian Relations: Hearings Before a Subcomm. of the House Comm. on International Relations*, 94th Cong., 2d Sess. 15 (1976).

synthetic natural gas exports to the United States, "and other energy-related tasks as may be appropriate."[158] This quite arguably would commit Canada to use the mechanism for consultations before making even basic decisions to restrict energy exports to the United States while the mechanism is in force, though it probably does not imply any commitment regarding price increases.

States enjoying oligopolistic power over export markets do not feel obliged to consult consumer states before raising prices. Thus, although various representatives of OPEC states have discussed prospective oil price increases with consumer states from time to time, there is no evidence that they felt under any legal compulsion to do so. In fact, at the 1977 North-South economic conference, the OPEC states adamantly resisted Western pressure to create a consultative mechanism for future oil price increases.[159] Similarly, though without comparable political motivations, Brazil has never recognized any need to consult before increasing coffee prices or imposing new coffee export taxes.[160]

These examples are sufficient to show that there is no overall duty to consult before a government restricts exports or increases their prices.[161] The closer the economic and political ties between the exporting and importing states and the greater the dependence of the importing state on the product, the stronger the argument is in favor of a duty to consult at least as to the manner in which a basic export control decision is to be implemented. This explains the Japanese expectation regarding American soybean exports, the American expectation regarding Canadian energy export restrictions, and the norms developed among some close neighbors when they establish a liberal trade regime among themselves.[162] As the OPEC case shows, however, the mere dependence of importing states on the con-

[158] *See* the Joint Communique, Mar. 3, 1979, 15 Weekly Comp. of Pres. Doc., No. 10, at 381–82 (1979).

[159] *See* N.Y. Times, June 3, 1977, at A1, col. 6 (city ed.). OPEC is the Organization of Petroleum Exporting Countries.

[160] *See, e.g.,* Financial Times, Nov. 23, 1976, at 27, col. 2.

[161] That there is no such duty, but that there should be (as to export restrictions), see C. Bergsten, Completing the GATT: Towards New International Rules to Govern Export Controls 27–28 (1974). The Tokyo Round did not produce rules on export restraints.

[162] *See* the intra-Community consultation provision in Council Reg. 2603/69/EEC, *supra* note 151, art. 8; Treaty Establishing the Caribbean Community, *supra* note 57, art. 18(5); Trade Agreement Between South Africa and Malawi, *supra* note 95, art. 12.

trolled product is not enough to create a binding consultation norm.

5. Trade Measures for Conservation or Environmental Purposes

Since 1969 the United States has had legislation restricting imports of endangered or threatened fish and wildlife species. The legislation was revised in 1973. In its original and revised forms, it has required the Executive Branch to consult interested foreign governments before designating restricted species.[163] When each bill was in the committee stage, the State Department urged that the listing of species be preceded by international consultations in order to avoid complaints from foreign governments.[164] Although the State Department stopped short of saying that the United States would be under an international duty to consult, it clearly believed that governments interested in harvesting the species would have legitimate complaints if the United States closed its market without listening to their viewpoints.

As events transpired, a list of endangered species was drawn up multilaterally in 1973, when the Convention on International Trade in Endangered Species of Wild Fauna and Flora was drafted at a conference attended by eighty states. Under the Convention, a party may import designated species only if they are accompanied by export certificates, which may be issued only under stipulated conditions. This is so whether the export is from a party or a nonparty to the Convention.[165] Since only twenty-five of the eighty states originally signed the Convention, some states were imposing their wills on others insofar as the nonsigners wished to continue exporting the designated species to them. They did so in consultation with the fifty-five nonsigners, whose views were considered in preparing the list. But they did not make it clear, in the Convention or otherwise,

[163] *See* the Endangered Species Conservation Act of 1969, 16 U.S.C. § 668cc-3(a)(1970), repealed by the Endangered Species Conservation Act of 1973, 16 U.S.C. § 1533(b)(1) (1976 & Supp. III 1979).

[164] *See Endangered Species: Hearings Before a Subcomm. of the Senate Comm. on Commerce*, 91st Cong., 1st Sess. 17, 18 (1969); *Predatory Mammals and Endangered Species: Hearings Before a Subcomm. of the House Comm. on Merchant Marine and Fisheries*, 92d Cong., 2d Sess. 15, 16 (1972).

[165] Convention on International Trade in Endangered Species of Wild Fauna and Flora, Mar. 3, 1973, arts. 2–6, 10, 27 U.S.T. 1087, T.I.A.S. No. 8249.

that they considered prior consultation mandatory, and it is not evident that all parties consider it so in practice.[166]

United States legislation requires individuals and firms to notify the appropriate federal regulatory agency before exporting hazardous products or substances, including toxic wastes. The agency then notifies the government that is to receive the exports, allowing it to make an informed decision on whether or not to permit their entry.[167] Although the legislation does not expressly require consultation, it serves a consultative purpose by relinquishing the decision-making authority to the foreign government while enabling it to receive the information it needs. Nevertheless, the U.S. legislation does not reflect an international norm regarding the export of hazardous products or substances. At most, it may presage the development of state practice relating to the export of toxic wastes, since other countries have shown some interest in emulating the United States only as to such wastes, and only as to them does the United States still regard the notification requirement as important.[168]

6. Trade Externalities

This book is about externalities—those effects on others that are not necessarily weighed at full value when governments make self-interested decisions. This subsection will consider what might be called second-order trade externalities. These are the indirect effects on third states of governmental decisions that are designed to affect directly the decision making state's trade with another state or states. For example, when state *A* grants preferential tariff treatment to state *B*, it indirectly may make it harder for state *C*'s exports to penetrate state *A*'s market; or

[166]Article 14(1) of the Convention, *supra* note 165, permits parties to enact stricter domestic measures than the Convention requires, and does not mention prior consultation. The British Endangered Species (Import and Export) Act 1976, ch. 72,§ 3(c), gives the Secretary of State authority to add to the British endangered species list, without requiring prior international consultation.

[167]*See* 15 U.S.C. § 2611(b) (1976); *id.* §§ 1202(c), 1273(d), 2067(b) (Supp. II 1978) (toxic substances, flammable fabrics, hazardous substances, consumer products). *See also* H.R. Rep. No. 1164, 95th Cong., 2d Sess. 7 (1978), for pertinent legislative history. On hazardous wastes, see also Interview with Douglas A. Costle, 6 Envt'l Pol'y & L. 88, 89 (1980). The Governing Council of the U.N. Environment Programme has urged member states to adopt essentially the U.S. practice regarding toxic wastes. *See* Report of the Governing Council, 35 U.N. GAOR, Supp. (No. 25) 119–20, U.N. Doc. A/35/25 (1980).

[168]*See* Washington Post, Sept. 9, 1981, at A1, col. 1.

when state *A* subsidizes its exports to state *B*, it indirectly may make it harder for state *C*'s exports to compete in state *B*'s market. We have already considered whether state *A* must consult state *B* when its measure is directed at trade with *B*. The question now is whether it must consult state *C*.

Most industrialized countries have granted tariff preferences to a variety of goods from developing countries as a form of development aid. These may be generalized preferences, available to all developing countries, or specialized ones available only to some. In addition, preferences are inherent in the customs union and the free trade area, involving the elimination of tariffs among member states without eliminating them as to the outside world. All of these preferences may harm exporting interests in nonpreferred states, and the free trade area may also harm import-competing interests in some of the preferred member states. This could happen when one member state reduces its tariff rate on some primary or intermediate products from outside the area, but others do not. The first state could then use those products to manufacture finished products less expensively than the others, and could export them to the others free of any duty. Such trade deflection would not happen in a customs union, since the external tariffs of all member states would be uniform.

Preferential tariff treatment not associated with a genuine customs union or free trade area runs afoul of the most-favored-nation clause in the GATT and other trade agreements. Consequently, GATT parties wishing to grant such treatment have had to invoke a clause permitting the plenary body to waive any GATT obligation. The early waivers for tariff preferences were given before the applicant state applied the preference (thus constituting the waiver process as a form of prior consultation) and required notification to GATT and an opportunity for consultation before the granting of any further preference not expressly authorized by the waiver.[169] But the 1971 GATT waiver for a generalized system of preferences requires notification and an opportunity for consultation only after a preference has been introduced or modified.[170] The Tokyo Round Framework text on preferences is similar.[171] Ap-

[169] *See* the waivers granted to the U.K. and Australia, respectively, in BISD 3d Supp. 21, 25 (1955) and 14th Supp. 23, 25 (1966).

[170] See BISD 18th Supp. 24, 25–26 (1972).

[171] Decision on Differential and More Favourable Treatment, Reciprocity and Fuller Participation of Developing Countries, Nov. 28, 1979, BISD 26th Supp. 203 (1980).

parently, preference-giving parties have sometimes consulted interested nonpreferred states before widening their preferences, although there is no evidence that they have felt obliged to do so in the absence of a treaty.[172]

GATT article XXIV(7) sets forth procedural requirements for parties "deciding to enter into a customs union or free trade area, or an interim agreement leading to the formation of such a union or area." Any such party is to notify GATT and make relevant information available. If the plenary body finds that the agreement is not likely to result in the formation of a customs union or free trade area within a reasonable time, it is to make recommendations that the parties are required to follow if they are to maintain the agreement or put it into force, as the case may be. An interim agreement must include a plan for the establishment of the customs union or free trade area; any substantial change in the plan must be communicated to GATT, which may request consultations if the change seems likely to jeopardize or delay attainment of the goal.[173]

Any correlation between article XXIV(7) and actual practice is slight indeed. Although several agreements have been submitted, none have immediately created a customs union or free trade area, and only a few could reasonably be expected to lead to one. Despite this, no disapproving recommendations have been made.[174]

Nevertheless, preferential trade agreements often are submitted under article XXIV(7), GATT working parties are appointed to review them, and informal consultations are held.[175] These consultations are both written and oral, consisting of questionnaires answered by notifying parties and discussions at meetings of the working parties. It is another question, however, whether these consultations are held at a time when they could significantly influence the parties' decisions. Article XXIV(7) does not require notification or consultation before an agree-

[172]When the European Economic Community was considering an extension of its generalized preferences to new products in 1974, it apparently consulted at least the United States and Canada, and perhaps Australia and New Zealand. See EIGHTH GEN'L REP., *supra* note 114, at 226–29, 257, 259; 7 BULL. EUR. COMM., No. 9, at 58 (1974).

[173]GATT, *supra* note 46, art. XXIV(7)(a)–(c).

[174]*See* J. JACKSON, *supra* note 51, at 605. The BISD supplements contain the reports of working parties appointed under art. XXIV(7), but they are devoid of any recommendations.

[175]*See* Dam, *Regional Economic Arrangements and the GATT: The Legacy of a Misconception,* 30 U. CHI. L. REV. 615, 661 (1963); J. JACKSON, *supra* note 51, at 605–07.

ment is signed, and in practice notification always comes afterward (though often before it enters into force). Virtually all notified agreements must be considered interim agreements at best, since they do not immediately create customs unions or free trade areas within the meaning of article XXIV and only a few contain the mechanisms needed to create them over a period of time.[176] One might think, then, that the GATT consultations would be in time to influence the ensuing final agreements. The trouble is that there seldom are any ensuing final agreements, so the crucial time for effective consultation is before it is too late to make substantial changes in the interim agreements. Even when GATT consultation occurs between the interim agreement's signing and its entry into force, there is little to suggest that it ever results in an amendment to the signed agreement or otherwise influences imminent decisions.[177]

To deal with the trade deflection problem within a true free trade area, the parties normally devise a prior consultation system. The paradigm is the European Free Trade Association, which requires each member state to notify the EFTA Council not less than thirty days before a planned tariff reduction takes effect, if practicable, and to consider any representations by other member states that the reduction is likely to lead to a deflection of trade.[178]

Preferential trade agreements that reduce, but do not eliminate, tariff barriers among the treaty partners typically contain consultation provisions like those in free trade area agreements. Thus, the European Communities' preferential agreements with other Western European countries plus Iceland and Israel contain clauses modeled on the EFTA provision above.[179] The Lomé Convention among the EEC and the associated African, Caribbean, and Pacific states requires the EEC to consult, on re-

[176] J. JACKSON, *supra* note 51, at 605–06.

[177] Reports of working party consultations under art. XXIV(7), with relevant dates, can be found in all BISD supplements from the 18th (1972) through at least the 26th (1980).

[178] EFTA Convention, *supra* note 56, art. 5(4). Virtually the same provision appeared in the Agreement Establishing the Caribbean Free Trade Association, *supra* note 57, art. 6(4). The latter agreement has been superseded by the Treaty Establishing the Caribbean Community, *supra* note 57, which provides for a common market in which trade deflection would not occur.

[179] *See* the EEC agreements with Austria, art. 12; Iceland, art. 12; Portugal, art. 13; Sweden, art. 12; Switzerland, art. 12; Norway, art. 12; Finland, art. 12; and Israel, art. 6, note 94 *supra*.

quest, when it envisages a preferential agreement with third states.[180]

Current EEC agreements with Middle Eastern states, other than Israel, contain clauses that do not clearly require the consultations to precede the tariff reduction whenever possible, but they could reasonably be so construed. These clauses state that when the external reduction has "a direct and particular effect on the functioning of the Agreement, appropriate consultations shall be held within the Cooperation Council at the request of the other Contracting Party so that the interests of the Contracting Parties may be taken into consideration."[181] It would be difficult to take the interests of the other party into consideration if the tariff-reducing party consults only after the reduction has gone into force, unless the consultations deal with new trade barriers between the parties to counteract any deflection—but of course such barriers would run counter to the goals of the agreement, and therefore presumably are not the primary focus of the consultation provision.[182]

Sometimes a government stimulates imports of primary or intermediate products, not by lowering tariffs, but by subsidizing the imports. This practice could give that government a competitive advantage in the manufacture of goods made with those products; it could also drive up the price and reduce the quantity of those products to other importing states. Such was the case when the U.S. Department of Energy decided in 1979 to provide a five-dollar-a-barrel subsidy for imported heating oil. Other members of the International Energy Agency complained that they had not even been notified in advance.[183] The United States did not publicly confess error, but neither did it attempt to justify its lack of notification. Instead, it argued that it was just trying to assure itself of a fair share of heating oil for the coming winter. Consequently, the incident probably should be viewed as one in which members of a concerned

[180] Second Lomé Convention, *supra* note 96, arts. 2(2)(d), 16(4).

[181] *See* The EEC agreements with Tunisia, art. 48; Algeria, art. 47; Morocco, art. 49; Egypt, art. 42; Jordan, art. 39; Syria, art. 40; Lebanon, art. 40, note 94 *supra.*

[182] Under the Fisheries Jurisdiction Cases, 1974 I.C.J. 3 & 175, a duty to take account of another state's interests implies a duty to consult with it when proposed action could affect those interests. *See* chapter VII, section C *infra.*

Some non-EEC preferential agreements do contemplate new internal trade barriers and require consultations before they are erected. *See, e.g.,* the South Africa–Malawi and India-Egypt-Yugoslavia agreements, *supra* note 95.

[183] *See* N.Y. Times, June 1, 1979, at D2, col. 3 (city ed.).

international body asserted that another member at least must notify them (presumably so they could discuss the matter with it) before breaking ranks in a way that would harm their interests, and the "respondent" state failed effectively to rebut the assertion.

Another form of trade deflection can occur when a government protects its producers from competing imports that are then likely to be diverted to other markets, creating the same difficulties for producers selling there. The GATT does not require prior consultation with governments whose territories are likely to receive any diverted trade, and state practice is inconclusive at best.

For example, when the United States was drawing up its trigger pricing scheme in late 1977 for antidumping duties on steel, it discussed its intentions in the OECD as well as bilaterally with Japan, the European Communities, and perhaps Canada. The primary thrust of these discussions, however, was to assure exporting states that their interests would be considered.[184] At some point, however, consultations were held with Canada regarding possible deflection to Canadian internal and export markets.[185] To give another example, in late 1975 the European Communities persuaded Japan to limit its steel exports to them, and later explored similar restraints with other supplier states. This could have diverted Japanese and other steel to the U.S. market. Apparently the Communities' Commission did not consult the United States before acting, though the latter did press its concerns on the Communities and Japan later.[186] When the roles were reversed in 1981, with Japan agreeing to restrict its automobile exports to the United States, the Commission complained that it had not been consulted. The United States acknowledged that there had been ineffective consultation, but did not concede that it had violated any obligation.[187] A prior consultation duty may be germinating in these situations, but it does not yet exist as customary law.[188]

[184] *See* text at note 137 *supra.*

[185] *See* Financial Times, Feb. 22, 1978, at 5, col. 5.

[186] *See World Steel Trade: Current Trends and Structural Problems: Hearing Before a Subcomm. of the House Comm. on Ways and Means,* 95th Cong., 1st Sess. 29, 126, 134–35, 137–38 (1977) (hereinafter cited as *Hearing on World Steel Trade).*

[187] *See* Financial Times, May 8, 1981, at 20, col. 5; *id.,* May 14, 1981, at 4, col. 5.

[188] A proposed GATT Safeguards Code would include a right of third countries to be consulted concerning possible trade diversion from safeguard action by others. At this writing the Code had not been agreed to, and its negotiating history suggests that

Yet another form of second-order trade externality concerns the effect on already-preferred countries of a widening of import preferences to include new exporting states. There is some indication that preference-granting states feel compelled to consult the preferred states in such cases, if the number of preferred states to be consulted is manageable.[189] The latter condition implies that they would not feel compelled to consult all beneficiaries of a generalized system of preferences if, for example, a new state emerges and is added to the list of beneficiaries.

Second-order externalities on the export side could stem from practices as commonplace as government advice to exporters, as well as from outright subsidies. There is no consistent practice of consulting other exporting states before a government conducts an export promotion drive not involving direct subsidies. This appears to be so even when the export promotion effort extends to trade concession negotiations with importing states, at least until those negotiations get down to specifics.[190] Even when they do get specific, probably no duty exists to consult other exporting states unless there is a real likelihood that exports of goods that are major foreign exchange earners for a particular state will be displaced and there is a special relationship between it and the export promoting state. The point is illustrated by the United States' reluctance to commit itself to consult Latin American countries before it adopts any measure

the prospective parties did not regard themselves as under any obligation absent such an agreement. *See* 23rd ANN. REP. OF THE PRESIDENT ON THE TRADE AGREEMENTS PROGRAM, 1978, at 36–37 (1979).

[189]The United States has allocated meat import quotas among exporting states, giving them preferences in the large U.S. market over nonquota states, and has pledged that allocations to new entrants will be subject to consultation with existing supplier states. *See* HOUSE COMM. ON WAYS & MEANS, TRADE AGREEMENTS ACT OF 1979, H.R. REP. No. 317, 96th Cong., 1st. Sess. 144 (1979); *see also* H.R. DOC. No. 153, pt. 1, *supra* note 124, at 460, 510 (pledges to New Zealand and Australia), and *id.* at 433 (comparable pledge to Switzerland concerning cheese quotas).

Another example is provided by the extensive consultations within the European Communities before new preferential trade agreements are negotiated, and the European Commission's care to negotiate such agreements virtually simultaneously with states having competing export interests. Even in the instance of the EEC-Israeli agreement, which was signed before similar EEC agreements were signed with Arab states, there were simultaneous negotiations. *See* N.Y. Times, May 12, 1975, at 1, col. 5 (city ed.).

[190]Thus, for example, the United States felt no need to consult Canada before mounting an effort in 1971 to obtain trade concessions from countries that imported similar products from the U.S. and Canada. *See* N.Y. Times, July 10, 1974, at 11, col. 1 (city ed.).

that might adversely affect their exports to third countries,[191] tempered by its extensive consultations with Caribbean countries while it negotiated the removal of British import quotas on U.S. semitropical products that were important foreign exchange earners for the Caribbean states.[192] Clearly, the United States was sensitive to its special relationship with the far smaller, geographically proximate Caribbean countries.

In a comparable situation, Australia demanded consultations with the European Community—and even threatened trade retaliation if the discussions proved unsatisfactory—when the Community's 1980 decision to include lamb in its heavily subsidized common agricultural policy threatened displacement of Australian lamb exports to third countries (as well as reduction of lamb imports into the Community). Community officials, sensitive to the economic and political ties to Australia, entered into give-and-take negotiations.[193]

A particularly controversial form of export stimulant has been the officially sponsored export credit. The governments of virtually all industrialized nonsocialist countries provide some type of export credit, usually with repayment periods and interest rates better than those available in the market. There is a strong tendency for these governments to compete with each other, offering ever-greater subsidies in the form of credits in order to support their major exporting industries and bring in foreign exchange. To try to control these competitive subsidies, OECD states began in 1974 to negotiate common export credit terms beyond which they normally would not go. Some general ground rules were agreed upon in 1976. They were refined in 1978, when twenty-two OECD states joined in the Arrangement on Guidelines for Officially Supported Export Credits.[194]

The Arrangement is a set of guidelines, rather than a formal treaty, applying to officially supported export credits with repayment terms of two years or more. It covers the participating states' exports of all goods except military equipment, agricultural commodities, aircraft, nuclear power plants, and certain

[191] *See* note 106 and accompanying text *supra*.

[192] *See The Trade Reform Act of 1973: Hearings Before the Senate Comm. on Finance*, 93d Cong., 2d Sess., pt. 1, at 212–13 (1974).

[193] *See* Financial Times, July 21, 1980, at 3, col. 1. For an instance in which Canada demanded to be heard regarding possible U.S. displacement of Canadian exports to Japan, see *id.*, Dec. 8, 1977, at 7, col. 1.

[194] OECD Arrangement on Guidelines for Officially Supported Export Credits, Feb. 22, 1978, OECD Doc. TD/Consensus/78.4 (1st revision) (1978).

ships. It sets forth maximum repayment periods and minimum interest rates, as well as normal installment repayment practices, with the permissible repayment periods and interest rates becoming more lenient for poorer importing countries. There has been much disagreement among the participants regarding the proper repayment periods and interest rates, and these items have been changed at various times to reflect changing economic conditions.

Whatever the repayment periods and interest rates have been at any given time, the arrangement recognized (until it was redrawn in July 1982) that there might be some deviations from its terms and set forth a prior notification and discussion procedure for all deviations except certain well-defined ones.[195] For the latter, either prior notification (to allow other participants to match the terms) or prompt postaction notification was sufficient. The net effect was that the participating states—all the industrialized nonsocialist states except Austria, Iceland, New Zealand, and Turkey—pledged to consult on request, before deviating from the norm (except within specified limits) for export credits on all products except those often supported to achieve goals that are at least as political or social as they are economic (military equipment and agricultural commodities) or products so expensive that special repayment terms were to be offered.[196] A problem arose, however, because participants often did not give notification until they had committed themselves by signing a contract or a letter of intent.[197]

The OECD Arrangement does not apply to such export-related programs as insurance against inflation and exchange risks, offered by some European governments to protect their exporters against profit reductions from inflation or exchange rate depreciation between the time of contracting and the date of payment. When the United Kingdom initiated its inflation

[195] *Id.* para. 9. The relevant language was, "If a Participant intends to take the initiative to support terms not in conformity with this Arrangement, the Participant will notify all other Participants of the terms it intends to support at least ten calendar days before issuing any commitment. If any other Participant requests a discussion during this period, the initiating Participant will delay an additional ten calendar days before issuing any commitment on such terms." The 1982 version contemplates no deviations. *See* Financial Times, July 5, 1982, at 4, col. 5.

[196] Almost all agricultural commodities are sold for cash or very short-term credit, and therefore do not pose a major export credit competitive problem.

[197] *See* Duff, *The Outlook for Official Export Credits,* 13 L. & POL'Y IN INT'L BUS. 891, 949–50 (1981).

risk insurance for exporters in 1975, it did so only after having tried and failed to persuade other governments with such programs to abandon them. There apparently was no prior consultation with the United States or any other state having export-competing interests with no inflation-risk program.[198] Nor is there evidence of such consultation when other European governments have initiated inflation-risk programs.

Another sensitive form of export-engendering activity that could affect third states' commercial interests is the disposal of surplus commodities. Governments accumulate stockpiles as a result of price-support programs (primarily agricultural) or of national security precautions. If they dispose of any substantial part of a large stockpile at once, they may either depress the market in their own territories and squeeze out imports, or flood foreign markets in such a way as to preempt exporters in other countries.

In the case of price-support surpluses, the disposable surplus would always be exported. In practice, this is often done in the form of food aid to developing countries. In order to insure that governments planning to dispose of food surpluses in that way consider the interests of other exporting countries, the Food and Agriculture Organization has devised procedures for virtually all substantial food aid disposals other than those effectuated through private charities and those undertaken to assist in emergencies. The main procedure, adopted in 1969 by the FAO Council in the form of a resolution, specifies that before carrying out any nonexempt food aid transaction:

> [T]he supplying country shall
>
> (a) undertake bilateral consultations with countries substantially interested by reason of their exports of the commodity concerned to the recipient country;
>
> (b) notify CSD [the FAO Consultative Sub-Committee on Surplus Disposal] of the main features of the proposed transaction in order to provide other countries directly interested in exports of the commodity an opportunity for bilateral consultations, it being understood that this would not result in any lengthening of the total period of consultation.[199]

[198]*See* The Times (London), Feb. 21, 1975, at 8, col. 2; Financial Times, Mar. 7, 1975, at 36, col. 5.

[199]FAO Council Resolutions 1/53 and 2/55, Annex, para. 2, in FAO PRINCIPLES OF SURPLUS DISPOSAL AND CONSULTATIVE OBLIGATIONS OF MEMBER NATIONS 27 (4th ed. 1979). Another provision states, in precatory language, that prior consultations should also be held with countries supplying closely related commodities. Annex para. 9, *id.* at 30.

About ten food-aid–supplying countries plus the European Economic Community have indicated their adherence to this procedure.[200] In practice, the aid-supplying country develops a proposed food-aid transaction, consults bilaterally with other countries that normally supply the recipient country with the commodity, and then consults multilaterally in the CSD. Only then does the supplying country proceed with the transaction.[201]

A separate consultation procedure applies to proposed projects of the World Food Programme (WFP), which supplies developing countries with food products. As in the case of bilateral food aid, the procedure is designed to minimize any displacement of normal commercial sales. Thus, the CSD regularly reviews proposed WFP projects and gives its advice.[202]

Although the FAO, through the CSD, has been the focal point for food aid consultations, the GATT has become involved too. A 1955 resolution of the Contracting Parties "considered" that

> when arranging the disposal of surplus agricultural products in world trade contracting parties should undertake a procedure of consultation with the principal suppliers of those products and other interested contracting parties, which would contribute to the orderly liquidation of such surpluses, including where practicable disposals designed to expand consumption of the products, and to the avoidance of prejudice to the interests of other contracting parties, and that they should give sympathetic consideration to the views expressed by other contracting parties in the course of such consultations.[203]

This statement captured the essence of the prior consultation principle—the avoidance of prejudice to the interests of other states by giving sympathetic consideration to their views before a decision is made—and inspired the then-evolving FAO procedure.

[200] *Id.* at 1, 45–46.

[201] *Id.* at 4, 6–7; *see also* Warley, *Western Trade in Agricultural Products,* in 1 INTERNATIONAL ECONOMIC RELATIONS OF THE WESTERN WORLD, *supra* note 63, at 287, 356.

There are some "grey area" transactions that are not clearly food aid (consultation required) or purely commercial (consultation not required). Apparently consultation practice is inconsistent in the grey area. See the CSD's 26th Rep. to the FAO Comm. on Commodity Problems, FAO Doc. CCP/CSD/76/184, at 4–6 (1976).

[202] FAO PRINCIPLES, *supra* note 199 at 9, 41.

[203] BISD 3d Supp. 50 (1955). In late 1982, when the United States contemplated large-scale disposal of agricultural surpluses, it consulted not only within GATT, but in the OECD and bilaterally with the EEC. *See* Financial Times, Dec., 2, 1982, at 20, col. 2.

The GATT also has stepped into the picture with the International Dairy Arrangement, most recently revised as part of the Tokyo Round in 1979. Parties to this arrangement agree, within the limits of their capabilities, to furnish dairy products to developing countries by way of food aid. They are to notify the International Dairy Products Council in advance each year, insofar as they can, of the scale, quantities, and destinations of their proposed contributions and to exchange views in the Council in order to harmonize efforts and avoid interference with normal trade patterns. In addition, the Arrangement provides that noncommercial dairy exports to developing countries "shall be effected in accordance with the FAO 'Principles of Surplus Disposal and Consultative Obligations.' "[204] The FAO Principles contain the consultative procedures discussed above. Consequently, for parties to the International Dairy Arrangement contemplating food aid in dairy products, the FAO consultative procedures rise to the level of a treaty obligation.

The International Sugar Agreement provides for sugar export quotas among contracting parties in order to stabilize world sugar prices. It permits parties to donate sugar abroad without charging the donation against their individual export quotas, if they meet certain conditions. One such condition is prior consultation to safeguard normal sugar trade patterns.[205]

Parties to the International Tin Agreements have a treaty obligation to consult each other (in the International Tin Council) before disposing of tin from a noncommercial stockpile.[206] The United States, whose disposals from the tin stockpile have caused most of the concern about disrupting normal production and trade patterns, was a party to the Fifth Tin Agreement, and has made a practice of prior consultation even when it has not been a party to any Tin Agreement.[207]

[204] International Dairy Arrangement, Apr. 12, 1979, art. 5, BISD 26th Supp. 91 (1980). The Arrangement has a Protocol Regarding Certain Milk Powders and a Protocol Regarding Milk Fat. Each sets minimum export prices for the products covered. Each provides in art. 8 that a participant, if it is faced with lower-price competition from a nonparticipant, may safeguard its position if it notifies the others and participates in a meeting, in advance if that is feasible.

[205] International Sugar Agreement, Oct. 7, 1977, art. 28, T.I.A.S. No. 9664.

[206] *See* Fifth International Tin Agreement, June 21, 1974, art. 43, 28 U.S.T. 4619, T.I.A.S. No. 8607; Sixth International Tin Agreement, June 26, 1981, art. 46, U.N. Doc. TD/TIN.6/14 (1981). At this writing, it appeared that the United States would not become a party to the Sixth Agreement. Nevertheless, the United States apparently intends to continue its preexisting consultation practice.

[207] *See* the message from the President transmitting the Fifth International Tin Agree-

This practice is not limited to tin. The State Department invites comments from the governments of countries producing any materials the United States intends to sell from its strategic stockpile, pursuant to U.S. legislation calling for efforts "to avoid undue disruption of the usual markets of producers, processors, and consumers of such materials."[208] It appears, however, that consultations regarding stockpile sales sometimes have concerned only such things as the precise timing of disposals (including the timing of installments within large-scale disposals) rather than the basic decision to dispose, or the total quantity to be sold, or even the overall time frame for disposal.[209]

There have been at least two significant multilateral nontreaty assertions that states planning to dispose of any surplus primary products—not just food or tin—should consult other states whose exports might be affected. The first was a GATT resolution adopted at the same time as its 1955 resolution on surplus agricultural products. In similar language, it called for notification and consultation on request, when a contracting party plans to dispose of a substantial part of any stockpiled primary product.[210] In more forceful terms, the Latin American states in 1969 "demanded" that the United States participate in "the effective functioning of consultation machinery in regard to the marketing of surpluses and the disposal of reserves, . . . preventing the disruptions in Latin America's flow of trade caused by the AID tied loans and the dumping of surpluses."[211] The same principle was expressed by the Inter-American Economic and Social Council in 1970 and reaffirmed by the OAS General Assembly in 1975, with the United States reserving its position.[212]

ment to the Senate, June 23, 1976, 75 DEP'T ST. BULL. 179, 180 (1976), for U.S. practice before it became a party.

[208]Telephone interview with State Department official in Office of Regional Economic Policy, Latin American Bureau, June 18, 1982. The language quoted in the text appears in the Strategic and Critical Materials Stock Piling Act § 6(b)(2), 50 U.S.C. § 98e(b)(2) (Supp. III 1979).

[209]For example, when the United States was going through the legislative authorization process in 1979 to dispose of 35,000 tons of stockpiled tin, it had not yet fulfilled its consultation duty under the Tin Agreement. *See* Financial Times, Nov. 6, 1979, at 28, col. 3. It did hold some consultations with interested states, however, before the President signed the disposal authorization bill. Washington Post, Jan. 3, 1980, at A7, col. 5. All along, the United States conceded its duty to consult in the International Tin Council before it actually disposed of any stockpiled tin. It complied with its duty in February 1980. *See* 13 BULL. EUR. COMM., No. 2, at 66–67 (1980).

[210]BISD 3d Supp. 51 (1955).

[211]Latin American Consensus of Viña del Mar, May 17, 1969, para. 17, in 8 INT'L LEGAL MATERIALS 974 (1969).

[212]*See* notes 106–07 *supra* and accompanying text.

As the discussion has shown, most of the norms relating to second-order export externalities stem, not from formal treaty obligations, but from instruments in the legal "twilight zone" between technically binding agreements and promises that create no serious expectation of fulfillment.[213] Such instruments as the OECD Arrangement on Export Credits and the FAO Principles of Surplus Disposal clearly create expectations among the participants that their rules—which are set out with much of the specificity one would expect in treaty obligations—will be observed. This is, however, a two-edged sword. The closer the instruments are to treaty obligations, the more particularized their coverage, the fewer the participating states, and the more those states depart from the letter of the instruments, the more difficult it is to argue that they represent general custom for nonparties. Thus, although the OECD Arrangement probably establishes a legal norm for states that have joined in it, it cannot be said to create or reflect a custom that any state intending to grant concessionary export credits must consult other interested states. The argument for a general custom is considerably stronger in the case of surplus disposal, since the various instruments calling for prior consultation reflect a widespread consensus.

It also is arguable that state practice establishes a custom requiring prior consultation regarding potential trade externalities when proposed action could seriously affect one or a few states and the acting state has some special economic relationship with them. This would explain the ubiquitous prior consultation requirement relating to trade deflection among partners in preferential trade agreements. It explains also the persistent assertion by Latin American countries that the United States must consult them before it adversely affects their trade interests, and the disinclination of the United States to repudiate the asserted obligation.

D. Domestic Measures Affecting Trade

1. Technical Specifications

The 1979 GATT Agreement on Technical Barriers to Trade

[213] *See* Schachter, *The Twilight Existence of Nonbinding International Agreements,* 71 Am. J. Int'l L. 296 (1977), and chapter V at note 19.

tries to limit the adverse trade effects of domestic measures concerned with such things as health, safety, environment, and product content disclosure. It defines "technical specification" as follows: "A specification contained in a document which lays down characteristics of a product such as levels of quality, performance, safety or dimensions. It may include, or deal exclusively with terminology, symbols, testing and test methods, packaging, marking or labelling requirements as they apply to a product."[214] A technical specification might be binding or nonbinding. In either event, if it applies to internationally traded goods (in addition to purely domestic goods), it is a potential nontariff barrier to trade.

Technical specifications often exist for the protection of consumers or the environment—matters of particular concern to the industrialized countries in recent years—and often affect the kinds of products they produce, such as high technology items (including chemicals) and final consumer products. Consequently, much of the international norm-setting activity has been conducted by the industrialized countries in their dual capacities as producers and consumers.

The 1979 Agreement on Technical Barriers to Trade includes among its signatories all the nonsocialist industrialized countries. It contains a mandatory prior notification-consultation procedure to be applied whenever a party proposes a technical specification that does not implement an existing international standard, if the specification may have a significant effect on the trade of other parties. Except when urgent problems require immediate action, the proposing party must give the others time to submit written comments and to make oral representations if they request the opportunity to do so, and must take the comments and discussions into account.[215]

The 1979 consultation procedure did not spring full grown on the trading world. It was presaged by the 1957 European Economic Community Treaty,[216] the 1971 OECD mandatory notification-consultation procedure regarding proposed measures to control chemical substances in the environment,[217] a

[214]Agreement on Technical Barriers to Trade, Apr. 12, 1979, Annex 1, para. 1, BISD 26th Supp. 8 (1980).

[215]*Id.* paras. 2.5–2.6. Intergovernmental consultations are required only if the proposed specification would be binding; if it would not, consultations may simply be held with interested private parties.

[216]*See* chapter V at notes 166–69.

[217]*See* Resolution of the OECD Council Concerning a Procedure for Notification

recommendation in the 1972 Stockholm Action Plan for the Human Environment,[218] a 1973 European Communities internal procedure regarding proposed environmental measures,[219] 1964 and 1975 notification-consultation procedures within the European Free Trade Association concerning member states' proposed new product standards,[220] and the practice of such important trading partners as the United States, the European Communities, and Japan.[221] Thus, the prior consultation norm for technical specifications is well established.

and Consultation on Measures for Control of Substances Affecting Man or His Environment, May 18, 1971, Annex, OECD Doc. C(71)73(Final) (1971), in OECD AND THE ENVIRONMENT 74 (1979). The parties were free to take immediate action if urgently required. The procedure was experimental for two years, and was renewed. It has been followed, and has been regarded as binding under the OECD Convention. *See* OECD ENVIRONMENT DIRECTORATE, TRANSFRONTIER POLLUTION 1975–1978: MEASURES RELATED TO OECD RECOMMENDATION C(74)224 ON PRINCIPLES CONCERNING TRANSFRONTIER POLLUTION 6 n.3 (1979).

[218] *See* Recommendation 103, Report of the United Nations Conf. on the Human Environment, June 16, 1972, U.N. Doc. A/CONF.48/14 and Corr.1, *reprinted in* 11 INT'L LEGAL MATERIALS 1416 (1972). As usual, there was an exception for cases requiring immediate action.

[219] *See* "The Information Agreement" of Mar. 5, 1973, in 16 O.J. EUR. COMM. (No. C 9) 1 (1973); Close, *EEC Action to Protect Fresh Waters,* in ENVIRONMENTAL LAW: INTERNATIONAL AND COMPARATIVE ASPECTS 38, 43 (J. Nowak ed. 1976).

EC directives require member states to notify the Commission before they regulate products that create waste disposal problems, unless an emergency requires quick action. The implication is that the Commission is to have the opportunity to comment before the member acts. *See* the Council Directive on Waste Disposal, 75/442/EEC, July 15, 1975, arts. 2, 3, in 18 O.J. EUR. COMM. (No. L 194) 39 (1975); Council Directive on Toxic and Dangerous Waste, 78/319/EEC, Mar. 20, 1978, art. 12, in 21 *id.* (No. L 84) 43 (1978).

[220] *See* EFTA SECRETARIAT, THE EUROPEAN FREE TRADE ASSOCIATION: STRUCTURE, RULES AND OPERATION 69–70 (1969); Middleton, *Technical Specifications: A Case Study of Non-Tariff Barriers to Trade,* pt. 2, 12 EFTA BULL., No. 3, at 6, 7 (1971).

[221] For example, during the early, formative years of the federal government's concern with the environment in the United States, the Director of the Environmental Protection Agency regularly consulted European Community officials regarding proposed U.S. measures. *See* J. SCHAETZEL, THE UNHINGED ALLIANCE: AMERICA AND THE EUROPEAN COMMUNITY 133 (1975). Later, when the EPA was formulating potentially trade-damaging regulations under the Toxic Substances Control Act, extensive consultations were held bilaterally with the EC, and multilaterally within the CCMS component of NATO as well as under the OECD Complementary Information Exchange Procedure. *See* Ward, Kendall, & Bresee, *Ten Years of CCMS: The Record and the Future,* 27 NATO REV., No. 6, at 12, 16 (1979); 1 INT'L ENVIR. REP., CURRENT REP. 29, 161, 188, 200 (1978); 2 *id.* at 649 (1979); 11 BULL. EUR. COMM., No. 6, at 43 (1978); Letter to the author from an official in the Office of Toxic Substances, EPA, Oct. 9, 1979.

The EC adopted new toxic substances legislation after the discussions cited above. *See* Council Directive 79/831/EEC, Sept. 18, 1979, in 22 O.J. EUR. COMM. (No. L 259) 10 (1979). It is not clear that France consulted outside the EC before adopting its toxic substances regulations on May 31, 1979. *See* 2 INT'L ENVIR. REP., CURRENT REP. 711 (1979).

2. Production Subsidies and Related Measures

Domestic environmental measures sometimes take the form of subsidies to assist producers faced with significant pollution-control costs. Trade distortion can result if the subsidizing state's trading partners follow the principle that the polluter pays for such costs. Accordingly, the OECD Council has espoused the polluter-pays principle for all its members. Nevertheless, it has recognized the permissibility of governmental assistance for pollution control under limited conditions. It recommends prior notification of assistance programs whenever practicable and has said that, regardless of notification, "consultations, as mentioned in the Guiding Principles on the implementation of such systems, will take place at the request of any Member State."[222] This amounts to an authoritative interpretation of the rather general harmonization provisions of the earlier OECD Guiding Principles Concerning International Economic Aspects of Environmental Policies,[223] establishing that consultation is expected before a member state deviates from the polluter-pays principle.[224] Interestingly, at about the time the Guiding Principles were adopted, Japan was consulting the United States and others regarding its plan to subsidize its industries' pollu-

When the Commission of the European Communities was preparing an asbestos control program in 1978–79, consultations were held with Canada, the Communities' major asbestos supplier. *Id.* at 463. Similarly, European sunglass manufacturers were allowed to participate when U.S. eyeglass safety rules were being formulated. *See* chapter I, note 30 *supra*.

The English Control of Pollution Act 1974, ch. 40, § 100, permits the government to prohibit or restrict imports of damaging or polluting substances, after consulting representatives of persons whose activities are likely to be prohibited or restricted. On the other hand, before the 1979 GATT Agreement was adopted, the Commission of the European Communities took the position that it was not required to consult non-member states regarding proposed Community safety standards for industrial products. *See* 18 O.J. EUR. COMM. (No. C 86) 8 (1975) (answer to parliamentary question).

In December 1976 Japan decided to enforce stringent emission control standards for cars sold after April 1, 1978. The European Commission immediately requested consultations regarding European-built cars. The consultations were held in January 1977, resulting in a three-year grace period for European cars. 10 BULL. EUR. COMM., No. 1, at 53 (1977).

[222] Recommendation of the OECD Council on the Implementation of the Polluter-Pays Principle, Nov. 14, 1974, § III, para. 5, OECD Doc. C(74)223 (1974), in 14 INT'L LEGAL MATERIALS 234 (1975), and in OECD AND THE ENVIRONMENT 28 (1979).

[223] May 26, 1972, paras. 8, 10, 14, OECD Doc. C(72)128, 11 INT'L LEGAL MATERIALS 1172 (1972), and in OECD AND THE ENVIRONMENT 25 (1979).

[224] *See* A. LEVIN, PROTECTING THE HUMAN ENVIRONMENT; PROCEDURES AND PRINCIPLES FOR PREVENTING AND RESOLVING INTERNATIONAL CONTROVERSIES 3 (UNITAR, 1977).

tion-control efforts. Japan then adopted the polluter-pays approach instead.[225]

There is no explicit prior consultation norm in the OECD or GATT regarding other types of production subsidy for domestic industry.[226] Regional development subsidies (to induce industries to build or expand plants in depressed areas) and subsidies to struggling industries are apparently granted without any consistent pattern of consulting nations whose producers will face the subsidized competition. Thus, as we have seen, the Canadian government expressly denied any duty to consult the United States before investment incentive subsidies were offered to Michelin to construct plants in Nova Scotia.[227] To give another example, before the European Communities adopted the Davignon Plan in 1977 to assist the European steel industry, the discussions with the United States focused on the plan's trade incentives and disincentives, rather than on its production subsidies.[228] But within the Communities, a prior consultation and approval scheme applies to proposed national production subsidies.[229]

Domestic agricultural policies typically combine some form of production subsidy with trade controls. The Organisation for European Economic Co-operation (OEEC) adopted a policy in 1955 of annual confrontations over the domestic agricultural policies of its members, designed in part to induce national policymakers to consider the interests of others while formulating their own programs. The system did not work well and was abandoned when the OEEC was replaced by the OECD in 1961.[230] On the other hand, when the European Economic Community was formulating its highly protectionist common agricultural policy in the early 1960s, it did consult at various

[225] *See International Cooperation in the Human Environment Through the United Nations: Hearings Before a Subcomm. of the House Comm. on Foreign Affairs,* 92d Cong., 2d Sess. 29 (1972).

[226] GATT Art. XVIII § C permits developing countries to aid the establishment of an industry by means inconsistent with the Agreement if no consistent means would be practicable, subject to prior consultation. This would not apply to the usual production subsidy, however, since such subsidies are consistent with the Agreement. *See* GATT art. XVI.

[227] *See* text at note 144 *supra.*

[228] *See Hearing on World Steel Trade, supra* note 186, at 124, 143–144.

[229] *See* chapter V at notes 162–63 *supra.* Despite the system, some national subsidies are adopted without prior consultation. *See, e.g.,* 10 BULL. EUR. COMM., No. 4, at 32–33 (1977) (Danish regional aids).

[230] *See* Warley, *supra* note 201, at 359–61.

times with supplier states. The pattern was (*a*) some discussions with supplier states during the early stages of policy formulation; (*b*) design of the basic common agricultural policy without consultation as to its specific form; (*c*) consultations regarding its prospective details, including the important base internal prices; and (*d*) adoption of the details.[231] Of course, the formulation of the common agricultural policy was an event of exceptional importance to a few supplier states politically allied with Western Europe. Moreover, the policy did not have to be adopted on a crash basis. Such are the circumstances in which international trade consultations are most likely to flourish. As the European Communities have expanded their preferential trading arrangements to include a widening circle of largely agrarian societies, they have acknowledged an intention to consult regarding changes in the common agricultural policy, but their stated intentions do not always contemplate that the consultations will precede the changes.[232]

The EEC's common agricultural policy is just one (prominent) example of a domestic tax or regulatory scheme that falls heavily on specific imported goods or services. Insofar as such a domestic measure amounts to a disguised tariff or openly regulates imported goods more stringently than domestic products, it would be inconsistent with GATT article III. There is little evidence of a prior consultation norm as to measures that clearly would violate article III. As we have seen, there is adequate evidence of such a norm if a regulatory proposal involves technical specifications directed equally at domestic and imported goods. If the tax or regulatory scheme does not fall squarely within either of these categories—as when a tax is nondiscriminatory on its face, but in fact falls more heavily on imports than on domestic goods—the picture is less clear, but there is some evidence that states peculiarly affected by the proposed scheme and occupying a relatively close political and /

[231] *See* G. Patterson, Discrimination in International Trade: The Policy Issues, 1945–1965, at 198–206 (1966).

[232] Sometimes they have promised to consult before acting. They made such a promise to the African, Caribbean, and Pacific states in the second Lomé Convention, *supra* note 96, art. 2(2)(c). Similar provisions appeared in the first Lomé Convention. The agreements with Middle Eastern states, however, are less specific. They are cited *supra* note 94.

or economic relationship with the proposing state expect to be consulted in such cases.[233]

3. Extraterritorial Antitrust Enforcement

The United States' application of its antitrust laws to conduct abroad affecting U.S. commerce has been a foreign relations irritant on several occasions. This has been a matter of particular sensitivity to Canada and Western Europe. Tension with Canada on this point peaked with an American investigation of an alleged conspiracy between U.S. and Canadian companies in the 1950s. As a result, in 1959 the United States and Canada entered into an Antitrust Notification and Consultation Procedure by which each country pledges to consult the other when it appears that either's interests will be affected by the other's antitrust enforcement action. The pledge, however, is not absolute. As put by the U.S. State Department:

> The arrangement is termed a Notification and Consultation Procedure for the reason that the circumstances or time schedule may permit not consultation but only notification prior to the institution of an antitrust action. The normal course, however, is that each country notifies the other prior to the institution of an antitrust suit which involves the interests or the nationals of the other country and permits time for consultation concerning the contemplated suit. While not required by the understanding, notification is given during the investigative phase whenever possible. In all cases each Government keeps the other informed of significant developments in negotiations with the parties and in litigation.[234]

The loophole apparently is rarely used, if ever, and the Procedure—as broadened somewhat in 1969—has functioned well.[235] It has been emulated in a 1976 agreement between the United States and the Federal Republic of Germany, and in a 1982

[233] *See, e.g.*, 23rd ANN. REP. OF THE PRESIDENT, *supra* note 188, at 49, 51, 52 (examples of U.S. practice with Austria, Canada, and Finland). Note also the EEC practice, text at note 231 *supra*.

[234] 6 M. WHITEMAN, DIGEST OF INTERNATIONAL LAW 160 (1968). For the events leading to the 1959 understanding, see Kindred & Biggs, *supra* note 116, at 123.

[235] *See* Henry, *International Aspects of Competition Policy*, in CANADIAN PERSPECTIVES ON INTERNATIONAL LAW AND ORGANIZATION 756, 785–86 (R. MacDonald, G. Morris, & D. Johnston eds. 1974); Campbell, *The Canada–United States Antitrust Notification and Consultation Procedure*, 56 CAN. BAR REV. 459, 463–69 (1978).

agreement between the United States and Australia.[236] Moreover, despite the absence of a U.S.-U.K. agreement, the British government has asserted that "British sovereignty must be respected and we must be consulted about any proposed [antitrust] steps by U.S. law enforcement authorities which will affect the United Kingdom."[237] This has not engendered any visible American objection.

In 1960 the GATT adopted a recommendation that "at the request of any contracting party a contracting party should enter into consultations on such [restrictive business] practices on a bilateral or multilateral basis as appropriate."[238] This was regarded simply as a "mild exhortation;"[239] its significance has been primarily as the forerunner of far more important OECD recommendations in 1967, 1973, and 1979.

In 1967 the OECD Council recommended to member governments:

> That insofar as their laws permit, when Member countries undertake under their restrictive business practices laws an investigation or a proceeding involving important interests of another Member country, they should notify such Member country in a manner and at a time deemed appropriate. Notification should, where appropriate, take place in advance in order to enable the proceeding Member country, while retaining full freedom of ul-

[236] Agreement Relating to Mutual Cooperation Regarding Restrictive Business Practices, June 23, 1976, art. 4(2), 27 U.S.T. 1956, T.I.A.S. No. 8291, *reprinted in* 15 INT'L LEGAL MATERIALS 1282 (1976); Agreement Relating to Cooperation on Antitrust Matters, June 29, 1982, United States–Australia, arts. 1–2, 21 INT'L LEGAL MATERIALS 702 (1982). The agreement with Australia is more detailed than the others.

Since World War II the United States has included in several of its bilateral friendship, commerce, and navigation treaties a clause contemplating consultations on restrictive business practices, but the clause does not expressly require consultation before enforcement action. It does not appear to have played a major role in shaping U.S. prior consultation practice. *See generally* Haight, *The Restrictive Business Practice Clause in United States Treaties: An Antitrust Tranquilizer for International Trade*, 70 YALE L.J. 240 (1960); State Department letter, Aug. 22, 1967, in C. FULDA & W. SCHWARTZ, CASES AND MATERIALS ON THE REGULATION OF INTERNATIONAL TRADE AND INVESTMENT 102–03 (1970).

[237] Speech by the British Secretary of State for Trade, Sept. 14, 1979, in Los Angeles. In 1980, when the United States began an antitrust investigation of freight rates on shipping from Australia and New Zealand, it consulted the interested governments. At least one government (Australia) seems clearly to have regarded this as a duty, and expressed its displeasure when it was not notified at the very outset of the investigation. *See* Financial Times, Aug. 18, 1980, at 1, col. 3.

[238] BISD 9th Supp. 28 (1961).

[239] Kintner, Joelson, & Vaghi, *Groping for a Truly International Antitrust Law*, 14 VA. J. INT'L L. 75, 90 (1973).

> timate decision, to take account of such views as the other Member country may wish to express and of such remedial action as the other Member country may find it feasible to take under its own laws to deal with the restrictive business practice.[240]

In 1973 the Council added a consultation and conciliation procedure.[241] In 1979 it made clarifying changes in the language quoted above and in the consultation-conciliation procedure. The most significant change in the quoted language substituted notification in advance "if possible" for notification in advance "where appropriate," and added that the notification in any event should be "at a time that would facilitate comments or consultations."[242] This had the effect of tightening the standard somewhat.

The notification-consultation process has been actively applied by member states since its 1967 inception.[243] It does contain some obvious loopholes, which are not quite as broad as they might appear. For example, the OECD Committee of Experts on Restrictive Business Practices narrowed one of them by saying that "important interests of another Member country" will generally be involved "when such investigations or proceedings involve enterprises of another Member country."[244]

As for the loophole permitting a member government to argue that notification in advance was not "appropriate" (1967 version) or "possible" (1979 version), the United States, in the

[240] Recommendation of the OECD Council Concerning Co-operation Between Member Countries on Restrictive Business Practices Affecting International Trade, Oct. 10, 1967, para. 1(a), OECD Doc. C(67)53(Final) (1967), in 8 INT'L LEGAL MATERIALS 1309 (1969).

[241] Recommendation of the OECD Council Concerning a Consultation and Conciliation Procedure on Restrictive Business Practices Affecting International Trade, Oct. 3, 1973, OECD Doc. C(73)99(Final) (1973). In 1978 the Council recommended that member governments "make use as far as possible of the OECD procedures on co-operation between Member countries in the field of restrictive business practices affecting international trade so as to facilitate consultation and resolution of problems." Recommendation of the OECD Council Concerning Action Against Restrictive Business Practices, July 20, 1978, para. 1(5), OECD Doc. C(78)133(Final), *reprinted in* 17 INT'L LEGAL MATERIALS 1527 (1978).

[242] Recommendation of the OECD Council Concerning Co-operation Between Member Countries on Restrictive Business Practices Affecting International Trade, Oct. 5, 1979, para. 1(a), OECD Doc. C(79)154(Final) (1979).

[243] Interview with U.S. State Department official, June 30, 1975. Between 1967 and 1975, the procedure was applied 137 times. On 14 of those occasions, the notified state requested (and obtained) consultations. OECD Report on the Operation of the 1967 Council Recommendation . . . During the Period 1967–1975, at 1, 3–5 (1976).

[244] OECD Doc. C(67)53, at 4 (1967).

role of protagonist in antitrust enforcement, has said only that it endeavors to consult "whenever feasible."[245] Nevertheless, the State Department has sometimes held up antitrust proceedings by other U.S. government agencies in order to consult fully.[246] On at least one occasion, foreign governmental objections aired in consultations with the State Department apparently influenced a Justice Department decision to drop felony antitrust charges against foreign companies.[247]

Despite some Justice Department equivocation,[248] the combination of the OECD consultation procedure, the U.S.–Canadian, U.S.–West German, and U.S.–Australian procedures, the British assertion of (and apparent American acquiescence in) a consultation duty, and the extensive consultation practice establishes a norm binding the nonsocialist industrialized nations to consult each other before their public authorities launch into extraterritorial antitrust enforcement, unless some bona fide exigency requires quick action. This includes consultation before pretrial discovery is attempted as to witnesses or documents in the territory of a foreign country.[249]

[245]The Views of the United States Government Concerning the Report of the [U.N.] Group of Eminent Persons on "The Impact of Multinational Corporations on the Development Process and on International Relations," Nov. 6, 1974, at 11, U.S. St. Dep't File L/EB, *summarized in* U.N. Doc. E/5595/Add.5 (1974). The Group of Eminent Persons recommended that formal consultative machinery be established pending substantive antitrust enforcement agreements. *See* U.N. Doc. E/5500/Add.1/(pt.1), *reprinted in* 13 INT'L LEGAL MATERIALS 800, 829 (1974).

[246]*See, e.g.*, Financial Times, June 5, 1979, at 6, col. 7 (consultations concerning proposed Civil Aeronautics Board [CAB] action against restrictive practices of transnational airlines). The CAB later held its own international consultations. *See id.*, Aug. 21, 1979, at 1, col. 7. For a case in which the State Department did not have time to consult effectively before antitrust proceedings were brought, see J. SCHAETZEL, *supra* note 221, at 134 (Justice Department proceedings against British Petroleum in an apparent attempt to head off imminent effects on retail gasoline distribution of BP acquisition of Sohio).

[247]*See* N.Y. Times, Dec. 4, 1979, at A1, col. 5 (city ed.) (alleged uranium cartel). In the mammoth private uranium antitrust action brought by Westinghouse, the Justice Department told the presiding judge that the views of foreign governments "are entitled to appropriate deference." At least five foreign governments submitted their views. 6 INT'L L. PERSPECTIVE, No. 5, at 12 (1980).

[248]*See* 1977 DIGEST OF UNITED STATES PRACTICE IN INT'L LAW 767, 768 (Attorney General viewed prior consultation as one way to exercise "comity" in extraterritorial antitrust). The State Department has said, however, that the Justice Department and the Federal Trade Commission regularly give notice to other governments before they begin antitrust enforcement affecting the other governments' interests, and that they "likewise regularly consult with foreign governments concerning particular enforcement activities." 82 DEP'T ST. BULL. Oct. 1982, at 35, 37.

[249]*See* Shenefield, *The Perspective of the U.S. Department of Justice*, in PERSPECTIVES ON THE EXTRATERRITORIAL APPLICATION OF U.S. ANTITRUST AND OTHER LAWS 12, 21 (J. Griffin ed. 1979).

4. Macroeconomic Policies

Macroeconomic policies in market-oriented economies are designed to stimulate or restrict aggregate demand for goods and services through the exercise of the government's taxing and spending power (fiscal measures), or its control over the money supply and interest rates (monetary measures), or, occasionally, through direct regulation in the form of wage-price controls. In a few close-knit international bodies, where member states have tried to integrate their economies, members are obligated to consult each other on these matters. Thus, in the European Economic Community, consultations are required before member states adopt significant short- and medium-term macroeconomic policy measures, though there is doubt whether the consultations often influence the policies adopted.[250] The Nordic countries have agreed to consult each other on questions of economic policy and to try to coordinate measures designed to lessen cyclical fluctuations.[251]

Beyond these instances, states have not formally obligated themselves to consult before they adopt macroeconomic measures; however, there is one pertinent GATT provision, and there have been at least two nontreaty statements that could have normative significance. GATT article III(9) provides: "The contracting parties recognize that internal maximum price control measures, even though conforming to the other provisions of this Article, can have effects prejudicial to the interests of contracting parties supplying imported products. Accordingly, contracting parties applying such measures shall take account of the interests of exporting contracting parties with a view to avoiding to the fullest practicable extent such prejudicial effects."[252] Although this provision does not expressly require prior consultations, it does imply such a duty—that being the only way in which the interests of exporting parties could be taken adequately into account.[253] The duty, however, would be subject to the common exception based on a need for secrecy

[250]*See* chapter V at notes 193–97 *supra.*

[251]Treaty of Cooperation (Denmark, Finland, Iceland, Norway, and Sweden), Mar. 23, 1962, *as amended*, art. 18, in COOPERATION AGREEMENTS BETWEEN THE NORDIC COUNTRIES 7 (1976).

[252]GATT, *supra* note 46, art. III(9).

[253]*See* chapter VII, section C *infra.* Kass, *Obligatory Negotiations in International Organizations,* 1965 CAN. Y.B. INT'L L. 36, 45, includes article III(9) in a list of GATT consultation obligations.

or quick action. For example, the United States apparently did not consult its trading partners before imposing a ninety-day wage-price freeze along with its closing of the "gold window" and its temporary import surcharge on August 15, 1971.

The Managing Director of the International Monetary Fund discreetly suggested in 1974 that consultations in the Fund "could be of great importance" when member governments plan reflationary measures to stem a recession,[254] and the OECD member governments have issued a statement on consultation in formulating and implementing their economic policies. The OECD governments said: "Member Governments agreed that the high degree of interdependence among their countries, their recognition, in a spirit of solidarity, of each other's problems and their dedication to the same basic principles demand close consultation and cooperation among themselves in formulating and implementing their economic policies."[255] Statements like these, stopping short of an assertion or acknowledgment of legal duty, nevertheless could be legally significant if they reflect or generate state practice according to their terms. But there is very little indication that states consistently consult during the formative stages of their macroeconomic policies unless, perhaps, a proposed measure would execute an irrevocable, major policy shift of particular concern to a small group of interdependent states.

Such a case was the French revaluation of its gold reserves in January 1975. Before it acted, the French government consulted the United States and the members of the European Communities.[256] On the other hand, the United States apparently did not consult internationally before it decided in December 1974 to begin periodic sales of its gold reserves.[257] The

[254] Statement of Mr. Witteveen to the U.N. Economic and Social Council, Nov. 26, 1974, in 3 IMF SURVEY 380–81 (1974).

The Fund Agreement, *supra* note 23, art. IV, sets forth general standards of good conduct for members in the formulation of their economic and monetary policies, but contains no prior consultation requirement.

[255] Communique of OECD Ministers' Meeting, June 22, 1976, in 15 INT'L LEGAL MATERIALS 961 (1976).

[256] *See* Communique of the U.S.-French Martinique Summit, Dec. 16, 1974, in 72 DEP'T ST. BULL. 42, 43 (1975), *reprinted in* 14 INT'L LEGAL MATERIALS 231 (1975); *see also* Le Monde, Dec. 20, 1974, at 1, col. 3.

[257] The Secretary of the Treasury announced the decision in a Congressional hearing on Dec. 3, 1974, and discussed it at some length without mentioning any consultation. *See Delay Until July 1, 1975, The Date for Removing Restrictions on Private Ownership of Gold: Hearings Before a Subcomm. of the House Comm. on Banking, Currency, and Housing,*

U.S. decision was irrevocable only as to the first installment and did not have the impact on the other Western states that the French action in 1975 had. France not only substantially increased the value of its reserves, but solidified the reserve role of gold at a time when the IMF and the other Western states were trying to diminish that role.

E. Domestic Measures Affecting Foreign Investment

1. Regulation of Incoming Direct Investment

Restrictions on incoming direct investment have obvious adverse effects on potential investors from capital-exporting countries. Incentives for direct investment also can have effects undesired by other countries, in much the same way as export credits can. They create pressures in other countries to keep up by matching or exceeding the investment subsidy in order to maintain the inflow of foreign exchange. The OECD has devised a consultation mechanism to deal with both types of investment measure:

> Consultations will take place in the framework of the Committee on International Investment and Multinational Enterprises at the request of a Member country which considers that its interests may be adversely affected by the impact on its flow of international direct investments of measures taken by another Member country specifically designed to provide incentives or disincentives for international direct investment. Having full regard to the national economic objectives of the measures and without prejudice to policies designed to redress regional imbalances, the purpose of the consultations will be to examine the possibility of reducing such effects to a minimum.[258]

93d Cong., 2d Sess. 4–13, 37–56, 65–73 (1974). Newspaper reports of foreign official reactions gave no hint of prior consultation. *See* N.Y. Times, Dec. 5, 1974, at 71, col. 3; Financial Times, Dec. 18, 1974, at 6, col. 4.

[258] Decision of the OECD Council on International Investment Incentives and Disincentives, June 21, 1976, para. 1, OECD Doc. C(76)119, 75 Dep't St. Bull. 88, *reprinted in* 15 Int'l Legal Materials 980 (1976). This provision was left unchanged when the decision was revised in 1979. *See* OECD Doc. C(79)145, *reprinted in* 18 Int'l Legal Materials 1175 (1979). It has limited application because it applies only to measures aimed specifically at international direct investment. Most investment incentive measures are equally available to domestic investors. *See* OECD, Review of the 1976 Declaration and Decisions on International Investment and Multinational Enterprises, OECD Doc. C(79)102(Final), *reprinted in* 18 Int'l Legal Materials 986, 1020 (1979).

This provision, of course, does not purport to apply beyond the OECD and does not make clear whether the consultations are to precede adoption of the incentives or disincentives. If anything, the language ("measures taken") suggests that consultation may follow action. This interpretation is supported by the absence of any requirement that the OECD or other member countries be notified of the proposed measures during the planning stages.

OECD members, as well as nonmembers, do sometimes consult bilaterally before incentives or disincentives are enacted, but not consistently and not under a recognition of duty. We already have seen Canada's denial of such a duty in connection with an investment subsidy in Nova Scotia.[259] On the disincentive side, when Canada was considering legislation directed against foreign (American) takeovers of Canadian banks, U.S. government protests were considered and rejected on the merits.[260] When Canada was preparing its 1973 Foreign Investment Review Act (establishing a screening mechanism for incoming investment), informal consultations were held with the United States as part of the normal, ongoing exchange of views between the two neighbors, but not under a claim of right or an acknowledgment of duty.[261] In 1980, Canada announced its intention to adopt a national energy program that would contain some burdensome or discriminatory requirements affecting foreign investors. While the legislation was pending, consultations were held bilaterally between the United States and Canada, and multilaterally in the OECD.[262]

There were informal consultations before the Andean Foreign Investment Code was adopted in 1970,[263] though not before Argentina adopted its restrictive Foreign Investment Law in 1973–74. In fact, in the latter case the Argentine government

[259] *See* text at note 144 *supra*.

[260] *See* Kindred & Biggs, *supra* note 116, at 119–20.

[261] Letter to the author from the Counsellor (Economic) in the Canadian Embassy in Washington, Dec. 20, 1973. The United States was keenly interested, since 24 percent of its foreign investment went to Canada. *Canadian Foreign Investment Screening Procedures and the Role of Foreign Investment in the Canadian Economy: Hearings Before a Subcomm. of the Joint Econ. Comm.*, 94th Cong., 1st Sess. 134 (1976).

[262] *See Issues in United States–Canadian Economic Relations: Hearing Before Subcomms. of the House Comm. on Foreign Affairs*, 97th Cong., 1st Sess. 5, 36, 41 (1981).

[263] Interview with U.S. State Department official, June 25, 1975. When Venezuela enacted a decree implementing the Code in 1974, it apparently did not consult the United States. In any event, the United States would not assert a duty to consult in such a case. *Id.*

asserted that the U.S. ambassador was interfering in Argentine affairs when he presented his views in writing while the law was being prepared.[264] There is no record of consultation before Australia and New Zealand enacted foreign investment screening legislation, although Australia apparently consulted Japan just before it announced its guidelines on foreign equity in the mining (uranium) industry.[265]

Frequently, the host government wishes to be consulted before a substantial foreign direct investment is made. This is the principal effect of most foreign investment screening laws, insofar as they apply to sectors not strictly reserved for domestic investors. The interest in consultation rises with the size and the degree of foreign governmental participation in the prospective investment. The latter point is reflected in the widespread (though not universal) treaty practice requiring governmental and quasi-governmental investment financing and insuring agencies to clear prospective direct investments with a host government before participating in them.[266] The point similarly is reflected in the U.S. response to the massive outflows of dollars to oil-producing nations beginning in 1974. Among other things, the United States embarked on a program to obtain assurances from foreign governments that they would consult before making significant investments in U.S. firms. Saudi Arabia has given a public assurance to this effect, and the State Department has informed all foreign governments (not just governments of oil-producing countries) that it expects them to consult before making any major investment, other than a portfolio investment, in the United States.[267] As of mid-1979,

[264] *Id.*

[265] *See* Parry, *Australia's Foreign Investment Policies: In Search of an Objective,* 8 J. WORLD TRADE L. 529 (1974); Tedeschi, *Legal Controls on Foreign Participation in the Australian Economy,* 9 *id.* 573 (1975); 46 AUSTL. FOREIGN AFF. REC. 672, 675 (1975); Neil, *Some Restrictions on Overseas Investment in New Zealand,* 1 AUCKLAND U.L. REV. 53 (1967); Paterson, *Legal Restrictions on Foreign Investment in New Zealand,* 9 J. WORLD TRADE L. 177 (1975).

[266] *See Extension of the Overseas Private Investment Corp.: Markup and Hearings Before the House Comm. on Int'l Relations,* 95th Cong., 1st & 2d Sess. 46–50 (1978); OPIC INVESTMENT FINANCING HANDBOOK 5 (1979); OPIC INVESTMENT INSURANCE HANDBOOK 5 (1979).

[267] The Saudi Arabian commitment is in the United States–Saudi Arabia Joint Communique, Feb. 27, 1975, 72 DEP'T ST. BULL. 369, 370 (1975). As to expectations concerning other governments, see *Foreign Investment Legislation: Hearings Before a Subcomm. of the Senate Comm. on Commerce,* 94th Cong., 1st Sess. 79, 90 (1975); *The Operations of Federal Agencies in Monitoring, Reporting on, and Analyzing Foreign Investments in the United States: Hearings Before a Subcomm. of the House Comm. on Government Operations,* 96th Cong., 1st Sess., pt. 3 at 288–91 (1979).

there had been three instances in which the United States had invoked the consultation procedure, and in each case the foreign government cooperated fully.[268]

Canada has gone further than the United States has in this area. Reacting to the large inflow of U.S. direct investment, Canada in 1973 enacted the Foreign Investment Review Act, requiring notice and prior governmental authorization of investments that would result in acquisition of control or establishment of new businesses in Canada by foreign governments or nongovernmental aliens.[269]

The Canadian approach, going beyond consultation and extending coverage to nongovernmental as well as to governmental entities, tends to reinforce the narrower practice involving foreign governmental investments. This would lead governments to expect consultations before a foreign government makes or participates in a major equity investment in the territories they govern. The practice is not yet sufficiently widespread, however, to declare confidently that a general custom to that effect already has been established.

2. Measures Affecting Existing Direct Investment

These measures may range from a minor increase in a regulatory burden, through substantial increases in the cost of doing business (by way of taxes or otherwise), to outright expropriation. Absent a treaty or other binding agreement, there is no duty to consult either a foreign government or its investors before enacting relatively minor increases in regulatory or tax burdens, even if the burdens fall peculiarly on foreign investors. Neither is there a customary duty to consult before enacting a law of general application (one that falls equally on domestic and foreign investors, in fact as well as in form) that substantially increases the burdens of doing business. An example of the latter would be the West German codetermination bill, providing for equal shareholder-employee representation on the supervisory boards of large German companies. Although this was of concern to American stockholders with sizeable German investments, the German government regarded American

[268] *Hearings on Foreign Investments, supra* note 267, at 69–70. The three cases involved France, Iran, and Romania.

[269] Canadian Foreign Investment Review Act, §§ 8–13, Can. Stat. 1973–74, ch. 46.

investors' opposition to the bill as intervention in German internal affairs; there is no record of U.S. State Department intervention.[270]

The OECD has established an intergovernmental notification-consultation procedure to be applied when its members make an exception to the basic national treatment standard for foreign-controlled enterprises in their territories. Although the consultation provision, standing alone, might be read to contemplate talks before an exception is enacted, it does not clearly say so. Moreover, it applies only at the request of a member state. Before a state can make a request, it must know what exception the other state is considering. The notification provision simply requires that exceptions "be notified to the Organisation within 30 days of their introduction together with the specific reasons therefor and the proposed duration thereof."[271] Since there is no duty of advance notification, there often will be no request to consult in advance. Even if there is such a request, it would strain the consultation provision to say that it requires a give-and-take discussion before even the duty to notify comes due. That is true as well of the rather common consultation provisions in bilateral friendship, commerce, and navigation treaties, relating to national treatment clauses.[272]

In practice, intergovernmental consultations are rare when national authorities are planning measures that would increase the burdens of foreign-controlled enterprises.[273] But discussions with the enterprises themselves are not so rare, especially

[270] *See* CCH Euromarket News, Oct. 22, 1974, at 4; *id.*, Oct. 29, 1974, at 3. The law was enacted in 1976, and took effect on July 1, 1978.

Compare the State Department's rejection of Canadian assertions that changes in Canada's tax law denying business expense deductions for advertisements in U.S. media directed at the Canadian market were domestic tax matters not subject to international negotiation. *See* 1977 DIGEST OF UNITED STATES PRACTICE IN INT'L LAW 778–79.

[271] Revised Decision of the OECD Council on National Treatment, June 13, 1979, para. 2, OECD Doc. C(79)144, *reprinted in* 18 INT'L LEGAL MATERIALS 1173 (1979). The consultation provision, para. 6, says: "The Committee [on International Investment and Multinational Enterprises] shall act as a forum for consultations, at the request of a Member country, in respect of any matter related to this instrument and its implementation, including exceptions to 'National Treatment' and their application."

[272] *See, e.g.*, the U.S. FCN treaties cited in Note, *The Rising Tide of Reverse Flow: Would a Legislative Breakwater Violate U.S. Treaty Commitments?*, 72 MICH. L. REV. 551, 568 n.63 (1974).

[273] One case in which such consultations did occur involved a bill before the U.S. Congress to require foreign banks to operate under the same rules as U.S. banks. The Federal Reserve Board consulted the Commission of the European Communities. *See* EUROPEAN COMMUNITY, Sept. 1975, at 11.

when the planned measure would affect a preexisting license, concession agreement, or other special relationship between one or a few enterprises, on one hand, and the host government, on the other. Thus, when the OPEC governments decided in 1970 to increase their income tax rates on the profits of foreign oil companies, they resolved to do so through negotiations with the companies if possible;[274] Jamaica imposed its stiff bauxite levy in 1974, after negotiations with the bauxite and aluminum companies had failed;[275] before Peru cancelled Braniff's operating permit in 1974 and then issued a more restricted one, it talked with Braniff (and with the U.S. government);[276] when Norway planned a "windfall profits tax" in 1974 on certain oil company earnings, it discussed the proposal with them and then revised the tax to take account of their objections;[277] when the United Kingdom was working out its participation in North Sea oil profits in 1974–75, it did so in consultation with the oil companies;[278] and the investment incentive laws enacted by several African states in the 1960s typically provided some form of hearing for the investor before its preferential treatment could be withdrawn.[279]

When there is no special relationship, the likelihood of prior discussion with foreign enterprises is reduced;[280] and even when

[274] *See* OPEC Resolutions XXI.120, Dec. 12, 1970, XXII.131, Feb. 4, 1971, and related documents, in 10 INT'L LEGAL MATERIALS 240–51 (1971).

[275] *See* the arbitral award in Revere Copper & Brass, Inc. v. Overseas Private Investment Corp., 17 INT'L LEGAL MATERIALS 1321, 1325–27 (1978).

[276] Interview with U.S. State Department official, June 25, 1975.

[277] *See* Financial Times, Dec. 4, 1974, at 6, col. 6; *id.*, Dec. 12, 1974, at 6, col. 8; CCH Euromarket News, Dec. 17, 1974, at 4; *id.*, Jan. 2, 1975, at 6.

[278] *See* Cmd. No. 5696 (1974), in 14 INT'L LEGAL MATERIALS 460, 461 (1975); Financial Times, Nov. 20, 1974, at 1, col. 3; *id.*, Nov. 30, 1974, at 1, col. 3; *id.*, Dec. 28, 1974, at 1, col. 5; *id.*, Jan. 24, 1975, at 22, col. 5; *id.*, Feb. 26, 1975, at 1, col. 3.

[279] *See, e.g.*, Dahomey Investment Code, Dec. 31, 1961, art. 24, in 7 INT'L LEGAL MATERIALS 334 (1968); Common Convention on Investments in the States of the Customs and Economic Union of Central Africa, Dec. 14, 1965, Pt. 5, *id.*, 221; Gabon Investment Law, Mar. 23, 1967, arts. 30, 37, 56, *id.* 1071; Niger Investment Code, Julv 31, 1968, art. 13, in 8 *id.* 598 (1969). *But see* Libyan Law on Investment of Foreign Capital, Aug. 4, 1968, art. 7, in 7 *id.* 1376 (1968); Moroccan Dahir of Aug. 13, 1973, art. 23, in 13 *id.* 406 (1974).

[280] For example, when Switzerland reimposed a prohibition against interest payments on Swiss franc accounts held by nonresidents, as well as a penalty charge on large nonresident accounts, it apparently acted without prior consultation. *See* Financial Times, Nov. 21, 1974, at 28, col. 2, and 44, col. 6; *id.* Jan. 24, 1975, at 6, col. 5.

When Belgium restored a five-year limit on its special tax deduction for foreign executives in 1974, it apparently did not consult beforehand. It later relented, after threats by several multinational corporations to move their European headquarters out of Belgium. *See* CCH Euromarket News, Apr. 30, 1975, at 3; Financial Times, Apr.

such a relationship exists, there is considerable doubt whether the discussions are motivated primarily by a perception of duty. In the OPEC and Jamaican cases mentioned above, a strong flavor of ultimatum pervaded the discussions, and in most of the others, the government's reliance on the enterprises dictated that an effort be made to reach agreement with them. When a government's short-run self-interest could explain its willingness to talk, and no pertinent resolution of an international body or other normative assertion calls for the talks, the requisite opinio juris will normally be lacking.

The scenario is quite similar when a government contemplates outright expropriation. The procedure surrounding Latin American expropriations of U.S. investors' properties is particularly revealing. When the State Department is aware that such an expropriation decree is pending, an embassy diplomat may enter into informal talks with representatives of the host government, but he or she does not assert a duty to consult.[281] On at least one occasion, when the United States ambassador to Venezuela recommended that the U.S. government play a greater role in negotiations on the nationalization of American oil companies in that country, the State Department rejected the recommendation.[282] Its attitude in such cases has been described as aloof.[283]

It is revealing, too, that the 1967 OECD Draft Convention on the Protection of Foreign Property, which reflects the views of the capital-exporting states, does not mention a duty to consult either the home government or the investor before foreign-owned property is expropriated.[284] As in the case of burden-increasing measures, governments often do negotiate with foreign investors when an expropriation is planned, but it is difficult to conclude that they do so because of any perceived international duty. Self-interest again explains what they do.[285]

22, 1975, at 7, col. 1.

[281] Interview with U.S. State Department official, June 25, 1975. Often the State Department does not find out about an expropriation until the decree is adopted. It does not assert a prior notification duty. *Id.*

[282] *See* N.Y. Times, June 30, 1975, at 43, col. 6, and 45, col. 1 (city ed.).

[283] *See* Lowenthal & Treverton, *U.S. Policymaking Toward Latin America: Improving the Process,* in *U.S. Relations with Latin America: Hearings Before a Subcomm. of the Senate Comm. on Foreign Relations,* 94th Cong., 1st Sess. 224, 231 (1975).

[284] OECD Draft Convention on the Protection of Foreign Property, Oct. 12, 1967, 7 Int'l Legal Materials 118 (1968).

[285] Examples abound. Some prominent ones include the "Mexicanization" program

When expropriation follows a radical change in government or is retaliatory, there usually is no prior negotiation even with the investor.[286]

3. Capital Movements

A final area of concern to transnational investors involves governmental restrictions on the flow of capital. Again, the OECD has entered the field, without requiring prior consultation. It has called for the progressive abolition of restrictions on capital movements, but it has adopted an escape procedure that recognizes certain exigencies in a member state's economic or financial situation (including its balance-of-payments position) that may not permit its compliance. If a member invokes the escape procedure, it need only give notification "forthwith," supported by reasons. The Organization may then consider the matter.[287]

When the United States adopted its Foreign Direct Investment Regulations on January 1, 1968, restricting the outflow of U.S. capital in order to improve the balance of payments, it had consulted Canada because of the unique economic relations between the two countries, but it did not even explain its action to other governments until immediately after the regulations

in the 1960s, E. BAKLANOFF, EXPROPRIATION OF U.S. INVESTMENTS IN CUBA, MEXICO, AND CHILE 47–49 (1975); "Chileanization" under President Frei beginning in 1969, *id.* 77–82 (and see President Frei's statement of June 26, 1969, 8 INT'L LEGAL MATERIALS 1073, 1075 (1969)); Peru's nationalization of Cerro Corp. properties in 1974, 8 LATIN AMERICA 1, 12 (1974); Saudi Arabia's takeover of Aramco in 1974–75, Financial Times, Dec. 11, 1974, at 42, col. 2; Malta's acquisition of control over local Barclay's Bank operations in 1975, *id.*, Mar. 27, 1975, at 6, col. 1: Trinidad and Tobago's acquisition of oil company holdings in 1975, *id.*, May 1, 1975, at 5, col. 5; Venezuela's nationalization of oil companies in the same year, Washington Post, July 6, 1975, at A10, col. 1; and Kuwait's similar action later that year, Financial Times, Nov. 27, 1975, at 5, col. 5.

There were preimplementation consultations between the U.S. and Canadian governments concerning the latter's "Canadianization" program in 1981. Washington Post, Sept. 10, 1981, at A1, col. 1.

[286] Examples include Cuba in 1960, E. BAKLANOFF, *supra* note 285, at 118, 161–66; Peru's expropriation of the International Petroleum Company in 1968, 7 INT'L LEGAL MATERIALS 1201–62 (1968); Chile's expropriation (under President Allende) of the copper companies in 1971, E. BAKLANOFF, *supra* note 285, at 87–106; Ethiopia's nationalization of financial institutions in 1975, Financial Times, Jan. 2, 1975, at 7, col. 5; and Nigeria's nationalization of British Petroleum's 20 percent interest in Shell–B.P. Petroleum Development Company of Nigeria in 1979, *id.*, Aug. 1, 1979, at 1, col. 3, and Aug. 2, 1979, at 1, col. 7.

[287] OECD Code of Liberalisation of Capital Movements, arts. 7 and 13, OECD Doc. C(61) 96 (Final) (1961). Canada did not adhere to the Code.

took effect.[288] The regulations did not restrict capital flows to developing countries nearly as severely as to industrialized countries. Nevertheless, the regulations seem to have spurred the Inter-American Economic and Social Council into including among the functions of the OAS Special Committee for Consultation and Negotiation: "To hold consultations on measures that might adversely affect the access of the Latin American countries to the capital markets of the developed countries."[289] This does seem to contemplate consultations regarding prospective measures. The United States acquiesced in the resolution, presumably in recognition of Latin America's special dependence on the U.S. capital market.

The U.S. State Department also has cooperated with foreign governments when they wish to object to draft legislation that would restrict business acquisitions in their territories. When the State Department forwards their objections to Congressional committees, however, it apparently does so as a courtesy rather than as an acquiescence in any asserted duty to consult.[290]

As noted in chapter V, the European Economic Community has developed procedures for restrictions in response to large capital inflows or outflows. Although the procedures contemplate prior Commission authorization as the norm, they recognize exceptions in urgent cases or when secrecy is required. Not even prior consultation is necessary in such cases.[291] Since secrecy often will be required to prevent speculative capital flows, the norm may be swallowed by the exception. Moreover, Commission authorization would not necessarily involve consultation with interested governments outside the Community. Consequently, although United States practice might suggest a developing custom of consulting specially affected states before capital outflows are restricted, European practice seems not to support any such general custom. There may be a developing special custom in the Americas to that effect.

[288] *See* the letter from the U.S. Secretary of the Treasury to the Canadian Minister of Finance, Mar. 7, 1968, 7 INT'L LEGAL MATERIALS 455 (1968); Press Conference, 58 DEP'T ST. BULL. 135–42 (1968).

[289] Inter-American ECOSOC Res. REM-1/70, para. 9(b), *supra* note 106.

[290] *See Energy Antimonopoly Act of 1979, S. 1246: Hearings Before the Senate Comm. on the Judiciary,* 96th Cong., 1st Sess., pt. 2 at 717, 1015–22, 1034 (1979). *See also id.* at 705 (direct contacts between Congressional staff and representatives of interested foreign governments).

[291] *See* chapter V at note 230 *supra.*

F. Synthesis: Economic Relations

State practice requires intergovernmental consultation before one government intervenes unilaterally to frustrate another's reasonable expectations regarding the price or quantity of goods (including money) or services moving in noncapital international transactions, unless the intervention is in the form of a subsidy or restraint affecting the intervening country's exports, or (even though no export measure is involved) there is a significant risk of (*a*) market speculation if the government's plans become known, or (*b*) nonminimal harm to the government or to an appreciable segment of the society it represents if the delay inherent in prior consultation is incurred.

The duty would not arise if the foreign government has no objective basis for its expectations, as would usually be the case if a tariff is increased on an item bound neither in the GATT nor by any other promise and not relied upon heavily by the foreign state for its economic development or foreign exchange earnings. If the intervention simply enforces an international standard, even against a state that has not expressly agreed to the standard (as could occur with restrictions on trade in endangered species), it is not an independent, unilateral act and would not necessarily trigger the duty to consult.

A borderline case is that in which an exporting state—usually a developing country—has obtained only a toehold in a particular product market in an industrialized country, and the latter wishes to protect its producers primarily from stronger competition originating in some third state(s). Unless one of the "significant risk" exceptions (above) applies, the protecting state normally will consult the third state(s). But there seems to be no consistent practice, absent a treaty obligation, of consulting the less competitive state, even though the protection will extend to its exports and even though the newly protected market might have been prospectively lucrative for it. The likelihood that the less competitive state will be consulted increases with the protecting government's awareness that it reasonably expects to increase its share of the market.

In the years since the creation of the Bretton Woods system in 1945, the two "significant risk" exceptions (especially the first) have nearly swallowed the rule in the case of noncapital monetary transactions. Thus, the risk of speculation now excuses the duty to consult when an exchange rate float or adjustment is planned and when an import quota, surcharge, or deposit scheme for balance-of-payments purposes is in the offing. But the duty is not automatically excused when an exchange restriction is contemplated, or when members' currencies or reserves are to be used in Fund-related transactions.

In the case of international trade measures, the exceptions are a bit less voracious.[292] The export exception is an established, though relatively confined, anachronism. Although it is more difficult to determine on any given facts whether the other two may properly be invoked, these exceptions have not managed to swallow the rule. In the absence of a third-party adjudication system capable of building a body of case law, about the most one can say is that the closer the economic interdependence of the states involved (or the stronger the economic dependence of the affected state on the acting state) and / or the more squarely the primary burden of the proposed measure would fall on an identifiable state or small group of states, the less likely it is that the exceptions will be invoked successfully. That is, they either will not be invoked at all, or if they are, the justification for their invocation will be examined critically by the affected states, and the acting state either will admit error (sometimes tacitly) or will feel constrained to set forth facts sufficient to justify its nonconsultation.

A similar sliding scale combining economic interdependence (or dependence on the acting state) and weight of burden determines whether there will be prior consultations concerning second-order trade externalities.[293] There appears to be no basic consultation norm for second-order externalities, however, so the sliding scale is not a means of gauging whether an exception applies. Rather, it determines whether an unwritten consultation norm exists in a given instance. In effect, consultation is less likely to be required in a close case than it would be when the sliding scale triggers an exception to an otherwise applicable consultation norm.

In a few instances involving trade, prior consultation norms

[292] Consultation expectations within GATT have been strengthened somewhat by the GATT ministerial undertaking "To give fullest consideration, in the application of measures falling within the GATT framework, and in the general exercise of their GATT rights, to the trading interests of other contracting parties." Final communique of the 1982 GATT Ministerial Conference, para. 7(ii), in 7 U.S. IMPORT WEEKLY (BNA) 301 (1982). *See also* chapter VII, section C *infra*.

[293] Second-order trade externalities are defined and discussed in subsection C6 *supra*.

have developed without being subject to quite such elastic qualifications. The norm has been established regarding surplus disposal, and governments have refrained from asserting any exception. The only real question would arise if the surplus commodity has a speculative market. If so, the "risk of speculation" exception might apply. The norm also has been established regarding new technical specifications. Here the only potentially troublesome exception stems from the need for quick action. That exception has been kept under control so far.

There are, in addition, a few special prior consultation norms limited to the industrialized, nonsocialist states. These apply particularly to some export credits for a relatively well-defined category of goods, pollution-control subsidies, and antitrust enforcement measures. They apply only to those OECD members that did not opt out when these norms were formulated.

In some cases—such as those involving exchange restrictions proposed by Fund members—the duty to consult is discharged by consulting the relevant international organization. The principle remains the same, however, since the organization represents the affected states.

In the area of international direct investment and capital transfers, there seems to be a developing norm that would require consultation with a host government before a foreign government participates in a substantial incoming direct investment, and it may already be the custom to consult states peculiarly and significantly affected by a proposed restriction on capital outflows. Neither of these putative customary norms is well established yet.

Chapter VII

Prior Consultation Practice in a Broad Perspective

A. Introduction

Previous chapters have identified prior consultation norms relating to a variety of specific circumstances. Those norms will not be reiterated here. Instead, the present chapter elevates the level of generality in order to identify, first, some broad contours of the prior consultation principle; second, an implied duty to consult, drawn from a broader duty to consider other states' interests; and third, a number of factors that tend either to nourish or to suppress prior consultation practice, but that do not by themselves definitively establish or negate the presence of a prior consultation norm in any given case.

B. Contours as Developed in Practice

First, there is no across-the-board requirement in international law that governments must consult others whenever they contemplate taking or permitting any unilateral action that might adversely affect the interests of nonnationals or of the international community as a whole. It is necessary to examine the relevant state practice in each case in order to decide whether a prior consultation (or, sometimes, a prior consent) norm attaches to the proposed conduct.[1]

When state practice does establish a prior consultation norm, it is usually limited to cases in which the risk of harm is signif-

[1]This is so despite broad language in the North Sea Continental Shelf Cases drawing on U.N. Charter article 33 as a source of a duty to negotiate the settlement of disputes. *See* 1969 I.C.J. 3, 47. The Court was dealing with a specific situation—continental shelf delimitation. *See* chapter III at notes 62–64 and 152–53 *supra*. Article 33, on its face, applies only to "any dispute, the continuance of which is likely to endanger the maintenance of international peace and security." It would stretch the language of article 33, and the Court's use of it, too far to find in it an across-the-board duty to consult before any dispute could arise.

icant. (If it is too significant, the contemplated activity may well be prohibited, in which case prior consultation becomes a moot point.) To evaluate the risk of harm, one must use a two-factor equation: The magnitude of the risk times the magnitude of the conceivable harm equals the risk of harm. Thus, a high risk of moderate harm might yield the same product as a moderate risk of devastating harm.[2] It is impossible to be precise as to when that product becomes "significant." It will be significant whenever there is a *substantial* risk of *appreciable* harm, but of course these italicized adjectives are not precise either.

Since a "significant" risk of harm cannot be mechanically determined, one must ask who makes the assessment. Clearly, there is no duty, absent a specific treaty obligation, to submit the matter to third-party settlement. The Lake Lanoux tribunal provided some guidance by making the state that is liable to suffer the repercussions of the proposed action the sole judge of its interests.[3] Thus, the acting state cannot simply decide arbitrarily that the risk of harm is insubstantial. On the other hand, the tribunal surely did not mean to say that the "suffering" state may decide arbitrarily that its interests are so great (or are so greatly endangered) that the risk of harm is significant—thus triggering a consultation duty that effectively delays the proposed action while the parties consult.[4]

The dilemma is alleviated somewhat by the customary duty of each side to act in good faith.[5] This, taken in conjunction with the Lake Lanoux dictum, would seem to require the acting state to notify potentially affected states of its plans in sufficient time to permit consultations if the risk of harm is arguably

[2]*See* Handl, *The Principle of "Equitable Use" as Applied to Internationally Shared Natural Resources: Its Role in Resolving Potential International Disputes over Transfrontier Pollution,* 1978–79 REV. BELGE DE DROIT INT'L 40, 61.

[3]*See* chapter II at note 67 *supra.*

[4]The Lake Lanoux tribunal found that a duty to refrain from operations prejudicial to the nonacting state's interests was implicit in the duty to negotiate. *See* chapter II at note 67 *supra. See also* the OECD Recommendation on Principles Concerning Transfrontier Pollution, in chapter II at note 204 *supra.*

[5]*See* Kass, *Obligatory Negotiations in International Organizations,* 1965 CAN. Y.B. INT'L L. 36, 42. Judge Richard Baxter, shortly before his untimely death, asserted that a duty to negotiate "in good faith" is an empty one, in the absence of appropriate adjudicative machinery. Baxter, *International Law in "Her Infinite Variety,"* 29 INT'L & COMP. L.Q. 549, 552 (1980). The assertion is puzzling. In many cases the presence or absence of good faith is quite apparent; even when that is not so, the standard is no more illusory than many other standards combining fact and law, and its application may be clarified through the usual international processes of assertion, counter-assertion, and acquiescence.

significant, and to engage in consultations if the potentially affected state or states make a plausible case that the risk of harm is indeed significant. In some cases, the very nature of the activity probably would produce such a plausibly significant risk of harm that the duty to notify, and to consult on request, could not reasonably be denied. For example, a project to alter the course of a river where it crosses an international boundary, or to engage in an activity that would inject a substantial amount of a known, untreated pollutant into a confined international watercourse, would, by its nature, meet the test. So would a plan by a state or international organization that would disrupt an ongoing, close relationship between itself and another international organization or state.[6]

Prior consultation is not synonymous with prior consent. A prior consultation duty does imply that the proposed activity will not be pursued, or at least will not be carried to a point at which it becomes a fait accompli, while good faith consultations are being conducted. But it does not imply that the state being consulted may block or indefinitely delay a project simply by withholding its consent. Only a reasonable delay, to give time for good faith consultations, is required in the absence of a treaty obligation or state practice requiring actual consent.[7]

A duty to consult in good faith implies that the states involved must be forthcoming about their intentions and about communicating any relevant, nonsensitive information they either have or could reasonably obtain, in order to make the consultations meaningful. In some cases, this would mean delaying a proposed project while relevant information is developed regarding its effects.[8] Sensitive data relating to such matters as national security or business secrets normally need not be produced.[9]

As previous chapters have shown, decisions to act unilaterally are frequently made in stages rather than all at once. A common

[6] *Cf.* Advisory Opinion on Interpretation of the Agreement of 25 March 1951 Between the WHO and Egypt, 1980 I.C.J. 73, 92–94, *reprinted in* 20 INT'L LEGAL MATERIALS 88, 98–99 (1981).

[7] *See* chapter II at notes 175–79 *supra*.

[8] *See* The U.S.-Canadian Int'l Joint Comm'n Report on Water Apportionment in the Poplar River Basin, discussed in chapter II at note 138 *supra*.

[9] Note, for example, the exception in NATO practice for fallback positions in SALT bargaining, chapter V at note 88 *supra*, and the exception for confidential business data in prior consultation practice relating to countervailing and antidumping duties, chapter VI at notes 129–33 *supra*.

situation involves a basic governmental decision to accomplish a certain objective—an extension of maritime jurisdiction to a specific distance, a reduction in military spending, a sale of surplus goods—which must be implemented by detailed decisions regarding timing, precise magnitudes, and the like. In such cases the tendency is to consult affected states after the basic decision, but before the implementing decisions are made.[10] In some instances, however, state practice calls for consultations before even a basic decision is made—if time permits. This is the norm when the basic decision, if irrevocable, could very significantly affect important interests of a discreet group of other states (or, occasionally, of the world community) no matter how it is carried out.[11]

Finally, there are situations in which a prior consultation duty exists, but no categorical statement can be made as to whether the consultations must precede the basic decision. The circumstances of the case will determine whether the initial decision threatens the type of detriment that could not substantially be alleviated by moderation in executing it. In this category, for example, are many decisions regarding activities that could pose environmental risks.

C. Implications of a Duty to Consider Other States' Interests

When a state is under a duty (imposed by treaty, custom, or any other source of international law) to consider the established interests of an identifiable group of states while exercising a right of its own, the state planning to exercise its right must consult those states before it acts, unless it is clear that the contemplated action would not significantly affect their interests. This could be deduced from a duty to consider other states' established interests, since consultation would be the only sure way to ascertain and evaluate the impact of the proposed action on those interests. But the duty to consult does not depend on deduction alone.

[10]This has been the practice in the three situations mentioned in the text. *See* chapter IV, section B (ocean jurisdictional extensions); chapter V at notes 27–47 (reductions in forces committed to NATO); chapter VI at notes 199–209 (disposal of surpluses).

[11]*See, e.g.,* chapter IV at notes 139–43 (disposals of radioactive waste at sea or on remote islands); chapter V, subsection B7 (confrontations that could lead to, or significantly escalate, a war); chapter V at notes 174 and 185 (exchange rate adjustments under the 1979 European Monetary System).

The principal source of the implied duty is the *Fisheries Jurisdiction* Cases. After finding that Iceland had only a preferential right to the fishery beyond twelve miles offshore, the International Court said this meant that "The coastal State has to take into account and pay regard to the position of [other states with important, established fishing interests in the area], particularly when they have established an economic dependence on the same fishing grounds."[12] The Court went on to say, "[T]he principle of reasonable regard for the interests of other States enshrined in Article 2 of the Geneva Convention on the High Seas of 1958 requires Iceland and [the United Kingdom or the Federal Republic of Germany] to have due regard to each other's interests, and to the interests of other States, in those resources."[13] In the same vein, the Court noted that "[B]oth States have an obligation to take full account of each other's rights and of any fishery conservation measures the necessity of which is shown to exist in those waters. It is one of the advances in maritime international law, resulting from the intensification of fishing, that the former *laissez-faire* treatment of the living resources of the sea in the high seas has been replaced by a recognition of a duty to have due regard to the rights of other States and the needs of conservation for the benefit of all."[14] After further discussion of the concept of preferential rights, the Court completed the connection between the duty to consider other states' interests and the duty to negotiate (or the lesser duty to consult) by pointing out, "The obligation to negotiate thus flows from the very nature of the respective rights of the Parties."[15]

It is immaterial for our purposes that events at the Third Law of the Sea Conference have overtaken the Court's notion that coastal states can assert no more than preferential rights to fisheries beyond twelve miles against states with established interests. We need to be concerned at this point only with the procedural consequences of preferential rights, not with determining when a right is preferential and when it is exclusive.

[12] 1974 I.C.J. 3, 28 and 175, 196.

[13] *Id.* at 29 and at 198.

[14] *Id.* at 31 and at 200.

[15] *Id.* at 32 and at 201. *See also* Advisory Opinion on Interpretation of the Agreement of 25 March 1951 Between the WHO and Egypt, *supra* note 6, and Judge Ruda's Separate Opinion in that case, 1980 I.C.J. at 114, 124, *reprinted in* 20 INT'L LEGAL MATERIALS at 109, 114 (1981).

What is important is that the Court found from the concept of a preferential right (as it found from article 2 of the Convention on the High Seas and—in different contexts—could find from other treaty norms or from state practice) a duty to take account of other states' established interests. Moreover, it contemplated that the duty could extend to states without quite as great an interest as the United Kingdom or the Federal Republic of Germany. The duty to consider other states' established interests defined the "very nature of the respective rights of the Parties," which in turn engendered the duty to negotiate. That duty encompasses the lesser duty to consult instead of simply acting unilaterally.

An express duty to take account of another state's interests has often been combined with an express duty to consult.[16] Since the drafters of such provisions thought it necessary or appropriate to pronounce the consultation duty expressly, one might ask whether it is justifiable to imply such a duty when nothing beyond the duty to consider other states' interests has been set forth. The *Fisheries Jurisdiction* Cases answer that question.

Article 2 of the Convention on the High Seas, which has a counterpart in article 87 of the Convention on the Law of the Sea,[17] is the most prominent instance in which the duty to consult must be implied from a duty to consider other states' interests. Less prominent examples include the trade agreements between the European Economic Community and the Arab states in the Middle East.[18]

It is arguable that Principle 21 of the 1972 Stockholm Declaration on the Human Environment is another example. This is so even though a companion principle, which would have

[16]*See, e.g.*, Outer Space Treaty, Jan. 27, 1967, art. 9, 18 U.S.T. 2410, 610 U.N.T.S. 205, discussed in chapter IV, note 185 *supra*. *See also* London Ocean Dumping Convention, Dec. 29, 1972, preamble and art. 5(2), 26 U.S.T. 2403, *reprinted in* 11 INT'L LEGAL MATERIALS 1294 (1972), discussed in chapter IV at notes 148–52; Nordic Convention on the Protection of the Environment, Feb. 19, 1974, arts. 2, 11, in 13 INT'L LEGAL MATERIALS 591 (1974), discussed in chapter III at notes 14–17; OECD Principles Concerning Transfrontier Pollution, Nov. 14, 1974, Titles C and E, 14 INT'L LEGAL MATERIALS 242 (1975), and OECD Recommendation on Implementation of a Regime of Equal Right of Access and Non-Discrimination in Relation to Transfrontier Pollution, May 17, 1977, Titles A and C, 16 *id.* at 977 (1977). The OECD instruments are reprinted in OECD AND THE ENVIRONMENT 106 and 115 (2d ed. 1979), and are discussed in chapter II at notes 204–09 *supra*.

[17]Dec. 10, 1982, U.N. Doc. A/CONF.62/122 (1982).

[18]*See* chapter VI at notes 181–82 *supra*. *See also* chapter VI at note 292 *supra* (final communique of 1982 GATT Ministerial Conference).

provided expressly for prior consultation, was deleted from the Declaration as finally adopted.[19] Principle 21 provides in part, "States have . . . the responsibility to ensure that activities within their jurisdiction or control do not cause damage to the environment of other States or of areas beyond the limits of national jurisdiction."[20] This is tantamount to saying that states have the responsibility to consider the environmental interests of other states that could be affected significantly and those of the world community when the international commons could be damaged. In the latter case, any consultation duty would be discharged within the relevant international organization.

Although the deletion of the express consultation provision would suggest that no implied consultation duty could have been found as of 1972, the law has evolved since then. The *Fisheries Jurisdiction* Cases were decided in 1974. In that same year the U.N. General Assembly's Charter of Economic Rights and Duties called upon states exploiting shared natural resources to cooperate through a system of information and prior consultation in order to make optimum use of the resources "without causing damage to the legitimate interests of others."[21] The U.N. Environment Programme's 1978 agreed text supplied procedural details to make the consultations meaningful.[22] These developments suggest that it would now be reasonable to read the World Court's implied consultation duty into the Stockholm principle on state responsibility.[23] Since the principle is not limited to "shared resources," the debate over the precise scope of that term would become academic.[24]

[19]*See* chapter II at notes 169 and 191 *supra*.

[20]Declaration of the United Nations Conference on the Human Environment, June 16, 1972, Principle 21, 11 INT'L LEGAL MATERIALS 1416 (1972). This principle gives some substance to the maxim, *sic utere tuo ut alienum non laedas*.

[21]*See* chapter II at note 194 *supra*. *See also* G.A. Res. 3129, chapter II at note 192 *supra*.

[22]*See* chapter II at note 196 *supra*.

[23]*Cf.* Suy, *Innovations in International Law-Making Process*, in THE INTERNATIONAL LAW AND POLICY OF HUMAN WELFARE 187, 193 (R. MacDonald, D. Johnston, & G. Morris eds. 1978) (tying shared resources resolutions to past practice). Note, though, that the General Assembly had not formally adopted the 1978 agreed text by the end of its 36th session. Some states still thought it premature to do so. *See* U.N. Docs. A/C.2/34/SR.57 at 6–7, and A/C.2/34/SR.58 at 3–4 (1979).

[24]Brazil has argued that a "shared resource" is one that is contiguous to two or more states, and would not include (for example) successive rivers. For the definition enjoying the greatest degree of consensus, *see* chapter II at note 197 *supra*.

Principle 21 does not settle the question of whether, in any given case, the consultation must precede the basic decision to develop an activity that could cause trans-

A promise or other duty to consider the interests of other states, absent an apparent way to distinguish those particularly affected from all others, or absent a relevant international organization to represent the common interest, would not imply a duty to consult. The implication arises, in other words, only when consultations would be practicable, as in the case of U.S. disposals of strategic materials from its stockpile.[25] An example involving no implied duty to consult arises from the undertaking by the members of the International Energy Agency to "give full consideration to the needs and interests of other oil consuming countries, particularly those of the developing countries,"[26] unless the proposed measure would uniquely affect an identifiable group of countries that could reasonably be consulted directly or through an international organization. In some cases involving special interests of developing countries, UNCTAD might provide an appropriate forum for consultation.

D. Practice-Influencing Factors

It is possible to identify a number of key factors, or circumstances, that tend to stimulate or deter prior consultation practice. The presence of any of these factors would not, in itself, establish whether or not a prior consultation duty exists in the usual case. To do that requires the kind of examination of state practice (including, of course, treaty practice) offered in the preceding chapters of this book. Identifying practice-influencing factors, however, does serve at least two purposes: (*a*) Those factors are signals to the decision maker or scholar that a careful examination is (or is not) likely to reveal a pattern of prior consultation practice; and (*b*) in a close case, involving some consultation practice that may not be clearly of sufficient quality or quantity to establish a norm, the presence of one or more of the factors could be determinative.

1. Factors Promoting Consultation

Starting at the highest level of generality, the greater the risk

national environmental harm, or whether consultation simply could take place before the basic decision is implemented.

[25] *See* chapter VI at note 208 *supra*. In this case the duty to consider the interests of particular states arises from a domestic (federal) statute.

[26] Agreement on an International Energy Program, Nov. 18, 1974, art. 45, 27 U.S.T. 1685, T.I.A.S. No. 8278.

of transnational harm from a nonprohibited activity, the greater the likelihood that prior consultation (if not prior consent) will be required. For example, the international community recently has placed considerable value on maintaining the integrity of relatively unspoiled areas of the international commons. Consequently, one finds an impressive, though not ubiquitous, body of prior consultation practice concerning activities that could deplete, or cause significant harm to, such areas. This practice applies to such things as nonprohibited disposals of hazardous wastes at sea[27] and outer space activities that could interfere with other states' space activities.[28] Arguably, it also applies to mineral resource exploitation in Antarctica (even though not all states recognize Antarctica as an international commons).[29] The United States in 1972 acknowledged a duty to consult before authorizing deep-seabed mining.[30]

Nonprohibited action that could encroach on another state's territory (or on its rights in an area geographically and juridically related to its territory, such as a coastal maritime zone) is at least as sensitive as action that could endanger relatively unspoiled areas of the international commons. Thus, one frequently finds a duty to consult the affected state. This applies, for example, to potentially overlapping maritime zone claims,[31] to seabed activities near coastal states' maritime zones,[32] to U.N. peacekeeping within a state's territory,[33] and to certain on-site

[27] *See* the discussions of *(a)* radioactive waste disposal in chapter III at note 117 and in chapter IV at notes 136–43; and *(b)* the London Ocean Dumping Convention in chapter IV at notes 148–52.

[28] *See* chapter IV at notes 176–92 *supra.*

[29] *See* chapter IV at notes 158–60 *supra.* The consultation norm does not apply to Antarctic krill.

[30] *See* chapter IV at notes 131–33 *supra.* Many states do not concede the lawfulness of deep seabed mining, with or without consultation, unless it is authorized by an established seabed authority. Nevertheless, the U.S. acknowledgment of a duty to consult is significant as a recognized limitation on an asserted freedom to act.

[31] *See* chapter III at notes 62–77, 93–98, 129–32 *supra.*

[32] *See* chapter IV at notes 129–30 *supra.*

[33] *See* chapter V at notes 246–50 *supra.* Compare IAEA practice relating to inspection of safeguarded nuclear facilities. To maintain the integrity of the safeguards, surprise inspections may be conducted, but they are the exception rather than the rule. IAEA inspection teams are selected in consultation with, and subject to the approval of, the states to be inspected. *See* D. KAY, THE FUNCTIONING AND EFFECTIVENESS OF SELECTED UNITED NATIONS SYSTEM PROGRAMS 154–55 (Am. Soc'y of Int'l L. Stud. in Transnat'l Legal Pol'y No. 18, 1980).

human rights investigations.[34] Prior consultation norms regarding the pollution of international watercourses[35] and transboundary climate modification[36] probably fall within the same category, since physical effects are felt in the other state's territory in those cases.

When an international norm requires or prohibits a particular course of action but contains an escape device for exceptional cases, the right to employ the escape device (and thus to act inconsistently with the basic norm) is usually hedged with a duty to consult the states affected or a representative international organization beforehand, unless the emergency justifying use of the escape device does not permit time for consultation. These escape devices are often attached to international environmental and trade norms.[37]

Two interrelated factors that tend strongly to nourish prior consultation practice are (*a*) existing or budding close political ties between the acting and potentially affected states, when the proposed action is important to their relationship; and (*b*) dependence by a discreet, identifiable group of states (or a single state) on a relationship, situation, or physical condition that could be changed significantly by the proposed action.

In the former category—proposed action affecting a close relationship—one could point to the extensive prior consultation practice between the United States and Canada,[38] practice

[34]The European Convention for the Protection of Human Rights and Fundamental Freedoms, Nov. 4, 1950, art. 28, 213 U.N.T.S. 221, EUROPEAN CONVENTION ON HUMAN RIGHTS: COLLECTED TEXTS 101 (1981 ed.), authorizes the European Commission of Human Rights to conduct investigations within the territories of member states, who "shall furnish all necessary facilities, after an exchange of views with the Commission."

The American Convention on Human Rights, Nov. 22, 1969, art. 48(1)(d), OAS Treaty Series, No. 36, at 1, is not as explicit, but implies advance consultation when it says that the Inter-American Commission "shall request, and the states concerned shall furnish to it, all necessary facilities."

[35]*See* chapter II at notes 26–40, 109–13, 135–36, 150–51, 160, 184–88, 191–209 *supra*.

[36]*See* chapter III at notes 100–105, 137–40, 162 *supra*, dealing with weather modification as well as climate modification. The consultation norm is clearer in the case of climate modification.

[37]*See* chapter II at notes 109–10 (African Convention on the Conservation of Nature and Natural Resources); chapter III at note 37 (European treaties on emergency dumping at sea of noxious substances); chapter IV at notes 148–51 (London Ocean Dumping Convention); chapter V at notes 187, 198–99, 216–18, 221 (monetary, transportation, and trade measures in the European Communities); and chapter VI at notes 70–73 (GATT art. XIX), 84–91 (textile arrangements), 105–10 (developing countries' assertions regarding safeguard action by industralized countries).

[38]*See, e.g.*, chapter II at notes 114–39 (watercourses); Chapter III at notes 100–102

among the NATO allies,[39] and that involving the members and nascent members of the European Communities.[40] Other examples, not covered elsewhere in this study, are available.[41]

In the latter category, proposed action involving an element of dependence, one could cite a number of instances concerning river pollution,[42] environmental risks to relatively confined areas other than rivers,[43] exploitation of nonrenewable resources straddling a boundary or delimitation line,[44] economic relations between developing and industrialized countries,[45] and (less consistently) trade relations affecting goods of particular importance to the nonacting state even though it is not a developing country.[46] Sometimes, of course, these instances involve

(weather modification), 105–08 (frontier issues generally), 131 (maritime boundary delimitation); chapter IV at note 117 (bottom trawling enforcement); chapter VI at notes 234–35 (antitrust enforcement). *See also* 80 DEP'T ST. BULL., June 1980, at 22 (assurance by U.S. Secretary of State of full consultation with Canada on law of sea issues).

[39] *See* chapter V at notes 5 (direct threat to any member's security), 24–47 (decisions to limit military commitments), 48–49 (use of tactical nuclear weapons in Europe), 71–72 and 87–93 (sensitive arms control negotiations), 95–107 (distinct rapprochement steps toward Eastern Europe), 123–31 (armed confrontations with the Soviet Union), 144–46 (sale of militarily useful goods to Communist states).

[40] *See* chapter V at notes 157–58 (new members before accession), 168–72 (nontariff barriers), 174 and 185 (European Monetary System), 186 (balance-of-payments borrowing), 193–97 (macroeconomic policies), 198–203 (common transport policy), 205 (nuclear energy), 224 (export credits), 225–26 (economic cooperation agreements), 231–34 (important foreign policy questions).

[41] For example: *(a)* When the U.K. was preparing its plans for a Rhodesian settlement in the summer of 1979, it consulted its Commonwealth partners. *See* Financial Times, July 11, 1979, at 1, col. 7; Washington Post, Aug. 2, 1979, at A26, col. 3. *(b)* When the United States was considering submitting a draft Security Council resolution to bring the Palestinian Arabs into the Middle East peace talks, it consulted Israel and then dropped the idea, at least temporarily. *See* Washington Post, Aug. 18, 1979, at A1, col. 5.

[42] *See* note 35 *supra*.

[43] *See* chapter III at notes 3–42 (European practice regarding relatively contained environments), 80 (African Convention on the Conservation of Nature and Natural Resources), 109–14 (U.S.-Canadian practice in ecologically fragile sea areas); chapter IV at note 143 (U.S. proposal to store spent nuclear fuel on South Pacific islands).

[44] *See* chapter III at notes 78, 99; *cf. id.* at note 133 (inconclusive practice in the Americas).

[45] *See, e.g.*, chapter VI at notes 106–10 and 289 (Latin American–U.S. relations concerning trade and access to capital markets), 178–82 (effect of across-the-board tariff reduction on preferential trade agreements), 192 (effect on Caribbean states of U.S. export promotion).

[46] Compare the U.S. insistence on prior consultation regarding Canadian changes in natural gas export policy with its nonassertive attitude toward Canadian oil export policy. *See* chapter VI at notes 155–57. The OPEC states feel no compulsion to consult oil consuming states regarding price and quantity decisions. See chapter VI at note 159. The United States consults consumer nations before it imposes short supply export

close political relationships as well as elements of dependence.

When an international forum (such as a joint commission) has jurisdiction to consider a proposed action by a member state, one is likely to find members asserting a duty to consult within the forum—especially if the agreement establishing it also expressly imposes on the member states a duty to cooperate with it. A member proposing to act will usually, but not always, acquiesce in these assertions.[47]

Occasionally it is appropriate to imply a prior consultation duty from an express duty to notify proposed action to interested states. In the usual case, however, a notification duty that does not mention consultation is intended simply to give affected states an opportunity to adapt to the new conditions. This is particularly apparent when the instrument calling for notification does not specifically require that it always precede the action. The exception—when a prior consultation duty could be implied—is likely to arise when notification clearly must precede action (especially if details of the proposed action must be included) and the contemplated action is such that the affected state or states probably could not adapt to it in the short run without substantial loss.[48]

Prior consultation duties often arise in transitional situations, when groups of states are moving from relatively unstructured relationships *inter sese* to the delegation of quasi-governmental authority to some representative organ. The paradigm is the European Community, where prior consultation has frequently been used as the procedural mechanism to ease transitions to the Community's exercise of decision-making functions binding

controls, unless secrecy is necessary to prevent speculation. *See* chapter VI at notes 148–50.

[47]Consultation practice is reasonably consistent when there is an international freshwater commission with jurisdiction over the proposed act. *See* chapter II at notes 22–24, 32–35, 40, 46–50, 61–67, 100–102 *supra*. Similarly, in the European Communities, prior consultation with the Commission of the Communities is required in a wide variety of circumstances. *See* chapter II at note 38, and chapter V, Section C. *But see* chapter VI at note 62 (U.K. did not acquiesce in its EFTA partners' assertions regarding consultation before the U.K. imposed an import surcharge in 1964).

[48]Notification duty not implying consultation duty: Chapter VI at notes 54, 56, 57 (trade measures for balance-of-payments purposes), 77 (provisional trade safeguard measures by developing countries), 195–96 (products not covered by express prior notification-consultation principle in OECD Guidelines for Officially Supported Export Credits). Notification duty implying consultation duty: Indus Waters Treaty, chapter II at notes 84–85; U.S. antidumping and countervailing duty regulations for proceedings by private parties, cited in chapter VI, notes 131, 134.

upon member states.[49] But prior consultation also may be seen as a transitional mechanism in some instances not involving a supranational organization. This appears to be so, for example, in the case of ocean dumping. What was once an unstructured regime lacking procedural safeguards has evolved into one featuring relatively elaborate consultation requirements for the dumping of those harmful substances that can still (sometimes) lawfully be dumped, and the trend is toward even tighter regulatory measures.[50]

Prior consultation norms flourish as procedural safeguards in international organizations when the member states delegate to a central organ functions normally regarded as the prerogatives of national governments. Often these norms connote transition toward greater international authority, at least if one looks at the long term. But they may also operate primarily as safety devices permitting sovereignty-conscious governments to relinquish limited authority to decision-making bodies with international constituencies, regardless of whether more extensive relinquishment is in the offing. Examples already discussed in this study involve the European Community,[51] the United Nations,[52] and the International Monetary Fund.[53] Other examples could be given.[54]

[49]*See* chapter V at notes 157–58 (relationship with prospective new members), 159 (antitrust), 175–85 (evolution toward monetary union), 210–20 (development of common commercial policy in relations with nonmember states). One might also view the essentially consultative role of the European Parliament as transitional in the movement toward development of fuller parliamentary authority. *See* chapter V at notes 152–53 *supra.*

[50]*See* chapter IV at notes 136–53 *supra.*

[51]*See* chapter V at notes 152–54 (important decisions regarding relations within the Community), 221, 223 (external relations).

[52]*See* chapter V at notes 240 (U.N. Charter art. 44), 246–50 (peacekeeping activities), 254 (international claims).

[53]*See* chapter VI at notes 35–43 *supra* (Fund decisions affecting members' currencies).

[54]Cases in point would include the procedures of the Food and Agriculture Organization and the International Civil Aviation Organization for the establishment of international standards in their respective fields. *See* 2 D. LEIVE, INTERNATIONAL REGULATORY REGIMES 439–56 (1976); Fitzgerald, *The International Civil Aviation Organization—A Case Study in the Implementation of Decisions of a Functional International Organization,* in THE EFFECTIVENESS OF INTERNATIONAL DECISIONS 156, 170–71 (S. Schwebel ed. 1971).

An analogous case involves the humanitarian functions of a Swiss organization, the International Committee of the Red Cross (ICRC). The law of international armed conflict contemplates that protecting powers (neutral states) will be appointed to safeguard the interests of the parties to a conflict. The system is fallible, so provision has been made for the ICRC to act as a substitute, if it is willing to do so—but only after

2. Factors Deterring Consultation

Two related factors provide widely recognized yet often-abused excuses for nonconsultation in situations where consultation normally would be expected. One is the need for secrecy to prevent speculation, as in the case of imminent decisions affecting commodities or currencies in which a speculative market exists.[55] The other is the need to act quickly in an emergency—a pervasive factor that affects consultation practice in a number of fields.[56] The emergency excuse is particularly troublesome when a government is willing to concede a basic consultation duty, but wishes to avoid condemnation for failing to abide by it in a case in which reasonably prompt action is necessary or desirable. The absence of any authoritative international review body in such cases hinders assessment of the emergency's true extent.[57]

When important national political considerations are at stake, prior consultation is unlikely—except to the extent that decisions in such cases directly affect the sensitive interests of close allies to whom the acting state is bound by a formal alliance. Even then, the perceived need for secrecy or immediate action sometimes takes priority. Thus, although consultations within NATO are expected before decisions are made that go to the heart of the alliance's defensive capability,[58] the United States did not feel obliged to consult Japan or its NATO allies before the initial shift in its China policy toward recognition of the

consultations with the parties to the conflict, and only after taking into account the results of the consultations. *See* Protocol I Additional to the Geneva Conventions of 12 August 1949, and Relating to the Protection of Victims of International Armed Conflicts, June 8, 1977, art. 5(4), U.N. Doc. A/32/144 (1977), in THE LAWS OF ARMED CONFLICTS 551 (D. Schindler & J. Toman eds., 2d ed. 1981).

[55] *See* chapter V at note 230 (restrictions on certain capital movements by European Community member states); chapter VI at notes 6–25 (IMF practice concerning exchange-rate alterations), 149–50 (U.S. export controls on soybeans).

[56] *See* chapter IV at note 148 (ocean dumping); chapter V at notes 27, 102, 109, 114–16, 123–25 (responses to crises by NATO members), 187, 198, 220 (economic crises within the European Communities); chapter VI at notes 70, 84, 94 (emergencies requiring import safeguards), 198–99 (emergency food aid exception to FAO consultation procedure), 234–49 (antitrust enforcement).

[57] Cases in which doubtful "emergencies" were claimed include the U.S. increased duty on sugar in 1977, *discussed in* chapter VI at notes 108–09, and the French import quotas in 1968, *discussed in* chapter VI at notes 120–21.

[58] *See* chapter V, section B *supra*, for the specific circumstances in which NATO consultations are expected.

People's Republic.[59] Military responses to perceived threats have not always been preceded by consultations even within NATO, but a norm has now been established requiring such consultation as is practicable when a military deployment would increase the allies' vulnerability to attack from the Soviet Union.[60] Outside the alliance context, decisions directly related to national security usually are not preceded by consultations.[61]

Prior consultation is less likely to occur when unilateral action is in the form of a legislative enactment than when it results from governmental decisions implementing preexisting legislation or taken without any direct legislative participation. This is particularly true in countries such as the United States, where the political party of the chief executive does not necessarily control the legislature and where party discipline is relatively weak. The result is that the officials responsible for the conduct of foreign affairs may not be able to consult effectively about pending legislation, since they may not be in control of the legislative process.[62] Even in countries where the cabinet or

[59]*See* Katzenbach, *Foreign Policy, Public Opinion and Secrecy*, 52 FOREIGN AFF. 1, 13 (1973); Christopher, *The U.S. and Japan: A Time for Healing*, 56 *id.* 857, 859 (1978); chapter V at note 137 *supra*. The United States also neglected to consult either the Republic of China (Taiwan) or its NATO allies when it decided to grant formal recognition to the People's Republic. *See* Washington Post, Dec. 29, 1978, at A1, col. 5; chapter V at note 138 *supra*.

[60]*See* chapter V at notes 123–33 and at subsection B7.

[61]*See* chapter IV at notes 98 (air defense identification zones), 164–66 (nuclear tests). The General Agreement on Tariffs and Trade contains a national security exception, as have the International Tin Agreements. GATT art. XXI, in IV GATT, BASIC INSTRUMENTS AND SELECTED DOCUMENTS 1 (1969); Fifth International Tin Agreement, June 21, 1974, art. 44, 28 U.S.T. 4619, T.I.A.S. No. 8607; Sixth International Tin Agreement, June 26, 1981, art. 47, U.N. Doc. TD/TIN.6/14 (1981).

[62]Note, for example, the incomplete (but not entirely futile) consultations by the U.S. Department of State while the Clean Water Act of 1977 was pending, chapter IV at notes 78–79. Note also the ineffective NATO consultation while Congress was considering its arms embargo against Turkey, chapter V at note 60.

There were some consultations by the United States while the Fishery Conservation and Management Act of 1976 (establishing a 200-mile fishery zone) was being considered, but the significant consultations occurred after Congress had completed its work. *See* chapter IV at notes 93–95 *supra*. This appears also to have been the case regarding the "buy and hire national" provisions of the Outer Continental Shelf Lands Act Amendments of 1978, Pub. L. No. 95-372, § 208, 43 U.S.C. § 1356 (Supp. II 1978). *See* 124 CONG. REC. 2048 (1978); *Contemporary Practice of the United States Relating to International Law*, 73 AM. J. INT'L L. 669, 679 (1979).

When the executive branch proposes legislation that foreseeably would affect the important interests of a particular country, reasonably thorough consultations in response to a claim of right may be expected. A case in point is the proposed revision of the U.S. Clean Air Act, chapter III at note 124 *supra*.

executive has relative control over legislation, consultation while legislation is pending may well be deterred by the delays and uncertainties of the legislative process.[63]

When proposed unilateral action would affect foreign interests only in the sense that it encompasses aliens within the acting state's own territory, air space, or maritime zone, consultations with foreign governments are much less likely than when the action would affect their nationals in an international commons or in their own territories. The contrast is well illustrated by comparing coastal states' authority under the Convention on the Law of the Sea to establish total allowable catches for fish within their 200-mile economic zones with their authority to establish the catches for anadromous fish even beyond the 200-mile zones. They need not consult in the former case, but must consult other interested states in the latter.[64]

Finally, there are situations in which potentially affected states do not wish to be associated with a particular state's proposed action and, thus, tend to reject any tendered role in the matter. The typical case involves politically sensitive action by the proposing state that could create "second-order externalities"[65] for allied governments whose major interests are not directly at stake, but whose image may be tarnished (or who may fear retaliation by those whose interests are directly at stake) if they appear to have participated in the decision-making process. Examples include the British reaction to the proposed Truman Proclamation on the Continental Shelf in 1945,[66] and the NATO allies' disengagement from the United States' use of military force in cases not involving direct confrontations with the Soviet Union.[67]

E. Conclusion

State practice establishes that prior consultation is a widely utilized, but certainly not universal, procedural mechanism serving

[63] For further discussion, see OECD Secretariat, Information and Consultation on Transfrontier Pollution, OECD Doc. ENV(79)23, at 11, 14–17 (1979).

[64] After it establishes the total allowable catch within the zone, the coastal state must consult other interested states before allocating any surplus beyond its own harvesting capability. *See* chapter IV at notes 99–105 *supra*.

[65] *See* chapter VI, subsection C6 *supra*.

[66] Although the United States consulted the U.K. before issuing the Truman Proclamation, the British Embassy in Washington responded, "His Majesty's Government do not wish to be associated with this Decision and would prefer that, when it is announced, no reference should be made to prior consultation with His Majesty's Government. . . ." 1945 [2]Foreign Relations of the United States 1527.

[67] *See* chapter V at notes 116, 118–22 *supra*.

to inject into national decision-making processes the extranational effects of proposed decisions. Its use as a dispute-avoidance device is growing, as assertions of a right to be consulted are increasingly made by directly affected states and are increasingly honored by other states as they decide how to proceed.

Despite the growth of prior consultation norms, it is unlikely that there will be any all-encompassing prior consultation duty in the foreseeable future. Thus, to the extent that formal procedural structures for prior consultation may be desirable, they should be tailored to recurring, relatively well-defined, troublesome situations. Several international consultative bodies of this sort already exist, ranging in size and scope from bilateral river or boundary commissions through relatively small multilateral bodies (such as the NATO Council or the Commission of the European Communities) to multilateral organizations with wide membership but relatively narrow focus (such as the International Monetary Fund and the General Agreement on Tariffs and Trade, which perform consultative functions as to some matters within their spheres of interest). Any of these bodies might serve as a useful model, depending on the circumstances, though it should be stressed that no formal structure is necessary for prior consultation norms to develop. The familiar process of assertion and acquiescence occurs here as in other fields, with or without formal structures, and may be expected to continue.

As the process does continue, new consultative forums inevitably will be devised for the purpose of regularizing the consultation process among interested states. As indicated above, each forum should have a circumscribed focus. Because these forums must differ according to their differing memberships and concerns, this study has not attempted to set forth an ideal structure for them. I hope, however, that the study has not only identified existing and developing prior consultation norms for the guidance of decision makers in the give and take of state practice, but has suggested those areas in which practice has developed sufficiently to justify efforts to construct new or improved consultative mechanisms.

Afterword

Brief mention needs to be made of a few events that occurred or were reported too late for inclusion in the preceding chapters.

International watercourses and the environment (chapters II and III). At its 1982 Conference, the International Law Association accepted a report of its Committee on International Water Resources Law, containing Draft Articles on Water Pollution in an International Drainage Basin. In addition, the I.L.A. adopted the Montreal Rules of International Law Applicable to Transfrontier Pollution.

Article 5(b) of the Draft Articles on Water Pollution says that basin states shall "notify the other states concerned in due time of any activities envisaged in their own territories that may involve a significant threat of, or increase in, water pollution in the territories of those other states." Article 6 adds, "Basin states shall consult one another on actual or potential problems of water pollution in the drainage basin so as to reach, by methods of their own choice, a solution consistent with their rights and duties under international law."[1] The language is mandatory. It is buttressed by the assertion of the I.L.A.'s Committee on Legal Aspects of the Conservation of the Environment: "With respect to the use of the waters of international drainage basins the principle of consultation and negotiation has become a rule of customary international law."[2]

The Montreal Rules are not limited to water pollution. They are intended to restate general international law relating to transfrontier pollution, i.e., that which originates wholly or in part within the territory of one state and which has deleterious effects in the territory of another state. The rules include a duty to give prior notice of planned activities that might entail a significant risk of transfrontier pollution, and say that "States should make environmental assessments before carrying out such activities."[3] They continue, in article 8:

[1] REPORT OF THE 60TH CONF. OF THE INT'L LAW ASS'N, 1982. *See generally* chapter II of this book, at notes 191–209.

[2] REPORT OF THE 60TH CONF. OF THE INT'L LAW ASS'N, 1982.

[3] Montreal Rules of International Law Applicable to Transfrontier Pollution, art. 7, REPORT OF THE 60TH CONF. OF THE INT'L LAW ASS'N, 1982. *See generally* chapter III of this book at notes 143–48.

(1) Upon request of a potentially affected State, the State furnishing the information should enter into consultations on transfrontier pollution problems connected with the planned activities and pursue such consultations in good faith and over a reasonable period of time.

(2) States are under an obligation to enter into consultations whenever transfrontier pollution problems arise in connection with the equitable utilization of a shared natural resource as envisaged in [a previous article].[4]

The Comment to article 8 says that although prior consultation has become an obligatory custom regarding the use of international watercourses, state practice is still developing toward a rule of international law regarding air pollution. Nevertheless, according to the Comment, "Whenever transfrontier pollution can be categorized as a use of a transfrontier medium [shared natural resource], to which the rule of equitable apportionment laid down in [a previous article] applies, States are under an obligation to enter into consultation."[5] Since this would often be the case with proposed uses of confined air sheds, semienclosed seas, and similar resources, the duty would often apply—even if one accepts fully the I.L.A.'s cautious approach toward air pollution.

Potentially overlapping maritime jurisdictional claims (chapter III). The Tunisian-Libyan Continental Shelf Case supports the proposition that agreement is required before a jurisdictional claim in a maritime boundary area is established.[6]

Military deployments by individual NATO member states outside the North Atlantic area (chapter V). In 1982 the representatives of NATO members taking part in the integrated defense structure declared,

[4]*Id.* art. 8. *See generally* chapter II of this book, at notes 192–98; chapter III at notes 134–36.

[5]Comment to article 8 by I.L.A. Committee on Legal Aspects of the Conservation of the Environment, REPORT OF THE 60TH CONF. OF THE INT'L LAW ASS'N, 1982. The reference is to instances in which the pollution of a resource, e.g., air, interferes with a beneficial use of the same resource on the other side of the frontier. See the comments to article 5, *id.*

[6]Case Concerning the Continental Shelf (Tunisia v. Libya), 21 INT'L LEGAL MATERIALS 225, 249–50 (I.C.J. 1982). *See generally* chapter III of this book, at notes 163–64.

> Noting that developments beyond the NATO area may threaten our vital interests, we reaffirm the need to consult with a view to sharing assessments and identifying common objectives, taking full account of the effect on NATO security and defence capability, as well as of the national interests of member countries. Recognising that the policies which nations adopt in this field are a matter for national decision, we agree to examine collectively in the appropriate NATO bodies the requirements which may arise for the defence of the NATO area as a result of deployments by individual member states outside that area.[7]

This reinforces the NATO norm requiring consultation, insofar as it is feasible, before a NATO member deploys forces outside the North Atlantic area, when the deployment could appreciably increase the allies' vulnerability to attack within that area.[8]

[7]Document on Integrated NATO Defence, June 10, 1982, in 30 NATO REV., No. 3, at 27 (1982). *See also* Defence Planning Comm., Final Communique, May 7, 1982, para. 8, *id.* at 30, 31. *See generally* chapter V of this book, at notes 7–12 and 113–33.

[8]*See* chapter V, section B(7).

Index